The Distemper
of Our
Times

THE DISTEMPER
OF
OUR TIMES

Peter C. Newman

With an introduction by Peter Regenstreif, and
a new Preface by the Author

The Carleton Library No. 112

Published by McClelland and Stewart Limited
in association with the Institute of Canadian Studies
of Carleton University, Ottawa

Contents

Introduction to the Carleton Library Edition

It is impossible to appreciate the Canada of the middle and late 1960's without reading *The Distemper of Our Times*. Better than anything written about any other period (save perhaps Bruce Hutchison's *Incredible Canadian*, the evocative biography of that ultimate Canadian politician William Lyon Mackenzie King), this narrative reflects the very essence of a critical time of transition for an exceedingly complex country.

At the outset, a few comments about Peter Newman are in order because it is difficult to separate the man and what he wrote from the times. There are some who still claim that rather than reflecting the atmosphere of those years, Newman was one of those largely responsible for creating it. During the period covered in this book, he was Ottawa columnist for the *Toronto Star*, his writings syndicated virtually everywhere else in the country. At one time, thirty newspapers carried his every word. For Canada, this was, and is, a phenomenal number.

So pervasive was his influence – and it was so perceived by notables, especially in that in-grown little town of Ottawa – that one of the leading topics of conversation in cabinet on any given day was his latest piece. Newman, like anyone, had his favourite sources, of course, and their whisperings along with his own predilections coloured his accounts as well as this book. Still, as someone who was engaged in political writing, polling, and consulting during the same period and in dealing with many of the same people, I can personally attest that his contacts inside cabinet, the bureaucracy, and the corporate world were unsurpassed.

Along with an undoubted capacity for hard work, what helped Newman penetrate the inner workings of the machinery of government was the apparent remarkable openness of the system for journalists and commentators. Compared to the middle 1950's, when cabinet ministers were tight-lipped and deputy ministers inaccessible, the 1960's were the heyday of insider reporting.

Perhaps this new situation was the result of the coming of John Diefenbaker whose style, attitudes, and behaviour so upset the establishment that after a while it seemed its members would talk to almost anyone who would listen. It was also probably a reflection of minority government and the latent instability and potential for excitement that accompany such circumstances. From 1962 until 1968, much of which period is covered here, no government had a parliamentary majority. But perhaps the relative openness was due to Newman too. If he dug deep and wrote some account exposing the maneuvering behind the scenes, this prompted other insiders to speak out so that their side would be reflected in his writings or in those of another columnist. In that fashion, much of the goings-on in Ottawa became common knowledge not only among a privileged few in the capital but in the livingrooms of the country. By the end of the era of Diefenbaker and Lester Pearson, so developed was the rumour machine in Ottawa that the Japanese ambassador to Canada was reported to have commented that the Canadian ship of state was the only one he knew of that leaked from the top.

Some of those leaks were frivolous or purely self-serving for those who were responsible for them, but others helped add substantially to our knowledge of how the Canadian cabinet system or decision-making in the civil service operates. For example, Newman's descriptions of the standing committees of cabinet in Chapter 15 and in one of the appendices is the only accurate reference to those groups and their responsibilities available outside cabinet minutes. When the book was published, it provided the first glimpse of a new system of collegial decision-making which Pearson began and which his successor, Pierre Trudeau, institutionalized as standard procedure. What appears in this book, therefore, is not only the work of a superb essayist and observer, but also a work with an authenticity found in few other commentaries on Canadian politics.

A final word about Newman and his perspectives before I discuss some of the events of the years covered by him here. This book is something of a continuation of two previous ones – *Flame of Power*, an account of the lives of some successful Canadian entrepreneurs, and *Renegade in Power*, a devastating critique of Diefenbaker in office – in that Newman is still fascinated by power and its exercise. Moreover, along with Walter Gordon, he was, early on, a confirmed nationalist, one of the first of a group who only came into prominence later in the middle of the 1960's. At the time he was writing both this book and the one on Diefenbaker, Newman seemed to me to be taken with the belief that what Canada really needed to achieve its destiny – whether as proclaimed by Sir Wilfrid Laurier or anyone of his and my generation – was a leader who could lead. We were all looking for someone who could and would mould the inchoate, heterogenous population scattered across a vast and formidable land into a unique and self-confident society. Mackenzie King was regarded as a waffler; Louis St. Laurent simply as a kindly chairman-of-the-board who was satisfied merely to maintain the status quo. Newman and a record number of Canadians gave Diefenbaker his unprecedented majority in 1958 and placed great hopes in the Tory chief. But Diefenbaker let them down.

Now, it was Pearson's turn. Already he had been flawed by one of his very first actions as new head of the Liberals. On his first day in the House of Commons as leader of the opposition, he moved a motion of non-confidence in the minority Diefenbaker government, calling for its resignation and the installation of the Liberals in its stead without an election. Diefenbaker was savage in his ridicule of the motion – justly so – and the episode began a ten-year relationship of animosity between the two men that coloured virtually everything in Canada's national political life. Despite this initial misstep, hopes were high that under Pearson the government installed in the spring of 1963 would fulfil expectations of restoring competence and rationality to the practice of government at home, and respect and admiration for the country abroad.

Right from the start there was miscalculation; followed by ineptitude; succeeded by incompetence; accompanied by scandal. Then came idiotic planning; stumbling, bumbling execution. The Pearson government was precisely the opposite of what its supporters anticipated. The first budget, which was supposed to demonstrate the old Liberal competence of the St. Laurent era, was a fiasco. The nationalistic provisions authored by Finance Minister Gordon had to be retracted in the face of determined opposition from financial circles. Gordon had used three non-civil-service economists from

Toronto to help prepare the budget, but only admitted having done so in the House of Commons after first denying it. But worst of all, the budget debacle all but discredited Gordon, thereby depriving the new government of the much needed talent of the chief architect of its coming to power. Gordon and a few of his friends and associates had almost single-handedly revived a moribund Liberal party after its defeat in 1957.

It seemed that everything the government turned its hand to became tainted. Pearson kept trying to find a lieutenant who could stand at his right as his man from Quebec. He was unable to do so until near the end of his office, but in the pursuit, featured an array of inappropriate and some-times tragic personalities: Lionel Chevrier, Maurice Lamontagne, and Guy Favreau. It was not until early 1967 that Jean Marchand succeeded to the position. Meanwhile, behind the scenes, in subordinate roles, but engaged in a fierce contest for control of the province were two groups: the remnants of an unbelievably corrupt operation which had been feeding off patronage and spoils since Confederation, known as the "Montreal garbage can"; against it were the forces of the new Quebec that were to produce both support for full participation by French Canadians in Canada and separatism. The same impulses that impelled Trudeau, Gérard Pelletier, Maurice Sauvé, and Marchand toward federalism underlay the separatist orientation of Claude Morin and Réné Levesque, to mention but a handful of the key figures of that period and of today.

While Pearson searched for his Quebec lieutenant, one French-Canadian notable in his government after another became embroiled in scandal or tainted by its suggestion. Minister-Without-Portfolio Yvon Dupuis was convicted of having accepted a $10,000 bribe to help obtain a licence for a new racetrack in his home constituency near St. Jean (the conviction was successfully appealed in 1968). Secretary of State Lamontagne and Immigration Minister Réné Tremblay were found to have bought furniture on suspiciously easy terms from a store that subsequently went bankrupt. The administration failed to launch an investigation of allegations of bribery involving an executive assistant to a cabinet minister in a conspiracy to obtain the release on bail of notorious narcotics smuggler Lucien Rivard. Justice Minister Favreau eventually was chastized for showing poor judgment by investigating Judge Frédéric Dorion; and Pearson's own Parliamentary Assistant Guy Rouleau was found to be involved in an attempt to influence the Crown Prosecutor in the case and was forced to resign. Other petty scandals abounded: failure to prosecute Hal Banks, the head of the Seafarers' International Union; the inordinate length of time it took to deport a convicted robber and murderer, Onofrio Minaudo; the huge profit made by back-bench Liberal MP Eddy Asselin in a land deal in Montreal, a profit he made by virtue of inside information. Asselin eventually resigned before the 1965 election because he had become a liability to his party. Pearson and his government were so accident-prone that when the Prime Minister brought in his suggestion for a new flag in the spring of 1964, it was regarded by many as just another partisan ploy. Many months of scheming and acrimonious debate and finally the invocation of closure had to be undergone before the flag was finally passed by Parliament.

With Diefenbaker, ever hopeful of regaining power, in full cry, these incidents seemed to obscure the accomplishments and new beginnings the administration achieved: record wheat sales to the USSR; the Canada-Russia Plan; the automobile agreement with the United States; the establishment of the Royal Commission on Bilingualism and Biculturalism. By the spring and summer of 1965, Pearson and his advisers came to the conclusion that many of their government's misadventures were the result of being in a minority situation in the House. Urged on by Gordon, Pearson decided to hold an election basing his campaign on the need for a majority government.

As in the campaigns of 1962 and 1963, the Liberals began the election that fall with a solid lead in the public opinion polls. And just as they did in those previous elections, they proceeded to lose support as the campaign progressed. One of the most remarkable elements of political life during the sixties was the contrast in feelings about Pearson between the elites in Ottawa and the average voter. Throughout his life, Pearson was held in the highest esteem by insiders; on the other hand, he was never able to achieve a very high standing with the common man. Survey after survey in those years would show the Liberals ahead of the Conservatives in popularity, while in both 1962 and 1963, Diefenbaker was preferred over Pearson as the man people wanted "to lead the country, party considerations aside." By 1965, Pearson finally pulled ahead of Diefenbaker in this dimension but he was still unable to arouse Canadians, many of whom, even while voting for candidates bearing his party's label, continued to regard him as "too political" or "only out for himself."

Throughout Pearson's tenure as leader, the Liberals were unable to make any inroads on the Prairies. In their traditional bastion of Quebec, they were so badly organized and so unwilling to deal with problems of economic development, poverty, and social deprivation that between one-fifth and one-third of French-Canadian voters in the province were supporting Créditiste candidates. The Liberals had become the party of Central Canada, of young people, and residents of the metropolitan areas, leaving the Conservatives with the aged, and with residents of small towns, farms, and the Prairies. The new Democrats, who grew to almost 18 per cent of the vote in 1965, had support predominantly among the working class and in primary producing areas in English Canada. The Liberals seemed to be winning not because of strong positive feelings in their favour but because the alternatives were worse.

As is well known, the 1965 election was regarded as a disaster for the Liberals. Pearson failed to win his coveted majority, and the bitter confrontations between the Liberals and the Conservatives across the floor in the House of Commons continued. After the absurd Munsinger affair, things appeared to settle down. With the Conservatives preoccupied with trying to rid themselves of Diefenbaker and choosing a successor, the Liberal government completed its extraordinary legislative program begun in 1963: both an Old Age Security Act and a Medical Care Insurance Act were passed, and a bill to unify the armed services was approved.

Diverting though Newman is in his depiction of events, he is at his best describing the character and style of the major protagonists – or antagonists – of the period, Pearson and Diefenbaker.

People commenting on Pearson's career even today seem unwilling to portray him as the supremely political man that he was. They excuse his failure to mobilize his countrymen as simply "his way" of doing things. The conventional attitude of insiders – in particular of the establishment group of which Pearson was clearly a charter member – toward him is of a man detached from such nasty political necessities as patronage or as a "nice guy" who was reluctantly "willing" to "do his duty" and take over the Liberals in 1957 when "only" Paul Martin was left to lead the party. With the Liberals still in office and with therefore so many people who know better lacking any incentive whatsoever to betray confidences, it is unlikely that Newman's thorough exposition will ever be matched.

The truth is that Pearson was a man who knew the political game intimately and played it to the hilt. He rewarded his friends and punished his enemies – sometimes not even bothering to reward his old friends if new, for the moment more useful, ones were around. His treatment of Gordon, Favreau, and Lucien Cardin, to name just three cabinet ministers, was disgraceful. His Senate appointments were no different than any of his predecessors' in their emphasis on the basest of political qualifications. His use of patronage and his reliance on criteria not remotely related to competence places him in the front ranks of accomplished manipulators. The public perceived all these things in time, while so many close to him continued to close their eyes to these facets of their beloved leader. In the end, Pearson emerged from active political life covered with glory, because, through all the scandals, miscalculations, and mistakes, he always managed to protect himself.

It was not so with Diefenbaker. Newman's previous book, devoted almost completely to him, is a classic of character dissection, but there is plenty left over for this volume. Most insiders abhorred or feared Diefenbaker relatively early on because he was so difficult to pin down, was badly organized, and was given to hearty, sometimes irrational, likes and dislikes. His style was confrontation rather than compromise and of course, he never could bring himself to let go of whatever power he had. He had fought too hard to achieve it, whereas for Pearson it had come so easily. The tragedy of those years of hostility between Pearson and Diefenbaker was that instead of trying to understand the needs and feelings of those to whom Diefenbaker appealed, the Liberals denigrated their values and ignored their sense of isolation. By so doing, the Liberals and Pearson, far more than the Conservatives, contributed to the fragmentation of the country.

But by the end of 1966 and the beginning of 1967, everything seemed to be turning around. Economic conditions were good, and, with the good feelings engendered by the Centennial and the marvellous experience of Expo 67, Canada appeared to be coming into her own; certainly she was becoming very attractive compared to the United States with her violence and assassinations, racial disturbances, the war in Vietnam, and the breakdown of presidential leadership.

Now, the country's political system seemed to be getting in step. In September 1967 the Conservatives managed to hold their leadership convention, emerging not only relatively unified, but with a highly reputable and intelligent man, Nova Scotia Premier Robert Stanfield, as their new leader. Since the 1965 election all sorts of cabals had formed as potential successors to Pearson, and were scrambling for position. Within three months after the Conservatives chose Stanfield (and with polls showing the Conservatives ahead of the Liberals in popular support), Pearson announced his resignation, effective in April after the Liberals held their convention to select their new leader.

The rise of Trudeau, within two months, from 2-per-cent public recognition in January 1968 to the most popular candidate of all the contenders in April is one of the most improbable developments in Canada's or any other country's political history. Newman's account is first-class and his capturing of the spirit of things is superb. Trudeau seemingly had it all and as the man of destiny appeared ordained to bring to Canada everything we all wished for it. It takes nothing away from Newman to note that there was obviously a dark underside to the hope that so many felt then but which so many wanted to overlook. Newman, in fact, mentions some of the potential difficulties, although sometimes only in passing. There is ample material here on the interplay of personalities and policy as the struggle for the province of Quebec gets under way. The discontent in the West, first reflected in a political style and historic legacy different from

Central Canada's, was to be reinforced by economic developments in the 1970's. While he was Prime Minister, Pearson presided over a considerable devolution of federal authority to the provinces, thereby helping create the circumstances in which the federal government no longer has the capacity to act decisively to ameliorate economic difficulties or to mitigate regional disparities. On the question of foreign ownership, Newman astutely notes that many of Gordon's opponents saw his activities as a bold attempt to establish the business dominance of Toronto. At the same time, he recognizes that French Canadians were more upset by English managers than by American capital.

The only criticism anyone could possibly have with this book is that it emphasizes personalities too much. There is a case to be made that the problems which were beginning to confront Canada in the 1960's – most of which are still with it but in enlarged form – were not to be solved by changing elites but only by fundamentally reordering the country's institutions. More than a new flag was required; Canada needed a new constitution, new values, and new forms. But as Newman so effectively suggests (if only obliquely) if Canada's leading men of affairs took almost a year to adopt something as simple as a flag, or had to resort to Byzantine subterfuges to settle on a pension plan, what then were the possibilities for change of a far-reaching and fundamental character? Precious few. Therein lay the hope so many people had in Trudeau. He seemed to offer the potential for basic innovation.

It is clear now that the Canada of Newman's and his generation's aspirations is not to be. But an author is not to be blamed for living in hope rather than despair. However, from this vantage point almost a decade after the book was written, it is perhaps more accurate to represent this marvellous period mood-piece as being not a chronicle of hope but a freeze-frame of the mid-point in the dissipation of a great dream. Whatever the perspective, I submit that this book is far more valuable and interesting today than when it first appeared.

Peter Regenstreif
April 1977

Author's Preface to the Carleton Library Edition

The Distemper of our Times must be read against the three volumes of Lester Pearson's own, subsequently published memoirs. Unfortunately, the manufacture of those tomes involved so many consultants, editors, literary executors, and ghost writers in the sky that what came out was a thin and curiously tasteless stew. The prime-ministerial recollections contain few hints of anger, no revealing tid-bits, little bite when they should be tangy. Too many cooks have spoiled the wrath.

Pearson uses ladles of butter to baste even those underlings who served him worst. A 1965 RCMP report strongly implicated Guy Rouleau, his own parliamentary secretary, as a "linchpin" in the conspiracy to spring Lucien Rivard, the heroin smuggler, out of jail, but the former PM issues no rebuke: "It was a sad and sorry business and Rouleau (who may have been weak but never evil) was broken up about it all."

Probably the most unintentionally revealing paragraph in these surprisingly tedious books is Pearson's confession that "the Liberal Party, in opposition or in government, included one group anxious to move to the right and a second group to steer to the left. This dichotomy is an essential characteristic of Liberalism."

Holy Mackenzie King! It's perfect: the Liberal gavotte — you take two steps left and two steps right, while moving sideways into an uncertain future. And that is how we got social security without socialism and biculturalism without having to learn French. Obviously, in the Liberal order of things, extremism in the defence of moderation is no vice.

In its Liberal incarnation, moderation seems to be not just a safe course between extremes, but the first principle of state, a mandate for the conduct of individual and collective affairs. Under this system of governing, the instinctive response to the call of the passing hour supersedes all pursuits and priorities; unlimited faith is allocated to reasoned discussion ("kicking things around"); history is trusted as a healer against the potentially injurious effects of men's baser natures. The Protestant Ethic reigns supreme. Such an approach tends to inhibit any political leader who carries with him into office the courage of his convictions, or even of his intentions. The prime minister who must deliberately deploy his inner forces so that he can succeed at the stodgy while failing at the glorious leaves himself no private proving ground for the soul, no moment when passion clambers up to endow his ideas with something more illuminating than necessity.

Yet this was very much Pearson's way. To be light on both feet, ready to move in every direction; to advance not according to any schedule of pre-ordained progress, but through a series of glandular gooses, most of them prompted by the shadow of angry voters gathering beyond the ramparts. Like most of our successful PM's, Pearson was not corrupted by power because he so seldom used it. Not even when he should have.

Though he was superficially gregarious, I always found Lester Pearson to be possessed by a profound sense of detachment which allowed him to move through many worlds without fully belonging to any but his own. Even when he finally withdrew from the prime ministership there was little hint of sadness or regret, just the cool civility of a man who has done his duty, stood the watch that ends the night: "So Trudeau won, and we all gathered weeping and laughing around the platform, slapping each other on the back. And it was all over in time to get home for the face-off of *Hockey Night in Canada*."

Throughout *Distemper* as well as his own books, Pearson emerges as the quintessential Establishment Man. He goes to London a week after he's been sworn into office and knows half the Macmillan cabinet by their first names; hops over to Paris and has a tête-à-tête with Chip Bohlen; flies to Washington for tea with Dean and Alice Acheson, then excuses himself to join Scotty and Sally Reston for cocktails. He nominates "Rolly" Michener to be governor-general because they played hockey and tennis together at Oxford. The February 19, 1968, Commons defeat of his government catches Pearson in the middle of a rubber of bridge at the Jamaica villa of

Senator Hartland de Montarville Molson. You feel the suffused glow of a hundred Rideau Club dinners as he lists the comrades of the Old Boy network that made the Pearsonian diplomacy tick: Norman Robertson, George Ignatieff, John Holmes, E.L.M. "Tommy" Burns, Dana Wilgress, Geoff Murray, Bert MacKay, Arnold Heeney, and Hume Wrong. (Typical was the message he sent to Hume Wrong, then Canadian Ambassador in Washington, on March 16, 1949, after both men had helped negotiate the original NATO pact: "Without your skilful and experienced help, we would certainly not have had as satisfactory a treaty as that which you will be signing for Canada. I am happy that my name will be associated with yours in that signature. It marks another stage in our joint progress from the days when we used to put our initials, together, on first year pass-papers in history at U of T.")

Like most men of his generation and persuasion, Pearson recognized very little if any barrier between politics and the senior civil service, since they both presumably belong to what Jack Pickersgill liked to call "The Government Party." This came out most vividly when Pearson reminisced about his first day in the Commons after his switch from having been a deputy minister. "The change to me did not seem startling," he said. "It felt like being promoted from general manager to president in the same company: 'External Affairs Ltd.'"

Even as Prime Minister, Lester Pearson seemed always a man of Ottawa more than of the nation, but he never lost his self-deprecating sense of humour. There is a story, for example, of the farmer who made what must stand as the shortest political introduction on record: "I have been asked to introduce Mr. Pearson who has been asked to speak to us. I have. He will." And a glimpse of the little boy with an "I LIKE MIKE" sign hung around his neck, a little uncertain about his instructions, who kept yelling, "I like Milk." Through it all, Lester Bowles Pearson remained always true to himself. A good and reasonable man incapable of adding even a faint hint of fanaticism to his cautious convictions. Although he spent a long career having to react to the exigencies of the moment, he never allowed his basic instinct for decency to be subverted.

Throughout his abnormally normal existence – which saw him rise from the obscurity of a manse in the Ontario heartland, and of his first job as a sausage-stuffer in Hamilton, to win the Nobel Peace Prize and become prime minister – Pearson led something of a charmed life, with circumstances conspiring to push him ahead at every turning point. It was this quality that made him such an appealing (and successful) diplomat. During the nine years he spent as Canada's secretary of state for external affairs, he took the striped pants and frown out of our foreign policy and replaced them with a tilted, polka-dot bow tie and a small-town Ontario grin on a face as comforting as a bowl of apple butter. His approach allowed Canada to exercise an influence quite out of proportion to the country's real stature. At the same time, it found ready response at home because there was something in the national character of Canadians that clung to sweet reasonableness as the only possible posture in the face of the country's geographical, social, and economic problems.

Pearson's lifelong quest for peace abroad and unity at home produced neither, but he did as much as any man to bring us closer to these ideals and became a model against which we could assess our collective future. He was the *beau idéal* of international statescraft. During that brief flowering of diplomacy between the innocent past when ambassadors still wore handkerchiefs up their sleeves and the darker present when presidents tape their conversations, L.B.P. set an exuberant style all his own. Light on both feet and ready to move in any useful direction, he came to be regarded as an immensely capable talisman whose powers of positive negotiations kept the Cold War cold. As chairman of the NATO Council, president of the United Nations Assembly, the main moving spirit behind the Colombo Plan, the new Commonwealth, the Korean Peace talks, the 1956 Middle East UN emergency force, and on half a dozen other major occasions, he became the "honest broker," an eternal seeker of the middle ground, testing the infinite contingencies that might lead to a way out. His interventions somehow seemed to spark a progression of crises that precipitated their own solutions, like thunderclouds that send down the rain to clear a sultry day.

The quality that stood out in everything Pearson did never

changed. Whether he was engaged in hushed bargaining with world statesmen or addressing a rowdy meeting of bush workers in the Algoma-East constituency he loved, he never for an instant pretended to know the answers to the intractable and ambiguous problems of his time. He was simply a man bent on trying to get the questions straight, and it was this honesty of approach that will be missed most by those who knew him, however slightly. That and the warmth of his wit. It was no accident that the most memorable aspect of the Pearson style was a wry, defensive sense of humour that flourished under stress. A politician, like a clergyman, is wise not to jest too freely about his vocation, but Pearson could make his puns work for him, both as a way of puncturing his opponents' rages and as a means of maintaining his own equilibrium. During a question-and-answer period at a Canadian University Liberal Federation convention, held in Ottawa on February 2, 1967, he told a story to illustrate the point. It was about the Indian-fighter who crawled into a frontier fort with three arrows in his back and was asked whether it hurt.

"Only when I laugh," he replied.

"My job," Pearson added, "only hurts when I *don't* laugh."

Despite his lightheartedness, Pearson's apparent detachment was due not to the fact that he cared too little, but to the fact that he cared too much and found it was only through jokes that he could compose himself for a world that was filled with disorder and anguish. When he became prime minister in the spring of 1963, Pearson never forgot that the great movements of history hinge not on day-to-day triumphs or setbacks, but on the conversion of ill-defined problems into great moral issues, and he tried to cast Canada's problem of French-English relations into such a context.

His persuasive powers were not always adequate to match his performance with his intentions, but his gift of being able to soften collisions and smooth tempers and his unwillingness to draw drastic conclusions from the temporary tactics of his opponents became considerable assets in the struggle for national unity. His stewardship as Canada's fourteenth prime minister, which is chronicled in this book, was a mixture of triumphs and failures, though he did bring his party into power after the great Diefenbaker sweep of 1958 which had left the Liberals with the smallest (49) parliamentary contingent since Confederation.

His rivalry with John Diefenbaker grew during the ten years the two men faced each other across the Commons until it extended even to their leisure hours. They were both avid fishermen, but neither had much luck at Harrington Lake, the official summer residence of Canadian prime ministers. When Pearson moved in, he kept hearing rumours that the Prince Albert politician had caught a 4½-pound trout. Unable to match that record Pearson insisted on tracking the story down to a local farmer, and was delighted to discover that while Diefenbaker had indeed hooked such a fish, he had never managed to get it into his boat.

Pearson was at his best in times of great stress when his diplomatic training let him underreact to the torrent of events threatening to engulf him. "We'll jump off that bridge when we come to it," he would airily announce to nervous aides as they fretted about the next catastrophe that could befall the government.

During the five turbulent years he presided over the Canadian government, there was constant speculation about Pearson's ideology. But the motives that chiefly guided him were disarmingly simple. They were as uncomplicated as the need to avoid a third world war and the necessity to preserve Canadian unity. He saw history not as an orderly succession of events but as an accumulation of tumbling paradoxes, in the midst of which anything might happen. He regarded politics as having the formidable mission of trying to cope with the resultant chaos and saw himself as a creative improviser possessed by the capacity to put disappointments aside, place them in a new perspective, and move on.

To shrug your shoulders and smile sometimes remained the only sane response to the preposterous incongruities of human existence.

From these observations, it may be clear that my assessment of the Pearson stewardship has softened somewhat since I wrote *Distemper*. I now recognize that the unrealistically ideal expectations I had of the men who occupy this country's highest political office have to be tempered by my acknowledgment of the dreadful difficulties involved in governing this country. In retrospect, the Pearson years appear to have been a kind of hiatus before the storm over national unity that has since engulfed us all.

Finally, as a note on sources I must repeat a disclaimer I wrote for the Introduction to the Carleton Library edition of *Renegade in Power: The Diefenbaker Years.* I had three main sources for both of these books: my own observations of events as they happened; tape-recorded, off-the-record interviews with most of the principals involved in the many political crises I described; and a set of diaries kept for me by many of the major participants in these crises. Some of my critics claim I should reveal my sources. But I believe that though it is the historian's duty to list sources, it is the journalist's obligation to protect the privacy of those who have befriended him with information. I wrote this book as a journalist.

In the past, academics could challenge journalists trying to write contemporary history because the release of documents of a prime minister and other important political figures was needed before his record could be fairly judged. The process has changed radically with the revolution in the technology of communications, especially the use of the typewriter and the telephone. In Sir John A. Macdonald's time, historians could depend on handwritten documents which contained a government's record almost in its entirety. With a quill pen, a prime minister could write only a limited number of letters. The use of the typewriter has vastly increased the flow of paper out of a prime minister's office, while the telephone has greatly decreased the importance of written documentation. There are more documents, but there is less in them. If a contemporary statesman has something to communicate, if speed and secrecy are of the essence, he will confide his messages not to a letter but to the telephone. Until wiretapping becomes a recognized skill of the Canadian Historical Association, there can be no permanent record of these transactions. (One of the first things Pierre Elliott Trudeau did when he moved into the prime minister's office in the spring of 1968 was to install an intercom which connects him with all of his important assistants, individually or simultaneously, for hurried on-the-spot conferences. There will be few inter-office memos in his legacy to the national archives.) In compiling their documentations, historians – both of the academic and journalistic variety – nose about in chaos, defining their themes, organizing their narrative, setting scenes, dramatizing conflicts, evoking characters and atmosphere. In this process there are limits to their capacity for invention, but there need be none to their capacity for insight.

A fuller list of suggestions for further reading on the Pearson years appears at the end of this volume.

Peter C. Newman,
Toronto, July, 1977

FOR *Ralph Allen*
(1913-1966)

Foreword

JUST AFTER PIERRE ELLIOTT TRUDEAU WAS SWORN IN as the fifteenth Prime Minister of Canada, I left his House of Commons office, a tape-recording of a long conversation with him under my arm, and walked into an April evening feeling the exhilaration of expectation that was so common in Canada that spring. I was working on this book at the time so the events of the previous five years were very much in my mind and it suddenly occurred to me just how long it had been since I, or anyone I knew, had felt this optimistic quickening of interest in national affairs. For half a decade, most of the people I talked to, not just journalists and politicians, but Canadians I encountered at dinner parties and in hamburger stands, in airport buses and on docks along the Rideau River, had been voicing – some eloquently, some awkwardly – a kind of dismay at and frustration with our politics that was hardening into cynicism and despair. They seemed to be experiencing an alienation they had never known before.

In its limited way, this book is a chronicle of the alienation between the politicians and the people that marked Canadian history from the collapse of the Diefenbaker administration in February of 1963 to Trudeau's assumption of power in April of 1968.

During that unsettled period Canada, which had always been blessed with more geography than history, fell at last into the grip of both. We had spent a hundred years trying to become a nation; now we *were* a nation and it was hell.

Some astute historian of the future will be able to discern a pattern in and attach a meaning to these five years of political turmoil. But to those of us who were there, it was a time of national distemper, a time when the political affairs of the country were in such a state of disorder that there was something faintly absurdist about their unfolding, a time when many Canadians were left with the feeling that much of what was happening had no meaning and that all they could do was ask themselves a series of unanswerable questions: Is the country being governed by fools? Or is it ungovernable? Has our good luck, taken for granted for so long, run out? Can't we just forget about the politicians and get on with our lives? Oh God!

We were only dimly aware that we were enduring the pains of passage from the safety of the past to we knew not what. The politics of the period was essentially a politics of transition.

The most visible public figure of the era – and chief victim of its turmoil – was the Right Honourable Lester Bowles Pearson. Although he could not know it at the time of his hopeful beginnings, Pearson was to be caught throughout his stewardship between a New Canada quixotically seeking a political midwife to be born and an Old Canada stubbornly refusing to disappear. For five hectic years he found himself suspended between two worlds, a moderate confronted by radical facts.

His term in power coincided with a profound shift in the country's social, economic, political, constitutional and moral climate. Although his government pushed through the House of Commons many useful, if ill-co-ordinated, new laws, the impact of each legislative accomplishment was obscured by yet another spectacular failure of spirit or method. So Lester Pearson, instead of being able to govern wisely and well (as Canadians had every reason to believe he was capable of doing) had the misfortune to appear during most of his tenure in office as a confused and inept politician, harassed by the acceleration of events beyond his capacity for decisive action.

Many of the tensions that plagued Lester Pearson's time in office were legacies from his predecessor, John Diefenbaker. But the two seasons in Canadian politics were as different as the men who gave them their labels. The Diefenbaker Years resembled nothing so much as the voyage of the *Titanic* – an inevitable rush to disaster, with the ship of state sinking at the end in a galaxy of fireworks, brass bands playing and the captain shouting hysterical orders to crewmen who had long since jumped overboard. The Pearson period, in contrast, was more like the voyage of some peeling, once-proud, now leaky excursion steamer, lurching from port to port, with the captain making up the schedule as he went along, too busy keeping afloat to spend much time on the bridge.

Canadian politics between 1957 and 1963 was essentially the story of what happened to one gigantic figure, John Diefenbaker. But Canadian politics between 1963 and 1968 was dominated by a tumble of events rather than by the personality or fate of any one man.

It was these events – some important in themselves, some merely indicative of the personalities and moods of the time – that gave the period its flavour and this book its structure. It was not a political era that lent itself to tidy chronological narration. Events shaped men and events in conflict shaped one another: Lester Pearson did battle with John Diefenbaker; the Conservative Party endured internal intrigues almost Byzantine in their flavour; the French rose up against the English; provincial governments challenged the federal authority; Walter Gordon lashed out against American domination of the Canadian economy; and Pierre Trudeau conquered the Liberal Party.

At the same time, nearly every aspect of Canadian life was in ferment. The church, our long-praised phlegmatic stability, the old idea of allegiance to Empire, all the comforting touchstones of the familiar past were being displaced by the urgent demands of a disquieting present. The trade patterns that had shaped the country's economy began to alter; the exodus from the farms went steadily on as Canada became a strung-out collection of city states beset by the pressures and neuroses of urban existence. Technological breakthroughs changed the nature and tenure of most jobs. The Pill and the flourishing ecumenical movement transformed the moral values of a generation. Television revolutionized public thought and with it the political process.

Instead of leading the people through this maze of change, the Pearson-Diefenbaker generation of politicians droned on, caught up in the vain hopes of a long-gone epoch, viewing their own peculiar Kiplingesque world through the rear windows of flag-fluttering limousines in the age of moonflights, mass marches and mod.

During this time of change and confusion, I laboured as do all reporters, by necessity and by choice, on the other side of the barricades from the politicians and so can offer here only an outsider's view of the governmental process. With a certain sense of melancholy, I realize also that the heavings of history are too complex and too subtle to be chronicled on the run with any pretense of absolute authority. But I continue to believe that a contemporary journalist's resolutely non-partisan observations can make a valid contribution to the history of his country. Even though the events recorded here are not yet cold, we are, as a nation, already locked into their ramifications.

PART ONE   *Presumption of Power*

CHAPTER 1

A Sizzling of Fuses

O N THE SUN-WASHED MORNING of April 22, 1963, Lester Bowles
Pearson, riding in a borrowed blue Buick and dressed in a well-
worn morning coat, drove up to the front door of Government
House to be sworn into office. When he drove away again a little more
than an hour later as the fourteenth Prime Minister of Canada, he
turned for a moment to his press secretary, Richard O'Hagan, and said,
as their car slid down the manicured drive, "You know, Dick, somehow
I feel like myself again."

In that hour took place the change of government the nation's
voters had barely approved in the election of April 8. In that sentence
was summed up the Liberals' reaction to their return from a political
wilderness they had wandered for six uneasy years.

POLICIES UNENFORCED, DECISIONS too hastily taken and choices dodged
too long would quickly dim the high expectations of the Pearson takeover. But in those days of optimistic beginning, a feeling of renewal and
rare excitement accompanied the new government into office.

The immediate post-election mood among the members of the
nation's various establishments had been one of chagrin that Pearson
was not granted the majority mandate they were sure he deserved.
Seldom if ever before had the country's vested interests been so unanimous in their political preference. Canada's financial, academic, bureaucratic and journalistic élites were united in an obsessive dislike of John

3

Diefenbaker and an unshakable conviction that the only way to rescue the country from its state of political and economic chaos was to elect a sturdy Liberal majority. On election morning, the Establishment newspaper, Toronto's *Globe and Mail*, normally conservative in tone and Conservative in politics, had editorialized: "The one clear need of Canada on this election day is for a sound, stable majority government. . . . In the circumstances the question of Conservative Party loyalty should not arise. Mr. Diefenbaker has destroyed the Conservative Party. . . . Canadians will serve their country best if they rise above partisan loyalties, if they put aside protest and vote into office a Liberal majority government."

The *Globe* was reflecting the widespread belief that if only Lester B. Pearson could be boosted into power, things would return to the calm pace and rational planning of those happy years before John Diefenbaker had come thundering out of Prince Albert.

The financial community was certain that with the government once more in the efficient hands of the Liberals, fiscal sanity would be restored. The Ottawa bureaucracy had no doubt whatever that with Pearson in office ("You must understand, one is entirely impartial in these things – but we all love Mike"), they would regain their rightful place in the decision-making firmament. The intellectuals saw Pearson as one of their own and believed that his return would bolster Canada's sinking prestige abroad. The journalists, entranced by the Kennedy mystique, somehow convinced themselves that Canada could, with the Liberals in office, have a northern version of the New Frontier.

Because they were united so unanimously behind him, these establishments found Lester Pearson's failure to obtain a clear majority galling, irrational and, as they were fond of telling each other, "beyond belief." They had *willed* an end to the nightmare of the Diefenbaker Years, and the people had only partially followed their direction.* It was typical of the time that instead of blaming Pearson for not having gained his majority, they blamed John Diefenbaker for denying him one. This curious attitude was to prevail during the Pearson regime, with someone or something else usually held responsible for the Liberal Leader's failures.

Throughout most of the Pearson stewardship, the nation's élites continued to regard John Diefenbaker as a kind of evil magician, who in all due reason should have vanished from Canadian life, but who somehow was able, in swirling cloak and howling rhetoric, to pull votes

---

*In the 1963 election, the Liberals received 41.1 per cent of the popular vote and 129 seats; the Conservatives 32.8 per cent of the vote and 95 seats; with the NDP (17 seats) and Social Credit (24 seats) splitting the balance.

and support like shabby rabbits out of a top hat. They were never more irritated with him than during those first long hours after the 1963 election when he refused to let go of power gracefully and ominously hinted that he might hang on until Parliament could meet and some form of coalition might be negotiated for his support.

Finally, on April 15, Governor General Georges Vanier was privately notified that the Tory leader would resign after all, and when the bitter truth finally possessed the Conservatives, they began at last to act like a deposed regime. Out of their ministerial offices moved the defeated, taking with them their personal secretaries and their private files. Green Government of Canada panel trucks trundled papers by the ton away from Parliament Hill, bound for either the incinerator or the Public Archives. Tories in minor and some major posts began to look about drearily for jobs. At least eight of the former ministers left town as quickly as TCA could carry them. The others got together for a subdued farewell dinner, given at the Rideau Club by Davie Fulton. After his final cabinet meeting, on the morning of April 18, John Diefenbaker came out to greet some 4-H agricultural youth club members who had been invited to his prime ministerial office. He looked around, blinking a little as if to re-orient himself, then asked if there were any delegates present from Saskatchewan. Melvin Solvason stepped forward and explained that he came from the Quill Lakes community of Kandahar. "Is that Chinese cafe that has those wonderful steaks still there?" the Conservative Leader asked. Assured that it was, he gently dismissed the group of fresh-faced youngsters who, as it turned out, were to be his last official visitors.

ALMOST AT ONCE THE MOOD, the very rhythm, of Canadian politics began to change.

The new administration's prime mission, as its activists saw it, was to provide an antidote to the Diefenbaker brand of government: to identify and quickly meet those national problems whose solution had resisted the capacity of the preceding regime. The outgoing Conservatives had left office with twenty-three uncompleted bills on their final Commons order paper. The newcomers set out to challenge such a sloppy approach, buoyed up by their confident belief that although much in government might be difficult, nothing was impossible.

Riding the Liberal campaign plane earlier that spring, it was possible to sense the itch of Pearson's lieutenants to be at work on the many national problems left in abeyance during the declining months of the Tory regime. As far as most Liberals were concerned, the great issue in the election had been John Diefenbaker's congenital inability to resolve the contradictions that his own indecision had produced in the nation's defence, trade, fiscal and external policies.*

Lester Pearson began the campaign flushed with certainty that he would be granted a majority mandate. But despite the dramatic resignations from the Conservative Cabinet that had set off the election and the disarray among his followers, it was evident as polling day approached that John Diefenbaker was still a devastatingly effective campaigner. By the last week of March, Pearson's inner circle felt that something dramatically out of the ordinary was essential to emphasize their candidate's assets. Since Pearson couldn't hope to match Diefenbaker as a campaigner, it was decided to concentrate on building up the Liberal Leader's decisiveness – the one trait that would most clearly contrast him with the vacillating Old Chief.

Walter Gordon, the Liberal Party's campaign chairman, flew to Halifax for a hurried conference with Pearson. He suggested that the voters might be galvanized into supporting the Liberals if they were promised "a hundred days of unprecedented action." As soon as the Liberal Leader's wife, Maryon Pearson, heard the idea, she pointed out that the "Hundred Days" slogan had first been applied to the period following Napoleon Bonaparte's return from exile at Elba – an interval that ended with his rout at Waterloo. The notion of setting himself deadlines was not in character for a politician who preferred to keep things vague, but it was Lester Pearson himself who suggested revising the slogan to "Sixty Days of Decision." On March 25, at an election rally in Hamilton, the Liberal Leader first promised that "more constructive things will be done in the first sixty days of a new Liberal Government than in any similar period of Canadian history." On April 1, Pearson tried to subdue a rowdy crowd in Vancouver by shouting: "The first sixty days of a new Liberal administration will be SIXTY

*Renegade in Power: The Diefenbaker Years (McClelland and Stewart Limited, 1963), chapters 23, 24 and 25, describes the Conservative Government's disintegration and the 1963 election campaign. The issue that had come to symbolize the Conservative Government's lack of resolution was the emotionally charged question of whether or not Canada should acquire nuclear warheads from the United States. This hesitation was not politically significant until Pearson (prompted by a confidential memorandum from Paul Hellyer [NOTE: The text and circumstances of this memorandum are reproduced in Appendix A.]) gave a speech on January 23, 1963, in which he reversed his party's position and called for the acceptance of the warheads. This dramatic switch, enhanced by John Diefenbaker's continued inability to articulate any defence policy of his own, led three weeks later to the breakup of the Conservative Cabinet and to the party's defeat in the Commons.

DAYS OF DECISION!" In the two weeks before polling day the future prime minister crossed the nation, making twenty-one specific policy pledges for action by his government during its first sixty days in office.

WHEN PEARSON FAILED to gain his majority, most Liberals rationalized that nothing much had been lost, because to put the nation's business back in order would require only the remedy of some swiftly applied managerial competence, and managerial competence was what the Liberal Party was all about. "Pearson and his ministers will come to power equipped with sheaves of policy papers, priority lists and agendas which they expect will enable the quickest take-off of any new Government in Canada's history," wrote Tim Creery in the Ottawa *Citizen*, accurately reflecting the mood of the moment.

In three campaigns Lester Pearson had placed before the electorate not a personal image for their beguilement but the pledge that he could field a competent team of associates who would give sound, progressive government.

Pearson recruited this team from the study of Stornoway, the opposition leader's official residence, while his two faithful secretaries, Mary Macdonald and Annette Perron, manned the phones and sent the telegrams to summon the chosen. His selections followed to the letter the Canadian tradition of naming a minister from each province (except Saskatchewan, which had denied the Liberals a single M.P.) plus representatives of such minorities as Protestants in Quebec and Catholics in Ontario. The twenty-six-member cabinet was neatly balanced between Roman Catholics and Protestants, with thirteen of each. Senior appointments were virtually automatic, since they merely involved moving Pearson's associates into the portfolios they had held in the Liberal Opposition's shadow cabinet. In this category were Finance Minister Walter Gordon, Trade and Commerce Minister Mitchell Sharp, External Affairs Secretary Paul Martin, Justice Minister Lionel Chevrier, and Defence Minister Paul Hellyer. Pearson allowed two other colleagues, Jack Pickersgill and Maurice Lamontagne, a choice of the remaining portfolios. Pickersgill took the relatively light Secretaryship of State (so that he could concentrate his talents on the management of Parliament as his party's House Leader) and Lamontagne requested the Presidency of the Privy Council (so that he could devote most of his attention to the problem of French-English relations, which both he and Pearson regarded as the new administration's greatest challenge). Some of the other appointments (William Benidickson to Mines; Arthur Laing to Northern Affairs; Jack Nicholson to Forestry; Jack

Garland to Revenue; Roger Teillet to Veterans Affairs; J. Watson MacNaught to Solicitor General; Azellus Denis to Post Office; Jean Paul Deschatelets to Public Works; Hédard Robichaud to Fisheries and George McIlraith to Transport) owed more to party loyalty than individual talent. Harry Hays, the former mayor of Calgary, was moved into Agriculture for the very good reason that he was the only Liberal elected between Winnipeg and the British Columbia border. A minor surprise was the sudden elevation to the relatively senior Immigration portfolio of Guy Favreau, a Montreal lawyer who had yet to make his maiden speech in the Commons.*

NO GROUP WAS MORE PLEASED about the coming changeover than Ottawa's senior civil servants. They had tried hard, often valiantly, to serve the Conservative Government, but John Diefenbaker's unrelieved suspicion of their motives had worn thin their loyalties. Although they made a remarkable effort to restrain their relief over the Pearson win within days they had begun to refer among themselves to the six Diefenbaker years as "the duration," like men who'd come safely through a long and painful war.

Despite this mood of elation their first contact with the new administration was strangely disturbing. It came on a weekday evening, just before the new government was sworn in, when several key civil servants were invited to attend a secret meeting at the Fourth Avenue home of Tom Kent. Their host, a self-contained, taut, intellectual Englishman who had joined the Pearson entourage in 1961, had since become the Liberal Leader's most important policy adviser, and had been largely responsible for drafting the party's 1962 and 1963 election platforms. No one at the time knew what his role in the new government was to be, but Kent cleared up any doubts that it would be a major one when he began the meeting by stating that it had been called on Lester Pearson's orders and that his intention was to outline the new government's policy objectives. He went over in detail exactly what the Pearson administration intended to accomplish before its sixty-day deadline, partly, he said, because he wanted to get the reaction of the civil service, but mostly so that some of the government's senior planners would make the necessary preparations for formal implementation of the ambitious proposals at hand. As Kent unfolded the long list of government intentions (in-

---

*Favreau had originally been offered the even more senior job of Transport Minister, but turned it down because he felt the job might create a conflict of interest with one of the clients in his former Montreal law firm.

cluding the broad outlines of Walter Gordon's first budget) he was met by strongly worded opposition, particularly from George Davidson, then head of the Bureau of Government Organization, Dave Golden, a former deputy minister who would shortly rejoin the government service, and Simon Reisman and Claude Isbister, two assistant deputy ministers of Finance.

These four contended that the Liberal program was not realistic, that the sheer mechanics of translating the many proposals into solid legislation simply could not be completed in sixty days. Kent reacted just as strongly, pointing out that he was not asking what might be done, but stating what *had* to be done. The exchange grew sharper when Kent let slip the remark that he had known the civil service was tired and disillusioned, but that until this meeting he hadn't realized how deeply the rot had set in.

After the conference was over, half a dozen of the bureaucrats stood around in the cool April evening on the sidewalk beside their cars. Their low talk reflected a disconsolate feeling that was all the more disquieting because it was so unexpected.

CHAPTER 2

Sixty Days A-Go-Go

T HE MOOD WAS ANYTHING BUT DISCONSOLATE at noon on April 22, 1963 – that first and most buoyant day of decision – when the Pearson Government was sworn into office. Reporters had been standing around like mendicants on the red-carpeted stairway just inside the Governor General's residence since shortly before 10 o'clock waiting to be given the names on the new cabinet roster, gossiping, speculating, laughing, feeling despite their touted cynicism and objectivity much the same kind of optimism that pervaded the more partisan precincts of Ottawa that day. Finally, at 11:45 the ministers-designate began to arrive.

The familiar figures were easy to pick out. The old debating team of Pickersgill and Martin came happily in together: Paul Martin, with his own special patina of old-world statesmanship laid on thick for the occasion, and Jack Pickersgill, exuding the deceptive amiability of a crocodile in the sun. Mitchell Sharp was there, his face beaming like that of a very intelligent orange monkey. Walter Gordon, Pearson's trench-coated proconsul, materialized out of a Red Line cab, moving awkwardly through the door almost unnoticed in the crush, because there were too many new faces nobody could put names to. Finally, Mike Pearson arrived, and the new boys followed their leader into Governor General Georges Vanier's "Willingdon" bedchamber, where he was recovering from a slight heart attack, for the formal ceremony. (In the newspapers next day, the new ministry was called everything from "the most impressive array of brains and professional experts ever assembled in a Canadian Cabinet" by University of Toronto political economist J. T. McLeod in the *Toronto Daily Star* to "a line-up of drones and bores and inadequates" by Douglas Fisher, the NDP M.P. and columnist for the Toronto *Telegram*.)

While the excitement was going on in Rideau Hall, downtown on Parliament Hill the final phases of the changeover were taking place. Promptly at noon, the switchboard girl in the External Affairs wing of the East Block stopped answering the telephone with "Mr Green's office" and began to say "Mr Martin's office" instead. On the second floor in the Prime Minister's suite, Pearson's longtime secretary, Mary Macdonald, stood at a window, watching the Peace Tower clock strike twelve, in what she later described as "a funny, lonely moment." Then she went back to processing answers to the many congratulatory telegrams that Pearson had received from statesmen on every continent.

That afternoon at three the new cabinet held its initial meeting. Lester Pearson walked into the Privy Council chamber for the first time as prime minister and hesitated a symbolic second before sitting down in the uncomfortable red leather chair that has been used by every prime minister since the time of Sir John A. Macdonald. The fanfare was over now, and the new government set about its business, which was to provide political leadership through a period Pearson described on national television in Kennedyesque terms as "not an easy time . . . but a time to excite the daring, to test the strong and to give new promise to the timid . . . a time of direction and decision."

When Cabinet broke up, the ministers dispersed to take over their departments. Some were so new to office they got lost. (Walter Gordon wandered into the Confederation Building which houses the Department of Finance offices and told the inquiring elevator operator: "I don't know where I'm going.") Paul Hellyer was still so stirred by the animosity of the election campaign that he refused a briefing on defence problems from Gordon Churchill, his predecessor. But most takeovers were uneventful and for the next three weeks ministers and their staffs were busy preparing for the opening of Parliament on May 16. Under the impact of the Sixty Days of Decision slogan, Ottawa crackled with activity. When Liberals met, their conversations were shorn of lengthy explanations and cautious definitions. Everyone was dedicated to action. Cabinet sat in virtually continual session, mapping legislation and carefully rationing out daily parcels of press releases to heighten the Sixty Days atmosphere. For a while, friends greeted new ministers with the quip: "Made a decision today?" But the line soon grew tiresome.

11

THE PRIME MINISTER'S immediate concern was to repair, at least on a personal level, the damage he felt the Diefenbaker Government had inflicted on Canada's external stature. On May 1 he flew to London for an official call on Harold Macmillan. He addressed the British Cabinet, dined with the Queen, and though nothing specific was accomplished, the visit was judged a success. "Mr Pearson has at a stroke restored the sense of intimate and understanding partnership that Britons used to associate with Canada," wrote Nicholas Carroll, diplomatic correspondent of the *Sunday Times*. "All trace of the quarrels and tension that unhappily characterised Mr Diefenbaker's Conservative rule seems to have been swept away by his visit."

Five days after returning from the United Kingdom, Pearson went to meet President John F. Kennedy at Hyannis Port, Massachusetts. Over lunch and dinner, before the family fireplace, the two men talked for most of ten hours, obviously enjoying each other's company. By the end of their conversation, Canadian-American relations seemed to be set on a new path. Pearson agreed, as he had pledged during the election campaign, to negotiate a nuclear warhead agreement with the Americans.* Talks on the Columbia River Treaty would be resumed. The U.S.-Canadian cabinet committees on defence (which had not met since 1960) and economic affairs were re-activated. "The general effect of the meeting at Hyannis Port," wrote Walter Lippmann, dean of American commentators, "has been that of a good scrubbing and a cool shower after a muddy brawl."

One direct result of Hyannis Port's pleasant afterglow was that Lester Pearson let Walter Gordon know, soon after his return to Ottawa, that it seemed as good a time as any to go ahead with the Canadianization measures the Finance Minister was planning for his first budget, on the theory that relations with the United States were at such a friendly pitch they could stand the minor disruption of a few nationalistic laws.

Gordon, at this point, was in undisputed command of the Liberal policy apparatus. Nearly every initiative taken during the Sixty Days was inspired by the Minister of Finance. Gordon epitomized the political and fiscal competence the Liberals were pledged to provide and Pearson's faith in him was hard to exaggerate. During the 1963 campaign he had confided to a reporter, only half in jest: "If I had my

*These negotiations were finally completed with an exchange of diplomatic notes on August 16, although the warheads were not installed at the North Bay Bomarc site until 2300 hours EST on December 31. The missiles were declared operational at 1349 hours EST on January 16, 1964, and have been rusting in their cradles ever since.

choice, I'd go away on a long holiday to Florida after we're elected, and let Walter run the country."

WALTER GORDON, WITH THE UNLIMITED CONFIDENCE his past record had inspired, was facing with equanimity the self-imposed task of tabling a budget within eight weeks of taking office. To meet his objectives, the budget would have to perform three major functions. It would have to move the national accounts significantly toward a balance (the Diefenbaker administration's uninterrupted string of deficits had added nearly three billion dollars to the national debt); it would have to reflect Gordon's conviction that Ottawa must interfere actively to halt the American takeover of Canadian business assets; and, finally, it would have to stimulate the economy in a way that would relieve what he thought were abnormally high unemployment rates. More important than any of these, the document was meant to affirm that management of the nation's finances had been returned to competent, responsible hands. John Diefenbaker hadn't exposed his administration to a full-scale budget debate for two years; international confidence in Canada's economy still had not fully recovered from his 1962 devaluation crisis.

These would have been ambitious objectives even for a budget prepared in normal circumstances, which allow for a four-month gestation process of hearing briefs, consulting officials, formulating laws, and drafting and redrafting the speech itself. But circumstances were far from normal.

IDEALLY, THE DEPARTMENT OF FINANCE should be the synthesist of creative policies within the federal bureaucracy, since all ideas that require the expenditure of money are funnelled through its officials. But Gordon came to Finance at a time when this was no longer true. Under the ultra-conservative stewardship of Gordon's predecessor, Donald Fleming, Finance had been forced to expend most of its energy documenting why some of the Diefenbaker Government's more grandiose fiscal visions were impractical. As a result, by the spring of 1963 Finance had earned a reputation for caution that delustred its customary eminence. Most people in the department felt that their deputy minister, Ken Taylor, was an exhausted and dispirited man. After more than a quarter of a century of dedicated public service, Taylor no longer seemed to have either the energy or the commanding presence that his job demanded. Unhappily he and Walter Gordon were not, and never had been, compatible. As early as 1957 when he was heading the

13

Royal Commission on Canada's Economic Prospects, Gordon had suggested to his friend Mike Pearson that Taylor should be moved out of Finance, and Pearson had tentatively agreed to open up an ambassadorship for the deputy. But the election intervened, and six years later, when Gordon realized he'd soon be coming to Ottawa as Minister of Finance, he pleaded with Pearson to put in Taylor's place Bob Bryce, the superman of the civil service who was then Clerk of the Privy Council. Pearson agreed but refused to make the transfer effective until after the budget, because he felt that during the first few weeks of taking over the administration he would need Bryce's advice too urgently himself. It was then – during the period between the election and the swearing in of the new government – that Gordon informed the Prime Minister-designate that since he couldn't have Bryce, he would take the unusual step of introducing into the budget-making process his own group of advisers.

What he wanted was vigorous, action-oriented economists unsullied by the caution that he felt the Ottawa bureaucracy demanded of its members. He chose three young Torontonians: David Stanley, an investment executive with Wood, Gundy and Company; Martin O'Connell, a municipal finance expert from Harris and Partners Limited; and Geoff Conway, a tax specialist studying for his doctorate in economics at Harvard.* Gordon was so sure of himself and his triumvirate that he originally thought they wouldn't be needed for more than three weeks. This was why Stanley and O'Connell didn't ask for leave of absence from their companies' payrolls.† On May 8, a memo arrived on Gordon's desk from Ken Taylor. It was a submission to the Treasury Board, requesting funds for the recruitment of twenty-one new finance officers. The note confirmed Gordon's suspicion that the department was inadequately staffed and seemed to justify his need for outside help.

Despite openings at the bottom and grave weakness at the top, the Finance Department had at its middle rung three strong assistant deputy ministers, Wynne Plumptre, Simon Reisman and Claude Isbister, who were individually brilliant and collectively effective. All three knew Gordon well, but Reisman, a spirited economist with strong convictions tempered by a wry sense of the possible, was the only one who had worked with Gordon before, while serving as assistant director of research for the Royal Commission on Canada's Economic Prospects.

*There was also a fourth Gordon adviser, R. J. Anderson of Clarkson, Gordon and Company, who went to Ottawa from May 7 to May 16 to carry out a study of government spending estimates.

†Conway was paid $50 a day plus expenses, for a total of $5,164.66 from April 21 to July 1, 1963.

On May 15 Walter Gordon took a minor decision that turned out to be a major irritant in his relations with the department. Instead of working on the budget in his permanent office in the Confederation Building, he decided to move into his Commons office on Parliament Hill. Civil servants who wanted to confer with him had to trudge a long way for an audience. This wouldn't have mattered except that it prevented the establishment of the climate of after-hours intimacy that usually develops between a minister and his officials during the writing of a budget. Had this rapport developed, the assistant deputies might have been able to head off, over Dixie cups of midnight coffee, some of the disastrous events that followed. They might have had the opportunity of dispelling the Minister's prejudice that the department was full of drones.

The three outside advisers, meanwhile, moved into the Minister's departmental office. They did so only because it was empty and air conditioned, but their presence in a place normally associated with authority, coupled with Gordon's physical separation from his officials, underlined the growing estrangement between Gordon and his department.

The object that came to symbolize this mood was a bright red IBM typewriter that Gordon ordered for his private secretary, Nancy Burpee. His initial request for the machine produced only a closely reasoned, six-page memorandum from the Treasury Board explaining why government-issue typewriters had to be grey. But Gordon insisted and arranged to get the scarlet machine himself. There it sat, right outside his office, and every passing civil servant glared at the saucy typewriter, as if enough dirty looks aimed at it could somehow repress the highly developed sense of the irregular that possessed this strange new minister.

ON THE TWENTY-FIFTH DAY OF DECISION – May 16 – Parliament opened with an emotional Throne Speech, outlining an avalanche of legislative measures. Lester Pearson was a happy man that afternoon. He played ball with his grandchildren Paul and Barbara on the lawn of 24 Sussex Drive after the ceremonies. Then the whole family drove to the official summer residence at Harrington Lake, where the Prime Minister and his brother Vaughan went fishing while everyone else played croquet.

In retrospect that day of the Throne Speech was the new administration's last golden moment. Almost immediately afterwards, the Liberals' grand Sixty Days design began to fall apart. The mechanics of Commons procedure meant that the combination of the Throne Speech debate, a supply motion and the government's motion to set up a special committee on defence would exhaust Parliament's time until June 7 – the forty-seventh day of decision. This interval not only prevented the government from introducing new legislation, it also gave John Diefenbaker a chance to rally his party.

The Conservative Leader, who according to all the rules of politics ought to have behaved like a humble has-been, emerged instead as an angry gladiator intent on toppling Pearson's minority administration. His presence continued to dominate the Ottawa scene. In the House of Commons, Liberal frontbenchers, including Jack Pickersgill and Paul Martin, still occasionally addressed him (to their own chagrin and the Opposition's guffaws) as "the Right Honourable the Prime Minister" and when Ormond Dier, an External Affairs official, was briefing Pearson on the protocol for his London visit, he began one set of instructions with the phrase: "And after that, sir, you and Mrs Diefenbaker . . ."

All this time, work on the budget was proceeding in the Finance Department. Gordon held his first plenary budget meeting on May 25. Twelve senior officials outlined their pet policy suggestions, only to have most of them contradicted by the three outside advisers with Gordon's silent but implicit approval.

After this meeting Stanley, O'Connell and Conway were regarded by the normally imperturbable Finance officials with something close to horror and referred to sarcastically in their conversations as "the bright boys," or even more bitterly as "the carpetbaggers." Such resentment was not unnatural. At that first budget meeting there were half a dozen of the best economic minds in the country. Their collective experience was a distillation of a quarter-century of guiding the Canadian economy through every imaginable crisis including depression, war, recovery, and boom. Yet their advice was being peremptorily discarded for that of what seemed to them three well-meaning but untried youths.

When the meeting broke up at midday, Bob Bryce (who had been sitting in as the PM's representative), Louis Rasminsky, Governor of the Bank of Canada, Simon Reisman and Claude Isbister had a gloomy lunch together. They agreed that this budget had every prospect of becoming the least articulate statement of the country's financial position ever produced but no one seemed quite sure what, if anything, could be done about it.

That afternoon, when Walter Gordon tried to close off the discussion by saying he would have his advisers draft the budget speech, Reisman broke in to remind the Minister that whatever else he thought the Department capable of, it certainly knew how to draft budgets. Gordon agreed to give the officials a chance and seemed delighted when they assured him they'd have a draft ready in two days. The document, a group effort written largely by Wynne Plumptre, landed on Gordon's desk on schedule and the following morning Ken Taylor proudly informed his assistant deputies that the Minister liked the draft and intended to follow it. For a few hours the mood at Finance changed. The whole budget operation now seemed to be in its proper context: the Department would write the budget, with the "bright boys" acting only as personal assistants to the Minister.

But on May 29 Gordon called Taylor into his office quixotically to reject not just the departmental draft but also its whole philosophy and approach. "It isn't different enough," he said. "It doesn't reflect the spirit of Sixty Days." There would be no more general meetings on the budget. It would be written by Gordon's own helpers. The "bright boys" had taken over.

From that moment relations between the Minister and his department went on a cold-war footing. The officials retreated, each performing only the minor tasks assigned to him. Since none of his subordinates in the Department knew what Gordon thought, they could not do what he wanted. "We all got our own little dog's breakfast of crap to look after and that was that," one assistant deputy later recalled.

The budget's main fiscal measures came under the command of the Gordon advisers. Stanley was assigned to work up a plan for the Canada Development Corporation, O'Connell to supervise the details of the municipal loan fund, Conway to formulate a tax designed to prevent the takeover of Canadian corporations by foreign investors. The Department faded into a passive, background role. Even the budget White Paper, usually an uncontroversial document reviewing the previous year's fiscal trends, had to be rewritten on Gordon's orders because he felt the original draft was too apologetic for the policies of Donald Fleming.

At one point, when an assistant deputy found his way into the Minister's office barred by the "bright boys," he gave them a scathing lecture on protocol. What really bothered the Finance officials was that the three young men not only had direct access to the Minister but that they went out of their way to mobilize the opinion of other government department heads behind their point of view, so that they were, in effect, acting as three deputy ministers, while freezing out all the permanent officials. The atmosphere didn't improve when David Stanley, in an interview with Clive Baxter of *The Financial Post*, boasted that "businessmen will be a little shaken by some of our legislation." Senior

Finance officials began vaguely to discuss their resignations, but with their own deputy minister unwilling to take a lead or even make objections, they felt nothing could be done. Isbister and Reisman submitted detailed memoranda, attacking the development corporation and the takeover tax as premature and not well enough thought out. Justice Department officials took a look at the takeover tax proposal and declared it an administrative monstrosity. One assistant deputy minister of Finance even broke protocol and cornered Gordon in private to warn against the practicability of the takeover tax. "I don't believe you can do this and stay in office," Gordon was told during that particular confrontation. The Minister of Finance was polite but unyielding.

One reason for Gordon's self-confidence was the enthusiastic response the budget had prompted from the Prime Minister. He had been shown a preliminary draft on June 3 and the penultimate version on June 7. "He saw it all the way through," Gordon later recalled. "While they were my ideas, he knew all about them, and as a matter of fact he thought it was a better budget than I did." The controversial takeover tax proposal, taken out of the budget and put back several times, finally stayed in when Pearson (emboldened by Gordon's assurance that it was workable) suggested it would give the budget "some kick."

The final version of the budget was dictated by Gordon from a draft prepared by David Stanley, and at 8 p.m. on June 13, the Finance Minister, dressed in a charcoal-grey suit with one button missing, delivered his maiden budget.* The document appeared to fulfil all the objectives Gordon had set for himself. He moved the nation's finances $360 millions a year closer to balance by removing the 11 per cent federal sales-tax exemption for building materials and production machinery. He began the process of reversing the American acquisition of Canada's corporate assets by instituting a 30 per cent takeover tax levied on sales of shares in listed Canadian companies to non-resident corporations and individuals. To further encourage Canadian ownership, the 15 per cent withholding tax on dividends paid to non-residents was reduced to 10 per cent for companies whose shares were at least a quarter Canadian owned, and increased to 20 per cent for firms with

*An unusual precaution taken that night was that Wynne Plumptre flew to Washington and just as Gordon rose to speak in the Commons, he began to brief U.S. Undersecretary of the Treasury Robert Roosa on the document's contents. Roosa made no comment, but next morning when Plumptre called on the American State Department, he found himself confronted by angry men.

a lower proportion of domestic ownership. To help combat unemployment, Gordon established a special allowance to employers hiring workers over forty-five years of age who had been out of work for six months and provided for a faster depreciation allowance to companies with the requisite 25 per cent Canadian ownership. The budget speech was an unusually partisan document, containing such statements as: "Canada is beginning to recover from the loss of confidence resulting from the financial and economic mismanagement of the previous administration."

That night in his parliamentary office Gordon threw a glittering cocktail party. His family was there, as were most of the cabinet, the administration's favoured journalists and, of course, Stanley, O'Connell and Conway, gracefully accepting everyone's congratulations. On that first night few people seemed to understand the budget's implications. The only unhappy note in the festivities was heard when E. J. Benson, the Liberal M.P. for Kingston and Gordon's parliamentary secretary, together with a few Finance officials broke away from the main party for a more sober discussion of the budget's effects. Benson was shocked when one of the men from Finance, who had drunk more than his colleagues, solemnly declared: "This is an ignorant budget prepared by ignorant people. Your victory party is premature. Just you wait till this hits the fan."

THE DISINTEGRATION OF GORDON'S BUDGET began the very next day. During the Commons question period Douglas Fisher, the M.P. for Port Arthur and deputy leader of the NDP, asked Gordon "to assure us that he and his government officials alone prepared the budget speech without the assistance of outside consultants or ghost writers from Toronto." Fisher's suspicions had been roused by the partisan nature of the budget speech, the fact that Stanley (whom he'd known while studying at the University of Toronto) had been in Ottawa all through the budget preparations, and rumours he'd heard about dissension in Finance. Gordon didn't know how to handle the question, and when Jack Pickersgill urgently whispered "Don't answer!", he merely said: "As Minister of Finance I take full and sole responsibility for everything which was contained in the budget." At five o'clock the same day, after a hurried conference with the Prime Minister, Gordon interrupted House proceedings to admit that the three advisers had indeed helped him and for the first time made their names public. He apologized for his previous hesitancy in naming them but pointed out that since they had all taken an oath of secrecy, there was no reason for Opposition alarm. John Diefenbaker got up, lectured Gordon for a while, then accepted his explanation. In the officials' gallery, Tom Kent, who had been moved in by the PM to handle the sudden crisis, made a surreptitious "V for Victory" sign to one of the "bright boys."

But the NDP wasn't satisfied. Fisher came back to the offensive and soon won an admission from Gordon that two of the advisers had remained in their companies' employ while working on the budget. This exchange rekindled Diefenbaker's interest and suddenly the Opposition sensed it had hold of a major issue.

While the House and the nation mulled over the intelligence that two of the budget's advisers had remained on private payrolls, Eric Kierans, then president of the Montreal Stock Exchange, was preparing a letter to the Minister of Finance, which he released in Ottawa on June 18. He condemned the budget's 30 per cent takeover tax as "utter nonsense," and wrote: "The financial capitals of the world have just about had enough from Canada. Last Friday, the initial reaction to the budget was one of bewilderment and dismay. Yesterday, it was anger and scorn. Today, our friends in the western world fully realize that we don't want them or their money and that Canadians who deal with them in even modest amounts will suffer a 30% expropriation of the assets involved. And their reaction? If that's what Canadians want, let them have it!" Although Howard Graham, head of the Toronto Stock Exchange, cautiously maintained that the takeover tax was "administratively feasible but inconvenient," Kierans saw it only as "an axe to murder the record of trust and confidence between Canada and other countries."

Under close scrutiny large questions began to be raised about the problems of administering the 30 per cent levy. The difficulty of identifying the real owners of shares traded and the impossibility of preventing sales through foreign exchanges were some of the more obvious difficulties. Kierans came to see Gordon in the late afternoon of June 18 along with some senior members of his board of governors and demanded the Minister withdraw the measure immediately. He advised his associates in front of Gordon to sell short their stocks in Canadian companies to force immediate action.

Horrified, Gordon realized that he could have a full-scale stock market panic on his hands by next morning, and the market did in fact begin to plummet as soon as trading opened. Gordon hurriedly arranged a conference with Pearson, still convinced that the takeover tax could be made to work, but aware that he couldn't demonstrate its administrative feasibility if one of the country's major stock exchanges refused to co-operate. When Pearson urged him to withdraw the measure, Gordon agreed and so informed the "bright boys," who had formulated the tax, on his way into the Commons on June 19. As he rose to make his announcement, it was 2:41 p.m., still nineteen minutes before eastern stock markets closed, and many traders made a considerable profit as shares roared upward as much as ten points. This was a blunder of major proportions, since it is an axiom of parliamentary procedure to save any announcements that might affect stock prices until after the markets have closed. As news of the takeover tax's withdrawal came in over the Dow-Jones ticker, traders on the floor of the Montreal Stock Exchange marched into Kierans' office, hoisted him on their shoulders, and singing "He's a jolly good fellow," paraded around the Exchange floor.

In the House of Commons, Walter Gordon was compounding his error by assuring John Diefenbaker that he had informed no one of the impending withdrawal of the tax "other than the Prime Minister and certain members of the cabinet," although he had, in fact, notified his three young consultants. Late that afternoon, the "bright boys" were riding in a taxi, heading for an Ottawa department store, where Geoff Conway planned to buy his eldest daughter a bicycle for her birthday. The cab driver started to sound off about "the three sharpies who'd made a killing on Bay Street" that afternoon and looked puzzled when his passengers roared with laughter. "If this ever gets back to Bay Street, we'll lose our union cards," one of them remarked.

But there was little to laugh about. The whole budget, not just the takeover tax, was coming under attack from every source of informed Canadian opinion. The quips circulating at Ottawa's Rideau Club that noon reflected accurately the national mood: "Donald Fleming's budgets may have been pre-Keynesian," went one punchline, "but Walter Gordon's are positively pre-Cambrian." Russell Irvine, research director of the Canadian Labour Congress, declared that Walter Gordon was "unfit to manage the economic affairs of Antarctica, let alone Canada." John Meyer, financial editor of the Montreal *Gazette*, quoted a St James Street broker as commenting: "More harm has been done to Canada's reputation by this one budget than by all the actions of the Diefenbaker Government put together." The *Globe and Mail*, the Victoria *Daily Times* and the Winnipeg *Free Press* editorially called for Gordon's resignation.

The next day was June 20 – the sixtieth day of decision. But the distance in spirit from the gay expectations of April 22 seemed more than the sum of sixty days in time. The platform with which the Liberal Party had gained office – a promise of lucid, managerial competence to contrast with the bungling and indecision of John Diefenbaker – had largely been forfeited. With his budget falling apart and his political ineptitude revealed for all the world to see, Walter Gordon decided that morning he would resign. He went to the Prime Minister's office at 9:15 a.m. and declared that he intended to resign if the PM felt he was causing the government embarrassment. Pearson replied he would accept the resignation only if Gordon felt he couldn't carry on, though a transfer to another portfolio might be appropriate. This Gordon refused to consider and the two men parted, both acutely uncomfortable in their unaccustomed roles.

Pearson immediately called Mitchell Sharp and asked him to take over Finance if and when Gordon resigned. After a few more conversations with key colleagues, the PM telephoned Gordon at 10:15 to ask the crucial question: had the Finance Minister lost confidence in himself? The answer was a firm "No," though Pearson never did indicate the state of his own confidence in Gordon.

It was a brief encounter and it settled nothing. Yet from that day on the relationship between Lester Pearson and Walter Gordon – a thirty-year association that perhaps more than any other single factor set the original tone of the Pearson Government – was irrevocably changed. Each man had been tested and each to some degree found wanting.

COLIN CAMERON, THE NDP MEMBER for Nanaimo, B.C., spoke for the nation that afternoon in the Commons when he looked over at the Liberal front benches and fiercely exclaimed: "For heaven's sake, pull yourselves together! We cannot afford any more of these follies, any more of these ineptitudes, because all the rest of us Canadians have to cringe along with you at the ridiculous spectacle you are presenting to the rest of the world."

Rumours about the resignation of Walter Gordon were fanned again next day (June 21) when several newspapers published stories predicting his impending departure. This speculation was based on the fact that Richard O'Hagan, the PM's press secretary, had polled some members of the Parliamentary Press Gallery on whether or not they thought Gordon should go. Later in the morning, when Pearson interrupted a cabinet meeting to deny the resignation rumour, the industrial average on the Toronto Stock Exchange dropped four points – a cruel indicator of the business community's verdict about Gordon's worth. In the afternoon, under intense questioning from Stanley Knowles of the NDP, Gordon admitted (contrary to his previous statement) that he *had* informed his three outside consultants about the withdrawal of the takeover tax. To his other blunders, Gordon now had added the very serious charge of having misled the House of Commons. "Inexperience is one thing," editorialized the *Ottawa Journal*, "bad judgment is something else. But open and knowing defiance of Parliament and its traditions is too much."

That day, Walter Gordon sat in lonely reverie in his parliamentary office. Not one of his cabinet or parliamentary colleagues called or came near to offer either advice or sympathy. His telephone, which had been ringing almost continuously since budget day, fell silent.

Probably the most unusual aspect of the unusual budget debate which followed for most of the next two weeks was that so few important figures in the Liberal Party rose to the Finance Minister's defence. His cabinet colleagues, sensing that he had withheld the real nature of his budget from them, demonstrated little feeling of responsibility for his downfall. They resented his failure to live up to his billing as a fiscal wizard; even the younger members of Parliament were annoyed because his behaviour seemed to discredit the whole progressive wing of the party.

The Liberal Old Guard, led by Jack Pickersgill, was something less than distraught over Gordon's fate. After the 1961 policy rally, the party's old-line establishment had faded in significance, as the extent of Pearson's trust in his friend Walter Gordon forced them out of one position of influence after another. Now, the Pearson Cabinet began visibly to split into pro-Gordon and anti-Gordon factions as ministers in private sessions with their supporters hurriedly dissociated themselves from Gordon's policies and methods. The only colleagues who remained loyal to Gordon were Guy Favreau, C. M. "Bud" Drury, Judy LaMarsh, Jack Garland and, to a lesser extent, Mitchell Sharp.

Tom Kent, who had not been involved in the budget's preparation, had been appointed by the PM to head the rescue squad. He had drafted notes for a speech defending the use of outside advisers, but nobody any more senior than Donald Macdonald, the M.P. for Rosedale and parliamentary assistant to the Minister of Justice, was willing to deliver it. When Sharp was told about the problem, he volunteered to make the speech and on June 24 he delivered a biting counter-attack. He challenged the Opposition Leader (who had been attempting to cast a shadow over Gordon's personal honour) to produce evidence or hold his tongue. It was Sharp's first chance to get back at the Conservative Leader for having used, on January 20, 1958, a confidential report on Canada's economic conditions (written by Sharp when he was Deputy Minister of Trade and Commerce) to ridicule Pearson and his Liberals. At the end of Sharp's speech, eleven harrowing days after the budget debate had started, the Liberals defeated, 113 to 73, an unprecedented

Conservative motion of non-confidence, not in the budget but in the Minister of Finance. The NDP abstained in disgust.

The Sixty Days madness had finally exhausted itself, and the Liberals could reckon the slim sum of their achievements. Legislation passed included only four important bills: establishment of a Department of Industry; creation of the Economic Council of Canada; setting up of the municipal loan fund; and expansion of the Atlantic Development Board's terms of reference. An avalanche of major and minor administrative decisions had also been pushed forward, but most of the government's election platform remained more promise than reality. In both the 1962 and the 1963 campaigns the Liberals had stressed that, if elected, they would implement a series of spectacular measures, including a national development corporation, a national scholarship plan, a municipal loan board, a national contributory pension scheme, a national medicare plan, and national marketing boards for agricultural products. The Liberal strategists had not given enough consideration to the fact that for constitutional reasons none of these pledges could be discharged without the support of the provincial governments.

More specifically, few federal Liberals were sufficiently aware of the vast changes that had been taking place in Quebec between the winter of 1962, when most of the Liberal platform had been written, and the spring of 1963, when it came up for implementation. In the interval, Jean Lesage had won a powerful majority mandate based on his *Maître chez nous* slogan, a group of supremely skilled, highly nationalistic intellectuals had moved into commanding positions within Quebec's civil service, and instead of being satisfied with sharing in Ottawa's initiatives, French Canada was now out to wrestle the national government for a new, meaningful equality. Most of the Pearson Government's brave legislative schemes foundered on provincial objections. The municipal loan fund was saved at an emergency federal-provincial conference through a complete surrender by Ottawa.*

The June 24 vote assured the government's survival and some of the pressure lifted. But the budget continued to crumble. Even some of its minor provisions weren't bearing up under close scrutiny. In one clause, for instance, Gordon tried to get at executives who use yachts for business entertaining by narrowing the 11 per cent sales-tax exemption on ship repairs to vessels used for commercial purposes. Embarrassed government lawyers were forced to report to the Minister that this meant taxes would have to be paid on fixing warships of the Royal

*The changes in Quebec and their implications for the federal government are discussed in Chapter 21.

Canadian Navy, which no one had thought to exempt. Serious protests were flowing in, at a peak rate of forty telegrams an hour, aimed at Gordon's proposal to lift the 11 per cent tax exemption on building materials and production machinery. The Canadian Construction Association estimated that projects across the country worth $120 millions would be cancelled; the printing trades complained that their industry would collapse because the measure inadvertently set a levy on typesetting. One enraged builder from northwestern Ontario called Gordon's office to ask for an appointment so that he could "shoot the minister," and was momentarily taken aback when a secretary calmly replied: "You'll have to get in line."

Gordon had chosen to lift the exemption (which brought the construction trades to the same tax level as other industrial sectors) because he preferred this alternative to raising either corporate or personal income tax. A similar suggestion for increasing government revenues had been worked out by Finance for the Diefenbaker Government but it provided for compensating cuts in corporation taxes that Gordon ignored. There was inadequate consultation with the Department of National Revenue, so that when the building lobbies started their pressure, they had the added force of legitimate grievances against imperfect laws.

Throughout the early part of the budget debate, Finance had cut Gordon loose. Instead of exercising the usual precaution of having two senior officials on call in the parliamentary galleries, it sent no one to lend him support. Now, the Department rallied for the salvage operation, with Claude Isbister carrying most of the burden. On July 8, Gordon made what was, in effect, a second budget speech. Nine major changes were included – the withholding-tax increase was abandoned; the sales-tax exemption was cut to an initial 4 per cent. Gordon had fought hard to retain the 11 per cent level but only two ministers would support him and by the time he gave in there was as much pressure from the Liberal benches behind him as from the Opposition.

Although he couldn't know it at the time (since there is always a considerable lag between what's actually happening to the economy and the publication of statistics about it) Gordon's first budget was based on an erroneous premise. He believed that unemployment was still the nation's main problem. Later statistical indices showed that by the spring of 1963 an economic recovery was well under way. Most of the Liberal platform had been written in the winter of 1962-63 when Donald Fleming was trying to "talk down" the dollar and unemployment was at a peak. Hypnotized by their neo-New Frontier slogans

("We'll get the Canadian economy moving again . . ."), the Liberals had planned most of their initial legislation to combat a disappearing business slump.

After tabling his revised budget, Gordon came down with a bad case of stomach flu, so that it wasn't until July 17 that he first exposed himself to national television. "I don't suppose many people would think I'm a very good politician," he told CBC interviewers Roy Faibish and Warner Troyer. "But perhaps I'm a little tougher than I may look. I've had an unpleasant time but I fancy that when people understand the budget they'll begin to think it has a good deal in its favour."

THE DAY AFTER HIS TELEVISION APPEARANCE, Gordon thought his ordeal was finally at an end and he planned a brief holiday. Instead, on July 18 there began a chain of events that was to put both Walter Gordon and the Canadian economy to an even more severe test than the budget fiasco just concluded.

A few minutes after 10 o'clock, Francis Linville, counsellor for economic affairs at the United States Embassy in Ottawa, phoned to request an immediate interview with the Minister for Merlyn Trued, head of the international finance section of the United States Treasury, who had flown up unannounced from Washington with news of "an urgent development." Gordon invited the American emissary and Linville to meet him at the Rideau Club for lunch and arranged for Bob Bryce, Wynne Plumptre and Bob Beattie (Deputy Governor of the Bank of Canada and Acting Governor during the absence of Louis Rasminsky) to join them. When they sat down, Gordon ordered a drink, read Trued's message, jumped up and rushed back to his office, trailed by his advisers, to prepare a statement for Parliament.

The news that had upset Gordon so much was the end result of a meeting that had taken place about two weeks earlier in the hushed inner sanctum of the White House between John F. Kennedy, Defense Secretary Robert McNamara and Robert Roosa, the Undersecretary of the Treasury for Monetary Affairs. McNamara was congratulating himself on having cut $30 millions from his overseas defence budget, but Kennedy shrugged his shoulders, and said "What's the use?" He showed the Defense Secretary a *New York Times* article on the floating of a large Hydro-Québec bond issue on Wall Street. The President then instructed Roosa to draw up a program that would halt or slow down this kind of drain on the United States balance-of-payments position. During the first half of 1963, the outflow had become a flood. Drastic action was required to protect the American dollar. Half the

1963 deficit was accounted for by foreign borrowing in the New York money market, where Canadian firms, municipalities and provincial governments had, during the year's first six months, sold $607 millions' worth of new stocks and bonds – 67 per cent of all new foreign securities taken up during that time.* To help halt this fiscal haemorrhage, the Kennedy administration proposed to establish an interest equalization tax, which would raise the effective interest cost to foreign borrowers by about 1.25 per cent. Since Wall Street had previously offered the advantage of interest rates about 1 per cent lower than those on other money markets, the effect of the tax would presumably be to drive foreign borrowers back into domestic lending operations.

At precisely the same moment that Gordon was rushing across Wellington Street to assess the impact on Canada of the new United States measure, Secretary of the Treasury Douglas Dillon was briefing Washington reporters on the implications of the new tax. It would apply to twenty-two nations, he noted, but Canada would be the most severely affected. In the House of Commons Gordon conceded this point, but added that it would be unwise for him to comment further until there was more time to study the U.S. proposals. Gordon hurried back to his office and as he passed Brian Land, his executive assistant, he shouted over his shoulder: "This time we've got a *real* crisis on our hands."

The first concrete reaction to the Kennedy proposal came from the shrewd floor traders on the Toronto Stock Exchange. Between noon and one o'clock, a selling wave hit the market, pushing the industrial index down 8.36 points. The downward pressure reflected their fear that the tax would drive United States investors out of their substantial ($457 millions in 1962) Canadian stock purchases, and that to escape the tax Americans would sell off all their Canadian portfolios. That evening in Ottawa, Louis Rasminsky was hurriedly recalled from a fishing holiday in the Saguenay country and Paul Martin sent for American Ambassador Walton Butterworth to inform him that Canada would apply for an exemption from the new law.

Next morning panic set in. On the Toronto Stock Exchange the stampede to sell pushed the industrial index down 15.29 points, one of the sharpest declines in the market's recorded history. The combination of Gordon's nationalistic budget and the Kennedy measure had so frightened the financial managers of some American subsidiaries in Canada that they hurriedly began to move dividends and accumulated

*Most of this amount was due to the Hydro-Québec loan taken out to finance the cost of nationalizing the province's electricity-producing firms, although the full amount of the loan was drawn down over the following fifteen months.

cash reserves out of the country. Much of this fiscal hysteria was based on the business community's conviction that a jump in Canadian interest rates would be required to re-attract American investment into Canada over the barrier of the new tax. Higher interest rates would also have meant a slowdown in capital expansion and a resultant leap in unemployment. To ward off that particular political evil, businessmen feared Ottawa would either impose foreign exchange controls or cut the value of the dollar further. As investors began to hedge against such a devaluation by buying U.S. currency, the selloff of Canadian dollars accelerated to unprecedented levels. Between Thursday noon and Friday evening, Canada's foreign exchange reserves were depleted by $110 millions – a run that surpassed even the shattering drain on the exchange fund of any two days during the 1962 devaluation crisis. By Friday night, Bank of Canada agents across the country were teletyping Ottawa that unless emergency action was taken an even bigger outflow could be expected Monday morning. National bankruptcy had become a possibility. Now it was essential for Canada to win an exemption from the Kennedy proposal over the weekend.

A council of desperation gathered in Gordon's office on Saturday morning, while Charles Ritchie, Canada's ambassador in Washington, was asked to arrange, as tactfully as possible, that senior United States Treasury officials remain on call throughout the weekend. After their briefing from Gordon, Louis Rasminsky, Wynne Plumptre and Ed Ritchie (an Assistant Undersecretary of State for External Affairs specializing in American-Canadian relations) flew to Washington in a Department of Transport Viscount. Their confrontation with the Americans took place in the Treasury Building office of Secretary Douglas Dillon, who was flanked by George Ball, the American Undersecretary of State, Stan Surrey, Assistant Secretary of the Treasury for Tax Policy, and Robert Roosa. It didn't seem altogether inappropriate to the Canadian officials that an eclipse of the sun darkened the sky and unnatural shadows melodramatically skipped on the White House lawn across the street as the two sets of experts argued about Canada's economic viability.

The Canadian case was put forward by Louis Rasminsky, an old hand at international finance who'd served his apprenticeship in the financial secretariat of the League of Nations and had gained the confidence of Washington monetary circles during his terms as executive director of the International Bank for Reconstruction and Development. With the ruminative manner of a professor sharing discoveries at an economics seminar, the Bank of Canada Governor pointed out that his country's trade deficit with the United States had for many years more than balanced the sales of Canadian securities to Americans. Canada therefore had helped to strengthen American balance-of-payments accounts and any discouragement of Canadian borrowing in the U.S. might eventually require a drastic reduction in Canadian imports which, in turn, would harm the American economy.*

The American officials were impressed by the weight and urgency of Rasminsky's case. They agreed to grant Canada a conditional exemption, admitting that they hadn't been fully aware of how closely the capital markets of the two countries had become integrated.† The revision did exempt new Canadian security issues from the tax, but only up to about $350 millions' worth a year. Significantly, the actual amount could be set at the President's discretion. In return, Canada undertook not to use the exemption to build up its exchange reserves beyond $2.7 billions.‡ On Monday the Toronto Stock Exchange industrial index climbed back eight points by one o'clock in the afternoon and monetary conditions returned to normal.§ The crisis had ended; only its implications remained to be studied.

These were considerable.

The fact that the President could exercise a veto over the extent of Canada's access to U S. capital meant that the country's prosperity had, in effect, come to depend not on the impersonal forces of the market but on American goodwill. The combination of a fixed exchange rate for the Canadian dollar and the agreement that exchange reserves

*Between 1952 and 1962, despite capital inflows from the U.S. of $8.5 billions, Canada's current-account deficit with the U.S. was $14 billions. The $5.5 billion difference (covered by Canada's current-account surpluses with the rest of the world and by Canadian gold production) helped to assist – not hinder – the U.S. balance-of-payments position.

†The agreement also set up the framework for future consultations. On February 10, 1965, when Lyndon Johnson imposed new curbs on direct U.S. investments abroad, he first telephoned Lester Pearson to check the wording of a paragraph in his announcement that applied to Canada and asked for an immediate reaction. When Pearson replied that he couldn't assess its implications by himself, Johnson told the Prime Minister: "O.K., I'll stall at this end, and if you have any changes, phone them to Doug Dillon within the next thirty minutes." Pearson called in Gordon, Rasminsky and Bryce, who rewrote the paragraph and telephoned Dillon. He accepted the Canadian draft with one inconsequential change. It was probably the first time in history that part of an American regulation had been drafted by Canadians.

‡This ceiling was reduced to $2.6 billions in December of 1965 and in May of 1966 it was cut again to $2.550 billions.

§To let Americans trade in Canadian securities despite the interest equalization tax, the Montreal and Toronto stock exchanges set up a "Z," or U.S. Curb, market in August of 1963. Ironically, this was exactly the kind of operation that might have made Walter Gordon's takeover tax administratively possible.

be limited reduced the flexibility of the country's monetary policy to an extent that made it only a slight exaggeration to call Canada "the 13th Federal Reserve District of the U.S." It meant monetary policy could not be effectively applied to restrain inflation. The supply of money could not be appreciably tightened when that process might force interest rates to a level that would attract U.S. funds, thereby adding to the Canadian exchange reserves beyond the permissible level. Monetary policy was, in fact, made largely subject to what the Federal Reserve Board was doing in the United States. John Diefenbaker was right when he told the Commons that such an arrangement was "not in keeping with the sovereignty of this nation." Scott Gordon, head of the Carleton University economics department, was even harsher in his criticism. "With one act," he said on the CBC-TV program *Explorations*, "we have put into the hands of the U.S. President more control over our economy than the past twenty years of growth of American investment in Canada represent." The strongest condemnation came from Fraser Robertson, financial columnist for the *Globe and Mail*, who wrote: "The major implication of the agreement is this: the Canadian Government now agrees that for the future Canada will be an economic satellite of the United States. Our financial stability, the level and direction of our trade, the capacity of our business to develop, the right of a private citizen even to take a trip to Buffalo, all are handed over to the safekeeping of Uncle Sam."

The interest equalization tax was finally signed into law by Lyndon Johnson on September 3, 1964. It was followed by increasingly tight restrictions on U.S. dollar exports, including the laying down of at first voluntary and later mandatory guidelines for direct United States investment abroad. By the late Sixties it was all too clear that Canada's ability to make economic policy suited to its own conditions had been gravely jeopardized by the events of July, 1963.

AT 10:56 P.M. ON AUGUST 2, 1963, PARLIAMENT finally adjourned for a summer recess. Thoughtful Liberals looked back, with barely concealed disbelief, on the record of their first three months in office. The round of legislative retreats, taken on the floor of the Commons in full view of a puzzled nation, seemed to have robbed the Pearson administration of the most valuable asset with which it had launched its stewardship on April 22: a supreme confidence in its own abilities. The dogma of the Liberal efficiency cult, so carefully nurtured during the late King and early St Laurent years, had been dissipated. It seemed as if the government remained in office not because it deserved to survive but only because no acceptable alternative administration was available.

A strange malaise gripped Ottawa. A sense of hopeless drift had replaced the exuberance of the Pearson Government's debut.

Every political regime has a dominant mood, a particular touch and tempo that sets it off and makes it distinctive. The trials and responses of the Liberal Government's first three months accurately foreshadowed its whole term in office. The sixty days of decision had unaccountably turned into ninety days of disaster, and the character of the man who was to be Prime Minister of Canada for the next five years was thrown into cruel relief.

PART TWO   *Paradox in Power*

It very often happens that the names of Canadian prime ministers become the political labels for the moods of their periods and the men themselves are eventually, if unfairly, held responsible for nearly everything that occurs in the country under their stewardships. In this process they acquire retroactive stereotypes: Mackenzie King is remembered as an occult manipulator and the King era as the time of our unawakened provincialism; Louis St Laurent is widely caricatured as a bloodless chairman of the board and the St Laurent period as the time of our smug prosperity; and John Diefenbaker continues to be thought of as a populist procrastinator and the Diefenbaker Years as the time when our pretentious pomposities exploded.

Although there was little difficulty in identifying the Pearson years as Canada's age of anxiety, the search for an appropriate tag to describe the man who lent his name to the period baffled and eluded his contemporaries. No journalistic formula seemed inclusive enough to capture adequately the real person behind the laugh-lined face and breezy exterior of Lester Bowles Pearson, the extraordinary, superordinary politician who for five turbulent years presided over Canada's government.

Because he was at the centre of national attention as Prime Minister, frustrated journalists were constantly attempting to invent a character for him and were perpetually discovering different versions of yet another "new Pearson." But the hunt for his real identity remained forever ungratified because Lester Pearson seemed deeply engaged in the same quest himself.

Circumstances formed the man. An idealist without any fixed goals, Pearson displayed a public personality that altered according to the pressures generated around him. Had the nature of his opposition been different, for instance, his behaviour in office and his government's record almost certainly would not have been the same. If George Hees had been the Leader of the Opposition during his tenure, Pearson might have frolicked his way through power; had it been Davie Fulton, Pearson would no doubt have tended to be more professorial. But because he had to face John Diefenbaker, Pearson became a nervous reformer and highly partisan Liberal.

Pearson's psyche was so difficult to penetrate because he behaved like a distracted actor, able to detach himself from whatever might be ravaging his mind without for an instant betraying the relevant emotions in his public performance. There was a mood of chameleonic detachment about everything he did. At once solitary and convivial, cynical and idealistic, profound and gay, Lester Pearson was easy to caricature, impossible to paint. Those who knew him best believed the outward paradox mirrored accurately a paradox within.

The curious gap between Pearson's glowing reputation before he became Prime Minister and his flawed performance in power left many Canadians concerned about his capacity to exercise political authority, his ability to judge men and occasions, and the nature of his ultimate goals. The trouble was that in any given situation Lester Pearson never managed to become greater than the sum of his virtues, even if he was less disappointing than the total of his defects. More a means than a source of action, his half-hearted acts and desultory gestures, halting assertions and hesitant rebuttals made him appear to be a politician defying his private doubts as much as those of the public.

CHAPTER 3

A Good Man in
a Wicked Time

THE POLITICAL DEEDS AND MISDEEDS that account for a prime minister's legacy to history flow as much from luck as from his character. Lester Pearson came to office at a perilous moment in his country's history. A good man in a wicked time, he refused to subvert his decent instincts or abandon his quest for world peace and Canadian unity. A slightly different turn of events might have marked him for greatness. He was not a politician corrupted by power, if only because he so seldom used it.

In a way, Pearson's timidity and vacillation in office accurately personified the confused state of the country he was trying to govern, a Canada grown uncertain of its domestic and external purposes in a rapidly changing world. Although most of the economic, social, cultural and political forces that burst into the open during the mid Sixties were already in train before 1963, their impact accelerated so swiftly soon after he took office that his world blew up under him. Unlike most political leaders in times of rude change, Lester Pearson was less the agent of revolution than its victim.

If there was a unifying theme to Lester Pearson's curious behaviour in office, it was his fatalistic approach to history not as an orderly progression of events, but as an accumulation of tumbling paradoxes in the midst of which anything might happen and almost nothing was foreseeable. He regarded politics as the formidable mission of trying to control that chaos, a province of infinite contingencies which no doctrine could encompass and no grand design could subjugate. He recognized that the essential issues would always remain insoluble (that's why they were important) and saw himself as a creative improvisator possessed by the capacity to put disappointments aside, place them in new perspective and move on. All that a sensible man could do was try and work through his destiny with as little unpleasantness to himself as possible. To shrug your shoulders and smile sometimes remained the only sane response to the preposterous incongruities of human existence. To Mike Pearson there was nothing wrong, and much that was right, in the British tradition of muddling through.

It was no accident that the most memorable aspect of the Pearson style was a wry, self-depreciating sense of humour that flourished under stress. On November 25, 1964, when the Lucien Rivard case was breaking in the House of Commons and it looked as if his administration might be swept out of office on the scandal allegations of Erik Nielsen, Pearson was due to make a speech to a municipal banquet in the Prairie city of Lloydminster. This was his first public appearance since the serious charges had been raised against his government, but Pearson de-fused the situation with this opening: "I am grateful, Mr. Mayor, for your welcome, because in your local weekly paper – which was kindly sent to me in Ottawa by air mail before I came here so I could get into the atmosphere of the community before arrival – I noticed the headline on the front page. The headline read, and I took it down, "WELCOME PRIME MINISTER" and then underneath, another headline "SEWER INSTALLATIONS PROGRESSING" . . . Well, I warn you, I don't intend to go down the drain yet."

A politician, like a clergyman, is wise not to jest too freely about his vocation, but Pearson could make his puns work for him, both as a way of puncturing his opponents' rages and to help maintain his own equilibrium. During a question-and-answer period at a Canadian University Liberal Federation convention on February 2, 1967, he used an Adlai Stevenson story to illustrate this point. It was about the Indian fighter who crawled into the frontier fort with three arrows in his back and was asked whether it hurt. He answered: "Only when I laugh." Stevenson would tell the story and quip: "My job only hurts me when I *don't* laugh." Pearson added: "I sometimes feel the same way."

Pearson's amiable and irreverent lack of pretension was noticeable even in the trivia of his office arrangements. John Diefenbaker had always kept in full view as a symbol of his power the red NORAD emergency telephone that connects the Prime Minister of Canada directly to the President of the United States. "I can get Ike any time," he would boast to visitors. Pearson not only removed the instrument from his desk, but hid it so carelessly that one morning during the winter of 1964 when it rang, he couldn't find it. Paul Martin, the External Affairs Secretary, was in the PM's office at the time. The two men heard the NORAD phone buzzing, couldn't locate it and began to chase each other around the room like a pair of Keystone Kops.

"My God, Mike," said Martin, "do you realize this could mean war?"

"No," Pearson puffed, "they can't start a war if we don't answer that phone."

The instrument was finally located behind a curtain and the caller – who wanted to know if "Charlie" was there – turned out, by incredible coincidence, to have both the wrong number and accidental access to one of the world's most private hot-lines.*

Pearson was fussy about personal matters, sometimes displaying a cranky peevishness toward the small errors or omissions committed by his staff. On one occasion during the centennial summer of 1967 he got into a snit over a glorified portrait of himself done by the Vancouver artist Joyce Devlin. After he had mildly criticized her work, he finally told her that his likeness didn't appear to make him look strong and decisive enough. "Who do you think you are," the artist demanded in exasperation, "Winston Churchill?" The Pearsons never took delivery of her canvas.†

Such displays of temper were rare and if Lester Pearson brought little grandeur to his office, neither did he occupy it with any sense of pompous pretension. In fact, becoming Prime Minister changed Mike Pearson very little. His personal tastes remained simple and surprisingly unsophisticated considering the number of years he had spent in the supercivilized environment of the diplomatic circuit. After a breakfast of toast with cheese and marmalade he would be driven to the office in his Buick Wildcat, arriving about 8:15. He'd work alone until nine, then see his main advisers to scan the day ahead. This daily session, known to his personal staff as "the prayer meeting," was the most important element in planning the Pearson Government's initiatives, deferring its decisions, and trying to react to the various events that were always threatening to overwhelm it.

*Pearson used the hot-line only once. On April 21, 1967, while he was being driven to his summer residence at Harrington Lake, his car struck a rock and broke its transmission. The hot-line was the only telephone available, so Pearson called Washington to arrange for a tow truck to be sent out from downtown Ottawa.

†The commission ($2,500) for the official portrait to be hung in the House of Commons went to Hugh Mackenzie, a Toronto artist and brother-in-law of Pearson's son Geoffrey. Pearson described it as "orthodox enough to be acceptable, yet different enough to be interesting."

Pearson would usually eat lunch (oysters or clam chowder, poached eggs and apple pie) in his office and leave at six with at least three hours of work in his briefcase. He could master complicated briefs and memos very quickly, signing most of his comments with the initials PM (for Prime Minister) instead of a plain LBP. He could be tough in dealing with the advice proffered in some memos, dismissing it with the marginal comment "This won't do," but more often he left the memo writer puzzled about his intentions. One senior adviser recalled ending his memorandum on an important political problem by suggesting alternative courses of action. Pearson sent it back, with a notation beside the two suggested options that merely read: "I agree."

Pearson rarely attended (or gave) cocktail parties and when he did go, he usually lingered briefly, sipping a weak rye and ginger ale. His official residence in no way became the capital's social or cultural centre. He liked listening to Brahms, occasionally tinkled on the piano, and went to view the offerings of touring theatrical companies that came irregularly to Ottawa, but his great relaxations were watching television westerns and sports.*

Pearson loved sports both as spectator and as participant. His father had been a baseball buff and as a young man Lester spent one summer in the Ontario semi-professional league, with the Guelph Maple Leafs. While he was studying at Oxford in the Twenties he played fullback in rugger, defence in hockey, and won a half-blue for lacrosse. He was on Britain's 1922 Olympic hockey team and on the Oxford squad that beat Cambridge by an unprecedented score of 27-0. Later, as a young history instructor at the University of Toronto, he coached the Orphans in the ORFU and replaced Conn Smythe as coach of the University of Toronto Blues hockey team. In later years he was still a good tennis player.†

Pearson's passion for baseball, hockey and football was intense. On one occasion when he met two Ottawa Rough Riders in mufti, walking along a Chateau Laurier corridor, he not only recognized them but

*The rivalry between Lester Pearson and John Diefenbaker even intruded into sport. They both enjoyed fishing but neither had much luck at Harrington Lake, the official summer residence of Canadian prime ministers. Pearson kept hearing rumours that Diefenbaker had fished a 4½-pound trout out of the lake. Unable to match this record, he tracked the story down by talking to a farmer who lived nearby and was delighted to discover that while Diefenbaker had hooked such a fish, he had never got it into his boat.

†On September 21, 1967, he and Governor General Roland Michener beat 27-year-old King Constantine of Greece and Marc Landry, a young Government House aide, 6-4 in the first set. Michener and Pearson had first played together at Oxford and in 1923 entered the Canadian Open Doubles Championships, but were eliminated in the first round.

knew what positions they played and what their records were. After a crucial game in the 1965 Stanley Cup play-offs, he was taken to visit the Maple Leaf dressing room. Even though the exhausted players were sitting around in sweaty underwear with their numbers off, he knew each man's name and could discuss his scoring history.

Earlier, during a dismal political journey into rural Saskatchewan in 1958, Pearson was slumped in the back of a car, listening to the rasping tones of an old political colleague, Jimmy Gardiner, as he held forth on the iniquities of Tory agricultural policies. Pearson said nothing for mile after dusty mile, but as they drove through a small elevator town he suddenly came to life and interrupted Gardiner by abruptly exclaiming, "Hey, that was Floral we just passed through. That's where Gordie Howe was born."

Pearson always followed the World Series with fascination no matter what crisis might be claiming his attention. He could name the starting line-ups and batting averages of most American teams. On May 10, 1963, during his first official call on President John F. Kennedy at Hyannis Port, his knowledge was put to the test by Dave Powers, the resident White House baseball expert. While Kennedy listened, the two men traded managers' names, World Series statistics and other diamond lore. It was Powers, not Pearson, who tripped up on some southpaw's 1926 earned-run average. "He'll do," Kennedy remarked, and the two leaders proceeded to equip Canada with nuclear warheads.

INVARIABLY WARM, CHARMING AND GENUINE in private conversation or intimate gatherings, Pearson often came across as cold, disdainful and remote on the hustings where the effectiveness of a democratic politician must be tested. Whenever he led the Liberals into electoral battle, he marched them backwards, snatching defeat or near-victory from what should have been certain triumph. Just before the 1962 campaign got under way, for example, the Gallup Poll showed that 45 per cent of the nation's electors intended to vote for the Liberal Party. By the time Pearson had campaigned across the country for six weeks, Liberal support had slumped to 37 per cent, allowing the discredited Diefenbaker administration to come back as a minority government. When the 1963 election was called, the Diefenbaker Cabinet was in chaos; the Liberals' popularity stood at 47 per cent and their fortunes were rising. But again, after six weeks of Pearson-style campaigning, the party's vote had dropped to 42 per cent by polling day. As a result the Liberals fell short of the majority that by all odds should have been theirs. In the 1965 campaign, facing a split Conservative Party and bolstered by the fact that he was going into electoral battle as the Prime Minister, Pearson began the campaign with a rating of 48 per cent. By the time the votes were cast, his party's public support had been reduced to 40 per cent. Denied a parliamentary majority, Pearson was deprived of any political leader's most valuable asset: a clear mandate from his people.

The reason Lester Pearson stirred so little mass emotion at election time was due to a basic shyness. There was about him an air of reserve, a feeling that he should not be drawn into situations where his prestige would be risked in routine encounters. He confessed to close friends that he just couldn't walk up to strangers and pump their hands without being afraid of either invading their privacy or compromising his own dignity. He acted always within the consciousness of his own limitations and of the voters' awareness of them. The simple fact was that he didn't like people in large groups, because he thought they didn't like him.

At the start of the 1963 election, party organizers had worked hard to mount a successful campaign kickoff in London, Ontario, traditionally a poor territory for the Liberals. They succeeded so well that they not only filled the city's largest arena but were left with an overflow of two thousand potential supporters outside the hall. When Pearson drove up, David Greenspan, a bright young Toronto lawyer who had headed the local organization drive, pushed his way toward the limousine, shoved his head through the car window, and shouted: "Mr Pearson! These people outside can't get in. They've been waiting for two hours in the cold. Here's a bullhorn; you have to say something to them." Pearson shrank back, and with an emphatic head-shake said: "I can't do that." Finally, Gordon Edick, then the Ontario Liberal Party's assistant director, physically barred Pearson's way into the arena until he had grasped the bullhorn to mutter an awkward acknowledgement of the crowd's enthusiasm.

This absence of communicable political passion confirmed him in the public mind as a curiously disengaged politician who could not be brought to bay by the urgencies of the moment. Although he had the advantage of great national issues to make the country hang upon his words, on few occasions did passion burst through to reveal the extent of his emotional commitment to his own policies. In an age of image politics, when inspiration was replacing identity as the link between voter and candidate, Lester Pearson could seldom project any sense of personal goals.

THIS FEELING WAS REINFORCED by the fact that during the first three years of his time in office while his government reeled from mishap to misfortune, few, if any, of the Liberals' legislative measures resembled the original proposals on which they were based. The Canada Pension Plan went through at least four mutations; the 1963 compromise with the provinces over the municipal loan fund made it into something very different from what had initially been put forward. Pearson's method of government often seemed to consist of engaging the nation in a horrendous rescue operation, made necessary by the Liberal Leader's precipitate tackling of some hitherto insoluble national problem. Each time, Pearson's own political back-tracking raised national frustration to such a peak that public opinion finally solidified behind him in order to help the government find some way out of its self-generated crisis. Almost as a side effect, the issue itself would have been reduced to reconcilable proportions. While this method achieved some impressive new laws, each time it was used, Pearson's credibility diminished in the process.

The most spectacular example of the method's success was Pearson's crusade for adoption of a distinctive Canadian flag. When he abruptly produced a red-white-and-blue pennant with three maple leaves in May of 1964, only a few Canadians felt particularly involved in the flag issue. Seven months later, so much public pressure had been built up that a majority of Canadians were hotly in favour of resolving the flag debate one way or another, and when the Liberal Government applied parliamentary closure to cut off the Conservative anti-flag fili-buster, there was hardly a ripple of resentment. The fact that the flag adopted had one less colour and two fewer maple leaves than the initial Pearson design didn't really matter – least of all to Pearson himself, who regarded the flag as his greatest accomplishment.

While he always appeared as the conciliator seeking a consensus, most of Pearson's achievements came about through a procession of crises that precipitated their own solutions, like thunderclouds that send down rain to clear the sultry air. He was at his best in times of great stress when his diplomatic training let him under-react to the torrent of events threatening to engulf him. "We'll jump off that bridge when we come to it," he would airily say to nervous aides, as they fretted about the next catastrophe that could befall the government. The late Grant Dexter, editor of the Winnipeg *Free Press* and a reporter of wisdom and tender conscience, once wrote of his close friend: "Mike is happiest when he's clinging to a precipice and just about to fall off."

During the crunch of a crisis, Pearson would launch himself on two or three different courses of action at the same time, agreeing with advisers who offered conflicting opinions, reserving his own decision until everyone else had shown his hand. His government's legislative proposals were treated like position papers presented at the beginning of international conferences, statements of basic intent open to revision as negotiations proceeded. He would allow events to play over possibilities, forcing the outlook now one way, now another. Then, just as the conflicting sets of options seemed about to collide, he would move in with a compromise that left all those involved free to claim partial victory. As the quintessential diplomat-politician he was always more concerned with the consequences of failure than the rewards of success.

BECAUSE LESTER PEARSON FELT CERTAIN that his inelegant fumblings at the negotiating table would be proved irrelevant by the long sweep of history (which would tend to correct the appearance of his errors) he was never overly concerned with press and public criticism of his style.

But to a nation in trouble, the *appearance* of poised, responsible political leadership was not a factor of marginal consequence. To look wise was nearly as essential as to be wise. Television had made the average citizen more aware of process; the mastering of technique had become the mark of modern man.

Even if it achieved some of his objectives, the Pearson method was undignified, creating the impression of a bumbling, incompetent administration making the worst of each bad situation. Pearson's manner left the residual impression of a prime minister who could not grip events on the move and was continually sprinting toward greatness only to stumble over self-erected barriers.

PEARSON'S WHOLE PERFORMANCE IN OFFICE was an unsettling combination of high purpose with inability to lead. His negotiable approach to the major issues of the day marked him as a politician drifting with the tide of events – an unusual prime minister who did not seem so much to be governing Canada as presiding over its survival.

Yet it was the great paradox of the Pearson stewardship that even if his government was worse than it should have been, it was better than it appeared to be. Although Pearson's achievement seemed limited to the civilizing of the *status quo*, an impressive stream of useful reforms somehow was squeezed through the minority parliaments.

Pearson's remarkably long legislative record included: a new Canadian flag, important reforms in parliamentary rules and the committee system, a reorganization of government departments, the foundations of a bilingual federal civil service, the redistribution of constituency boundaries by an independent commission, important changes in federal-provincial relations, the beginnings of constitutional reform, a new bank act, new regulatory agencies for transportation and broadcasting, a new labour code, the Canada Pension Plan, the Canada Assistance Plan, a guaranteed minimum income plan for old age pensioners, medicare legislation, the setting up of a health resources fund, youth allowances, the liberalization of divorce laws, industrial research incentives, provision for technical and vocational training schemes, a doubling in the External Aid program, the abolition of capital punishment for a trial period of five years, new bankruptcy, company and consumer legislation, the unification of the armed forces, collective bargaining for the civil service, establishment of the Order of Canada, new feed grain and crop insurance legislation, a fund for rural economic development, a new immigration act, and the setting up of several important new agencies, including the Economic Council of Canada, the Science Council, a corporation to encourage the Canadian film industry, the Company of Young Canadians, and a corporation to manage and phase out the Cape Breton coal industry.

Prompted by the progressive activists who were his main advisers, Pearson let loose a torrent of new forces and pressures. In a way, Pearson was like a man walking through an apiary, punching a stick into beehives. He seemed chagrined when the bees, instead of just buzzing around briefly and settling into new life patterns, stung the very man who had set them free.

By setting in train a series of fundamental social changes, but failing to explain them or to channel them into some rational sequence of priorities, Pearson missed the political advantages that might have accrued to him and eventually lost control of the society he was trying to govern. The residual impression of the Pearson Government was one of undiscerned direction and missed opportunity. The impact of the Liberal administration's many achievements was so diluted by the time it reached the public's consciousness that in a Canadian Institute of Public Opinion poll taken near the end of Pearson's rule, an overwhelming 70 per cent of respondents could not think of anything beneficial the Pearson Government had accomplished.*

Pearson's main policy preoccupation was his attempt to sponsor some kind of accommodation between Quebec and the rest of the

*The only specific achievements mentioned in the survey, published on March 11, 1968, were new social security measures (10%), handling of the Quebec problem (4%), and the adoption of a Canadian flag (4%).

country, a task to which he brought more sympathy and comprehension than any other politician on the federal scene. Only the unfolding of history can pronounce the final verdict on Pearson's efforts to meet the potentially explosive aspirations of French Canada, but certainly it was on this crucial issue that he expended the most concern.

ALWAYS THE NIMBLE-FOOTED DIPLOMAT trying to find some political base to stand on, Pearson never really had any root constituency of his own. His views reflected the aspirations of no particular region or group, except perhaps the narrow horizons of the Ottawa Establishment. This alienation included even Pearson's own riding of Algoma East, for although he won re-election with easy majorities, he was not *of* it. It seemed perfectly natural to call John Diefenbaker "The Man from Prince Albert," but it would have been patently silly to label Lester Pearson "The Man from Algoma East."

Though he applied much goodwill to the task, Pearson could never genuinely involve himself with Canada at its grassroots political level. He had existed for too long outside the country, his ideas having been formed at universities, in embassies abroad, and in the hermetically sealed environment of bureaucratic Ottawa. Unlike most of his predecessors in the office of prime minister, in the public mind he had been nurtured away from the backroom involvements and partisan skirmishes that combine to endow most Canadian politicians with recognizable contours. This prompted Douglas Fisher to write that "Mr Pearson was somehow born out in the North Atlantic and is not a Canadian at all."

Diplomats live in an artificial cocoon of ritualistic exchanges into which real people and their mundane problems seldom intrude. "His External Affairs experience, his years abroad, and his association with Mackenzie King combined in quite a consistent way to put Pearson out of touch with the realities of Canada," wrote Professor Denis Smith, associate professor of politics and vice-president of Trent University. "Some of his views were intelligent and tolerant and compassionate but they were often views held in a vacuum, hardly related to the real passions and complexities of the Canadian character, either English or French."

Although he loved the idea of Canada, Pearson remained something of a foreigner in his own country, a man without permanent roots who lived in eighteen different houses during his period of public service. Having spent the wrong years in the faith, he came to the nation's highest political office too late in life to feel that vital rapport with the average citizen that nourishes all successful politicians. As a result, the image of him imprinted on the public mind remained confused and vague.

The fact that the many blurred pictures the public had of him sometimes didn't even add up to the simple act of recognition was amusingly illustrated by a minor incident that occurred at the time of the royal visit to Prince Edward Island in the fall of 1964. Pearson and his entourage, including Jim Coutts, his appointments secretary, were quartered overnight at the official residence of the province's lieutenant-governor in Charlottetown. Back in Ottawa, an aide got his time zones mixed up and placed a call to Coutts that rang in Charlottetown long before breakfast. A local waiter, brought in to act as a manservant for the occasion, put down the phone and went sleepily upstairs to shake Pearson awake, demanding: "Are you Mr Coutts?" When he heard the emphatically negative reply, the man, still unaware he was addressing the Prime Minister, persisted: "Well, look, fella, you've got to help me find him. This is important." The anecdote may have reflected as much on the lack of formality among Charlottetown waiters as on the vagueness of Pearson's public image, but it was not an incident that could conceivably have involved a strong public personality like John Diefenbaker, Louis St Laurent or even Mackenzie King.

LESTER PEARSON WAS PROBABLY THE FIRST MAN to serve as Prime Minister of Canada whose public and private personalities were one and the same. Unlike most of his thirteen predecessors, he wasn't noticeably enlarged by his arrival at the peak of Canada's political system.

By treating the prime ministership like a job that he was trying to do rather than an urgent mission he longed to fulfil, Pearson inspired familiarity without the undercurrent of mystery and excitement that people yearn for in their leaders. He would come into a room, and the room was the same.

The exercise of political power at the summit means more than sitting in a hushed office with a crammed appointments schedule. Every hour a prime minister spends in that office is an hour in his country's history. He is not a functionary, but a man chosen by the people to embody the national direction. Lacking a resident monarchy, Canadians have elevated their prime minister to a position of prestige as high as that found in any parliamentary democracy. The energies he releases, the standards he sets reveal the character of the country to itself. His office is an immensely important command post with a large internal decision-making potential which can alter the march of great events. He is the centre of gravity in the nation's political system and everything that happens in Ottawa swirls around his single powerful figure.

From a distance, the government of Canada seems an impersonal institution, its responsibilities divided among squads of faceless experts. But this doesn't hold true for the really important decisions of state. It is the prime minister, acting in isolation, who must make the final commitment on major policy shifts. He can recruit expert assistance in the exercise of his authority, but he cannot delegate its substance. To perform his supreme task a prime minister needs three qualities: knowledge, power and purpose. Lester Pearson had the knowledge, did not use the power, and failed to supply a purpose.

The office of prime minister demands of its occupant some special quality, a dimension of unrealized potential, to maintain a distance between himself and the people. Pearson's personality was fatal to any sense of awe.

More than that, Lester Pearson's record identified him as a statesman-politician without much potential for greatness. Greatness in a man implies a clear commitment to the future, a stone-truth conviction that the right thing must be done, no matter what; it involves the perception and making of enemies and the recognition of causes more important than men. Pearson was dedicated to the proposition that all things are relative and he remained in most circumstances the disengaged observer.

A nation, to be great, even to have a conviction that it is able to survive, must have a feeling of movement toward something better, a vision of itself larger than its present-day realities. Pearson could give no such direction to Canada because this would have involved a decision in favour of one clear course of action, a declaration that there is a right way, and that other approaches must be closed off.

At the core of Lester Pearson's disappointing performance was the fact that during his time in power he behaved as if he would rather be himself than a memorable prime minister. His tragedy was that he could not be both.

CHAPTER 4

The Seminal Influences

A STUDY OF LESTER PEARSON'S LIFE reveals less the making of one individual than of a procession of men – the soldier, the historian, the bureaucrat, the diplomat – all favourites of fortune. His abnormally normal existence was elevated into something of a charmed life by a combination of his own sheer likableness and circumstances conspiring to push him ahead at every turning point.

Always ready to exploit these happy accidents, yet never apparently self-seeking, Pearson took his philosophy of living from the atmosphere of the manse into which he was born. "My family," he liked to recall, "would always say: 'Well, now, the Lord will provide. If you can't have milk tomorrow, you can have buttermilk. If you can't be first in your class, be second.'" He was ambitious but he had few definable goals. "When I look back on my career," he said in an interview shortly after assuming the prime ministership, "it's most amazing how everything has happened. I was always alert for any opportunities, new responsibilities, or interesting work, but if I didn't take them on, it didn't worry me. I'd do something else. I've never hewn to any particular line. It was only pressure, really, that got me into this."

Pearson's father was a peripatetic Methodist minister, moving through the parishes of rural Ontario in those halcyon days before World War I. Methodism's concentration on welfare and reform (as contrasted with the more rigid, sin-oriented theology of the Baptists and Presbyterians) allowed young Lester to grow up in an atmosphere that developed his social conscience. The family soon moved away from his birthplace at Newton Brook* to a succession of small Ontario towns, including Aurora, Chatham and Peterborough. At sixteen, he enrolled in Victoria College at the University of Toronto (where his uncle, Richard P. Bowles, was Chancellor) but in 1915 he decided to volunteer for service in World War I.

The war had a profound influence on his life. He spent his eighteenth, nineteenth and twentieth birthdays overseas, and saw the cream of his generation destroyed. It was the memory of those days that led him to inquire into the causes of wars, to study history, and eventually to become a diplomat. Like most other sensitive survivors of that terrible war, Pearson felt ever afterwards that he had been granted a second life. This accounted in part, at least, for his wry humour and his fatalistic view of human existence.

He began his wartime service as a medical orderly in the Balkans, taking part in the Salonika campaign. Though there was little fighting, disease of plague proportions swept the troops, but Pearson himself never suffered a day's illness. After he volunteered for the infantry, he was sent to a training camp at Wadham College, in Oxford, England, and was so impressed with the university that he vowed he would try to go back after the war. He won a commission and was due to be shipped off to France as a front-line platoon commander when he volunteered for the equally hazardous Royal Flying Corps. Making his first solo flight at Hendon Aerodrome, after only ninety minutes of instruction, he was trying to land his Grahame-White "boxkite" when it stalled and crashed. Slightly injured, he was sent to a London hospital. Released a week later, he was hit by a bus during a blackout and after another month in hospital was invalided home in April of 1918.

Back at the University of Toronto he was given his third year for war service and completed successfully his fourth year through a stroke of very special good fortune. Pearson had always been stumped by the subject of mathematics. On his final exam he answered the only two questions that looked possible to him, then worked himself up to such a nervous pitch that his nose started to bleed over his exam paper. He had to leave the room, overwhelmed by the realization that he would fail the paper and his final year. A few days later he went to see the head of the mathematics department to inquire what might be done. The professor turned out to be a baseball fan. When after an hour's discussion of the sport Pearson offered his explanation of what had happened, the professor replied with happy largess that it didn't matter at all, the

*Now part of the Metropolitan Toronto borough of North York. Lester Pearson was born on April 23, 1897.

whole thing was perfectly understandable and he would be marked only on that part of the paper he'd written. That was how Lester Pearson got his Bachelor of Arts degree with a close-to-perfect mark in mathematics.

Unsure of what he wanted to do following graduation, Pearson tried law school for a few weeks, then decided to go into business. His uncle, Edson White, President of Armour and Company, the Chicago meat packers, stepped in at this point and got him a job. He worked briefly in the Armour plant in Hamilton, Ontario, shooting meat into sausage casings, but was soon promoted to a clerkship in the company's fertilizer division in Chicago. But his dream of going to Oxford was still with him and luck intervened once again. Vincent Massey, who had known Pearson while Massey was Dean of Residence at Victoria College before World War I, recommended him for a Massey Foundation Fellowship, tenable at Oxford.

Pearson spent the next three years at St John's College, earning his MA. He then returned to the University of Toronto as a lecturer in the history department. On August 22, 1925, he married one of his students, Maryon Elspeth Moody of Winnipeg, and settled into the academic life. Hume Wrong, a fellow member of the university's history faculty and a good friend of Pearson's, resigned in 1927 to join the newly formed External Affairs Department in Ottawa.* Wrong had recommended Pearson to Dr O. D. Skelton, the influential Undersecretary of State for External Affairs, so that when Pearson went to Ottawa in 1927 to do some research at the Public Archives on the United Empire loyalists, Skelton suggested he join the department. Pearson wrote that year's External Affairs entrance examinations and was appointed a first secretary.†

---

*Wrong (who died in 1954), Pearson and Norman Robertson, a longtime External savant, (who died in 1968), became the powerful triumvirate that dominated the Department after Skelton's departure. In the late Forties the three men bought, for ten dollars each, plots at Maclaren's Cemetery near Wakefield, Quebec, in the Gatineau Hills, where Wrong and Robertson are already buried and Pearson plans to make his final resting place.

†Unknown to Pearson at the time, his luck very nearly ran out. According to Professor James Eayrs of the University of Toronto, one of his examiners was Vincent Massey, then Canadian minister to the USA. Though Massey liked Pearson, he questioned the wisdom of his admission to the Department on the grounds that there was "something curiously loose-jointed and sloppy about his makeup which, as a matter of fact, is reflected in some measure in his physical bearing." But Skelton overruled Massey and Pearson headed the list of sixty applicants.

DURING THE NEXT TWENTY YEARS of his service in the middle and upper reaches of the External Affairs Department, Pearson came under two definitive influences that would have great bearing on his later behaviour as prime minister: his personal contacts with Mackenzie King and his membership in the Ottawa bureaucratic Establishment.

Mackenzie King was a man of strong will who reserved his greatest personal commitment for keeping unwanted things from being done. His political philosophy was probably best summed up by two entries in his diary. The first, written in January of 1938, reads: "In politics one has to do as one at sea with a sailing ship; not try to go straight ahead, but reach one's course having regard to prevailing winds"; the other, from September of 1940, states: "I really believe my greatest service is in the many unwise steps I prevent."

Hugh MacLennan, the Montreal novelist, once quoted Mackenzie King's belief that a prime minister should model himself on the ram in a flock of sheep. Most of the time the sheep nibble at the grass or rest in the shade and the ram stands by, keeping his eye on them. But every now and then the sheep begin moving to one of the pasture gates. When this happens, King explained, the ram trots up to the head of the flock and leads them out.

Although Pearson never had this sixth sense for the shift of power from one place to another, he did try to model himself on many other precepts of the King leadership style. He often recalled a conversation he'd had with King (who acted through most of his tenure as his own Secretary of State for External Affairs) on a train going to New York City in the Thirties. "My boy, you may one day have some responsibility," King told the still youthful-looking External officer. "I would just give you one bit of advice, to remember that in the course of human history far more has been accomplished for the welfare and the progress of mankind in preventing bad actions than in doing good ones."

King was able to govern Canada for such a long time, despite his uninspiring presence, because he had an uncanny ability for finding the point of political balance in any situation and then perching on it until a national consensus had formed behind him. By the time he was finally ready to move on a given problem, the political hazards of his position had been minimized. (King also had the advantage of presiding over a somnolent nation which was still in thrall to the idea of Empire, largely uninformed, pastoral and politically unsophisticated.)

Pearson prided himself on his King-like attempts to straddle the spectrum of Canadian political ideology. After the Kingston Study Conference of 1960 which moved the Liberal Party noticeably to the left, C. D. Howe, then in political retirement as a Montreal business executive, voiced some public criticisms of the direction his old party was taking under Pearson's leadership. When Pearson attended a testimonial dinner for Howe at Port Arthur later that year, he took the former Trade and Commerce Minister aside and told him: "Please stop sniping at me. This is practical politics. I don't intend to let the New Democrats steal the popular ground of the left. Besides, this is exactly the line Mackenzie King would have taken if he were alive today."

FROM THE BEGINNING PEARSON was an adept and competent foreign service officer. Since he had arrived at External Affairs just before the tremendous expansion that reflected Canada's multiplying international responsibilities, he moved rapidly up the departmental ladder.

By 1934 he had attended four international conferences. His first overseas trip was to the Five-Nation Naval Limitations Conference. Though Mrs Pearson had only one long dress at the time, they attended twenty-nine formal dinners during the thirty-one days they spent in London. Pearson's wry humour proved a diplomatic asset even then. In 1932 he was the Canadian representative on a League of Nations subcommittee charged with dividing armaments into offensive and defensive categories. Discussions had ground to an impasse when Pearson suggested that the offensiveness or defensiveness of any weapon depended on whether you were in front of it or behind it. His most searing experience during the Thirties was his assignment on November 2, 1935, to succeed Dr W. A. Riddell as Canada's permanent representative at the League, after Riddell had been publicly disowned by Mackenzie King for advocating a blockade of oil shipments to Italy in retaliation for Benito Mussolini's attack on Ethiopia. Pearson had to occupy Canada's seat at the League without daring to say anything. Riddell's downfall had been a harsh lesson in the price of personal commitment.*

Appointed secretary in the office of the High Commissioner for Canada in London later the same year, Pearson was recalled to Ottawa in 1941 to become an Assistant Undersecretary of State, and a year later was given the grandiose title of Envoy Extraordinary and Minister Plenipotentiary to the United States. In January 1945 he became Cana-

---

*Referring to the League of Nations Geneva meetings, Hume Wrong once described the ideal Canadian representative as "a delegate who would have a name, even a photograph; a distinguished record, even an actual secretary – but he would have no corporeal existence and no one would ever notice that he was not there." This description was quoted in *What's Past is Prologue* by Vincent Massey (Macmillan Company of Canada, 1963).

dian Ambassador to Washington. By September 1946, he had reached his department's highest civil service position, Undersecretary of State for External Affairs.

All this time Pearson was a key figure in the Ottawa Establishment, that group of intellectually sophisticated, like-minded individuals in the top echelons of Canada's public service who set the style and outlook of official Ottawa in the Forties, Fifties and early Sixties. Recruited and led by Clifford Clark and O. D. Skelton, the long-time deputy ministers of the Finance and External Affairs departments, the Establishment's members were bound together not so much by any conscious desire to manipulate the politicians as by their conviction that somebody had to restrain democracy from running wild, and that power was far safer when lodged with experts rather than demagogues. They viewed their mission as a ceaseless vigil against both the unbridled selfishness of the populace and the opportunistic shortcuts of the politicians.

They had an uncanny ability to reach consensus on daily problems through casual exchange of gossip over Rideau Club luncheons, the sharing of silences, the homogeneity of their backgrounds, and a marked similarity in their habits of thought and action. They were cultivated, clever, hard working, dedicated to public service and cordial. But just as their talents lacked definite doctrine, so their passions seemed isolated from the everyday concerns of most citizens. Existence for them held few sensations and no surprises. Substituting good manners for compassion, they viewed life as an intellectual tumbling exercise. Better conversationalists than authors, they much preferred the impermanence of talk to the commitment of prose.

Pearson was the beau ideal of the Ottawa Establishment, a proud generalist who believed in resolving situations as they came up. Reacting magnificently was always more important than anticipating or reaching out for problems.

Light on both feet, ready to move in any direction, Pearson epitomized the quantitative small-l liberalism that dominated the thinking of his Ottawa contemporaries. Like his confrères, he saw power in Canadian society dispersed among competing institutions that always managed to balance each other, producing "the national interest" by osmosis. An enlightened government's function in this context was limited to supplying the stark necessities of life to the underprivileged. This was in marked contrast to the qualitative liberalism that would emerge as an important force during the mid Sixties. Here was a new kind of social involvement that questioned the *kind of life* people led, the individual's capacity for self-fulfilment within his society. Although

Pearson intellectually understood this new, broadened concept of liberalism and in the last few months of his stewardship did push through some legislation that was concerned with social, moral and political justice, he was caught up with the old Ottawa Establishment credo that governments should limit their function to economic justice and that the duty of the responsible man in public life was to exercise a restraining influence on political risk-taking.

THE MOST INFLUENTIAL PHASE of Pearson's career before assuming the prime ministership was the nine years he spent as Canada's Secretary of State for External Affairs. He took the vest and the frown away from Canadian foreign policy and replaced them with a tilted, polka-dot bow tie and a small-town Ontario grin on a face as comforting as a bowl of apple butter.

For most Canadians, the period in the country's history when Pearson had the most impact on the national conscience was the decade after 1948, when he transformed the dormant External Affairs portfolio into a creative enterprise that allowed him to bring more prestige to his country than any other living Canadian. A bright, ingratiating personality who chose to detach himself from the drab protocol of his trade, Pearson became the darling of the international mandarins.

A typical example of the informality that characterized the Pearson approach was a brief encounter he had in 1948 with James Patrick Manion, the son of a former Conservative leader who served as commercial secretary of the Canadian Embassy in Paris. In his memoirs, Manion described an occasion when he called on Pearson at the Hôtel de la Paix. "Mike met me at the door, and after a hearty handshake I asked how things were going. He said 'Shhh,' led me into the room, locked the door, looked into the cupboards, under the bed, behind the curtains, then came back to me and whispered, 'Everything's all right.' To illustrate the conspiratorial atmosphere still further, he explained that if one did not whisper, one was considered of no importance, with no secrets and therefore no significance in the scheme of things. 'Thus, if you see two diplomats buttonholing each other and earnestly whispering to each other,' said Mike, 'they are probably asking each other what they had for lunch.' "*

In the loosely organized postwar world, Pearson's unflappability and flair for constructive conciliation earned him nearly every honour the diplomatic community could bestow: the council chairmanship of

* *A Canadian Errant* by J. P. Manion (Ryerson Press, 1960).

NATO (1951-52), the presidency of the United Nations Assembly (1952-53), two dozen honorary degrees, and the Nobel Peace Prize. Walter Lippmann wrote that Pearson "incarnates the hope of building a true community of the Atlantic peoples." Gunnar Jahn, chairman of the Nobel Prize committee, declared that at the time of Suez, Pearson had "saved the world." Even if the majority of Canadians weren't aware of exactly what Pearson was doing, every citizen could feel part of his crusade for world order.

Pearson set the postwar style of Canadian diplomacy. Always the rational man in an irrational world, forever trying to make the best out of a bad situation, he epitomized the concepts of quiet diplomacy and middle-powermanship, then the twin cornerstones of Canada's foreign policy. This approach allowed Canada to exercise an influence quite out of proportion to the country's real stature. At the same time, it found ready response at home because there was something in the national character of Canadians that clung to sweet reasonableness as the only possible posture in the face of the country's geographical, social and economic problems.

In practice, the Pearson policy meant that Canada devoted most of its external energies to acting as a kind of Dale Carnegie mediator between nations threatening to upset the international balance. This sublime mission of Pearson's as the eternal seeker of the middle ground often worked international wonders. As the "honest broker," unhampered by convictions on substantive issues, Pearson could bring together competing world powers by persuading them to subtract a little from their preconceived positions. As the neutral mediator he didn't really care where he ended up – any settlement was successful because something less than disaster was bound to emerge, moving the world back a little further from the precipice.

Certainly the outstanding example of the method's success was Pearson's handling of the Suez crisis in the fall of 1956. When Britain and France entered the war between Israel and Egypt, they split the western alliance, brought the Commonwealth to the brink of dissolution, and came close to starting World War III. Pearson took personal charge of the Canadian delegation to the United Nations and used all his mediating skills to press for a UN emergency force that would establish a cease-fire on the Gaza Strip.* It was the classic demonstration of the value of Canada as a middle power. Although John Foster Dulles, the United States Secretary of State, supported a similar

*The details of Pearson's accomplishment are ably documented in *Crisis: the Inside Story of the Suez Conspiracy* by Terence Robertson (McClelland and Stewart Limited, 1964).

settlement, he felt that his government could not advance the scheme because any American-sponsored resolution would bring on the automatic opposition of the Soviet bloc and the uncommitted nations who were suspicious of any proposals put forward by the super-powers. While the support of the American State Department was essential to Canada's success, it was Pearson who emerged as the one man trusted by all the parties involved because of his obvious disinterest in the outcome. The UN Assembly finally voted (57-0, with the Communist bloc and the combatants abstaining) to set up the UN police force. Within a fortnight the UN troops, including Canadians, were on the spot restoring an uneasy peace. The Pearson manoeuvre is still regarded as one of the most skilfully organized coups in United Nations history. But the real nature of his contribution was not so much to devise a solution as to fog up the details without abandoning his main objective of reducing the tensions of the moment. The parties that agreed to the Pearson compromise realized they were subscribing to something very unclear and each of them had his own understanding of what Pearson was actually proposing. Pearson knew that this was the way it had to be. His triumph was to keep everybody talking and to prevent the irreversible escalation of the crisis into general war.

The Pearson method in the Suez affair, repeated many times in lesser contexts, depended on his abstinence from personal commitment. It allowed him to draw a consensus out of almost any group or committee. By then adopting this consensus as his own view, he would enlist the support of the original disputants. He had a congenital reluctance to permit antagonism of any kind, a compulsion to "find a way" out of any acrimonious situation. He seldom allowed himself to get into a confrontation that denied his opponents an honourable exit, but always managed to come up with something that kept those involved bargaining and compromising until the impasse had been broken.

As a diplomat, Pearson could be counted on never to embarrass another nation publicly; even if he did so, he always warned its diplomats in advance. He seldom dealt absolutely with any international issue, no matter how serious; he preferred to handle each problem relative to the strains it was causing and to the sensitivities of the nations involved. He could walk through the corridors of the United Nations building in New York and effortlessly, it seemed, whisper the right thing to the right person at precisely the right moment. His long association with international affairs taught him the rhythm and vocabulary of political terminology so that he knew how to recognize the trigger words in another man's rhetoric.

Pearson's favourite description of the diplomatic ideal was contained in an essay by Sir Harold Nicolson, the British author and former diplomat, who defined the diplomat as someone who "must be a naturally patient man, willing to spin out negotiations and to emulate the exquisite art of procrastination. He must be imperturbable, able to receive bad news without manifesting displeasure, or to hear himself maligned and misquoted without the slightest twinge of irritation. He must be tolerant of the ignorance and foolishness of his home government and know how to temper the vehemence of the instructions he receives. Finally, he should remember that overt diplomatic triumphs leave feelings of humiliation behind them and a desire for revenge: no good negotiator should ever threaten, bully or chide."*

FEW SENIOR EXTERNAL AFFAIRS COLLEAGUES had been surprised when Lester Pearson, at the urging of Louis St Laurent, abandoned the civil service in the fall of 1948 to become Secretary of State for External Affairs. He had always been regarded as the most politically sensitive member of the Department. "A civil servant can only go so far in determining policy. When the essential decisions are made, you're not even in the room. I want to be able to argue my points in Cabinet," he told a friend at the time, to explain his move.

Though he entered the arena of politics, Pearson never detached himself from the methods of diplomacy. His modes of thought, his approach to negotiation, his private sense of priorities were all formed by the long apprenticeship he had served in international councils. When he became Prime Minister he remained ever conscious of the fact that the great movements of history hinge not on day-to-day triumphs or setbacks but on the conversion of ill-defined problems into great moral issues, and tried to cast Canada's problem of French-English relations into such a context. His persuasive powers were sadly inadequate to match his performance with his intentions. But his gift of being able to soften collisions and smooth tempers and his unwillingness to draw drastic conclusions from the temporary tactics of his opponents became considerable assets in the struggle for national unity.

In other situations, however, the skills that had created Pearson's towering reputation as Secretary of State for External Affairs proved to be only vaguely related to the exercise of prime ministerial power. For one thing, his diplomatic training resulted in an incongruous configuration of skills: he could *observe* without feeling the muffled uncertainty that became his trademark when the time came to *act*.

*From *Diplomacy* by Harold Nicolson (Thornton Butterworth Ltd., 1939).

Similarly, Pearson tried to apply his honest broker approach to domestic issues, often with disastrous results. He was never able to recognize the fundamental change in his status: that as Prime Minister he could not meaningfully mediate national problems without inevitably compromising his own position. Agreements that he achieved, such as the 30 per cent wage increase to government workers on the St Lawrence Seaway during the summer of 1966, may have averted an immediate crisis, but they also fatally weakened his government's credibility. (Ottawa was at the time urging a national policy of wage restraints.)

In an international context Pearson's task had been not to defend any position of his own, but merely to subtract enough from the convictions of each of the disputing parties to achieve a compromise settlement. But as Prime Minister of Canada, Pearson was by definition no longer a neutral outsider but leader of one of the sides involved in any domestic quarrel. Yet he was still attempting to reconcile the various points of view involved by reducing them to a weak mixture of attitudes that he could support. In the process, he often compromised his own and the federal government's position on vital issues. By acting as his own middle man, he inevitably ended up as an appeaser.

During his term as Prime Minister, all of Pearson's actions were affected by the seminal influences of a long, varied lifetime: his upbringing in the manse, the memory of the horrors of war, his apprenticeship in the Ottawa Establishment, and his flowering as the country's brightest diplomat. Having lived sixty-five years as one of the luckiest men of his generation, he was transformed by the parade of dire circumstances that haunted him from the first day he took office into the unhappy warrior of Canadian politics.

CHAPTER 5

The Captive Hero

A COMMONLY HELD MYTH among Lester Pearson's admirers, seeking explanations for his administration's many pratfalls, was that he spent his days as a kind of captive hero. They visualized him as a man who, instead of acting according to his own basic decency, allowed a retinue of self-interested, politically oriented advisers to subvert his finer instincts and blunt his potential effectiveness. They felt that somewhere within him he had the capacity to be great, but that he was constantly undermining himself on the advice of some partisan hireling.

"I think he needs to listen to himself a little more and not so much to some of his lieutenants," Professor Frank Underhill, the noted Canadian historian and longtime Pearson *aficionado*, told Douglas Fisher during a 1964 television interview. Whenever he made some particularly awful blunder, the explanation among Ottawa's bureaucratic in-group was that "Mike is not being himself."

The way prime ministerial decisions are taken ultimately remains impenetrable, but it was a tender misunderstanding of both Pearson and the political context in which he operated to regard him as the prisoner of his advisers. They did not possess Lester Pearson. They were not only his instruments but his creations. They existed in national politics only because Pearson had decided they should.

Pearson himself disavowed the importance of his advisers. "I was too long a civil servant not to respect the opinion of the experts," he said in a 1965 interview. "But I do what *I* want and while the government's tactics may often be those of others, its policies and strategy are mine." On many major issues, Pearson ignored the consensus of his inner circle. His sudden introduction of the flag issue in the spring of 1964, for instance, was his decision alone. The turnabout in the Liberals' nuclear policy, which split the Diefenbaker Cabinet in February of 1963, was his personal initiative pursued against urgent warnings from some of his most trusted aides.

While he was polite to his staff, he could move on from one set of advisers to the next with an equanimity bordering on indifference. Because he would change the composition of the group of people nearest to him in such an effortless, almost preoccupied manner, not one of his aides knew at any time how long his own influence might last. Particularly after 1965, Pearson's personal retinue was in a constant state of flux and while the appropriate farewell messages of personal loss and unflagging esteem were always issued, by next morning no wounds would show. "Mike heals awfully fast," a former aide once commented. "If he walked into his office and saw a completely new set of faces he'd probably say 'what's on the agenda for this morning?' I suppose this was a good thing because he didn't become overwhelmed with obligations to a lot of people. But you always wished for some reflection of warmth, some visible sign of feeling over your departure."

Pearson listened to everybody who gained access to his office but trusted no one all the way. He operated on the assumption that every difficult new situation should be reduced to its origins and component parts before a solution could be attempted. As a result, each new policy or governmental crisis became a separate equation, requiring a different consultative mix. On legislative problems, for example, he would usually call in George McIlraith, a deceptively bland parliamentary veteran, or Jack Pickersgill, who could be counted on to choreograph some tricky procedural pirouettes on the floor of the Commons.

In choosing which advice he would eventually act on, Pearson was less of a consensus reader than an eclectic, selecting what he thought was best from various sources of opinion rather than basing his decisions on the common denominator of the views he received. This was a carryover from his External days. His technique then had been to select half a dozen sensitive points in international relations around the world, and call into his office the appropriate experts for a daily gab session. He would throw out some stimulatingly negative remark, listen to the recommendations and warnings that followed, then abruptly close off the discussion without stating his own views. Everyone left the room feeling that he had influenced Pearson's thinking without knowing exactly how but later in the day, when his dispatches were written, they realized that he had taken the best of their assessments while not fully accepting any single point of view.

One of Pearson's problems was that he was too much attracted by lucidity in others, and would often reach out for acceptable abstractions without thinking through the practical political consequences. An equally serious drawback was the absence of efficient communications within the PM's own office. Since they never knew exactly where they stood with their boss, his aides would jealously guard the prerogative of their shared confidences with him, frequently keeping his decisions away from the people they were supposed to affect. Time was always running out on Lester Pearson. He seldom had the opportunity to apply all of the necessary dispassion and weighing of options that most problems deserved.

THE MOST IMPORTANT SINGLE SOURCE of Lester Pearson's lieutenants and advisers was the Study Conference on National Problems, held at Queen's University in Kingston between September 6 and 10, 1960, when the small Liberal band that had survived the Diefenbaker land-slide of 1958 was desperately searching for new directions and fresh ideas. Billed as a non-partisan assembly of "liberal-minded" Canadians, the meeting was organized by Mitchell Sharp, then a Toronto-based vice-president of Brazilian Traction, Light and Power Company. The Kingston Conference's policy conclusions (endorsed at a national Liberal rally held in Ottawa in June 1961) moved the Party significantly to the left and away from the St Laurent preoccupation with the gross national product.

But the meeting's main endowment to the Liberal Party was the new-wave Liberals it provided to man the command posts of the Pearson Government. An analysis of the delegates' list shows that, of the 196 men and women who attended, 48 were later named to senior appointments in the Liberal administration.

It was yet another paradox of the Pearson incumbency that even if the machinery of government often broke down and the administration seemed, at the beginning at least, to stagger from one ineptitude to the next, the individuals who were the prime minister's main advisers were nearly all capable, highly intelligent individuals. What was lacking was not so much intellectual input as the kind of coalescing leadership that might have been able to extract co-ordinated achievements from their efforts.

During Pearson's first term, from 1963 to 1965, apart from his close confidants in Cabinet, three men – Tom Kent, Keith Davey, and Richard O'Hagan – emerged as the most important backstage influences within the prime ministerial entourage. They saw themselves as the Canadian equivalent of Kennedy's company of New Frontiersmen, and they had a special feeling both for the Prime Minister and for each other. In part, what bound them together was the fact that they had all given up interesting jobs elsewhere to serve Pearson during his bleak years as Opposition Leader, from 1958 to 1963.*

O'Hagan, an astute pragmatist with a contemporary outlook, came to Ottawa from MacLaren Advertising in Toronto to act first as Pearson's press secretary and later as his special assistant. His dress was a source of controversy in the Establishment because he resolutely remained, in outward trappings anyway, a vivid Toronto ad man in the grey Ottawa landscape. (The Prime Minister once told him to stop wearing his British warm but O'Hagan went right on sporting it.) He had his hair cut in Toronto, his shirts with his initials sewn into the neck were made by an Egyptian shirtmaker, and he loved to do all the things that were *in*. As the Pearson stewardship sped on and the terrifying spiral of error swirled about the PM, O'Hagan became an inner circle confidant. He could be seen smoothly ducking out of airplanes and limousines, just behind or just ahead of Pearson, protecting, cajoling, persuading, trying to motivate the frightened man who so unaccountably had found himself in professional difficulties for the first time in his life.†

Keith Davey, O'Hagan's best friend in the Pearson entourage, was appointed by Pearson in 1961 to be the Liberal Party's National Director. Davey supplied the personal enthusiasm that kept the organizational apparatus alive, willing and loyal. A big, hunched, handsome Eagle Scout in politics, Davey was one of the most dedicated partisans in Ottawa, but also one of the warmest and most widely liked men ever to hit that cold town and bounce his enthusiasms off its icicled back. A former radio station sales manager, he had been a Pearson supporter from the beginning (he delivered 96 of a possible 105 votes from the Toronto delegations to him at the 1958 leadership convention) and his faith in his leader never faltered. Davey had been a central figure in a group of progressive young Liberals in Toronto who began meeting after the 1957 defeat on Wednesday evenings in the Board of Trade dining room at the King Edward Hotel. These dinners provided the first serious sharing of the ideas that would eventually form

*For a description of Lester Pearson's performance in Opposition, see *Renegade in Power: The Diefenbaker Years,* Chapter 25.
†On September 1, 1966, O'Hagan was named Minister-Counsellor (Information) at the Canadian Embassy in Washington.

the Pearson Government's style, particularly after Walter Gordon joined the sessions in November 1957. The most important members of the group, who went into politics partly as a protest against the patronage-oriented policies of the St Laurent Government, were: Keith Davey,* John Aird,† Richard Stanbury,‡ Paul Hellyer,§. David Anderson,‖ Gordon Dryden,# Royce Frith,** Andrew Thompson,†† and Daniel Lang‡‡.

Keith Davey remained the most politically active member of the group. An unabashed worshipper of the political techniques of John F. Kennedy, he tried – without too much success – to transplant the shimmering style of the New Frontier to the colder latitudes of Ottawa. Theodore H. White's *The Making of the President, 1960,* was his bible and he was the first Canadian political organizer to base his decisions on the sophisticated new polling and motivational research techniques imported from the United States. Although he had been guilty of some poor judgements in the 1963 campaign by resorting to the gimmickry of the anti-Diefenbaker "Truth Squad" and "Colouring Books," he communicated a sense of involvement to party affairs that kept the Liberals united in the face of legislative and electoral setbacks.

THE MOST CONTROVERSIAL – AND IMPORTANT – of Pearson's staff members when he took office in 1963 was Tom Kent, his policy co-ordinator. An austere, cerebral Englishman in his early forties, Kent had come to Canada in 1954 to edit the Winnipeg *Free Press* with a brilliant record as a scholar at Oxford and a writer on the Manchester *Guardian* and the *Economist*. He had left the *Free Press* in 1959 after disagreements with its management to serve briefly as a vice-president of a Montreal chemical firm. He joined Pearson's office as a full-time policy adviser in 1961, wrote the party's platform in the 1962 and 1963 elections and ran himself as an unsuccessful Liberal candidate in 1963 against NDP Leader T. C. Douglas in the Vancouver riding of Burnaby-Coquitlam.

*Later appointed the party's national organizer and a senator.

†Later appointed a senator.

‡Later appointed a senator.

§Later appointed Minister of National Defence.

‖Later appointed a director of Canadian National Railways and Air Canada.

#Later appointed a member of the commission inquiring into costs of federal election campaigns.

**Later appointed a member of the Royal Commission on Bilingualism and Biculturalism.

††Later appointed a senator.

‡‡Later appointed a senator.

When the Liberals moved into power, Kent turned himself into a new breed of public servant on the Ottawa scene. Not quite politician, not quite administrator, not quite bureaucrat, but a little of each, he derived his authority directly from the Prime Minister whose personal ambassador-at-large he became in dealing with members of the cabinet, deputy ministers, lobbyists, and even the representatives of other governments. The span of his influence was a personal achievement, built on his superior intellect, his talent for clear, trenchant analysis, his ability to move fast and keep his head in the heat of crises. He was, in the deepest sense, the organizer of the process of prime ministerial decision-making, and this made his position within the Pearson power structure supreme. "I've never worked with anybody in all my years of public service who has had greater devotion and ability," Pearson said of Kent at a press conference on April 15, 1965.

Kent's ideological influence on Pearson was easy to exaggerate but difficult to pin down. His speech to the Kingston Conference, "Towards a Philosophy of Social Security," contained many of the more radical ideas that became the Liberal Government's policies, and Pearson's critics tended to blame Kent for the administration's excesses. But even Kent was a creation of Lester Pearson and when his reputation for shrewdness was diluted by his advice on the 1965 election, he quickly moved out to become Deputy Minister of Manpower and Immigration. Still, if the first Pearson administration had an *éminence grise*, it had to be Tom Kent. His irreverent juniors in the party even made up a song (to the tune of "Over the Rainbow") to commemorate his austere stature:

Tom Kent thinks in the East Block,
Way-y-y-y up high,
If Tom Kent thinks in the East Block,
Why, oh why, can't I?

Four other prime ministerial aides played an important part in the Pearson entourage: Jim Coutts, a young Alberta lawyer of zest and wit who enlivened Ottawa's cocktail circuit with his imitations of Jack Pickersgill and Paul Martin; Hal Dornan, a former Vancouver newspaperman who added much grace and integrity to the operation of the PM's office; Don Peacock, a radically inclined and perceptive former reporter turned speech-writer; and Torrance Wylie, who succeeded Coutts as Pearson's loyal appointments secretary. Outside his office Pearson relied on the friendship and solid counsel of John Nichol, a Vancouver businessman of good humour, considerable elegance and firm realism whom he eventually named to the Senate.

The civil servant who had the most influence on Pearson's decisions was Gordon Robertson, Clerk of the Privy Council. A Rhodes Scholar and former deputy minister of Northern Affairs, Robertson had served an important apprenticeship (1945-49) in the cabinet secretariat under Mackenzie King. A secretive man who seemed to reject the notion that there was a political aspect to the leadership of the country, he was one of the most competent bureaucrats in Ottawa, but he revered the state of the unrocked boat and had little willingness to experiment. Backing him up in the Privy Council office was a corps of unusually intelligent young men headed by Michael Pitfield, a Montreal constitutional expert, one of the most formidable intellects introduced into the Canadian public service in a generation.

What vigour of style was possessed by the Pearson administration came largely from two men not associated with the Prime Minister's office. They were Bill Lee, a former RCAF group captain who was Paul Hellyer's executive assistant, and Michael Joseph McCabe, who performed the same function for Mitchell Sharp. While Lee limited the daily tempest of his activities to hustling hard for his minister, McCabe's concerns ranged much wider. His appetite for power, his disregard for protocol and his instinct for novelty marked him as a young and very different kind of politician in a city that was still used to equating bald heads and cigar smoke with the kind of power that counts. McCabe was one of the very few men associated with the Pearson administration who understood and exploited the news media. His national network of contacts provided him with a reading of the national mood and in turn, he involved a large group of regionally influential citizens across the country in the process of governmental decision-making. McCabe and his wife Nora, a gorgeous American girl, formed the nucleus of a young group of executive assistants who held Saturday night parties to trade ideas, do the watusi, and plan the future.

AFTER THE HUMILIATION of the 1965 election, the staff of Pearson's office underwent a gradual transformation. The Kennedy-inspired activists dropped away and Pearson, tired of playing at Lochinvar, became determined to find his own style again: that of a seasoned public servant reluctantly in politics, a quiet man, a proud compromiser, an administrative patriot. The most important change in his staff in this final period was the replacement of Tom Kent by Marc Lalonde as the PM's chief policy adviser. Lalonde, an Oxford graduate and former law professor at the University of Montreal, was the first of a new breed of brilliant French-Canadian technocrats to move into a position of high influence within the Ottawa hierarchy. Along with his friend Pierre Elliott Trudeau, he was a charter member of that small group of Quebec intellectuals who believed that the province's best interests lay within Confederation, and that the only way to beat the country's Anglo-Saxon Establishment was on the grounds of competitive excellence.

IN THE MYTHOLOGY THAT DEVELOPED around the ebb and flow of influence within the Pearson circle, no figure remained a source of more conjecture than a friendly spinster with sparkling blue eyes called Mary Elizabeth Macdonald, the PM's executive assistant. Born in North Cobalt, Ontario, she had joined External Affairs in 1946, was posted to Pearson's office as a staff assistant a year later and stayed at his right hand ever after. Her emotional loyalty to her boss was legendary. She would sanction no criticism of Pearson in her presence and was reputed to hide memoranda that questioned the wisdom of his actions so that he would not get upset. During the 1966 Liberal policy convention, for example, a high-ranking member of the ministry had worked hard on a memo outlining some of the necessary, if slightly unpleasant, things the PM should mention in his closing speech. Mary Macdonald intercepted the document and asked another member of the Pearson entourage what he thought of it. Her colleague read it and replied that some of the points cited might make trouble for the PM but that others were highly relevant and useful. "I have my own way of taking care of these things," said Miss Macdonald and she tore up the memo and crumpled it into her handbag.

The source of Mary Macdonald's power was her close control of the avenues of access to the Liberal Leader. Critics, no matter how mild or how constructive, seldom could get past her to present their case. She was, in the mediaeval meaning of the word, the Prime Minister's chamberlain, the guardian at the monarch's door. Frustrated Liberal advisers devised all sorts of schemes for bypassing her, the most successful of them being the recruitment of M.P.'s to deliver messages to Pearson during the sittings of the Commons, the one time of the day that he and his faithful executive assistant were separated.

Because her insistence on handling every piece of paper bound for the PM's desk eventually threatened the efficiency of the whole office, an attempt was launched in the winter of 1964 by Walter Gordon and several of the PM's aides to have her relegated to taking care of

Pearson's constituency affairs. But the conspiracy fizzled when several others in the PM's office tipped her off and sided with her. The compromise finally reached was the appointment on January 6, 1966, of John Hodgson, an assistant deputy minister of National Defence, to be the PM's principal secretary. But Hodgson could never establish much meaningful influence and Mary Macdonald remained queen bee of the Pearson entourage until the very end.

Another dominant influence on Lester Pearson was that of his wife Maryon. Unlike Olive Diefenbaker, her predecessor at 24 Sussex Drive, Mrs Pearson won few converts to her husband's cause. Shy and stiff in public, clinging to her dark glasses when seated on the speakers' platform, she was the possessor of a manner too tart for the cautious clichés of Canadian politics. At the end of an exhausting day on a campaign trip to Algoma East during the 1962 election, Pearson was attending the last of five coffee parties, and at the end of a brief question period asked his constituents: "Now, is there anything else anyone wants to bring up?" Mrs Pearson replied, in a whisper loud enough to chill the room: "Yes, the last five cups of coffee." On another occasion, when the members of Pearson's staff in Opposition presented her with a cup and saucer set as a mark of their esteem, she acknowleged the gift with the ungracious comment: "Well, I guess this will be one more dust collector in our house."

There were many similar anecdotes to illustrate Mrs Pearson's lack of political tact; but she remained the centre of Pearson's life. He enjoyed her shrewd wit and was fond of recalling that she, the intrinsically non-political woman, had told him not to make the ill-fated no-confidence motion of January 1958 because it was ridiculous and politically unsound. Both Pearsons were happiest when they had their grandchildren tumbling around them. In fact there was something almost bourgeois in Pearson's love of *gemütlich* gatherings; he had a sort of summer-picnic simplicity about him that never faltered. Mrs Pearson was somewhat more sophisticated in her tastes; she liked elegant clothes, read English novels, collected paintings and enjoyed entertaining people she knew well. At one farewell party for a member of Pearson's staff, she pinned *New Yorker* cartoons all over the main drawing room at 24 Sussex Drive and required the guests to play an elaborate, funny game of identifying themselves in the drawings. She always photographed badly but seeing her in person one caught frequent glimpses of the pretty, witty girl she'd been, now trapped by an official life she disliked.

THE TASK OF CREATING A FAVOURABLE PUBLIC IMAGE for the Pearsons occupied the energies of a long line of earnest and frustrated public relations and television specialists. While in Opposition, Pearson seemed willing to put up with practically any indignity to create some kind of rapport with his television audiences. Expert after expert was given complete freedom to make him look as warm on TV as he was with small groups of friends. A voice coach was brought in from Toronto and writers were hired to remove as many sibilants as possible from his scripts so that he could hide his speech problem. Toronto's Mac-Laren Advertising Company exhausted its considerable resources trying to improve his television manner. The TV manipulators tried a dozen different settings – intimate soirées, crowd scenes, living-room shots, interviews with academics – but nothing really worked. Lester Pearson emptied many a living room in his time. "They're trying to make me look like 'Danger Man' but I feel more like 'The Fugitive'," Pearson complained to a friend about his TV advisers.

Unfortunately for him, Pearson's political ascendancy coincided with the breakthrough of television as the most important medium through which politicians communicate with the voters.* The adroit exploitation of television made it possible to maintain the nation in a constant state of political mobilization. The whole country became a whispering gallery, with political triumphs and errors flashed from coast to coast as they happened. Just as few TV comedians could survive more than two seasons (when they used to go on for twenty years on the vaudeville boards), there was a constant demand for new faces and new ideas in politics. "Television has made democracy workable," wrote Roy Shields, television critic for the *Toronto Daily Star*. "Gone, or going, are the phony rhetoric, the wheeling and dealing, the rule of the oligarchy. To gain power these days, a politician has to present himself to the people through TV, a medium that tears the mask from all who dare to appear before it."

Pearson could not cope with this revolution in communications.

His frantic image-makers recognized the problem but their diagnosis for his failure was shortsighted and inadequate. They blamed his high-pitched voice, his persistent lisp, the total absence in him of a sense of occasion. These were relevant liabilities but the real reason he could not communicate with the people was that fundamentally he didn't wish to do so. The legacy of both his diplomatic and his bureaucratic background was an aversion to the very idea of open government.

*By 1970, Canada's population will be 50 per cent higher than it was in 1951, the year before national TV began in Canada, creating a new television generation.

He was far more concerned with his professional prestige among the Ottawa bureaucratic savants who had formed his circle of intimates through the formative years of his life than with his public reputation in the country at large. Throughout his time in office, Pearson remained obsessed by the idea of administrative secrecy, telling the people only the end result of his government's deliberations. He tried, with a glaring lack of success, to apply a closed-door information policy to most of his government's actions, preferring behind-the-curtains machinations to open debate.

This attitude reflected the fact that Pearson was the product of a school of government that truly encompassed an élite, a group of politicians and bureaucrats nominally the leaders of a democracy, who really held power over a quiescent public. In the Teens and Twenties of the twentieth century Canada had an electorate that was still largely uneducated, still plagued by class differences; in the Thirties, an electorate that was numbed by depression; in the Forties, an electorate that was diverted by war; and in the Fifties, or most of them, an electorate that was fat and groggy with boom. But in the Sixties, Pearson and his ministers were balancing on top of an electorate in turmoil. What Pearson was dealing with – even if he didn't realize it – was a true democracy, an electorate that figured it had a *right* to know, that demanded to know not just what was being decided, but how it was decided; an electorate that wanted genuinely to participate in government, that was interested not in unctuous words but in facts. Canadians, particularly the young generation, were increasingly demanding to know not just the news, but the action. They didn't want excuses, or even reasons. They wanted results.

Because he was not prepared to entrust the public with the facts of most situations, Pearson was, in turn, instinctively mistrusted by the voters and failed to enlist their loyalties. He never seemed to realize that every democratic leader must speak *to* as well as *for* his people. There was no communicable style, no correlating of policies, no pinpointing of arguments. Pearson had an almost comic inability to instill his public utterances with any flashes of insight or inspirational perspectives. Not a single memorable phrase survived his stewardship except perhaps the "sixty days of decision," which was always used in a derogatory way.

Pearson worked and re-worked the drafts of the speeches supplied by his assistants, favouring strings of carefully shaded adjectives and complex sentences with triple subjects and triple predicates. While he put a great deal of energy into polishing his texts, he delivered most of his addresses as if they had been written by someone else in another language that he barely spoke or understood. Only before small groups, preferably in university common rooms, did he speak with feeling and style, without the self-consciousness that was so punishing to him on television or before large audiences.

A senior aide recalled taking the draft of a speech to the PM at his summer residence where, to his horror, the Pearsons' poodle started to play with it, tearing a page or two. When he tried to rescue the manuscript, Pearson tiredly waved him away with the comment: "Oh, let him have it; he'll have more fun with it than I will."

The absurd lengths to which Pearson's advisers went to improve his public personality culminated in a National Campaign Committee meeting just before the 1963 election. There were only two items on the agenda: one dealt with the selection of a campaign portrait of the Leader, and the other with whether he should continue to wear a bow tie. After exploring the various points of view, Keith Davey, the discussion chairman, asked George Elliott, a vice-president of MacLaren Advertising, for his comment. Elliott, a sophisticated man who believed in Pearson but not in the possibility of remaking him, gave this caustic reply: "If the Liberal Party could afford to take an inventory of new tie sales, it might discover that 97% of all ties are four-in-hands; 3% are bow ties of which half are given as gifts and never worn. Therefore, when a party leader wears a bow tie, he is getting a positive response from only about 1½% of the male population. If the party could afford to hire Ernest Dichter, the big name in motivation research in the U.S., it would pay him $10,000 to make his report that the man who wears a bow tie is the man who is afraid of growing old and would recommend against Pearson wearing a bow tie. However, if Pearson likes to wear a bow tie, I see no reason why he should stop."

Although Elliott's tongue-in-cheek analysis didn't answer the tie question (Pearson continued to wear both kinds), it did dampen the enthusiasm of the men who sought to remould the Pearson image.

Near the end of his time in office, when the image-makers had long since departed in despair, Pearson was talking to a friend about the problem. "It's just too late to make any changes in me," he said. "The best thing would be for people to accept me as I am, strengths and weaknesses, and stop trying to make me into something I am not."

Unfortunately for him, as Prime Minister of Canada Pearson found himself holding one of those great offices of state in which style can be as significant as substance. The way he acted was often as important as what he did. Canadians demand of the man they elect to lead them that the strength of his personality become a unifying influence to the nation at large. This Pearson was never able to accomplish. The picture he left imprinted on the public mind was that of a good man, a kindly man, but a man without the political juices, acting as if he were not presuming to be a leader in his own right.

CHAPTER 6

The Politics of Utility

O NE OF THE MINOR PREROGATIVES of a Canadian prime minister is to hang in the East Block office where he works the official portrait of his party's patron saint. Within hours of being sworn in, every Conservative incumbent has followed custom by dispatching the painting of Sir Wilfrid Laurier, done by J. Colin Forbes (1846-1925), to the building's basement and ordering up from storage a companion Forbes portrait of Sir John A. Macdonald. Liberal prime ministers have just as swiftly reversed the process.

But in April of 1963, when Lester Pearson moved into the office he broke precedent by ordering both paintings to be hung, and received callers with Laurier behind him and Macdonald on his left. The gesture no doubt reflected his feeling for Canadian history, but it also represented Pearson's curiously ambivalent attitude to politics.

Although he held the highest political office in the land and had been an active politician for fifteen years before he became prime minister, Pearson did not see himself as a partisan and hoped the country would regard him as a diplomat-statesman who happened also to be the leader of a political party.

He talked derisively about opponents who spent their time "politicking" and there seemed to exist in his mind a strange dichotomy between public and political morality. "We have got to be concerned with enduring moral values," he said at an election rally in Winkler, Manitoba, on October 7, 1965. "I feel as strongly about that in *political* life as in *public* life."

In place of patronage-based, old-line partisanship, Pearson advocated a new kind of politics. "What I mean by the 'new politics'," he told the Toronto and District Liberal Association on March 14, 1964, "is the dropping of narrow and nasty, short-sighted and selfish partisanship. The times are too serious for us in Canada to afford the luxury."

This was a commendable objective. But in fact partisan considerations pervaded the PM's office, sometimes preventing the desirable, always testing the acceptable.

While it was true that his approach to life held *politics* to be a mere fraction of existence, Lester Pearson was a highly *partisan* prime minister. His was a politics of utility. He could, on occasion, dispense patronage with blithe disregard for the qualifications of his appointees, all the while wrapping himself in a cloak of statesmanship, condemning the very system he was perpetuating.

The real test of Pearson's sincerity about his "new politics" was the standard of his appointments to the Senate, since these are the sole prerogative of the Prime Minister. Instead of taking the emphasis off partisanship, Pearson used Senate seats as straight political payoffs more blatantly than most of his predecessors. "Mr Pearson," wrote Arthur Blakely, the political columnist of the Montreal *Gazette*, "managed to put together a series of Senate appointments more appalling, if that is possible, than any of his prime ministerial predecessors including, in the primitive Confederation period, Sir John himself." G. Alex Jupp, a leading Liberal riding association executive from Calgary, accused the Prime Minister of transforming the Senate into a political garbage can, a depository for political leftovers with the shabbiest of credentials. Of the thirty-nine senators Pearson appointed, twelve were either ministers whose incompetence had become embarrassing to the administration or M.P.'s whose seats were required for Pearson favourites; another ten were party bagmen; while the balance was made up of various party hacks, organizers and one personal friend, Dr Norman MacKenzie of the University of British Columbia.

Possibly Pearson's strangest appointment of all was that of Hazen Argue, the former CCF House Leader who defected to the Liberals in 1961. Argue had always been a fierce critic of Pearson (he once called him "the Liberals' greatest mistake in history") and his conversion did little to help the Liberal cause on the Prairies during the 1962 and 1963 campaigns. Pearson named Argue a senator without even consulting Saskatchewan's Liberal Premier Ross Thatcher. In fact, Argue was so unpopular in Saskatchewan at the time that his appointment had to be held up until after a provincial by-election in Bengough, because reports from the province indicated the Liberals would lose it if news of

Argue's appointment became known. In a bitter speech attacking the Argue appointment, David Lewis of the NDP told the Commons: "We have made progress in our civilization. The thirty pieces of silver have now become half a million dollars, which is what Mr Argue has been paid for being what he was."* A. M. Nicholson, a former CCF cabinet minister in Saskatchewan, complained that "never in history has any person been appointed to the Canadian Senate whose main qualifications were that he betrayed the thousands of hard-working people who trusted him."

On February 17, 1966, when Acting Prime Minister Paul Martin brought a list of ten Pearson senate appointments which included Argue's name to Cabinet, there were loud groans of protest around the Privy Council table and the necessary cabinet minute was not signed. At the next meeting of Cabinet, Pearson, his face red with fury, told his colleagues: "I just want you all to know I'm signing this!"

It was bad enough that not a single distinguished Canadian was honoured by a senate appointment during the Pearson incumbency except for his services to the Prime Minister or the Liberal Party, but even worse was the occasional extension of this patronage into the federal public service. On March 5, 1966, Pearson appointed as chairman of the Dominion Coal Board J. Watson MacNaught, a gentle nonentity from Summerside, P.E.I., who had earned a reputation as the Liberal Government's least effective minister and was known by the irreverent in his party as "J. Watson MacZero."

While chairmanship of the Dominion Coal Board hardly ranked as one of Ottawa's more important positions, it was not a trivial appointment either. At the time, the chairman of the coal board (paid $20,500 a year) was responsible for a $22 million yearly budget. It was essentially a technical department of government, concerned with administering coal subventions and recommending policies to the government on the production, import and distribution of coal.

An active Liberal since he was a law student at Dalhousie University in the late Twenties, MacNaught had won a Liberal seat in the 1945 election, lost it in 1957 and won it back in 1963. When he picked his first cabinet, Pearson put MacNaught into the Solicitor-General's office, the most junior of portfolios. During a private dinner given at Ottawa's Country Club, shortly after the government was sworn in, MacNaught interrupted two Quebec ministers deep in animated conversation and repeatedly asked them to speak English.

*Appointed to the Senate at the age of forty-five, Argue had thirty years to serve before compulsory retirement. At the current annual stipend of $15,000 a year he would collect $450,000.

The government used him for routine assignments, such as representing Canada at the inauguration of a new president of Mexico (on December 1, 1964). Official Ottawa was baffled when, in the summer of 1965, MacNaught was suddenly promoted to the Mines and Technical Surveys portfolio. This seemed particularly illogical since P.E.I. happens to be the only province in Canada that has no known mineral resources. "I'm going into the department with a very open mind," MacNaught stated firmly at the time and while he was being sworn in, when asked what he intended to do about the Dominion Coal Board, he replied: "I guess I'll have to look into it, if that's the word."

In the 1965 election, MacNaught probably had more going for him than any other cabinet minister; shortly before the campaign started, the government had pledged $148 millions toward the construction of the long-promised P.E.I. causeway. But he lost the two Liberal seats on the island, including his own. He managed this feat by deliberately neglecting to invite Walter Shaw, the Premier of P.E.I. (and a Conservative), to the sod-turning ceremonies for the causeway, which MacNaught had thoughtfully arranged for just three days before the November 8 vote.

The MacNaught appointment was a particularly cynical gesture because it was made by a prime minister who had himself spent twenty years in the public service and was aware of the objections to political appointees. It was final proof, if any was needed, of the gap between the intent and the reality of the Pearson brand of "new politics."

SUCH OBVIOUS PARTISANSHIP did much to destroy Pearson's credibility as being somehow removed from the shadier side of politics. But there was nothing accidental about his paradoxical pose of sounding like a statesman while behaving like a ward boss. Paying off political debts was his method of maintaining the loyalty of the hard-core Liberal Party apparatus.

The Liberal Party membership during the Pearson period could be divided roughly into two categories. There were the new, idealistically inclined amateurs who had come into politics because of their personal admiration for Pearson (and for Walter Gordon), and there was the still powerful residue of tough professionals who manned most of the regional power outposts. By appointing his cabinets strictly according to seniority and recognizing party services through his senate and other appointments, Pearson was able to keep the pros from turning against him. Each potential rebel knew that if he continued his loyal support for the Prime Minister (despite Pearson's inability to obtain a majority and the many errors of the Liberal government) his personal reward would not be forfeited.

The less hardened newcomers to politics, particularly the eighty M.P.'s who came into Parliament after Pearson assumed the leadership, needed no such inducement. Their loyalty to Pearson was real, "a mystical bond," as Bryce Mackasey, the M.P. from Verdun and one of the most loyal of his caucus members, called it.*

"It was Pearson's sincerity, his lack of deceit, his openness which made him so popular with the backbenchers," Mackasey explained. "There were no angles with him, no hidden motives, he was never trying to undermine anybody. Also, he always found time to talk to us, while most ministers claimed they were too busy." Pearson's tolerance of human weaknesses (including his own) inspired a mutually protective attitude among his supporters. Always sympathetic, approachable and understanding, he made M.P.'s feel that they could come up to him at any time to ask how they were doing. Paul Martin told a 1963 meeting of the Ontario federal caucus: "You're lucky you have a leader who cares. When I was a freshman M.P., it was two years before King even spoke to me."

Pearson was consistently popular with most of the public servants who came into close contact with him. They believed that Pearson's critics were mistaking the man for his method. "Mike is a diplomat," said one of them. "He slides things through when they are least expected. He compromises where he thinks he can, in order to win the goals he really believes are worthwhile. It is only the unperceptive who imagine that he doesn't know where he is going."

Unlike John Diefenbaker, who got the blame for everything that went wrong while his government was in office, Pearson was seldom criticized, even when his government was in deep trouble. Errant cabinet ministers deflected most of the anger away from him. Only occasionally a journalist would find some disillusioned Liberal M.P., muttering in the midnight privacy of his office over a glass of Scotch: "Tell me again why I'm for Pearson. I keep forgetting."

Despite such stirrings, the genuine affection in which Pearson was held stirred more loyalty in his followers than either Mackenzie King or Louis St Laurent had commanded; they had always generated more fearful respect than warm esteem. In this sense, at least, whatever Pearson's failures may have been as a national figure, he was a successful party leader in the eyes of most of his Liberal confreres. To substantiate this contention, they made much of the point that Pearson had been left, in 1958, with a parliamentary rump of fifty-eight mem-

*For another explanation of this mystical "bond," see Appendix B.

bers, but his parting gift to the Liberals was a strong party of more than twice that number, a new leader who could capitalize on the nation's urban strongholds, and enough momentum to win the 1968 election.

ONE AREA OF THE COUNTRY where Pearson's charm made no impact whatsoever was Western Canada. Under his leadership the Liberals displayed a total lack of rapport with the territory west of the Lakehead. It was one of the ironies of the Pearson period that the Liberals, while flailing away at the Conservatives for being unresponsive to the aspirations of Quebec, themselves remained equally insensitive to the ambitions of the three Prairie provinces and British Columbia. Nearly every political blunder that John Diefenbaker committed in French Canada had a near equivalent in Lester Pearson's attitude toward the West.

Ever since the Liberals had assumed power in April of 1963 without Western support, a "to hell with the boondocks" attitude pervaded the Pearson high command, an attitude that arrogantly dismissed that part of Canada outside the main population centres of the industrial East as a politically insignificant hinterland. Canada, like Caesar's Gaul, was divided by the ruling Liberals into three parts. The division, both geographical and psychological, was into Upper Canada (Ontario), Lower Canada (Quebec), and Outer Canada (the rest of the country). It was Outer Canada, both East and West, that Pearson simply did not understand and never really governed.

During the five years of Liberal rule the government made few decisions which had enough favourable political impact to span the Prairies or scale the Rockies.

Like the French Canadians under the Conservative Government, westerners during the Pearson administration felt their isolation from the centres of national decision-making. Both regions wanted to develop their societies and economies in their own ways, and resented the Ottawa politicians who took them for granted, awarding their provinces only minor portfolios and little policy consideration.

Outer Canada, particularly the Prairie provinces, responded by rejecting Lester Pearson's leadership. In the campaigns fought under his command, the Liberals won only six of the grand total of 192 Prairie seats that were at stake in the four contests. The Liberal attitude was probably best summed up in an unusually frank speech given by Health and Welfare Minister Allan MacEachen to the Winnipeg South Liberal Association on March 16, 1966. "We suffer from what I would call a lack of sympathy with the Prairie approach to life, a lack of identification," he said. "In our efforts to rebuild the party after the 1958 defeat, we concentrated on Quebec and Ontario. The West became an afterthought. When it came to regional planning it was almost as if we said: 'Oh, yes, we almost forgot the Prairies; we must include something on western agriculture.' Like the Tories, who publicly proclaimed they could win without Quebec, we've tried to get along without the Prairies; the only difference is that we've done it by default rather than by design."

Walter Gordon made the definitive pronouncement on the government's attitude toward the West during the 1965 election campaign, when he refused to make policy concessions attractive to the Prairies with the comment: "I'm an accountant in these things. The Toronto area has more seats than Saskatchewan, and we can win them."

Jack Davis, a Vancouver Liberal, proposed at one parliamentary caucus in 1965 that the occasional cabinet meeting be held in Western Canada to demonstrate the administration's interest in the region. He was met with derogatory hoots from the ministers present, and the idea was dropped. In the early summer of 1965, Dr Pat McGeer, an articulate and politically astute Liberal MLA from British Columbia, came to Ottawa on his own, determined to make the Liberal ministers take notice of western problems. He compiled a "policy for the West" with five specific and relatively simple suggestions that might have won the Liberals some additional B.C. and Prairie representation in the election that fall. McGeer was received politely enough but not a single one of his ideas was followed up.

In August of 1966, when western Liberals organized their own symposium in Saskatoon to prepare for the Liberal Party's national policy conference, they urged, indeed begged, Pearson to attend. But he chose instead to spend a holiday with his friend Philip Chester, a Winnipeg business executive, in Algonquin Park. "That the delegates were disappointed is not quite accurate," reported Peter Regenstrief, the political pollster, in the *Montreal Star*. "They were angry and hurt. Here was a chance for the Prime Minister to play his role as national leader among people crying out for leadership. Had he showed up, they would have accorded him a stupendous welcome. Instead, he reinforced their belief that he just doesn't care."

Such deliberate neglect of the West represented an abrupt change in attitude by the Liberals. During the Mackenzie King and St Laurent periods, the West, particularly Saskatchewan and Manitoba, had been a Liberal stronghold. National attention had been focused on the Prairies and B.C. with the discovery of the huge petroleum and gas deposits, the building of the trans-Canada pipeline, the carving out of the city of Kitimat, the emergence of giant forest product complexes, and discovery of new mineral wealth. But when the federal focus shifted to the struggle for national unity, the West seemed suddenly to become irrelevant as a major factor in Ottawa's policy planning. The Pearson Government gave the impression that it believed all it had to do was sell wheat to keep the West happy, or at least quiet. What the Ottawa Liberals never seemed to realize was that the Western economy had become broadly based, with petroleum, potash, pulp and power rapidly displacing agriculture as the main source of income. Even in Saskatchewan, by the mid Sixties farming was providing less than 50 per cent of the gross provincial product.

Wheat sales didn't have that much to do with the West's alienation. The citizens of the Western provinces had a gut feeling that the Liberals just didn't *care* about their particular problems, and they were right.

In one election campaign after another the Liberals put forward in Western ridings the wrong kind of candidates: city slickers in overalls, machine-tooled to the dictates of the party's Toronto power group. The people of the prairies were never given any good reason for voting Liberal, and they obeyed their instincts by sticking with John Diefenbaker and Alvin Hamilton. The Western viewpoint was best expressed in a thoughtful article by Andrew Snaddon, the editor of the *Edmonton Journal*, on April 4, 1966. "This Western area is not a land of conquered and unconquered," he wrote. "It is a land purely populated by people whose forefathers came, or who have recently come themselves, to seek new freedoms and new opportunity. Some left their homelands because of persecution and fear, but most came because this land offered both a challenge and a chance. Their love for their old lands is not forgotten in a love for the new. Succeeding generations think first of Canada. They may remember the lands of their forefathers but they are Canadian, not something else first and Canadian next. . . . A central government which is going to run under the old rules with nine provinces and deal with a new, virile government in the tenth almost as an equal won't do. Other regions in Canada will also have to find their new status. We, too, have our special interests and concerns and it is clearly time we defined them and then chose the course we must follow. It is time for discussion and concern and it is time for leadership which no longer will come from Ottawa."

Because Lester Pearson remained oblivious to the aspirations of the greater Canada away from the glare of the big-city lights, throughout his time in office he acted not as the leader of his nation, but as the effective prime minister of only that golden triangle formed by Montreal, Toronto and Ottawa.

80

CHAPTER 7

The Puzzle Inside
the Chinese Boxes

CANADA'S MOST SERIOUS PROBLEM during the mid Sixties was not the French-English confrontation, not the paralysis of Parliament or the continuing takeover of a major share of the country's resources and factories by the Americans. It was the growing disbelief that something meaningful could be done to solve the nation's problems through political action. Lacking the unity of purpose that allows a people to think together on fundamental issues, Canadians became citizens of a country that seemed no longer to believe in itself.

Just as the hunger of the Thirties was for material resources, so the hunger of the Sixties was for strong resolve, some assurance that the political system was not a senseless clash between self-seeking men, but a process that would lead somewhere and accomplish something.

It was Lester Pearson's bland, uninspiring leadership that caused much of the malaise and this must stand as the real criticism of his time in office: that despite his good intentions, he failed to provide any frame of reference in which his own government and the people of Canada could reach a consensus on national issues. As more and more Pearson proposals became law, no clear pattern emerged. Canadians could not discern what kind of society was being constructed in the process, and what forces beyond mere political survival were at work in the endless Liberal manoeuvrings.

The academics and journalists who attempted to analyse the man and his motives were split on the question whether there existed some hidden rationale behind Lester Pearson's actions, or whether he was merely reacting to the pressures that built up around him. One school of thought, of which the most eloquent spokesman was Bruce Hutchison, the dean of Canadian political journalists, portrayed Pearson as a man of indecipherable complexity. Hutchison wrote, in one of the vivid sentences for which he's justly famous: "Beside him the cryptic Mackenzie King was a sphinx without a riddle, the courtly St Laurent an open book, and the gaudy Diefenbaker a public meeting." In his profile of fourteen Canadian prime ministers, Hutchison described Pearson's mind as being "constructed layer by layer in a series of Chinese boxes [which] had never revealed its inner content to any colleague, perhaps not even to its owner."*

An entirely different assessment came from James Eayrs, the perceptive University of Toronto political scientist, who described Pearson in a column in the *Montreal Star* as "one of the most scrutable Canadians ever to attain high public office" and ascribed his prominence to "a talent for conciliation, good luck, a sunny, uncomplicated temperament, and a disposition to take things as they come."

The real Pearson existed somewhere between these extremes, a unique politician possessed by a profound sense of personal detachment that allowed him to move through many worlds without fully belonging to any but his own. The fabric of his political commitment was like a veil, translucent but not transparent, serving to protect the inner man. There was always a part of himself that he withheld from any situation, so that he could be participant and onlooker at the same time, viewing from the vantage point of his self-containment events on the outcome of which he had risked something less than his entire fortune. "You must draw limits in your political commitment," he once remarked, "otherwise you become uncivilized."

LESTER PEARSON'S PERSONAL CONVICTIONS did not anchor him in any specific position on the Canadian political spectrum. He never seemed to be in debate with himself about the distinctions between the political left and right. During one 1963 election rally he correctly predicted: "When the Liberals assume office, the government will make changes which may justify the opinion that we are left of centre. But we may also have to resist changes which would be harmful and premature, and this may leave us at times open to the charge that we are being right of centre."

Mr. Prime Minister, 1867-1964 by Bruce Hutchison (Longmans Canada Limited, 1964).

82

Despite, or perhaps because of, this ambiguity, most left-wing Liberals felt that he was really on their side and that without him the party might fall into the hands of its reactionaries. At the same time, the party's right-wingers were just as certain that he was their best buffer against a takeover by its socialist-minded progressives. It was Pearson's intention to spread a large umbrella over the "centre" of Canadian politics, then try to pull the majority of the electorate under it with him. ("A Liberal," he explained in a television interview on October 20, 1966, "is a man of the centre, moving forward.")

While he never openly took sides in the left-right split within his own party, there was little doubt that on most issues his reform instincts placed Pearson in the company of its progressives. He allowed his left-wing ministers great latitude, all the while disarming the party's reactionaries by constantly lecturing the nation on the need for restraint.

The Pearson government's Canada Assistance Plan, amendments to the Old Age Security Act and similar schemes raised federal welfare expenditures to an unprecedented level so that by March 31, 1965, for the first time, their grand total exceeded the nation's defence bill. But the Prime Minister recognized little ideological content in such government initiatives as medicare and the Canada Pension Plan, regarding them merely as administrative and constitutional problems. "We are well beyond the point where it is even a matter of debate whether governments should assume any responsibility . . . for social adjustment, for individual welfare and the basic nature of our society," he told the House of Commons on May 9, 1966.

Pearson regarded his party as espousing a kind of "consensus Liberalism" that made it an instrument for the accommodation of Canadian differences, instead of an apparatus for implementing coherent sets of ideas. Like Mackenzie King, he believed it was desirable during election campaigns to aim party appeals at a wide variety of special interest groups and then act as a broker among them in the actual process of governing.

IT WAS DIFFICULT TO JUDGE how much of Pearson's ideological disengagement was merely a self-protecting, instinctive response to the call of the unpredictable circumstances in which he found himself. Here was a puzzling prime minister, who by temperament and inclination seemed the most traditional of men; yet he touched off a whole series of reforms and social explosions that altered Canada's political landscape.

To use a chemical analogy, Pearson seemed most often to be acting like a true catalyst – a substance that without undergoing change itself enters a mixture and converts it, creating by-products without synthesis.

Lester Pearson was a pragmatist in the purest meaning of that term. He believed that progress flowed not from commitments to any central, synoptic goals, but from the pursuit of a wide range of policy alternatives through adjustable tactics that permit the gradual reconciliation of differences. He had an open-ended attitude to politics that renounced passion for patience, the grand design for the minute ploy. "Rock the boat, it's exhilarating," Pearson told the national convention of the Young Liberal Federation of Canada on April 15, 1966. "But remember that a capsized boat gets nowhere. We don't want to have to swim merely because we've been sunk."

The litmus test of Pearson's political pragmatism was that he assayed the meaning of each new proposition purely by its consequences. More committed to existence than to essence, he was bored by philosophical discussions and his whole performance was a flight from any metaphysical involvement in the political process. From Mackenzie King, Pearson had learned that any politician anchored in the bedrock of his own convictions is less free to move with the tides of power than a leader who maintains an approach coherent enough to give his party momentum, yet fuzzy enough to permit a variety of interpretations. Jack Pickersgill, who worked closely with King, St Laurent and Pearson, maintained that Pearson was the least ideological of the three.

This ideological void expressed itself in Pearson's ability to smudge all the major issues, so that he appeared to be on both sides or on neither side of most controversies.

In any confrontation of ideas, Lester Bowles Pearson was quick to adopt a protective coloration, like some Darwinian survivor in a harsh landscape. On the issue of nationalism, for example, he told a joint service clubs luncheon in Calgary on March 29, 1967, in what must stand as one of the least meaningful of Canadian political pronouncements: "Just as Canadian unity must be based on diversity, so our nationalism must be international." He recognized no problems in reconciling the different ideological outlooks of his colleagues. During the 1965 election campaign he simultaneously recruited into the Liberal Party Robert Winters, an ultra-right-wing Bay Street tycoon, and Jean Marchand, a socialist-minded Quebec union organizer, two men so incompatible in their ideas that in any other country they would have been dedicated to each other's political destruction.

Except for his basic conviction on the need to improve French-English relations, Pearson seldom defended very strenuously the policies of his own government. On the CBC-TV program *Twenty Million*

Questions of October 6, 1966, host Charles Lynch asked the Prime Minister: "Are you sure that what you're going to get at the other end of the armed services unification program – at the business end of it – will be effective?" Pearson calmly replied: "Well, if it's not effective, then the policy will have failed."

This kind of limp answer, and many similar responses, gave the public the impression of a prime minister constantly trying to square the circle of political leadership, seeking consensus at the expense of conviction.

MANY COMMENTATORS AND ACADEMIC PROBERS who tried to fit Pearson's behaviour into some orderly, recognizable school of political thought inevitably came away frustrated, convinced that he was a man quite devoid of philosophy. A more useful approach was to weigh his motivations. Viewed from a distance they might be grouped into these major themes:

PEARSON'S MAIN THRUST seemed to be away from fanaticism and toward compromise, conciliation, tolerance and diversity. He regarded the grip of ideology as a dangerous trait in politicians and encouraged the kind of scepticism, even about himself, that discounts hero-worship. In place of ritual, hierarchy and demonology, he stressed the systematic cultivation of unrestricted inquiry. Lester Pearson's world was not black and white like John Diefenbaker's. It was shaded in a wash of ever-changing pastels. He regarded compromise as a positive virtue and seldom allowed himself to become the protagonist in any situation.

THE CONCEPTS THAT CHIEFLY MOTIVATED HIM were as uncomplicated as the need to avoid World War III and the necessity to preserve Canadian unity. These sentiments were probably most warmly expressed in a personal note Pearson sent his daughter Patricia in 1954 when his grandson Paul was born. "A warm welcome to my little grandson," he wrote, "who by now no doubt has already expressed vocally his opinion of the world into which he has been ushered. We will have to work harder to make it a better one than it is now."

The intensity of Pearson's feeling about national unity rarely came through to his audiences. One exception was in a little-noticed speech he gave in Timmins, Ontario, on October 5, during the 1965 election campaign, when the Conservatives were trying to blame him for jeopardizing national unity by condoning the many scandals that had marred the record of his government. "They can call me corrupt if they want to," he declared, quivering with rare conviction. "They can call me stupid. They can call me anything they like. But to suggest that I would do anything to divide our country hurts me and cuts me to the quick. If I have one overriding passion in my life it is to do what I can to make our country strong and united. . . ."

On another occasion during the same campaign, in a small high school auditorium at Ridgetown, Ontario, on November 4, Pearson told the students a gentle story that illustrated his deep commitment to peace:

A few years ago, when I was visiting Moscow as the Secretary of State for External Affairs, Mr Molotov, who was the Foreign Minister of the Soviet Union, asked me what I wanted to do on Sunday, and I said I wanted to go to church. This sort of shook him for a minute because churchgoing is not an approved activity in the Soviet Union, at least it wasn't then. However, he said there was a church in Moscow, a Baptist Church, and they would be very happy to take me. The place was crowded with people, and this surprised me and interested me. The Russian Baptist minister knew that we were coming and was ready for us. When we entered the congregation was singing, as Russians know how to sing. I thought the words were strange but the melody was very familiar because it was *Rescue the Perishing*. They were singing it in Russian and I wondered whether they were referring to me or not. Anyway, I felt at home even though I didn't know the words. Then the minister started to – what I thought – preach a sermon. It was in Russian so I didn't expect to get very much out of it, but my translator nudged me and said, "Do you know that the minister is just announcing to the congregation that you're going to preach the sermon." So I said, "I can't speak Russian." He replied, "Well, you speak English and I'll translate. That's what I'm here for." So I gave my first and only sermon in a Communist country, and I had to have a text. I searched frantically for a text and I used words which I thought would be very useful in Russia at that time: "Blessed is the Peacemaker." I talked for a few minutes about peace and brotherhood in the world and they seemed to think that was all right. I got the impression then that all the people in this world want peace. They want to be able to live in peace and bring up their children in peace and improve conditions for their children. Surely, out of this spirit of peace, which is in the hearts of ordinary people, we will be able to bring about a situation in the world where peace will prevail and we will not be destroyed by atomic warfare.

His diplomatic training had left Pearson forever the internationalist, and despite his involvement in an endless procession of domestic crises, his personal sense of priorities was always attuned to the larger questions of war and peace. At the Liberal Party's 1966 national policy conference, for instance, after the British economist Barbara Ward had finished speaking and while the delegates were still applauding her remarks on the causes of world tension, Pearson was heard by those listening in hotel rooms over closed-circuit television, whispering to his seatmate: "That should take their minds off their mundane problems." During the 1966 Munsinger affair, Pearson complained in disgust to John Turner, "Here we are caught up in this sordid silly mess while NATO's going down the drain."

PEARSON'S POLITICAL POSTURE was so pragmatic that he seemed to believe the only way for a politician to remain consistent amid changing circumstances was to change with them. The essential thing was to take each situation as it came, never to make facts conform to one's ideas, but to let ideas emerge from the facts. Pearson's view of Canadian society was based on three assumptions: that the value of the individual must be maximized through the primacy of law; that increasing material prosperity would dissolve most strains resulting from social inequality; and that the continuity of experience would provide solutions for most problems.

THESE WERE ALL WORTHY IDEAS, the fruits of a well-spent life, but they served only to mask Lester Pearson's political purposes, reducing the arc of power along which he could operate. There was little here to inspire loyalty, to illuminate the Prime Minister's view of his country and its people. Pearson was never able to translate his yearning for a better Canada in a better world into terms to which the ordinary citizen could respond.

Adolf Berle, the American lawyer-philosopher, once noted that all political priorities must flow from an over-all system of philosophic values. "Only when a political system has decided what is good and what is beautiful can it take the intermediate steps and set the priorities for reaching its goals," he wrote. No such sequence of priorities ever existed in the government headed by Lester Pearson.

Every modern political leader must be a pragmatist, but the great ones have also championed a common faith to guide their people through the convulsions of social change. Because Pearson failed to identify any meaningful, unifying Canadian theme, by default individuals began to search out their own purposes, and the country's political structure was atomized into groups of grumbling, politically apathetic citizens, intent on their own objectives.

Pearson's entire psychic energy seemed devoted to fostering his vague concept of national unity. But the question never answered – or even asked – was, national unity for *what*? Canada's federal government could not become a relevant institution without evolving some meaningful national purpose, what Professor Frank Underhill called the moral equivalent of building the CPR.

"Our root trouble in the 1960's," he wrote, "is that we never agreed on any great nation-building policies to take the place of the original Macdonald-Laurier policies of transcontinental railway-building, industrial tariff protection and immigration. A Liberal government is not going to save Confederation in this present crisis of English-French relations unless it shows a passionate commitment to some specific positive programs to be carried out by the national authority, programs in which French-Canadians will co-operate with enthusiasm. . . . People do not conceive of a common purpose spontaneously. They need leadership. A nation is a body of people who have done great things together in the past and who hope to do great things together in the future. The function of political parties is to give the lead in realizing these hopes. What causes widespread doubts about the Liberal party is its failure to communicate to the Canadian public what its specific ideas are about the things which it wants us to do together."

This had not always been so. In the Thirties Canadians were busy getting out from under British influence and trying to survive the Depression. World War II was, for English Canada at least, a deeply unifying experience. Postwar reconstruction and the "middle power" initiatives of the Fifties gave Canadians a sense of mission. John Diefenbaker's personality and northern "Vision" briefly appeared to supply a similar impetus. A positive reconciliation of the French-English problem might have provided a similar cause for the Sixties. But instead, under Lester Pearson's leadership, all the great political problems seemed to exhaust themselves, not by the catharsis of solution, but through repetition and the absence of decisive action. This "end of ideology" situation drained the electoral process and the parliamentary system of the vitality that flows from a confrontation with great issues.

PART THREE   *Renegade out of Power*

*S*o much of what Lester Pearson did, so many of the Liberal Government's pratfalls, were reactions to the strange strength and compelling political instincts of John George Diefenbaker, that it seemed, at least from 1963 to 1966, as though the Pearson period in Canadian history might be little more than an extension of the Diefenbaker Years.

Diefenbaker's prominence was all the more remarkable because during his tenure in Opposition he was beating off the most sustained attack on his leadership ever mounted against a Canadian party leader by his followers.

The succession of backroom insurrections that shook the Conservative Party, between the time of John Diefenbaker's defeat as prime minister in the turbulent spring of 1963 and his final dethronement as party leader in the centennial autumn of 1967, appeared to fit the pattern of a mediaeval fairy tale. Here was the classic story of a fiery monster who devoured his victims and terrorized his challengers, until the forces of enlightenment triumphed, and Dief-the-Dragon was slain.

Yet this was only a surface impression. In reality, John Diefenbaker's downfall involved more pity than terror; more agony than triumph. There was no joy in his political assassination, only necessity.

When he was PM his circumscribed view of the political process had been clearly evident only to those who sat with him in the cabinet chamber. It never really penetrated to the back benches or the Conservative Party at large. It was only during the Pearson period that one layer of his party adherents after another was exposed to the real character and limitations of the man. As this process took hold, disillusionment with Diefenbaker began to be translated into ever-widening circles of abandonment.

To the old-line Tories of the party, John Diefenbaker had always been an upstart, even in victory. Now that he was both an upstart and a loser, they wanted to be rid of him. But this proved far from a simple assignment. In 1964, the party élite staged a badly managed rebellion that only helped strengthen his hold. In 1965, ineptly led by Léon Balcer, a more serious challenge to his leadership was turned away and it wasn't until Dalton Camp, the party's president, tackled him at the 1966 annual meeting that the shell of his self-confidence was really penetrated. Yet it took one more convulsion – the dramatic leadership convention of 1967 – to finally unseat him.

The Old Chief must have wondered why so many Conservatives turned against his assertive leadership at a time when the weakness and confusion of the Liberal Government invited defeat. The trouble was that instead of measuring him against the political frailties of Lester Pearson, his one-time disciples were remembering with a sense of profound disillusion the inspired Diefenbaker they had followed out of the political wilderness in 1957 and 1958. By the mid Sixties, his vision of Canada, once so relevant to their demands, no longer fitted into the mainstream of responsible Conservative thought.

Like many another political hero, John Diefenbaker was frozen in history at the moment of his triumph. His great electoral victories condemned him to a permanent sense of anti-climax. The spontaneous affection which had erupted across the nation in 1957 and 1958 imbued him with the kind of self-esteem that can shield an aging man from the terrors of mortality. Everything that followed his 1963 defeat was only dimly perceived in the inner recesses of his explosive nature, and attributed to the dark forces that had always haunted his days.

While he continued to be possessed by a capacity to feel his ideas as if they were passions, Diefenbaker's political responses could not cope with the radically changing modern world. Through a dark decade of spreading disenchantment, Diefenbaker's stand against the forces of change isolated him as an obsolete figure, intoning a litany of obstruction against the twentieth century.

In the end, John Diefenbaker succumbed not to the wounds inflicted by his petty defectors, but to the shades and passions in his own character. This stubborn, yearning man, plunging on in the loneliness of the long-distance runner, contrived his ruin with truly spectacular grandeur. It was not the conspiracy of his enemies that bested him, but the dreadful predicament of having outlived the time of his time.

CHAPTER 8

The Waltz of the Party Pashas

D URING THE 1963 ELECTION CAMPAIGN that followed the Conservative Government's downfall, those highly placed Tories who had become disillusioned with his leadership were already hopefully writing dirges and composing John Diefenbaker's political obituaries. But he surprised them all by winning ninety-five seats, and when the pashas of the Conservative Party returned to Ottawa from the electoral wars, they found him standing on what was to have been his political grave, eyes on fire, assaulting all comers. He vowed revenge against those disloyal Tories who had robbed him of his unexpired mandate from the Canadian people, and made clear his intentions of retaining the leadership.

To keep his sense of self-importance from dwindling, he listened only to the retinue of die-hard loyalists with which he surrounded himself. This palace guard included his executive assistants Tommy Van Dusen and Greg Guthrie and his private secretaries Marion Wagner and Margueretta Pound. In the Senate, he could depend on unflagging support from David Walker, his former Public Works minister, and Harry Willis, a florid Ontario backroom Tory. He also continued to receive the wily counsel of Senator Allister Grosart, who in retrospect appeared an even more remarkable political manipulator as the main creator of the Diefenbaker legend.

As his chief lieutenant in the Commons Diefenbaker counted on Gordon Churchill, the veteran member from Winnipeg South Centre. Churchill, who served as Tory House Leader from July 1959 to April

1965, always deferred to "the Chief," but he had his own peculiar interpretation of Parliament's functions. He did not regard the House of Commons primarily as a place where legislation should be enacted, except as a sort of afterthought to the study of departmental estimates. "Parliament is assembled in order to determine taxation and the granting of supply," he said on June 25, 1964. "If, incidentally, it passes legislation for the good of the country, that is a gain. But it is quite conceivable that Parliament could assemble, go through the preliminaries, pass supply, and do nothing else."

Gordon Churchill's grasp of the social and cultural forces transforming contemporary Canada could not even be described as tenuous. During a June 9, 1966, debate over the incorporation of the National Arts Centre in Ottawa, for instance, he proposed that the new theatre concentrate on presenting such non-controversial works as *Oklahoma!*, *My Fair Lady* and Gilbert and Sullivan operettas. "I hope that in this project," he said, "we will not, certainly in the early stages – I do not suppose it can be avoided altogether – attempt to stir up public interest by putting on performances that are a little out of the ordinary, or are calculated to make people think. We have been subjected to enough of that type of thing on radio and television to last us for our lifetime."

This was the man who, as House Leader for the official Opposition, occupied the key position in setting the Commons' legislative pace during most of the Pearson period.

A troop of lesser lights, including Erik Nielsen (Yukon),* J. Waldo Monteith (Perth), Michael Starr (Ontario), Wallace Nesbitt (Oxford), Terry Nugent (Edmonton-Strathcona) and the rambunctious Horner brothers from Alberta, were always prepared to carry out John Diefenbaker's bidding, even when it involved a diminution of their own reputations. They were rewarded by key appointments as chairmen of caucus committees – Monteith for Finance, Nesbitt for External Affairs, Nielsen for the Solicitor-General's department – which honoured their loyalty more than their talents.†

*For a description of Erik Nielsen's role, see Chapter 20.
†Other Diefenbaker die-hards included: A. D. Alkenbrack (Prince Edward-Lennox); F. J. Bigg (Athabasca); A. C. Cadieu (Meadow Lake); George Chatterton (Esquimalt-Saanich); Drummond Clancy (Yorkton); Robert Coates (Cumberland); Lloyd Crouse (Queens-Lunenburg); Walter Dinsdale (Brandon-Souris); F. J. W. Fane (Vegreville); H. J. Flemming (Victoria-Carleton); R. E. Forbes (Dauphin); W. H. Jorgenson (Provencher); C. F. Kennedy (Colchester-Hants); L. E. Kindt (Macleod); John Loney (Bruce); H. R. MacEwan (Pictou); Donald MacInnis (Cape Breton South); J. A. MacLean (Queens); Nicholas Mandziuk (Marquette); R. J. McCleave (Hali-

These men, collectively known on Parliament Hill as Diefenbaker's cowboys, felt and demonstrated total devotion to the Chief. Half a dozen or so other Conservative M.P.'s were never actively against Diefenbaker but simply opted out of all political involvement except for their constituency affairs. A few, notably Eldon Woolliams (Bow River) and Marcel Lambert (Edmonton West), started as Diefenbaker die-hards and became rebels. At least two Privy Councillors – George Hees (Northumberland) and R. A. Bell (Carleton) – tried, after their return to the House in 1965 but without much success, to straddle both factions. Watching the Tory Opposition in action between 1963 and 1967, it was all but impossible to credit the fact that it included sixteen former cabinet ministers – men who had been running the country only a brief time before.

Diefenbaker's power throughout the opposition period was rooted in his parliamentary caucus which, as he incessantly pointed out, was larger than any other Conservative Opposition since the days of Macdonald. Despite its size it was hardly a group accurately representative of Canadian society. The one million citizens of Saskatchewan, for example, had seventeen votes in the Tory caucus, while the nearly five million inhabitants of Metropolitan Toronto, Montreal and Vancouver had only one.

Gradually there emerged a small band of rebels within the Tory parliamentary group. Timidly at first, they began to voice their objections to Diefenbaker's behaviour and policies. The most impressive member of this band was Gordon Fairweather, a gentle and learned former attorney-general of New Brunswick who talked of his political commitments with solemn deliberation, as if he were reading what was written on his mind. Although his New Brunswick riding of Royal was faithful to Diefenbaker (and in the 1965 election Fairweather had the distinction of being picketed by Tories in his own constituency carrying placards pointedly reminding him that "Royal is LOYAL!") he could not swallow his leader's anti-intellectual bias, and spoke out on many

fax); Jack McIntosh (Swift Current — Maple Creek); R. D. McLelland (Rosetown-Biggar); Melvin McQuaid (Kings); K. H. More (Regina City); Ed Nasserden (Rosthern); P. V. Noble (Grey North); J. N. Ormiston (Melville); J. E. Pascoe (Moose Jaw — Lake Centre); D. V. Pugh (Okanagan-Boundary); Reynold Rapp (Humboldt-Melfort-Tisdale); Roger Régimbal (Argenteuil-Deux Montagnes); Théogène Ricard (St-Hyacinthe-Bagot); Dr P. B. Rynard (Simcoe East); Robert Simpson (Churchill); W. M. Skoreyko (Edmonton East); C. S. Smallwood (Battle River-Camrose); R. R. Southam (Moose Mountain); Eric Stefanson (Selkirk); Lawrence Watson (Assiniboia); R. A. Webb (Hastings-Frontenac); Eric Winkler (Grey-Bruce); and after 1965, Dr Lewis Brand (Saskatoon) and R. J. Keays (Gaspé).

issues, bravely and sometimes alone. He was despised by the Diefenbaker cowboys and eventually the point was reached that whenever he made some innocuous remark in the House (such as "humbug is no longer an adequate substitute for fact and Canadian parliamentarians who do not understand this have a doubtful future"), he would immediately find himself under severe attack in the caucus for having delivered "an anti-Diefenbaker tirade."

Later on, it took little courage to be a Diefenbaker dissenter but in the early opposition years only fourteen Tories besides Fairweather were daring enough to urge policy reform and leadership review when this was still heresy.*

The treatment which the Diefenbaker loyalists meted out to these non-conformists was always petty and sometimes brutal. Douglas Harkness, for example, who had resigned from the Conservative Cabinet over Diefenbaker's nuclear indecision, returned to the Parliament Buildings after the 1963 election, and as the third most senior Tory in the House (only Diefenbaker himself and Elston Cardiff had exceeded his eighteen years of service), chose to settle in one of the comfortable two-room Centre Block parliamentary offices reserved for senior Opposition M.P.'s. But a few weeks later while Harkness was delivering an out-of-town speech, Eric Winkler, the Tory Whip and a Diefenbaker die-hard, ordered that his files and personal belongings be removed and unceremoniously dumped on the floor of a tiny, attic-like office on the third floor of the West Block.

More serious was the fact that Harkness and most of the other rebels could seldom get their names on the parliamentary speakers' lists that the Whip drew up in consultation with the Leader. In the House itself, Harkness had been tucked away on the very last seat of the Tory front benches, so that he'd be as far removed from Diefenbaker – and the centre of Commons attention – as possible. But this turned out to be something of an advantage. Harkness' ostracism put him directly under the dais of Alan Macnaughton, the Speaker of the House. Harkness and Macnaughton were old friends and the former defence minister never had any trouble catching the Speaker's eye before the next member on the official Tory speaking list could rise in his place.

*They were: Gordon Aiken (Parry Sound-Muskoka); G. W. Baldwin (Peace River); Tom Bell (Saint John-Albert); S. J. Enns (Portage-Neepawa); Heward Grafftey (Brome-Missisquoi); A. D. Hales (Wellington South); Douglas Harkness (Calgary North); Heath Macquarrie (Queens); Heber Smith (Simcoe North); Mrs Jean Wadds (Grenville-Dundas); and after their election in 1965, Davie Fulton (Kamloops); David MacDonald (Prince); Patrick Nowlan (Digby-Annapolis-Kings); and L. R. Sherman (Winnipeg South).

This practice infuriated Diefenbaker so much that on October 29, 1963, when Harkness popped up to take part in a supply motion debate on national defence, the Conservative Leader forced a House vote in an attempt to shut him up. When all the other parties had voted to hear Harkness, Diefenbaker rose on a question of privilege and insisted that Harkness (although he had been in charge of Canada's military affairs for most of the preceding three years) not be allowed to take part in the defence debate. He was overruled by Speaker Macnaughton and Harkness was finally unleashed to deliver a prosaic condemnation of the fact that the acquisition of nuclear warheads had become a partisan issue. (It was an interesting footnote to the dislike for Diefenbaker that was felt by most of the foreign emissaries to Ottawa that after he moved into Opposition, the city's diplomatic corps frequently picked Harkness, Fairweather and some of the other rebels to represent the Conservative Party at their national day celebrations.)

JOHN DIEFENBAKER'S SUPPORT WITHIN his own caucus was substantially weakened for the first time during the 1963 parliamentary session over the Pearson Government's proposal to increase the indemnity of members from $8,000 to $12,000 a year and tax-free expense allowances from $2,000 to $6,000.

Parliamentary pay had not been reviewed since 1954, although in the interval being an M.P. had become a year-round job. Because raising their own salaries was bound to be a touchy political issue, M.P.'s of all parties agreed they would support the Pearson Government's plan to push the legislation through the House on a strictly non-partisan basis in a single sitting day. Before proceeding, Jack Pickersgill had called in the other House leaders and asked them to sound out their party chiefs on the idea. The measure would be introduced, he warned, only if there was a guarantee of no opposition. The House leaders of the NDP (Stanley Knowles) and Social Credit (Alex Patterson) brought Pickersgill the required assurance, but Gordon Churchill of the Conservatives returned to demand more details, particularly about the increase in pensions that was concurrently being granted prime ministers who had served four years in office. Two days later, after George Nowlan had interceded on behalf of Tory backbenchers who badly wanted the pay raise, Churchill finally assured Pickersgill that his party would not oppose the pay increase. But that afternoon in the Commons, when Pearson tabled his formal intention to move the measure, Diefenbaker made procedural objections, and Pickersgill immediately broke off negotiations. When Tory backbenchers, who had been forced to finance two election campaigns in the preceding eleven months, angrily objected to their own party's tactics, Churchill enlisted Stanley Knowles as an intermediary to re-establish contact with Pickersgill. But the Liberal House Leader refused to resume the discussions until he could get written assurance there would be no Conservative opposition to the bill. Churchill then sent a note to Pickersgill across the floor of the House which read: "JACK: If you put the indemnity measure on votes and proceedings, we will pass all three stages on Monday. G.C." The Tory Opposition thus seemed to be committed to supporting the bill.

But on Monday (July 29), when it came up, Diefenbaker launched an angry attack on its provisions and led six of his fellow Prairie Tories in voting against the proposed pay increase.* There was a hush in the House as W. H. A. Thomas, the mild-mannered Conservative M.P. from Middlesex West (and a longtime Diefenbaker loyalist), explained that the Leader had not been speaking for the party.

THIS AND OTHER INSTANCES of John Diefenbaker's disregard for the private sanctions of the parliamentary "club" had the cumulative effect of undermining his reputation as a House of Commons man. The sequel to his stand on the pay increases came on June 4, 1964, during the early days of the Tory filibuster on the flag. The previous evening, addressing a dinner-dance of Toronto's York-Scarborough Progressive Conservative Association, Diefenbaker had dismissed Liberal threats of an election over the flag resolution by saying: "The Prime Minister knows he stands in no danger from his allies – the Social Credit, Créditiste and New Democratic parties – because the government voted M.P.'s a pay increase of $18,000 a year. It had a wonderful effect on third-party support. . . . On the flag vote, the attitude would be, not that I love the Red Ensign less, but $18,000 more." Next afternoon, when the Commons met, furious members of the three major parties demanded that Diefenbaker withdraw his charge. Colin Cameron, the grandfatherly NDPer from Vancouver Island, put the case most succinctly. "I do not propose," he said, "to sit quietly under a slanderous lie stated by any preposterous mountebank who will seize upon anything in his desperation. . . . If a case of this kind occurs again outside the House, I shall take the matter to the courts."

*Tories voting with John Diefenbaker against the pay increase were Ed Nasserden, Drummond Clancy, D. R. Gundlock, A. R. Horner, J. E. Pascoe and Reynold Rapp. Three Socreds – Réal Caouette, C. E. Dionne and Raymond Langlois – also opposed the measure. Unlike Diefenbaker, all these men accepted the higher remuneration after it became law on October 1, 1963.

This was probably as strong language as has ever been used to condemn any party leader in Canada's Commons. Diefenbaker quickly withdrew his remarks. For once, the menace seemed to drain out of him as he found himself humbled by the institution he had served for a quarter of a century.

BY THE FALL OF 1963 the upper echelons of the Conservative Party had become restless and a few Conservative constituency organizations had passed motions in favour of turning the Association annual meeting (due to be held in Ottawa from February 1 to 5, 1964) into a leadership convention. But this remained a minority view, held mainly by the pashas of the Conservative Party – the Tory élite of another day who had been ignored by Diefenbaker while he was in power, and now wanted to re-assert their authority.

The loyalists, sure in their faith, welcomed a showdown, in the hope that a solid reaffirmation in John Diefenbaker's leadership would halt the whispering campaign against him. Since every annual meeting had traditionally included a vote of confidence in the party leader, the confrontation between the pro- and anti-Diefenbaker factions centred on whether or not this vote (which ordinarily amounted to little more than a formality) should in 1964 become a secret ballot in which Diefenbaker's leadership could be tested.

Before the annual meeting of the parent association got under way, the PC Student Federation shocked their elders by supporting the secret ballot on a close vote. The YPCs gave Diefenbaker a narrow expression of confidence with many abstentions, and passed a resolution calling for the leader to restore Douglas Harkness to a position of respect within the party. On Monday, February 3, 1964, some fifteen hundred delegates gathered at Ottawa's Chateau Laurier and broke up into provincial caucuses to debate the secret-ballot issue. The Atlantic provinces, Saskatchewan and Manitoba quickly rejected the idea, but Ontario balked, with only John Robarts' intervention on behalf of Diefenbaker preventing a floor fight.

The Chateau Laurier ballroom, where the debate on the confidence motion was to take place on the afternoon of the following day, would hold about nine hundred people. This meant that six hundred of the attending delegates would be disfranchised in any standing vote. Diefenbaker's strategists – mainly Senator Grosart – quietly passed the word that the Chief's supporters should skip the scheduled Tuesday morning breakfast parties and by 9:30 a.m. the hall was jammed, mostly by elderly delegates sporting determined looks and Diefenbaker buttons. Just before the Conservative Leader rose to speak, teams of newsboys darted into the hall, distributing free copies of the previous day's Toronto *Telegram*. Although that newspaper had editorially opposed Diefenbaker's re-election in 1963, it now urged delegates not to weaken the party by withdrawing their support from the Chief.

Diefenbaker began his 53-minute oration at 2:30 p.m. with a slashing attack against Lester Pearson for "introducing an era of bunk masquerading as diplomacy." He poked fun at the Liberals' disastrous sixty days of decision. ("They introduced a budget which they said was the finest budget ever. By the time they were through, they still had Walter Gordon, but almost everything else had disappeared.") Then he leaned into the tangle of microphones before him and enunciated his credo: "I come before you today as a defender of the faith of the Fathers of Confederation in *One Canada*. I come to you to unite, not to disunite. I come to heal, not to wound. To raise up your eyes to the future, to build, not to tear down. . . . I have no ambition that is unsatisfied, everything that one could have has been given to me. . . . We have a responsibility as a party which Macdonald and Cartier tried to achieve – bringing about a new unity in this country. . . . I do not come before you to ask you, to appeal. I come before you knowing you will decide a question I want decided. No leader can ever march forward facing the foe, knowing somebody is behind him who is going to interfere."

The meeting was his. Ovation after ovation punctuated his rambling discourse, including a sudden aside – that since the Liberals had come to power the price of cattle had dropped five cents a pound. "Those in opposition to me are still faceless and nameless," he continued. "Some say the vote should be an open one. Others say a secret vote. I will not say what that will mean in the years ahead, but I don't want you leaving here saying that if the vote had been secret, the result would have been otherwise. If it's a secret vote, that's fine with me. I want to know where I stand. I want to know where *you* stand too!"

The rest was anticlimax. After Diefenbaker left the hall there followed a ninety-minute wrangle on the secret-ballot motion, with twenty-one of the thirty-three speakers supporting the idea. But it was easily defeated and on the open vote of confidence fewer than fifty Tories stood up against Diefenbaker. Douglas Harkness was the only M.P. to do so, an old soldier with his regimental tie at the ready, standing at ceremonial military attention against the catcalls of the crowd. Near him stood the proud ramrod figure of Hon. James Macdonnell, in his eightieth year and still his party's most revered symbol of dedication to public service. Allister Grosart silently slipped out of the hall and telephoned Diefenbaker the news of his easy victory.

But two concessions had been wrung out of the Conservative Leader. He had agreed to follow the wishes of Dalton Camp, the PC Association's newly elected president, for the holding of a party policy conference. He appointed Léon Balcer as his Quebec lieutenant and the party's deputy leader. To quiet the rumbles of discontent shaking the French-Canadian wing of the party, Diefenbaker had gone in front of the Quebec caucus, embraced Balcer and called him "the greatest living Canadian Conservative from Quebec – a second Sir George Etienne Cartier!"

The party delegates went home, with the leadership issue pushed into the background though still unresolved. But the rebels had learned their first lesson in the difficult art of political lion-taming.

CHAPTER 9

A Dark and Bellowing Presence

ALTHOUGH JOHN DIEFENBAKER WAS BRANDED an Anglo-Saxon separatist in Quebec and regarded by many people in the rest of the country as the political field marshal of the thin red line protecting British Canada from the French fact, his attitude toward Quebec was more a matter of political strategy than the result of any personal prejudice. He viewed the Quebec problem not as a social phenomenon with deep moral significance but as a partisan issue, one he could exploit by appealing to the deep-rooted *status quo* feelings of the nation's majority while ignoring or misrepresenting the aspirations of its militant minority. Though Diefenbaker's public discourses seldom betrayed any explicit anti-Quebec bias, neither did they hint that he possessed the slightest understanding of what the root causes of and possible remedies for the French-English confrontation might be. Although he had fought all his life against racial and sectional prejudice, his drive for power became based on an appeal to hard-rock Anglo-Saxonism.

There was nothing mysterious or complicated about his view of Quebec. He regarded French Canadians as just another ethnic group,* one that happened to get here first, and all Quebec's initiatives as a kind of subversive dynamism that could be tamed by strong words from Ottawa.

*On June 28, 1966, for instance, while attacking a parliamentary amendment requiring that three of the nine directors of the National Arts Centre be French speaking, Diefenbaker referred to the clause as "an ethnic formula."

102

Diefenbaker's ideal of nationhood was his Prairie-bred pan-Canadianism – the vision of a wide-open society in which citizens overcome the burden of their origins to join its great mainstream, which, in turn, accepts them without any barriers of race, creed or religion. When he kept repeating in his speeches how much easier his life would have been had he borne his mother's name, Campbell-Bannerman, Diefenbaker was not only referring to his Anglo-Saxon origins. He was voicing the anguished cry of a man who had suffered the tacky prejudices, the deliberate snubs of small-town social establishments where he had grown up, because his name had a foreign ring. He best expressed this attitude in a 1958 interview with *Maclean's* when he said: "I am the first prime minister of this country of neither altogether French or English origin, so I determined to bring about a Canadian citizenship that knew no hyphenated consideration. . . . It's the reason I went into public life." But for the 37 per cent of the country's population that was French-Canadian, the hyphen symbolized an essential part of their identity. Similarly, the Conservative Leader's often repeated clarion call for "One Canada" found easy response in most of rural Ontario and the West. But in Quebec, it rekindled folk memories of the assimilation doctrines of Lord Durham, the 1840 Act of Union, and the centralized regimentation that Ottawa imposed on the province during two world wars.

None of this seemed to bother Diefenbaker very much. His calculations were based on the politics of the situation and it was evident there were far more votes to be gained in the country as a whole by questioning French Canada's motives than by defending Quebec's aspirations. Diefenbaker was very much aware that in the 1957 and 1962 elections it had been Quebec's disaffection which had robbed him of his majority, that in 1963 the province's desertion from his cause had cost him his power, and that even in 1958 (when Quebec gave him fifty seats) he had achieved his parliamentary majority without needing French-Canadian support.

Even though his statements on French Canada had the ring of candour and courage, they were clothed in an ambiguity that permitted him to charge misinterpretation if he should be accused of voicing anti-Quebec sentiments. But his implicit meaning was clear to the more thoughtful members of the Conservative Party, and gradually they began, with great circumspection, to express their objections. "Are there those in our party who consider valid the mathematical possibility of forming a government without substantial representation from Quebec?" Gordon Fairweather rhetorically demanded during a 1965 Montreal address. "I for one will not give allegiance to a party that will tolerate a Canada without Quebec." Senator Wallace McCutcheon detected similar dangers in Diefenbaker's tactics. "I do not want the word Liberal to mean French, and the word Conservative to mean English," he told the Progressive Conservative Association of Manitoba on November 14, 1964.

The Diefenbaker cowboys, anxious to show their chief that they had understood his message, freely expressed their disdain for the French fact. Typical of such outbursts was the reaction of Douglas Alkenbrack, the Tory backbencher from Napanee, Ontario, to the modest Liberal proposal of paying a 7 per cent salary bonus to lower- and middle-echelon civil servants who were fluently bilingual. Part of "a devilish plan that day by day is dividing Canada," Alkenbrack called it in the House of Commons on November 24, 1966, and accused French Canadians of "fanatical racist and linguistic demands." R. A. Bell, the member for Carleton, who led the parliamentary battle against bilingualism, summed up his reaction in one sarcastic quip: "Pretty soon it'll be compulsory to be bilingual to empty a wastebasket." These and similar bleats of immoderation were accorded the approbation of silence by John Diefenbaker at a time when attempts to reinforce the image of Ottawa as a meaningful seat of government for the citizens of Quebec had become a matter of national survival.

THE POLITICIAN WHO FINALLY ROSE UP to challenge Diefenbaker was Léon Balcer, a man of few intellectual pretensions and little knack for leadership, but with a large love of his country and a capacity for patience that had finally been exhausted after sixteen frustrating years of trying to make Quebec's views felt within the Tory hierarchy. Balcer had first won the Trois-Rivières seat in 1949 and had held it through five more elections – a record unmatched by any other Quebec Conservative in this century. At a time when it meant very little to be a federal Tory in French Canada, Balcer had stubbornly adhered to his political faith, insisting that it was possible to be both a useful Conservative in Ottawa and a good Quebecker. Balcer became the first French Canadian to be president of both the YPC's and the party's parent association, but when he was forming his first cabinet in 1957 Diefenbaker appointed him to the trivial Solicitor-General's post while leaving five more important ministries vacant. Balcer later served as a competent minister of Transport and became a Diefenbaker supporter to the extent of telling a Conservative rally in Quebec City on March 4, 1961: "Ninety per cent of the Kennedy administration's proposed legislation has been inspired by Canadian legislation of the Diefenbaker Government."

In the winter of 1964, shortly after Diefenbaker had hailed him as "a second Sir George Etienne Cartier," Balcer found to his chagrin that instead of being treated as the party's deputy leader he was more than ever frozen out of any position of influence or even consultation. During the next thirteen months, Balcer was not once invited into the Leader's parliamentary office. His fellow Tory M.P.'s from Quebec were constantly being advised by Diefenbaker to ignore him, and he was not allowed the slightest influence on party policies even when they exclusively concerned his home province. An empty symbolic gesture was made to Balcer's new status when he was moved to become Diefenbaker's seatmate in the House of Commons. "During the months that followed, the two men never spoke to each other," Pierre Sévigny reported in his political reminiscences.* "Actually, the Leader did ask his deskmate on one occasion if it had snowed in Three Rivers. The latter answered politely that he did not know. On another occasion, having overheard a rather unpleasant remark about himself made by Diefenbaker to Gordon Churchill, the Quebec leader told the Honourable Member from Prince Albert to go to hell."

The banishment of Léon Balcer would not have been particularly significant had not Diefenbaker's 1964-65 stands on various national issues simultaneously lost him the support of many powerful party members across the country, including most of the Conservative provincial premiers. The first of these policy confrontations occurred in the fall of 1964 over the amending procedure for bringing the British North America Act under exclusive Canadian jurisdiction. Because constitutional amendments excite politicians more than voters, this issue never really had much public impact. But inside his party it provided one of those rare moments of cruel illumination when John Diefenbaker's habit of bending and curving the facts to fit his purposes of the moment was revealed for all to see.

The problem about bringing home the BNA Act had always been to devise an acceptable domestic amending process, once the power to change the 1867 statute was removed from the British Parliament. Seven federal-provincial conferences over forty years had tackled this question and been defeated by it. Disagreement arose mainly over Sections 91 and 92 of the Act which allocate powers between federal and provincial jurisdictions. Because he wanted to be remembered as a nationalist who

*This Game of Politics by Pierre Sévigny (McClelland and Stewart Limited, 1965).

had patriated the Canadian constitution, Diefenbaker gave the project high priority during his time in office and together with his Justice minister, Davie Fulton, worked out an amending formula, which was debated at a series of federal-provincial meetings during 1960 and 1961. It finally foundered on objections from the province of Saskatchewan, but Guy Favreau revived the patriation idea as soon as he became Justice minister. Alberta's Premier E. C. Manning provided some of the early initiative and at meetings with Prime Minister Pearson in Charlottetown (September 1, 1964) and Ottawa (October 14, 1964) the provincial premiers unanimously agreed to accept the Fulton-Favreau amending formula. Manning called it "the most progressive piece of constitutional legislation in Canadian history." W. A. C. Bennett of British Columbia was "elated"; Duff Roblin of Manitoba was "gratified." Jean Lesage of Quebec said that it "opened the door to propose all the constitutional changes Quebec could desire." The usually unflappable John Robarts of Ontario outdid them all by stating: "God help the man who holds up agreement."

What the Fulton-Favreau formula proposed was to give each province an absolute veto on amendments in certain areas of exclusively provincial jurisdiction. At the same time, it provided for the delegation of powers by the provinces to Ottawa (and vice versa) with the mandatory support of the federal government and at least four of the provinces. The formula's critics pointed out that this rigid approach left the federal government in a weakened position. They claimed it established the questionable principle that national ends can be met by provincial means. The formula's supporters argued that it represented the best practical solution to a tough problem and that experience with the new domesticated constitution would eventually produce a useful document.

The premiers pledged themselves to pass the enabling legislation* and for a while it seemed as if Canada's constitution – the framework within which its people live and govern themselves – would at last come under domestic control. Just after agreement on the Fulton-Favreau formula was reached, John Diefenbaker had a chance Ottawa encounter with Davie Fulton (then leader of the moribund Conservative Party in British Columbia) and asked him to prepare a memorandum comparing his original amending formula with the Favreau version. Fulton dictated a five-page letter immediately after he returned to his home in Kamloops on October 26.† He concluded that the latest

---

*They all did except Jean Lesage, who rejected the formula in a letter to Prime Minister Lester Pearson dated January 20, 1966.

†For a text of the Fulton memorandum, see Appendix C.

Favreau approach did not "alter in principle or effect the amending formula as embodied in the 1961 proposal." He also stressed that the all-important delegation provisions "do not confer any new jurisdiction or power on the provinces, nor do they have the effect of diminishing the federal jurisdiction or power in the slightest."

Between October 28 and November 2 – even though he had the Fulton memorandum in his pocket – Diefenbaker publicly stated three times that the new Liberal formula differed substantially from the amending procedure his own administration had been enthusiastically advocating only three years before. Each of these pronouncements came not under pressure, but in circumstances allowing Diefenbaker to choose his words carefully. The first was delivered on October 28 in a scripted free-time CBC political broadcast. The second was made on October 29 in the House of Commons, as a contradiction to Prime Minister Pearson's contention that there was, in fact, no essential difference between the two amending formulas. The third was given on November 2 at the Ontario Conservative Association annual meeting in Toronto, where Diefenbaker charged that alteration of his original formula would "allow the balkanization of Canada."

As news of the Fulton memorandum leaked out, the worth of John Diefenbaker's word came into question. The country's Conservative provincial premiers found themselves having to defend before their own legislatures a measure that their party's national leader had branded as dangerous to the national future. Inside the Conservative caucus, a group of Tory rebels led by Léon Balcer and Gordon Fairweather began to attack Diefenbaker's opposition to the Fulton-Favreau formula.

HAVING NO FRAME OF REFERENCE within which to fit the inexorable impulse toward change that was shaking Canadian society during the Sixties, John Diefenbaker interpreted each of the Pearson Government's mild reforms as the hot breath of revolution. A majority of the NDP and Socred members of Parliament, as well as a dozen or more Conservatives, realized that no matter how poor an opinion they had of the Liberal Government, restoration of John Diefenbaker to office would be infinitely worse. For much of the Pearson period it was mainly the spectre of Diefenbaker's return that retained the minority Liberal Government in power.

As leader of Her Majesty's Loyal Opposition, Diefenbaker in his attacks frequently left the Pearson Government in disarray and obscured most of its achievements. Yet seldom did he manage to convey the idea, through the barrage of his vague and violent words, that he could offer constructive policy alternatives.

The man who leads the parliamentary opposition has a higher duty than the destruction of the government in power. Operating away from the compromising pressures of office, he must draft and advance his own version of the country's future. This Diefenbaker could not or would not attempt. "The duty of the Opposition," he told a Kiwanis Club luncheon in Ottawa on March 13, 1964, "is to turn out the government."

Because it was the main source of power left to him, Diefenbaker concentrated most of his energies on his performance in the House of Commons. Even though the range of his concerns seemed limited to exploiting the destructive potentials of every situation, most of his speeches had an impressive lyric quality about them – sometimes deliberately comic, sometimes unintentionally sad, but always spellbinding and somehow mystical in their impact.

His language was a splendid artifice. His every parliamentary appearance let loose a hundred verbal balloons, tangled together in wild confusion. One minute Diefenbaker would be contemplating the indiscretions – real or imaginary – of some squirming Liberal frontbencher, portraying the errant minister as an irredeemable disgrace to his office, his country and mankind in general. The next instant Diefenbaker would glance across the aisle, including on the distant horizon of his civility the tense face of his victim – and smile. It was the best show in town, and even constant repetition did little to soften its debilitating effects on the Pearson ministry.

Excited by small gains, unshaken by major reverses and ever partial to the slashing, massive retort, Diefenbaker used the parliamentary question period to badger the administration on a succession of irrelevancies while many of the essential national problems remained untouched and unresolved. Even on the kind of politically charged issues that he might have used to defeat the government, Diefenbaker fumbled and threw away his chance. In the late fall of 1964, for example, with the Pearson administration reeling from the succession of revelations about the involvement of some of its members with the dope smuggler Lucien Rivard, a determined, shrewdly led opposition might have been able to topple the government. But on November 30, Diefenbaker directed J. Waldo Monteith, the Conservative member from Stratford, to move an opposition amendment calling for a national flag plebiscite. The flag debate had already occupied dozens of parliamentary sitting days and six weeks of committee hearings. Tactically, the Monteith amendment meant that the debate would continue until the Liberals

re forced to cut it off through closure. But strategically, Diefenbaker's
istence on spinning out the anti-flag filibuster had much more serious
sequences. It granted the Liberals a two-week respite from the daily
estion period – precisely at a time when they were most susceptible
attack on the developing scandal accusations.

Diefenbaker was never able to unite the opposition parties on any
al issue. On the contrary, it was the violence of his attacks against
New Democrats and Social Credit that granted the Liberals the
rking majority denied them by the voters. Jack Pickersgill, who
ved as Liberal House Leader during the early Pearson period, gave
efenbaker most of the credit for keeping the government in power.
hen the Liberals had only fifty members in the Opposition," he once
narked, "we always consulted the eight CCFers and tried to get as
ch co-operation from them as we could to consolidate everything
inst the Government. But Diefenbaker never lost an opportunity to
ult Tommy Douglas, Bob Thompson or Réal Caouette. He really did
re, I think, than any member of the Government to create an effective
jority for us."

One reason the smaller parties refused to deal with Diefenbaker was
t he continually broke the Commons' unwritten rules, which hold
t certain things aren't done, even in the extreme heat of partisanship.
the spring of 1964, for example, when the terms of reference for
nada's Cyprus force were being debated in the Commons, Diefen-
ker privately approached Paul Martin with the suggestion that the
vernment should follow the United Kingdom parliamentary tradition
keeping the opposition confidentially briefed on world problems.
xious to foster a bipartisan foreign policy, Martin agreed immedi-
ly, although the practice had not been followed during Diefenbaker's
e in power. At a meeting of opposition party leaders in his office a
days after the Diefenbaker request, Martin explained that the
prus force would be operating under two sets of directives: a general
erence drawn up by the United Nations which was public and another
of orders given to the UN commander in the field which, the partici-
ing countries had agreed, would be kept secret. The External Affairs
nister briefed the party leaders on the outlines of both documents,
ing to satisfy their queries in private so that Commons questions
ght not endanger the touchy operation. As he listened, Diefenbaker
ddenly grew angry. Shouting, "You're trying to seal my lips. I won't
silenced!", he stomped out of the room. Later he used the data as
basis for some probing parliamentary questions and all attempts to
ef the opposition on foreign policy promptly ceased.

DISSATISFACTION OVER DIEFENBAKER'S LEADERSHIP broke into the open at the annual meeting of the party's executive on December 5, 1964, when J. Edward Murphy, a former mayor of Moncton, N.B., and a recently defeated candidate in the Westmorland by-election, bluntly declared that blame for the party's low state should be placed where it belonged: on the quality of its leadership. James Macdonnell stood up to echo Murphy's sentiments, and Léon Balcer jumped in to urge that the meeting pass a resolution calling on its parliamentary wing to end the anti-flag filibuster then under way. Half a dozen anti-Diefenbaker Tories tried to claim the floor and it was only the intervention of two Diefenbaker supporters – Ed Nasserden (M.P. for Rosthern) and Bill Macadam (the British Columbia vice-president of the party) – that prevented a vote on the flag issue from being taken.

During the parliamentary recess that Christmas, Macdonnell and Joseph Sedgwick, a distinguished Toronto lawyer and longtime party stalwart, considered a mailing campaign to caucus members in their home constituencies urging them to support a review of the party's leadership, but they were talked out of the idea by Senators Grattan O'Leary and Wallace McCutcheon.

Despite the growing unrest, Diefenbaker's position still seemed secure. The party constitution provided no machinery to force out an existing leader and no alternative figure around whom the dissidents could rally had dared to present himself. Convinced that only the loss of seats in another election campaign could dislodge their leader, the rebels by the end of 1964 expressed their feelings in the Marxist-sounding slogan "liquidation through defeat." As they whispered this confidence to each other, they seemed like some underground cell in the Leninist tradition, plotting the overthrow of legitimate but obsolete authority.

THIS INTERNAL DISCONTENT HAD GRADUALLY COME TO FOCUS itself on the escalating feud between Léon Balcer and John Diefenbaker. The Quebec Tory had already split publicly with his leader over the constitutional amending formula and as the flag filibuster ground on, their differences became irreconcilable. Finally, on December 9, Balcer rose in the Commons on a point of personal privilege, attacked the Conservative tactics of paralysing the business of the House, then invited the Liberals to end the flag debate by moving closure. Gordon Churchill immediately stood up to declare that the member for Trois-Rivières had not been speaking with the authority of his party.

Five weeks later, at a Montreal meeting of Quebec Tories, Balcer formally moved that the party issue the call for a leadership convention and set February 16, 1965, as his deadline. In a letter to the Progressive Conservative Association president, Dalton Camp, Balcer charged that Diefenbaker's influence had left the French Canadians "feeling ill at ease and uncomfortable within the Party" because "on every issue touching the taproots of Confederation, the hopes and aspirations of French Canada had been distorted, misinterpreted and ignored." Balcer's call was supported by the English-speaking rebels in the parliamentary caucus, but Diefenbaker dismissed the affair as "the work of the Liberal propaganda machine."

This was a particularly inapt description because many Liberals (in this time of multiplying scandalous revelations) were convinced that only the fact John Diefenbaker was its leader stood in the way of the Conservative Party's return to office. George Hogan, a former Diefenbaker supporter who had become the Conservative Party's most articulate young theorist, warned in his Toronto *Telegram* column that Balcer's ultimatum presented Canadian Conservatism with the greatest crisis in its history. "The survival of the Party itself is now at stake, and this transcends loyalty or hostility to any leader," he wrote. "If the Tories don't face up to this crisis of leadership, they are in danger of breaking up. . . . It is entirely possible that the Party will not survive the next thirty days." Hogan and Eddie Goodman (the Toronto lawyer who had broken with Diefenbaker on the nuclear issue in 1962) were telephoning all over the country, trying to mobilize the anti-Diefenbaker forces within the Progressive Conservative national executive. The few sources of responsible Conservative newspaper support still backing John Diefenbaker now began to turn against him. One of the most important switches was made by Winnipeg *Tribune* publisher Ross Munro, an ideological Conservative and a sensitive man with a large conscience who had consistently given John Diefenbaker editorial support when nearly every other major newspaper in the country had come out against him. He wrote in his February 3, 1965, issue that "the *Tribune* has come slowly and reluctantly to the conclusion that the Tories cannot meet their great opportunity under Mr. Diefenbaker. . . . There is a time for leaving for every man from any post. The Tories should call a national convention as soon as possible to select a new man to head the party."

Dalton Camp had meanwhile been polling the members of the party executive on how to deal with the Balcer ultimatum and Diefenbaker had called a parliamentary caucus for February 11 and 12, to coincide with the start of the parliamentary session. But when Camp switched his executive meeting to February 6, Diefenbaker promptly rescheduled his caucus to February 5. This tactic of rallying what Gordon Churchill called "the party's fighting troops" had worked once before for Diefenbaker, when he quelled a cabinet rebellion in February 1963 by first obtaining an endorsement of his leadership from the caucus.

Ninety-eight M.P.'s and Tory senators attended the parliamentary caucus which gathered in Room 16 of the West Block at 11 a.m. on February 5. Balcer had decided at the last minute to boycott the meeting and dispatched Paul Martineau, the member from Pontiac-Témiscamingue, to represent him. Martineau, who had served briefly as Diefenbaker's minister of Mines and Technical Surveys, had never attracted much attention; a rumpled figure with awkward limb movements, he was not known either as an orator or as a particularly passionate Canadian. But now, as the main target of Diefenbaker's wrath, he proved to be both. The caucus began with an hour-long speech by Diefenbaker. He attacked Martineau as "Balcer's plenipotentiary," and blamed the member from Pontiac-Témiscamingue for all of the party's difficulties, claiming that Martineau had opposed his leadership at the party conventions in 1942, in 1948, and in 1956, and undermined him during his time in power. Diefenbaker then carefully differentiated between his position as head of his party and his role as its parliamentary House Leader, demanding an immediate vote of confidence from the caucus in this latter function. When Martineau protested that he wanted a chance to speak before any votes were taken, the Diefenbaker loyalists shouted him down so viciously that Martineau began to walk out. But Ken More of Regina, a Diefenbaker supporter with a sense of fair play, called him back. "I am sick at heart to be here and play this part . . ." Martineau began, then stopped as the cowboy chorus, led by Diefenbaker, resumed its catcalls, forcing Martineau to sit down.

At this point Heber Smith, a leather-lunged Tory rebel from Barrie, Ontario, jumped up and shouted at an astonished John Diefenbaker, "We heard *you,* now let him talk!" Senator David Walker, a Diefenbaker die-hard, stepped over to Smith, started to punch him, and it took a brief scuffle to separate the two men.

If looks could kill, the glance Diefenbaker gave Heber Smith would have left him a dead man, but eventually order was sufficiently restored for Martineau to continue. It was not true, he began, that he had opposed John Diefenbaker at the three most recent leadership conventions. During the 1942 contest, when Diefenbaker had first run, Martineau had been serving with the RCAF overseas. During the 1948 convention he had been a law student not involved in politics. In 1956, he had actively supported the Prince Albert member for the leadership and had later served as his parliamentary assistant. Turning to Diefenbaker, Martineau pleaded: "You *know* I served you well," and won a reluctant nod of agreement. "During those years," Martineau continued, "I witnessed with anguish the gulf developing between the leader and wide sections of his following, in particular the almost complete alienation of the ground swell of support that was gained in Quebec during the 1958 election." He told of how, after the flag filibuster had continued beyond the point of sensible debate, he had walked up to his leader in the lobby of the Commons and advised him that his call for a national flag plebiscite would be ruinous to Canada. Instead of replying or even acknowledging the comment, Diefenbaker had walked away from Martineau, shouting: "That man is crazy! That man is crazy!"

In calm, measured tones, gaining confidence as the cowboys gradually lapsed into sullen silence, Martineau went on to charge that under its present leadership the party had congealed into reaction, lacking the imagination and courage to express new ideas. "We are dedicated to a servile cult of leadership. Popular support is slipping away. Our leader is isolated from the mainstream of Canadian Conservatism and in the kind of election campaign he wants to wage – fought on issues of race and religion – the fragile plant of Confederation could not survive." Then, the emotions of the moment moving him close to tears, Martineau made his final appeal: "I put it to you. Is our historic party to become an instrument of division and reaction? The Conservative Party must now outgrow its fondness for internal dissent, rid itself of prejudice and find its soul. Let the party recognize Quebec's place under the sun, not grudgingly but generously. This party should be prepared to extend the Quebec members the hand of friendship in the name of equality. This is the historic role of the Conservative Party and if it refuses, it will fritter away its chances. The issue is clear, but the choice is yours."

Diefenbaker was silent now. There was applause in the hall, for Martineau the man, if not for his ideas. Senator Wallace McCutcheon, his October face glowing with excitement, got up to plead that the party follow Martineau's suggestions and not allow the leadership problem to split its ranks. He was supported in strong speeches by Heath Macquarrie, Senator Jacques Flynn, Gordon Aiken and Alfred Hales. But the Diefenbaker loyalists quickly counter-attacked, with Erik Nielsen,

113

Terry Nugent, and Senator Walker rallying majority support behind the Chief and against "the Quebec position."*

A standing vote was then taken on a carefully worded motion of confidence in Diefenbaker's Commons leadership. Only ten caucus members remained seated. When the meeting broke up Gordon Churchill, asked by reporters whether anyone had opposed the confidence motion, replied: "I saw nobody." John Diefenbaker declared that the endorsement had been "virtually unanimous." Drummond Clancy, M.P. for Yorkton, confided: "How to get rid of Mitchell Sharp, that's what we were talking about." And Senator McCutcheon summed up the morning's proceedings with the comment: "I'm waiting for a drink."

THAT NIGHT DALTON CAMP MET with some of the Conservative Party's principal officers to plan the agenda for the next day's meeting of the Conservative executive. The word was out that the rebels would move a motion of non-confidence in Diefenbaker's leadership from the floor, and that "no power on earth could stop it." Camp decided to try, because he realized that any attempted ouster of Diefenbaker as part of Léon Balcer's ultimatum would only turn the English-speaking sections of the party permanently against Quebec. Finlay MacDonald, a Progressive Conservative national vice-president from Halifax, came up with the compromise solution of disallowing any debate on the leadership issue from the floor and having members of the party executive fill out a questionnaire on both the Balcer resolution and the leadership question instead.

At 7:30 the following morning (February 6) Dalton Camp had breakfast with John Diefenbaker. He put forward the questionnaire idea, pointing out that it would merely allow for an expression of views. The Leader would be free to disregard the results of the questionnaire, because the national executive was strictly an advisory body with no authority to call a leadership convention. It was not clear afterwards what measure of agreement had actually been given by Diefenbaker but certainly Camp himself believed he had assurance of support for his proposal: that in exchange for not allowing any debate on the leadership issue, Diefenbaker and his supporters would not object to the

---

*The senator allowed his enthusiasm to run away with him. Comparing the integrity of the Diefenbaker administration with the ethics of the Pearson Government, David Walker proclaimed: "He's an honest man who ran an honest government, and I can say that nobody's ever found John Diefenbaker out." This unintentional slip of the tongue dissolved the caucus into loud titters – the first time that John Diefenbaker became the subject of laughter from his own followers.

handing out of a questionnaire. Its results would be kept confidential, with only Camp and two Diefenbaker supporters – National Organizer Dick Thrasher and National Secretary Ken Binks – as well as the Leader himself being informed of the outcome.

At the meeting itself, after some preliminary discussion the 137-member executive quickly endorsed Camp's suggestion that Léon Balcer and John Diefenbaker should speak before the luncheon adjournment, when the questionnaire was to be prepared for distribution in the afternoon. Balcer, his great opportunity at hand, chose to throw it away. He read the letter he had previously mailed to Camp complaining about the quality of Diefenbaker's leadership, looked around the room, said "My views are well known," and sat down.

The anticlimactic void was quickly filled by a ninety-minute oration from John Diefenbaker that began with a review of how previous Tory leaders had been destroyed from within their own party. He then rambled into a disjointed attack on Liberal corruption, President John F. Kennedy, Davie Fulton, "the Liberal press," Quebec, the American State Department, Léon Balcer's "support of the Liberals" and other assorted villainies and villains. He went on and on. His discourse gradually veered away from any pattern of orderly thought, dissolving into a fugue of self-pity. Everyone had always been against him. He had gained power all by himself. His enemies, the agents of Bay Street, had deprived him of it. Even here, he was surrounded by enemies.

All through that long, agonizing speech, Diefenbaker never stopped demanding from his audience some confession of betrayal. But his numbed listeners had nothing to confess, except perhaps the dawning panic seizing them that they had been supporting a cause they could no longer comprehend. The room was cold as a morgue. Diefenbaker pointedly mentioned that William Gladstone had won his last election at the age of eighty-four. Scanning the puzzled faces in his audience, he painted his enemies as "termites and chisellers intent on their personal ambition." Then he tremored his conclusion: "I say to those who are ambitious – wait, your turn will come."

The effect of the Diefenbaker harangue was intense. This had been a Diefenbaker most faithful party members had never seen before – an angry, persecuted, barely rational man about whom they had previously only heard guarded whispers. This was not the bonny slayer of Grits they had cheered during election campaigns, but a dark presence who had been bellowing not at some unruly mob of political enemies, but at his own shock troops, the men and women who made up the hard core of active Conservatism in Canada. Long after the lunch break had been called the delegates sat there, trying to read unspoken and unspeakable thoughts in each other's glances.

OVER LUNCH THE PRINCIPAL OFFICERS of the national executive drafted the final version of the questionnaire. It had four parts. The third and fourth questions, dealing with the setting up of a joint caucus-executive policy committee and whether or not the Leader should attend the flag-raising ceremonies scheduled for the following Monday, were diversionary matters, put in at Diefenbaker's request.

Only the first two questions really counted:

1. Please indicate which of the following statements is nearest to the advice you would give:
A. the interest of the Party would not be served in calling a leadership convention at this time,
   or
B. it would be in the general interest of the Party if a national leadership convention were called in the immediate future.

2. Please indicate which of the following statements is nearest to the advice you would give:
A. I give my full and unqualified support to the national Leader, the Rt Hon. John G. Diefenbaker,
   or
B. I believe it would be in the general interest of the Party that our national leader consider making way for a successor.

This clever device would permit delegates to vote both against Léon Balcer (on Question 1) and against John Diefenbaker (on Question 2). It would allow those Tories outside Quebec who had turned against Diefenbaker to express their views without appearing to be bowing to the ultimatum of the party's French-Canadian leader.

When the meeting reconvened, Diefenbaker's leadership was immediately attacked by Heath Macquarrie, Egan Chambers (Camp's predecessor as president of the Progressive Conservative Association) and James Macdonnell. "It is possible," Macdonnell calmly declared, staring at the Chief, "that I qualify for the term 'termite,' since a year ago I was among the few who stood up against the Leader. But since, in addition to being a termite, I am also an octogenarian, I doubt if I qualify for the Leader's suggestion that all termites are moved by personal ambition."

Flora MacDonald, the office manager at Conservative headquarters, then walked into the hall with the printed ballots and handed one to Camp, who began to read it aloud. Diefenbaker immediately muttered objections and when Camp reached the second question, he stood up to shout: "NO! that's completely unacceptable. Decide on your convention, but I'm not going to accept it. I have no regard for it. It's none of your affair. I'll have to go back to caucus, they've just given me a vote of confidence . . ."

Camp, his face flushed with anger, embarrassment, or both, said that there must be some misunderstanding and asked to be allowed to consult his principal officers. They withdrew and returned twenty minutes later to state that they would stand by the questionnaire. Eddie Goodman supported their decision from the floor.

Camp had by this time lost control of the meeting. The principal officers sat at the head table, frantically whispering useless instructions to each other. Diefenbaker, white-faced, stood rooted in his place, wheeling about like some latter-day Caesar expecting the first knife-thrust. While most delegates couldn't understand what was happening, Erik Nielsen, the Yukon M.P., shouted for attention. Claiming that the national executive should not set a precedent by dealing with leadership confidence, Nielsen moved an amendment to eliminate the offending second question. The issue of Diefenbaker's leadership was by this method altered from a secret ballot on the questionnaire to an open vote, with delegates standing up to support or reject the Nielsen amendment. There was so much noise and confusion that three votes were required. The counts, taken by National Secretary Ken Binks and National Vice-President James Doak, were close but all in favour of the Nielsen motion, with the actual tallies being 51-49, 53-49 and 57-55. Most of the executive members from the West (except British Columbia and parts of Alberta) and the Atlantic provinces (except New Brunswick and part of Prince Edward Island) voted with Nielsen, while most of the members from Ontario and Quebec and the YPC delegates lined up against him.

When the results were being announced, Eddie Goodman kept interrupting with shouts of: "How about you fellows up there?" National Vice-President Finlay MacDonald responded immediately that he was against the Nielsen amendment. Women's Association President Mrs H. S. Harrison Smith said: "We agreed not to vote." Ken Binks and James Doak just looked at each other, and Binks finally repeated: "We agreed not to vote." Camp immediately declared the Nielsen amendment carried, and when Goodman insisted: "What's the vote?", he ignored the question. The ballot was distributed, with instructions not to reply to the offending second question.

As delegates marked their ballots, they heard an impassioned plea from a member of the party's youth wing for long-term policy considerations. Mrs Patricia Fraser, president of the British Columbia Young Conservative Association, produced loud cheers in the room with her dignified appeal. "Our loyalty to the leader cannot come second to our loyalty to the nation," she said. "If we don't have positive programs to offer as an alternative to the present situation we have no right to ask the people to vote for us." She was cheered, and John Diefenbaker took the cue to align himself with the youthful yearners. "We need something in the nature of a national philosophy . . . a declaration," he said, in muted contrast to his morning performance. "Let's get together and understand each other."

By outmanoeuvring his own national executive, John Diefenbaker had won what he wanted: the right to lead his party in one more election campaign.

Dalton Camp announced the following day that Balcer's call for a leadership convention had been rejected, but the details of the questionnaire tally were never released. Diefenbaker meanwhile had transformed the challenge to his leadership from the reality of discontent within his own ranks into a threat from powerful but undefined outside interests. On February 17, on a CBC-TV network show, he so informed the nation. "I have been maligned. I have been condemned," he lamented. "No one since the days of Macdonald has gone through the like . . . They say they want to remove me . . . I have been told in the last few days that if I remain as leader of the Conservative Party, support for the party by certain interests will end. My friends, they believe that they will succeed in this way. I will follow the will of the people. Will it be the will of the people or those that are all powerful?"

The next day, Rémi Paul, one of the ten surviving Quebec Tories, crossed the floor of the Commons to sit as an independent. "I must leave the ranks," he said, "not of the Conservative Party but of the Diefenbaker Party." The rebels within the parliamentary caucus were growing bolder now, not only because the vote at the executive meeting had demonstrated that they were far from alone but because they had been able to attach their dissent to firm policy issues.

Diefenbaker was still demanding that the constitutional amending formula be killed, and his supporters were also trying to whip up Conservative opposition to the government's Bill C-142, which was to permit provincial governments to opt out of some federal-provincial cost-sharing programs – a right considered vital by the government of Quebec. Caucus also had to deal with Section 3 of the Canada Pension Plan Bill, which would acknowledge the right of provinces (Quebec was the only one interested) to set up their separate but integrated pension plans. Diefenbaker and his loyalists regarded these three issues as amounting to a surrender of the federal prerogative to French Canada. They dug in for a fight.

Erik Nielsen produced a secret memorandum summing up the Diefenbaker position.* After attacking Quebec's approach to Confederation, he stated that any Conservatives opposed to his ideas would have to leave the party. "Those who are not prepared to stand must be at least prepared to support or, failing that, to go where their convictions lead them," Nielsen wrote. "Their betrayal will not be forgiven or forgotten."

Léon Balcer and most of the rebel Tories from English Canada fought against the Nielsen-Diefenbaker policy, in effect lining themselves up with the Liberal position on the three issues. In a series of nine caucus confrontations they eventually won their point, and the Diefenbaker forces backed away from making much of a parliamentary issue out of any of the three bills. Significantly, all the Conservative premiers aligned themselves with the Balcer position. John Robarts led the debate in the Ontario Legislature which passed the constitutional amending formula by a vote of 71 to 7. J. Waldo Monteith, dispatched by Diefenbaker to forestall Ontario's approval, arrived in Toronto just in time to be met by Provincial Treasurer James Allan, who told him how the vote had gone, and with malicious pleasure commented: "See how your Leader likes *that*!"

Diefenbaker had by now lost the support of nearly half of his party's executive council and had been deprived of policy control over his parliamentary caucus. On March 14 he suffered yet another humiliation. Members of the Young Progressive Conservative Association, holding their semi-annual meeting, went to Diefenbaker's home and with much embarrassment and more courage pleaded with him to resign.

With so many forces conspiring against Diefenbaker, it now began to look for the first time as if Léon Balcer would inevitably win his fight for a leadership convention. Characteristically, he chose this moment to give up his struggle and when the Commons met on April 7, Balcer crossed the floor to sit as an independent.† "At first I thought that Mr Diefenbaker just didn't understand Quebec," he said following his

---

*For the text of this document see Appendix D. It constituted the only written attempt to define the terms and implications of the "One Canada" policy advocated by Diefenbaker and his supporters within the Conservative Party.
†Balcer later became the Quebec Government's Director of Centennial Projects. He ran as a Liberal candidate and was defeated in the 1966 Quebec provincial election.

resignation from the party. "Now, I'm convinced that he is genuinely against French Canada and that as a political expedient he is trying to whip up an English-Canadian backlash for an election campaign. I quit for honour's sake, so that I will not be ashamed to look myself in the face."

As Léon Balcer, his sense of dignity bolstered by the magnitude of the step he was taking, crossed the floor of the Commons, John Diefenbaker could be seen laughing and several Tory backbenchers banged their desks in approval. One Saskatchewan M.P. said to his seatmate, loud enough for the galleries to hear: "I feel as if our party has just had a bowel movement."

The glee of the Diefenbaker cowboys provided a rare public glimpse of how they and their leader really felt about Quebec. "Diefenbaker's response to Balcer shows that he regards the Quebec caucus as he would regard any other ten members from any province," wrote John Bird in *The Financial Post*. "In reality, the Quebec Ten are Diefenbaker's last lifeline to French Canada and to almost one third of the Canadian people." It was Balcer's friend, Paul Martineau, who paid him the most eloquent tribute in the Commons on April 12. "Surely," he said, "the departure of such a man from the ranks of any party must signify tragedy for the party that bears this loss. And the tragedy involves much more than just the person or personality of the Hon. Member for Trois-Rivières: it affects all of us. For if there is no room for such a man in the party, what kind of a man from Quebec or even elsewhere can the party accommodate?"

IN THE THIRD SESSION of Canada's twenty-sixth Parliament, which had begun the day before Balcer resigned, Diefenbaker seemed unable to focus on the important issues of the day, wasting himself instead on marginal excursions. On the session's opening day, for example, his main question to Justice Minister Guy Favreau concerned not national unity or even the Liberal scandals. He demanded instead, with all the outrage he might have mustered on the other two issues, whether the RCMP was being "divested of its stetsons, spurs, riding breeches and Sam Browne belts." Later in his Leaders' Day speech, Diefenbaker accused the Liberal Government of establishing a clandestine force of RCMP reservists. "Some kind of auxiliary force is being set up," he intimated. "Parliament has not heard about this auxiliary force, said to number eight hundred. We have been given no information. Why should Parliament not have this information? Is it true that a body of extra Mounties who will operate as irregulars has been set up?" He went on to imply that it would be some kind of secret service organization and that it was typical Liberal arrogance to create such a force without the consent of the Commons.

When Lester Pearson rose to reply, he calmly referred the Opposition Leader to Chapter 54 of the revised RCMP Statutes (passed by the Diefenbaker administration in 1959) which had set up the Mounted Police reserve force. The Liberal Leader pointed out that the Diefenbaker Government had established the force by order-in-council and that its creation had thus never been discussed in Parliament. It was a minor encounter in a long war, but for the first time – by simply sticking to facts and not trying to match him as an orator – Pearson had succeeded in chastening the Tory chief in front of his followers.

The Conservative caucus demonstrated its growing disenchantment with Diefenbaker during that session's Throne Speech and budget debates, when for the three important non-confidence motions first twenty-eight, then thirty-one and then sixteen Conservative M.P.'s stayed out of the Chamber. This was the rebels' ultimate form of protest: by deliberately absenting themselves from crucial Commons votes, they were depriving Diefenbaker of any chance of defeating the Liberal administration.

The most serious blow to Diefenbaker's self-esteem was probably the dramatic confrontation that took place in his parliamentary office on the morning of Tuesday, June 8, 1965. The Commons at that time was discussing the adoption of a new, streamlined set of rules that would permit time limits to be set on debates. Diefenbaker saw the issue not as an attempt to modernize archaic regulations, but as "a guillotine" menacing "the basic democratic rights of the average Canadian." He planned to filibuster the rules change, hoping it would eventually lead to an election campaign. But on June 8 there filed into his office the chairmen of his key caucus committees. They told their leader with unusual candour that they would not support him in his intended filibuster. The party could not, they informed him, afford to be tagged yet again with the obstructionist label, particularly when the issue at hand was the reform of Parliament. Significantly, the few anti-Diefenbaker rebels who headed parliamentary caucus committees stayed away; only the loyal core of Diefenbaker supporters came to voice their objections, as if to save their chief from himself. It was the first time Diefenbaker had been forced to back down not by his enemies within the party but by his supporters.

None of this alienation seemed to have much effect on John Diefenbaker's resolution to remain as party leader. At a private reception in his parliamentary office held in the spring of 1965 to commemorate his twenty-fifth year in federal politics, he remarked to one of his assistants that he had been touched by the tribute Lester Pearson had paid him that day (March 26) in the Commons. Turning to his wife Olive, he said: "I must do the same for Pearson on his twenty-fifth anniversary. Don't forget to remind me on the date." The quip was immediately passed along the Conservative Party's whisper-circuit. The realization that Pearson wasn't due to celebrate his first quarter-century in Parliament until October 25, 1973, left many of the Tories dismayed and angry.

By the late summer of 1965 it seemed that John Diefenbaker had dissipated beyond redemption the warm, high regard in which a political party must hold its leader. His political existence was comparable to the life-span of a picked flower: the blossom was still there, but the roots that must nourish it had been cut.

CHAPTER 10

The Year Dalton Camp
Blew His Cool

WITH THE GENIUS FOR SELF-AGGRANDIZEMENT that so seldom failed him, John Diefenbaker was able to salvage out of his party's defeat in the 1965 election a rhetorical victory for himself.* He led back with him into the Commons a strong Tory Opposition despite predictions of disaster, and it was hard to deny his claim that he had earned at least the right to choose the time and circumstances of his retirement.

But the Tory power brokers, sifting through their private graphs and surveys of the 1965 election results, realized that the rural electoral base which had provided their leader with its support was a rapidly depreciating asset. No political party can fight the population trends and hope to survive for long. Any future Conservative majority would have to recruit the allegiance of the young, the suburbanites and the citizens of French Canada. Yet these groups were, almost by definition, charter members of the informal anti-Diefenbaker coalition that had grown across the country.

The very idea that the Conservative Party of Canada might possess a future apart from John Diefenbaker had lost its currency during the decade since 1956. The Prince Albert politician had treated the party as his personal instrument for so long that Conservatism in Canada had, in effect, been split into two barely compatible political movements: a Conservative Party which had no leader, and a Diefenbaker Party which had little else.

*For a description of the 1965 election, see Part Six.

The internal struggle between these two factions, simmering for three years, now boiled over. Although it turned on a clash between the party's pro- and anti-Diefenbaker elements, at another, more significant level this was a classic confrontation of the old and the young, the painful passage of power from one political generation to the next.

On one side were ranged the men and women in their late fifties, sixties and seventies whose view of Canada was circumscribed by the Tipperary patriotism of World War I and the economic martyrdom of the Great Depression. Pressing up against this aging leadership were younger Tories who had come to maturity during World War II and had long since grown impatient to grasp the levers of political command. Ranged behind them, in turn, was a whole new generation of much younger Conservatives – their ranks depleted by the disillusionment of the Diefenbaker Years – who saw the anti-Diefenbaker struggle as a chance to express their beliefs through political action.

Ten years of policy neglect could not be redeemed by a single act of political blood-letting but if this revolution of the younger elements within Tory ranks did not succeed, the service of a whole generation of Conservatives would be forfeited. As they prepared to challenge John Diefenbaker, these younger Tories persuaded themselves, not without reason, that nothing less than the perpetuation of a meaningful two-party system in Canada was at stake.

IMMEDIATELY AFTER THE 1965 ELECTION, John Diefenbaker hinted that any parliamentary upset of the Liberals in the Commons would automatically return him to office. "If defeated in the House, it would be the bounden duty of the Prime Minister to advise the Governor General to call on the party holding the next largest number of seats," he declared. But this view was immediately challenged by NDP Leader T. C. Douglas, who put on record his intention of not "being manoeuvred into helping those transparently seeking to keep Parliament in a continual state of ferment at a time when there is so much work to be done."

In his Leaders' Day address, which opened the 1966 parliamentary session, Diefenbaker attacked the Liberals' Throne Speech as "a puerile, pusillanimous piece of repetitive propaganda." He labelled its authors "a floundering government" which had "bumbled, bungled, boxed and bewildered itself." But characteristically he offered no policies of his own beyond expressing grave fears about inflation, a concern he then proceeded to temper by calling for an immediate increase of twenty-five dollars a month in old age pensions. This move would have cost the already overstrained federal treasury an annual $825 millions.

Typical of Diefenbaker's partisan desperation – and parliamentary irrelevance – during this period was an incident involving a television interview Lester Pearson gave Pierre Berton on February 14, 1966. At one point, Berton asked the Prime Minister whether he sometimes envied the American president "who could theoretically work at his desk all day, because he doesn't have to go down and face Congress for several hours each day and use up that amount of time in discussion." Pearson replied:

> Yes, I used to think before I had this responsibility that there was no comparison between the parliamentary and the congressional system; that it was so much better to have the executive right there on the floor of the legislature exposing itself to parliamentary criticism every day; so that if it didn't retain the confidence of the House of Commons, we had an election. I thought that was the good old British way of doing things and it was the right way of doing things. I used to be a little scornful of the congressional system, where the executive were separated from the legislative side of government. They had four years and during that four years – I was going to say they could get away with anything. Now I think there is something to be said for a little more independence – I mean by that, the executive not being subjected every hour to parliamentary appearances. It is going to be difficult to reconcile the two things because parliamentary discussion is still, rightly, a very important part of our political lives.

When the Commons met the following afternoon, Diefenbaker was on his feet, ominously reading the text of Pearson's reply into Hansard. "That is a most unusual doctrine," he thundered. "I will suggest to the Prime Minister that his thinking as evidenced by his remarks does not have that regard for Parliament which those occupying the position of Prime Minister should have."

Although the occasion was a routine debate of Transport Department estimates, Diefenbaker continued his attack, accusing a bewildered Pearson of harbouring "an attitude that whatever the Government says is good and that the Opposition should not question the Government as to what it does." Pearson kept vainly interrupting to point out he had meant no such thing, and finally managed to blurt out a question: Where, in the text of his remarks, had he indicated that Canada should adopt the congressional system? Diefenbaker stared across the Commons aisle, and with all the considerable scorn he could summon shot back his triumphant reply: "If it was not to be adopted, why was it talked about?"

BOLSTERED BY HIS INTERPRETATION of the 1965 election results as a moral vindication of his leadership, Diefenbaker in the early months of 1966 proceeded to strengthen his personal hold on the Conservative organization. As loyalty to faction superseded loyalty to party, a purge was ordered of those few unwavering Conservatives who had remained active in order to provide the party with some continuity of purpose apart from glorification of the Chief. Early in 1966, Diefenbaker had moved into Progressive Conservative headquarters, as national director, James W. Johnston, a 39-year-old economist and former newspaperman who quickly became the Leader's faithful right hand. On April 19, acting on Diefenbaker's orders, Johnston abruptly fired Flora MacDonald, a dedicated Nova Scotia Tory who during her ten years in Conservative headquarters had come to personify the party to its workers across the country. She knew most constituency members by their first names and arranged their appointments with party bigwigs. Her political acumen was keen, her working hours legendary.

For a decade, Flora's allegiance to John Diefenbaker had run second only to her dedicated Conservatism. But that ranking in her personal priorities was enough to cause her purge. While her dismissal was hardly a major political event, its timing triggered the final phase of John Diefenbaker's overthrow.

It was Flora's abrupt firing that made Tory workers across the country doubt the validity of Diefenbaker's repeated accusations that he was being destroyed by Liberal-inspired traitors. Flora MacDonald was simply not credible as the agent of any anti-Conservative plot. More significant was the effect of the episode on Dalton Camp. Despite his position as president of the Progressive Conservative Association of Canada, he had been consulted neither on Johnston's hiring nor on Flora's firing and had seldom been invited into the Leader's office during the time he occupied his post.

DALTON KINGSLEY CAMP was uniquely fitted to challenge the stubborn myth of John Diefenbaker's infallibility. With his cool demeanour, his disdain for orthodoxy and the Kennedy cadence of his words, Camp represented the new and growing sophistication of urban Canada, light-years away from the buffalo-bone country that had produced John

Diefenbaker. His opponents derisively dismissed Camp as nothing more than "an ambitious Toronto ad man," but his instincts had been honed by a more demanding tutorship than that available in the asphalt canyons of Toronto's advertising community. Born in 1920 at Woodstock, N.B., the son of a Baptist minister, he had attended the Horton Academy at Wolfville, N.S., and later remembered that on one of the several occasions when he was being considered for expulsion for some minor misdemeanour, the school's headmaster told him: "Camp, there are just as many trains leaving Wolfville as there are coming into Wolfville." This mundane advice became one of his lifetime guideposts: "To me, it meant that there's no such thing as permanent station or rank, that in all life one can achieve success or failure by the same means; only the direction is different, and each of us has as much capacity for good as for wrong, as much energy for success as for failure."

Camp went on to enroll in biology at Acadia University ("but science enraged me, or eluded me, or both") and he left to join the army before graduating. After the war he returned to the University of New Brunswick, where he caught the eye of Lord Beaverbrook. He helped Camp get a scholarship to the London School of Economics. There he came under the influence of Harold Laski, who implanted in him the streak of radicalism that set him apart from most of his contemporaries within Canada's Conservative community.

While at university, Camp was briefly a Liberal and attended the party's 1948 leadership convention as national treasurer of the Young Liberal Federation. There were rumblings of discontent among the party's younger elements that year but at the evening session of the convention's second day, young Camp did his best to dispel them. "I see by today's headlines," he declared, "that the young Liberals are supposed to be fed up. I want to assure my friends in this convention that they don't speak for the Young Liberal Federation of Canada when they say that. We are not fed up – we can't get enough!" The enthusiastic young Grit then went on to praise Canadian Liberalism so lavishly that at the end of his impromptu address Mackenzie King called him over, approvingly patted his shoulders and warmly congratulated him.

Camp's disillusionment set in the next night when a series of resolutions on Maritime development he had helped draft were perfunctorily dismissed by Robert Winters, then a fast-rising Liberal M.P. from Nova Scotia who was slated to join the cabinet later that year.

"Being basically a radical, I couldn't stand to be suffocated by the Liberal establishment," Camp recalled. "I've always felt that there's a massive weight of authority at the top of the Liberal Party, and no way for an ordinary regional politician to get either near it or around it. The

Liberal Party has a congenital capacity to exist only within the limits of its own experience."

Camp turned Conservative with a vengeance. During the next decade, as a rising young Toronto advertising executive specializing in political accounts, he stage-managed the election campaigns that deposed provincial Liberal governments in New Brunswick (1952), Nova Scotia (1956), Manitoba (1958) and Prince Edward Island (1959). While Diefenbaker was in power, Camp was put in charge of the campaign for the Maritimes and ran Progressive Conservative headquarters during the 1963 federal election.

Although he remained loyal to the Conservative Leader throughout this period, there was always conflict between Camp and the hard-core Diefenbaker followers. Their ways were not his ways, and even when he seemed wholly committed to the Prince Albert politician, Camp stood out in his exquisitely tailored Ed Provan suits and monogrammed shirts as a rare bird among the dull fowl then roosting in the organizational wing of the Conservative Party.

In the fall of 1964 Camp set up a National Conference on Canadian Goals at Fredericton, N.B., as a final attempt to orient the Conservative Party toward policy concerns. But Diefenbaker only derided those who attended the conference for "wasting three or four days on intangibles." During a gathering of young Conservatives at McMaster University in the spring of 1966, Camp heard his party and its leadership severely castigated, particularly by Fraser Kelly, an articulate young journalist later named Political Editor of the Toronto *Telegram*. "Listening to the attacks on the party and its leadership," Camp said later, "were members of the caucus, privy councillors, senior party officials – and the response was absolute silence. You can't live with division like that."

Then came Flora MacDonald's dismissal and Camp knew that he had no choice left about involving himself in the leadership issue. On May 19, in a private after-dinner talk to a group of gently rumbling old-line Tories at Toronto's ultra-conservative Albany Club, he quietly inaugurated his campaign for reassessment of the party leadership. Camp urged potential successors to make their views and intentions known to avoid a repetition of the 1942 convention, when the party found itself confronted by a stranger (John Bracken) and indicated that a leadership convention ought to be held by the spring of 1968. It was an off-the-record affair but in the audience, chewing a dead cigar, sat Senator David Walker, one of Diefenbaker's closest confidants. Word of Camp's bold challenge was conveyed to the Chief minutes after he had finished speaking, although it was weeks before its full import seeped through to party members.

128

At this point only a few of the party's most senior officials were aware of any impending confrontation and neither faction took the possibility of an ultimate showdown very seriously. Most Diefenbaker supporters regarded Camp as either a politician ridden by intense personal ambition or a slick front man for those interests who wanted to return the Conservative Party to its old role as the political arm of Toronto's Bay Street barons. The party's anti-Diefenbaker rump, meanwhile, had lost heart about any further attempts to dislodge the Chief. Under the party constitution no appropriate mechanism seemed realistically available. One group of young Quebec Tories led by René Dionne and Jean Sirois even drafted a half-serious motion for presentation to the 1966 annual meeting that would have called for "the Rt Hon. John George Diefenbaker to hold the position of Leader of the Progressive Conservative Party of Canada for the rest of his natural life," in the hope that the bizarre quality of the proposal might point up the desperate nature of the leadership impasse.

In the early autumn, the *Ottawa Journal*, the last major metropolitan daily still faithful to Diefenbaker, cut him loose. "The grinding intellectual work ahead will call not so much for Mr. Diefenbaker's undoubted platform skill and political acumen, as for long trying hours of study attacking the stubborn facts and figures of this nation's problems," wrote that Tory paper's editor, I. Norman Smith. "Mr. Diefenbaker will surely see the wisdom and honour of asking the party to seek a successor."

It was Diefenbaker himself, on the innocent occasion of an office party given on September 16, 1966, to celebrate his birthday, who finally forced his enemies openly to defy the bravado of his years. With one gusty whoosh he blew out the seventy-one blue candles on his birthday cake and pointedly reminisced about how Sir John A. Macdonald had won two elections in his late seventies. As he fingered his gifts (including a book called *Sex and the Single Dog* which some pet-lover had sent his Labrador pup, Happy) Diefenbaker confided to his well-wishers that he intended to celebrate his next anniversary once more comfortably ensconced in the prime minister's parliamentary office.

Now there could be no doubts remaining, no longer any basis for prolonging the fiction, promulgated by Diefenbaker's supporters, that if left unchallenged the Old Chief would retire gracefully of his own free will.

His own options having thus been exhausted, Dalton Camp decided, just four days after Diefenbaker's birthday festivities, that he now had to risk an ascent into full public view of his underground demands for leadership assessment. In a dramatic speech to the Toronto Junior Board of Trade on September 20, he outlined the burden of his self-imposed mission: "I believe I speak for many in calling for a reassessment of policy, a reform of party organization, and the reconfirmation – or otherwise – of leadership. If I am wrong, then the usual penalties of politics will apply. But it is important that we no longer perpetuate instability, indecision and expediency. If our politics are to be renewed, then we must renew our political parties. It is time to speak and time to act. Procrastination, putting things off, is the art of keeping up with yesterday. In all the unfinished business of the nation, nothing is more necessary than that we resume the art of politics, for it is the art of keeping up with the challenges of tomorrow."

This was the opening salvo of a campaign that would end with John Diefenbaker's overthrow, but the Conservative Leader's initial reaction was sheer disdain. Tommy Van Dusen, his executive assistant, reported the Chief's "monumental indifference," and commented: "Why, in the last election Camp spent $43,000 and still couldn't beat Mitchell Sharp. . . . If he thought that was going to be hard going, he'll be finding out now just how hard a fight can get." To this assessment, the Tory national organizer James Johnston added his own nonchalant observation: "So what else is new? This kind of thing always helps the registration of delegates at annual meetings."

Diefenbaker flew to Toronto on September 22 to deliver a previously scheduled Albany Club address of his own. "Are you planning to meet Mr Camp while you're in town?", reporters demanded as he strolled east along King Street toward the club. "I thought he had decamped!" was the only retort.

"Will you be offering your resignation at the party's annual meeting in November?" one reporter insisted.

"Ha-ha-ha," mocked the Tory leader, then dispersed his journalistic retinue with a final "Ha!"

Inside the club, Diefenbaker spoke for eighty minutes, but there was more wit than fire in his words. He predicted that the Pearson Government would face a great lawsuit, because its new green unified armed services dress was modelled on "the outfits worn by Coca-Cola company truck drivers." He invoked the past glories of Macdonald, Borden, Meighen and the other party saints whose busts decorate the dusty reaches of the Albany Club. He talked about his mail, always his mail, and the growing ground swell of support for him across the country. The only tough question came from Allan Lawrence, the member of the Ontario legislature for the Toronto riding of St George, who bluntly demanded whether Diefenbaker was willing to face a leadership convention. Diefenbaker slapped him down with a non sequitur, "Oh, I know you well enough, I know who you are. . . ."

The next day, Mr Justice Wishart Spence issued his long-awaited report on the Munsinger affair in which he whitewashed the Liberals for introducing the incident, while condemning Diefenbaker for not having been harsher with Pierre Sévigny, his errant Associate Minister of National Defence.* Spence's harsh verdict immediately bolstered Diefenbaker's position within his party. No matter how they felt about their leader, most Conservatives were enraged by the Liberals' vengeful resurrection of an incident involving the prerogatives of the prime minister – six years after the event.

But at this crucial moment in his career, John Diefenbaker was betrayed yet again by his incapacity for moderation. Instead of accepting the Spence findings at their dubious value, he tried to link his own action in forgiving Pierre Sévigny's indiscretions with the precedent of Lester Pearson's backing of Herbert Norman, though the two cases were totally dissimilar. (Norman, a distinguished Canadian diplomat, had jumped off a roof to his death in Cairo in 1957 after having been hounded by undocumented allegations that youthful Communist associations had turned him into a security risk.)

It had been one thing for the Tories to rally around their chief in the face of what they considered to be the grossly unfair and partisan Spence report. But it was quite another matter to be asked to endorse the same kind of mud-slinging tactics that Diefenbaker was ascribing to the Liberals. The Conservative Leader had been guilty of many political extravagances, but it's doubtful that anything he ever said was quite as unfair as his linking of the Munsinger affair with the Norman case.

Many Diefenbaker supporters had originally given their loyalty because they recognized him as a man who championed individual rights and stood for a sense of fairness for the individual in a bewildering and impersonal age. It had been John Diefenbaker in the mid Fifties who had attacked Senator Joseph McCarthy as "a destroyer of justice." Now Diefenbaker was using McCarthy tactics of his own. To many Conservatives, his actions provided a rare flash of self-revelation. They realized not only that Diefenbaker had changed but even more important that he seemed to be losing the sure touch which had carried him such a long way during a lifetime of political in-fighting. This absence of his usual political acumen also showed up in the fact that the Tory Leader was using massive retaliation tactics against the Spence report, though the prevailing mood of the nation was to forget about it as a temporary aberration of Canadian public life.

*For a description of the Munsinger affair see Chapter 28.

131

THE DISPLACEMENT OF A PARTY LEADER reluctant to abandon power is always a dismal enterprise – wasteful, crude and unjust. By inaugurating his reassessment-of-the-leadership crusade, Dalton Camp was, in effect, attempting to stretch the fine-drawn limits of party democracy to stage a *coup d'état* against John Diefenbaker. Certain that history was on his side, Camp kept insisting that his aims were only to modernize and democratize Canadian Conservatism. But since neither objective could be achieved in the face of the incumbent's anachronistic, authoritarian style of leadership, it very quickly became inevitable that the golden fleece at the end of Camp's long quest would be Diefenbaker's crinkly political scalp.

Camp had gleaned some valuable lessons from the kamikaze attempts of predecessors bent on similar missions. Until the very end he kept both his private and his public campaigns divorced from personal attacks on the Leader. Instead, he transformed himself into the embodiment of an irrefutable cause: the reform of the Conservative Party. Not once – and the temptations were jabbed at him daily in the phallic thrusts of radio reporters' microphones and the journalists' pencils at the ready to jot down the incriminating words – not once during his entire campaign did Camp attack or even mention John Diefenbaker.

By insisting that the leader of every democratic party must, at some point, make himself accountable to its members, Camp enlisted in his cause a growing number of those Conservatives yearning for reform (and power), yet reluctant to oppose "John" openly. Camp's tactics also succeeded in placing the Prince Albert politician on the wrong side of the issue of internal party democracy – one of the charges he had hurled so effectively against the establishment of the Liberal Party during his triumphant 1957 and 1958 election campaigns.

Camp's strategy was simple. If he could drive home the point that his own re-election as Progressive Conservative Association president at the party's 1966 annual meeting would constitute endorsement of his reassessment policy, then a party leadership convention would presumably have to follow. The key to the success of the entire undertaking was that the party constitution called for the election of the association president by secret ballot, and thus differed from a motion of confidence in the leader.

Though Camp's itinerary during the six weeks after his original attack coincided with annual Conservative Association meetings in Prince Edward Island, Alberta, Nova Scotia, Newfoundland, Quebec and British Columbia, he concentrated his efforts on speaking over the heads of the party's regulars by addressing mostly service clubs and university audiences. But everywhere he went, private dinners were also arranged with key local Tories and gradually his message began to permeate beyond the tight circle of the anti-Diefenbaker rebels. He repeatedly called on Conservatives to "make party politics less of an occult science in the spirit of Mackenzie King, and more of a democratic exercise in the interest of a free society," and concluded his sermons with variations on his theme, that "if the Party to which I give my allegiance is not the first to reform, it will become an artifact of history."

The main logistic and organizational support Camp received during this crucial period came from Lowell Murray, then serving as executive assistant to Senator Wallace McCutcheon, who handled Camp's liaison with the parliamentary wing of the anti-Diefenbaker movement, and Flora MacDonald, who did much of the recruiting involved. Through the quickening twilight of those fall evenings, as the time zones changed across the country, Murray sat by the telephone in the senator's outer office, cajoling delegates at both ends of the country to support Camp's reassessment bid.*

Camp prowled the country for support, looking like the very model of a sleek and social advertising man with all the command of cool that this implied. Gradually his gutsy plea began to produce results.

Throughout his passionate journey, he held few formal strategy meetings. The most important of them was a secret rendezvous at a Kingston, Ontario, motel on September 28. It was attended by Norman Atkins (Camp's brother-in-law), Lowell Murray, Flora MacDonald (then attached to the political science faculty at Queen's University) and David MacDonald, an ardent young anti-Diefenbaker Tory M.P. from Prince Edward Island. The group was astonished to learn that Camp had not thought out any strategy beyond trying to win the Association presidency. He seemed undecided whether he ought then to confront the party's annual meeting with a motion calling for a leadership convention, or to attempt the same procedure through a complicated series of constitutional amendments. "I'm not prepared to settle on a strategy until I see the size of my army," Camp kept insisting. The meeting ended inconclusively and its dispirited participants drove their separate ways through the nippy gusts of autumn rain.

The event that returned impetus to Camp's crusade was a remarkable ruse perpetrated by a group of young Quebec Conservatives at their annual meeting the following weekend. Recruitment of French-Canadian delegates to Camp's cause had been going badly. The provincial party was so loosely organized that few permanent constituency

*It was a minor irony of this cross-country telephone marathon that it was financed by a recent Pearson Government directive allowing senators and M.P.'s unlimited long-distance telephone tolls.

organizations existed and Conservative headquarters had been able to pack some riding delegations to the annual meeting with pro-Diefenbaker people. National organizer James Johnston had even appointed his own agent to recruit the Diefenbaker delegates.*

Diefenbaker was due to address the Quebec Progressive Conservative annual meeting at the Motel des Laurentides in the Quebec City suburb of Beauport on October 1, and it was part of Johnston's assignment to make certain that the Chief be shown appropriate homage upon arrival at Ancienne Lorette airport. To swell the airport crowd, Johnston decided to take with him most of Diefenbaker's French-Canadian supporters. Just before climbing into the airport limousine, Johnston took aside some of the party's Young Turks who seemed to be running the session and told them patronizingly that they should keep the meeting discussing non-controversial matters until he returned with the Chief. Unfortunately for Johnston, the three young Tories he chose – Michael Meighen (grandson of the former Conservative prime minister), Brian Mulroney (the young Montreal lawyer who had served as executive assistant to Alvin Hamilton in Agriculture) and Peter White (an executive assistant to Daniel Johnson) – were young in years but not in political experience. White had previously arranged for Diefenbaker to be driven from the airport to the provincial legislature for a courtesy call on the Quebec premier. This – plus the fact that most of Diefenbaker's supporters were at the airport – gave the young Tories and their friends enough time to rush back into the meeting and ram through a series of resolutions calling for the federal leadership to be reviewed every four years, starting in the fall of 1967.

A not insubstantial quantity of political power changed hands that day but in retrospect it provided one of the great comic scenes of Canadian politics. There was the trio of young Quebec Tories – all English-speaking and all in their twenties – using a set of pre-arranged manoeuvres to swing the meeting against Diefenbaker. Meanwhile, the Chief and his retinue of flacks, ensconced in rented black limousines, were being escorted by six motorcyclists of the Quebec Provincial Police, their sirens screaming, along a circuitous route to the premier's

---

*So barren was the province of politically experienced Diefenbaker supporters that the only man Johnston was able to find for the job was Paul-Emile Jacob, a former Quebec City barman who had once been mess sergeant at the Valcartier military camp. He was promptly disowned by the Quebec Conservative Association.

office. Johnson somehow managed to fill forty-five minutes exchanging pleasantries with Diefenbaker. By the time the Diefenbaker entourage finally arrived at the motel where the party meeting was being held, they found the province's delegates (274 strong) had been firmly pledged to support Camp's reassessment motion.

But even as political support was being removed from under him, Diefenbaker's personality had lost little of its power. That night, Camp and Diefenbaker confronted each other for the first time in a year.

"Hello, Mr President, how's your pilgrimage going?" Diefenbaker asked.

The normally poised Camp was rattled enough to reply: "Good evening, Prime Minister."

"Now, that's what I like to hear. You just keep that up."

"I always think of you as Prime Minister."

THE SHOCK OF QUEBEC'S OVERWHELMING SUPPORT for Camp finally alerted Diefenbaker's supporters to the fact that this latest challenge to the Chief's leadership had gone far beyond attracting the straggle of rebels involved in previous party rebellions. At last they began to counter-attack. Speaking over a national television network on October 26, Diefenbaker tried retroactively to align himself with the principle of leadership reassessment. "No leader can carry on unless he has a vote of confidence," he declared. "I have had it in the past and I will be asking again that the representatives who come to Ottawa determine by their vote a major question, answering once and for all the shoddy propaganda that is being spread across this country that I have taken a stand at any time against a reassessment." Then he added: "I have had everything that the Canadian people can give. Why have I stood? Why do I continue in the face of bitter criticism from certain interests which have attacked me from the beginning? I believe I yet have a contribution to make to Canada."

At the same time, Diefenbaker dispatched some of his loyal supporters into the field in an attempt to discredit Camp. Robert Coates, the M.P. for Cumberland (Nova Scotia), charged that "the forces from Bay Street" were behind Camp, and Erik Nielsen hinted bitterly that the whole affair was an elaborate Grit plot. "What," Nielsen demanded before a meeting of the Lakeshore Progressive Conservative Association in Toronto on October 24, "were the circumstances under which he [Camp] chose to leave the Liberal Party? Why doesn't Camp say what his relations are with Sinclair Stevens and the British International

Finance group, who named him a director within days of his opening attack on Mr Diefenbaker?"* Other Diefenbaker die-hards began to whisper stories about Camp that accused him, among other things, of being an operative hired by Washington's Central Intelligence Agency and an agent of the Vatican.

Such attacks only helped to strengthen the resolve of the party's anti-Diefenbaker forces. Camp's real fear was that he might be out-manoeuvred at the annual meeting. By simply not running a pro-Diefenbaker candidate for the party presidency and allowing him to win by acclamation, the pro-Diefenbaker elements could have prevented Camp from claiming that he had been granted a mandate for the leadership reassessment.

But Diefenbaker's supporters remained confident they still controlled the levers of power within the party and they saw the 1966 annual meeting as a chance to crush the rebels once and for all. At this point Gordon Churchill was trying to recruit a member of the parliamentary caucus (either Erik Nielsen or J. Waldo Monteith) to oppose Camp for the presidency. Finally, Senators David Walker and Harry Willis and M.P.'s Hugh Horner, Terry Nugent, Russell Keays and Michael Starr were able to persuade Arthur Maloney to contest the office and on October 27 he made his announcement: He would run against Camp on two planks – unqualified support for John Diefenbaker and opposition to any review of the party leadership.

Maloney, a highly capable Toronto lawyer, had supported Donald Fleming against Diefenbaker at the 1956 leadership convention, but he later was elected as a Tory backbencher and came to believe in the Prince Albert politician with the fierce emotional loyalty of which the wild Irish are capable. During the 1957 election, Maloney had declared that "any working man who votes against John Diefenbaker is voting against a man who wants to be his friend and advocate." It was never clear why Maloney's fervent devotion and distinguished legal record didn't win him a cabinet post in the Diefenbaker Government. He was defeated in the 1962 campaign and although there were rumours that he was offered a ministry five weeks before the 1963 election, he declined to run again. But his loyalty to Diefenbaker was unswerving and at the party's 1964 annual meeting he worked hard to defeat the proposed secret ballot on the leadership. After deciding to take on Camp, Maloney brushed off the issue of leadership reassessment: "I

*Stevens did contribute one hundred dollars toward Camp's travelling expenses, as did many others of his supporters, but Camp claims he explicitly forbade any corporate contributions and no individual donation was allowed to exceed one hundred dollars.

don't think the leader of our party with all the other burdens he must bear should be subject to the day-to-day or month-to-month whims of convention delegates."

Maloney ran an honest and courageous campaign, trying hard to sell himself as "the compromise candidate" whose election would re-unite the party. But his own fierce loyalty kept getting in the way. Because he could never escape his true label as a Diefenbaker man, the race for the Association presidency quickly polarized the party into pro- and anti-Diefenbaker factions, exactly as Camp had hoped it would.

The only humiliating defeat for Camp that fall came from an un-expected source. One of his main allies from the start of his crusade had been Finlay MacDonald, the Halifax broadcasting executive who was a Conservative Party national vice-president. Robert Stanfield, then Premier of Nova Scotia, had picked MacDonald as his candidate for the 1966-67 presidency of the Nova Scotia Progressive Conservative Association. By tradition the leader's choice was confirmed by acclama-tion at party annual meetings. But Stanfield had made his decision known during a meeting of the Nova Scotia Cabinet not attended by Welfare Minister James Harding, who, unaware of the Premier's wishes, had already received a pledge from Maurice Flemming (the incumbent association president and a Diefenbaker supporter) to run for re-election. Flemming, a merchant from Shelburne, not only defeated MacDonald at the association's annual meeting on November 5, but put through a resolution supporting John Diefenbaker's leadership. Finlay MacDonald, who had originated the Nova Scotia slogan for the 1957 federal election campaign ("Nova Scotia first to say, Diefenbaker all the way"), now twisted his words into a bitter jingle more fitting to the times: "Nova Scotia last to know, Diefenbaker's gotta go."

AS JOHN DIEFENBAKER PREPARED to confront the most serious challenge yet mounted against his leadership, he was faced with two separate but related problems. One was that to save himself from the series of revolts that had rocked his party since 1963, he had already been forced to cash in most of the political IOU's he earned during the six years he was prime minister. There was very little political credit left for him to draw on outside his home territory, and all three Prairie provinces were sending only 271 out of more than 1,300 delegates to the Conservative annual meeting. At the same time, each of the succeeding revolts over the style, substance and duration of his leadership had significantly reduced his estate within the Conservative Party. The first revolt in 1963, led against Diefenbaker's nuclear indecision by his Defence minister, Douglas

137

Harkness, had been confined to the inner circle of his cabinet. The next rebellion, at the 1964 annual meeting, had left a much wider circle of once committed Diefenbaker followers disillusioned. The much more serious rebellion of 1965, awkwardly field-marshalled by Léon Balcer, alienated most of French Canada's Tories and a large section of the national executive. This time, the circle of alienation was the widest of all. By providing an argument directed at an issue (the regular review of party leadership) rather than against a personality, Dalton Camp had infused a spirit of rebellion into the entire party apparatus.

This new mood had reached even the parliamentary caucus, which in past revolts had been the true-blue defender of the Chief's virtues. Until Camp had begun his crusade, the few M.P.'s who dared to question Diefenbaker's leadership had remained isolated figures without influence or leverage. But now, the anti-Diefenbaker faction in caucus was growing both in number and in daring. This was partly because the Tory leader's bizarre patronage system was no longer effective.

Any opposition leader has limited political rewards at his disposal. They include the appointment of M.P.'s as opposition representatives on parliamentary junkets to NATO, the UN, etc., and – less tangible but more desirable – the promise of cabinet posts in any future administration. By the fall of 1966, Diefenbaker's shadow cabinet appointments had reached a stage of diminishing returns. Fellow M.P.'s always knew when one of their number had been in to see the Chief and received the "great-things-are-in-store" treatment from the look of destiny that decorated the would-be minister's face following his interview. But when this favoured group began to compare notes, they often discovered that others had already been appointed to portfolios the Chief was supposed to be keeping warm for them. (One satirist in the Tory caucus claimed that a quiet survey yielded him a list of forty-two future Diefenbaker cabinet ministers.)

As knowledge of such tactics drifted around the Tory caucus his circle of unquestioning supporters diminished still further, and even his most ardent adherents were desperately attempting to arrange some face-saving compromise with the Camp forces. In late October Gordon Churchill had approached George Hees to ask that Eddie Goodman act as an intermediary for negotiations. Camp agreed to several compromises but on November 10, when Goodman saw Diefenbaker to sound him out on the suggestions, the Tory Leader shouted "No! No! No!" and ordered him out of his office.

Two of Diefenbaker's closest friends in the party – Leon Ladner, the Vancouver lawyer, and Bill Macadam, the Conservative vice-president from Campbell River, B.C. – personally pleaded with him to make some kind of conciliatory gesture that would encourage the annual meeting to give him a vote of confidence. One of Camp's agents even approached a Diefenbaker aide with the pledge that Camp would drop the reassessment campaign providing the Leader gave a private pledge that he would consider retirement at some unspecified future date. But Diefenbaker was beyond the reach of any advice. "It's war," he muttered at his staff. But, strangely, he made few preparations to do political battle. He remained confident, as always, that the magic of his personal appeal to the party's shock-troops would quickly disperse the rebels.

Instead of being concerned with the logistics of preserving his own position, Diefenbaker was engaged in some curious crusades of his own. When the government announced its intention (on September 14, 1966) of putting up to auction the horses that the RCMP no longer required at its Regina training centre, the Conservative Leader launched a bitter, prolonged tirade against the move. During the month that followed he tried to work up storms in Parliament over the fact that the coat of arms had been dropped from the cover of the *Labour Gazette* (and placed instead on the front page) and that Postmaster General Jean-Pierre Côté wanted to drop the coat of arms from mail trucks. Even though it was the week of a crucial federal-provincial conference on tax-sharing, Diefenbaker rose in the Commons on October 19 to demand that the Commons adjourn its regular business for an emergency debate on the mail-truck decorations. He interpreted the issue as "a form of underground revolution, mounted in the silent precincts of the Prime Minister's office and the Cabinet . . . a derogation from the sovereignty of this nation and the usurpation of the rights of Parliament."

It was this kind of immoderation that prompted responsible Conservative thinkers in the country to despair about the future of their party. "More than half way through the twentieth century," wrote John Harbron, an associate editor of the Toronto *Telegram*, "the Progressive Conservative Party finds itself on one side of a gulf separating it from the mainstream of Canadian life. On the other move the new realities and the deep-set patterns of social and cultural change which, for the moment, are passing it by."

DALTON CAMP ARRIVED IN OTTAWA on November 7, a week before the annual meeting was due to start, and promptly called a press conference. Looking contained and unworried, sipping a beer and puffing a cigarillo, he jousted with reporters.

"How many delegates did you meet today in your hotel room?" he was asked.

"Didn't count them."

"Is James Coyne backing you financially or otherwise?"

"I'm not interested in someone else's paranoia."

"Is your aim to unseat Mr Diefenbaker?"

"Certainly not. I've said that often enough. The issue at this meeting will be the degree to which the national association is prepared to take risks for democracy."

"Why are you raising the matter of leadership at this particular time?"

"Why not?"

"How did you get a copy of the proposed agenda for the meeting?"

"In the mail."

"Who signed it?"

"It was unsigned."

"How do you think it was made up?"

"I don't have a suspicious mind."

While constitutional authority for drawing up the agenda of annual meetings was not clearly defined, the 1966 document mailed out by national organizer James Johnston had been drafted to give the Diefenbaker forces a tactical advantage. By scheduling the election of officers for the final day and John Diefenbaker's main speech for the convention's opening meeting, the Diefenbaker supporters clearly hoped that they could stage-manage a voice-vote of confidence in the Chief early, so that the Camp-Maloney confrontation – whatever its outcome – would become a meaningless anticlimax. Johnston, on the other hand, claimed quite rightly that he had attempted to contact Camp for consultation on the agenda but his letter had remained unanswered.

As the last-minute preparations for the annual meeting were being made, Camp's problem remained the actual mechanics of how to translate his potential re-election as party president into the calling of a leadership convention. Article 11 of the party constitution was very clear on the point that it must be the national association (not the president) who "shall call any convention for that purpose." Unlike the vote for the association presidency, such a motion would be decided not by secret ballot, but by an open, standing vote, which Camp realized could well go down to defeat.

As late as the week before the meeting was to start, it still looked possible that the Conservatives would both endorse Diefenbaker's leadership (on the Monday night) and re-elect Camp (on the Wednesday afternoon). Camp, badly needing a confrontation to demonstrate the broad base of his support, decided to attack the headquarters-sponsored agenda and called a meeting of the party's national executive

140

for the Sunday evening (November 13) preceding the meeting. His intention was to alter the order of business so that the election of officers would take place on Tuesday afternoon, giving him time, if he won, to carry through the motion for a leadership review the following day.

Late into Saturday night Camp met with his chief strategists – Lowell Murray, Brian Mulroney, Flora MacDonald and Norman Atkins – to discuss their tactics for the executive meeting. The consensus of the gathering was that they would probably carry the agenda change by a margin of sixty-nine to sixty. Senator Wallace McCutcheon publicly declared his support of the Camp position on Sunday afternoon, a not insignificant move because it added a measure of old-line legitimacy to what was, after all, an attempt to usurp the party leadership.

By Sunday evening the customarily sleepy Chateau Laurier Hotel had been transformed into a political battle circus. A four-piece band established itself in the main lobby, swingingly proclaiming Arthur Maloney's virtues – a performance highlighted when Elizabeth Blaikie, a 69-year-old Diefenbaker loyalist from Economy, N.S., did a torchy twist for the Chief. The Camp supporters acted subdued and confident.

At the executive meeting the Diefenbaker partisans – mainly Terry Nugent, Erik Nielsen, Ed Nasserden, George Chatterton, Mrs H. S. Harrison Smith, Lewis Brand, and Gordon Churchill – attempted to turn the session into a condemnation of Dalton Camp. The National President's supporters – mainly Egan Chambers, Heath Macquarrie, Davie Fulton, Elmer Bell and Heward Grafftey – stuck to the agenda issue. The key amendment, to alter the time of voting for the association presidency, was finally passed by the astonishing margin of eighty to forty-one. Most significantly, the three Conservative provincial premiers all supported the Camp position.*

It was the first time in the ten years since he had assumed the leadership that a party vote had gone against John Diefenbaker. Everything now depended on the keynote speech he was to make the following evening. Recalling the way Diefenbaker's supporters had packed the same Chateau Laurier ballroom at the 1964 annual meeting, Camp's strategists this time made certain that their troops showed up early to claim the first ten rows of the hall's nine hundred chairs. Their main worry was that the Conservative Leader would deliver a masterfully rousing oration at the end of which one of his supporters would jump up and call for a spontaneous voice-vote of confidence in the Chief.

To forestall this possibility, one of Camp's advisers on his own

---

*Robert Stanfield voted himself, while John Robarts cast his ballot through the proxy of Stanley Randall (his minister of Economics and Development) and Duff Roblin through Walter Weir (his Highways minister).

initiative hired a pianist to sneak into the ballroom. His instructions were to hit the first bars of the national anthem right after Diefenbaker's speech so that, frozen at attention, no delegate could use the occasion for motions from the floor. The pianist showed up on schedule, but he didn't have to play a note.

THE EVENING BEGAN IN HIGH GOOD CHEER. The hall was jammed to overflowing two hours before proceedings were to begin and many delegates had to watch through closed-circuit television sets mounted in the corridors outside. The room seemed to be a forest of blue-and-white Camp banners, waved by young boys and girls who cheered lustily as their lion-tamer made the opening address. It was a thinking ad man's speech, delivered in both measured English and dubious French, and Camp was heckled often and loudly by men with hog-callers' voices. "My friends," he pleaded, "this is surely not going to be an exercise in democracy by applause meter. . . . We are all united by a common bond as Conservatives."

Camp went on about how he had done his best and how he had tolerance for all and malice toward none but suddenly the attention of the hall was fixed on John Robarts, striding up to the stage and warmly shaking Camp's hand before taking his assigned seat. Robarts, who had been in the hotel since the early afternoon, appeared to have staged the timing of his entrance as confirmation of his support for the National President at a critical moment.

The preliminaries over, Joel Aldred, a longtime Diefenbaker loyalist, rose to introduce his leader. Aldred began by praising himself and continued to say nothing much, but to say it surpassingly well in the resonant voice and with the cardboard charm that had made him the highest-paid reader of television commercials in the country. "Some things are considered old-fashioned," he intoned, "and to some even loyalty has entered that category." This line caused one long-haired Camp boy to whisper to his companion: "Doesn't that make you sick?" which in turn prompted an elderly matron seated behind him to snap: "Listen to that kid! He's still wet behind the ears!" Though the distance between the two was only one row of Chateau folding chairs, the gulf of their misunderstanding was as wide as the forty years that separated them.

Diefenbaker then began to speak. Almost immediately the crowd sensed that something was not quite right. What had gone wrong was that the lectern (which Diefenbaker always liked to have at exactly four feet six inches so that he could lean over it into the microphones) was placed too low. This threw him off stride. He crouched over it, looking awkward, shuffling his papers, putting on his glasses, whipping them off again. "I come to you to deal with issues, not personalities," he began, and a front-row heckler shouted: "Get on with it, then."

The speech was a ragbag of past triumphs, tragic lyricism and vanished appeals. Some of the mercurial touches were still there, in his pouting half-smile, his flashes of self-assurance, the devastating scorn for his opponents, and his voice continued vibrant and strong. But the total effect was that of a stuck record.

Dying of repetition, John Diefenbaker could no longer endow his passions with the practical force and symmetry of ideas. The only policy passage of his speech turned out to be a pathetic attempt to update Sir John A. Macdonald by proposing the construction of new railways to the Maritimes and British Columbia. When he trotted out the old memories and the older clichés, he left his audience dazed and indifferent. Tom Hockin, a young Conservative political scientist, turned to a friend and mockingly demanded: "David, do you suppose he's going to tell us about Lord Salisbury?"

Diefenbaker reminded his audience how far they'd come under his leadership. ("Oh I remember through the years . . . I am able to come before you now and say that I kept the faith.") And an old lady in a black crepe dress and white fake-fur hat and a *diamanté* pin murmured, "You tell them, John. That's right; these kids are wet behind the ears and why don't they get their hair cut."

In a kind of frenzied desperation, trying to create some different reality to which his listeners would surrender themselves, Diefenbaker then began to lash out blindly, words tumbling out in a cascade of malapropisms and non sequiturs: "All my life, human values have been uppermost with me. Disunity and self-criticism and division are a sweet sympathy to the Liberal Party." Making no progress, he turned his attack on Dalton Camp, seated a scant ten feet away. He quoted Camp as once saying: "I would rather fight Grits than Tories." He quoted Camp as criticizing the practice of blaming party leaders for the failures of individual candidates. He quoted Camp as saying that the Conservatives under his leadership had enacted "an astonishing amount of legislation." As he read these quotes, he turned and faced the association president, pointing a stiff left index finger at him. Camp quietly stared back. Dief demanded to know how Camp's views of "two years ago and one year ago and two months ago could suddenly change during the month of September."

The audience was restive and hostile. His patience exhausted, Diefenbaker wheeled like a cornered leopard and snarled "Is this a Conservative meeting?" The shouts came back "Yes! Yes!"

Then a surprising thing happened. Diefenbaker came close to casting some light on his intentions. "Do not tell me I have not looked forward with my wife to the day when my work is ultimately done . . ." At this point, he was interrupted by such a barrage of shouts that he never finished the sentence. "I've had a long life from the days of my youth when I dreamed of the opportunities to serve this country," he said, voice quivering. He reminisced about "the Dinosaur Days" when the party had thirty-nine seats or forty-one seats under Bennett and under Meighen and under Drew (and a heckler shouted, "Don't talk about the past, we want to go forward!"). He implied that his enemies were Liberals at heart ("Why do they attack me? – for the benefit of the party, they claim, yet thousands of Grits, too, are willing to say a new leader is what we need – Why? They hope to carry us back to the days of forty-one seats").

He charged that the Liberals were "a government that has been arrogant in its arrogance." He kept harking back to his successes, but to the kids in the audience, 1957 might as well have been 1857. They belonged to *now*. They were impatient and yearning and they hadn't come to follow John but to bury him.

Most people in the hall were barely suppressing yawns. A Camp supporter carefully lettered on the back of an old Diners Club envelope, "I was a teenage Diefenbuddy," and held it up over his shoulder.

Diefenbaker rambled on, returning again and again to the past, as though it were full of promise for the future.

There on the platform behind him were the lesser party chieftains, still confident in their power: Robarts of Ontario, looking as bored as a company president at his annual staff picnic, and Stanfield of Nova Scotia, his skull-formed face drained of emotion.

They watched as Diefenbaker claimed of the 1965 election: "We were right, but the people didn't follow us," and presented himself as the incarnation of the party and the sole interpreter of its will. For fifty-one minutes he talked on, his forehead corded with excitement, searching for the key phrase that would reactivate his magic.

But his gestures were the gestures of a drowning man, slowly sinking into his private pool of quicksand, daring no one to throw him a lifeline. His whole nervous system seemed to be disconnecting itself from central command. His fists went limp and the jabbing forefinger merely floundered. Each of his sallies had at first been greeted by rising moans of disbelief from the Camp kids, but now they stopped listening altogether. For the first time in his life, John Diefenbaker had lost his audience. In the corridor outside there were sounds of cocktail glasses clinking, cash registers ringing and Arthur Maloney's band (miscued by some anonymous misanthrope) suddenly striking up *When the Saints Come Marching In*.

The music made Diefenbaker's head snap back. Struck by some glimmer of reality, he looked around and said, as if to himself: "I must watch my time."

"Your time is running out," came a heckler's reply.

But still he went on and on. His enemies were the Grits, the press was Grit, but he stood, he would stand, he would not falter, he had followed the course. Finally, mercifully, it was over and the old man sat down, finished.

THE EVER-GALLANT OLIVE BY HIS SIDE, John Diefenbaker left the hall and it seemed somehow a smaller, meaner place. There was in the sight of him the painful recognition of a human being cruelly abused, by himself more than others. Here was a great man, a former prime minister, Freeman of the City of London, reduced to a state where young men and women unborn when he first took his seat in Parliament could challenge him openly. Not even his severest critics could help feeling how sad his story was, how terrible his lost opportunities, how really dreadful it was for a politician to be unintelligently indomitable.

Women with Maloney badges were weeping, while the youthful victors pranced a graceless victory march down the hotel corridors. Allister Grosart was shaking his head and asking no one in particular: "What will arise from the ashes of this once-great party?" John Bassett, publisher of the Toronto *Telegram*, which had editorially campaigned against Camp's reassessment crusade, went directly to his hotel room and began to dictate his paper's leading editorial for the following day: "The Diefenbaker Years of the Conservative Party are over. They ended here tonight when the former Prime Minister's appeal for continued support fell on deaf ears and was greeted time and again with boos and jeers. . . . "

Later that evening Diefenbaker came to plead privately with John Robarts. "You've got to help me save the party. . . . " But the Ontario premier threw up his hands, said "What can I do?" and walked away. In the now empty Chateau ballroom sat Alberta Tory Jack Horner, clenching his fists and blubbering, "I care! I care!"

THE SOUR SMELL OF DEFEAT hung over the Diefenbaker-Maloney forces the following day as Dalton Camp and his young crew took over the convention. John Diefenbaker retreated to his parliamentary office during the voting for the new officers. Camp won re-election, but his margin (564 to Maloney's 502) was surprisingly narrow.

It started to snow that morning and the delegates began to worry about getting home. Eddie Goodman had made one final effort at reconciliation by trying to bring Camp and Diefenbaker together at a private meeting, but the word came back through Joel Aldred that the Chief had scornfully replied: "Tell Camp to go to hell."

The Prince Albert politician's own supporters were in disarray and were not even contemplating any counter-moves of their own. It was as if Diefenbaker's Monday night performance had robbed them not only of momentum but of purpose. Camp's partisans spent most of Tuesday plotting their strategy on the various confidence votes scheduled for Wednesday morning, trying to make certain they would be able to translate their victory into the calling of a leadership convention.

Camp himself, exhausted by his efforts of the past three days, now left the detailed planning to Elmer Bell, a lawyer from Exeter, Ontario, and Eddie Goodman. Goodman wanted to bring on first the report of the Constitutional Committee, which was to include an amendment calling for the regular reassessment of the party's leadership eighteen months after general elections. Consideration of the Constitutional Committee report was supposed to follow review of the Organization and other committees, so that it would probably be delayed until the early afternoon. The session was to have been chaired by Roy Deyell, the party's national treasurer, while Goodman was to steer the Resolutions Committee to follow.

Shortly after ten o'clock, Deyell telephoned Goodman that word had come from Parliament Hill: Diefenbaker would arrive at the hotel within the hour, vowing he would sweep the convention. Goodman rushed down to the ballroom, grabbing on the way out of his room a shoe horn to use as a gavel. After hurried consultation with Camp and Elmer Bell, Goodman called the meeting to order, blithely announced that there had been a change in the order of business and that the report of the Resolutions Committee would precede consideration of the Constitutional Committee's report. By this time, the sound of the welcoming bagpipes could be heard down the hall and Diefenbaker partisans began streaming out of the meeting to greet the Chief.

Goodman quickly set out the procedural ground rules for the leadership resolution. By obvious pre-arrangement, he recognized Elmer Bell as first speaker on the leadership motion and Bell promptly moved that the vote of confidence be made a secret ballot. The motion passed easily on a standing vote. Ben Cunningham, a Kingston lawyer and longtime political ally of both Bell and Goodman, then (again by pre-arrangement) was immediately recognized. He moved that the original motion ("That this Party expresses its confidence in its Leader, the Rt Hon. John G. Diefenbaker") be amended to read: "That this Party expresses its support of the Rt Hon. John G. Diefenbaker, its national leader, and acknowledges its wholehearted appreciation of his universally recognized services to the Party; and in view of the current situation in the Party directs the national executive, after consultation with the national leader, to call a leadership convention at a suitable time before January 1, 1968."

The few remaining Diefenbaker supporters left in the room suddenly became aware of what was happening. They began to move amendments against the Cunningham motion and Goodman realized that enough amendments could talk out the proposal. When Lionel Schipper (Goodman's own law partner) got up to move a sensible but debate-prolonging amendment of his own, Goodman gave him such a dirty look that John Bassett leaned over and whispered to Schipper: "How are you going to enjoy working for Blake, Cassels?"* Schipper sat down. After forty minutes of desultory discussion, Goodman cut off debate and declared that a vote would be taken on the original confidence resolution and its suggested amendment, but that only if the amendment were lost would the straight confidence vote be announced. The Cunningham motion eventually carried by a margin of more than two to one.† The first stage of the down-with-Dief putsch was over.

BUT NOBODY HAD TOLD JOHN DIEFENBAKER. He had arrived as heralded at the Chateau Laurier, squired by his palace guard – Joel Aldred, Fred Hadley (a Prince Albert organizer), brother Elmer, Gordon Churchill, Waldo Monteith – just as Eddie Goodman was banging his shoe horn for order. As word of his presence spread, the faithful bunched around him in a small drawing room across a narrow corridor from the ballroom where his political fate was being sealed.

This was John Diefenbaker's private army, their violent loyalty tempered by an animal shyness that now burst its tolerance as women wept openly and men dabbed their eyes. They clustered in front of him – two hundred strong – chanting, cheering, yearning for his marching orders.

"My friends, I deeply appreciate this," Diefenbaker began, his head

*A distinguished Toronto law firm.
†Ironically, the motion dealing with the regular reassessment of leadership, on which Dalton Camp had based his campaign, was never passed or even properly debated.

bowed, voice breaking with emotion. "I read in the press that the old magic has waned. But I don't know how one could practise that with the trained seals that stood in front of me the other night and were placed there in advance."

He had come down, he said, to see his friends for one more time "because this may be the last opportunity that I'll have the privilege of speaking to you."

"No. We want you. You're the only honest man we've got!"

The crowd quivered, hanging on his every breath. The restorative potion of their response made his whole being swell, his shoulders squared, the gooseberry eyes found their focus again. His sense of timing returned, so that he began to play the chants of homage as a counterpoint to his theme:

"All through the years . . . "

"We need you . . . "

"I've fought on behalf of principle for this Party . . . "

"You're an honest man, John . . . "

"What comes to mind are the immortal words of one of the great ballads of the other Elizabethan era. In that era there were men who *stood*. One of them was Sir Richard Barton. His words have been, through the years, a constant source of inspiration to me. 'Fight on, my man,' quoth Sir Richard Barton . . ."

"Attaboy, John!"

" 'I am wounded, but I am not slain . . .' "

"Three cheers for John!"

" 'I'll lay me down and rest a while and then I'll rise and fight again.' "*

Three cheers and a tiger resounded through the drawing room, interrupting only momentarily the serious enterprise being concluded across the hall.

"We've marched together," Diefenbaker went on, "we've won over and over again. The reason is the rank and file, you men and women in the constituencies. And as long as you remain true to the faith, this party, even though predictions are made to the contrary, shall not die."

"You'll never die, John."

---

*The quotation was from the traditional ballad *Sir Andrew Barton*, by an unknown author. The accepted version, first published in a collection of Scottish and English ballads called *Percy's Reliques* in 1765, reads:

"Fight on, my men," Sir Andrew sayes,
"A little Ime hurt, but yett not slaine;
Ile but lye downe and bleede a while
And then Ile rise and fight againe."

"Thank you, thank you one and all. Go back to your constituencies and build."

"Not without you . . . "

"I wish you could read the telegrams I am receiving from across this country from the ordinary, the average Canadian. They were not deceived the other night, even though the commentators were."

Loud cheers.

"They were not deceived in any way. I've spoken to all kinds of audiences through the years. I ask you how can you move those who are immovable by intention and by direction . . . "

"That's right. . . . We'll support you . . . "

"I owe much to every one of you. I'm sorry my wife cannot be here today."

"Three cheers for Olive."

"She won't be here, she can't be here, but she gives me this message to you. Thank you from the bottom of her heart and my heart. God bless you all . . ."

That was the end of it. Diefenbaker's assistants passed the word. The Chief would not be attending the convention's closing banquet (dubbed by Camp partisans "The Last Supper").

BACK IN HIS PARLIAMENTARY OFFICE studying the messages from his supporters, Diefenbaker bubbled: "They're coming in from everywhere. It's the most fabulous reaction that has ever taken place in this country." To reporters he boasted: "Look, here's one from Calgary that says 'WE CAN SMELL SKUNKS ALL THE WAY FROM HERE.' Here's another: 'THE COUNTRY'S FULL OF DALTON CAMPS. THERE IS ONLY ONE JOHN DIEFENBAKER.' Here's one describing Camp's punks as 'HITLER YOUTH' . . . "

THEIR INDIVIDUAL FURIES EXHAUSTED, their emotions spent, the Conservatives returned home. Camp decided to let tempers settle before calling a leadership convention for the fall of 1967.

Outwardly, John Diefenbaker seemed unaffected by the traumatic meeting, hinting that under the British parliamentary system the caucus (and not the Party meeting in convention) determines who will lead.* To back up his claim he referred to Sir Winston Churchill, who had at

*The Canadian Conservative Party had given up the practice of having the parliamentary caucus choose its leaders in 1927.

one time sat for thirty months as prime minister before his selection as party leader had been formally confirmed. But privately he toyed with the idea of quitting politics, and even wrote out a draft resignation.

When word of Diefenbaker's intended resignation began to spread among his senior lieutenants, they met in the office of Eric Winkler, the party whip, to find a way of changing his mind. Gordon Churchill dispatched a Saskatchewan M.P. to his office with instructions to look in the centre drawer of his desk to fetch a "loyalty pledge" he had drawn up. The document, which urged Diefenbaker "to continue as leader of our Party," was promptly signed by seventy-one of the ninety-six Tory caucus members. One week later, the caucus majority removed from the party's national executive five of the M.P.'s who had refused to sign the pledge. But these were only rear-guard acts of desperation.

An isolated Diefenbaker sat in his office that Christmas, pawing through the great pile of cards he had received, claiming that they represented a resurgence of support. Not even his loyal associates could plumb his intentions. Occasionally he would tell visitors to his office that he intended to resign. But this was more a test of loyalty than a statement of intent. If the visitor agreed that this might indeed be the most advisable course, Diefenbaker would immediately note the man's name down as yet another traitor.

It was through a procession of individual torments that one by one his disciples arrived at the awful realization that their leader was something less than a prophet, and that there was really nothing left in his cause worth the sacrifice of keeping it alive. The imperatives of each man's own political survival gradually took precedence over his personal devotion to the Chief. And so they dropped away, leaving only those hangers-on who had loyalty to offer and nothing else.

Trapped between his eroding authority and his haunting desires, John Diefenbaker by the end of 1966 had become a politician without a party.

CHAPTER 11

The Struggle for Succession

D URING 1967 ALL THOSE MYSTERIOUS FORCES and influences that he claimed had always been persecuting him finally combined to grant John Diefenbaker his political martyrdom.

Despite the undiminished roaring of his words, his admitted transformation of Canadian Conservatism, and the loyal affection he still commanded from a substantial following, the Diefenbaker myth proved to have little validity when tested at the party's leadership convention in the early autumn of the year.

The main result of the leadership contest that took place during the first eight months of 1967 was to rid the party of John Diefenbaker. But what was going on, in essence, was a continuation of generations of guerrilla warfare between the party's radicals and reactionaries to possess the soul and voice the purpose of a political movement that since the days of Sir John A. Macdonald had never properly defined its place in the Canadian ideological spectrum.

At the heart of the Tory dilemma was the cruel fact that at this point in their history the Conservatives had to seek a man with the capacity both to unite his party and to win the prime ministership of Canada. Yet the lessons of recent Conservative history dictated the difficulty of the choice. In the preceding thirty-two years, the Tories had captured power only under John Diefenbaker, a man who in party terms was an outsider and not really an ideological Conservative at all. He had gained office by pressing for welfare-state policies his party had bitterly opposed for decades. His minority wins of 1957 and 1962 and his overwhelming mandate of 1958 were all based on the attraction his personality and policies had for non-Conservatives, particularly in the Prairies and the Maritimes. The prospect was that much of this element of Conservative support would depart with Diefenbaker, reducing the Tories to the minority party they were before he arrived on the scene.

With this background, it was not difficult to understand why John Diefenbaker viewed the turbulent events of 1967 not as the beginning of a legitimate leadership contest, but as a plot by reactionary elements to recapture Canada's Conservative Party. While it was a fact that, with the exception of Alvin Hamilton, all the serious candidates who presented themselves as his potential successors made policy declarations that sounded reactionary compared with some of Diefenbaker's early rhetorical efforts, it was also true that the Prince Albert politician had long before lost any legitimate claim to behaving or even sounding like a genuine radical.

Instead of pressing social and economic reforms on the Pearson Government during this terminal phase of his political career, Diefenbaker seemed entirely preoccupied with defending the *status quo*, particularly in such areas of marginal national concern as the monarchy and its symbols. Why had the pipe band been eliminated from the changing-the-guard ceremonies on Parliament Hill, he demanded, as if it were the seminal issue of the day. Who had dared to remove the lion and the unicorn from the official coat of arms appearing on Centennial medallions?*

Even when he was debating major problems, Diefenbaker was so little able to discipline his thoughts that at times he became almost incoherent. On April 11, 1967, while attacking Paul Hellyer's armed forces unification bill, for example, he somehow managed to cover in his discourse the appointment of Liberal bagmen to the Senate, Paul Martin's cool reception on a visit to Paris, Benito Mussolini's entry into Rome, the inadequacies of Canada's "Liberal" press, interference by the U.S. Ambassador in Canadian affairs, the Duke of York's marching men, the absence of a French guard of honour at Vimy Ridge memorial ceremonies, and the Central Intelligence Agency's alleged involvement in the 1963 defeat of his government.

Probably Diefenbaker's worst parliamentary performance was his Leaders' Day speech of the 1967 session. On such occasions in previous

---

*This terrible deed, it turned out, had been perpetrated by Diefenbaker himself. A simplified version of the Canadian coat of arms (minus the lion and the unicorn) had been approved through an order-in-council by the Diefenbaker Cabinet on September 5, 1957.

years, the House of Commons invariably took on the expectant tension of a theatre at curtain time, with hushed parliamentarians, filled galleries and a phalanx of appreciative Tories ready to thump desks at the Chief's every sally. But as the stale phrases rolled out in 1967 ("I am not one of those who over the years . . . ") he couldn't hold his audience and at one point during his speech thirty-four Tories were absent from their seats. Only four bored ministers were holding down the government's front benches and they didn't even bother to heckle him. He attacked those who urged that "we should think only about the present," and praised again and again the glories of Sir John A. Macdonald and other fabled heroes in whose company he numbered himself.

By early spring, Diefenbaker was acting as if he were contriving ruin with a finality his most dedicated enemies could hardly have hoped to achieve. Faced by the desertion of all but the tightening inner circle of his one-time followers, John Diefenbaker now was concerned only with the rude chance of his own political survival. A man of lacerated ego and exhausted sensibilities, famished for popularity and denied understanding, he turned himself into a kind of ideological nomad in his own land, romanticizing the soaring windmills in the blazing frescoes of his imagination. He retreated into a world of his own which he roamed vainly searching for the elusive touchstones of power.

Diefenbaker's decline was most graphically demonstrated by the Gallup Poll assessments of his popularity. Although 51 per cent of Canadians polled had praised his political performance in the hopeful spring of 1958, by February of 1967 (although his party then held 36 per cent of the seats in the Commons) Diefenbaker had dragged the Conservatives down to only 25 per cent of popular support – ranking the Tories third behind the Liberals (37 per cent) and the New Democrats (28 per cent). In Vancouver, Frank Bernard, the hotel operator who had originated the FOLLOW JOHN slogan in the 1958 campaign, now coined a new version: JOHN PLEASE GO.

As these and other signs of public disaffection over Diefenbaker's leadership began to grow, he lost the final vestiges of control over his parliamentary caucus. In the eight months after the reconvening of Parliament in the fall of 1966, he attended only two regular caucus meetings. The anti-Diefenbaker rebels asserted themselves by deliberately staying away from crucial Commons votes. On March 2, 1967, during a supply motion dealing with old-age pension amendments, thirty-two Conservative M.P.'s stayed out of the chamber, though a later tally showed most of them were in Ottawa at the time. On May 17, a vote of non-confidence in the Pearson Government's agricultural policies was lost by 107 to 90, with twenty-five Tories deliberately absent. The Pearson Government might have been defeated by a fully attended Opposition on either occasion. On May 23, Diefenbaker had agreed with his caucus chairmen that the Conservatives would support the government's Vietnam policy, but later in the Commons he broke ranks to support an anti-government motion on the issue sponsored by the NDP. Only ten Tories stood with him.

In those last sad months, when Diefenbaker's entire energy was devoted to the shoring up of his own tenure, he seemed to be a man immersed in the flux of nebulous, evil events of his own construction, scrutinizing his environment with even more suspicion than usual.

No remembered insult was small enough to claim his forgiveness and dissent was always equated with disloyalty. On April 4, 1967, when the Prime Minister announced that he had named the former Conservative Speaker, Roland Michener, to be Canada's twentieth governor general, Diefenbaker alone on the opposition side of the House failed to applaud the appointment, presumably because Michener had ruled him out of order during a 1959 procedural wrangle.

The result of four by-elections held in early June was yet another humiliation. Conservative candidates ran a bad third, garnering only a token 9 per cent of the votes cast. On July 7, the wind-up day of the 1967 session and the last occasion on which he was to appear in the Commons as Party Leader, only twenty-four Conservative M.P.'s bothered to turn up. Most Conservatives were by this time engaged in the much more relevant enterprise of choosing John Diefenbaker's successor.

THE CONVENING OF A PARTY CONVENTION had been accelerated by a TV broadcast on January 18, 1967, in which Diefenbaker unexpectedly demanded that the leadership issue be settled as soon as possible. His tactics were presumably based on the fact that since the two men he considered his most potent rivals – John Robarts of Ontario and Robert Stanfield of Nova Scotia – were both tied down by impending provincial election campaigns, he might be able to maintain his hold on the party by beating down the lesser competitors within his parliamentary caucus. In his television appearance, Diefenbaker made it clear that he intended to be a candidate himself. "I know," he said in measured tones, "that some will interpret what I am saying as being a swan song. Let me say at once, this is no swan song. Those who will interpret it that way do not know me. I have never in the past and I shall not now desert the course of a lifetime, of at all times upholding principle and standing for those things which in my opinion are good for Canada, for this nation – never forgetting the humblest of our people."

MEANWHILE, CAMP HAD DECIDED he would work through the much smaller executive committee to determine the logistics of the leadership convention, instead of using the party's national executive (which had given Diefenbaker a slim majority at its Ottawa meeting in 1965). Only five of the committee's twenty-five members were known Diefenbaker supporters.

During a Toronto meeting of the executive committee on January 28 and 29, Gene Rheaume, a former Tory M.P., moved a key motion which called for delegates to be appointed on the basis of new riding associations set up according to redistributed constituency boundaries. This meant that many of the entrenched Diefenbaker-appointees would be disfranchised. The committee also decided to reform convention voting rules by forcing the low man to drop off after each ballot. Eddie Goodman (a longtime supporter of George Hees) was neutralized by being appointed convention co-chairman while Dalton Camp accepted no official function and thus was set free to swing his influence wherever he chose to apply it. The convention was set for September 5-9 in Toronto's Maple Leaf Gardens.

AS CANADA'S CONSERVATIVE PARTY at last began to disengage itself from the shadows and the echoes of the Diefenbaker era, a dozen candidates – ambitious men of vastly different demeanours and remarkably diverse persuasions – came forward to bid for the succession.*

*Two of the earliest entries were the darkest of dark horses: John Maclean, a Brockville, Ontario, Hertz dealer, and Hugh Horner, the physician-M.P. from Barrhead, Alberta. During the convention itself a Toronto housewife, Mary Walker-Sawka, became a last-minute contender, but mustered only the votes of her nominator and seconder. John Maclean turned out to be an earnest and engaging young Tory of forthright manner, though he too was strictly a first-ballot phenomenon. Hugh Horner soon abandoned the contest to run provincially in Alberta but while it lasted, his candidacy provided some badly needed comic relief. The policy platform for a Horner government, worked out by Hugh's brother Jack, featured the immediate abolition of tariffs on lariat rope. If nothing else, the Horners demonstrated a truly spectacular faith in each other's abilities. Asked what role Brother Jack would be playing in his campaign, Brother Hugh replied: "Well, you've heard of Bobby . . . take it from there." Asked how serious Brother Hugh's candidacy really was, Brother Jack allowed only that "people laughed at Edison when he invented the light bulb."

The most mysterious candidate of all was Michael Starr, a loyal Diefenbakerite who ran without money, purpose or effort and finished up accordingly.

THE FIRST SERIOUS CONTENDER to hoist his colours was Edmund Davie Fulton, the one-time minister of Justice and Public Works in the Diefenbaker Government who had returned to federal politics in the 1965 election after a brief, unhappy period as leader of the British Columbia Conservative Party. Fulton had always been a hybrid among the Conservatives of his time. He brought to everything he touched both the excellence of a first-class mind (which helped to set partisan issues properly against national aspirations) and the natural mistrust of the intellectual for the glib answer (which tended to embalm most of his declarations in unbecoming pomposity).

Although he had a habit, rare for politicians, of turning inward for comfort rather than outward for assurance, Fulton saw himself as a man fated to influence beneficially the course of Canadian history. Gradually he began to overcome the restraints of his upbringing, and his quest for power became progressively more purposeful. In terms of both its logistics and its intellectual content, he ran the best leadership race of any of the contestants, although he was severely impeded by recurring money problems.

Fulton's close advisers, Brian Mulroney, Joe Clarke, Dan Chilcott and Lowell Murray, were the first to recognize the new reality of Conservative politics in Quebec. Unlike most of the other Conservatives they realized it was no longer possible for political bosses to deliver the Quebec vote. It remained desirable to recruit the influential Montreal power-broker lawyers, but now their mandate had been reduced with most delegates making up their own minds and ignoring the dictates of once-powerful political overlords. The best way to capture the Quebec vote was to stump the province, riding by dusty riding, and this was what Fulton proceeded to do.

Some of Fulton's men resorted to less orthodox methods. Ian Pyper, who was responsible for recruiting his British Columbia support, was infuriated when Alvin Hamilton walked away with most of the delegates elected in the Vancouver-Quadra riding. When Pyper realized that the Hamilton forces were also drawing a bead on his own Vancouver South Association meeting, he rushed around looking for possible delegates. He discovered that a drum and bugle band would be marching by the meeting hall on the way to practise and by some fast talking persuaded them to stop en route. The band members trooped in, put their instruments down, paid a dollar to join the Association, voted for the delegates Pyper had indicated to them, picked up their instruments and marched out again. And that was the way Fulton's men carried Vancouver South.

By the end of his long campaign, Davie Fulton had become a politician at last.

A VERY DIFFERENT MAN and a very different candidate was the next Tory standard-bearer to declare his intentions: George Harris Hees. As a young veteran-candidate in the 1945 election, as president of the Progressive Conservative Association in the arid early Fifties, as a noisy backbench Tory M.P. during the St Laurent period, as an able minister of Transport and Trade and Commerce in the Conservative Government, as the man who swore to support Diefenbaker and forty-eight hours later resigned from his cabinet, as a former president of the Montreal Stock Exchange fighting his way back into politics during the 1965 election in rural Ontario – in all of these incarnations George Hees had always been a unique phenomenon in Canada's public life.

While the inner philosophy and driving force of most politicians is difficult to set down, Hees' ideology was relatively simple to diagnose. Canadian politics, he seemed to believe, was open to the palliative of the bored: razzle-dazzle.

George Hees, who descended on most of his political meetings out of the clouds (courtesy of a rented helicopter), saw himself as the great ringmaster of Canadian politics – or at least as the man who could best create the aura of excitement that enlists people's political passions. His approach seemed to exude the simple idea of love, served up with the famous Hees smile, and the delight in himself that marked all his personal encounters.

Hees' advisers were convinced the technique would work ("They go for ham out there, and George can cut the slices"). But Canada's problems in the mid Sixties were too serious to be entrusted to any man who began most of his rallies with the singsong: "As we say in merchandising circles – as you ladies really *know* – this is the chance to really sample the goods!" Hees had answers for everything ("The big bad wolf of foreign domination is simply a myth created mainly by politicians to win votes at election time!"), and solutions for nothing. Because he was possessed by none, he could never project any definable ideology or even self-limiting purpose to his quest.

By the end of his campaign, Hees was handing out Polaroid photographs of himself with delegates he'd just met, signed: "Best wishes to my good friend . . . from George Hees." He claimed these were "passports to the prime minister's office." But their currency had become questionable.

THE NEXT TWO CANDIDATES to declare themselves – Wallace Mc-Cutcheon (on May 11) and Alvin Hamilton (on May 26) – provided the party with its most striking alternatives. While neither man fitted into the mainstream of contemporary Canadian political thought, they represented opposite but authentic strains of Canadian Conservatism.

McCutcheon's campaign was easy enough to caricature. Here was an aging senator, his fleshy face flushed with good humour as he stumped the boondocks, trying to rouse a complacent nation against "creeping socialism." The veteran of many a boardroom power play (he had resigned twenty-seven major corporate directorships to enter politics), McCutcheon seemed to see the problems of government entirely through the eyes of the unfettered entrepreneur. Yet there was something valiant about this old Bay Street lion, straining every ounce of commitment that he could wring from himself in a hopeless cause.

Alvin Hamilton's candidacy went back to the six months of lonely anguish he had spent debating his future following the party's 1966 annual meeting. He couldn't forgive Dalton Camp for having wounded the Chief and seriously considered sitting as an independent in the Commons. "But suddenly it came to me," he told a friend, "that it wasn't their party; it was my party, and I decided to fight for it." He gathered a small cadre of highly competent and compatible part-time workers (Roy Faibish, his brilliant former executive assistant; Ken Binks, the party's ex-national secretary; Don Johnson, a Toronto executive of Trans-Canada Pipe Lines; Bill Whiteacre, a Toronto lawyer; and David Sinclair, a Vancouver chartered accountant) and began the long search for delegates.

Although there was a distinctly old-fashioned air about the man himself – the small moustache, the hand-knit diamond socks, the thick leather watchband – Hamilton's campaign provided the party with its most important source of unorthodox ideas. Instead of merely recognizing the problems that existed and coming up with policy answers, he was trying to establish new issues not yet perceived by his fellow politicians.

What he was asking the Conservative Party of Canada to do, in effect, was to collaborate with him in its own liquidation. He wanted to establish a new, broadly based political alliance of city workers, union members, farmers, young people and intellectuals who recognized the creative potential of the state.

Hamilton controlled few important pieces of political machinery within his party and had few favours to grant or withhold. But Conservatives all over the country turned out to hear him, because – well, because he was Alvin. Because he had been the most successful and the most popular of the Diefenbaker ministers. Because he had never compromised himself nor pretended to be anything but an honest school teacher out of the West. Because he had never lost his optimism.

His grappling-hook approach to Canadian politics, his leaps between the administrative and the idealistic, his endless discourses about that industrial complex somewhere near James Bay, in brief, his untrammelled imagination had always attracted audiences to his cause. Alvin Hamilton could have qualified as a straight socialist except for the fact that he never abandoned his intellectual commitment to Conservatism with one part of his mind while expressing personal compassion for all the country's downtrodden minorities with the other. The compartments never stayed closed and the result was an inconsistent view of life which called for fewer government handouts accompanied by massive intrusion of the bureaucracy into the nation's everyday affairs.

Hamilton's campaign had an impact on his fellow Tories quite disproportionate to the convention voting support he eventually received. No matter what happened to the Conservative Party in the unpredictable future, it seemed there would always be a touch of Alvin in the night.

LIKE SOME GEOLOGICAL RELICT of a forgotten age, there strutted onto the national scene, in early June of 1967, the improbable figure of Donald Methuen Fleming, by his own admission the great unity candidate that the Conservative Party and the country had been waiting for all along. Persuaded by Gordon Churchill and other Diefenbaker supporters that he should contest the leadership (presumably so that he would further fragment delegate support and give Diefenbaker a greater chance of winning), Fleming quickly surrounded himself with a retinue of expiring Tories whose collective misjudgements had done much to discredit the Diefenbaker Government. With his campaign being managed by Ellen Fairclough, R. A. Bell, J. Waldo Monteith, Raymond O'Hurley and B. T. Richardson, his prospects would have frightened any less self-confident man. But not the redoubtable Donald. "I have decided to accept the challenge," he told a press conference, announcing his availability. "Those who know me know there will be no half-hearted approach." He then handed out to reporters his biographical résumé ("the bare bones of a misspent life") which ran on for 1,200 words through 27 chapter headings and included his honorary membership in an RCMP officers' mess and mention of a parliamentary junket to Nairobi.

159

Donald Fleming had fought many a speech to a draw in his time and during the next four months he proceeded to do so across the country, expounding the doctrines of a Canada that had begun to vanish before he was born. At one point, he demanded that all of his fellow candidates take an immediate oath of loyalty to the Queen. His retinue, meanwhile, laboured tirelessly to merchandise his virtues. Raymond O'Hurley made the most astonishing breakthrough of all (would it deliver Quebec?) when he discovered Fleming's grandfather's name had been Flamand and that he had lived right in Lotbinière County.

Donald tried hard to become one of the boys, and even told funny stories in his best Harry Lauder dialect, but his impact on most people was that of an old-fashioned Sunday School teacher with values and virtues much admired in an era long gone. His candidacy surely must rank as one of the really spectacular miscalculations of Canadian politics – which is taking in a lot of territory.

EVEN THOUGH THE TORY LEADERSHIP CANDIDATES in the field by the early summer of 1967 were claiming large blocks of support among the party's M.P.'s, most of the original anti-Diefenbaker rebels within the parliamentary caucus were carefully remaining aloof from the declared contenders. Davie Fulton, for example, who was more or less openly attacking Diefenbaker, could muster only one M.P., Tom Bell, to his cause. The other rebels, led by Gordon Fairweather and David MacDonald, were still searching for a man who would not only replace John Diefenbaker but would become a freshly minted influence to purge the party of its Diefenbaker mentality. Because every sounding they had taken indicated that Robert Stanfield would not volunteer and could not be drafted, and since John Robarts had deliberately taken himself out of contention, the group turned its persuasive efforts on Duff Roblin. If none of the premiers could be persuaded to enter the race, they were determined to back Dalton Camp for leader.

In the provincial election on May 30, Stanfield became the first Tory in Nova Scotia history to win a fourth consecutive mandate from his people – a landslide, with the Conservatives claiming forty of the legislature's forty-six seats. Even though he'd repeatedly declared during the campaign that he would rather "take up ski-jumping" than enter federal politics, the pressures for him to enter the race began to build up again. Unlike Roblin or Camp, Stanfield had always remained a party regular, keeping his credentials in good standing with both the pro- and the anti-Diefenbaker factions. Although he had voted with Camp at the 1966 party executive meeting, he had generously supported Diefenbaker during the 1965 election.

Stanfield's entry into federal politics was a gradual thing, ruminated over like a cud of new-mown hay. Dalton Camp explained it this way: "I suppose it was partly the Nova Scotia landslide, which was so overwhelming, so emphatic and so personal. As a result Bob found it more credible to believe what people said to him about his federal potential, that he really did have some kind of capacity, some worthwhile contribution to make."

During a brief visit to Ottawa in mid June, Stanfield had paid a call on Diefenbaker. He left persuaded that the Old Chief intended to run against all comers, and that such a move would wreck the party's long-term prospects. At the same time, Stanfield realized that if neither he nor Roblin entered the contest, Camp would have to declare himself, and that his candidacy might similarly create irreparable splits in the future. Stanfield had planned to gauge Roblin's personal intentions at the Centennial dinner tendered the provincial premiers by Queen Elizabeth and Prince Philip aboard the royal yacht *Britannia* at Kingston, during the July 1 weekend prior to the premiers' being sworn into the Privy Council. But the sudden death of Stanfield's brother Frank cancelled his trip. No direct contact between the two premiers was ever established, though each assumed that he would not end by running against the other.

Senator Grattan O'Leary, who at seventy-eight was supposed to be the Conservative Party's "grand old man" but in reality remained one of its most impatient activists, had stepped into the picture by this time. Convinced that the Tories had yet to come up with a credible candidate, he had been trying to persuade Stanfield to change his mind and finally, on June 26, he went to meet the Nova Scotia premier in Toronto. He saw John Robarts first and received a warm response to the idea of the Stanfield candidacy. Then, during a two-hour session at the Park Plaza Hotel, O'Leary told Stanfield it was his clear duty to preserve party unity by running for the leadership. For the first time he was rewarded with a glimmer of interest. On July 7, when Stanfield came to Ottawa to be sworn belatedly into the Privy Council, a reception was set up by Pat Nowlan to demonstrate that his candidacy would receive widespread caucus support. Stanfield flew back to Halifax and the next morning decided to run, though the actual announcement was delayed until July 19. Asked at his press conference whether he now intended to take up ski-jumping, Stanfield replied: "No. I don't think so. One bit of foolishness at a time is enough."

Stanfield's declaration instantly transformed the nature of the Conservative leadership race. It suddenly came alive as the candidates realized they were engaged in hand-to-hand combat for the allegiance of the convention's 2,350 delegates.

THE DAY AFTER STANFIELD'S ENTRY, his main strategists met at Dalton Camp's summer cottage on Grand Lake, near Fredericton, New Brunswick.* Between sets of tennis they plotted the anatomy of the preconvention campaign. It would begin with a tour of the Maritimes (to consolidate Stanfield's power base), then swing through the major population centres; the emphasis would be to avoid enunciating definite stands, because the group felt it would be less dangerous to be accused of not having policies than "to collect a series of albatrosses." "What we have to preserve," said Camp, "is Stanfield's credibility. A provincial politician doesn't come rocketing out of the Maritimes full of national policies. People aren't looking for salvation in policy anyway, they want to judge the quality, the substance of the man."

Atkins proudly presented to the meeting organization charts he'd already drawn up for a national campaign, which could have served a Roblin or Camp candidacy equally well. The most important decision taken at Grand Lake was that the leadership would be won or lost not during Stanfield's national tour but at the convention itself, where the organization's major efforts would be concentrated.

On July 28, twenty members of the federal caucus declared for Stanfield. Early in August he moved into Ontario. While he generally impressed party power brokers at private luncheons and dinners, in public his non-declarations of non-policy failed to electrify or even awaken the delegates. The only obvious breakthrough he seemed to make was in Quebec, where his enlightened analysis of French-English relations drew high praise from Claude Ryan, the influential editor of *Le Devoir*.

Although he was billed as "the man with the winning way," Stanfield's manner of brooding diffidence marked him more as a man who seemed always waiting for something that had already happened.

*Attending this important meeting were: Dalton Camp, Norman Atkins, Flora MacDonald, M.P.'s Gordon Fairweather and David MacDonald, New Brunswick MLA's Richard Hatfield and Cyril Sherwood, Nova Scotia Progressive Conservative Association director Joe Clarke (not to be confused with the Joe Clarke who worked for Fulton), Paul Weed (a Camp worker from Toronto), and Finlay MacDonald.

"Maybe I shouldn't campaign at all," he told an associate at one low point of his tour. "Maybe I should have stayed home, and maintained my mystique." Laconic at his private best, seemingly cold at his public worst, Stanfield was analysed by a man who knew him well with the statement, "Bob's always unable to say what he means because he suffers from a kind of internal stutter."

DUFF ROBLIN, THE LAST OF THE PRE-CONVENTION CANDIDATES, entered the race reluctantly, ran it well until the last week when his organization faltered badly, and lost it through an accelerating succession of blunders. This was a pity, because in terms of both his political personality and his record of achievement in Manitoba, he seemed at the point of his entry into the race the man best suited to take up his party's national leadership.

Dufferin Roblin had never been a provincial premier like the others. Since leading his party to victory over a strongly entrenched, reactionary provincial administration in 1958, he had managed to lift Manitoba out of the Depression psychology that had so long hampered its economic and social progress. Roblin had also proved himself to be a premier striving to transcend parochial problems and concern himself with national issues, though he continued to shrink back from the widening political commitment that his conscience seemed to be dictating. During the first half of 1967 he remained a much-wooed but coy political maiden, frustrating suitors to an extent that turned most of them to less capricious pursuits.

While Roblin himself remained aloof, his supporters were trying to put together the kind of national political base that would precipitate his federal entry. During a four-hour interview with Daniel Johnson on May 29, Cam MacLean, president of the Manitoba Progressive Conservative Association, and Sterling Lyon, the province's Attorney General, won the Quebec premier's pledge to make some of his top Union Nationale organizers available to Roblin. To emphasize his commitment, the Quebec premier telephoned Roblin's wife, Mary, on June 16, asking that she urge her husband to go national. Johnson later repeated his private endorsement to Roblin, suggesting that Roblin's leadership (and the help of the Union Nationale) would "guarantee" the Tories twenty-five Quebec seats in the next federal election.*

*When Roblin visited Quebec during his campaign, Jean Bruneau, a leading Union Nationale organizer, chauffeured Roblin to a meeting at the Renaissance Club in Premier Johnson's limousine and left it parked where incoming members would notice it and, it was hoped, appreciate its significance.

Cam MacLean had also been favourably received in Ontario, where Ernie Jackson, one of John Robarts' chief organizers, told him that the forthcoming provincial election would force Robarts himself to remain neutral, but that he was certain Roblin could carry most of the Ontario delegation. Roblin had also personally called on Leslie Frost, the former premier; who was still an important force in Ontario politics. Frost had assured him that none of the declared candidates could hold the party together and that he would win, no matter how late he declared.

On June 11, two of Roblin's longtime Winnipeg friends, Ralph Hedlin and Merril Menzies of the Hedlin-Menzies firm of economic consultants, went to see Alvin Hamilton in Ottawa. Acting not as politicians but as concerned Canadians who thought Roblin would make the best Conservative leader, they tried to persuade the former agriculture minister to pledge his support to their man. But Hamilton had by then recruited an impressive following of his own and invited Roblin to support *him*. That the Roblin people considered such a proposal unworthy of serious consideration was confirmed on June 25, when Hamilton went to Winnipeg and asked the Manitoba premier whether he would consider accepting the External Affairs portfolio in his government. Roblin's point-blank refusal so insulted Hamilton, he decided not to support Roblin at a crucial moment during the convention that followed.

Well into the summer Roblin insisted that he would enter the Tory leadership stakes only if he could be drafted by a public coalition including John Robarts, Alvin Hamilton, Robert Stanfield, and Dalton Camp, and with the tacit support of Daniel Johnson. The fact that he felt he could tackle John Diefenbaker only with such powerful allies behind him indicated how seriously Roblin had over-estimated the Prince Albert politician's remaining influence in the party. An overwhelming anxiety not to anger Diefenbaker dominated Roblin's campaign, and it was this attitude as well as his long delay in declaring himself that cost him the support of the Dalton Camp organization.

When Camp arrived in Winnipeg, at Roblin's express invitation, on June 20, he was treated like some dark harbinger of bad news. Camp was whisked from the Winnipeg airport to the home of Wally Fox-Decent, one of Roblin's executive assistants. The Premier entered later by another door. They met again that evening in the home of Sterling Lyon, but discussions between the two men remained cool and inconclusive. To emphasize his non-involvement with Camp, Roblin's office leaked stories to the *Winnipeg Tribune* on how "uneasy" the Manitoba premier felt about Camp's visit.

During their talks the Conservative Association president assured Roblin that if he came into the federal race by mid July he could be sure of a clear field as well as his personal support. But Camp also cautioned Roblin that neither guarantee would hold much past July 10. When Camp realized that the main preoccupation of the Roblin people was to line up Diefenbaker's support, he warned them that "Charlie" (the code name for Diefenbaker then being used by Roblin's workers) would never support any candidate other than himself. He suggested that their best bet was to recruit Arthur Maloney as Roblin's campaign manager and angrily flew off to Edmonton for a speaking engagement.

The pressures for Roblin to declare himself now escalated almost beyond endurance but he continued to preserve his options. What none of his backers realized was that the Premier's wife had just been advised she might have a serious ailment that could permanently affect her eyesight. It later turned out to be an inexact diagnosis but it was Duff Roblin's concern for her welfare that prompted the long delay and allowed Robert Stanfield to declare ahead of him.

A few days after Stanfield jumped into the race, Camp telephoned Winnipeg. "I hope you people have finished wiping your eyes," he quipped, sure that Roblin was now out of the running. Instead, Roblin regarded the Stanfield entry as having made the race "respectable." Now that he had the protection of another premier, he felt Diefenbaker could at last be legitimately challenged. His announcement had originally been timed for July 26, but that was a week when Canada was preoccupied with the after-effects of Charles de Gaulle's *"Vive le Québec libre!"* shout, so Roblin waited until August 3 to become an official candidate.

He immediately gathered about him a staff of loyal helpers, including most members of his Manitoba cabinet. But they were more of a retinue than an organization and their first decision – to conduct the national campaign from Winnipeg – proved a costly one. Because of Camp's involvement, Stanfield ran most of his campaign out of Toronto. This meant that he had a ready-made cadre of well-drilled supporters available for the convention, while Roblin had to move his platoon of dedicated amateurs to Toronto at the last minute.

During the month left to him before the convention, Roblin zigzagged across Canada in a rented jet, making impressive inroads into delegate commitments wherever he landed. He immediately seemed to become the party's most acceptable compromise candidate and it was being widely predicted he would receive between six and seven hundred votes on the first ballot. His sudden appearance on the national stage revealed him as the proponent of a new Conservative doctrine that included a dynamic concept of equal partnership for Quebec in Canadian society. Unlike most of the other candidates, he did not moderate his views during the campaign but sharpened them to give himself the image of an exciting new alternative to the spent leadership of his party.

"I think I'm going to make it," he confided to reporters accompanying him on a triumphant lightning tour of Quebec's Eastern Townships. By convention time, his jet had logged twenty-three thousand miles and Duff Roblin had become the palpable political presence against whose stature all the other Tory hopefuls had to measure themselves.

THROUGHOUT THEIR LEADERSHIP CAMPAIGNS, each of the Tory contenders found himself constantly having to look over his shoulder at the shadow of John Diefenbaker. The Old Chief had spent the first half of 1967 throwing out mysterious hints that he intended to succeed himself. The Diefenbaker supporters still believed their champion could afford to ignore the details of the situation and sweep everything aside with a speech or a glare.

Diefenbaker himself was meanwhile making various demands of the convention committee, trying to manufacture an emotional case for his belief that he was being gagged. At its meeting in Victoria on June 24, the committee received a request from Diefenbaker that he be allowed to speak on the Thursday evening of the convention, whether or not he decided to stand as a candidate.

The committee agreed, even though many of its members felt this would give him an unfair advantage over his competitors. When James Johnston telephoned Diefenbaker that his wish had been met, he was asked to pass on the further request that nominations remain open until Friday, instead of Thursday, of the week of the convention. Again, the committee agreed, depriving Diefenbaker of a target.

In mid August, meeting at a thinkers' conference at Montmorency Falls near Quebec City, party delegates had unanimously passed a resolution describing Canada as being composed of two founding peoples (*"deux nations"* in the French translation) with "historic rights who have been joined by people from many lands." To Diefenbaker this was heresy. It ran directly counter to his long-cherished "One Canada" concept. On September 1, he called a press conference to attack the "two nations" resolution. "When you talk about 'two nations,' " he declared, bristling at the very audacity of the idea, "that proposition will place all Canadians who are of other racial origins than what is wrongly described as English and French in a secondary position. All through my life one of the things that I've tried to do is to bring about in this nation a citizenship which was not dependent on race or colour, on blood counts or racial origin, but a citizenship whereby each and every one of us was a Canadian. I'm not going back on that – and support a proposition that will place those Canadians, six or seven million strong today, in a position of being a kind of secondary, second-class citizen in a nation that we're trying to build strong and united."

During his press conference, Diefenbaker displayed both his evocative power ("I've been across the country and I've seen something of that tremendous sentiment that has built up for your Canada and mine . . .") and his woefully anachronistic approach. (His quotations were nearly all from Sir John A. Macdonald, although he did bring in one 1899 speech from Sir Wilfrid Laurier and briefly skipped into the twentieth century to read a 1904 statement from Henri Bourassa.)

At this point it still seemed uncertain whether Diefenbaker would accept the verdict of the convention. Asked about the leadership question, he only replied: "Vacancy doesn't arise by the desire of others." At the end of August, two of Diefenbaker's agents, James Johnston, the party's national organizer, and Laura Mann, an Ottawa Tory appointed to the convention's Ontario Committee, had launched an attack on Eddie Goodman, charging that he tried to pack the choice of Ontario's delegates-at-large in favour of George Hees. But when Goodman called a meeting of the party's executive committee to investigate the accusation on the Sunday before the convention, Johnston was unable to substantiate his claims. The mood of the gathering was so overwhelmingly against him that at one point Johnston pleaded: "Look, I don't want to be a black bastard about all this."

The room squirmed as all eyes focused on Lincoln Alexander, a dignified Negro lawyer from Hamilton who had been chosen the convention's Elections Committee chairman. Alexander looked hard at Johnston, and said with deliberate irony: "Watch it, baby." The tension drained out of the meeting and Johnston, the Diefenbaker man, suddenly looked an irrelevant, foolish figure.

CHAPTER 12

Convention

Politicians measure out their lives in terms of conventions and elections—and of the two, conventions are the more intensely exciting. There never had been in the history of Canadian political parties anything quite like the Progressive Conservative Convention of 1967 which took place in Toronto during the sultry September week after Labour Day.

Like other democratic happenings, it developed its own mood and generated its own momentum, leaving on those who were there an indelible impression compounded of heat, noise, razzle-dazzle, the taste of hospitality suite liquor, the sight of sweaty men blowing up balloons, pretty girls handing out badges, the sounds of loud laughter, bad quips, easy promises, big talk. It was a convention that could only have taken place in the go-go Toronto of the era – at any other time or in any other Canadian place it would have had quite a different feeling.

The voting machines, the television technicians looking like moon-men staggering under the load of their apparatus, the fancy identification badges, the whirring air conditioners in the hotel rooms, the candidates' mock-rock bands with their transistorized guitars, gave the convention an atmosphere in which machines appeared more crucial than men. Most of the candidates' campaign managers behaved as though they believed that if only they were clever enough in engineering the mechanics of the occasion, the delegates could be dazzled into consent.

After it was over, most of the professionals still believed that this was so, that the victory of the Camp-Stanfield coalition had been inevitable all along. What they forgot was that on Labour Day as the first of the delegates, still brown from the late summer sun, began to pour into the city's downtown hotels, the smart money was still on Duff Roblin rather than Robert Stanfield. Men who on the following Saturday night would be saying confidently they had always known Stanfield was a sure winner were privately admitting Monday afternoon that it was "still anybody's ball game."

Only hours after the delegates began registering at the Royal York Hotel on Monday, the convention came alive. What took hold of it was the fever that always grips politicians when power is changing hands, a curious euphoria reflected in the flushed faces of matrons with dimpled arms, in the glazed eyes of garrulous men of late middle age recalling past conventions, and in the endless, disjointed theorizing of the young recounting the latest inside-inside stories. Down the long carpeted tunnels of hotel corridors delegates, reporters and onlookers jostled each other in constant, verbose confrontation. Still in evidence were the senators, the wringers of hands, the anxious, glad-to-see-you toothsuckers who promenaded up the hotel lobbies as if bent on some essential mission. But in fact, most of these old pols were already far removed from the real sources of power in the party and the astute among them realized that after this convention even their presence would become redundant. This meeting belonged to that lost generation of Conservatives who had come of political age after World War II.

ALL OF THE HOOPLA AND MOST OF THE ATTENTION was focused on the candidates themselves, as they strained to satisfy the yearnings of their followers. Tired men, they had talked too much and travelled too far, their pronouncements had begun to multiply back in April, and through the long, uncertain summer (would Dief run or wouldn't he?) they had criss-crossed the country, exhausting mental and physical energies, lacerating the sense of self that sustains even the most extroverted of men.

The first and loudest convention arrival was that of George Hees, tanned and handsome, rolling up to the Royal York in a rented London double-decker bus. (Hees' claque filled only the bottom deck of the bus which prompted an onlooker to crack, "Just like George – nothing upstairs.") Hees bounced into the hotel lobby, accompanied by the rhythms of Jim McHarg's Metro Stompers beating out *Muskrat Ramble*. Sporting a plastic boater, which he raised every few minutes to fan the cheers of his supporters, Hees registered, then led the parade to his hospitality suite. Momentarily breathless, he called for a drink. To prove he was a sober fellow after all, he held up the glass and declared to the accompanying retinue of reporters: "Gentlemen! I want to assure you this is plain, unfluoridated Toronto water!" Badly briefed to the end, Hees blushed when Robert Macaulay, his campaign manager, leaned over and whispered: "It *is* fluoridated, George."

Davie Fulton came next, gayer and younger than he had looked in years, bathed in an aura of self-confidence that tended to dispel his image as a stuffy politician. Michael Starr never officially "arrived," but his supporters tried to grab the limelight by registering a trained chimpanzee, who held a sign that read "LEAD US OUT OF THE JUNGLE MIKE." The animal could perform an Irish clog to the tune of *Mc-Namara's Band*, but wasn't accredited as a delegate since he couldn't sign his name. (The chimp roamed the hotel for the next four days, prompting a drunk delegate slumped in the corner of an elevator late one night to gaze intently at the strange apparition and utter the definitive comment: "I know Mike Starr from way back, and you're *not* MIKE STARR!")

Roblin flew in from Winnipeg on Tuesday morning but most of his supporters didn't arrive until Thursday so that his presence really wasn't felt in the convention's important early days. Stanfield cannily came to the convention refreshed after a three-day weekend at the Moonstone, Ontario, farm of Don Guthrie, a Toronto lawyer. He had met there with Dalton Camp, who came to discuss the final drafts of the policy speeches the Nova Scotia premier would have to deliver at the convention's Tuesday and Friday evening sessions. The Stanfield campaign had, from the beginning, been operating out of the Westbury, the closest hotel to Maple Leaf Gardens, and Camp, although he never once during the convention's run attended any strategy meetings, had a suite of rooms directly above the Stanfield headquarters and maintained constant telephone contact with the organization's key members. Besides Camp, the Stanfield strategists' main advantage over other candidates was a list, drawn up by Flora MacDonald, that identified the delegates who would be casting their ballots at each of the convention's twenty voting machines. A poll chairman was appointed for every machine, his assignment to soft-sell delegates the idea that Robert Stanfield should be their second or third, if not their first choice.

THE FIRST FULL PARADE OF CANDIDATES took place on Tuesday evening with ten-minute speeches to the convention's policy committee at the Royal York. All the contenders – except George Hees, Robert Stanfield and Duff Roblin – ran true to form, neither advancing nor hurting their causes. But Hees came on too strong, sweating profusely as he expounded a grandiose, semi-coherent scheme for expanding Canadian export sales. Even his close friend and one-time fervent supporter, John Bassett of the Toronto *Telegram,* wrote Heesy-baby off that night.

Roblin, who was without personal representatives on the convention's executive committee, had been ill-advised on the nature of the meeting. Told that it would consist only of brief statements followed by question periods, he made no preparation and for a time even considered not attending at all. When his turn to speak came, Roblin in confusion retreated into a raucous, over-righteous political style. He sounded like a fundamentalist political preacher of the Diefenbaker school, bearing the complexities of the twentieth century only as a thin veneer.

Stanfield, buoyed up by the Camp text before him, made the most of the occasion, and the audience, packed with Stanfield supporters on Camp's advice, interrupted his discourse seven times with waves of applause. He talked persuasively about the "quality" of Canadian life and attacked those ignoring the fact that the citizens of Quebec "cannot feel satisfied with a union which they believe denies them the right to be themselves." The poor showing of his competitors plus the reverberating effect of the news media's choice of Stanfield as the best performer made that Tuesday evening speech the convention's turning point.

JOHN DIEFENBAKER FLEW IN FROM OTTAWA on Wednesday morning to defend his title. The delegates who turned out to meet him in the Royal York lobby seemed more curious than committed. In an environment suited to the throbbing klieg-lit meeting halls and mini-skirted teeny-boppers, the old man's political sorcery appeared to have little voltage. His very presence seemed to be something of an embarrassment.

AS SOON AS JOHN DIEFENBAKER had been ensconced in the Royal York's sixteenth-floor viceregal suite, five of the candidates – Fleming, Roblin, Stanfield, Hamilton and Starr – came to pay him homage. The corridor outside was lined with newsmen and elderly matrons incongruously sporting "YOUTH FOR DIEFENBAKER" buttons on their ample bosoms. Vera Graves, a 76-year-old music teacher from Courtland, Ontario, read an epic poem (to be sung slowly to the tune of the Salvation Army hymn, *Sound the Battle Cry*) she had composed for the Chief:

> *Onward, forward, shout for Diefenbaker,*
> *Christ is his captain, he will lead us on.*
> *He's no doped-up mind; he's no drunken swine;*
> *And bribery cannot bind him to wrong.*
> *He's no renegade, no fault-digging spade,*
> *He a path has made 'twixt right and wrong.*
> *Let him lead us on, join our victory song;*
> *Make our Canada a land to love.*
> *Get beneath the weight, open wide the gate,*
> *Help our leader great to lead us on.*

By Wednesday noon it was already obvious that the Stanfield-Camp machine had severely rocked the Roblin bandwagon, though Martial Asselin, M.P. for Charlevoix and George Hees' Quebec lieutenant, still thought enough of Roblin's chances to approach him with a breakaway proposition. Jean Bruneau, a Roblin supporter, was meanwhile passing the word to Quebec delegates that Daniel Johnson wanted them to "vote Duff." When Fulton heard about the ploy, he phoned Johnson and won a pledge that the Quebec premier would stay out of the fight, although two prominent Union Nationale organizers did work for Roblin throughout the Toronto convention. Wednesday's most frequently repeated rumour was that Senator McCutcheon was serving free Chivas Regal Scotch in his hospitality suites. When the mobs began to arrive, a cheaper brand was substituted.

TO THOSE WAITING FOR JOHN DIEFENBAKER to address the convention's first plenary session on Thursday evening, Maple Leaf Gardens felt like an arena before a bullfight. There was the same kind of excitement in the crowd, the same kind of combined terror and blood lust, and it was easy, though fanciful, to cast the Tory leader in the role of the bull, with the nine leadership candidates as the waiting toreadors, bandy-legged but game.

It took almost two hours of dolorous introductions before Diefenbaker rose to speak, and by then the once eager-for-sport crowd had wilted into a sweaty, sullen, sodden mass, fanning itself with copies of candidates' pamphlets. Chairs scraped as the wind-up orators dared the delegates to disregard them and the audience took up their challenge.

Finally, Eddie Goodman started the main proceedings of the

evening by presenting Diefenbaker with a silver tray that once belonged to Sir John A. Macdonald.

Diefenbaker was weak and surrounded by powerful adversaries; all that remained to him now was the power to say "no." That was the essence of his roaming, rambling fifty-minute speech. He said "no" a dozen different ways to a variety of propositions and vistas. His was a tale of public betrayal, party betrayal and the fatal consequences to his country's future.

At times Diefenbaker's discourse achieved its familiar resonance, but it was filled with echoes of past victories, faded visions, forlorn hopes. The melodic line of his gestures, his murmurs and his asides were unchanged, but he could no longer transmit or transfer his emotions to his listeners. When he intoned such sentiments as: "They criticize me for too much concern with the average Canadian, but I can't help that, ladies and gentlemen, for I am one of them," there was only embarrassed silence in the hall.

It was an event out of joint with the times. Here was John Diefenbaker talking about how French Canada "had stood in 1776 . . . and in 1812." Yet two blocks away on the nightclub strip of Yonge Street, half-naked go-go girls were pulsating in their neon-burnished cages.

The ebb and flow of his words, the murmur in an old man's throat, divided his listeners into two main groups: the young, whose country he could not hope to enter; and the elderly women in print dresses and men in suspenders, weeping as much for themselves and their vanished world as for their one-time champion.

As the speech wore on, and the response was obviously less than he had expected, Diefenbaker's voice grew harsh and insistent, his demands imperious. He began to blaze away against the "two nations" concept of Canada, already endorsed by the convention's policy committee.*

"I couldn't," he quavered, "I couldn't accept any leadership that carried with it this policy that denies everything I stood for throughout my life. . . . They say I don't understand the meaning of 'nation,' that it means something different in French than in English. Laurier said it was 'one nation,' Cartier said it was 'one nation.' I'm not going to go back a hundred years or more and borrow a policy that proved to be wrong in order to get votes in 1967."

*On Monday the convention's policy committee had passed the "two nations" Montmorency resolution. Only 240 of the 400 eligible policy delegates had attended the sessions. The controversial resolution had passed by a vote of 150 to 15.

John Diefenbaker had always fought alone, and now at the end of nearly half a century in politics he found himself truly alone, with only the tragic lyricism of his rhetoric for comfort. Long gone was his power to destroy anyone but himself. Time had always been John Diefenbaker's great enemy. And at Maple Leaf Gardens that steamy Thursday night, he was fighting it to the end.

THE DIEFENBAKER SPEECH had done nothing to resolve the question enthralling the delegates: Would the Old Chief run to try and succeed himself? By hinting that he would not want to lead any political movement that followed the "two nations" resolution, he managed to make it sound as if he were about to repudiate his party, instead of the other way around.

On Friday morning, just fifteen minutes before deadline, Joel Aldred, the TV pitchman, and Hugh Arscott, a gallant, longtime supporter from Saskatoon, deposited Diefenbaker's nomination papers. Tension and dismay swept the convention. Some delegates half-admiringly remarked, "The Old Man's stonewalled us again," but the much more general reaction was one of anger that Diefenbaker should continue to play with the party.

Just why Diefenbaker chose to run was never clear. It may well simply have been the reflex action of a man who had never backed away from a political contest, or a genuinely angry response to the party's deliberate snub on the "two nations" resolution. Because he was by then surrounded only by hard-core, unreconstructed admirers, he may even have believed that he had a chance of carrying the race. Arscott, for example, estimated the Chief would receive 1,300 votes on the first ballot. His advisers kept referring to the deadlock that might develop, and how Diefenbaker would emerge as "the compromise candidate." This was a grave misreading of the convention's rules, which provided for the low man to drop off after each ballot, so that no deadlock was conceivable. The most likely explanation of the Diefenbaker candidacy was that he had intended to run all along – that he had been seeking a plausible way into the contest and the "two nations" resolution provided a handy excuse. Throughout his political career John Diefenbaker had accepted only one judgement, that of the ballot box. Now it would deliver its final verdict.

His supporters immediately began to lobby for their candidate, with sentiment as their main weapon. At one point a Diefenbaker aide ushered into the convention press room an elderly widow, introduced as Mrs Ross from Richmond, B.C., whose husband had died three weeks before. "His last words," she sobbed in a sad testimonial, "were, 'Get out, Mae, and fight for the Chief.' "

Most of the anti-Diefenbakerites in the party were delighted by his candidacy. The Chief had finally given them the means of his political destruction, and they intended to use it. An exception was Donald Fleming. He had been promised support from the Diefenbaker loyalists, and now had to watch them removing his badges ("Only Fleming Is Ready Now") and substituting "Keep the Chief" buttons.

With Diefenbaker once again the centre of the convention's concern, the Friday afternoon demonstrations on behalf of the candidates turned into a lame anticlimax. McCutcheon's girls were the prettiest, the Fulton girls the gayest, Hees' the noisiest, Stanfield's the peppiest and the Starr monkey the saddest. Only twenty-nine placards followed the Diefenbaker band up the Gardens aisle, a group hired at the last moment by a Diefenbaker loyalist from Calgary, George Cloakey, the son of R. B. Bennett's campaign manager.

THAT EVENING THE CANDIDATES, for the first time, came before the massed convention to deliver their nomination addresses. The speakers were notably more right-wing than the western populism of John Diefenbaker, but for the most part they enunciated an enlightened conservatism which could rally major support across the country. While every speaker came out against universality in welfare, higher taxes and the guaranteed annual income, each also fashioned his appeal to the young, French Canada, and the nation's poor.

Davie Fulton was more logical than moving, but he maintained his natural dignity without having to reach for it. He sounded neither radical nor reactionary and there was an unspoken confidence in this man that, should the time for leadership come, he would rise to the occasion and serve his nation and his party truly and well.

George Hees bounded onto the platform, full of vinegar, a booster and a boaster ("I want a happy country"), a political football coach, a lucky man wanting to be luckier. Hees' personality was his only marketable asset and he stood there, staring into the blinding television lights like a sun worshipper, certain that this was his deity and that he would receive its blessing.

A florid personage, Wallace McCutcheon, addressed the Maple Leaf Gardens rally as though it were a meeting of his board. ("I know Canada. I've done business in every province.") He wanted to see the party move openly to the right and the country revolt against the overdose of government interference ("We're all being fed into computers").

The real surprise was that this man of serious mien turned out to be the wittiest speaker of the evening. His humour sparkled especially brightly because it was so unexpected, like finding a pun in the telephone book.

Donald Fleming had the look of a banker about to foreclose a mortgage as he delivered his stuffy proclamation. "I offer you no tranquillizers," he declaimed soporifically. His speech sufficed.

Michael Starr came off as a sincere and simple man ("I have not wined and dined you . . . "), his very presence a tribute to the changes Diefenbaker had wrought in the Conservative Party. John Maclean declared he was no crackpot candidate, and proceeded to demonstrate it.

Then came Alvin Hamilton, this fervent hour worth the anguish of his long campaign. Completely unself-conscious, totally without coyness, *avant-garde* in this company (he wanted to recognize Red China), he was talking, as always, in his private shorthand, his visions too high flown for his listeners.

Duff Roblin, constrained by his advisers not to distract delegates with superfluous hand motions, gave an uninspiring speech on the essential issues ("Let us move forward, united in our comradeship; united in the vision of our future – many cultures, two languages, one nation") and met head-on Diefenbaker's challenge on the "two nations" resolution: "We must not let words divide us. We must make their meaning clear so they become a source of strength."

John Diefenbaker's speech was surprisingly brief, touching, yet pathetic. For once, he seemed to recoil from the occasion of the moment. Most of the audience felt the chill of watching a man who had finally realized that nothing could arrest his terrible slide. It was like the collapse of some great papier mâché temple, built for a Hollywood spectacular, when the rains come down and wash the whole Technicolor structure into the sea.

Robert Stanfield was the only contender shrewd enough to wear television makeup that night, but even untouched his face was a political dream, so honest it made one feel sheepish. His text, written by Dalton Camp, was slick ("There is a time for advice and a time for action") but because Stanfield himself remained so unslick, the speech and the man meshed and his performance sounded as if it came from the heart – a rational well-ordered heart with few purely partisan impulses. His restraint and the feeling that his friendship could not be easily earned lent him the opaqueness that has characterized so many successful Canadian political leaders.

That night Duff Roblin still felt confident enough of his chances to cancel his Sunday morning return flight to Winnipeg and begin drafting his acceptance speech. In his hotel room, Alvin Hamilton, whose eventual support the Roblin strategists were taking for granted, was discussing his future with three of his closest advisers. Lying on his bed, puffing a ten-cent cigar, he was saying: "Duff *has* to come to me, and when he comes, I'll be waiting. I've been waiting ever since that conversation in Winnipeg to give him my answer . . . "

BY SATURDAY MORNING, VOTING DAY, the Tory convention was in an advanced state of hysteria. The candidates and delegates had talked too much, drunk too much, slept too little. There were stories that John Diefenbaker, fuming over the "two nations" resolution, would walk out to form a rump "One Canada party; that Gordon Churchill and other Diefenbaker supporters would disrupt the balloting to argue the convention had been illegally called; and a dozen other improbable yarns, all peddled as inside intelligence.

All that was really happening was the negotiation of a quiet, face-saving compromise to salve John Diefenbaker's pride. Gordon Churchill and Joel Aldred had sought out Eddie Goodman to suggest that the policy committee recommendations, instead of being voted on by the convention's plenary session, merely be tabled. Goodman consulted the policy committee chairman, Ontario Education Minister Bill Davis, and agreed to make the change. This allowed Diefenbaker to claim vindication, although Tory Party platforms, even when adopted, have traditionally had little influence on incoming leaders.*

WHILE PUBLIC ATTENTION WAS still focused on the antics of John Diefenbaker, Dalton Camp, who had engineered the holding of the convention, was quietly preparing in his Westbury Hotel room for the final showdown. He had been an invisible, if pervasive, influence all week, keeping in constant telephone touch with key Stanfield organizers. What he and his group of young activists had contributed to the Stanfield campaign, in addition to the texts of every Stanfield declaration, was a professional ability to feel the convention's environment, to provide both a superb sense of timing to Stanfield's every move and the image-maker's true comprehension of what he had to appear to be during that hectic week in Toronto.

*After Diefenbaker's own selection as party leader in 1956 he not only ignored most of his convention's resolutions, but actually ordered all the extant policy papers burned. Alvin Hamilton retained copies for his own use and later circulated them to a select group.

It wasn't exactly that consent was manipulated by the Camp-Stanfield coalition but that the combination of Camp's cleverness, Stanfield's integrity, the other candidates' tactical errors, the shimmering heat and the mind-stunning noise all conspired to make the delegates reach out to the coolest man there.

By Saturday noon Camp's work was done. He sat relaxing with his wife Linda in the Westbury suite, telling friends how a bottle of her strawberry preserves had burst inside his flight bag in Montreal airport. He turned on the hotel television set, poured himself a Martini, and watched Stanfield arrive. He confessed that he'd been praying every night for Diefenbaker to enter the race and was obviously delighted with the Chief's increasingly isolated position. "Now he's an albatross too," he said to no one in particular, put on his delegate's badge and walked over to the Gardens.

Duff Roblin was already there, still scribbling away at his acceptance speech in a Gardens corridor. Jean Bruneau, one of his chief supporters from French Canada, rushed over breathlessly to report: "We'll get Hees' and Fleming's vote from Quebec. There's no question. We've made a deal." Impatient and tense, Roblin left the building for a walk, chatting with his retinue of journalists.

George Hees' men were frantically testing their walkie-talkie back-up system. "We've been out-razmatazzed," Hees' campaign manager Bob Macaulay was complaining. "Christ, we only have a couple of bands and buses. Roblin has more, and Stanfield had the whole damn navy down there tooting *Anchors Aweigh* this morning in front of Union Station."

Stanfield already had two hundred organizers moving around the floor, all plugged into a master switchboard. The Stanfield scrutineers wore blue jackets and tall black, numbered hats, so that binocular-equipped spotters high up in the Gardens gondola could relay messages to them quickly, and kill or spread the appropriate rumours and news.*

BY ONE O'CLOCK MAPLE LEAF GARDENS was stifling hot. Delegates were fanning themselves with newspapers, scraping their chairs, shuffling their feet. Party hacks, sporting specially-coloured badges and puffed

---

*One persistent story was that John Robarts would declare for Roblin. (Actually, he voted for Senator McCutcheon on the first ballot.) By keeping a man glued to the Ontario premier throughout the afternoon, the Stanfield people were able to deny the rumour authoritatively, and they also were able to communicate immediately the news of Bill Davis' gesture of pinning on a Stanfield badge.

up with secretive self-importance, were running about on inconsequential missions. Old men in shirt-sleeves, hoarse-voiced, drenched with perspiration, sat stolidly listening to the warm-up proceedings. The candidates' handlers were making desperate last-minute checks of wavering delegates, breathing instructions into portable transmitters, while paper placards proclaiming each contender's virtues bobbed above the human sea, adding a splash of colour to the drabness of the hall. A thousand urgent conversations on the convention floor seemed to make the huge building throb, like the muted turbines of a big liner's engines.

CHAPTER 13

Done For

JOHN DIEFENBAKER MUST HAVE KNOWN that he was beaten, his brand of politics dying, but custom and courage can outlast reality. When he walked into Maple Leaf Gardens that Saturday, he was going out on his particular path to the end. All of the sweetness and all of the bile that he inspired had by now been expended, so that he had become one of history's truly irrelevant figures and the whole elaborate drama of his candidacy was pointless, even as a gesture.

Through the long afternoon he sat in a tier of box-seats, just left of the stage, with his wife Olive and her ten-year-old grandson, while his aides, Gordon Churchill, David Walker and James Johnston, came to report the fragments of conversation and miasma of rumours enveloping the Gardens. Directly in front of him, an arm's reach away, two dozen reporters, television cameramen, and radio beepers watched his every gesture, their metallic voices demanding his comments, flashing lights and thrusting microphones at their victim. Diefenbaker's face showed the strain; his eyes were hooded in apprehension. But he remained composed throughout the ordeal, talking during the two-and-a-half-hour delay before the first ballot the way a hungry man eats, for comfort as well as nourishment.

"You've done what you had to do," Olive is saying.

"When does the vote begin?" Diefenbaker replies, just as a convention official makes an announcement in French.

"He's speaking in the language of the second nation," remarks Olive.

"Yes. The Queen's picture isn't even here."

"What d'you think of the convention?" asks a radio man, pointing to the voting machines, holding up his mike to catch the reply.

"Remarkable. In past conventions things moved faster without all those gadgets. But they do *look* impressive."

"Will all this hoopla rejuvenate the party?"

"If the balloons that are up there attached to the ceiling bring on rejuvenation, bring on more balloons!"

"Watcha gonna do when this is over?"

"Go fishing in the north of Saskatchewan. I haven't had a successful fishing trip in years."

"You like fishing with a bamboo pole?"

"What about you," Diefenbaker is suddenly angry. "Do *you* have a bamboo pole? Are you a bambooer or a bamboozler?"

"You gonna write your memoirs?"

"I never think of memoirs. I'm still making history."

"What about the voting delay?"

"Everything's electrified today. But they can't find the plug. That's for sure."

"You read anything by Marshall McLuhan?"

"Oh, that's a very interesting thing. When I was in Regina the other day . . ."

A reporter interrupts: "When did you *really* decide to run today?"

"When I knew that the decision was reached, determined upon, that this two-nations resolution would be quietly put away."

Finally, at 3:21 Eddie Goodman announces that voting can start. Diefenbaker makes his way toward the machines. He gets bursts of applause along the way. He has trouble with the machine, has to be shown how to use it, and when he returns to his seat is asked about the experience. "If that be not complication, I know not what complication is," he answers.

"Do all those telegrams you've received reflect Canada's opinion of your view of the two-nations policy?"

"Oh yes, oh yes, there's no question about that. And that applies to the province of Quebec, with the exception of a vociferous minority."

"You won't change your mind?"

"Absolutely not. To do so would be to deny the trust of every prime minister and leader of this party since Confederation."

"Have you tried to get support from other candidates?"

"I've never discussed support with anyone. I've never spent any money on this convention. Accept me. Here. That's all."

"Didya get a chance to look at your tray? Is it engraved, the silver tray they gave you?"

"It's not engraved."

"It's not, eh? D'ya know where they got it?"

"I don't. They say it's a Macdonald tray."

"How much d'ya think it's worth?"

"I don't look at it from a collector's eyes. It's a question of value, intrinsic value, not a matter of consideration of dollars, when the smallest of things have behind them tradition."

It is time, now, for the results of the first ballot, and the circle of reporters tightens: "How d'ya feel, Mr Diefenbaker?"

"I'm one of those who believe in the democratic process. You have never heard me exult in victory. I was never craven in defeat . . ."

"You never were WHAT?"

"Craven in defeat. If you stand for a principle and the principle is right, ultimately you triumph."

"There's a gorgeous colour story in the old boy," says a smooth radio voice.

Davie Fulton comes, for a moment, to perch beside Diefenbaker, and asks: "How did you like the voting machines?" There is no reply and Fulton, looking like a spoiled boy caught trying to curry favour from his school principal, sneaks away.

Gordon Churchill follows with a fistful of telegrams. "FOR CANADA'S SAKE KEEP FIGHTING" he reads, and passes it on. "GLAD TO SEE YOU BACK IN ACTION. KEEP ON KEEPING ON." The two men smile, and give each other a playful elbow poke.

There is yet another delay, and a reporter asks again: "What about the two-nations policy?"

"I have a great sense of satisfaction today. If it hadn't been for me, we would have had that resolution that went through the subcommittee two hundred, what was it, to one, and then through the program committee, with the platform committee. They didn't dare bring that before the convention. They had it all arranged. It was going to be done well."

"How d'ya mean, 'done well'?"

"Put through, and everything was going to be dandy. Macdonald or Borden or Bennett or Meighen. If they looked down here, they would say: 'What is this?' And Langevin and Cartier . . . No, great principles must never be subverted to the hope or expectation of political gain. In 1948 I was alone in this party standing against outlawing communism. I said: 'You can't outlaw thought!' They brought it in as a policy. They said you can't do it; I was booed for that. You can in-law wrongdoing but you can't outlaw thought. Once you start outlawing thought, you place everyone in a position who has association with a communist of having to swear that he isn't a communist. You can't get votes on a principle that's all wrong. They were going to sweep the province of Quebec – two other provinces were mentioned – if the people wanted it. I said whether they want it or not, it stands. Does anyone talk about outlawing communism any more? You've got to take your stand. Oh, here we are. . ."

It is Eddie Goodman, announcing the results of the first ballot: "Diefenbaker, 271; Fleming, 126; Fulton, 343 (CHEERS); Hamilton, 136; Hees, 295; Maclean, 10; McCutcheon, 137; Roblin, 349 (CHEERS); Sawka, 2; Stanfield, 519 (CHEERS); Starr, 45. That's it, thank you, ladies and gentlemen."

John Diefenbaker leans forward, writing the figures on a pad. They show that after eleven years of leading his party, he has retained less than 12 per cent of its support. Just for an instant, a frozen flutter in time, he sits staring at the figures, caught up and held in some stillness of insight. The pouches under his eyes seem suddenly heavier, like purses containing the remnants of a played-out life.

"How d'ya feel now, Mr Diefenbaker, huh? How d'ya feel right at this minute? Huh?" a voice persists.

The Old Chief draws himself together. "I feel as I've always felt," he begins. Then he asks the reporters his one question of the afternoon: "What would be your summary of me, if you were being entirely objective?"

The same voice but in subdued tones: "I'd say you're bearing up extremely well under the strain."

"I've served my country. I shall continue to take those stands that I believe to be right."

Pierre O'Neill of *Le Devoir* turns to a colleague: "Ours is a disgusting trade. We watch a man die slowly and every now and then we say 'You've had it. Now, how do you feel since the last time we asked you?' "

Diefenbaker leaves his seat to fetch some soft drinks for Olive and her grandson. An elderly delegate reaches out for him. "John, you'll always be *my* Chief," he cries, trying for a little while longer to keep alive the legend of John Diefenbaker as the defender of society's underdogs.

Maple Leaf Gardens is filled with average Canadians who may still believe the legend. But they can no longer support the man.

THE SECOND BALLOT. Diefenbaker goes to vote and when he comes back, there is joy in his gloating. In silent mime he shows how he pushed and pulled the voting machine's lever, and comments sarcastically on the long time it takes to count the ballots: "Well, it certainly shows what technical advances can do." Then he suddenly seems distracted and tells Gordon Churchill beside him: "Nasser says, next time his people are going to understand who to vote for."

The microphones and the lights are still there, but the questions have stopped. The reporters are looking at Diefenbaker as if they expect him to begin haemorrhaging at any moment. It is now Diefenbaker who leans forward, trying to engage their attention with the story of a Tory convention held in the late Twenties: "That was the first time they ever had loudspeakers. There were about twelve hundred delegates, as I recall it . . . that was the occasion when the big fight took place between Meighen and the Premier of Ontario, Ferguson. It was the first time any of us had ever seen loudspeakers. The loudspeakers were just horns, oh, eighteen inches in diameter, placed at strategic points around the walls, mainly behind the audience. And in the audience, there would be about three thousand. They filled the rink portion of the amphitheatre in those days. There were joint chairmen. One was Senator Beaubien, who had a very large, loud voice. And Tommy Church, who was Mayor of Toronto several times.

"Tommy was the only person who could make a speech that was totally incomprehensible when it was delivered that was a literary masterpiece when it came out in Hansard. Because nobody knew what he was talking about. Every now and then he'd put in 'British Navy,' 'Empire,' and so on. The matter before the assembly was resolutions on the tariff. Tommy got up, way back, oh, possibly sixty feet from the podium. 'I'm entirely opposed to this business,' he said, 'of a navy for Canada. The *Rainbow* and the *Niobe,* that's all we've got. One's in a garage in Halifax and the other's in a garage in Esquimalt. I'm entirely opposed to that.' The chairman said: 'You're out of order, we're dealing with the subject of protective tariffs.' 'Oh,' Tommy said, 'oh, that's what we're on. Then I can tell you immediately. Let this be perfectly clear. This idea of sending ambassadors. . .' "

The monologue is interrupted by an announcement from Eddie Goodman.

Diefenbaker picks up the story exactly where he left off. "He said, '. . . as far as I'm concerned, this sending representatives down to Washington is nonsense. I wouldn't. . .' "

Again there is an interruption, this time for an announcement by Roger Régimbal, the convention co-chairman.

Diefenbaker picks it up again: ". . . he said: 'It's the biggest nonsense I ever heard in my life.' The chairman replied, 'You are out of *ord-eur*.' That was Senator Beaubien with his big voice. 'We are dealing with the tariff. You are out of *ord-eur*.' 'Oh,' Tommy said, 'it's a simple thing, this business of social security.' He said, 'I'm opposed to that a hundred per cent.' He said, 'This idea of giving pensions to the old. I'm against that. Not yesterday, today and tomorrow . . .' And with that Beaubien became very annoyed and he said, 'You are out of *ord-eur*.' From out of this loudspeaker up there comes 'You are out of *ord-eur*.' Tommy turns around to the audience and says: 'Shut your damn mouths, you're not even delegates here!' "

The reporters laugh, a little too loud, and the group waits for the announcement of second-ballot results: Diefenbaker, 172; Fleming, 115; Fulton, 361; Hamilton, 127; Hees, 299; McCutcheon, 76; Roblin, 430; Stanfield, 613; Starr, 34.

Now the Diefenbaker smile becomes a grimace, without its adornment of the afternoon's brave joy. He has dropped a hundred votes. He is asked if he will withdraw.

"I have no observations to make."

"Well, never mind, Chief," says Senator Walker gently, "maybe we'll go for a little walk and maybe you can get a glass of ginger ale."

Walker and Churchill lead Diefenbaker out to a room under the Gardens galleries. After quick, dismal consultation, Diefenbaker decides to withdraw. Douglas Bassett, a young Hees supporter, flashes in to say that George will give the Chief anything for his support, but finds himself rebuffed.

AS ALWAYS, DIEFENBAKER HAS WAITED TOO LONG to act. It is too late to withdraw. The third ballot has started. Diefenbaker goes to vote, and the applause he gets is thin, the polite clapping of a cricket-match crowd. Back in his seat, he looks at the reporters and they look at him. No one says anything. Then Roger Régimbal is announcing the results of the third vote: Diefenbaker, 114; Fleming, 76; Fulton, 361; Hamilton, 106; Hees, 277; Roblin, 541; Stanfield, 717.*

John Diefenbaker is down to 5 per cent of his party's support. "That's it," he says, and suddenly he is going.

*Although seventy-one M.P.'s had signed the loyalty oath to John Diefenbaker the previous November, an analysis of the voting-machine results showed that only sixteen M.P.'s remained faithful to the Chief on this ballot.

He is still somehow holding himself together, like a sheet of broken safety glass. The conductor of the house orchestra catches the occasion and begins playing *Hail to the Chief*. But there is no music left in the old man, as he makes his way out of that hot hell of a hall, jammed with shamefaced reporters, ungrateful Tories and shattered illusions.

CHAPTER 14

The New Leader

I T TOOK TEN HOURS FOR THE CONVENTION to pick Robert Stanfield as John Diefenbaker's successor and the transfer of power was accompanied by more than the expected quota of wheeling, dealing and high-jinks.

The first-ballot results had been a disappointment to all of the candidates, particularly John Diefenbaker (who had expected more than 600 votes), Davie Fulton (well below his first-ballot estimate of 450 at 343 votes) and Donald Fleming (who had refused to believe he might run fifth, and actually ran eighth). Stanfield led easily with 519 votes.* Mrs Walker-Sawka and John Maclean withdrew after the first ballot. After the second, Michael Starr was dropped and Senator McCutcheon swung his support to the Stanfield group.

Fulton's people kept trying desperately to dislodge Fleming's Quebec support, while the Roblin strategists were trying to do the same to

---

*After the convention Scott Young and David Slocombe reported in the *Globe and Mail* that a breakdown of voting statistics showed Stanfield leading right from the start on the first nine voting machines, those assigned to the power brokers, the arm-twisters of the party. On the machines where constituency delegates voted, Duff Roblin comfortably outran the Nova Scotia premier. A fuller analysis of the voting-machine results is contained in an excellent thesis, written for the political science department of McGill University and entitled "Mother and Father" (the code names used for Camp and Stanfield respectively by the Stanfield communications network), by Michael Vineberg, a young Conservative who worked for Davie Fulton during the convention.

Hees, but both groups decided to hold tough for one more ballot. Ernie Jackson was vainly trying to persuade John Robarts to put on a Roblin button. George Hees, disappointed beyond smiles, was being urged by his two chief handlers, Robert Macaulay and Lionel Schipper, to withdraw while he still had "some marbles left to roll." Dalton Camp, seated in front of a colour television set in the Maple Leaf Gardens Directors' Lounge, directed the Stanfield supporters to begin negotiations with the Fulton men. Duff Roblin took the returns in his backroom Gardens office. "It's still a horse race," he mused, and bounced back into the arena, singing a few bars of *With a Little Bit of Luck* with the house band.*

DONALD FLEMING, BELLIGERENT TO THE END, was dropped after the third ballot; John Diefenbaker withdrew; George Hees marched into the Stanfield compound and raised the Nova Scotia premier's hand in a mock victory salute.

Halfway through the balloting the really decisive edge of the Stanfield organization began to shove Roblin's hard-working amateurs into the ground. Ralph Hedlin, who was the key link between Roblin and Alvin Hamilton, could find no way to pry loose the former Agriculture Minister's support, which was needed to give the Manitoba premier his last chance to win. (Hamilton also rebuffed an approach made by Finlay MacDonald on behalf of Stanfield.) Roblin had never managed to establish any chain of approach to Davie Fulton. He was isolated while Stanfield's men were fanning out, consolidating the carefully nurtured contacts they'd long ago established with Davie Fulton, who now held the balance of power.

Because Fulton's support had held firm but not grown through three ballots, his backers realized that the convention had become a Stanfield-Roblin contest. It was Tom Bell, the New Brunswick M.P., who first suggested to Fulton that, with his own chances gone, he should begin

---

*The Vineberg study makes this interesting comparison between the commitments Stanfield and Roblin received from their home provinces: "The wounds of the 1966 Annual Meeting had not been healed in Manitoba. The Diefenbaker loyalists were prepared to support Duff Roblin but let it be known that they preferred an authentic Prairie spokesman. Unlike their Nova Scotia counterparts, they did not feel a comparable identification with their Premier and their political survival did not hinge upon their votes. While the tightly organized Nova Scotia organization ensured complete attendance and support of provincial delegates, five Manitoba MLAs were absent from the convention and no more than 70% of its delegates voted for Roblin on the first ballot."

considering his alternatives. Bell, Fulton's closest friend in the Commons, stated that his own preference was Stanfield.

The Fulton strategists met, a grim, tight-lipped gathering by now, and decided that they would withdraw on the next ballot, if their support failed to grow. Sidney Spivak and Joe Martin, two key men in the Roblin entourage, contacted Brian Mulroney of the Fulton team, to say that the Manitoba premier would like to meet the former Justice Minister. But they were told that there would be no concession until after the fourth ballot.

Duff Roblin's candidacy was now at its crucial moment. He had expected Alvin Hamilton to swing in behind him, but even though he had not moved significantly upward from the first ballot, Hamilton remained silent and aloof from all attempts to woo his support. Bitterly disappointed that John Diefenbaker had decided to contest the race, Hamilton stuck through to the fourth ballot in the hope of inheriting the Chief's support, but he received only sixty-one of his votes. Had Hamilton withdrawn after the third ballot, he would probably have given the Manitoba premier enough of an edge to lead on the fourth ballot. Stanfield still had very little Quebec support. Stranded without the expected Hamilton votes, Roblin's managers now began an eleventh-hour bid for an alliance with Davie Fulton.

The decisive meeting of the Fulton organizers took place immediately after the fourth ballot, which showed Fulton, 357; Hamilton, 167; Roblin, 771; Stanfield, 865. To throw off pursuing reporters, they met in a Maple Leaf Gardens conference room (really a dressing room) that had originally been assigned to Donald Fleming. Present were all of the key members of the Fulton organization. Dan Chilcott, an Ottawa lawyer and longtime Fulton worker, briefly reviewed the statistics of the contest, which showed that the Fulton strength formed a solid core but had no potential for growth. He concluded that at this stage in the race Fulton support could put either Roblin or Stanfield over the top. There was a long debate over whether Fulton should now withdraw unconditionally or cast his support to either of the premiers.

Only now did Roblin's key strategists hold out a vaguely worded promise of a cabinet position to Fulton and desperately try to arrange a meeting between the two men. (In making their offer they were reflecting Roblin's thinking, but not acting on any specific instructions. When they had asked the Manitoba premier whether he would consider having Fulton in his cabinet, Roblin had merely replied: "What do you think?" and, when they had acknowledged that Fulton would certainly be a member of any Tory cabinet, the Manitoba premier merely said: "Well, there's your answer.") At the same time, Fulton had not been directly approached by any of the Stanfield lieutenants except Pat Nowlan, who was trying to woo British Columbia delegates away but had never mentioned any possible offers from the Stanfield camp. Faced with the choice of saying nothing (as Alvin Hamilton had done) or supporting either of the premiers, Fulton now told his lieutenants: "I have a responsibility. Personally, I prefer Mr Stanfield."

Although Roblin was waiting across the hall from the Fulton dressing room, the two men never met. Fulton went out, shook Stanfield's hand, and most of his Quebec, British Columbia and Alberta support, which was fanatically loyal, swung to Stanfield. Lowell Murray and Brian Mulroney, Fulton's campaign managers, immediately moved onto the floor of the Gardens to hustle for the Nova Scotia premier.

The fifth ballot (Stanfield, 1,150, Roblin, 969) ended the convention. "That's nice," was Stanfield's initial victory comment. He then made a dismally anticlimactic acceptance speech, refusing to follow tradition by praising his competitors, vowing with somewhat wry humour only to "get along with that fellow Camp."

JOHN DIEFENBAKER, WHO HAD RUSHED back to the Gardens less than two hours after his dramatic exit, rescued the occasion.* "My fellow Conservatives," he began, as if nothing had really changed. But when he called for "loyalty in the rank and file to the new leader," the audience knew that he was performing the closing rites for easily the most spectacular and certainly the most tragic career in Canadian politics. Here, on display for one final, luminous moment, was the greatness and the courage, the rhetorical ardour of the man. Yet it was also a poignant occasion, full of regret for the less self-destructive course he might have chosen and the opportunities he had missed.

In the end a politician's greatness must be judged as much by his impact on the country's conscience as by what he did or left undone. Most men lead short political lives and leave few followers. But John Diefenbaker's name would be reckoned with long after the circumstances that gave birth to his brief flowering had been forgotten. What would survive in the nation's folk memory would be the stride and stance of the man, the quality of his courage, the biblical cadence of his rhetoric. Here was a politician who filled the space around him; whatever ground he stood on was *his*.

*As his parting gesture, John Diefenbaker the next morning directed the Royal York to send his hotel bill (for approximately eighteen hundred dollars) to the Conservative Party of Canada for payment.

Now he was standing there in front of the convention, a loser about to become a relic, and he said: "My course has come to an end, and I have fought your battles, and you have given that loyalty that led us to more victories than this party has had since the days of Macdonald . . . Now, taking my retirement, I say this to you, with the deepest of feeling: my country, I have nothing to withdraw in my desire to see Canada one country, one nation – my country and your country . . . From the bottom of my heart, I thank you for having given me this opportunity to serve in my day and generation."

The Diefenbaker Years of the Conservative Party were over.

PART FOUR   *Exercise of Power*

IF John Diefenbaker had not held tenaciously to the leadership of the Conservative Party until the fall of 1967 but had been replaced earlier, the history of the Pearson period would have been very different. As it was, the relationship between him and Lester Pearson was anything but the distant connection that normally links the prime minister and the leader of the opposition. Exchanges between them soon developed into a full-fledged political feud conducted on one side with outright gusto and on the other with nervous disdain.

In the exercise of federal power Pearson and his ministers always considered, as one of the main factors to be taken into account, the question: "What will Dief say?" It was this pressure from the Conservative Leader coupled with the relentless urgency of events that turned the Liberal Government into a driven, harassed administration, perpetually on the edge of avoidable disasters.

The passage of time to most Liberal ministers seemed less a continuum than a progression of fits and false starts, a theatre-of-the-absurd production without predictable plot or final denouement. Overwhelmed by the immediate problem of doing something to frustrate the fury of John Diefenbaker, and contain the rush of circumstances, the Pearson ministers found little time to consider exactly what they were doing.

That the ministry could, when its collective will was fired, accomplish much was established by its impressive feat of pushing through a reluctant Parliament the design for a new Canadian flag. How badly the same group of men reacted under the panic of opposition attacks was vividly demonstrated by the way the Pearson Government fell apart during the Rivard affair and its associated scandals.

Cabinets function efficiently on the tacit understanding that the prime minister will provide the cohesive agent of firm leadership while the ministers, having once pledged themselves to certain courses of action, will collectively support those policies, their leader and each other.

During most of the Pearson period the cabinets that managed the nation's affairs were sadly deficient in these important elements of leadership and loyalty. With a leader who commanded affection but not fear, who sought not to impose his own will but to placate the strong wills of those around him, the Liberal Cabinet endured five years of barely concealed disarray. At the same time, some of the ministers let their leader down badly by their semi-public bickering, alarming displays of ineptitude and strange reluctance to defend their beleaguered confreres in or out of Parliament.

It seemed at times that what held the Pearson Cabinet together was the ministers' collective fear of John Diefenbaker and the instinctive desire to endure that unites a group of men under prolonged siege. There was little esprit de corps because that would have required a unity of purpose that could not be supplied by the mere desire for political survival.

CHAPTER 15

The Acrobats in
the Empty Circus Tent

IN MANY WAYS THE HISTORY of the Pearson administration is a re-counting of its cabinet deliberations, schisms and peregrinations. Most of the government policies formulated in the years from 1963 to 1968 were group decisions involving the sometimes reluctant consensus of twenty-seven individuals rather than the strong opinion of one man.

Members of the Pearson ministry were nearly all well intentioned and hard working separately even though they only sporadically functioned effectively as a group. They had gone into office determined to end the disorder of the Diefenbaker Years. But the humiliation of the sixty days of decision began an accelerating series of emergencies that never let up.

As the succession of crises dulled its sensibilities, the government became increasingly introverted. Most ministers lost their zest for public occasions, retreating more and more into the seclusion of the cabinet chamber, where they rationalized their actions to each other, behaving as though only the small clique of equals to which they belonged had to be satisfied with the efficacy of their choices. Observed at a distance, they resembled a troupe of shy acrobats, performing in a half-illuminated circus tent before the audience is admitted. Here in unassailable privacy they did their tricks for one another, then basked in their own applause. When their elaborate ploys were tested in Parliament before a live audience the acrobatics seldom worked, and many ministers ended up doing a flop-dive into the safety nets.

ALTHOUGH ITS COMPOSITION was frequently altered (only four ministers – Paul Martin, Bud Drury, Hédard Robichaud and Roger Teillet – retained their original portfolios) the Pearson Cabinet could be divided roughly into seven main categories, with a few ministers fitting more than one classification.

1. THE MOST PROMINENT GROUP, at least at the beginning, was the old managerial élite left over from the St Laurent era made up of self-possessed, confident men who felt certain that left alone they could revive those halcyon days of smooth competence that had marked the Liberal Government of the mid Fifties. The politician who epitomized this blithe band of brothers was Jack Pickersgill,* but it also included Paul Martin, Bob Winters, Lionel Chevrier, Senator John Connolly and George McIlraith. They had been stunned by their expulsion from office in 1957 and humiliated by two further electoral defeats; they had despised their time in Opposition, acting all the while like sober men at a masquerade. Now they had inched their way back into power and had no intention of hazarding their hard-won estate by taking unnecessary risks. Unqualified by temperament and experience to understand the changing Canada they were governing, they remained, in Professor A. R. M. Lower's phrase, "Whigs; people who in general were on the side of righteousness, took a benevolent attitude towards it, but felt no urge to advance interests other than their own or those of the group with which they identified themselves."† The ministers in this category were locked into intellectual positions based on Canada as it had been. They ignored most political or social portents that seemed to them imponderable or elusive and regarded themselves as being not so much responsible *to* the people as responsible *for* them.

2. THE SECOND GROUP consisted of former senior public servants who had gone into politics in response to both their dismay at John Diefenbaker and their admiration for Mike Pearson. They might have been new to the Privy Council chamber but they were prepared by both training and background to fit very well into the managerial style of the first group. Ministers in this category included Mitchell Sharp, Bud Drury, Guy Favreau, Maurice Lamontagne and Jack Nicholson. They were hybrids, owing their allegiance to the very different disciplines of politics and the bureaucracy. Talented technicians, they seemed confused by a world whose prob-

*For a description of Pickersgill's role, see Chapter 17.
†*Canadian Forum*, October, 1963.

lems no longer lent themselves entirely to administrative solutions. Among this group, the most influential adviser to Pearson turned out to be Bud Drury. Abrupt and distant in public, Drury could be witty and razor sharp in his private insights. Not politically ambitious himself, he brought much common sense to cabinet deliberations and became a kind of talisman of stability within the Pearson entourage.

3. THE THIRD GROUP was that platoon of secondary ministers who form the majority of most administrations and become footnotes to history – names that flare up briefly like thin flames in the wind. This category included Azellus Denis, William Benidickson, Jack Garland, Jean-Paul Deschatelets, J. Watson MacNaught, Roger Teillet, Harry Hays, Arthur Laing, Senator William Ross Macdonald, and Léo Cadieux. Larry Pennell by force of circumstances also belonged to this classification though potentially he was among the best men in the Pearson Cabinet.

4. THE FOURTH GROUP consisted of promising young ministers in their thirties and forties who made some impact – in a few cases a considerable impact – under Lester Pearson, but who would probably make an even larger mark in the succeeding Trudeau administration. This contingent comprised Trudeau himself, Paul Hellyer, Jean Marchand, E. J. Benson, Allan MacEachen, John Turner, Jean-Luc Pépin, Bryce Mackasey, Joe Greene, Jean Chrétien and Jean-Pierre Côté. Of these men, Allan MacEachen was closest to Lester Pearson, who treated him at times almost as a son.

5. THE FIFTH SUBDIVISION included the New Guard - Old Guard ministers from Quebec who expended most of their energies fighting each other: Lionel Chevrier, Maurice Lamontagne, Guy Favreau, Maurice Sauvé, Yvon Dupuis and Jean Marchand.*

6. JULIA VERLYN LAMARSH. The word "Judy" in any newspaper headline during the Pearson period almost always indicated a lively, mind-boggling story to follow. Miss LaMarsh was the only woman in the Pearson Cabinet, first as Minister of National Health and Welfare and then as Secretary of State, and she operated both portfolios with a flair for publicity and a tendency to indiscretion unmatched in the grey annals of Ottawa. She was partisan in the extreme (what was good was Liberal), awkward in her handling of

*For a description of this feud, see Chapter 18.

the two major problems that came her way (the pension plan in Health and Welfare and the CBC in Secretary of State) and joyously adolescent in her pleasures (which encompassed white convertibles, poodle dogs, curly wigs and net stockings). But for all that, she was the most popular publicly of the Pearson ministers and among the most contemporary of them in her thinking. She fought hard for imaginative appointments to the various government agencies under her aegis, she consistently showed guts and frequently showed gallantry, and her friends, who far outnumbered her enemies, were in complete agreement with Robert Fulford when he wrote in the *Toronto Daily Star*, "She is better than genteel, she is alive."

7. WALTER GORDON, the most important and least easily classified of the Pearson ministers.*

ONLY A MAN WITH AS OPTIMISTIC A NATURE as Lester Pearson possessed could bring together such a motley group and expect it to function amicably. In a way it was a tribute to his conciliatory skills that for more than two years he was able to control his ministers to the extent that they maintained publicly nothing was wrong with *them* but that division was being imagined by an irresponsible press and fostered by an opposition made up of partisan blackguards.

After the 1965 election, however, the Liberals ceased pretending theirs was a smooth cohesive cabinet and became a nervous group of self-centred men no longer hoping for triumph as a team but only for survival as individuals. The various factions resolutely battled each other in and out of the cabinet chamber; ministers and their executive assistants leaked stories to the press favourable to their particular points of view and cabinet solidarity was almost a forgotten concept.

The schisms revealed in these last two years had been inevitable from the beginning. Pearson originally set out to run a government with policies supplied mainly by two rabid progressives, Tom Kent and Walter Gordon. But when he came to choose his first cabinet, he was unwilling to support these radical impulses by picking vigorous young talent from his back benches. Instead, he appointed his ministers according to party seniority and expected old hands to fall in line with new ideas. Later on, when Gordon's errors discredited the progressives' approach, Pearson began to rely more and more heavily on such cautious colleagues as Jack Pickersgill, Mitchell Sharp, Bud Drury, Senator

*For a description of Gordon's place in the Pearson administration, see Chapter 16.

John Connolly and Paul Martin, whose point of view was easy to accept and whose philosophy was in no way unsettling. But the Left-Right, Old Guard - New Guard feud continued unabated.

Walter Gordon refused to acknowledge his decreasing power and inside the cabinet, supported by Larry Pennell, Jean Marchand, Allan MacEachen, Judy LaMarsh and E. J. Benson, continued to fight for reforms. He was strenuously opposed by Jack Pickersgill, Arthur Laing, Jack Nicholson, Mitchell Sharp, John Connolly and eventually by Robert Winters.

Probably the most adroit infighter was Jack Pickersgill. In the fall of 1966, for example, Pickersgill as Transport Minister wanted to appoint Norman MacMillan, the CNR's executive vice-president, to succeed Donald Gordon as head of Canadian National Railways, but he knew that the cabinet's Quebec ministers were determined to name a French Canadian. Although Donald Gordon wasn't due to retire until December 31, 1966, Pickersgill brought the subject up on a day during the last week of September and pushed his nominee through when all the important Quebec ministers were away.*

Cabinet disagreements eventually became common gossip in Ottawa and it sounded to the outsider as though the atmosphere of the Privy Council chamber was peculiarly like that of a country schoolroom full of unruly boys flicking spitballs at each other and paying no heed to the likable but bumbling teacher who was supposed to be in charge. Pearson took to lecturing the cabinet ministers on their indiscretions to the press. At one point he set up a committee on cabinet secrecy but its make-up and purpose were known to a journalist that same afternoon. In the final eighteen months of his administration, with eight ministers more or less openly jockeying for his job, Pearson's lectures became totally ineffective.

To spread the load of responsibility over the whole cabinet and in the hope of improving its team spirit, Pearson revamped the cabinet committee system. There were ten standing committees – external affairs and defence; legislation; sessional; finance and economic policy; resources and trade; communications and works; manpower, social development and labour; agriculture, forestry and fisheries; culture; and

---

*Favreau was ill with pneumonia at the Ottawa General Hospital; Sauvé was in Scandinavia touring rural development sites; Pépin was in Venezuela with the chairman of the National Energy Board; Marchand was in Japan on Immigration business; Cardin was in Sorel resting from his heart attack; and Cadieux was in Europe on NATO business. The only Quebec minister present was Jean-Pierre Côté, who was firmly in Pickersgill's corner and said nothing.

federal-provincial relations – as well as a large number of special committees.* This system was designed to streamline the cabinet's policy-making process. It helped, but there was too much pressure, constantly the feeling of "How do we get out of this one?", to allow the calm appraisal of policy alternatives.

IN POLICY TERMS, the Pearson Cabinet's most disappointing performance was in the field of external affairs. Here, after all, was a government headed by the most successful practitioner of diplomacy Canada had ever produced, yet during the five years that Pearson was in power the country's external affairs posture did not alter in any imaginative way and indeed was scarcely altered at all. It was true that Canada did manage to regain some of the prestige in world councils that had been forfeited during John Diefenbaker's erratic grandstand plays for personal publicity. But not one of the hopeful objectives that External Affairs Secretary Paul Martin outlined on assuming his portfolio – the recognition of mainland China, membership for Canada in the Organization of American States, the development of a more meaningful relationship between Canada and the West Indies, Canadian leadership in the reform of the United Nations – had been implemented.

When Martin was named to the External post neither his supporters nor his detractors in the Liberal Party were particularly pleased. His friends claimed that he would be pushed into obscurity under a prime minister who regarded foreign relations as his personal prerogative (although External was what Martin personally wanted); his enemies thought his highly partisan habits would be a dangerous influence on a government department that prided itself on hermetic aloofness from political involvement. Both groups were wrong.

Martin spent five years gliding around Ottawa, his right arm constantly at the ready to pump an outstretched hand or pat a back, and in conducting his constituency affairs he remained as partisan as ever. But in public he was careful to claim non-involvement in domestic issues. "I am not concerned with political matters," he once explained primly to a guffawing House of Commons. In Parliament he sat hunched in his seat, holding himself with the tired pride of a man who daily meets Herculean claims on his resources, and was seldom reduced to the indignity of making a factual reply. Using half a dozen vague, circumlocutory sentences where six short words would do, he spun out the smooth skein of Canada's foreign relations into webs of verbiage that he

*The chairmanship and membership of these cabinet committees often changed but Appendix E shows a typical distribution of ministerial assignments.

himself could not possibly have unravelled. Although each of these occasions served Martin's purpose of transmuting the rasping realities of a troubled world into comforting generalizations, they did little to enhance his reputation.

All the while he was perpetuating the outmoded concept of Canada as a "middle power," his main principle seemed to be that by venturing nothing new he was bound to make few mistakes. He became a creature of the careful External officials and their Merchant-Heeney approach.

There was much going and coming; the texts of Paul Martin's speeches could have papered the Peace Tower; but there were no structural changes in Canada's relations with the rest of the world, or even an articulated realization that Canada had a choice between "the comfortable, safe path of a quiet, gentlemanly but less effectual policy" or "the more dynamic, more demanding path of an effective independent role," as Professor Stephen Clarkson wrote.* Clarkson's definition of the foreign policy style inherent in the independent approach hardly sounded revolutionary but it would have represented a radical departure from Paul Martin's *status-quo* attitude. "A hush-puppy style may be proper for our diplomats but is not the manner that our political leaders should adopt if they want to reinforce the Canadian identity. Without having to bang their shoes on the United Nations podium they could adopt a more assertive stance that makes clear Canada's existence as a bicultural nation with a unique set of policies," Clarkson wrote.

Because it was the touchstone international problem of the times, the Vietnam war proved the most frustrating foreign policy issue. Professor Thomas Hockin of the political science department at York University noted in the 1966 edition of the *Canadian Annual Review*: "A staggering number of airplane flights, communiqués, diplomatic conferences, agonizing appraisals and evasions went into Canada's search for some contribution to a solution to the war in Vietnam." But the results were meagre and Canada's presence on the International Control Commission provided a rationale for the government's inactive ambivalence. Only the journeys to Hanoi of Chester Ronning provided hopes of a useful Canadian intervention, but few concrete results were achieved. Though the Canadian government attempted in various ways to present itself as a potential Vietnam mediator, the Liberals came under increasing attack, particularly from the nation's academic community. "Our policy in what must be regarded as an unjustly provoked, clearly illegal and barbarous war raises grave doubts not just about the

*In *An Independent Foreign Policy For Canada?* edited by Stephen Clarkson for the University League for Social Reform (McClelland and Stewart Limited, 1968).

worth of our policies in themselves, but also more general questions about the usefulness of quiet diplomacy in the present circumstances and the reality of our foreign policy independence," wrote Professor James Steele of Carleton University. Steele and other critics of the Liberal Government's Vietnam position questioned the validity of Canada's mandate with the International Control Commission, particularly in view of the fact that Canadian industry sold an annual average of $300 millions' worth of arms to the United States, much of it destined for the Vietnam battlefields.

The absence of genuine neutrality in Canada's participation in the ICC was documented in a series of articles by Gerald Clark, an associate editor of the *Montreal Star*, who reported that Canadian officers on the commission had been "acting as informants for U.S. intelligence agencies." The accusation was denied but never successfully refuted by the External Affairs Department.

Lester Pearson's major Vietnam conciliation effort was a speech he delivered at Temple University in Philadelphia on April 2, 1965, in which he suggested "a suspension of air strikes against North Vietnam at the right time" to "provide Hanoi authorities with an opportunity, if they wish to take it, to inject some flexibility into their policy, without appearing to do so as a result of military pressure." This call for "a measured and announced pause" was coolly received by President Lyndon Johnson at a meeting with Pearson the following day.

Similarly, Canada took only limited initiatives toward realizing its announced intention of helping to sponsor mainland China for a seat at the United Nations. In 1967, for the seventeenth year in a row, a motion to seat Communist China at the UN was defeated. During the 1966 and 1967 balloting on the controversial issue, Canada for the first time abstained instead of voting against the motion and participated in some intense backstage efforts to overcome resistance to China's admission. The *People's Daily* in Peking described Canada's involvement as "an undisguised move in the service of the United States' imperialist two-China scheme."

The most dramatic event involving the External Affairs portfolio was, of course, the speech made by Charles de Gaulle in Montreal in the summer of 1967 but for political reasons of his own, Paul Martin continued to down-grade the seriousness of the General's intrusion into Canada's domestic affairs.*

Martin's greatest success in External Affairs was the speed with which he helped organize a United Nations force for Cyprus in the

*For a fuller discussion of this controversy, see Chapter 29.

spring of 1964 to avert the threat of war between Greece and Turkey. The one section of his department where Martin gave real leadership was in the area of external aid. He fought stubbornly to increase the budgetary appropriations for foreign aid programs and brought Maurice Strong, a highly intelligent and dedicated Montreal businessman, into the government service to head the External Aid Office.

Because the pressures of domestic politics kept him so preoccupied, Pearson himself found little time for external initiatives. But he demonstrated the magic of his old diplomatic skills at the Commonwealth Prime Ministers' Conference in the fall of 1966, when he solved the tricky problem of drafting a communiqué on the Rhodesian situation that was acceptable to the many varied interests represented at the meeting. Still, the failure of his government to pioneer a single dramatic new approach to world problems must rank as one of the great disappointments of Lester Pearson's time in office.

THE ONE ASPECT OF DOMESTIC POLICY that made some international impact was Canada's experiment as the first western democracy to carry through the unification of its armed forces – something that many other countries had discussed but lacked the political nerve to put into practice. National Defence Minister Paul Hellyer's efforts – and more particularly his brusque methods – met with understandable resistance from the members and ex-members of Canada's proud armed services. Part of the problem was Hellyer's personality.

He was a difficult man to know. Refusing to practise the hearty arts of phony camaraderie, he gave all those who came in brief contact with him an impression of stand-offish pomposity. But beneath an imperturbable surface he was both personable and impassioned. He once described his choice of a political career as "my kind of Christian ministry." Religion played a decisive part in Hellyer's life. Brought up as a zealous Baptist at Waterford, Ontario, he later organized Bible classes for young people at Westmoreland United Church in Toronto, sang bass in its choir and remained one of the most active church laymen in the country. "I pray every night," he told Kenneth Bagnell of the *United Church Observer*. "I know that problems are in stronger hands than mine, and my own weakness is reinforced again."

Known mainly as a young man who threw bad puns across the floor of the Commons during the opposition years, Hellyer took absolute charge when he was moved into the Defence Department, acting, as one disillusioned admiral privately put it, "like some bush-league McNamara." Within weeks of his arrival, he cancelled the weapons contracts for the army's Bobcat personnel carrier, the RCAF's replacement for the CF-104 fighter-bomber and the navy's expensive general-purpose frigate. In March of 1964 he tabled a White Paper on defence which outlined in precise detail his plan "to integrate the armed forces of Canada under a single chief of defence staff" as a first step "toward a single unified defence force." The legislation creating the integrated command structure was passed July 16 and Air Chief Marshal Frank Miller, previously Chairman of the Chiefs of Staff Committee, became the first chief of the Canadian Defence Staff. Hellyer was careful to point out that this meant "the three services [were] no longer independent entities for the purpose of control and administration." The issue didn't become controversial until the summer of 1966. The Conservative Opposition, which had a high proportion of veterans, did not seem to grasp that Hellyer was really serious about doing away with the individual services until he reiterated his intention in the Commons of establishing "one force with one common name, a common uniform and common rank designations."

Rear-Admiral William Landymore, a dedicated, articulate and much decorated war hero, led the opposition to the scheme because he believed that the ramifications of unification had not been thought through carefully enough. Ordered to relinquish his post as chief of Maritime Command in Halifax, he produced before the Commons Defence Committee several well-documented attacks on the Hellyer proposals. He summarized his arguments in a biting article published in the September 17, 1966, issue of *Maclean's*:

Within the services the threat of this single force is devastating. The single force threatens the psychological basis of military life. The confusion and insecurity already caused among career-conscious officers and men is the immediate reason why so many more are leaving the service and not being replaced by recruits. The concept of the single force is based on a naive and limited view of the armed services – not as forces to defend the nation in time of war, but primarily as a special peacetime force to undertake small police actions in foreign countries. Historically, police actions form an insignificant part of the life-and-death tasks of the armed services in protecting the nation. Yet Canada is being asked to dismiss her armed services as they are now, and form a new force to concentrate on police work.

The frightening thing about this aspect of the single-force plan is that it assumes present conditions among the nations of the world will remain basically as they are. But what happens when the *status quo* alters? And we can be sure that it will, for international conditions and military planning have changed several times since the end of World War II. Instead of the flexible military organization we have at present, are we to be left with no more than a contingent of unemployed constables, in green suits? The absurdity is that our armed services have shown their existing organizational framework is eminently competent in fighting police actions. The new force does not derive from military necessity, but from political expedience. . . . We know from experience that our armed services work well in all phases of military operations, but we really don't know whether the new force will work at all.

Seven admirals and several air marshals and generals joined Landymore in condemning the Hellyer unification idea and extensive hearings of the Commons Defence Committee were held to air their complaints. But Hellyer was unyielding. "The minister," wrote George Bain, the *Globe and Mail* columnist, "has got to the point of being tough merely for the sake of being tough – or perhaps for the sake of the image he hopes will propel him into the Liberal leadership, that of a strong, resolute, decisive man." It will take a decade to evaluate the real worth of Hellyer's unification program but viewed strictly as one of the more daring attacks on the *status quo,* the plan should be judged as one of the really imaginative experiments of the Pearson ministry.

ANOTHER MINISTER WHO ATTEMPTED TO INNOVATE within his department was Mitchell Sharp, who took over the Finance portfolio from Walter Gordon late in 1965. Sharp became the most effective parliamentarian in the Pearson Cabinet, one of the few ministers who refused to panic in the face of John Diefenbaker's ferocious onslaughts. Because he was temperamentally so different from his predecessor, there was a temptation to picture him as an unreconstructed right-winger, standing against social reforms. While he did reflect the Establishment's fiscal values, preferring sound budgeting to social welfare innovations, the extreme poverty of Sharp's youth in Winnipeg, where as a young boy he had seen his family's furniture repossessed, had left an indelible impression. No adventurer, neither was he afraid of change. He had little ideology or prejudice to confine his mind in the search for solutions to problems. His apprenticeship in the Department of Finance during the post-Depression and postwar periods had made him a fastidious administrator and deprived him of the creative urge that produces the kind of intuitive leaps distinguishing the inspired politician. But he did maintain some strong social feelings and, despite a stint on Toronto's Bay Street, he remained outside the business ethos that regards man's acquisitive impulse as his highest virtue.

Sharp's most remarkable political asset was his looks. His jaw structure had set his lips into permanent lines of good humour which bespoke a kind of folk-wisdom. He looked wise without appearing intellectual, with a strong, decent face, tough as the rubber in a handball, its effect enhanced by red hair and piercingly honest eyes. His problem as a politician was that his rise was unaccompanied by the usual reminiscences of friends and as he grew in eminence he moved without any attending anecdotes, a man without shadows.

Sharp was a very different finance minister from Walter Gordon, who threw himself into all sorts of battles figuratively carrying his signed resignation in his pocket at all times. Sharp was not without strong principles but his supreme sense of the rational caused him to assign priorities to the many demands on the government's fiscal assets, which prevented him from escalating most issues to the confrontation stage. Probably his greatest failure was to reject in what appeared an almost off-hand manner the many creative taxation reforms suggested by the Carter Commission.

Mitchell Sharp's first budget, tabled on March 29, 1966, was a complex, adroitly fashioned document that demonstrated both his competence and his unwillingness to enter into any fiscal adventures. Its main purpose was to reduce aggregate consumer demand and induce Canadian businessmen to slow down their capital investments and import purchases. Despite the document's inherent caution, Sharp rejected the old-fashioned idea that governments increase taxes only to raise money. Instead, he established his intention of using taxation in its more creative application as an instrument for modifying the nation's economic trends. Significantly, neither this budget nor the three others Sharp wrote contained even one sentence that enhanced the economic nationalism that had been Walter Gordon's main concern.

Despite his first budget's economic damper, the tempo of business activity – and government spending – continued to accelerate, adding new momentum to rising prices. Because labour costs continued to go up in almost every industry faster than productivity gains, the price increases were proportionately much higher than during the great resource boom of the Fifties. The factor that made this period of incipient inflation dangerously different was that Canada no longer had unlimited access to the American money market, so that it couldn't easily attract investment capital to compensate for the growing balance-of-payments deficit.

Sharp's second budget, brought down on December 19, 1966, reflected an approach he had described previously (on September 8) in the House of Commons: "We have now reached a position that is unstable. The present trends just cannot continue for long into the future. . . . If this kind of boom goes on, many will suffer as a result of higher prices and from the inevitable upset that will follow. All Canadians will suffer if a continued boom should lead to a bust. We must moderate our pace so that we can continue to grow in a steady way, with a continually increasing standard of living and with the economic and social improvements that we can afford year by year."

To help ward off this threat of inflation and to raise the $275 millions required to pay for the government's guaranteed income plan for old-age pensioners that was about to go into effect, Sharp produced a meticulously orthodox document. It raised taxes so that the extra yields would equal almost exactly the expected outflow of cash to senior citizens.

Sharp's third budget, produced on June 1, 1967, was written at an uncertain moment in Canada's fiscal history. With the economy poised delicately between expansion and contraction, Sharp was caught in the dilemma of recognizing the threat of inflation, yet not daring to move massively against it. In the preliminary drafts of this budget he had opted for applying some fiscal brakes through a tax increase, but the final version was aimed at mildly stimulating the economy. It predicted a record peacetime deficit of $740 millions. The budget cast a harsh light on the Pearson Government's spending habits. It showed that since the Liberals had assumed power federal expenditures were up by $3,115 millions – from $6,585 millions for the fiscal year ended March 31, 1963, to the $9,700 millions forecast for the 1967-68 fiscal period. According to the fourth annual report of the Economic Council of Canada, total government expenditures in Canada had risen 35 per cent between 1963 and 1965 compared with a 25 per cent jump in the United States, even though the Americans were spending $2 billions a month fighting the Vietnam war.*

---

*It was Ottawa that got all of the blame for increased government spending. But this kind of accusation neglected the proportionately greater multiplication of provincial and municipal expenditures. In a study done for the Canadian Tax Foundation, Professor R. M. Burns, the director of the Institute of Intergovernmental Relations at Queen's University, pointed out that "in 1950, which is a reasonable year for measuring immediate postwar 'normalcy,' federal non-defence expenditures on goods and services were equal to 2.7% of the gross national product. In the same year, provincial expenditures were 3.0% and municipal 4.6%. But between 1950 and 1965, the

THIS KIND OF FISCAL EXCESS was due directly to the absence of decisive control inside the Liberal ministry. Events made the cabinet spin swiftly, with the ministers all sprawled about its rim and no strong presence in the power-supplying centre. Lacking a focal point, cabinet discussions were often as inconclusive as academic seminars. Because his colleagues never knew what Pearson's own position might be, they could not support him even when they wanted to: the PM acted merely as a presiding officer, a committee chairman with a brittle mandate.

Except in the area of French-English relations, where he had some strong ideals of his own, Pearson often gave the impression that he really didn't care too much what decisions were made as long as they represented an acceptable consensus. "The trouble was," said one close observer of cabinet deliberations, "that Mike would go into a cabinet meeting and confess that he really had no views on the subject, say, of some labour relations problem. He'd turn to MacEachen on the ideological left and say 'What do you think?' and to Bob Winters on the ideological right and ask the same thing. After some decision had been hammered out between the two extremes of opinion, Pearson would have to rationalize it in terms of principles and defend it – when the only real principle involved had been that this was the only compromise to which both MacEachen and Winters could subscribe. This kind of thing was pretty significant in understanding what went on in the Pearson Cabinet."

Senator Grattan O'Leary described Pearson's relationship to his cabinet as a kind of misguided sincerity. "No one doubts [the PM's] sincerity," he wrote. "The trouble is that no one can be sure from day to day what he is going to be sincere about. On Monday he may have a good word for his old friend, Walter Gordon. On Tuesday, he may be extolling Robert Winters. On Wednesday, he has a pat on the back for the humanitarian Allan MacEachen. On Thursday, he comes down solidly for the cold efficiency of Mitchell Sharp. As Laurier said of the Conservative-Quebec nationalist alliance, what a salad!"* An even rougher assessment came from the constitutional expert Dr Eugene Forsey, who once commented: "We were virtually assured, when the

federal share of non-defence expenditure on goods and services rose to 3.3% of the gross national product or by 22%. The provincial percentage rose to 4.3% or by 43% while that of the municipalities went to 7.9% or up by 71%. Total government expenditures (exclusive of intergovernmental transfers) rose from 22.1% of the gross national product in 1950 to 31% in 1965. The federal share rose from 11.5% to 13.4% or by about 17%. The share of provincial governments went up by 59% from 5.6% to 8.9%. The municipal share increased from 5.0% to 8.7% or by about 74%."
*In the *Toronto Daily Star,* October 8, 1966.

Liberals took office, that the heavenly choir had come down to administer the affairs of Canada. Everybody was given to understand that pure intellect was now going to preside over our destiny. One of the signs of the hash they've made of things is that George McIlraith, who himself would say he is not the reincarnation of Einstein or Churchill, has really become one of the most eminent members of the Pearson government – largely by virtue of the fact that he can get from here to the corner of Metcalfe Street without falling flat on his face six times and knocking over seventeen people."

The Pearson Cabinet lurched on from one crisis to the next, avoiding catastrophe through a series of hastily patched-up compromises. But each crisis left it a little weakened, a little less credible as a government, so that eventually only the succession of a new prime minister could repair the damage.

CHAPTER 16

Walter Gordon:
Troubled Canadian

T HE MOST CONTROVERSIAL MEMBER of the Liberal ministry – both at the beginning of the Pearson period, when his abilities were grossly inflated, and at the end, when they were sadly underestimated – was that eccentric pursuer of lost dreams and gallant advocate of unlikely causes, Walter Lockhart Gordon.

It was Gordon's philosophy and influence on federal government policy between 1963 and 1968 that marked the real difference between the St Laurent and Pearson brands of Liberalism. Even his enemies were willing to admit that his role in revitalizing the Liberal Party after its defeats in the late Fifties was crucial; certainly the influence he had on Lester Pearson in the early years of his administration was hard to overestimate. As the key left-wing member of a mildly reformist government, he stood for policies which made his less committed colleagues feel vaguely guilty and despite the steady decline of his prestige after the disaster of his first budget, Gordon managed to maintain the moral leadership of the Pearson administration almost to the conclusion of its tenure. In fact, for most of the decade from 1958 to 1968, Walter Gordon was so inextricably linked with Lester Pearson that it was difficult to discuss one without the other. It was as though the two men absorbed from each other the kind of knowledge and strength they lacked separately.

At the beginning, their mutual dependence was based on a common lack of political experience and a friendship of more than twenty-five years' duration. They had met first in January 1935 when Pearson was serving as secretary of the Inquiry into Price Spreads and Mass Buying and Gordon was brought in to do a research study for the inquiry. At the time Gordon was twenty-nine, a partner in his family's Toronto accountancy firm and by birth and training (if not by temperament) a charter member of Toronto's powerful financial establishment. The son of Harry Gordon, who had commanded a Canadian unit at Vimy Ridge, he had been educated at Upper Canada College and the Royal Military College.

He could easily have spent his life in the languid pursuits of the very rich but a strong social conscience, which was activated by the discussions he had with farmers during the time he spent travelling the Depression-ravaged prairies during that winter of 1935, led him to an involvement in public affairs. He soon became a kind of roving ambassador of efficiency, moving from one government problem to the next with imperturbable ease and widely admired results.

Gordon first came to Ottawa in 1939 as a dollar-a-year man to help establish the Foreign Exchange Control Board and stayed on to become special assistant to the Deputy Minister of Finance. He played a key role in negotiating the 1942 dominion-provincial tax agreement and worked on the first wartime budget. Immediately after the war he was asked to conduct a royal commission on administrative classifications in the federal civil service and set a precedent by producing a quick report that was only thirty pages long.

When Walter Harris in his 1955 budget speech suggested the setting up of a major royal commission to inquire into the nation's economic future, Pearson recommended Walter Gordon to be its chairman. The project had been bitterly opposed by C. D. Howe, who regarded any investigation of the Canadian economy as an investigation of C. D. Howe. Many of Howe's colleagues, however, hoped that out of the commission's deliberations would come badly needed fresh ideas for their 1957 election campaign. Gordon and his four commissioners travelled 21,000 miles hearing 330 submissions on the outlook for every Canadian industry including undertaking. When it became apparent that the job could not be completed in time for the election, a preliminary report was issued early in 1957 but it rejected too many attitudes and policies sacred to the old-line Liberals. Asked in the House about accepting certain of its recommendations, Louis St Laurent shot back testily that the Gordon suggestions surprised him because "they indicate a conception of the existing situation . . . that does not fit in with my conception."

Some Liberals later believed that the immediate and wholehearted adoption of the Gordon proposals might have prevented their 1957 defeat at the polls. But Louis St Laurent was displaced by John Diefenbaker, and the final version of the Gordon Report was submitted to a Conservative administration. (Diefenbaker didn't release it until the week after his 1958 electoral victory, although it was ready for distribution five months earlier. It was never tabled in the House of Commons.)

In the fall of 1957, when Pearson still had grave doubts about whether or not he should contest the Liberal leadership, he turned to Gordon for advice. Gordon not only urged him to run but became his campaign manager for the 1958 leadership convention. Not quite three months later, Pearson suffered the most shattering electoral defeat a Canadian Liberal leader has ever had to face and Gordon, feeling partly responsible, turned his energetic efficiency to the rebuilding of the moribund Liberal Party organization. "Walter was the real architect of our party's renaissance," Keith Davey, the Liberals' national organizer brought in by Gordon, said afterwards. "He was the man who made all the tough decisions."

In 1961 Gordon published *Troubled Canada*, in which he outlined the essence of the Liberal campaign platforms for the 1962 and 1963 elections. In the 1962 campaign he moved into active politics by contesting and winning the Davenport seat in downtown Toronto. In that election, John Diefenbaker helped Gordon to national prominence by attacking him from coast to coast as "the Toronto taxidermist who fills Mr Pearson with flossy economic ideas."

Pearson and Gordon grew ever closer in this period not only because they were confreres in combat but because Gordon was Pearson's kind of person – civilized, not essentially political, a man one could talk to.

His very closeness to the Leader left him open to charges of Machiavellian intent and scarcely endeared him to old-line Liberal politicians either before or after the victory of 1963. They may have reluctantly accepted him as a political organizer but they never approved his policies, particularly the economic nationalism that was his most urgent concern. When he got into trouble, as he did so spectacularly so often, many longtime Liberals were secretly glad, or at least openly amused. Walter Gordon conquered the Liberal Party without ever convincing it.

He never did conquer the Canadian people, in part because the kind of man he really was tended always to be obscured by the kind of man he seemed to be. Witty, intelligent, contemporary and humanitarian, he looked merely overprivileged, the very model of an upper-middle-class WASP in pin-striped suit and regimental tie. To most people he seemed to be a dilettante, forever playing at politics, a crackpot millionaire with mischievous aims and obscure resources.

He liked good food, fine wines, paintings, antiques, travel, and the company of his peers. He could be warm and amusing with close friends, but remained an intensely private person who abhorred the little arts of popularity that are the touchstones of politics in western democracies. His language was that of his class – cool, reasonable, passionless. He could never transform himself from an ideologue into a revolutionary and in the conduct of his nationalistic crusades he remained a sort of Garibaldi without a horse. Even his books, with their revolutionary implications for Canadian society, read like dry texts on bee-keeping.

The emotions that move most politicians to spend their waking hours mouthing platitudes had no place in his make-up. "If you have too highly developed a sense of the ridiculous," he once explained to a friend, "you can't get through daily political life in Ottawa without laughing, and that's not allowed." In a town where ministers seldom make even a minor point without first taking a *tour d'horizon* of all the rumours they've heard in the previous twenty-four hours, Gordon stood out as a man incapable of diversionary small talk. He made lists of what he wanted to discuss with the people who came to call on him, and expected them to do the same. A typical opening move was to lay the appropriate list in front of him and ask his visitor, "Who'll go first?" The traits that isolated him most from his fellow politicians were his decisiveness ("I think in straight lines") and his willingness to delegate power to people he trusted.

Whenever he appeared in public, Gordon diluted his impact by invariably assuming one of two facial expressions: mild boredom or superior amusement. Though his manner was rooted more in shyness than in arrogance, his offhand behaviour left a feeling of aloofness and failed to impress most of the visitors to his office. He never even tried to give the appearance of appreciating the advice constantly poured onto his desk by lobbies of angry businessmen.

A sceptical man with a highly developed sense of individual responsibility and accountability, he abhorred pretence of any kind. As Minister of Finance he often had to fly to Washington, but he would invariably have his assistants phone ahead to request that no official representative of the Canadian Embassy meet him at the airport. He especially enjoyed this freedom when there was another minister on the incoming plane, and he could watch the flunkies bowing to, say, Paul Martin, while he would climb off the aircraft, zippered overnight case in hand, unattended and carefree. His dislike for empty formalities was also apparent in his refusal to allow his aides to insert into his budget speeches the two or three perfunctory French sentences that finance ministers normally use.

He did not speak French and considered it an insult to French Canadians to pretend that he could.

He was indifferent to the procedural ritual of the House of Commons and was always getting it wrong. In May of 1963, as he walked down a parliamentary corridor with Pat Carney, business columnist for the *Vancouver Sun*, he pointed to the Commons chamber and confided: "I find this terribly time-consuming." During one debate on federal-provincial relations, when he began by staunchly defending the government's record, he was interrupted by Michael Starr of the Conservatives, who shouted: "Cut out the politics, Walter!" Gordon disarmed Starr by replying: "Well, I had to have *some* sort of introduction . . ."

Gordon always expected the worst from his encounters with the public. During a visit to England on July 1, 1964, he addressed the London Canada Club to mark the ninety-seventh anniversary of Confederation. The flag debate was just beginning in Canada at the time, with Lester Pearson still committed to his original three-colour, three-maple-leaf design. But Gordon, who had little patience with symbols, had forgotten the colours and kept referring to the new Canadian flag as being "red, white and gold." Every time he made the mistake and said "gold," a few voices in the audience would shout back "blue." But Gordon thought they were yelling "boo," and the fifth time he was interrupted he smiled and said sadly: "I was afraid of that."

His friendship was hard to win, but once gained it was enduring, even in the most trying of circumstances, and his unheralded kindnesses to friends in good times and in bad were many. His personal popularity with the progressive elements in the parliamentary caucus was always high. He was the only minister who tried to encourage and bring along new cabinet talent (particularly Ben Benson, Larry Pennell and Joe Greene) and was always precise and honourable in his dealings with backbenchers.

Gordon had always felt a warm sense of rapport with Guy Favreau because they were both dedicated amateurs in politics. On November 26, 1964, in the bearpit of the debate over the Rivard scandal, Gordon was the only minister to come to Favreau's defence in the strongest possible terms. "I can only say, Mr Chairman," he told the Commons, "that if a man like my honourable colleague, the Minister of Justice, were ever forced to resign for the kind of political reasons suggested, I for one would not be happy to remain in this House." What no one knew at the time was that a few hours before the debate, Gordon had received word that his son, John, a student at Ridley College in St Catharines, had been struck in the eye by a flying puck and that his sight might not be saved. The weather had grounded all planes that afternoon, so Mrs Gordon set off for St Catharines by bus. But her husband, who wanted to accompany her, stayed behind to defend his friend, Guy Favreau. The boy recovered, and Favreau was never even told of the accident.

WALTER GORDON'S MAIN PROBLEM as a politician was his impatience. He could never wait until public opinion crystallized, and boredom usually overcame him before the full implications of a complex political issue were clear. He preferred to put forward alternatives to be tested in the crucible of actual experience. "My inclination is to ask 'Why not?' if I hear what sounds like a good suggestion," he once commented.

His working habits were acquired during the twenty-five years he spent as the moving spirit of Woods, Gordon and Company, Canada's best known firm of management consultants. It may be significant that he practised a profession in which a man earns his living by recommending alternative solutions to corporate problems, with the understanding that the client will reject those ideas that prove impractical. He was never satisfied with things as they were and liked to experiment. The most precise statement of his views was contained in a key passage of his first book, *Troubled Canada.** "Neither governments nor individuals," he wrote, "should ever be satisfied with conditions as they are. They should strive continually to improve things and to give a lead in the introduction of reforms. It is well to remember that all changes and all reforms are likely to provoke opposition to begin with. Perhaps unfortunately, that is a natural reaction of human beings to anything that is new. But once people become used to some new measure, especially in the sphere of social security, they will complain even more loudly if it is discontinued."

In contradiction to the classic economists of the past, Gordon didn't recognize the free market-place as the most appropriate mechanism for allocating the nation's assets. He believed instead that the central government should be charged with a vital role in deciding how Canadian resources ought most fairly to be exploited. In effect, he did not consider successful businessmen as necessarily possessing the best brains or being the best company. He saw them as a faction to be placated, not a force to be followed. Because he was personally a rich man, Gordon was not afraid of tackling established power blocs. Politics to him was an end in itself only in so far as it could translate human necessities and moral obligations into legislative accomplishments.

---

*Published by McClelland and Stewart Limited in 1961.

In many important ways, his attitudes ran directly counter to the view of Liberalism prevailing during the St Laurent - C. D. Howe period, which held that corporate capitalism was at the very centre of Canada's social order. "The Liberal Party," Gordon told a meeting of the Hamilton and District Liberal Labour Group on April 14, 1967, "must always stand for the average Canadian, for the unorganized and the inarticulate, and not for special occupational groups or social classes." Such an approach implied that the major share of the benefits flowing from economic growth should not go to the investors, risk-takers and corporate managers, but should be distributed by the government to less privileged individuals. It was this philosophy that made Gordon a very unusual minister of finance. Instead of deliberately casting himself as the villain of the cabinet – the man who traditionally holds up the spending estimates of his colleagues until they prove to him that their pet schemes are really essential – Gordon was always the chief advocate of bold spending proposals. Since this left no minister in the role of defender of the public purse, the Pearson Government's growing budgetary deficits and serious overspending eventually led to a fiscal crisis. The Canadian cabinet system makes no provision for a minister of finance who happens also to be an evangelist.

ALL OF GORDON'S PECULIAR PASSIONS for causes and all of the paradoxes in his character were illuminated by the way he went about mounting the major crusade of his public career, his fight to repatriate the Canadian economy.

Like the Northern Vision of the Diefenbaker Years, his economic nationalism provided the Pearson administration with its most imaginative, and most disappointing, policy venture – imaginative because, like the Diefenbaker vision, it had the potential of endowing Canadian life with a sense of shared national purpose; disappointing because, as in the case of the Northern Vision, words and intentions far outran accomplishments.

The economic benefits of American investment in Canada were so overwhelming that any appeal to stop – or in any way control – the influx of such funds ran squarely against the self-interest of many influential citizens, particularly members of the business community. They brought down on Gordon's head one of the most vicious personal campaigns ever mounted against a Canadian cabinet minister. The businessmen were all the more enraged because they regarded Gordon as a traitor to his class.

Because Gordon was obsessed with formulating solutions to the problem of foreign ownership rather than trying to persuade Canadians that a problem existed, economic independence remained an abstruse issue. Gordon never effectively replied to those who saw nationalism as an anachronistic evil and failed to make clear his firm conviction that nationalism is an expression at a group level of the very essence of humanity, its belief in individualism.

His theories for the economic repatriation of his country had about them the violent, charcoal beauty of early Picasso prints, leaving much of their originator's intent to the beholder's imagination. "We can do the things that are necessary to retain control of our economy and thus maintain our independence," he summed up in his second book, *A Choice for Canada*.* "Or we can acquiesce in becoming a colonial dependency of the United States, with no future except the hope of eventual absorption." He believed that this was the central issue of the Canadian future and that it should be acted on without equivocation or emotion. His aim was statesmanlike: to alter the Canadian economic setting and gradually draw the people behind him in an all-out attempt to recapture control over the nation's economic destiny. But he could never get enough cabinet ministers on his side to make economic independence a definite plank in his party's platform and was constantly haunted by the fear that if the issue were once rejected by Canadian voters, American business corporations would interpret the result as giving them a permanent mandate to expand their operations.

Gordon's policy demands were not extravagant. No developed nation in the world had set fewer limits and regulations on foreign investment than Canada. Gordon only wanted to begin the repatriation process so that at some future date more stringent measures might not be needed to protect what was left of Canada's vanishing economic independence. He believed with President John F. Kennedy that "those who make peaceful revolution impossible, make violent revolution inevitable."

Boldly, if at times superficially, Gordon challenged accepted beliefs about the place of the nation state in an increasingly interdependent world. He attempted to head off criticism of his thesis by equating nationalism with patriotism. "In wanting to retain our independence," he insisted, "we are no different from the British, the French, the Swiss, or the people of other countries, including the United States. Some may call this nationalism, and so it is. It amounts to a proper respect, loyalty, and enthusiasm for one's country, and a legitimate optimism and confidence about its future."

*McClelland and Stewart Limited, 1966.

Typical of his low-key approach was a speech Gordon made to some students at Simon Fraser University on September 26, 1966. "If you are content – as far too many of my generation seem to be content – to see us go on as we are, you should be able to live out your lives in some comfort, some security and considerable boredom," he said. "You should be able to find jobs working for the absentee owners of Canadian business. Naturally it will be they who will take the responsibility for making the important decisions. And, naturally, it will be they who will take most of the profits. . . . But you should be safe – or as safe as the subjects of any satellite or colonial state can ever be. But this does not need to be the fate of the members of your generation. You should decide that we can develop Canada ourselves."

Gordon's suggested cure was a strong dose of government intervention. He wanted to pit the authority of the Canadian state against the power of foreign capital. What gave the whole issue its cutting edge was Gordon's awareness of the fact that the essence of national independence had become economic power, which in the Sixties consisted not only of capital investment but also of control over new technology. "Gordon had intuitively perceived the import of the new political landscape," wrote Professor Abraham Rotstein, an astute University of Toronto political economist, in the *Tamarack Review* in the fall of 1966. "The age of affluence is only another name for the technological society which is the source of our abundance. . . . The economy is the home of this new technology and what goes on in corporate board rooms has a public significance far exceeding the fate of each individual enterprise. The politics of the new technological society increasingly turns on the question of who makes these crucial corporate decisions." What Rotstein meant (and Gordon realized) was that the effect of the new technology was to upgrade economic life to the level of a vital national interest, and that to lose control over corporate decision-making (as Canada was rapidly doing) implied loss of the nation's ability to exist in meaningful independence. "The survival of indigenous social institutions and cultural values in the face of technological pressures," Rotstein concluded, "becomes a concern transcending class interests, and a matter for action by the most powerful of our political institutions, the nation state. It remains only to invest our nationalism with the social tasks of the Sixties."

This was precisely what Walter Gordon failed to accomplish. He could not reconcile the two main strains of Canadian Liberalism: the party's concern over social reform and its barely suppressed desire for economic integration with the United States.

IT WAS NOT THAT GORDON LACKED EVIDENCE of the extent of American economic penetration. By the mid Sixties the conquest of Canada's economy by American businessmen had left Canadians in control of a smaller proportion of their productive wealth than the citizens of any other industrialized nation on earth. Foreign investment in Canada by 1968 amounted to more than $34 billions (the bulk of it American), a sum so huge that it ceased to be only money, but had become a force in its own right that created its own magnetic fields and multiplied through its own vitality.*

American investment had been cascading into Canada at a net rate of about three million dollars a day since 1947. By the end of the Pearson period, nearly two-thirds of the country's manufacturing capacity was owned outside the country, while the percentage of foreign ownership in such key industries as automobiles, petroleum, mining, chemicals and rubber ranged up to the high nineties. Nine out of ten factories in Canada important enough to have at least five thousand names on their payroll were controlled by parent corporations in the United States. Because Canada's natural resources boom had come at a time when most Canadians were still unwilling to gamble on their own country's future, most of the profit from the great economic undertakings was accruing to the more venturesome investors of the United States. Since the American investment was largely in the form of equity (ownership) stock, the proceeds could never be reclaimed by domestic interests.

These foreign investment funds provided the steam that drove the economy and gave Canadians the world's second-highest standard of living. But it was Gordon's contention that American capital, if unchecked, would eventually threaten the collective freedom of Canadians by turning the country into a political as well as an economic satellite of the United States. What Gordon seemed to be saying, in effect, was that foreign investment was harmful simply because it was foreign and owed its prime allegiance to an outside sovereignty; that even if American capital in Canada were the best-behaved foreign capital in the world, it still deprived Canadians of the power of national economic decision-making.

He was supported in this view by a study in which eight academic economists, commissioned by the federal government, had investigated

*This Dominion Bureau of Statistics estimate of foreign investments was well below their real worth because it was based on historic "book" values rather than market value.

221

the problem.* The report stressed that foreign investment is not simply the movement of capital between two countries, but also a political phenomenon. "Foreign control," it concluded, "means the potential shift outside the country of the locus of some types of decision-making. To the extent decision-making is eroded, national independence – being, in a broad sense, the ability to make decisions in the national interest – is reduced." It also warned about the use by foreign governments of the parent-subsidiary relationship as an instrument of their foreign policy. "The Canadian-based subsidiary," the report noted, "is confronted with two peaks of sovereignty; it must choose and might be expected to defer to the higher peak. In the nature of the case, the higher peak will typically be the home country."

Gordon's complaints about the behaviour of foreign subsidiaries in Canada included such things as the absence of a minority Canadian interest in their equity stock distribution; little meaningful Canadian representation on these firms' boards of directors; the fact that export policies were set by parent organizations, often against the domestic Canadian interest; and the reluctance of most American firms to process their raw materials before shipping them to the United States, so that most of the employment in the manufacturing process would be American. Beyond this level of corporate policies were some even more significant issues, particularly the extraterritorial application of United States laws. American tax laws made it difficult for Americans to give up a significant share of their stock holdings to Canadians. Losses on Canadian operations, for example, could be consolidated with American income for tax purposes only if the parent company retained at least 80 per cent ownership of the subsidiary. In the oil and mining industries. U.S. depletion allowances were granted for foreign as well as domestic operations, providing full corporate control was maintained. The anti-trust laws also put pressure on American firms to maintain a total hold over their Canadian operations. At least one important prosecution under these laws (the Timken Roller Bearing case) had established the precedent that if a U.S. company attempted to direct the production and sales policies of a subsidiary in Canada that was not wholly owned

*Report of the Task Force on the Structure of Canadian Industry, January 12, 1968. This was the most impressive study compiled about the influence of foreign investment on the Canadian economy, but the trouble was that by the time it was published, Walter Gordon's reputation as the Peck's Bad Boy of the Liberal Party had made all his enterprises a subject of suspicion in the business community. As a result, the Task Force report was not taken nearly as seriously as it deserved to be.

it would be acting "in restraint of trade." The simplest protection against such charges was to turn the subsidiary into an outright branch because no firm can conspire with itself. Similarly, the Antitrust Division of the United States Department of Justice did not hesitate to prosecute American companies when their Canadian subsidiaries entered into agreements, perfectly legal by Canadian law, that offended its view of American law. In 1960, Washington pressure had broken up a Canadian radio patents pool that was not only legal but arguably even mandatory under the Canadian Patents Act.

The most obvious extraterritorial application of United States laws in Canada was the Trading with the Enemy Act which prohibited the subsidiaries of American firms abroad from selling any goods or services to Cuba, mainland China, and North Korea, even though these sales were perfectly legal under Canadian law.* The American regulations employed powerful sanctions: the executives of a parent corporation whose foreign subsidiaries engaged in such trade were held directly responsible and liable to ten-thousand-dollar fines and/or ten years in jail. There were many examples of this law being applied to stop potential Canadian export sales and only a few instances of the United States granting special permits for small transactions with the Communist countries involved.

All these business considerations aside, Gordon recognized that the main harm inflicted by the overwhelming fact of American ownership was not economic but social, cultural and even political. Because the American subsidiary operating in Canada owed its prime allegiance to its corporate headquarters in the United States, it inevitably became a vehicle for spreading American ideas and policies in Canada. "While we like you, we are also worried about you," Beland Honderich, editor-in-chief and later publisher of the *Toronto Daily Star*, a staunch Gordon supporter and a leading Canadian nationalist, told his predominantly American audience at a Quebec City meeting of the International Press Institute on March 12, 1965. "American cultural, economic and political influences so pervade our way of life that we have begun to wonder if our relatively small nation can retain its independence in face of the strong pressures generated by our giant neighbor to the south. It is against this background that we Canadians consider the question of foreign investment."

---

*When the late U.S. Secretary of State John Foster Dulles was asked just who would qualify as an "enemy" within the context of this law, he replied: "An enemy is anybody the State Department says it is."

A PRIME EXAMPLE OF THE LENGTHS to which the American government was willing to go in protecting United States investment against Canadian laws involved the successful intervention by both the White House and the State Department to win an exemption for *Time* and *Reader's Digest* from the measure in Walter Gordon's 1965 budget that disallowed advertising in foreign-owned newspapers and periodicals as a tax deduction.

The position of the so-called Canadian editions of *Time* and *Reader's Digest* had long been a controversial topic in American-Canadian relations. During the 1960-61 hearings of the Royal Commission on Publications, Lawrence Laybourne, then the managing director of *Time Canada*, had pleaded that his magazine be considered "in all essential respects a Canadian periodical, having regard to the character and quality of its contents and the nature of its publishing operation." But this application for Canadian corporate citizenship was rudely demolished by no less a witness than Henry R. Luce, the co-founder and then editor-in-chief of *Time*, who appeared before the commission on January 17, 1961. Prompted by the probing wit of Commission Chairman Grattan O'Leary, the mighty Luce declared: "I may be in some disagreement with my colleagues. But you said, Sir, you want me to be very plain. I do *not* consider *Time* a Canadian magazine."

Despite this admission, the Pearson Government's 1965 budget endowed *Time* and *Reader's Digest* with honorary Canadian citizenship by exempting them from the new tax provisions. Since they were the only two foreign-owned publications actually operating in Canada at the time, the 1965 law granted these two American magazines protection from competition, because no other United States publications could launch similar "Canadian" editions in the future. There was so much dissatisfaction over the paradoxical exemption for the two magazines within the Liberal caucus that the government was forced to declare that it regarded the issue a matter of confidence and would "stand or fall" on the *Time-Digest* resolution. The motion came to a vote on June 28, 1965.* The Pearson Government's attitude on this issue reflected the effectiveness of the American magazine lobby in both Ottawa and Washington. The *Time* and *Digest* organizations had been actively lobbying in the Canadian capital ever since 1957, when the St Laurent government attempted to bolster the country's declining domestic magazine industry by imposing a 20 per cent tax on advertising in their Canadian editions. During the initial meeting between Dwight Eisenhower and John Diefenbaker, one of the American President's

---

*Thirty-one Liberals refused to back the bill and stayed out of the Commons during the vote. Thirty-six Conservatives were also absent.

first questions was, "What are you doing to our *Time* magazine up here?" Shortly afterwards, the Tories rescinded the 20 per cent tax. Diefenbaker then established the Royal Commission headed by Grattan O'Leary to examine the problems of Canadian periodicals. Its report, tabled on June 15, 1961, concluded that "Canadian periodicals are denied competition on an equitable basis with foreign publications publishing the so-called 'Canadian editions.' " It recommended measures that would have closed down such operations.

Just nine hours after the O'Leary Report had been tabled, a senior representative of the White House was on the telephone to Ottawa, warning that implementation of the commission's findings would result in the immediate cancellation of a major United States aircraft-components contract then in the process of being geared up at Canadair Limited in Montreal. Nothing was done about the magazine problem during the Diefenbaker Years. When Lester Pearson came to office, he was told that Henry Luce was such a powerful influence in Washington that the White House would vigorously resist any laws aimed at the American magazine's Canadian operations.

The vehemence with which the American State Department expressed its opposition was a shock to Ottawa officials used to the give and take of most United States policies. One senior Canadian civil servant reported privately to the Prime Minister that he had never seen the State Department so unyielding. "There seems nothing, but nothing, that we could do which would upset Washington more," he wrote. "I had the impression that if we dared touch the Canadian operations of *Time* and *Digest*, the State Department would view it as far more serious than if, for instance, we sold armed tanks to Fidel Castro."

The American State Department made some not very subtle threats that unless *Time* and the *Digest* were exempted from Gordon's regulation against foreign-owned publications, Canada's quotas on exports of oil to the United States would have to be reviewed and congressional approval of the auto pact with Canada would be placed in jeopardy. A pro-American magazine lobby developed inside the cabinet, led by Bud Drury, member for the Montreal constituency where the *Digest* operates. He was joined by Maurice Sauvé and Paul Martin, who were upset by the idea of a possible rupture in Canadian-American relations over the issue. *Time* and the *Digest* meanwhile were putting tremendous pressure on ministers and individual M.P.'s. Douglas Fisher, then the NDP M.P. for Port Arthur, was subjected to a constant barrage of letters and telephone calls from the employees (and employees' wives) of the Provincial Paper Limited mill in his home riding, which supplied *Time* and *Reader's Digest* with paper. Although he was directly threatened with a loss of votes if he didn't relent in his campaign on behalf of Canadian magazines, Fisher persisted.

In describing the situation later,* Pauline Jewett, director of the Institute of Canadian Studies at Carleton University and a former Liberal M.P. for Northumberland, noted that most of the caucus was against the exclusion of *Time* and the *Digest* from the legislation, "but the Cabinet was a bit more split, being closer no doubt to political reality. The 'political reality' in this instance was, quite simply, fear of American retaliation."

The American pressure proved so great that the Pearson Government capitulated and Walter Gordon brought in a law that exempted the only two publishing operations it might have affected. It was Grattan O'Leary, speaking in the Senate on June 28, 1965, who had the final word. "If this House votes for this legislation," he told his fellow senators, "it will be voting for the proposition that Washington has a right to interfere in a matter of purely Canadian concern, and voting a probable death sentence on Canada's periodical press, with all that this can entail for our future voyage through history."

THE SATURATING FORCE of the cultural, political and economic compulsions of American civilization was the dominant factor in world politics during the Sixties. The Pearson Government's response to this pressure, which could be felt in Canada more than in any other country, was always to avoid trouble, even if the national psyche was damaged in the process.

Lester Pearson's concept of Canada had been formed during his nearly thirty years with the External Affairs Department, whose overriding concern at the time was to move out of the shadow of the British Foreign Office. The whole thrust of his policies in those years was to help sever the nation's umbilical dependence on the United Kingdom by strengthening ties with the United States. While not anti-British, he was convinced that Canada's future belonged to the North American continent, probably in some form of eventual economic alliance with the United States. In any case, he was a firm anti-nationalist. "I am an unrepentant and insistent internationalist. Any other position seems to me a rejection of reality as absurd as relying on the bayonet for defence," he told a Private Planning Association seminar at Montebello, Quebec, on November 16, 1966.

*In *An Independent Foreign Policy For Canada?* edited by Stephen Clarkson (McClelland and Stewart Limited, 1968).

His attitude was even more precisely stated in the first speech he made as a private citizen following his retirement in 1968. Addressing that summer's Couchiching Conference at Geneva Park, Ontario, he advocated that Canada "should be in the forefront of every move to widen and deepen political internationalism – even if it means accepting, through international treaty arrangements, limitations on our own independence."

For many years Pearson had been one of the senior Canadian diplomats who had served in Washington and reached the conclusion that the cardinal factor of Canadian foreign policy ought to be good relations with the United States. This attitude was set out most clearly in the Merchant-Heeney report, which the Pearson Government never disowned.* It urged that relations between the two countries should be conducted in private by their diplomats and that "Canadian authorities should have careful regard for the United States government's position in the world context" and "so far as possible avoid . . . public disagreement especially upon critical issues." The document was one of those rare instances when a frank declaration froze a senior member of Ottawa's bureaucratic establishment for an instant in time, staring straight into the camera of history. Arnold Heeney reflected perfectly the sincerely held but previously unstated continentalist views of the Pearson-vintage Ottawa public servants. "What Mr Heeney and Mr Merchant have agreed on," wrote Frank Walker, the ironic editor of the *Montreal Star*, "is that Canada is in fact a satellite of the United States, that Canada must never make trouble for the United States in its major international policies, that we will be good boys."

Throughout his time in office, even when Walter Gordon was his most trusted adviser, Pearson remained suspicious of nationalism, viewing it in its nineteenth-century context as a destructive, self-inhibiting force. He believed that the facts, the compulsions, and the opportunities of the contemporary world lead inexorably toward closer international association and away from the self-sufficient sovereignty of the nation state. Pearson seemed, in fact, to have abandoned the very idea that Canada could have any meaningful economic independence. "We can maintain our economic sovereignty," he said during the annual meeting of the Canadian University Liberal Federation in Ottawa on February 11, 1966, "if we are willing to pay the price, and the price would be nationalistic economic policies which would reduce our standard of living by perhaps 25% to 30%. Not many Canadians are willing to do that, and I don't think Canadians should have to do that."

Canada and the United States: Principles for Partnership by A. D. P. Heeney and Livingston Merchant, June 28, 1965.

Because his own fight for the Canadian identity had been concentrated on helping to reduce the old ties of empire with Great Britain through the forging of a closer link with the United States, Pearson had little sympathy for the Gordon point of view. "No two men could have stood further apart in all their principles and all their instincts," correctly editorialized the Winnipeg *Free Press*.

The idea of economic nationalism had little place in the Prime Minister's notion of middle-powermanship, which was based on the illusion that it was possible to balance diverse foreign interests on Canada's behalf, if only there were sufficient goodwill and lots of smooth, quiet diplomacy.

Because Pearson was made uncomfortable by absolutes, he never could subscribe to the kind of platform rhetoric that idealizes greatness in nations. The feeling of rightness implicit in greatness carries with it the conviction of the wrongness of others. It is not possible for a man – or a nation – to be great if he (or his country) is not set against some other human force or community. There can be no greatness for Canada, indeed no Canada, unless it is a country somehow set apart from the United States.

But Pearson was a politician dead set against the proposition of the rightness of some men and the wrongness of others, rigidly against the idea of one country being set apart from, and if necessary against, all others. It was not enough to label Pearson as a man who was not a Canadian nationalist. For Pearson, Canada was not so much a country set apart from the United States as part of a continent dominated by the United States. He set this course for his country in the joint communiqué that was issued following his meeting with President John F. Kennedy in May of 1963, which stressed "the vital importance of continental security . . . bilateral defense arrangements . . . fulfillment of Canada's existing defense commitments to North America and Europe . . . rational use of the continent's resources: oil, gas, electricity, strategic metals and minerals and the use of each other's industrial capacity for defense purposes in the defense production-sharing programs . . . a positive and cooperative manner with developments affecting their international trade and payments . . . cooperative development of the Columbia River . . . joint cabinet-level committees on trade and economic affairs and defense."

Nearly everything in the Pearson regime followed from this communiqué. It defined the development of Canada in terms of an American hinterland. In the bargaining, Canada was to gain some industrial development (as with the auto pact) in return for American control of Canadian resources (as with the Columbia River Treaty). Many of the

Pearson-sponsored developments were built on north-south lines, cutting across the international boundary, through the east-west backbone of Canada. The Columbia River would be harnessed to serve the Pacific Northwest to the south; at the same time the possibility of routing Columbia waters west through Canada to the sea via the Fraser River and east to the Canadian prairies would be denied. Defence contracts and the auto pact would concentrate industrial development in Canada in the Great Lakes - St Lawrence basin. And if industry was to be dispersed across Canada, it would be done through the establishment of other north-south, across-the-border pacts.

That despite Pearson's obvious distaste for economic nationalism his government became the sponsor of several nationalistic laws was either strong evidence of Walter Gordon's truly gargantuan influence on the Prime Minister or a remarkable admission of Pearson's weakness in not even championing one of his few strongly held views. The situation was all the more surprising because the Liberal Cabinet bristled with Walter Gordon's enemies.

THE HARSHEST OPPOSITION to Gordon's nationalistic ideas came from the cabinet's right-wing ministers and its western members plus another group of non-ideological ministers, who simply regarded Gordon as an irresponsible dilettante whose ideas were jeopardizing party support across the country.

Outside the cabinet, he was constantly being attacked by Liberals as the man most responsible for the party's inability to attain a parliamentary majority. Because of his economic nationalism, he was referred to at party meetings in British Columbia as "that tab-collar Castro" and Stuart Keate, publisher of the Liberal *Vancouver Sun*, told a meeting of American businessmen: "It's true that we have some economic nationalists, but any country that can survive three wars, floods, rockslides and other natural disasters, can survive Walter Gordon." Ross Thatcher, the Liberal Premier of Saskatchewan, labelled Gordon "the worst and most dangerous Socialist in Canada." His very name produced a flush of anger in most businessmen, who privately went beyond the socialist label and seriously debated among themselves whether he might not be "some kind of Commie nut." E. P. Taylor, speaking from Lyford Cay in the Bahamas, labelled Gordon's insistence that subsidiaries be forced to sell 25 per cent of their equity stock to Canadians as "absolute nonsense, contrary to good business principles, unnatural and monstrous."

Throughout the West and to a lesser degree in the Maritimes, Walter Gordon's theories of economic nationalism were regarded as a thinly disguised coverup for Toronto protectionism. The influx of foreign capital had done much to rid the citizens in both extremes of the country from the detested yoke of the Bay and St James Streets brand of capitalism. In Gordon they thought they recognized the grip of the Toronto-Montreal industrial establishment which through its tariff and price-fixing policies had long exploited the resources of their areas with minimal returns to the inhabitants, and was now attempting to reassert its dominance. They feared Gordon's protectionist tendencies as a type of state socialism running directly counter to their idea of the open society and their longing for freer trade with the United States.

Neither was there any significant support for Gordon's policies in French Canada. The Quebec nationalist tradition, with its cultural and social roots, was not compatible with Gordon's economic thesis. The target of French-Canadian nationalists had never been American investment but the economic influence of Montreal's English-speaking managers. In fact, American dollars were welcomed in Quebec to offset the power of the province's own English-speaking community. Most of the Quebec ministers in Ottawa, particularly Pierre Elliott Trudeau and Maurice Sauvé, had been fighting Quebec nationalism all their political lives. They could not do battle against one kind of nationalism in their home province without at the same time opposing the Canadian nationalism implied in Gordon's economic doctrine.

PERHAPS WALTER GORDON'S INABILITY to move the nation in his direction was due to the historic accident that Canada matured into nationhood at a time when the human race was moving, as the eminent critic Northrop Frye pointed out, "towards a post-national world." In the long jostling of their history, Canadians had never been able to settle the nagging question whether their northern subcontinent could retain its political sovereignty while espousing only indistinct and not always compatible brands of nationalism. Still, despite the limited success of his nationalistic crusades, Walter Gordon's time in public life enlarged not just his party but the nation as a whole. He had three qualities rare in politicians – courage, simplicity and selflessness; they made him for a time the conscience of his country.

CHAPTER 17

A Footnote on "Sailor Jack"

JUST AS WALTER GORDON EPITOMIZED what was fresh and different in the Pearson regime from the King-St Laurent era, Jack Pickersgill stood for everything that was the same. He interpreted each new suggestion not in terms of its future potential but merely by how it tallied with the past. He judged policy initiatives on the basis of their administrative acceptability and regarded all reforms with suspicion.

John Whitney Pickersgill's approach to government was so uniquely his own that his name found a place in Canada's political dictionary. The expression "Pickersgillian" came to signify any partisan ploy that was too clever by half. His strong personality, encyclopaedic knowledge of Ottawa and its ways, his mastery of Commons rules and intense loyalty to Lester Pearson allowed him to exercise a decisive and not always benign leverage on the course of federal events. But his violent partisanship, dated view of Canadian society and erratic political judgement made him a doubtful asset to the hard-pressed government.

"Jack is so firmly hooked on the past that I sometimes think he's wearing cement boots," commented one of his colleagues. Another minister swore that rare indeed were the meetings of the Pearson Cabinet during which Pickersgill failed to mention the way Mackenzie King used to solve the crises of his day. Pickersgill readily billowed forth irrelevant historical data (such as the fact that John Bracken's Manitoba cabinet of 1922 was composed entirely of Presbyterians) but had little feeling for contemporary events.

Part of Pickersgill's problem was that he really had no contact with modern Canada. He had grown up on a Manitoba farm, attended university and then, except for summer holidays on the coast of northern Newfoundland, had spent the rest of his life entirely in Ottawa. "Metropolitan urban society is just outside my human experience. What the great majority of Canadians regard as a normal environment has not been my environment and this undoubtedly colours my outlook," he once admitted.

What allowed Pickersgill to prosper so long at such high levels of influence within the Ottawa hierarchy was his uncanny ability to manipulate the gears of bureaucratic control. His thirty years within the Ottawa power structure had taught him all the tricks both of how political control of the civil service could be exercised and of how bureaucratic methods could be used to drain the will of the politicians.

He had the habit of power and knew the mechanics of the game.

Jack Pickersgill's unusual career spanned four political eras and left a deep imprint on each. Between 1937 and 1948 he had functioned as Mackenzie King's chief adviser and it was during this epoch that the phrase "clear it with Jack" first became a password to power in Ottawa. He was an even more important arbiter of influence during the administration of Louis St Laurent and he emerged, full-blown, in 1953 as a cabinet minister and M.P. for Bonavista-Twillingate. His next guise was as one of the most effective Liberal opposition frontbenchers during the Diefenbaker Years. After the Liberals regained power in 1963, Pickersgill emerged once again as a prime ministerial confidant. Near the close of the Pearson period, when he could sense the draining away of his political power, Pickersgill smoothly slid into a self-created job as head of the Canadian Transport Commission.

It may not have been exactly a noble career but it was – well, cohesive.

Like Mackenzie King, Jack Pickersgill could not see much scope for public service away from power. Probably more than any other Liberal he considered his party not so much an organ of the people as an organ of the state and in private would often refer to the Liberals as "the government party." His career and opinions made him the incarnation of the Ottawa Liberal Establishment. He acted as though he really believed that, by accepting the burdens of office, the Liberals were bestowing a benefaction on the nation at large and that any criticism of Liberalism was an unpatriotic activity. Just before the 1957 election, Pickersgill declared with a straight face: "It is not merely for the well-being of Canadians but for the good of mankind in general that the present Liberal government should remain in office."

His party affiliation seemed so close to a religion that one wondered whether faith alone and not reason informed him. Questioned by a reporter about the characteristics of Liberal prime ministers, he replied: "They never, any one of them, ever told a conscious lie or allowed anything that was calculated to give a false impression. Mackenzie King, for instance, was meticulous to the point of being tiresome about it, putting in all sorts of qualifications so that nobody in any conceivable circumstances could ever show that there was anything about his statements that was untrue."

If the Liberals were lily white in the Pickersgillian lexicon, the Tories were jet black. "The real trouble with the Conservative Party," he once said, "is that basically it has been a party of Anglo-Saxon racists. They really don't believe in the equality of all Canadians. They really don't believe the French have any right in this country, unless they act like a conquered people." On another occasion he remarked that Conservative governments are "like having the mumps – something you have to endure once in your lifetime, but when it's over you don't ever want it again."

THOUGH PICKERSGILL'S INFLUENCE was exercised in the hush of his office and the privacy of the cabinet chamber, he was best known for the displays he put on in the House of Commons. His penguin shape was constantly bobbing up and down during the excitement of debates. Physically clumsy, he was utterly incapable of sitting still. When he was a youngster, his grandmother had made him a standing offer of five cents for every five minutes he could keep quiet. "I needed the money badly, but I never earned a penny of it," he recalled.

The thrift he learned growing up on a prairie homestead dominated his life in the expenditure of both time and money. He never parted easily with the coins he carried in a woman's black, clasp-type change purse stuffed into his right hip pocket. He used pencils until they were inch-long stubs that could barely be gripped. He once complained at length in the House of Commons about the fifteen cents he had lost in an airport stamp-vending machine. On a twelve-day trip to British Columbia in 1952, as Clerk of the Privy Council, he submitted an expense account of $30.35. He wore only two kinds of tie – his Oxford New College brown-and-silver stripe and a blue-and-white polka dot – depending on friends to notice when the ties became frayed and send him new ones.

Pickersgill's father had died in 1920 of wounds suffered at Passchendaele. He had to help run a small lumber business managed by the family to supplement the income from their quarter-section homestead at Ashern, near Lake Manitoba. Both before and after the death of the senior Pickersgill, politics was the family's main dinner-table topic. The father had been a hard-bitten Tory who gave his eldest son the middle name of Whitney after Sir James Pliny Whitney, a Conservative who became Premier of Ontario in 1905. Young Jack grew up such an ardent Tory that at ten he converted to his faith two school chums who happened to be the sons of Ashern's leading Liberals. When the boys in turn tried clumsily to convert their families, the angry fathers called the elder Pickersgill and demanded that he order his son to give up the schoolyard politicking. "That didn't stop me," Pickersgill recalled. "I swore the little buggers to secrecy, took them into the woods at lunchtime, and instructed them on the evils of giving the franchise to women and the glories of the Conservative Party."

Pickersgill's own conversion to Liberalism occurred in the fall of 1925 when, as a University of Manitoba history student, he went to hear Arthur Meighen, then Conservative party leader, speak at the Winnipeg Rink. "I was a Tory when I went in and a Liberal when I came out," he remembered. "I felt that Meighen was on the wrong side of three issues – racial tolerance, tariffs and colonialism. The Tories had not really accepted the implications of self-government; they were reluctant to see Canada become an adult nation." The young student's ideological transformation was further strengthened during his two years of studying nineteenth-century history at Oxford on an IODE scholarship. He qualified for two degrees at the end of his studies there but hadn't enough money to pay his diploma fees.

Pickersgill spent the eight years after his return from Oxford as an obscure lecturer in European history at Wesley College in Winnipeg. When he still hadn't received a salary increase or promotion by 1936, he wrote exams for the External Affairs Department, topping his group, and joined the civil service on October 14, 1937, at $2,280 a year. Mackenzie King was then in the habit of seconding to his office bright young men from the department, and O. D. Skelton, the Undersecretary of State, nominated Pickersgill for the job. "You won't last more than six months," a colleague predicted. "Nobody ever does."

But the posting lasted eleven years and grew into a relationship unique in the history of Canadian politics. As King's main speech writer, private secretary and general confidant, Pickersgill grew closer to the Prime Minister than any other man in Ottawa. King, as he got older, found contact with new faces increasingly distasteful and learned to depend more and more on his trusted assistant to maintain touch with the political world. One reason Pickersgill's help was so acceptable to

King was the younger man's instant realization of how useless it would be to attempt any alteration of the Prime Minister's style and vocabulary. "His language," Pickersgill said later, "appeared to have been frozen in the latter part of the nineteenth century. Mr King didn't like flamboyant phrases. He detested the word 'challenge' and would never use the adjectives 'sober' or 'decent.' " Pickersgill became such an expert in gauging King's reactions that he could point out to the other assistants who helped draft paragraphs for the Prime Minister's speeches exactly which words would be stroked out.

The relationship wasn't always smooth. The two men quarrelled openly during the 1945 meeting in San Francisco that established the United Nations. Pickersgill had suggested to King that a good way of solving Canada's dilemma over a national flag would be to replace the Union Jack flying on Parliament Hill with the Red Ensign on VE Day and then pass a law adopting it as the official flag. King agreed to hoist the distinctive emblem for VE Day but insisted that Pickersgill tell Ottawa it would be removed the next morning. "If you once put it up, you'll never be able to take it down," Pickersgill snapped irritably at the Prime Minister. King angrily ordered him to do as he was told, and when after King's death Pickersgill read the diary entry for that day, he found himself referred to as "an impudent upstart."

To protect himself Pickersgill maintained his job classification as a foreign service officer, temporarily assigned to the Prime Minister's office. He admired King, but doubted that the admiration was mutual. "To an extraordinary degree," he once remarked, "Mr King regarded me as part of the furniture."

His relationship to Louis St Laurent was vastly different. The obscure fixer of the King era became the true grey eminence of Canadian politics under King's successor. When he was sworn into office on November 15, 1948, St Laurent had spent most of the preceding two years in the politically insulated External Affairs portfolio. He depended on the "special assistant" he had inherited from King for direction on how to operate the prime minister's office. Political observers in Ottawa insisted that for the first three months of St Laurent's term at least, the country was to an astonishing degree run by Jack Pickersgill. "I had a very great influence on Mr St Laurent," Pickersgill admitted. "He had more confidence in me than in any cabinet minister or anyone else." During the 1949 election St Laurent made a pact that he would commit himself to no appointments or public appearances that weren't "cleared with Jack."

Most Canadians first heard of Pickersgill in June 1952, when St Laurent appointed him to succeed Norman Robertson as secretary to the cabinet and Clerk of the Privy Council. This was a non-political job, but Pickersgill had become a political creature and St Laurent soon saw that it might be more useful to have Pickersgill in the cabinet. That meant not only promoting him over the heads of 160 Liberal back-benchers but also finding a constituency he could win.

This problem was solved by Joey Smallwood, the Premier of Newfoundland, who had become friendly with Pickersgill during the negotiations leading up to confederation. At one critical moment it was Pickersgill's quick thinking that had saved the whole project. Mackenzie King had felt that Newfoundland should join Canada only if a substantial majority of her people voted for confederation. The first plebiscite ended in a stalemate. When Pickersgill heard on the morning news that a bare 52 per cent had supported union in the second vote, he dug up the percentages of the popular vote received by the Liberals in every election under King. At ten o'clock that morning King placed his first daily phone call to Pickersgill. "Well, did you hear the Newfoundland result?" he asked coolly, implying that the vote wasn't high enough to warrant confederation. "Yes. Isn't it wonderful!" Pickersgill shot back gleefully. "Do you realize, sir, that the Newfoundlanders want union with Canada by a considerably higher percentage than Canadians voted for you in any election except 1940?" King, obviously surprised, replied with a snort, but the plebiscite figures suddenly became acceptable.

When Smallwood first suggested to Pickersgill that he should run in the Newfoundland seat about to be vacated by Gordon Bradley, the Secretary of State, who was being retired to the Senate, Pickersgill didn't think it could be done, but Smallwood assured him: "Don't worry. When I'm through with you, you won't recognize yourself." Pickersgill agreed to run, providing he could limit his electioneering on the island to five days, so that he could spend the rest of the campaign at St Laurent's side. He was appointed Secretary of State on June 12, 1953, and a week later opened his brief campaign by sailing into Twillingate aboard the coastal steamer *Glencoe*. The local fishermen saluted him with a blast from thirty sealing guns, while on the flag-decked wharf a brass and drum band whacked out the hymn *Hold the Fort, For I Am Coming*.

Pickersgill found himself hailed more as a hero than a vote-seeker. Smallwood would get him up on a platform, point to him and thunder: "This is Pickersgill! Isn't that an incredible name?" Then the Premier would lean down and confide to his audience: "You'd better like him despite his name. He's the second most important man in Canada . . . some day he'll be prime minister!"

Pickersgill won his seat with a 7,500-vote margin and earned the nickname "Sailor Jack" by buying a 115-foot schooner to make the rounds of his constituency. But Smallwood's assurances that Pickersgill would become prime minister were received less enthusiastically in Ottawa. C. D. Howe acidly remarked to a reporter: "I don't think the newest member of the cabinet should aspire to leadership right away." In the House of Commons, the Conservatives were delighted that they could finally taunt the man so long dedicated to advising prime ministers on how to keep them out of office. They treated Pickersgill as something of a performing animal. Tory hecklers called him, among other things, "Jumping Jack with springs in his trousers" and "Poor Old Pick," and asserted that he was "deaf in one ear and dumb in the other." Pickersgill didn't help matters by replying to every opposition thrust with a smart-aleck retort. On July 1, 1954, St Laurent astonished Pickersgill's critics by appointing him to the important and sensitive Immigration portfolio.

The best-remembered legacy of his term in office is the report of a speech he made to a group of Liberals in Victoria quoting him as saying that no immigrant is as good as a Canadian-born baby. He insisted that the Victoria *Colonist* had ripped his words out of context, leaving out his vital qualification that a child born and raised in this country is naturally better adapted to the Canadian way of life than any new-comer. But his denials never did catch up with the original headlines.

Pickersgill's most controversial contribution to the St Laurent Government was to plan, along with Walter Harris, the disastrous Commons strategy of the 1956 pipeline debate. When C. D. Howe moved closure on each of the pipeline bill's three readings he was acting on the instructions of Jack Pickersgill and seemed himself hardly aware of the significance or long-term legacy of what he was doing. After the Liberals moved into opposition, Pickersgill's advice proved equally bad but it was still taken. It was Pickersgill who drew up the ill-fated non-confidence motion which Lester Pearson moved on January 20, 1958, asking, in effect, that the Diefenbaker Government resign and turn power back to the Liberals. This allowed John Diefenbaker to produce his so-called "hidden report" and to launch the 1958 election that won him such a landslide.

During the rest of the Liberals' opposition period, Pickersgill's performance improved. Dedicated to the destruction of the Conservative Government, he became one of the party's best infighters, taking the floor to hurl barbs across the House more often than any other opposition member. He once broke into a sonorous speech by Donald Fleming sixty-two times with interjections that ranged in rudeness from the inelegant to the vulgar. He regularly called John Diefenbaker "utterly incompetent" and used every device to accuse him of lying without actually saying the word, which would have been against parliamentary rules. In one 1959 debate he summed up the Diefenbaker record, then in a sweep of anger declared that Diefenbaker and his promises were just like Humpty Dumpty – broken. The Prime Minister laughed, agreeably surprised by Pickersgill's mildness. Then Pickersgill bore in. Referring to Allister Grosart, the former vice-president of McKim Advertising in Toronto who had been Diefenbaker's campaign manager, Pickersgill chanted: "Yes. Just like Humpty Dumpty. And all McKim's horses and all McKim's men can never put him together again." Diefenbaker was furious. During the 1960 debate on the Bill of Rights, Pickersgill hesitantly asked Immigration Minister Ellen Fairclough whether the government intended to deport a Chinese woman who had emigrated to Canada illegally two and a half years before and subsequently given birth to a child. As soon as Mrs Fairclough had admitted that the deportation was proceeding, as Pickersgill knew she would, he reared up to ask Diefenbaker: "Can the Prime Minister tell us how the government squares its conduct, in attempting to exile a Canadian citizen, with the Bill of Rights?" The Prime Minister, obviously caught without an answer, could only mumble: "The Bill of Rights hasn't been passed yet."

Pickersgill's authority within the Pearson retinue continued to expand and when the Liberals moved back into power he was named to the key post of House Leader. One of the few ministers Mary Macdonald would unhesitatingly put right through to the PM any time he called, he was a key influence throughout the Pearson period, particularly after Walter Gordon (following Pickersgill's whispered advice) proved so inept in defending his first budget. Pickersgill was able to create a parliamentary majority for the Liberals by his continuous negotiations with the Social Crediters. He also steered through the House the controversial constituency redistribution bill and plotted the Liberals' defensive strategy during the scandals debates.

Pickersgill extended his power by adopting Guy Favreau as a kind of political protégé. It was Pickersgill who persuaded Favreau to bring Léo Cadieux and Jean-Pierre Côté into the cabinet, mainly because they were colourless, politically neutral French Canadians who would cause no trouble but would back the Pickersgill-Favreau axis. In the winter of 1964, Pickersgill recommended to Pearson that Guy Favreau succeed him as House Leader because it would enhance his prestige when he became Quebec lieutenant. This was a disastrous appointment, for both Favreau and the Liberals, but despite these and other errors

238

in judgement the Prime Minister continued to heed Pickersgill's advice.

Part of the reason may have been that to Pearson, Pickersgill represented those happy placid days when the government had been really in charge of Parliament and Parliament seemed in control of the country. Surely this man who had advised Mackenzie King and Louis St Laurent in the delicate art of keeping the political lid on could do the same for him. The trouble was that while Pickersgill remained the same, the country in which he was operating had altered. In terms of the federal administration this meant the unruly, sometimes agonizing passage from the old, interest-group, élite-conducted approach to government (which had allowed a Pickersgill to thrive) to a new and very different kind of politics. Mild welfare plans, tailored to keep the voting public at bay, were no longer effective. Issues and challenges became more sophisticated, far less amenable to the old calculus of behind-the-scenes deals conducted by a self-selected hierarchy, of which Jack Pickersgill had been the most experienced member.

His world was vanishing, but Pickersgill was shrewd enough to recognize it and proceeded to plan himself a new career. His longtime acquaintance with John C. Doyle, a fugitive from American justice, and Geoff Stirling, the Newfoundland broadcaster, had cast a shadow over his reputation, particularly when the Conservative Opposition accused him of being involved in Stirling's attempt to move the Channel Three television outlet from Barrie, Ontario, to the more lucrative Toronto market.*

In the summer of 1967 Transport Minister Pickersgill was busy piloting through the Commons the National Transportation Act, designed to rationalize Canada's obsolete railway system. Few M.P.'s noticed that the presidency of the new Canadian Transport Commission set up by the legislation was made particularly attractive. The annual salary was set at $40,000 a year and the retirement age (Pickersgill was then sixty-two) was not the usual sixty-five, but seventy. The position was never advertised by the Civil Service Commission. Having written himself a job description, Pickersgill on September 5 resigned from

*A major interest in the Barrie station had been acquired by Stirling, a well-known Liberal and Pickersgill supporter, who expected permission from the Board of Broadcast Governors to move its antenna closer to Toronto. The BBG was deadlocked 7-7 on the issue when on June 20, 1967, Ian Stott (a former vice-president of the Nova Scotia Liberal Association) was appointed to the board. The same day, though he had heard none of the submissions leading up to the vote, Stott broke the tie in favour of the Stirling application. A group of ministers, led by Mitchell Sharp, went to Pickersgill's office and objected to the move as patronage of the rankest kind. It was eventually killed by the cabinet.

Cabinet and recommended himself for the opening. Pearson accepted and "Sailor Jack" launched himself on his fifth Ottawa incarnation, showing no qualms whatsoever about having left the public service, staying fourteen years in politics and now re-entering a bureaucracy which, in theory and practice, ought to be non-partisan.

The circumstances that allowed Jack Pickersgill to flourish were part of a cynical old-style approach to politics in Canada. But even in that context he was one of a kind.

CHAPTER 18

The Exploding Epaulettes

AS THEY TUMBLED DARKLY ACROSS THE POLITICAL STAGE during the mid Sixties, the ministers Lester Pearson relied on to represent French Canada inspired, both within and without the province of Quebec, disappointment, disbelief, despair and, not infrequently, laughter. During the first four years of the Liberal regime eight French-Canadian ministers disappeared from active politics, an average of one every six months. Without exception, their leave-taking was considerably less heroic than their coming. It was all somehow reminiscent of a hoked-up silent film about the Foreign Legion where in reel after reel, disgraced lieutenants have their epaulettes ceremonially ripped off before being sent tottering alone into the desert.

It was not an easy time to be a French-Canadian minister in Ottawa and to be a Quebec lieutenant was very hell. In his dealings with French Canada, Pearson was eager to adopt and adapt the new ideas stirring in the province. But until the Marchand-Trudeau-Pelletier entry into federal politics in 1965, Pearson tried to mix his philosophical attraction to the new Quebec politicians personifying these ideas with his commitments to the Old Guard figures who still manned the province's federal machine. As a result, both groups were edgy, neurotic, conspiratorial and driven by excesses of Gallic emotion to declare war on each other, dedicating themselves not to the advancement of a common cause but to each other's political destruction. They were unhappy in Ottawa, a WASPish town alien to the vivacity of French-Canadian life, and unhappy at home, where they were considered sell-outs from the Quebec cause.

As a consequence the man who wore the epaulettes of Quebec lieutenant in the Pearson Cabinet was always trying to keep afloat on a sea of impulses, with most of his actions dictated by intra-party considerations instead of external circumstances. He had to spend so much time and energy appeasing everyone within his own caucus that he lost the capacity to make much of an impact outside it. Yet each successive Quebec lieutenant knew that his performance as the chief representative in Ottawa of Canada's French element would reflect not only on himself but on his people and that at this point in Canada's history, it was crucial both for English Canadians to understand the French dilemma and for Quebec to respect the federal system.

The post of Quebec lieutenant to English-speaking prime ministers had long roots in the province's political traditions. The run-of-the-mill Quebec M.P. accepted the fact that English-speaking politicians and civil servants made the decisions that really counted in Ottawa. By delegating his authority to a "chief," who was also the PM's right-hand man, he could feel that he had at least indirect access to the inner sanctum of power. In the pre-Trudeau period there was little demand by Quebec M.P.'s to participate in formulating national government policy. They came out of a system that chose political emissaries, according to Pierre Trudeau, "not so much for their ability to serve democracy as for their ability to make democracy serve their party, their main qualifications being familiarity with machine politicians and schemers."*

English-speaking prime ministers, particularly Liberals, found in their French lieutenants valuable proconsuls who kept the electoral machinery in Quebec sufficiently oiled so that votes by the hundred thousand were delivered by it every election day. In return these men were awarded the stature and patronage control that gave them their power. The Liberal Party's prototype Quebec lieutenant was Ernest Lapointe, Justice Minister under Mackenzie King, and for twenty-five years after his death in 1941 Liberals still hopefully referred to every promising Quebec politician as "another Lapointe." Lapointe had been in the Commons thirty-seven years, the unquestioned Ottawa spokesman for a quiescent Quebec, simultaneously transmitting the complex King personality to the people of his province.

Lapointe was followed by Louis St Laurent, who served as King's Quebec lieutenant until 1948 when he became prime minister himself. His aristocratic conception of both roles prevented the evolution of a

*Canadian Journal of Economics and Political Science, August, 1958.

democratically based party organization in Quebec or the emergence of potential successors. When he finally recognized this just before the 1957 election, instead of promoting any Quebec M.P.'s, St Laurent reached into Ontario and to the surprise of his colleagues and the consternation of French Canadians, named Lionel Chevrier President of the Privy Council and parachuted him into the safe Montreal seat of Laurier.

Chevrier had been born just after the turn of the century in the Seaway Valley town of Cornwall, had served as secretary of the local board of trade and was first elected an M.P. in 1935. A decade later he became Mackenzie King's Minister of Transport and in 1954 left politics for three years to head the St Lawrence Seaway Authority. Chevrier, not unnaturally, was regarded as a carpetbagger in Quebec but St Laurent confidants frequently remarked that the PM was so fond of him that he treated him almost as a favourite nephew.

In August of 1957, when St Laurent met Pearson at his summer home in St Patrick, Quebec, to discuss his resignation as Liberal Leader, Chevrier was asked along to relieve the impression that an English-speaking politician was hurrying the old man's departure. Chevrier's presence established his claim to the Quebec lieutenancy and his position was strengthened after June 13, 1958, when Jean Lesage, the only other prominent French-Canadian Liberal M.P. still in Parliament after the Diefenbaker triumph, left the federal house to enter provincial politics.

During the next six and a half years Lionel Chevrier acted as Pearson's chief Quebec lieutenant. Nicknamed "the silver fox," he was a smooth caricature of the old-fashioned WASP's idea of what a *bonne entente* Quebec politician should sound and look like. His French was easily comprehensible to the English ear, he had a splendid mane of white hair and carried himself with the air of the minor government functionary in an ancient French film who, after solving some young couple's romantic difficulties with grandfatherly concern, bursts into a song about *amour* and turns out to be Maurice Chevalier.

But the realities of the political world of French Canada in the Sixties were too large for Lionel Chevrier. He had drifted into Quebec politics from very different pastures and displayed little evidence that he was aware of the truisms, much less the subtleties, that formed the foundations of the new Quebec. The character of the advice Chevrier tendered Pearson was inevitably coloured by the nature of his personal connections in the province. Since he had no power base of his own, he became the Ottawa agent for the Montreal Old Guard clique of machine politicians who were deliberately standing clear of the reforms Jean

Lesage was by then putting into effect among provincial Liberals. These reforms, which culminated in Lesage's electoral victory on June 22, 1960, never managed to trigger the faintest response in Chevrier, who gave most observers the impression that he imagined Quebec's awakened aspirations might be satisfied by the federal government's advocacy of bilingual signs on the doors of airport washrooms.

Through Pearson's opposition years Chevrier's seigneurial approach distressed the younger, progressive elements of Quebec's Liberal Party. They wanted to apply the democratic reforms they had won in provincial politics at the federal level. In November 1960 a delegation of young Lesage supporters led by Maurice Sauvé, who had been director of public relations in the victorious provincial campaign, came to Ottawa on a day when they knew Chevrier would be out of town. They suggested to Pearson that he hold a policy conference on French-Canadian problems and democratize the federal party in Quebec by transferring control of future election campaigns away from patronage-conscious party hacks and into their hands. Pearson seemed to agree but when Chevrier threatened to resign if any such action were taken, he retreated and later named Chevrier his Quebec chairman for the 1962 campaign. As a token to the province's New Guard element, Sauvé was made a member of the key organizational committee, but the appointment wasn't effective until two months before the election was called.

Under Chevrier the Liberals waged a standard old-fashioned campaign with no attempt to formulate the kind of social policies that might fit the mood of the new Quebec. As a result, on June 18, instead of getting the fifty Quebec seats they had expected, they won only thirty-five, allowing the vacuum to be filled by Réal Caouette's rampaging Social Credit movement. At an election post-mortem in Montreal's Windsor Hotel Chevrier led the party's Old Guard in blaming the failure on Sauvé, who had himself been elected federal member for Iles-de-la-Madeleine.* This tactic set the pattern for all of Pearson's Quebec lieutenants: each political catastrophe within their jurisdiction was followed not by an examination of its real causes but by an attempt to shift the blame.

---

*Only Bryce Mackasey, the newly elected M.P. for Verdun, stood up to Chevrier. Mackasey, an intense and tough-minded former union organizer, had been one of the first Quebec Liberals to buck the Old Guard machine. Mackasey managed to win his nomination at a democratically conducted convention but he was not the machine choice and $3,500 in central party funds was spent in helping Leonard Poitras, a Liberal Independent candidate, run against him.

During the ten-month interval until the 1963 election Maurice Lamontagne, then a member of Pearson's opposition office staff, tried to bypass Chevrier by swinging the party toward a reorientation of policy through a series of informal discussions held at the home of Gérard Pelletier, the editor of *La Presse*. Participants in these talks included such Montreal intellectuals as Pierre Elliott Trudeau, André Laurendeau and Jean-Louis Gagnon. It was here that preliminary suggestions were discussed for the important speech Pearson delivered in the House of Commons on December 17, 1962, in which he proposed the establishment of a royal commission to investigate and advance the causes of biculturalism and bilingualism in Canada. But the group abruptly dissociated itself from the Liberals when Pearson committed his party to the acquisition of nuclear weapons and supported the NDP during the 1963 election instead. That campaign, also run by Chevrier, produced forty-seven Quebec M.P.'s for the Liberals, among them such newcomers as Guy Favreau and Maurice Lamontagne.*

Despite Chevrier's repeated failure to deliver Quebec seats, Pearson named him official Quebec lieutenant, Minister of Justice and acting prime minister in the new government. Chevrier promptly began to push his own protégés in Ottawa. They included Yvon Dupuis, Guy Rouleau and Raymond Denis, who were all major figures in the scandals that rocked the Pearson administration in the fall of 1964 and early winter of 1965. By the time these scandals broke, Chevrier was thousands of miles away, snugly ensconced in the most distinguished of Canada's overseas diplomatic posts as High Commissioner to the United Kingdom. The high regard in which Chevrier was held by two prime ministers and the plummy rewards he garnered at every turn of his career always seemed mysterious to dispassionate observers since his contribution to his party consisted of a legacy of troubles.

When Chevrier left the cabinet in January 1964 another Old Guard figure, Azellus Denis, the Postmaster General in the original Pearson Cabinet who had been caught using a list of defeated Liberal candidates for patronage recommendations, resigned as well and was named a senator. These two cabinet vacancies gave Pearson an opportunity to revitalize his Quebec contingent.

*To get Favreau a seat, Chevrier opened up the Montreal-Papineau riding by promising to name its incumbent, Adrien Meunier, a judge. Meunier was appointed to the Quebec Superior Court six months after the 1963 election despite objections from members of the Montreal Bar Association. He was removed from the bench a year later when he was sentenced to two years in jail for perjury. He was acquitted on appeal in 1967. To make room for Lamontagne, the sitting member for Outremont, Romuald Bourque, was promised a Senate seat and was appointed on July 16, 1963.

IN THE NERVOUS GROPING FOR ALTERNATIVES that followed Chevrier's departure, the name that dominated many discussions was that of Maurice Sauvé, the federal Liberal most in tune with the rapidly changing politics of Quebec.

Though Sauvé was a dedicated social and political reformer, it was never clear whether he was really the torch-bearer of a new political generation or if his position – a man on his knees in a land of midgets – just made him appear so. A big man with a ruddy face, combative instincts and lusty appetites, Sauvé was once described by Ron Collister of the Toronto *Telegram* as looking like "an Irish pug with his back to the bar." Always easier to respect than to like, Sauvé had as his most obvious flaw an intensely self-centred view of the world. Without any pretense of piety, he measured most events in terms of their effects on him. He not only felt everything very deeply, which is bad enough for any politician, but he was always willing to say exactly what he thought, which in a town where discretion is the ultimate virtue was unforgivable.

That he ended up a casualty of the Ottawa power struggle was probably more a criticism of Ottawa than of Sauvé, but he did lack what might best be called docility. He refused to go along with the accepted way power worked in the capital. He would not concede that the transfer of authority from one political generation to the next was a difficult process which could not be unduly rushed. He refused to acknowledge that political pre-eminence must be achieved through slow rings of growth, each larger in circumference, until power is finally passed on in painless, natural succession. He saw fate as a force made to be altered, and battered himself against it. He became so uncompromising that he seemed to be not only pushing himself ahead but trying to create his own environment as he went along. Few politicians trusted him and even those who did were reluctant to feed the furnace of his ambition.

Driven on by a barely concealed presumption of his intellectual superiority, Sauvé deliberately ignored another cardinal rule of power politics in Ottawa: that since power is based on personal relationships which are constantly changing, they must steadily be multiplied. Instead of attempting to enlist allies for his many reform causes, he made enemies effortlessly. He became a politician who was always negotiating but could not be readily negotiated with.

But even if Sauvé failed, he did become a pivotal figure in the transformation of the Quebec Liberal Party's federal wing. Simply by continuing to exist within it and stating his enlightened demands with uncompromising harshness he broke a whole complex of traditions and successfully challenged the orthodox assumptions and vested interests of the Old Guard manipulators. Like most iconoclasts in advance of their time, Sauvé was reviled for his trouble. Prime ministers seldom forgive advisers for being right, particularly when their counsel is ignored.

The earliest indication of Sauvé's difficulties came in April of 1963, when Pearson left him out of his first cabinet. At thirty-nine, Sauvé had impressive qualifications: degrees in law and economics, including a term at the London School of Economics and a Ph.D. from the University of Paris, and a period as assistant secretary of the Gordon Commission on Canada's Economic Prospects. His participation in the 1960 provincial campaign had given him valuable experience and contacts in Quebec politics. He even had some claims on the basis of seniority, since he was one of four senior M.P.'s from the Quebec district, which traditionally had cabinet representation. Many influential Liberals (including Walter Gordon, Senators Chubby Power and Maurice Bourget and National Organizer Keith Davey) interceded on Sauvé's behalf, but the counter-lobby, led by Lionel Chevrier, won out. Three members of this Quebec Old Guard – Yvon Dupuis, Guy Rouleau, and Alexis Caron – felt so strongly that they agreed to forgo cabinet expectations of their own, providing Sauvé was left out.

The next year, when Chevrier left Ottawa for London, Sauvé was moved into Cabinet in the junior Forestry Department, but to balance the ticket, Pearson also appointed Yvon Dupuis as a Minister without Portfolio.

WITH SAUVÉ CONSIDERED TOO DIVISIVE A PERSONALITY to be named Chevrier's successor as Quebec lieutenant, the natural heir-apparent seemed to be Maurice Lamontagne, Pearson's old friend and one-time staff adviser on Quebec policy. When the Liberals had come to power Lamontagne as much as any man on the new front bench – and far more than most – personified the promise of the Pearson ministry. He was a recognized intellectual, a man who looked as a cabinet minister should – handsome, with grey at his temples, thought lines in his forehead and urbanity in his eye. He gave the impression of being a man of the world, above all, a sophisticate who by raising one eyebrow could convey to a friend the refinements of a whole way of life.

Lamontagne had come to Pearson with enviable credentials. He had been one of the most articulate disciples of Father Georges Henri Lévesque's School of Social Sciences at Laval University, which provided the founding ideology of Quebec's anti-Duplessis revolt. He had fought the authoritarian methods of Maurice Duplessis at a time when it took personal courage to do so, had eventually become chairman of

Laval's economics department and was a major force for social advancement in the province.

His second, no less valuable quality was as an economist. He had earned a master's degree from Harvard, had sat on several royal commissions dealing with economic subjects, and in 1946 and 1948 had come to Ottawa to be special adviser to the economic research branch of the Department of Trade and Commerce. During the stewardship of Louis St Laurent, he had served with distinction as chief economic adviser to the Privy Council – the most influential economic post in Ottawa.

His third qualification was that he was a cultured politician, a rare bird in Ottawa's longitudes. It had been Lamontagne who had persuaded Louis St Laurent to establish the Canada Council, and later he had drafted the original legislation setting it up. During the bleak opposition years, Lamontagne won the admiration of Lester Pearson. At a time when most Liberals vanished into more profitable lines of endeavour, Lamontagne remained at Pearson's side, acting as one of his chief economic and cultural advisers.

At the Liberal Party's Kingston Conference in the autumn of 1960, Lamontagne's paper, "Growth Price Stability and the Problem of Unemployment," set new economic directions for the future regime. His thesis was contained in his opening paragraph: "The ultimate objective of economic activity is the maximum common welfare. The great majority of the Canadian people want to achieve that objective within a mixed economic system where the direction and composition of the public and private sectors are determined by the democratic process and free markets. The requirements of general welfare are varied. They can partly be expressed by three secondary objectives, namely sustained and balanced growth, price stability and minimum unemployment." He went on to document his case with the off-hand brilliance of a Lord Keynes or a J. K. Galbraith.

Unhappily none of these impressive qualifications really fitted Lamontagne to be either a successful politician or a spokesman for post-Duplessis Quebec. He had run twice in Quebec East, only to be defeated in this traditionally Liberal seat which had elected Laurier, Lapointe and St Laurent. After 1963, when he was parachuted into the Outremont constituency, he demonstrated in his brief stint as Secretary of State a startling ineptitude in the Commons and his advice on how to deal with the Lesage Government had proved embarrassingly wrong. It had been Lamontagne who had pushed the federal municipal loan fund and student loan plan, both of which had to be drastically changed under pressure from Quebec. By the winter of 1964, Lamontagne had been away from French Canada for a decade and was no longer in tune with the social changes he had himself helped to bring about.

Before the Liberals came to office, Lamontagne had been a gay spirit, fighting the Diefenbaker government (as he had once fought Duplessis) with wit and imagination. But the assumption of power changed him. He became distant, arrogant and tactless. Because he owed his seat to the Old Guard manipulators who had arranged his entry into the Outremont riding, he gradually forged an informal alliance with the less idealistic elements of the Quebec Liberal Party. He backed Dupuis' elevation to the cabinet and Guy Rouleau's appointment as parliamentary secretary to the prime minister. In February of 1964 he helped to bypass democratic nominating conventions in two Quebec by-elections to pick Old Guard successors to Azellus Denis and Lionel Chevrier.

Because Old Guard adherents in Ottawa realized that Lamontagne was not tough enough to stop Maurice Sauvé from expanding his powers, they began to search for another candidate to succeed Chevrier in the Quebec lieutenancy. Pearson himself tried to establish an interim triumvirate to fill the post, consisting of Guy Favreau, Lamontagne and Sauvé. That scheme collapsed on March 28, during a secret conference held in the Prime Minister's railway car at the Windsor Station in Montreal, where Pearson had gone to watch a hockey game. The three men could not agree on how their jurisdictions might be split and the Quebec caucus, led by Guy Rouleau, decided that it wanted a single leader: Guy Favreau. Rouleau circulated a letter in mid March, written on prime ministerial stationery, claiming it was the will of the Quebec caucus that Favreau be immediately named Pearson's Quebec lieutenant. When Lamontagne found out about the document, during a federal-provincial conference in Quebec City, he had a violent quarrel with Rouleau and for nearly a year afterwards he refused to attend meetings of the Quebec caucus. Even before his private furniture deals got him into public trouble, Maurice Lamontagne had been rejected by both factions of his party's Quebec contingent.

GUY FAVREAU WAS NAMED Lester Pearson's Quebec lieutenant at a closed-door meeting of the Quebec Liberal Federation held in Montreal's Queen Elizabeth Hotel on April 25, 1964. Although he was a member of Quebec's progressive element by personal instinct, the manner of Favreau's promotion left him indebted to Rouleau and the party's Old Guard. At the same party meeting the idea of establishing an organization separate from the provincial Liberals was discussed. The Lesage

Liberals, much more nationalistic than their federal counterparts and fed up with their anti-democratic machinations, were delighted. On July 5 they voted to drop their affiliation with the federal party.

Only three unhappy years after he became Lester Pearson's Quebec lieutenant, Guy Favreau was not only out of politics, he was dead. The official cause of his death at the age of fifty was described as uremia, but there was little doubt that his shattering experiences in Ottawa had much to do with the deterioration of his health. He was an honest man caught up in a traumatic confluence of circumstances that seemed to immobilize his sense of self-preservation. Every time he tried to break out, he collided with himself. Eventually his behaviour became a kind of political self-immolation, set off by spontaneous combustion.

Joseph Albert Guy Favreau had risen to prominence in Montreal courts as government counsel in the tricky postwar deportation cases against Count Alfred de Marigny (Sir Harry Oakes' son-in-law) and Count Jacques de Bernonville (the French collaborationist). In 1951, Louis St Laurent invited him to Ottawa as special counsel to a parliamentary committee studying price-maintenance legislation. A year later he was named a member of the monopoly-hunting Restrictive Trade Practices Commission. Although Favreau had been appointed by a Liberal government, Diefenbaker's Justice Minister, Davie Fulton, named him an associate deputy minister in 1958. He left Ottawa in 1960 to join Montreal's largest law firm, Howard, Cate, Ogilvy, Bishop, Cope, Porteous and Hansard.

Favreau first became politically involved through his membership in the Jean-Marie Nadeau Society (named for a promising Montreal intellectual killed in a car accident), which met to discuss liberal ideas. Jean Lesage had offered him a cabinet post but it was Pearson who persuaded him that it was his duty as a French Canadian to enter public affairs. "I thought I had no right to refuse," Favreau said later.

Campaigning with the slogan "GUY'S OUR GUY" he handily won the safe Montreal Liberal seat of Papineau in the 1963 election and was immediately named Immigration Minister in the new Pearson government. He was an instant success. He would stride through an incredibly crowded day with the impatient attitude of a tugboat skipper who wishes his ship would go faster and he seemed to have that indefinable but invaluable quality of political stage presence that allows a politician to claim followers with little apparent effort. The first French Canadian to occupy the touchy Immigration portfolio, he handled the assignment with quiet confidence and compassion. One hot Saturday in July of 1963, for example, he interrupted a weekend with his family in

Montreal to intercede personally for Herbert Hemberger, a waiter from Belleville, Ontario, who needed a passport to fly home to Germany where his father had been killed in a car crash. Favreau had dazzled Parliament by drafting amendments to a bill while it was being debated on the floor of the Commons and had his changes approved by the Opposition. He was being touted as another St Laurent, with predictions being freely made that he would succeed Pearson in the party leadership.

This happy period came to an end on February 3, 1964, when Favreau was promoted to the Justice ministry and named government House Leader in the Commons. Together with his appointment two months later as Quebec lieutenant, these jobs imposed on him a work schedule that no man could survive. Throughout that summer and fall he was at the very centre of the Pearson Government. As Justice Minister, he was in charge of the negotiations on bringing home the Canadian constitution; as the senior Quebec minister he was consulted on all party matters as well as handling arrangements for the upcoming visit of the Queen; as House Leader he had to attend every parliamentary sitting and eventually took charge of the party's strategy in the flag debate.

Each of these responsibilities was taxing, but none more so than the House leadership. During this period Gordon Churchill was crustily refusing to co-operate with the other party House leaders and Favreau had to meet him separately. Unlike Ernest Lapointe, who had been in the Commons twenty years before he was named Mackenzie King's Quebec lieutenant, Favreau was an untried parliamentarian. He stumbled over the rules, exasperated the Opposition and gradually lost his accumulated goodwill. André Letendre, his executive assistant, determined to make Favreau the next Liberal leader, kept booking him to make at least one major speech a week and Favreau insisted on writing all of his own texts. He worked a fifteen-hour day but his desk was never clear. Unlike most ministers who sign their correspondence, drafted by departmental officials, as if they were blindfolded, Favreau carefully scrutinized the nuances of every sentence that went out over his signature.

As he grew busier, he became untidy and forgetful. During the first week that he lived in a rented house in Rockcliffe, for instance, he had to break in twice because he'd misplaced his keys. He owned four pairs of glasses but never could find any of them and even left one pair behind on the witness stand at the Dorion Inquiry. By October 1964, Pearson finally recognized how badly he had overloaded his loyal lieutenant and relieved him of the House leadership by assigning it to George McIlraith. But the eight-month stint in the job had been enough to start the wreckage of Favreau's career. His epic encounter with Erik Nielsen which began that fall and ended in the Dorion Report the following spring cost him the Justice portfolio and the last vestige of his reputation.* His former friends deserted him but Pearson, because he recognized that only the quality of Favreau's judgement, not his integrity, had been questioned in the Dorion Report – and possibly because he felt guilty for having placed Favreau under such a strain – persuaded his former Justice Minister to continue as his Quebec lieutenant for another eighteen months. Gérard Pelletier wrote the best analysis of Favreau's downfall in his syndicated political column: "Both his success and his defeats have their source in the man's character, which is a unique blend of honesty, candour, eagerness, devotion to his country and half-conscious ambition of the legitimate kind. He did make mistakes. One is described at length in the Dorion Report. It happened to attract attention; it brought the man down."

More a victim than a villain of the Liberal scandals, Favreau remained in Ottawa until shortly before he died in the summer of 1967.† He was a haunted and haunting figure in those last months and one of the saddest sights in the capital was a sign he bought in a joke shop and hung inside his parliamentary office. It read: I NEED ALL THE FRIENDS I CAN GET.

BY ACCEPTING HIS RESIGNATION as Minister of Justice but keeping him in the cabinet – first as President of the Privy Council and later as Registrar General – Pearson suspended Favreau in a curious kind of political limbo. Favreau had been shorn of his prestige and authority, yet his presence blocked the ascent of potential successors. He gradually and predictably lost control of the Quebec caucus. In February 1966, for instance, he had backed Gerald Laniel (M.P. for Beauharnois-Salaberry) for the job of caucus chairman, but H. "Pit" Lessard (Saint-Henri) was elected.

In his minor cabinet shuffle of July 7, 1965, Pearson had replaced Favreau in the Justice ministry with Lucien Cardin, a quiet-spoken lawyer from Sorel, Quebec. The scandals claimed the resignations of three more ministers – Yvon Dupuis, Maurice Lamontagne and René Tremblay – and Jean-Paul Deschatelets left of his own accord after a

---

*For details of this incident see Chapter 20.

†In the late spring of that year Pearson appointed Favreau to the Quebec Superior Court.

252

family tragedy.* Lucien Cardin resigned in April of 1967, broken by the aftermath of the Munsinger affair.†

LESTER PEARSON'S LAST QUEBEC LIEUTENANT, Jean Marchand, was very different from his predecessors. Unlike Chevrier or Favreau, he had genuine grassroots support and appeal in his home province, the result of an eighteen-year (1947-65) stint as general secretary and president of the Confederation of National Trade Unions (and its forerunner, the Confederation of Catholic Workers).

A thoughtful individual whose reserve easily dissolved into belly-pumping laughter, Marchand was a very different kind of man from his predecessors. Stocky, with a thatch of stand-up greying hair, he was the youngest of six children who were meagrely supported in the village of Champlain, Quebec, by the labour of an older brother. He had worked his way through Father Lévesque's social science school at Laval University and then became a professional labour organizer, spending two decades fighting union battles in the markedly anti-labour climate of Duplessis' Quebec.

In coming to Ottawa, Marchand immediately recognized that political parties are instruments for the exercise of power, not hothouses for ideological debate. It was his view, for instance, that Quebec's claims to special treatment within Confederation should be based not just on the concept of its rights as the domicile of a founding race, but also on the harsh reality that, as the home of the only minority in Canada which occupies its own territory, Quebec alone has the leverage to break up the country. While Marchand readily acknowledged that the idea of a Quebec lieutenant was basically an outmoded concept, he could see no practical alternative at a time when he felt Quebec M.P.'s had special problems and needed a senior spokesman who had the ear of the prime minister.

On April 4, 1967, French Canada received its strongest representation ever in a federal cabinet with the appointment of Pierre Elliott Trudeau as Minister of Justice. By promoting Trudeau, the Liberal Party's most articulate and impassioned advocate of federalism, to a place in his inner circle, the Prime Minister seemed to abandon his long-time policy of non-confrontation with Quebec, with results that neither Pearson nor Trudeau could foresee.

*Lamontagne and Deschatelets were appointed to the Senate. Tremblay, whose behaviour was exonerated by the Dorion Commission, died on January 22, 1968, at the age of forty-five.
†See Chapter 28.

CHAPTER 19

The Great Flag Debate

O UTSIDE, THE AIR ROLLED IN COLD from the Gatineau Hills and the tree limbs chattered with frost. Inside, Canada's Parliament was engaged in what would, in retrospect, become recognized as a debate marking a turning point in the evolution of Canadian sovereignty: the adoption of a distinctive national flag.

The great flag debate, which blew itself out in the Commons during the early morning hours of December 15, 1964, involved very much more than legislative approval of a piece of bunting with a maple leaf design. It represented a symbolic passing of the attitudes of a generation; a triumph of the Canadian present over the Canadian past.

Politically, the controversy was important for what it revealed about the character of its two leading figures: Lester Pearson and John Diefenbaker. Although they had been born within two years of each other and belonged to the same generation, they viewed the wide plain of public affairs from summits far apart. The thirty-seven angry days of the flag debate allowed the Liberal Leader to transcend his time while the Tory Chief remained a prisoner of his heritage.

Diefenbaker's flag oratory, enriched and emboldened by the obvious sincerity of his beliefs, revealed the Prince Albert politician as the undaunted defender of the British fact in Canada, perpetuating a stand he had taken thirty-eight years before during a 1926 campaign speech at Macdowall, Saskatchewan, when he had declared: "I want to make Canada all Canadian and all British. The men who wish to change our flag should be denounced by every good Canadian." Both the stances he took and the tactics he used in the flag debate irrevocably confirmed John Diefenbaker in the public mind as a figure out of the Edwardian past, inflamed by issues that no longer animated the majority of Canadians.

Lester Pearson's more contemporary outlook was expressed in the question he asked the Opposition Leader: "Am I supposed to be forgetting my British past because I look forward to my Canadian future?" With sure instinct if uncertain tactics, the Liberal Leader brought the nation's myths out in the open and helped alter their contents. Entombed forever was the image of a Canada depending for its greatness on a British connection which for generations had been based more on legend than on fact.

While the flag debate raged on, paralysing Parliament off and on for most of six months, it demonstrated – fortunately on a symbolic issue only – just how deep the gulf between French and English Canada had become. The crux of the controversy was not whether there should be a new flag but whether or not it should include the traditional symbols of Canada's mother countries.

The Liberals won the debate and the flag became one of Lester Pearson's most memorable achievements. But the process of transferring the nation's allegiance to the new ensign was not distinguished by dignity or decorum or softened by respect for the emotional roots of the generations who had laid the foundations of a new society in the broad and terrifying geography of the Canadian subcontinent.

THE VERY IDEA OF BECOMING THE SPONSOR of a flag seemed too emotional, somehow extraneous, to a politician of Lester Pearson's experience. But the Liberals' platform in both the 1962 and 1963 elections had specifically pledged that the party would, within two years of taking office, submit to Parliament legislation for a distinctive Canadian flag, while retaining the Union Jack as a symbol of Commonwealth membership. The Conservatives, who sensed it was an issue that might deeply embarrass the administration, kept prodding the Prime Minister about his plans.

By the spring of 1964, John Diefenbaker had managed to bring Parliament to a virtual standstill; thirty untouched bills were listed on the order paper and the Liberal Government, still reeling from the impact of its ill-contrived first budget and the many legislative reverses that followed, seemed unable to command the will of the Commons. Pearson realized that if he did not assert his authority, he soon would have very little left. Without consulting cabinet, caucus or even his retinue of personal advisers until he had made up his mind, the Prime Minister decided to grab the initiative by introducing a new flag design. He hoped the aura of bold resolution that might be created would allow him to carry forward the more essential parts of his program.

The flag question had been quietly shelved by every Canadian government since Confederation as an issue too divisive to permit legislative action. The Red Ensign, with its Union Jack in the upper left-hand corner and Canadian coat of arms in the lower right field, had first been authorized for use on Canadian ships by the British Admiralty in 1892. The flag had gradually acquired general acceptance throughout the country and an order-in-council issued in 1924 had permitted its use at Canadian diplomatic offices abroad. In 1945 another order-in-council allowed its display wherever appropriate, pending Parliament's approval of a distinctive Canadian flag. Various parliamentary committees had considered the question, but nothing had been done.

Inside the Liberal caucus the M.P. with the greatest interest in the flag issue was John Ross Matheson, a Brockville, Ontario, lawyer who had served with distinction in World War II as a forward observation officer in the 1st Field Regiment of the Royal Canadian Horse Artillery and was gravely wounded in the fighting at Ortona. Matheson, who had always maintained an interest in heraldry, wrote Pearson a twelve-page letter on May 23, 1963, outlining his idea for a flag. In it he suggested that the basis for the new design should be "a white field charged with three red maple leaves conjoined on a single stem." The historical precedent for this design was its appearance in the coat of arms proclaimed as Canada's national symbol by George V in 1921. A similar pattern had been used on the personal banner of Queen Elizabeth II for her Canadian visits.

To help him with technical details Matheson enlisted two Ottawa heraldic experts, Alan Beddoe, a retired naval commander who had illustrated the Book of Remembrance for Canada's war dead, and Colonel A. Fortescue Duguid, a retired army historian. Beddoe showed some preliminary sketches of the three-leaf design to Pearson, including one with blue borders along its vertical edges to represent the "sea-to-sea" motif. On the evening of May 14, 1964, Pearson called eight Parliamentary Press Gallery reporters to his residence and gave them a private briefing in which he announced his intention to proceed with the flag legislation and gave as his personal preference the three-maple-leaf pattern with blue borders. Three days later he flew to Winnipeg for a long-standing engagement to address the annual meeting of the

Royal Canadian Legion.* "It's time now for Canadians to unfurl a flag that is truly distinctive and national in character, as Canadian as the maple leaf which should be its dominant design," he declared. The hall broke into a pandemonium of protests as the Legionnaires shouted "No! No!" One leather-lunged veteran jumped to his feet, shook his fist, and bellowed: "You're selling Canada to the pea-soupers!"

Though crudely put, this interjection summed up the main issue of the national and parliamentary debate that followed. Those English-speaking Canadians who already thought of Pearson as being "soft on Quebec" were enraged that the Union Jack had been left out of his new flag design and interpreted his policy as yet another "sop to French Canada."

In mid June, when he opened the parliamentary debate on the flag, Pearson concentrated on trying to prove that the maple leaf design had a meaningful domestic tradition. John Diefenbaker, instead of supporting retention of the Red Ensign as expected, tried to shift the responsibility for the flag decision to the voters by calling for a plebiscite on the question. The Liberals strongly opposed this motion because the country's previous plebiscite – in 1942, on conscription for overseas military service – had exposed sharp cleavages between French and English Canada. Even Conservative newspapers were appalled by Diefenbaker's idea. "[A plebiscite] would feed an appetite for feud and hate on both sides that would cripple every process of government in our federal system," editorialized the *Ottawa Journal.*

The Liberal Government's parliamentary strategy during the debate that followed was appallingly amateurish. It helped turn the flag into a partisan issue. Pearson had initially called for a free vote, later stated the vote would be considered a question of confidence in the government and finally retreated from this position as well. If it hadn't been for Speaker Alan Macnaughton's diplomatic and skilful handling of the House, the debate would not only have been tedious but might have proved abortive as well.

Outside the Commons public interest in the issue quickly developed. In Toronto, night-club strippers were climaxing their acts by jiggling on stage with three strategically placed red maple leaves. In Regina, Ted Goodwin designed a maple leaf flag of his own that weighed a hundred pounds and had ten flashing lights to represent the provinces. On a more serious level, a group of distinguished academics including Eugene Forsey, Donald Creighton, W. L. Morton and T. H. B. Symons

*Less than four years earlier, on December 19, 1960, the Canadian Legion had been granted permission by the Queen to add the word "Royal" to its name.

addressed a letter to the Prime Minister applauding his decision to seek a new flag but condemning his choice. "We have a despairing feeling that this insipid flag, instead of promoting national unity, will produce only an indifferent response. . . . The very essence of this country's history, and the reason for our national distinctiveness, has been the long and often turbulent marriage of French and English heritages. We have faith that in their depths, Canadians pride themselves on this union, and on its parliamentary and non-revolutionary tradition. . . . The nation is strong enough to face its own past proudly, and to assert it. Whatever may be said about the use of the maple leaf as a Canadian emblem in the past, it has never gained anyone's vigorous allegiance, and it involves no commitment to the human fact of Canada."

Though most hard-rock Anglo-Saxons remained convinced that Pearson's abandonment of the Red Ensign represented an important concession to Quebec, many opinion leaders in French Canada saw the flag debate as less a French-English confrontation than an old-fashioned wrangle between English-Canadian nationalists and British imperialists. "Quebec doesn't give a tinker's damn about the new flag, it's a matter of complete indifference," Pierre Trudeau commented in an interview with the *Toronto Daily Star*.* Quebec had too many real grievances against Ottawa to regard Lester Pearson's hopeful advocacy of the new pennant as a meaningful instrument of national unity. Guy Cormier wrote in Montreal's *La Presse*: "Pearson's appeal for unity is a wish, it is not a reality. It is less than a reality. Things first come into existence, then the symbols they represent are created. Mr Pearson is proceeding by artificial insemination."†

In the Commons, Quebec M.P.'s of all parties (including the eight Conservatives from French Canada who were present) supported the new flag on the final vote. But the debate itself provided numerous examples to show that the twin founding cultures of Canada dwelt on either side of a wide barrier, all but oblivious of one another's aspirations. Russell MacEwan (PC, Pictou) tried to demonstrate his enlightened attitude by confessing that he enjoyed singing *Alouette!* with Quebec M.P.'s and Drummond Clancy (PC, Yorkton) generously interpreted the Conquest with this historical footnote: "Wolfe won the Battle of the Plains of Abraham by a fluke; Montcalm lost because he was asleep, and that's a fact." Another unusual historical interpretation came from F. J. Bigg (PC, Athabasca), who managed to bring Joan of Arc into the debate when he told the Commons: "They took Joan of Arc's flag down. They put her lily banner in the dirt, and she was only

*June 12, 1964.
†May 19, 1964.

258

a woman. But what a glorious woman she was. She put her lily banner out in front and never looked back, and with her very small army swept the ranks clear. She put the rightful heir, I am led to believe, on the throne of France. Then the king of France ratted on her, and you know the rest. Now she's a saint. Which of those opposite in their male pride will stand up and say that they think the lily banner of France or the cross of St George should be laid in the dirt?" Percy Noble (PC, Grey North) argued against the maple leaves on the grounds that Conn Smythe, the man who had named the Toronto hockey club the Maple Leafs, was really a strong Red Ensign supporter.

This kind of silly byplay by Tory backbenchers was designed primarily to prolong a debate the substance of which had been adequately stated during its first ten days. But to John Diefenbaker and his partisans within the Conservative caucus, the extension of the flag filibuster had a serious secondary purpose. The Conservative Leader was desperately anxious to force another election because he thought the ineptitude the Liberals had demonstrated during their first year in office combined with the increasing public concern about their integrity might bring him victory at the polls. Diefenbaker saw the flag proposal, and especially the manner in which Pearson had introduced it, as an ideal handle to force a snap election, particularly if he could maintain the filibuster long enough to force the Liberals into using the perilous closure rule to cut off debate.

Diefenbaker threw himself into the flag debate with a zest and conviction rare even to him. From his initial contention that the new flag would treat "all the milestones of our past greatness as irrelevancies" he soared into an attack on the administration's alleged atheism. "Why does the government insist that the Christian crosses, the spiritual elements, be removed from our flag?" he demanded in a *Nation's Business* telecast on July 22, 1964.

As Diefenbaker tried to orchestrate his party's filibuster he met with increasing resistance, particularly from the Quebec caucus led by Léon Balcer. In the end it was mainly Diefenbaker's Prairie cowboys who co-operated. Sixteen of them spoke four times or more during the debate. Eventually some thirty English-speaking Conservatives as well as the ten-man Quebec contingent refused to go along with prolonging the debate and most of them refused to attend the party caucus meetings where filibuster tactics were discussed.

WHEN IT BECAME OBVIOUS THAT NOTHING would be accomplished inside the Commons, a fifteen-member committee was appointed with a six-week deadline to submit its flag recommendation.* The committee held forty-five sessions, beginning on September 17, and reviewed more than two thousand designs submitted to it. Just before its crucial vote on the issue John Matheson had asked Beddoe, the heraldic expert, to draw a flag that had been mentioned to him in a memorandum from Professor George F. G. Stanley, Dean of Arts and head of the history department at the Royal Military College in Kingston, Ontario. It described an adaptation, using a single red maple leaf, of the red-white-red banner used by RMC. Without telling the non-Liberal committee members, Matheson had tacked up this design among the final few to be voted on. By October 22, the choice had narrowed to the Red Ensign, the Stanley design and the original Pearson pennant. The Red Ensign was defeated first, with only the four English-speaking Tories supporting its retention. Next up was the single-maple-leaf design. The Tories, who assumed that the Liberals were still committed to the Pearson pennant and that the NDP, Socred and Créditiste M.P.'s would probably prefer the non-government design, saw a chance to humiliate the Grits. They decided among themselves to vote for the new one-maple-leaf flag. To their horror, the vote was unanimous. They immediately demanded another vote on whether or not the design should be recommended to Parliament and cast four ballots against it. At the same time, the committee recommended (nine to five) use of the Union Jack as a secondary flag symbolizing Canada's membership in the Commonwealth.

Diefenbaker immediately declared the committee's new flag recommendation unacceptable and J. Waldo Monteith moved an amendment in favour of a national plebiscite. In a television interview Pearson reaffirmed his government's determination to "have a flag by Christmas." The flag debate staggered on for another six weeks with the Tories giving up all pretense that they were doing anything but carrying on a time-wasting blockade.

The man who finally broke the impasse was Léon Balcer, then still (at least nominally) Diefenbaker's Quebec lieutenant. Exasperated

*Herman Batten, Liberal member for Humber-St George's, was the non-voting chairman. The other Liberal members were Léo Cadieux (Terrebonne), Grant Deachman (Vancouver-Quadra), Jean-Eudes Dubé (Restigouche-Madawaska), Margaret Konantz (Winnipeg South), Joseph Macaluso (Hamilton West) and John Matheson (Leeds). Progressive Conservative members were Hugh John Flemming (Victoria-Carleton), J. Waldo Monteith (Perth), David Pugh (Okanagan Boundary), Reynold Rapp (Humboldt-Melfort-Tisdale) and Théogène Ricard (St Hyacinthe-Bagot). Reid Scott (Danforth), Raymond Langlois (Mégantic) and Marcel Lessard (Lake St John) represented the NDP, Créditistes and Socreds respectively.

beyond endurance by the Tory tactics, he rose in the Commons when it opened on December 9 and invited the Liberals to use closure as a means of halting the debate. "Freedom of speech must be respected," he said, "but we should not act in such a way that this House be deprived of its main duty which consists in making decisions."

The closure rule had last been used in the pipeline debate of 1956 with drastic consequences for the Liberal Government. But late in the afternoon of Friday, December 11, George McIlraith, the Liberal House Leader, gave notice that the closure rule would be applied at the Commons' Monday sitting. This meant members' speeches would be limited to twenty minutes and that at one o'clock Tuesday morning the flag motion would arbitrarily be put to a vote. The Diefenbaker Tories were jubilant. But the country, fed up with the transparent Conservative attempt to turn the flag debate to their partisan advantage, seemed to support the Liberals. There was hardly an editorial ripple opposing the introduction of closure.

Ironically, the best speech of the entire debate was given during its closing hours by Paul Martineau, the anti-Diefenbaker Tory member for Pontiac-Témiscamingue:

The new flag is the symbol of the future because it expresses unity, that unity to which so many of us have paid lip service during the course of this debate. I believe that in the maple leaf Canadians of whatever origin or background may find something in common. . . . In this debate many hard and bitter words have been spoken that it would have been better to have left unsaid. It is useless, futile and, I feel, mischievous to try at this stage to assess blame in this chamber or elsewhere. But the truth remains – and it is a bitter truth – that the embers of hatred and prejudice have been fanned, and if they should continue uncontrolled they could very well lead to disaster and the end of our nation. That is why this afternoon I approved and voted for the extreme measure that is closure; because I am firmly convinced that the continuance of this debate at this stage, after it has given rise throughout the land to so many utterances born of prejudice and hatred, could only achieve its normal course, the very destruction of this country. It may be well to look at others and learn a lesson from history. Almost a hundred years ago the United States of America, our great neighbours, today's leaders of freedom, were engaged in a murderous civil war. Fortunately, and I thank God, this has not happened in our country, and I trust and believe it will never happen.

As time for the closure deadline approached, the Commons grew tense. Several Tories defied the Speaker, hoping they would be "named" and thus turn themselves into political martyrs. Diefenbaker himself intended to speak in the closing minutes of the debate, planning to take up enough time so that the Liberal Leader would have no opportunity to answer him. But at 12:31, Réal Caouette was recognized and used up the next twenty minutes. Diefenbaker, Pearson and Douglas Fisher of the NDP rose to follow him. Because the last three M.P.'s to participate had been non-Liberals, Speaker Macnaughton recognized the Prime Minister. Eldon Woolliams angrily demanded that Diefenbaker be granted the floor, but his motion was defeated.

Hugh Lawford, a member of Pearson's legislative staff, noticed that the Woolliams motion had been prepared beforehand because it was typed. Convinced that the Tories were planning to disrupt the PM's speech, get one of their members named and drape his seat with a Red Ensign, Lawford scribbled a note to the Prime Minister suggesting he offer half of his speaking time to the Tory Leader. The parliamentary page boys had gone home for the night, so Lawford ran it down to the Commons lobby himself and had it passed up to the PM. Pearson interrupted his speech to suggest that the Leader of the Opposition could have his concluding ten minutes. The gesture was rejected with an angry wave. Diefenbaker sat in his seat, enraged to the point of incoherence. Near him, J. Waldo Monteith kept staggering to his feet and yelling: "Oh, nuts!" Gordon Churchill, his face flushed with anger, repeatedly demanded to be heard. The Commons was very close to spinning completely out of control. Pestered by interruptions and Tory catcalls, Pearson concluded his speech: "This is the flag of the future, but it does not dishonour the past." At 2:15 a.m. the final vote was taken. It passed, 163 to 78.

After a debate that had lasted through 308 speeches Canada had a new flag at last.* Yvon Dupuis led the Commons in singing *O Canada* and George McIlraith followed with a falsetto rendition of *God Save the Queen*. Three M.P.'s – Ralph Cowan, the maverick Liberal from York-Humber, Drummond Clancy and Chester MacRae (PC, York-Sunbury) – conspicuously stayed in their seats.

Fifteen minutes later Pearson was in his parliamentary office, receiving congratulations and preparing to go home. One supporter rushed in, pumped his hand and said: "That was a great speech; it must surely make up for January 20, 1958." Pearson paused and replied: "Yes, it really did." Next morning the *Globe and Mail* summed up the debate:

*The Conservatives had made 210 speeches, the Liberals 50, the NDP 24, Social Credit 15, and the Ralliement des Créditistes 9.

"Flags that have been torn in battle with a foreign enemy can still fly with pride. This will surely be the first flag in history that was shred by its sons."

THE OFFICIAL FLAG-RAISING CEREMONY took place on February 15, 1965, before a crowd of ten thousand shivering citizens gathered before Parliament Hill's Peace Tower. At noon, with a watery winter sun shining through the clouds, the muffled sound of a twenty-one-gun salute could be heard and moments later a sudden gust of wind gave the first flutter of life to the new flag. "If our nation by God's grace endures a thousand years, this day will always be remembered as a milestone in Canada's national progress," Pearson said in one of the most moving speeches of his career. John Diefenbaker stood on the platform and when the television cameras focused on him, took out a white handkerchief and dabbed his eyes.

Despite the trauma of its birth the flag was quickly accepted even by its most obdurate opponents. On April 16, 1966, the Canadian Legion passed a resolution supporting its adoption. It decorated the platforms of many Conservative candidates during the 1968 election.

Whatever history's final assessment of Lester Pearson might be, the flag would be one of his most imaginative accomplishments. Speculating about its impact on the Canadian people, A. R. M. Lower wrote in the Summer 1967 issue of the *Queen's Quarterly*:

Since the adoption of the new flag, something very interesting has happened to the Canadian psyche, something that probably cannot yet be put into words, but of whose reality sensitive minds are aware. One testimony to that is the universality of acceptance of the new flag, another is the evident satisfaction with which many people, especially plain people, regard it: being Canadians, they do not express themselves in words, they hide resolutely away any gesture or grunt that might conceivably betray emotion, but the sharp observer gets the signals all the same. There is nothing in this of turning backs on a hated past, nothing suggesting that old ties were irksome. The point is simply that the country is growing up, coming to see itself as an entity, taking the interest in itself that any organism, to be healthy, must. Each time, that is, that the average citizen looks at the new flag, he unconsciously says to himself "That's me!"

CHAPTER 20

The Temptations of Power

IN THE FALL OF 1964 and the long winter and spring of 1965, Ottawa was rocked by a series of scandalous allegations and revelations of corruption so remote from the Canadian ethos that at times the whole sordid business seemed absurdly like an old-fashioned, low-budget gangster movie scripted by some third-rate dramatist with no regard for the authenticity of his plots.

This ugly episode, known variously as the Rivard affair and the Dorion scandals, began on November 23, 1964, with highly insulting and partisan charges hurled across the Commons floor by the Tory M.P. from the Yukon, Erik Nielsen, and ended on June 29, 1965, with the publication of the report of Chief Justice Frédéric Dorion of the Quebec Superior Court, which meticulously documented most of the accusations.

During the intervening seven months, political man was exhibited at his most combative and least attractive. The capital was awash with rumours as suspicion became a self-accelerating process. The Liberals involved were made to look like fools or knaves, or both. The Prime Minister was revealed to his party and his people as a weak man afraid to face the consequences of his own actions. Most Canadians of conscience felt their pride in country diminished by the realization that what had taken place was not some trivial patronage matter but political involvement with men engaged in the most pernicious of criminal activities: the smuggling of heroin by a Mafia-connected drug syndicate. The revelations ceased to be fascinating and became repulsive when it turned out that these gangsters had been able to reach right into the offices of the Prime Minister and the ministers of Justice and of Immigration.

THE CENTRAL FIGURE IN THE CRIMINAL CONSPIRACY that triggered the scandals was Lucien Rivard, a stocky, arrogant Montreal thug with a certain panache and the terrifying amorality of his kind. Rivard had served a tough apprenticeship in the slums of Montreal, had done time for burglary, run a gambling casino in pre-Castro Cuba and become a ringleader in the Mafia-dominated North American drug trade through his connection with Paul Mondoloni, an inner-council member of *L'Union Corse*, the syndicate that controlled the refining of Middle East opium into heroin.

On October 10, 1963, a minor Montreal hood named Michel Caron and his wife Marie were stopped by a customs officer at Laredo, Texas, for a routine check of their car after crossing the border from Mexico. When the search turned up bags containing seventy-six pounds of pure heroin, the pair was arrested. Caron later confessed he was a courier in a network run by Lucien Rivard that was engaged in large-scale smuggling of narcotics into the North American market.

Acting on a warrant from the U.S. Attorney General, Canadian police arrested Rivard in Montreal on June 19, 1964, and took him to Bordeaux Jail. The United States government immediately applied for his extradition. Following standard procedure, Washington asked the Canadian Justice Department for the name of counsel to prosecute the extradition case. The Justice Department, also following standard procedure, looked up its approved list of lawyers who belonged to the government party and recommended Pierre Lamontagne, a bright young Liberal working for the Montreal law firm of Geoffrion and Prud'homme. So far, everything was normal.

Almost immediately efforts were launched to arrange bail for Rivard. Because he knew so much about its international operations, the Mafia was anxious to keep him away from the American authorities. Accordingly, Robert Gignac, a Montreal underworld character who described himself as "a contractor," contacted Guy Masson, a small-time Montreal Liberal organizer who claimed he knew "an Ottawa extradition expert," and offered him a thousand dollars for his help in arranging bail for Rivard.

Masson promptly went to Ottawa for three conferences with Raymond Denis, the executive assistant to Immigration Minister René Tremblay. A 32-year-old lawyer, Denis had been brought into the federal government by Lionel Chevrier as his own executive assistant

265

in the Justice Department. His power increased when he moved over to Immigration and found himself under the direction of a weak minister who took little creative interest in his portfolio and referred many touchy situations to his executive assistant.

In Montreal, meanwhile, on the advice of Masson, Rivard's wife Marie assembled $60,000, to be used either as part of a bribe or as bail money for her husband. She was aided by Gignac and Eddy Lechasseur, a dapper, cold-eyed ex-convict with no visible means of support, who described himself as an importer in partnership with Rivard. It was a remarkable show of Rivard's strength in the Montreal underworld that Mrs Rivard was able to raise the cash in two days. She later testified that $20,000 of the sum came from Ovide Gagnon, who worked as an $80-a-week handyman. (Gagnon never did corroborate her evidence since he was found dead shortly afterwards.) Masson came to Ottawa on July 13 to inform Denis that the $60,000 had been deposited with the Royal Trust Company in Montreal. The next morning Denis called Pierre Lamontagne, who was conveniently an old friend, and asked him to come to Ottawa that day on an urgent matter.

According to later evidence, Denis made Lamontagne two offers – one in his departmental office and one in Lamontagne's room at the Chateau Laurier – of $20,000 if he would withdraw his opposition to Rivard's release on bail. This was, at best, a naïve request. Lamontagne had already been instructed by his client, the United States government, to oppose bail strenuously because Rivard was known to have large bank accounts outside Canada and could easily skip the country. Lamontagne really had no discretionary power to grant Denis' request. Lamontagne later quoted Denis as saying that Rivard was a great friend and supporter of the Liberal Party, that his help might be needed in the election and that "it would help the party if he was let out on bail." The Montreal lawyer summarily turned down the executive assistant's offer and went on his summer holidays. Soon afterwards Lamontagne began to receive phone calls from Robert Gignac and Raymond Daoust, Rivard's lawyer, claiming that he had been paid and asking why he wasn't co-operating. Finally Lamontagne – who realized how dangerous his position was because the Mafia obviously thought he had taken the bribe – telephoned Denis to warn him that he would call in the RCMP if the threats didn't cease.

Even so he continued to be pressured by phone calls from important Liberals who seemed to have taken up the Mafia cause. On August 4 Guy Lord, a special assistant to Justice Minister Guy Favreau, telephoned Lamontagne about Rivard's bail dilemma. This was followed by more pointed requests for intervention from André Letendre, another

Favreau assistant, and Guy Rouleau, Prime Minister Pearson's parliamentary secretary. On August 11 Lamontagne, by this time thoroughly frightened, told the whole story to Inspector J. R. R. Carrière of the RCMP. The Mounties reacted quickly. Three days later Commissioner George McClellan passed on the details to Guy Favreau. Initially the Justice Minister was co-operative, urging the RCMP to interview Denis, Lord, Letendre and Rouleau. But on August 20, when Denis called on Favreau to beg him to inform René Tremblay of the investigation, Favreau did nothing. Denis finally told the Immigration Minister himself eleven days later and submitted his resignation.

The most significant exchange in the Rivard affair up to this point took place on September 2 between Guy Favreau and Lester Pearson on a government plane flying from Charlottetown to Ottawa. At noon that day the PM and the country's ten provincial premiers had completed meetings they were holding in Charlottetown to discuss patriation of the Canadian constitution. Around two o'clock in the afternoon, the PM's party boarded the Department of Transport's JetStar for the journey back to the capital. Aboard the plane with the Prime Minister and Mrs Pearson were Senator John Connolly, Justice Minister Guy Favreau, Solicitor General J. Watson MacNaught, Jim Coutts, the PM's appointments secretary, and Paul Gérin-Lajoie, Quebec's education minister, who was hitching a ride to Ottawa, where he was to preside over the Commonwealth Education Conference.

In mid flight, when Mrs Pearson left her husband's side for a few minutes, Favreau slipped into the seat next to the Prime Minister. There was no record of the conversation that followed but according to later testimony Favreau told the Prime Minister five facts in quick succession: that there were allegations of bribery involving the executive assistant to the Minister of Citizenship and Immigration; that these allegations were denied by the official in question; that they were being investigated by the RCMP; that the individual concerned had been sent on leave while the investigation was taking place; and finally, that the PM would be given the results of the investigation when Favreau felt they were complete. No names were mentioned and the key word "narcotics" was not used in describing the allegations.

Sixteen days after the airplane conversation, Favreau received the complete RCMP report on the case. With only a cursory examination of its contents, the Justice Minister decided not to send the police report to his department's criminal law section for further evaluation. Instead, on his own authority, he concluded the same day that there were no grounds for the laying of criminal charges. Even though the RCMP files strongly implicated Guy Rouleau, Favreau, curiously, did not even find it necessary to tell the PM that his own parliamentary secretary had been a key figure in the attempt to spring Rivard. An Old Guard Quebec politician, Rouleau had entered the House of Commons in 1953 at the age of thirty. Although Rouleau never achieved much in Ottawa, at Chevrier's request Pearson promoted him to be his parliamentary secretary in January, 1964. On July 17, 1964, Rouleau had written a letter (on prime ministerial stationery) asking the National Parole Board to transfer Robert Tremblay, serving twenty years in a Vancouver penitentiary for the attempted murder of a man by beating him with lead pipes, to Bordeaux Jail. Rouleau later admitted the request had been made on behalf of a constituent, one Lucien Rivard.

The RCMP report on the Rivard case included the opinion that "if there was a linchpin in this conspiracy at the top, it was probably Guy Rouleau." Yet for sixty-six days – from September 18 until November 23 – Favreau told Pearson nothing of Rouleau's involvement. When the Prime Minister finally saw the same RCMP report, he called Rouleau into his office and immediately demanded his resignation.

But as far as Guy Favreau was concerned, the case was closed once he had decided on September 18 that it did not warrant any prosecutions. He locked the police report in his desk. Its secrets would no doubt have lingered there had not Erik Nielsen been given his own briefing by a frustrated RCMP officer who thought the whole incident was being swept under a political rug.

A THIN MAN WITH GREY, BROODING EYES, Erik Nielsen had some of the attitudes of a fundamentalist preacher who believes that all men must sin before achieving forgiveness. Congenitally suspicious of bureaucracy and dedicated to the eradication of Liberal supremacy in Canada, he waded into every parliamentary debate determined to draw blood. Like John Diefenbaker he saw the Commons as a courtroom where he could advance his daily litigation against the Grits and waged his campaign with all the skill he had acquired while conducting some two hundred courts martial in the RCAF. Although Liberals referred to him sneeringly as "the Tory hatchetman," on November 23, 1964, he was cool in manner and not unfair in method when he put forward the case against Favreau's handling of the Rivard affair.

The great surprise of that chaotic day in the Commons was that the Liberals were so totally unprepared for an event nearly everyone else on Parliament Hill saw coming. For the previous month rumours about the Rivard affair had been drifting around the Commons corridors. The telephone network that links politicians and press had hummed for weeks. One syndicated columnist had an article in type waiting for the revelations he knew were forthcoming and a radio reporter – Ed Murphy of CKNW, New Westminster, B.C. – had even told André Ouellet, one of Favreau's executive assistants, exactly how much information Nielsen had in his possession. Keith Davey, the party's national organizer, had telephoned on November 17 to tell Favreau that he'd learned of the affair and the extent of Nielsen's knowledge. The most direct warning to the Justice Minister had come from Antoine Geoffrion, a senior partner of Pierre Lamontagne's Montreal law firm. He informed Favreau that Nielsen had visited Lamontagne on November 18, that he seemed to know the details of the case and that he intended to bring them up on November 23.

Consideration of Justice Department estimates, which would provide Nielsen with his needed opening, had been postponed four times. But on November 17 Gordon Churchill, the Conservative Party's House Leader, had offered the government a plan for allowing other departmental estimates through the Commons, if Justice were called on November 23. Churchill's unusual generosity made at least three ministers (Walter Gordon, Maurice Sauvé and Allan MacEachen) highly suspicious but they were overruled by the majority of Cabinet.

Up to this time neither the cabinet nor the PM had been briefed on the Rivard affair. Favreau himself seemed unconcerned. He spent the three days before the debate consulting departmental officials on the details of his estimates. "It did not reach my mind that Nielsen would do what he did," Favreau later complained. "We had already fired Raymond Denis and as judge and jury I could not convict him beyond reasonable doubt. I had co-operated fully with the RCMP and even offered to let them listen in on my office telephone." Favreau did mention the case to Pearson during a meeting at 24 Sussex on Sunday, November 22, but only in a general way and still without revealing Guy Rouleau's involvement.

It wasn't until Monday afternoon that the PM became aware of the full dimensions of the case. He heard the details not from his own Minister of Justice but from Erik Nielsen, in the House of Commons. Ignorant of the seriousness of the charges, the government had no opportunity to formulate a strategy to meet them. The fumbling that followed – the setting up of a commission of inquiry and the squabble over its terms of reference – were all matters a cabinet would ordinarily discuss in private. Instead, the narrow time margin dictated by Favreau's inexplicable delay meant that the government's every countermove had to be made in public, its awkwardness revealed for all the world to see.

When the Commons met on November 23, Tommy Douglas of the NDP asked whether the Minister of Justice had received any complaints that "persons in high places" had been trying to exert improper pressure to get bail for two men in Bordeaux Jail. Favreau replied casually that he would be making a statement on the matter later in the day. Jack Pickersgill was the only Liberal frontbencher to sense danger; he shot up in his seat and began whispering animatedly to Favreau. But it was too late. As soon as Favreau finished making his estimates speech, Nielsen was up, questioning him about "the offenders in this case" and mentioning executive assistants in Favreau's own office and that of René Tremblay. Favreau knew the charges were true but blurted out that they were "an absolute lie," standing on the technicality that since no charges had been laid there could be no "offenders." When Favreau was asked whether the case involved "anyone else higher up in the government," he denied it – even though he'd already been warned that Nielsen was aware of Guy Rouleau's role.

That night Pearson was finally given the full RCMP report and next morning he unceremoniously fired Rouleau as his parliamentary secretary.* When the House met, Favreau agreed that an inquiry would be held into the matter. Douglas Harkness, the former Conservative Defence Minister, then rose to ask the Prime Minister when he had first been informed about the affair. Pearson replied: "Mr Speaker, I think I was informed on the day before his [the Minister of Justice's] estimates were brought before the House." The PM then immediately left Ottawa to spend the rest of the week making a previously planned political junket through Western Canada.

Paul Martin, the acting Prime Minister, telephoned Pearson at the Prince Edward Hotel in Brandon, Manitoba, at 3 p.m. on Thursday, November 26. His news was devastating. Under questioning in Cabinet Guy Favreau had informed his colleagues about his September 2 in-flight conversation with Pearson. The Prime Minister was now in the unenviable position of appearing to have misled Parliament. After changing his mind several times, Pearson decided to continue his western politicking, leaving a leaderless, badly divided ministry in Ottawa to deal with the situation as best they could. Under opposition pressure, to which it yielded only because it was in a minority position and feared being overthrown, the Liberal administration agreed to widen the terms of the proposed inquiry into the Rivard affair to include an investigation into the conduct of the Justice Minister.

*Guy Rouleau resigned as an M.P. on July 6, 1965. He was allowed to post-date his resignation to July 31, permitting him to claim his full $1,500 salary for that month.

Pearson rationalized his absence from Ottawa during this crucial week on the theory that cancellation of his western tour would have inflated the scandals beyond what he then considered to be their true importance. Yet it was hard to comprehend why the Prime Minister would choose to go on a party fund-raising junket when his government's integrity was being challenged in Parliament. Instead of enlisting his prestige against the abrasive tormentors threatening the honour of his ministry, Pearson simply opted out. ("At the UN, delegates could vote four ways – yes, no, abstain, or go to the delegates' lounge. When the scandals broke, Mike chose the delegates' lounge," remarked one of Pearson's former External colleagues.)

Pearson returned to Ottawa on Sunday, November 29. At Cabinet next morning he agreed to rise in the House that day on a question of personal privilege and reveal the facts of his September 2 conversation. But when the House met, even though several questions of privilege were raised, including such trivialities as a complaint by Walter Dinsdale about the way contracts for servicing RCMP cars were being awarded in his riding, Pearson remained silent.

The crisis that evolved from the PM's hesitation was internal, fought out among his closest advisers, with one group (led by Mary Macdonald) reminding him that the airborne conversation could hardly constitute an "official notification" by the Justice Minister, while the other (led by Tom Kent) appealed to his Methodist conscience to tell the truth and face the consequences. It was the Methodist conscience that won. But it took a full two weeks and when Pearson finally acknowledged the earlier Favreau warning he did so in a curiously roundabout manner. Instead of making a straightforward statement in the Commons, he wrote a letter about his conversation of September 2 to Frédéric Dorion, who was then beginning his inquiry.

Asked in the House why he had previously said he had first heard about the case on November 22, Pearson replied lamely, "I had completely forgotten the earlier conversation." The opposition moved that the whole matter be sent to the Commons Committee on Privileges and Elections which, in effect, would have constituted a tribunal to determine whether or not the Prime Minister of Canada had lied. The Speaker ruled against this motion and was upheld 122-105.

PUBLIC HEARINGS OF THE SPECIAL INQUIRY into the government's involvement with Lucien Rivard began in the Board of Transport Commissioners' Ottawa courtroom on December 15, 1964. Dorion turned out to be a stern, unyielding presence, always fair even though his unusual mandate placed him in the position of having to be both judge and jury on the careers of the dozen men involved. During eleven weeks of hearings sixty-six witnesses and seventeen lawyers gave their testimony to the inquiry. Though proof in law requires the establishment of facts beyond reasonable doubt, this was not always possible and the judge often had to rely on circumstantial evidence. ("Where the version of one witness is contradicted by that of another," Dorion wrote in his report, "we must have recourse to circumstantial evidence to determine where the truth lies, and frequently circumstantial evidence constitutes a much more convincing proof of what actually occurred than are testimonies given by witnesses, particularly when they have an interest at stake in the litigation.")

The inquiry's most poignant moment occurred on March 24 when Guy Favreau entered the witness box. He had arrived in Ottawa only two years before, a man full of promise, his black hair becomingly touched with grey, his future golden. Now he was distraught, his hair nearly white, his future clouded. He had been unable (and never was able, as it turned out) to recover from the intense strain of those three weeks when he was allowed to shoulder full blame for the "forgotten" conversation of September 2. Ever since November 23 when Nielsen made his original charges, Favreau had been under fire in Parliament, harassed beyond endurance by angry Tories trying to deepen the guilt he already felt for involving the government in the whole shoddy business. Nearly every editorial writer in the country had called for his resignation at least once.

In his testimony before the Dorion Commission, Favreau displayed something of the irresolute alertness of a forest animal baffled by contradictory warning signals, strained to a point where normal reflexes were no longer his to command. The burden of his defence was that "this young man [Raymond Denis] was the head of a family. It was going to be in the order of things that he would lose his position. In my opinion it was not justified to take criminal action against him because I was convinced it would not lead to a conviction. It would have been so easy to have washed my hands of the affair and without regard of the consequences against him, to have caused charges to be laid." This was the compassionate position of a compassionate man. But it could also be interpreted less generously as the action of a Justice Minister anxious to save his government the political embarrassment of scandal.

ON MARCH 2, THE DAY HE WOUND UP his Ottawa sessions before moving on to hearings in Montreal, Mr Justice Dorion threw a party for the reporters who had been covering the inquiry. The festivities ended abruptly when Dave McIntosh of Canadian Press received a phone call from his bureau informing him that Lucien Rivard had just escaped from Bordeaux Jail. Dorion himself seemed unperturbed at the news. "I suppose," the judge quipped, "he was getting fed up waiting for his bail to be approved."

At 6:20 that evening Rivard with another prisoner, André Durocher, had received permission from Guard Sergeant Roger Beaupré to water the jail's skating rink – even though the outside temperature was 40 degrees above zero and the rink was already full of water. Rivard and Durocher used the hose to slide down the prison walls, hitched a ride with a passing motorist and disappeared.* Daniel Johnson, then opposition leader in the Quebec Legislature, commented that the escape has made "Quebec a laughing stock in all Canada, in all America and even in the whole universe."†

For a while, Rivard was a folk hero and his flashy wife Marie a gun-moll heroine in the manner of Bonnie of *Bonnie and Clyde*. Ann-Marie Fauteux even wrote a song about the "Gallic Pimpernel":

> *The search goes on relentless,*
> *Through valley, hill and dell,*
> *They seek him here, they seek him there,*
> *That Gallic Pimpernel.*
> *For years to come in Crooksville*
> *They'll tell the epic tale,*
> *How Rivard left his footprints*
> *On the walls of Bordeaux Jail.*

Though Bordeaux Jail is under provincial jurisdiction the escape prompted a fury of renewed attacks on the government, with Tory M.P.'s charging that Favreau was the man who "let Rivard go." Prodded by Jack Pickersgill, Favreau now began to use old Justice Department

*Although Rivard might have fled anywhere in the world, nobody took the trouble to notify Interpol, the international police organization, until a full four days after his breakout.

†It turned out later that Rivard and Durocher hid in the St Donat area of the Laurentians with a fugitive bank robber and his mistress. The robber and the woman were murdered. Durocher, who was suspected of the crimes, hanged himself in jail while awaiting trial. Rivard was recaptured on July 16. He was eventually extradited and sentenced in Laredo, Texas, to a twenty-year jail term for "masterminding a giant narcotics ring."

files to attempt a shoddy counter-attack of his own. He lamely tried to prove that the Tories had also attempted to subvert the course of justice by producing an irrelevant charge that Walter Dinsdale had once pleaded with the Justice Department to delay charges pending against one of his constituents. Favreau also dug out files against William Grant and Joseph Armishaw, two Indian agents in the Yukon on whose behalf Erik Nielsen had made representations.*

In the months after Nielsen's charges the administration's composure gradually disintegrated under the pressure of opposition attacks. The Liberal Government was not in real danger of falling, partly because few opposition politicians (including some Conservatives) could face the alternative of bringing John Diefenbaker back into office, and partly because scandals only bring down governments if they provide proof of a basic absence of integrity already suspected by the public. In this case, as Richard J. Gwyn pointed out in his excellent full-length study of the incident,† "It would be hard to imagine anything more remote from Lester Pearson himself, or from the group of experienced professional politicians and former university professors, civil servants and successful businessmen which constitutes his Cabinet, than the welter of squalid scandals that erupted during the winter of 1964-65. Yet they happened. A government with the foresight to devise policies as imaginative as 'co-operative federalism' was also blind enough to foster the worst political scandals Ottawa had known in more than thirty years."

Because the idea of being involved in shady manipulations with Mafia gangsters was so foreign to most Liberals, they reacted – at the beginning at least – by dismissing the scandals as a political commonplace, started by those dastardly Tories, and blown up by a headline-hungry press. They pretended both to themselves and to the public that the scandals really amounted to little more than a lifting of the lid on the kind of pork-barrel politics that has been practised in Ottawa under every regime since Confederation. "They're only little scandals, if you can say they're scandals at all," Judy LaMarsh said in a Vancouver interview.

Certainly the headline writers had a field day and there was little

*The men had used government relief funds for such non-regulation purposes as providing emergency housing for Indians. In a trial concluded in June 1965, Armishaw was acquitted. Grant was fined ten dollars, though the judge commended him as "an exceptional man who had risked his career to do what his conscience told him."

†*The Shape of Scandal: A Study of a Government in Crisis* (Clarke, Irwin and Company Limited, 1965).

doubt that John Diefenbaker and most of his colleagues reacted to the sordid outpourings with more delight than anger. If the Liberals behaved like a party whose morals were temporarily in petrification, the Conservatives acted as if their morals were in eruption. At the same time, the charges brought against the Pearson administration by the Opposition were very much more serious than partisan sallies.

THIS BECAME CLEAR ON JUNE 29 when Frédéric Dorion's report was tabled by the government. It was an unexpectedly harsh indictment of the Rivard affair's central figures. The judge found no difficulty in believing that a bribe had been offered to release Rivard. He wrote: "There cannot be any doubt that Lawyer Denis did offer Lawyer Lamontagne the sum of $20,000 to obstruct the course of justice." He also found that Marie Rivard, Eddy Lechasseur, Robert Gignac and Guy Masson "conspired to obstruct the course of justice." Guy Rouleau's conduct was termed "a reprehensible act." Guy Lord had "acted imprudently" and André Letendre's involvement was "reprehensible without malicious intent." René Tremblay was exonerated.*

The harshest verdict was reserved for Guy Favreau, not because it accused him of any wrong-doing, but because it questioned his judgement, and no man whose judgement is suspect can remain the country's Minister of Justice. In his summation Dorion maintained that on September 18, when he chose not to proceed with the case, Favreau "did not have sufficient knowledge to reach the proper decision about whether to lay charges" and he should therefore "have submitted the case to the legal advisers within his department."

The Pearson Government had a long time to prepare itself for the Dorion Report but its findings unaccountably caught the administration by surprise. George Street, chairman of the National Parole Board, was in Favreau's office when a Privy Council official gave him a copy

---

*Denis was charged on two counts – one of corruptly offering a sum of money to Lamontagne and the other of attempting to obstruct justice. His first trial, at which the Crown proceeded with the first count only, ended in a mistrial on March 30, 1966, in Ottawa. On December 15, 1967, also in Ottawa, he was convicted on the obstruction charge and sentenced to two years in prison. On December 22 an appeal was launched against the conviction. Gignac was sentenced in Montreal on October 18, 1966, to a prison term of two and a half years for perjury during the Dorion Inquiry. On January 18, 1968, the conviction was upset by the Quebec Court of Queen's Bench. Lechasseur was sentenced in Montreal on January 11, 1966, to seven months in jail and fined $1,000 for a fraudulent bankruptcy involving $40,000.

of the Dorion findings early in the morning of June 29. Favreau excused himself, read the section that applied to him, immediately dictated a preliminary letter of resignation to a weeping secretary and then went up to see his political mentor, Jack Pickersgill.

The day began in pathos and ended in confusion with a typical Pearson compromise which neither exonerated Guy Favreau nor cleansed the administration. Cabinet was hastily assembled for three hectic sessions. The final decision on Favreau's future was reached only an hour before the Prime Minister rose to announce its details to a hushed Commons.

Favreau had offered his resignation to Lester Pearson in mid morning, shortly after his consultation with Pickersgill. He stayed away from the eleven o'clock cabinet meeting, where there was a great deal of confused comment and advice, with the Quebec ministers unanimous in their view that Favreau should remain in Justice and fight for his political redemption. This was also Pearson's original stand. But in his meetings with Favreau, he found the minister determined to leave Justice. At the same time, Favreau expressed his willingness to remain a member of the ministry and his desire to stay in active politics. In a final effort to persuade Favreau that he should not move out of Justice, the Quebec ministers met independently and urged him to reconsider. The compromise – to accept Favreau's resignation from the Justice portfolio but not from the ministry – was approved by the cabinet over the objections of its Quebec members around six o'clock. At 7 p.m. Pearson announced to Parliament that Favreau was resigning but because he "remains a man and a minister of unimpeachable integrity and unsullied honour, I have asked him to consider the acceptance of another post."

In all this political uproar the personal tragedy of Guy Favreau had to take second place. The desperation of his situation could be measured by the fact that his retirement from politics would inevitably have been interpreted as a personal admission of guilt in the scandal that led up to the Dorion Commission; his dismissal from Cabinet would have amounted to a verdict of guilt from his colleagues. The choice he made left him shorn of his power yet struggling to retain his honour. His chief sin seems to have been a misguided attempt to protect minor political hacks, who took advantage of his incapacity for ruthlessness. It was in the service of this understandable, if not excusable, objective that Favreau refrained from allowing the full force of the Justice Department to come to bear on the events that were reported to him.

The Justice Minister's poignant letter of resignation summed up his position:

My Dear Prime Minister:

Since our talk this morning when my offer of resignation was discussed, I have given very serious consideration to your request, supported by our colleagues, that I continue in the Government.

As I have already stated to you, it is my view that the conclusions of the report, as far as I am concerned, are tantamount to no more than a statement on the part of the Commissioner that, had he been in my place, he would have exercised his discretion in a different fashion.

I wish to repeat that my resignation was tendered, not out of a feeling that I had done anything wrong, but because of the feeling that my usefulness as Minister of Justice had been impaired by the situation which has developed.

I need not say how deeply moved I am at the confidence which you, Mr Prime Minister, and my colleagues have shown me in suggesting that I carry on.

Therefore, while I must insist that my resignation be accepted as Minister of Justice, I would be willing to continue to serve in some other capacity.

May I take this occasion to say how very grateful I am for your kindness and consideration and for your unfailing support during difficult and, at times, even cruel days.

Yours faithfully,
GUY FAVREAU

When Favreau left the House that day he was mobbed by sympathetic Liberal members. Patting him on his broad back and joking as they swept him ahead of them, the parliamentarians flocked into the Justice Minister's office for drinks. It turned into a gay party which went on well past midnight. Outside, on the Parliament Hill lawns, a CBC crew was rehearsing for the annual July 1 extravaganza. As the party inside the Justice Minister's office grew more boisterous, its sounds were mixed with blaring of trumpets and thumping of drums from the Dominion Day rehearsal. The flashing television klieg lights threw the crazy shadows of scantily clad girls doing their dance routines on the grey walls of the Parliament Buildings as Guy Favreau's public trial came, at last, to an end.

ONE REASON THE RIVARD SCANDAL had such a far-reaching impact on public opinion was that the climate it created forced out into the open several other examples of questionable behaviour by the Liberals. Some of these dubious incidents actually happened before Pearson took office, others were part of the same climate of influence-peddling that had allowed Lucien Rivard to reach so far into important government offices. They included:

The Shadow of Hal Banks

IN MONTREAL, WHEN HAROLD CHAMBERLAIN BANKS was still functioning as the despotic head of the Seafarers' International Union, Canadian District, he always sent his thugs out to help Liberal candidates on election day. On June 30, 1954, when Banks was about to be deported from Canada, Walter Harris, then Liberal Minister of Immigration, personally reversed the ruling of his own department. In a television interview with Pierre Berton on November 22, 1964, Lester Pearson admitted that some of his Montreal M.P.'s had received electoral funds from the SIU. Banks himself, after a decade of investigation by the RCMP, was charged with the non-extraditable offence of conspiracy to commit assault and sentenced to five years in prison but in July 1964, while free on a paltry $25,000 bail, he skipped to the United States.

Banks had been brought to Canada by the Liberal Government in 1949 to drive the Communist-led Canadian Seamen's Union, then engaged in a lengthy strike that was holding back Marshall Plan supplies, out of the Great Lakes. Though he had a long criminal record, including a fourteen-year sentence to San Quentin prison (of which he served three and a half years), he was allowed to remain in Canada for the next fifteen years, gradually building up a personal empire based on terrorism and corruption which were more than adequately documented in the spring of 1963 by an inquiry into Great Lakes and St Lawrence shipping conducted by Mr Justice T. G. Norris of Vancouver. The RCMP sent the federal Justice Department two secret reports on Banks (on February 23, 1959, and June 14, 1961) but the Diefenbaker Government took no steps to prosecute him. In October 1963 the Liberals established a temporary trusteeship over the SIU. Banks himself disappeared until he was discovered on a yacht in Brooklyn harbour by Bob Reguly, a reporter with the *Toronto Daily Star*.

Exactly what hold Hal Banks had on the Canadian government was never clear but there could be little doubt that his charmed existence was not entirely accidental. Even when the Ontario government applied for his removal from the United States on perjury charges he was saved by the intervention of U.S. Secretary of State Dean Rusk, who overruled his own legal advisers and declined to issue an extradition warrant. The *Wall Street Journal* later revealed that Banks' union had contributed $100,000 to the Democratic Party. "I can buy any government," Banks once told an interviewer, and though he was by nature a boastful man this remark hardly seemed an exaggeration.

The Minaudo Intervention

ON NOVEMBER 30, 1964, JOHN DIEFENBAKER drew attention to a complaint, published by the Ontario Police Commission, that it had received no satisfactory reply to its urgent requests for Ottawa to supply information on "several immigrants living in Ontario with undesirable reputations and backgrounds of a criminal nature." The Police Commission had first written about the matter to Guy Favreau, then Minister of Immigration, on November 13, 1963. Four months later, on March 12, René Tremblay, who had meanwhile taken over the portfolio, wrote to say that Onofrio Minaudo, the most dangerous of these immigrants, had been deported from Canada the previous day. Apart from its confirmation of Favreau as a sloppy administrator, the issue seemed stillborn. But on December 16 Andrew Brewin of the NDP placed a long sequence of questions about Minaudo on the Commons order paper, including the query if anyone had made representations on his behalf.

The net had been cast and it yielded some strange fish. Minaudo's history reinforced the image of the government as being overly protective of certified hoodlums. Born in Sicily, Minaudo had been convicted of, among other crimes, murder, armed robbery and double murder. Sentenced in absentia to life imprisonment, he had emigrated illegally in 1924 to the United States, where he became a Mafia lieutenant and suspected murderer. A Detroit police commissioner had named Minaudo as a key figure in the Detroit-Windsor Mafia complex which grossed an estimated $200 millions a year from murder, assault, extortion, prostitution and bootlegging. Minaudo had come to Canada three times. After his final entry, on June 25, 1960, he had settled in Windsor, established a bakery, and applied for landed immigrant status. A deportation order had been issued against him on February 9, 1961, but it had not been acted on until more than three years later when the Ontario Police Commission brought his case to the public's attention.

The long delay could only be explained by the stature of some of the politicians who had made representations on Minaudo's behalf. They had included D. F. Brown, a former Liberal M.P. from Windsor, Richard Thrasher, a Conservative member from the district, and Paul Martin. The External Affairs Secretary proclaimed his innocence, claiming that he was not aware of Minaudo's character until he had read a story about his activities in a 1963 issue of *Maclean's*. Immigration Department files, however, showed that on December 7, 1960, after Martin had made one of his many telephone calls on Minaudo's behalf, F. D. Collins, a departmental administrative assistant, had written him to warn "that the history of this man as known to us and authorities in other countries isn't quite simply the one he makes out in the affidavit supplied through his solicitor." Martin continued his representations and was reported to have received five hundred dollars in legal fees.

Because the case involved members of both parties, the Conservatives refrained from making much of an issue of Minaudo's strangely delayed deportation order. Interviewed at Custonaci in Sicily following his deportation, Minaudo claimed that he had been thrown out of Canada to cover up payoffs he had made to high Ottawa officials. "Whether I paid members of Parliament or government officials, and I'm not saying which it was, certainly it was somebody powerful enough to push the Immigration Department around," he told Mack Laing of the Toronto *Telegram*. On May 17, 1965, Minaudo was found dead, a bullet in his heart, outside a farmhouse in Custonaci.

The Asselin Diversion

BEFORE HE WAS ELECTED A LIBERAL M.P. in 1962, Edmund Tobin "Eddy" Asselin was a real-estate operator and city councillor in Montreal. In 1961, together with a partner, he took an option to buy a property he knew was required by the Protestant School Board of Greater Montreal, at forty-five cents a square foot. Without purchasing the land himself, Asselin sold it to the board at sixty cents a square foot. The Montreal Catholic School Commission was buying up land in the same area at the time for thirty-five cents. Asselin and his partner realized a profit of $87,605 on the deal. The school board later complained that he was acting as its agent and was merely entitled to a nominal commission. A provincial inquiry into the transaction accused Asselin of having made an "unlawful and unconscionable" profit but when the board sued Asselin to get its money back, the Quebec Superior Court judge declared he had "searched in vain for some motive to cast any blame whatsoever upon the defendant [Asselin] . . ." and dismissed the action with costs against the board.

The fact that Asselin had, even though acting legally, made a large profit at the expense of a public body made him the target of attacks by members of the Canadian University Liberal Federation, which passed a motion demanding his resignation. When Pearson was confronted by the question of how he could reconcile Asselin's presence in Parliament with his own Code of Ethics,* he replied: "I won't even try. . . . Mr Asselin himself feels there is no irreconcilability." This prompted George Bain, the witty columnist for the *Globe and Mail*, to compare the Liberal morality code to "an insurance policy that they pay on only if you're run down by a left-handed Polynesian driving a Stutz Bearcat."

On June 1, 1965, Asselin tried to read into the Commons record the judgement that had exonerated him but it was too late. He had become a serious liability to his party and on July 22, still protesting innocence, he resigned his seat.

The Dupuis Case

YVON DUPUIS BECAME THE ONLY MINISTER in Canadian history fired from a federal cabinet to face criminal charges. Other public men had left under clouds but their departures were always masked in polite terms and presented to the public as resignations.

Unlike most of the defendants involved in the Pearson administration's scandals, Dupuis went down scratching and fighting. Elected to the Quebec Legislature when he was only twenty-six, Dupuis had led some of the first verbal attacks on the awesome Maurice Duplessis. Eventually defeated by the Union Nationale machine, he went into federal politics in 1958 and sat in the Commons for an uneventful five years. He first came to public notice during the 1963 campaign when the Liberals enlisted his loud stage presence to out-shout Réal Caouette on the rural hustings of Quebec. He did imitations of "Caouette's good friends – Hitler and Mussolini," threw fistfuls of play money into the crowd to mock Social Credit's monetary theories and generally harangued the crowds into supporting Liberal candidates. Even though he'd been warned by several Quebec colleagues of Dupuis' political shortcomings, Pearson accepted Chevrier's recommendation and promoted him into the cabinet on February 3, 1964. Dupuis' only recorded accomplishment was to represent Canada in a ground-breaking ceremony for Colombo International Airport at Katunayaka in Ceylon, built with Canadian external aid funds.

Two weeks after Dupuis had been appointed to the cabinet, Eric

*The document setting out Pearson's Code of Ethics was drafted by Tom Kent and Gordon Robertson, the Clerk of the Privy Council, and was sent to Liberal cabinet ministers on November 30, 1964. Its key paragraph stated: "It is by no means sufficient for a person in the office of a minister – or in any other position in the public service – to act within the law. That goes without saying. Much more is required. There is an obligation not simply to observe the law but to act in a manner so scrupulous that it will bear the closest public scrutiny."

Kierans, then Revenue Minister in the Quebec government, told Jean Lesage that he suspected the new federal minister of having accepted a $10,000 bribe in 1961 to facilitate the obtaining of a licence for a new racetrack in his home riding near St Jean, Quebec. Lesage passed on the information to Pearson. Nothing happened.

In the fall of that year, when the Rivard scandals broke, the Quebec administration became concerned that, weighted down by one more scandal, the Pearson Government would fall before it could pass the important opting-out legislation allowing Quebec to abstain from federal programs while receiving compensating payments. During a private meeting at the PM's residence on December 7, Lesage strongly urged Pearson to fire Dupuis before the charges were revealed and warned him that only the strike at *La Presse* was preventing their publication. He also pointed out that the provincial legislature would reconvene on January 21, 1965, when he expected the Union Nationale opposition to mention the Dupuis case.

After this meeting Pearson finally called Dupuis into his office and gave him two weeks to produce evidence why an RCMP investigation into the racetrack charges should not be begun. Kierans turned over some of his evidence on the case to Guy Favreau on December 17. When he was shown the letters that Dupuis had produced in his own defence, Kierans bluntly told Favreau they had to be forgeries.* The main point at issue was the claim by Roch Deslauriers, a St Jean chiropractor, that in 1961 he had passed "a present of $10,000" to Dupuis as a payoff to four Quebec City Revenue Department officials charged with chartering racetracks in the province. Kierans' private investigation had established to his own satisfaction that no members of his department had, in fact, been involved. When Kierans had confronted Dupuis with this conclusion on February 14, 1964, the Ottawa minister insisted he'd received a brown paper package containing money, which he had given to an unknown man claiming to represent the Department of Revenue in a hotel corridor. Kierans' parting shot was a revealing insight into both his integrity and his toughness. He warned Dupuis that if the $10,000 was not reported as part of his 1961 income, the Quebec government would assess him for the tax on it.

*During Dupuis' trial an RCMP sergeant testified that the correspondence, all relating to the alleged 1961 bribery attempt, had been written on a brand-new 1964 Royal typewriter. Roch Deslauriers, the racetrack promoter, told the court that Dupuis had dictated a series of "fake" letters to him on December 16, 1964, in an attempt to convince Favreau and Pearson that he was innocent. He also described how Dupuis had sent him out to rent a typewriter and the rental manager of an Ottawa office-equipment store corroborated that he had been given a 1964 Royal machine.

282

By Christmas 1964 Pearson finally agreed that the RCMP should look into the affair and put Guy Favreau in charge. On January 17, 1965, Pearson called Dupuis into his office, told him the preliminary RCMP reports were unfavourable and asked him to resign. Dupuis refused. But five days later, prompted by the partial disclosure of the facts in the *Toronto Daily Star*, Pearson fired his minister by issuing a press release that stated: "Effective today, Mr Dupuis is no longer a member of the Government." Pearson then telephoned Dupuis, who was at home in St Jean, and with uncharacteristic bluntness said: "I'm not calling you to argue. I'm asking for your resignation. I am the Prime Minister. I name my ministers. I am demanding your resignation. I have the right to do so." Dupuis hung on for the rest of the day, then sent in his resignation.

Early in March the former Minister without Portfolio was formally charged on three counts of influence-peddling. After six weeks of lengthy, often contradictory testimony, Dupuis was found guilty and fined five thousand dollars or a year in jail. The strangest moment of the trial occurred when Guy Favreau took the stand. At the conclusion of his testimony he walked over to Dupuis, shook his hand, and in a loud voice heard through the courtroom, wished his colleague *"Bonne chance."*

Dupuis appealed his sentence. On April 16, 1968, he was acquitted, mainly on the ground that during the first trial counsel for the Crown had brought "before the jury various matters which had no direct relation to the question of the Appellant's guilt but which might be expected to arouse prejudice against him in the mind of one or more of the jurors." Finished as a politician, Dupuis was easily beaten as an independent in the 1965 election.

The Stonehill Caper

HARRY S. STONEHILL was a blunt, beefy Chicagoan who had made a postwar fortune out of shady dealings in the Philippines and wanted to settle in Canada. Diosdado Macapagal, the Philippine President, who personally signed his deportation order on August 3, 1962, accused Stonehill of "economic sabotage, blackmail and corruption," claiming that his continued presence constituted "an immediate and continuing menace to the peace, welfare and security of the country." Because Section 61 (f) of the Canadian Immigration Act prohibits the admission of persons who have been deported, Stonehill's attempt to gain Canadian citizenship ought to have been a fairly simple matter for the Immigration Minister to decide. Yet Stonehill managed to get in on a visitor's visa and stay for eighteen months. But for the fact that his case became public and that a senior civil servant risked his job to keep the government honest, Stonehill would probably have succeeded in subverting the regulations.

Following his expulsion from the Philippines, Stonehill went briefly to Mexico but after he had been declared *persona non grata* there he decided to settle in British Columbia. He bought a $60,000 house in Vancouver and became friendly with the Social Credit Government. To help push his application for landed immigrant status, he hired Al Williamson, a Vancouver public relations consultant and confidant of Premier W. A. C. Bennett. Williamson contacted Hal Dornan, a friend from his days as a newspaperman then working as an aide in Prime Minister Pearson's office. Dornan arranged a meeting for Williamson with Raymond Denis, the executive assistant to René Tremblay, then Minister of Immigration. When the three men were sipping coffee in the parliamentary cafeteria on the morning of July 3, 1964, Williamson mentioned that Stonehill proposed to sponsor substantial business investments in British Columbia. Denis seemed interested and remarked, "It's too bad he [Stonehill] wouldn't invest $25,000 or $30,000 in us." Dornan, shocked by the implications of Denis' statement, replied: "I sometimes find it difficult to tell the difference between Quebec humour and Quebec politics."

The story, first published by *Time*, seemed to end there, though Denis later admitted he had passed on some departmental information about Stonehill to Senator Louis Gélinas, treasurer of the federal Liberal Party in Quebec. But efforts to grant Stonehill his citizenship continued. It was mainly the stubborn, incorruptible attitude of Claude Isbister, then Deputy Minister of Immigration, which brought these secret negotiations to an end. Isbister made it very clear that if Stonehill's application were approved he would resign and say why. It was under this pressure that Stonehill finally left the country in January of 1965.

One of the documents Williamson sent Dornan to support Stonehill's application had been a letter signed "W. A. C. Bennett." The British Columbia premier promptly denied that he had actually signed it and Williamson later admitted that he had written the body of the letter, transcribing it on a signed piece of stationery in his office. When Pearson was under pressure in the Commons to have the alleged forgery investigated, the Commissioner of the Royal Canadian Mounted Police had confided the fact to him that Williamson was a constable in the RCMP's civilian reserve who had been reporting to the force about Stonehill's activities. He begged the Prime Minister not to reveal that

Williamson was an RCMP agent in case this would shatter public confidence.

The matter was taken out of the federal government's hands when formal charges of forgery were laid against Williamson. On June 10, 1965, he was found guilty and sentenced to six months in jail. The judge went out of his way to comment that none of the evidence had reflected any discredit on Hal Dornan. The fact that Williamson was allowed to suffer for the involved machinations of the Social Credit Government prompted the *Vancouver Province* to describe the incident as "one of the most squalid and contemptible episodes in British Columbia's history."

The Furniture Deals

PROBABLY THE MOST DEPRESSING ASPECT of the proliferating Liberal scandals was the small-time ugliness of cut-rate furniture trading with questionable characters on the fringe of the Quebec underworld involving René Tremblay and the country's *ex officio* Minister of Culture, Maurice Lamontagne. In a way this was both the most damaging and the most petty of all the allegations. Max and Adolph Sefkind, the Montreal businessmen involved, had received nothing in return for granting the ministers compromisingly easy terms on their furniture. But because it was the kind of situation – the buying of furniture – familiar to everybody it was this scandal that probably undermined the administration most.

The affair started on November 30, 1964, when Donald MacInnis, the combative Tory from Glace Bay, N.S., acting on an anonymous note, placed on the Commons order paper a question regarding the involvement of unnamed Liberal ministers in the bankruptcy, earlier that year, of the Sefkind brothers' Montreal operation. MacInnis' question prompted George Brimmell of Southam News Services and Paul Akehurst of CHUM, the Toronto radio station, to make further inquiries, which eventually led them to the office of Maurice Lamontagne. He admitted that he had taken delivery of two lots of furniture worth $6,800 from Union Upholstering, a Sefkind company, and that he had made no payment until the Bank of Montreal (the Sefkinds' main creditor) had sent him a bill and arranged to receive two-hundred-dollar monthly instalments.

On December 8, the day the Lamontagne story broke in the newspapers, René Tremblay called a press conference to admit that he too had bought furniture worth $3,935 from Futurama Furniture, another Sefkind subsidiary. Although some of the furniture, including a loveseat, had still not been delivered, Tremblay had paid for his purchases in full to the Bank of Montreal. Tremblay compounded the unwarranted appearance of guilt by protesting (though no one had asked him about it) that there wasn't any connection between his furniture purchase and the fact that, as Deputy Minister of Industry in the Lesage Government, he had approved a $1.2 million loan to Rec-Stone Corporation, yet another Sefkind operation.

This was John Diefenbaker's favourite scandal. "The situation has all the appearance of political upholstery," he told the Commons on December 18 in mock seriousness. "Furnish us with the facts!" twitted another Conservative frontbencher, as the Liberals drooped in their parliamentary seats. Lamontagne and Tremblay rose to give their halting explanations. It was a sad spectacle to watch Maurice Lamontagne, the great anti-Duplessis reformer, reveal the untidy details of his personal finances, ending with this advice to his fellow M.P.'s: "Should you want to buy furniture, pay cash."

Lamontagne made a strong case proving that his intentions had in no way been dishonourable but his behaviour could not be made compatible with Pearson's own Code of Ethics. It had explicitly warned ministers that they must never "place themselves in a position where they are under obligation to any person who might profit from special consideration or favour on their part." Although both Tremblay and Lamontagne stayed in the cabinet for a year following the furniture transaction disclosures, their political careers had been forfeited.

THIS PROCESSION OF GRUBBY REVELATIONS and scandalous allegations that clouded the Ottawa scene for so many months revealed a great deal about Lester Pearson, both as a man and as a politician.

His reactions were based on a strictly legalistic interpretation of each scandal as it occurred. "I won't destroy a man just because he's made a mistake and I won't inflict injustice in the name of justice," he commented at the time. When he was finally forced into being ruthless, he was clumsy, ruefully aware that his own permissiveness had been partly responsible for the whole mess. He had delegated too much authority and freedom to ministers without the accompanying discipline.

Dodging unpleasant situations – however minor – had always been a Pearson characteristic. "Dad was a poor disciplinarian. When we got into mischief he was likely to melt away or disappear behind his newspaper," recalled his daughter, Mrs Walter Hannah.* As Secretary of

*In *Chatelaine*, September, 1963.

State for External Affairs, Pearson got his deputy, A. D. P. Heeney, to look after whatever firing of personnel had to be done. He was hesitant to judge people and consequently not perceptive about their weaknesses, preferring to like everyone until he had been given plenty of reason to think otherwise.

Two traumatic events in Pearson's own past had contributed to his reluctance either to act on accusations not fully established by law or to condemn men for making political mistakes. The suicide in 1957 of his friend and colleague Herbert Norman had taught Pearson the bitter effectiveness of innuendo. His own monumentally inept motion of no confidence of January 20, 1958, had made him deal with the political bloopers of his ministers with a modifying awareness of his own limitations.

This was a commendable humanitarian attitude but it removed from the governmental process one of the essential functions of the office Pearson occupied. "It is one of the sure signs of an able prime minister," wrote Professor MacGregor Dawson, the foremost scholar of Canadian politics, "that he will have the courage and toughness to get rid of men who have ceased to be assets."

Despite intermittent efforts by Erik Nielsen to revive the sport in which he had achieved such a high score, no further misdeeds were pinned on the Liberals. Probably the greatest long-term value of the whole episode was that for a concentrated instant of history the scandal investigations tore away the screen of discretion that usually hides the inner manipulations of political Ottawa, giving the nation a shuddering look at the underworld's ability to win friends and protectors in high places.

The wave of scandals passed. But it left a record of its stay. It would always remain on the charts of Lester Pearson's accomplishments, like a buoy that marks the position of a wreck.

PART FIVE   *Emancipation of Power*

It was one of the ironies of the Pearson period that even though individual Quebec politicians caused the Prime Minister considerable grief, his dealings with French Canadians collectively showed him at his diplomatic best. No matter how history finally judges him, there can be little doubt that Lester Pearson provided the essential moderating influence that helped bring under at least temporary control the centrifugal forces threatening to split English and French Canada apart during the mid Sixties.

By personally identifying himself with the broad goals of Quebec's social upheaval, Pearson helped hold the country together at a crucial time in its history, effecting an important national transition without a national convulsion. In the process he uncovered no magic antidotes to the toxins of Quebec separatism. But by yielding to most of their nationalistic demands, he deprived the province's separatists of the oppressive target they needed to give legitimacy to their militant claims.

It was a process without order or grandeur. At times Pearson's transactions with Quebec politicians had about them an air of desperation reminiscent of the cry uttered by the nineteenth-century French nationalist Alexandre Ledru-Rollin, who was heard to shout amid the confusion of a rioting mob during the February Revolution in 1848: "I've got to follow them – I am their leader!"

Because time, training and temperament prevented Pearson from portraying his own role in a politically appealing manner, critics in English Canada condemned him for staging what appeared to be a *badly managed retreat in the face of Quebec's demands. At the same time, many French-Canadian nationalists, dreaming big dreams and longing for the power to fulfil them, despised him for his fumbling appeasement.*

But Pearson knew very well what was at stake and what had to be done. Aware that in certain circumstances a policy of desperation can be quite as valid as a policy of confidence, he went about improvising new approaches, trying to find a way of allowing Quebec politicians to work out their problems within Confederation. Unable to champion a bipartisan approach to Ottawa-Quebec negotiations because of John Diefenbaker's intransigence, he even moved ahead of his own party on the issue. His dealings on national unity were essentially a Pearsonian activity rather than a Liberal enterprise. (The Liberal Party's most vocal anti-Quebecker was Ralph Cowan, the M.P. for York-Humber. When Harry Bruce of Maclean's during a 1964 interview remarked that it seemed to be fairly quiet in the Parliament Buildings, Cowan replied: "I'll tell you why it's quiet. It's quiet because Pearson's giving the Frenchmen every blankety-blank thing they want. They go home at night and dream it up. They ask for it in the morning and, in the afternoon, Pearson gives it to them.")

Pearson regarded the issue of French-English relations as transcending all others. He had the courage to stand out against the hysteria of prejudiced men in both language groups, skilfully propitiating their impulses until he had diverted their power to break up the country.

While he did fumble and he did appease, there was in Pearson's dealings with Quebec a reawakening of the skills that he had used with such impressive results in world councils before becoming a politician. He felt confident in his handling of Quebec-Ottawa relations because he regarded the bargaining involved as a contest between sovereignties, something that had become very familiar to him during nearly thirty years as a diplomat. By treating relations between Quebec and the rest of Canada as an exercise in foreign affairs involving the clash of nationalistic forces, he was able to make the large adjustments involved and to sponsor his own version of a political cease-fire. In much the same way as during the Suez crisis of 1956, he was the pivotal outsider keeping both sides talking and sponsoring a way out of each impasse, getting the antagonists to subscribe to his formula even though neither side had a very clear idea of exactly what it was accepting.

None of the tough problems of disunity were actually resolved. But just as in his Suez solution he temporarily prevented a shooting war, Pearson gained the vital time for a more enduring settlement of Canada's internal problems.

Instead of being the prime minister, defending the federal interest, he acted as a kind of secretary general of Canada, more concerned with reaching a modus vivendi among the provinces than any clear-cut exposition of Ottawa's pre-eminence. He acted as if he saw a clear parallel between Canada (a group of interdependent regions) and the United Nations (a group of interdependent nations).

Pearson applied his UN *methods and training at federal-provincial conferences where, far from the furious gaze of John Diefenbaker, he could cast himself as a mediator between Ottawa and the provincial premiers, drawing up "treaties" that participating governments would later ratify. In these negotiations, he banged no gavels and followed no charter. He would call the conferences to order by hitting a water glass with his fountain pen. Draft proposals were prepared and then amended to meet provincial objections. The simultaneous translation system added further to the international conference atmosphere.*

The Liberal administration's dependence on federal-provincial conferences was so great that the meetings turned into a kind of super-parliament, an extra level of government. Some form of federal-provincial bargaining went on almost every day. During its first eighteen months in office, the Pearson Government held 114 federal-provincial consultations at all levels, more than had been called during the entire six years of the Diefenbaker administration. "Federal-provincial conferences are becoming the real seats of power – the places at which national policies are set in private to guide eleven governments," wrote Anthony Westell in the Globe and Mail. "There is no legislature of equivalent authority and prestige to check and balance this exercise of executive power."

Pearson's methods may have been constitutionally questionable but in his quiet way he achieved a fundamental rearrangement in the national structure. A measure of how far Pearson was able to bring his government – and the nation – toward recognizing Quebec's aspirations was that near the beginning of his time in office (on July 8, 1963) George McIlraith, then Minister of Transport, rose in the Commons to explain that the name of Trans-Canada Air Lines could not be changed to Air Canada because the cost of repainting the aircraft fuselages was too high. This evasive statement was accepted without comment but everyone knew the real cause for the government's hesitation was that giving the national airline a new French-sounding name might produce serious resentment in English Canada. Only fifty-five months later, in January of 1968, not only had the relatively trivial matter of the Air Canada name long since been settled, but the eleven heads of the country's governments reached agreement in Ottawa for linguistic equality across the nation and for what amounted to the eventual redrafting of the British North America Act to take Quebec's special wishes more directly into account – all with the general acceptance of English Canada.

No definitive verdict on the Pearson legacy in the volatile area of French-English relations is yet possible. But in judging Lester Pearson's performance it is difficult to disagree with the assessment of George Ferguson, editor-in-chief of the Montreal Star, who wrote in the April, 1968, issue of Round Table: "It can reasonably be said that Diefenbaker's fall and Pearson's 1963 arrival at the summit probably rescued Confederation. Pearson, his sensitive antennae delicately tuned, knew trouble when he felt it. . . . It is no exaggeration to say that another year or two of the Diefenbaker stand-pattism would have ended in rupture. What Pearson gained was time, and time was all important."

CHAPTER 21

The Revolt That Tried
to Become a Revolution

ARTHUR KOESTLER ONCE WROTE that the meaning of a revolution only becomes clear after fifty years: "It is like a process of distillation – the fumes evaporate, while the essence of the brew slowly gathers at the bottom." Using this criterion, it is much too early to trace the origins, define the limits or predict the outcome of the so-called quiet revolution that first agitated French Canada in 1960, or even to state whether it was a genuine revolution. Certainly there was bloodshed on a scale rare in Canada's placid history.* But what gave the quiet revolution its meaning was how quickly it produced an evolution in Quebec from one kind of society to another.†

*Casualties between the spring of 1963 and the fall of 1968 included: the death by bomb blast of night watchman Wilfred O'Neill on April 20, 1963, at a Canadian Army recruiting centre; the wounding of army paymaster J. J. Marcel Ste Marie on April 30, 1963, during a payroll robbery; the maiming on May 17, 1963, of Sergeant-Major Walter Leja while dismantling a bomb planted in a Westmount mailbox; the beating up of a 19-year-old waitress on January 11, 1964, who was found at St Michel with the letters FLQ written in blood on her breasts; the shooting of Leslie MacWilliams and Alfred Pinisch during an August 29, 1964, gun-shop raid in Montreal; the suicide in a Montreal jail of separatist Gilles Legault; the death in a time-bomb explosion in east-end Montreal of Thérèse Morin and the wounding of eight others on May 5, 1966; and the death of a young separatist, Jean Corbo, on July 14, 1966, when a bomb he was carrying went off prematurely.

†For a brilliant summary of the ideological and constitutional background of Quebec's quiet revolution see *Canada and the French-Canadian Question* by Ramsay Cook (The Macmillan Company of Canada Limited, Toronto, 1966).

The surge of French-Canadian nationalism set off in the process was radically different from previous manifestations under Honoré Mercier in the eighteen-eighties, Henri Bourassa in the early years of this century and the *Bloc Populaire* movement of World War II. Before 1960, Quebec's nationalism had been nourished by two intimately entwined forces: an understandable will of the people to preserve their French culture and the provincial government's paternalistic, basically reactionary objection to unsanctioned change of any kind. Maurice Duplessis had manipulated the folk memory of the Conquest to maintain in the province what Gérard Pelletier called "a state-of-siege mentality." Pierre Elliott Trudeau described this strategy as a play of opposites: "Against an environment English, Protestant, democratic, materialist, commercial and later industrial, our nationalism elaborated a system of defence dominated by the French language, Catholicism, authoritarianism, idealism, the rural life and later, a return to the soil."

By 1960, when Jean Lesage overthrew the Union Nationale Government, Quebec society was throbbing with long-repressed desires for a life radically different from the parish ideal. His electoral victory brought a feeling of liberation, a dynamic impulse to progress. By that year only 9 per cent of the Quebec labour force (compared with 13 per cent in the rest of Canada) was still in agriculture. Television, which had begun in the province eight years before, had brought the world into Quebec living rooms. Suddenly industrialization, education, and equal employment opportunities with the English became the dominant issues. Jean Lesage and his small retinue of progressive ministers seized on this mood. They were determined to go beyond anything Duplessis had dared to do in order to guarantee the survival of French-Canadian culture in North America but at the same time they pledged themselves to use the powers of the state to interfere powerfully on the side of the ordinary citizen. More than that, they decided to challenge the federal authority, asking not – as Quebec had in the past – for minor, symbolic concessions but for a genuine sharing of fiscal powers and, eventually, constitutional authority. What Lesage set out to accomplish was nothing less than the creation of a situation in which the rest of the country would accept, in fact and not just in theory, Quebec's concept of Canada as a nation that was no longer a homogeneous entity but the political home of two quite separate though not necessarily incompatible societies.

This meant that a movement that had initially been a revolt or revulsion against the lost Duplessis years gradually turned into something more positive and more important. A vocal minority in Quebec seriously took up the doctrine that the province could achieve its long-term aims only through political independence.

The reaction of most English Canadians to this sudden release of energy, to an acceleration of domestic history that they did not expect or welcome, was at first ill-concealed hostility. Their fear was based in part on the fundamental difference in public philosophies that divides Canadians. "Because they are a conquered people and a minority, French Canadians have always been chiefly concerned with group rights. The English Canadian, as is equally befitting his majority position, is far more concerned with that characteristic North American middle-class ideal: equality of opportunity. The English Canadian has, therefore, tended to look upon privileges asked for or granted to groups as inherently undesirable, indeed, undemocratic," wrote Ramsay Cook, the Canadian historian, in the Winter 1964-65 issue of *International Journal*. The Quebec nationalist argument was that communities can be integrated but individuals can only be assimilated, so that until Quebec became its own community, efforts to integrate its citizens would necessarily imply assimilation.

EXCEPT FOR OUTRIGHT SEPARATISTS and such ideologically committed politicians as René Lévesque, it was never clear exactly how important preservation of French-Canadian culture and expansion of provincial autonomy really were in the initial phase of the quiet revolution. While Lesage and his ministers rationalized their actions on the basis of advancing these twin objectives, the immediate effect of the revolt was to create a new ruling class – the technocrat-politicians of Quebec City who used nationalism as a vehicle for their journey into power. They were agents of reform but nationalism was more their tool than their objective. The movement was essentially a bourgeois venture that never grew into a genuine proletarian revolution and once the new élite had consolidated authority, its enthusiasm for innovation and experiment waned. The high degree of government intervention required to reform the society of Quebec helped to expand the reach and the influence of this new power structure.

Economic reality and administrative responsibility soon replaced nationalistic adventures and ideological stances. Most problems were eventually reduced to the need for monetary resources to finance Quebec's leap into the twentieth century. By 1963, provincial expenditures had reached $954 millions, which was $91 millions more than available revenues.* In three short years repeated deficits had doubled the provincial debt and it was costing Quebec nearly $2 millions a month merely to pay the interest. Education costs alone had jumped 100 per cent and would double again by 1968. Efforts at cutting government expenditures had become so desperate that in the spring of 1963 Lesage ordered a temporary postponement on refills for the fire extinguishers in provincial office buildings. Despite the money that was being pumped into the Quebec economy, the province's standard of living in 1963 was still 27 per cent below that of Ontario and fully 40 per cent of Canada's unemployed lived in Quebec.

Jean Lesage's main concern, during the six years he presided over Quebec affairs, was how to obtain adequate funds to pay for the many social reforms required to make up for the fifteen years of Maurice Duplessis' dismal under-financing of the province's facilities. He strained Quebec's borrowing capacity to the limit and taxed his people to an extent that eventually drove him out of office. But the bulk of the money had to come from the only other available source: the coffers of the federal treasury. It was this fiscal assault on Ottawa and the Pearson Government's response that provided the political battleground in French-English relations during a stormy half-decade.

THAT CANADA'S FEDERAL SYSTEM seemed to undergo a basic reorientation in the process was not in itself particularly disturbing. A federation of regions widely separated geographically and wildly disparate economically like Canada must, by its very nature, undergo periodic strains as its members compete for fiscal and constitutional authority. Although the 1963-68 crisis was serious – probably the gravest since 1867 – it represented only the most recent swing of a pendulum that had been moving since Canada was born.

The Confederation of 1867 – which brought together Nova Scotia, New Brunswick and the already united colonies of Canada East and Canada West – was no grand design conceived in a sudden burst of patriotism. It was a desperate gesture by the British North American colonies to counter the mounting economic difficulties that were threatening the survival of them all. The problems of each colony reached crisis proportions at the same time, and only in the sharing of burdens did there appear to be hope of solution.

In the two Canadas, efforts to draw the trade of the American Middle West down the St Lawrence River had failed and the debts

*This compared with expenditures of $553 millions and revenues of $556 millions for 1959, the last year in office of the Union Nationale Government.

incurred for the improvement of the St Lawrence system had destroyed the colonies' credit on the London money market. In the Maritimes, an economy based on the age of sail was crumbling in a new era of steel and steam. Great Britain's switch from imperial preferences to free trade and the final termination of reciprocity with the United States endangered the commerce of the struggling colonies. The United States, recovering from the Civil War, was showing signs of territorial ambition toward Canada while Britain was withdrawing its North American garrisons.

By uniting the colonies under a single government ("From Halifax to Sarnia!"), the Fathers of Confederation hoped they could escape what one of them called "our impending misfortunes." The BNA Act failed to bring much immediate relief but it did provide the vital framework in which a national destiny could be worked out. To create a state with strong central authority but also expressive of the regional and racial differences of the existing colonies, the men who drafted the British North America Act conceived a new kind of nation. Neither a kingdom nor a republic, it was to be a self-governing dominion with constitutional ties to the British Crown. It was to combine the British principles of responsible government (in which the executive is responsible to the legislature) with the American system of federal organization (in which sovereign powers are divided between central and local administrations). All the powers not specifically granted to the provinces were left with the federal authority – exactly the reverse of the United States constitution.

From the beginning there was constant conflict between national and regional loyalties. The Liberal Opposition in Ottawa under Alexander Mackenzie strove to reassert provincial rights – a movement strengthened by the long depression that began in 1873, throwing the economic viability of Confederation into serious doubt. By the Eighties provincial premiers were openly challenging the edicts of the federal government and, in most instances, their positions were confirmed by the decisions of the Privy Council in London.

The boom of 1901-11 brought an about-face. Overseas demand for grain and Sir Charles Saunders' discovery of rust-resistant wheat spurred the development of the Canadian West. The million immigrants to the Prairies provided a great new purchasing force, and booming wheat exports gave Canada's east-west transportation network its first important cargoes. Confederation was working at last. Provincial demands faded as the central government became the engine of national development.

World War I cut short the depression of 1913 and the urgencies of the international conflict strengthened federal power even further. Provincial grievances grew through the Twenties but the Great Depression of the Thirties once again increased Ottawa's power. Saskatchewan and Manitoba had to be rescued from the edge of bankruptcy by the central government, which also helped with national relief payments amounting to $750 millions. World War II brought centralization to its peak. The provinces rented the major part of their tax-collecting powers and Canada became virtually a unitary state. The fear of a postwar recession maintained Ottawa's power into the early Fifties and the boom that followed left most of the provinces too prosperous to engage in jurisdictional disputes.

By the mid Sixties, however, the whole system had been placed in jeopardy by the large gap between the intentions and the effects of the 1867 terms of Confederation that had developed during nearly a century of rapid change. The provinces, for example, had been originally charged with the intellectual and material development of their citizens but since pioneering colonists staunchly believed that individuals could be expected to work out their own destinies, unrestrained and unassisted by the state, all the money the provinces spent on social welfare in 1867 did not quite reach a million dollars. By 1963 welfare spending had topped four billion dollars a year. In the same period the invention of the automobile had pushed the provinces into highway construction – another financial burden not contemplated at the time of Confederation. But what really strained provincial treasuries to the breaking point in the Sixties was the entry into the expensive upper levels of the educational system of so large a proportion of the huge crop of postwar babies. As a result of these and other changes, all of the provinces – but Quebec in particular because it had a decade and a half of neglect to overcome – had to find new sources of revenue to fulfil their responsibilities.

THE PEARSON GOVERNMENT'S RESPONSE to these pressures was to improvise a policy called co-operative federalism, which was aimed at disarming its opponents through flexibility, pacification and an unabashed willingness to compromise its own position. Co-operative federalism was one of those vague Pearsonian concepts whose definition varied according to its user. Eldon Woolliams, the Alberta Tory, regularly referred to co-operative federalists as "the assassins of Confederation." George Davidson, then Secretary of the Treasury Board and later head of the CBC, once defined the co-operative federalist approach as "flying by the seat of your pants over terrain where there's no place to land. You have to keep aloft in order to avoid crashing." Jean-Luc Pépin, who was co-operative federalism's resident guru, defined it as involving co-operation between Ottawa and the provinces at three levels: pre-consultation in the formulation of federal policies; collaboration in the drafting of these policies; and co-ordination in their implementation.

This was a laudable ideal but it was basically incompatible with both the theory of the parliamentary system (which demands that policies be drawn up within the secrecy of the cabinet chamber, enunciated in a Throne Speech and only then thrown open to discussion) and the particular situation in which the Pearson administration found itself. In both the 1962 and 1963 elections, the Liberals had stressed that if elected, they would implement an impressive series of national measures. All of these schemes touched areas with at least partial provincial jurisdiction. The Liberal priorities – for a municipal loan fund, a contributory pension scheme, and medicare – were set even before the government assumed office. Each of the election planks was subjected to provincial pressure and each became a very different piece of legislation from its original conception. Co-operative federalism thus degenerated into a woolly catch-all used occasionally to harmonize federal-provincial initiatives, though the actual area of joint decision-making remained predictably narrow.

The federal government's attempt to find an accommodation with French Canada was based not on any preconceived or carefully thought-out interpretation of constitutional subtleties but on a pragmatic reaction to Quebec's demands. It became a frantic, surrealistic situation, with Jean Lesage triumphantly coming to the rescue at the last moment by championing dramatic proposals to solve the many impasses he himself had created. For the first three or four years of this kind of bargaining, Ottawa's bureaucrats appeared confused about how to deal with Quebec. They had never before faced a provincial government that was bursting with initiatives in the form of brilliantly detailed position papers and could field teams of able negotiators to put forward its point of view.

But Pearson knew intuitively that the ferment was serving its purpose: Quebec was getting the money it needed, and it was getting it within the framework of Confederation. Despite the many concessions made to please Lesage, Quebec did not receive anything to which it was not constitutionally entitled under the BNA Act. All of the arrangements made with Quebec were available to the other nine provinces.

Co-operative federalism's main drawback was that it dealt more with the manifestations than with the sources of Quebec's problems. Although Pearson did much to advance the cause of bilingualism and biculturalism, he stopped short of sharing real power with French Canadians. Until the last months of his time in office there were no Quebec advisers in his immediate entourage, no Quebec ministers were named to the senior economic portfolios and no French Canadians were promoted into the mandarin class within the civil service.

The main dividend of Pearson's policy was that it gained the nation time, both for English Canadians to accustom themselves to the idea of accepting basic changes in the constitutional structure of the country to meet Quebec's legitimate demands, and for French-Canadian moderates to reassure themselves that their aspirations would be respected.

JEAN LESAGE'S ASSAULTS ON OTTAWA had about them a certain swash-buckling style but it was all on the surface; what was taking place was a well co-ordinated exercise in *realpolitik*. One day the Education Minister, Paul Gérin-Lajoie, would be demanding treaty-signing rights for Quebec; next day, Revenue Minister Eric Kierans would be lambasting the federal government for attempting to disallow provincial investment in chartered banks; then Labour Minister Carrier Fortin would decide that it was high time Quebec set up its own employment service; and Municipal Affairs Minister Pierre Laporte would voice his determination to establish a provincially run Central Mortgage and Housing Corporation. René Lévesque, meanwhile, would be off on half a dozen tangents, claiming family allowances – in fact, all federal spending powers – for his province.* Just as the federal government seemed about to collapse under the weight of this concentrated abuse, Jean Lesage would stride onto the national stage, stroking an imaginary moustache, and declare he could fend off all these guys, in return for some extra fiscal equivalents.

A HANDSOME, HIGHLY EMOTIONAL QUEBECKER with an almost luminous public presence, Lesage had first been elected to the federal House of Commons in 1945 for the rural riding of Montmagny-L'Islet. His work as chairman of the parliamentary committee that devised the plan for old-age pensions without a means test so impressed Louis St Laurent

*On February 8, 1966, the Quebec government even introduced a bill in the legislature known as the Official Time Act, which authorized the province to opt out of national time.

that he brought Lesage into the cabinet in 1953 as the first Minister of Northern Affairs and National Resources. Lesage tripled the government's spending on northern administration during his three and a half years in office and gained the self-confidence necessary for his entry into Quebec politics. He once referred to his job at Northern Affairs as "the premiership of Canada's unorganized territories." After the second electoral defeat of the federal Liberals, Lesage's ambitions switched to the provincial field and on May 31, 1958, at a virtually uncontested convention in Quebec City, he became the provincial Liberal leader. At the time, it wasn't much of a prize. The Liberals hadn't been in power since 1944.

Though he was conservative by nature, Lesage quickly became an anti-Duplessis reformer. He fell in love with an image of himself as the man chosen to lead his province out of the wilderness of political immorality. Many of the province's intellectuals dismissed him as *un homme de la situation*, a polite term for opportunist, and described him as a kind of Presbyterian Jesuit – a man who believes devoutly that the end justifies the means. But he was much more than that. In the early years of his regime, he brought to the government of Quebec both a consummate honesty and a sense of purpose that for a while made it the most exciting and forward-looking administration in any western democracy. Although it was the deaths of Maurice Duplessis and his enlightened successor Paul Sauvé that provided him with the possibility of an electoral victory on June 22, 1960, Lesage's own campaign was a superb effort, conducted against great odds and the shoddy tactics of his opponents.

Once in office, he took over with Napoleonic *grandeur*. His personal staff numbered twenty-eight, including a *chef du protocole* in morning coat. His appointments schedule was mimeographed two weeks in advance and he was such an imposing figure in his province that three Montreal dailies once solemnly reported how the Prime Minister had been bitten by a mosquito on the middle finger of his right hand. He abolished patronage, introduced an impressive series of social reforms and brought to Quebec City a cadre of brilliant young French Canadians to run the civil service.

The whole social structure of the province was altered, it seemed in retrospect, almost within months. The oppressive attitude of the Duplessis days was replaced by a dramatic surge in every aspect of Quebec life, with the educational system undergoing modernization and secularization, trade unions operating without the restraints of state intervention, and censorship and repression replaced everywhere by freedom and light. Suddenly French Canadians after two hundred years of introversion were proud to be French Canadians; they no longer felt the burden of inferiority and wanted to trumpet the glory of their superiority.

It was the final repudiation of the agrarian, clergy-bound view of Quebec society, as expressed in *Maria Chapdelaine*, and the emergence of an urban-industrial people who could compete within the North American environment. With television sets replacing double beds as the focal point of married life in French Canada, the birth rate dropped below the Canadian average. Quebeckers developed a new interest in their language and a pride in all expressions of their culture from their cuisine to their literature. The most dramatic visible change was the face-lift that made downtown Montreal into one of the world's most stimulating urban centres. Architecturally and psychologically, this transformation paved the way for the even more exciting venture of Expo 67.

NO MATTER HOW BITTER THE PUBLIC WRANGLING between Jean Lesage and Lester Pearson became, the two men never lost contact with or respect for each other. When Lesage made a speaking tour of Western Canada in 1965 and received a cool reception, he wrote a complaint to Pearson, who replied with a warm, fourteen-page letter. Very few of Lesage's demands were made without prior consultation with the federal Liberals. The key contact man was Gordon Robertson, Pearson's Clerk of the Privy Council, who had been Deputy Minister of Northern Affairs under Lesage. Senior Ottawa civil servants joked about the "Robertson-Lesage hotline" when they wondered what Quebec's next demand might be.

Typical of the difference between the public and private postures Lesage adopted in dealing with Ottawa was the performance he put on during a federal-provincial conference on July 19, 1965. When Pearson opened the meeting by announcing that the question of jurisdiction over offshore mineral rights would be referred to the Supreme Court of Canada, Lesage denounced the decision in abusive tones. "The federal government chose to take advantage of its privileged position in relation to the Supreme Court in order to impose its own solution," he declared, then added that he wouldn't recognize the ruling in any event. Later that day Pearson invited the premiers to his summer residence at Harrington Lake in the Gatineau Hills. As the premiers were standing on the lawn admiring the lake, one of them suggested they go fishing and another quipped: "What about the underwater mineral rights?"

Pearson caught Lesage's elbow and, pretending to be a policeman, said: "You can go to the edge of the lake, Jean, but no further."

Lesage drew himself up and with mock seriousness replied: "May I remind you that we are now in the Province of Quebec?"

Despite the ideological compulsions that forced the Quebec premier into increasingly more nationalistic pronouncements, his ambitions were tempered by his thirteen formative years in Ottawa. Jean Lesage could never make up his mind whether he wanted to be the next prime minister of Canada or the first president of Quebec.

CHAPTER 22

Nine Momentous
Days in April

FOR SHEER DRAMATIC IMPACT, none of the many confrontations that marked the relationship between Lester Pearson and Jean Lesage could match that frantic round of negotiations in the spring of 1964 through which Ottawa obtained Quebec's consent to participate in the Canada Pension Plan.

Those nine momentous days in April were a minor turning point in Canadian history. The pension plan itself was not that significant an issue. But the accord that made it possible also prevented the Quebec administration from exploiting impulses and following directions that might eventually have led to the break-up of the country. Jean Lesage had cornered himself in a position where an open break with the federal Liberals appeared inevitable. Lester Pearson seemed about to forfeit his reputation as the indispensable politician-statesman who was holding the nation together. "That issue," Pearson said later about the pension crisis, "could have broken up our country. If Quebec had gone ahead with a pension plan of its own that bore no relation to the national plan, it would have been a disaster."*

When it was done, when the pension formula had been settled and the politicians turned back to comfortable generalities, the climate for national survival seemed brighter and everything appeared possible again, at least for a crucial few months. Lesage had obtained the funds he needed for priority provincial projects without having to impose the double taxation that might have driven even Quebec's moderates toward

*In an interview with Alexander Ross, *Maclean's*, July, 1967.

separatism. Pearson was granted another chance to get a renewed grip on the country's problems. All Canadians were able to look forward to the benefits of a new dimension in social welfare. The nation had won a reprieve.

The *entente* that settled the complex impasse of the pension legislation was made to work by the fortunate coming together of five very different men, each of whom brought to the negotiations a highly specialized talent:

LESTER PEARSON contributed his superb sense of timing, honed during a lifetime spent in diplomacy, which had taught him that large problems can be solved by allowing them to ripen precisely to that point when decisive action becomes acceptable.

JEAN LESAGE took the occasion to demonstrate his sentimental attachment to Confederation, so that when he was presented with the chance of stoking the fires of Quebec nationalism, he held back and opted for a federal compromise.

TOM KENT used his cool ability for reducing explosive issues to manageable proportions to work out the details of the complicated formula that eventually satisfied both Ottawa and Quebec.

MAURICE SAUVÉ brought to the confrontation a tough-minded independence and provided the key link between the sources of real (as opposed to titular) power in both camps.

CLAUDE MORIN, Quebec's Deputy Minister of Federal-Provincial Affairs and as such the main provincial negotiator, contributed a sure instinct for the possible and a basic integrity of purpose that allowed him to compromise on means without abandoning objectives.

THE PENSION PLAN CRISIS THAT BROUGHT these five men together was the outgrowth of legislative proposals first drafted by Geoff Conway, David Stanley and Martin O'Connell, long before they became Walter Gordon's three bright boys. The trio had been working on policies for the Ontario Liberal party caucus in 1960 when the federal party, still smarting from John Diefenbaker's description of the St Laurent Government after its paltry pension increase as "the six-buck boys," asked them to devise a permanent federal-provincial scheme that would remove pensions from the political auction block. They wrote a 250-page report, which was reworked and turned into a major plank for the Liberals' 1962 and 1963 election platforms by Tom Kent.

The original Canada Pension Plan legislation, based on this approach and requiring provincial as well as federal participation, was presented to Parliament in a government White Paper on July 18, 1963, as part of the "instant legislation" of Pearson's first sixty days. It was promptly attacked from three quarters: John Diefenbaker demanded an immediate ten-dollar increase for old-age pensioners; John Robarts declared that Ontario might not participate because his province had recently enacted its own legislation requiring employers to set up private, portable pension plans; and Quebec sharply rejected the whole basis of the federal approach. The Ottawa legislation was a pay-as-you-go scheme; Quebec wanted a funded plan based on a compulsory savings idea with the provinces using the accumulated funds for public investment purposes. A provincial committee set up to study public assistance (including among its members Claude Morin, then a professor in the social sciences faculty of Laval University) had submitted a report along this line in June of 1963 and the Quebec government was quietly working out its own pension plan.

During the next eight months, Ottawa's pension scheme fell apart. At a federal-provincial conference in September, Pearson acceded to the Diefenbaker demand for an immediate pension increase of ten dollars, wrecking the actuarial basis of the original plan. At the same time Judy LaMarsh, then Minister of National Health and Welfare, noisily attacked both Quebec and Ontario for not endorsing the national plan. In the Ontario provincial election that followed, Judy waded in to charge that Conservative Premier John Robarts was reluctant to do anything that might upset powerful lobbies from private insurance companies. This, not unnaturally, strengthened Robarts' hostility to the Ottawa plan.

Reacting to provincial objections, the federal Liberals threw together two more legislative drafts. The second version, released in January 1964, pleased no one. A third version, made public on March 17, 1964, ignored Quebec's objections and concentrated on meeting Ontario's demands. But Robarts responded that if Quebec could have a pension plan of its own, so could Ontario. The three federal pension plans were now being referred to caustically by numbers (CPP #1, etc.); what had been an earnest attempt to help Canada's elderly citizens had turned into a national joke. The last opportunity to salvage the scheme seemed to be the federal-provincial conference scheduled for Quebec City from March 31 to April 2.

THAT CONFERENCE BEGAN IN A MOOD of chill foreboding, when Jean Lesage distributed a printed brief that demanded for his province 25 per cent of personal income tax revenues, 10½ per cent of income from federal corporation taxes and 100 per cent of succession duties. He also made it clear that Quebec would withdraw from most joint federal-provincial programs and asked for an estimated $150 millions as compensation for the revenues Quebec had not shared during the Duplessis period. "If there had been a war between the rest of Canada and Quebec, and Quebec had won, the peace terms would probably have sounded something like the demands placed on the table by Premier Lesage," wrote Charles Lynch, the chief of Southam News Services.

The conference convened in the chamber of the Legislative Assembly, heavily guarded, sound-proofed and wired for simultaneous translation. Lester Pearson, aware that pensions would be the agenda's most contentious issue, got agreement to deal with other matters first. But one of the ministers on the federal delegation jokingly told Lesage: "Provided, of course, you have something to discuss."

"Yes, I have," said Lesage, "and here it is." He melodramatically dropped on the table a five-hundred-page report from a provincial task force outlining Quebec's pension plan. The scheme, conceived by a group of experts that included Claude Morin and Claude Castonguay, a Quebec City actuary, ran directly counter to Ottawa's original pay-as-you-go approach. It proposed using pension contributions to create large capital sums under provincial control. Applied to the entire country, the plan would raise between $8 and $10 billions in provincial investment funds in ten years. Lesage read his outline slowly in French, allowing the translators time to emphasize its importance clearly and increase its impact on the premiers hugging their ear-pieces. The Ottawa delegation just sat there, numb with embarrassment. The Quebec plan was indisputably a better piece of social legislation than the federal version. Following the Lesage presentation, Pearson quipped weakly: "Maybe we should contract into the Quebec plan." Premiers Robarts, Roblin and Smallwood said as much without intending it as a joke.

The unhappiest participant in the conference was Lesage himself. His concern was not pensions: he knew he had the best plan. He had come anxious to negotiate for extra tax revenues and found to his dismay that Ottawa was not prepared to discuss his problems. (Quebec had been granted $42 million of an $87 million increase in equalization payments at a previous federal-provincial conference in November, 1963, and as far as Finance Minister Walter Gordon was concerned, the federal treasury was now locked. The Ottawa delegation was willing to offer its "contracting out" formula for shared-cost programs, and nothing more.)

That night student leaders from Laval University planned a march on the legislature in support of Quebec's demands. Lesage had sent personal emissaries to warn the students against using violent tactics but the more nationalistic René Lévesque called the parade marshals to Quebec City's Aquarium Restaurant. He ridiculed Lesage's caution and told them: "Go ahead with your march. But make it big." The next day two thousand students carrying anti-Ottawa placards stormed the conference.

Adjournment had been planned for noon of April 2. It had to be postponed when Lesage refused to endorse the mild, cliché-riddled communiqué drafted by federal officials. Late that afternoon Pearson made a bland statement saying, in effect, that everyone had been very amicable in deciding absolutely nothing. But Jean Lesage was not amicable at all. He held his own separate press conference and with the wrath of a jilted opera tenor declared: "We must say that the Quebec government is not satisfied and that we will have very soon to study much more carefully than ever before what we should state in the next budget." The implication was clear: Quebec, feeling that its demands for both revenue and a revised pension plan had been ignored, was about to impose double taxation, for which Ottawa's intransigence would be blamed.

When the dispirited federal delegation returned to Ottawa, Pearson declared, with the slight stutter that sometimes betrayed his nervousness, that the Canada Pension Plan would be implemented, with or without Quebec. But John Robarts of Ontario firmly pledged that his province would not join any national plan in which Quebec was not a partner.

The full gravity of the situation didn't hit most federal politicians for several days. Maurice Lamontagne, one of the few ministers who saw the danger, had stayed behind in Quebec City to begin a round of desultory negotiations with Bona Arsenault, the only provincial minister who would talk to him. Neither man spoke with the accent of power.

MAURICE SAUVÉ, NAMED MINISTER OF FORESTRY in the Pearson Cabinet that February, didn't attend the Quebec City conference but shortly after it began, he received a series of agitated telephone calls from Claude Morin. The Quebec Deputy Minister of Federal-Provincial Affairs told Sauvé that he was writing Lesage's budget speech, scheduled for April 17, and that he had been instructed to draft a violent attack on Ottawa to justify the province's imposition of double corporate and income taxes. The two men had first become friends in 1959 when Sauvé (then director of public relations for the provincial Liberal Party) was gathering policy ideas for the 1960 election platform. Morin, a graduate of Father Lévesque's social science faculty at Laval, had done graduate work at Columbia University in public administration and returned to Laval as a lecturer in economics. He wrote most of the social security planks for the 1960 Lesage platform and the same year was invited to speak on welfare trends at the Liberal Study Conference on National Problems at Kingston, Ontario. It was there that he both expanded his friendship with Sauvé and made the acquaintance of Tom Kent. Now Morin was appealing to the only Ottawa minister in whom he felt total confidence to help stave off what he feared might be national disaster.

Sauvé immediately informed Tom Kent, who had independently reached a similar conclusion and was already drafting a memorandum for the PM outlining a new pension approach that would incorporate Quebec's idea for a funded plan. On the morning of Tuesday, April 7, Kent's long memorandum landed on Pearson's desk. It described a daring formula which would allow Ottawa's requirements and Quebec's requests to be met in one package deal. Pearson decided to call a meeting of senior ministers at his home the following evening to discuss the proposals. But Sauvé, worried about the time element – Lesage's double-taxation budget was now only ten days away – and impatient to get Quebec reinvolved in negotiations, had already telephoned Morin to find out whether he would receive an informal delegation from Ottawa the following day. Morin had readily agreed.

When Sauvé and Kent walked, grim-faced, into Pearson's office late Tuesday afternoon to obtain permission for the flight to Quebec, they were greeted by a downcast prime minister asking: "So what's the new disaster?"

Kent explained that, because of the Wednesday night meeting at 24 Sussex Drive, Sauvé felt they should both go to Quebec City immediately. At first Pearson thought the journey would be too dangerous: "If word of your trip leaked out, we'd be accused of catering to Quebec, and we're in too much trouble now . . . " But after a brief exchange of views the Prime Minister made his decision: "All right. I don't want it said that I didn't do everything possible to save Confederation. Go ahead. But keep the trip secret." (This self-generated cloak-and-dagger atmosphere sounds absurd in retrospect but it was indicative both of the nervous temper of the times and the personalities involved.)

It was 6:40 p.m. by the time Kent and Sauvé left the PM. With only thirty minutes to pack, the two men caught the 8:10 Trans-Canada flight to Quebec City. Sauvé's secretary had made reservations for them at the Chateau Frontenac but in order to preserve the secrecy of their mission, she booked Kent's room in the name of Claude Frenette, Sauvé's executive assistant. When Kent and Sauvé switched aircraft in Montreal, they found themselves seated near Jules Lesage, the premier's son, who was full of discomfiting questions. "Just a routine visit," said Sauvé blandly.

Claude Morin came to Sauvé's hotel room at 9:30 the following morning, bringing word that Lesage would receive them at three that afternoon. By the time Morin left at 1:30, he had been briefed on Kent's compromise and reacted favourably to its terms. That afternoon the Ottawa emissaries slipped through a side entrance into Lesage's office. René Lévesque and Paul Gérin-Lajoie joined the talks. After Kent and Morin had outlined the formula, Lesage sprang out of his seat and on the spot postponed the date of his budget presentation to April 25 to allow more time for a settlement. He seemed willing to compromise on some aspects of the pension plan in return for new tax-splitting arrangements. Gérin-Lajoie and Lévesque supported Lesage's enthusiasm. Though many issues remained unsettled at 4:20 when the meeting broke up, Lesage shook hands with his visitors and there were tears of happiness in his eyes.

After the meeting, Sauvé and Kent were driven to the Quebec City airport in a government limousine and spirited back to Ottawa in a provincial aircraft. They rushed to the Prime Minister's home, where five senior ministers (Sharp, Gordon, Favreau, Martin and Lamontagne) heard the report of their journey. General shock at the magnitude of what was being proposed persisted until the meeting broke up two hours later. Walter Gordon paced the floor of his bedroom most of that night trying to find a way of agreeing with Pearson's dramatic action.

The next day (Thursday, April 9) Kent and Sauvé continued to work feverishly on the detailed terms of the federal offer. Sauvé phoned Morin and asked whether Quebec would be willing to send a delegation to Ottawa on Saturday for the final settlement. Morin called Sauvé back that night to say that Lesage had agreed to send him and Claude Castonguay with full powers to make the deal.

On Saturday Sauvé had breakfast with Morin and Castonguay in their hotel suite and described the federal position. He was in turn informed of exactly what Quebec would and would not accept. At ten o'clock, the Quebec emissaries were led into an office adjoining the

East Block's Privy Council chamber. On the federal side of the bargaining table were Sauvé, Kent, Joseph Willard, the Deputy Minister of Welfare, and Don Thorson, an assistant deputy minister of Justice. The bargaining began badly. There seemed no way to meld the two pension plans without one side's having to give in not only on details but also on principles. The meeting adjourned for a listless lunch in an Eastview hotel.

At four o'clock a messenger knocked on the door and said a DOT plane would fly the two Quebec delegates home. Morin and Castonguay pushed their chairs back from the bargaining table and prepared to leave. The conference seemed to be over; the package deal was dead.

It was Tom Kent who broke the impasse when he excused himself and went to the men's room. Sauvé caught the signal and also left the meeting. Over the basins of an East Block washroom Sauvé outlined the position that he knew from his breakfast conversation would win Quebec's acceptance. Kent agreed to try again.

Working rapidly the two negotiating teams isolated the fifteen main differences between the two pension plans, set aside the best features of each and, after both sides had made important compromises, agreement was finally reached by 7 p.m. It turned out to be a costly settlement, worth $200 millions out of the federal treasury over the next two years. The pension plan compromise was only part of the package. Its principal terms were these:

1. Quebec agreed to a constitutional amendment permitting federal pension benefits for widows under sixty-five, orphans and the disabled.

2. Quebec agreed to modify its pension plan, bringing it more into line with Ottawa's, mainly by cutting the transition period from twenty to ten years but including other significant alterations, among them the contribution rate.

3. Quebec agreed to take part in the federal-provincial tax structure committee.

4. Ottawa agreed to revise parts of its pension plan, mainly the investment of reserves, which was surrendered to provincial control.

5. Ottawa agreed to grant Quebec an additional 3 per cent of income taxes in lieu of the federal student loan and extended family allowance plans.

6. Ottawa agreed to double the rate of its withdrawal from the personal income tax field, giving the provinces 21 per cent in 1965 and 24 per cent in 1966.

7. Negotiations were to proceed on a federal-provincial agreement concerning contracting-out arrangements for shared-cost programs.*

The following Monday morning Kent telephoned Morin to double-check the details of their agreement. At 5 p.m. the same day, Pearson finally revealed the new proposals to his full cabinet. It was one of the most impressive performances of his career. Each of the objecting ministers – at one point the majority of the cabinet – found himself the target of a rare display of impassioned persuasion by the Prime Minister. Two days later the Pearson and Lesage cabinets approved the deal.

The next Saturday (April 18) Morin and Castonguay flew to Ottawa again for a final consultation with Kent. After their meeting was over, Kent gave them a dinner invitation from the Prime Minister. When they arrived at 24 Sussex Drive, Kent took Castonguay aside and Morin was left alone with Pearson, who was lying on a living-room sofa, looking old and exhausted. "I'm Prime Minister of this country and I can't sleep at night because I don't know what to do," he said, as much to himself as to Morin. "If I do one thing Diefenbaker's going to attack me. If I do something else Quebec's going to criticize me. I'm condemned in advance to be criticized. I don't think any other Canadian prime minister has been in such a situation. I just don't know what to do. I don't want to be praised. But I don't want to be criticized all the time either. Sometimes I wonder whether I'm really fit for the job."

"Listen," Morin spoke up. "Listen, you may be criticized now, but I'm sure that a few years from now they'll say: 'Well, Pearson was the man who had to be there at that particular time.' That's what I really think."

"You may be right. I may live another ten or twenty years and my reward will come when someone eventually really says that. If I live long enough to see that I'll think that I've done something really good."

Kent and Castonguay came back in. The mood broke. Pearson jumped to his feet, made a quick joke and began to discuss the pension plan details once more.

ON APRIL 20, WHEN PEARSON AND LESAGE publicly announced the pension settlement, they were hailed as heroes. Tommy Douglas said the

*There were sixty-six of these shared-cost programs in existence, including hospital insurance, old-age assistance and various vocational training and health grants. Quebec eventually opted out of twenty-nine of the programs, receiving in compensation a 20 per cent increase in its share of personal income tax revenues from Ottawa.

agreement was "a real victory for national unity," and even John Diefenbaker called it "a step forward." In the Quebec house, Paul Gérin-Lajoie provided a moving eulogy of the pension *entente* when he said: "April 20, 1964, will become an outstanding date in the annals of Canada and the men who have taken part in these events will see their names in the pages of history." Jean Lesage pulled out all the dramatic stops when he told a hushed legislature: "During the past month I have lived a terrible life. I worked for my province as no man has ever worked before. I used all the means that Providence has given me so that Quebec, in the end, would be recognized as a province with a special status in Confederation. And I have succeeded." The more cautious Claude Ryan, the influential editor of *Le Devoir*, wrote: "Are we at a turning point in the history of Confederation? It is too early to be able to make such a big statement. But at least a ray of light has appeared. Let us rejoice!"

CHAPTER 23

The Death of
Co-operative Federalism

Q UEEN ELIZABETH'S VISIT TO QUEBEC CITY in the autumn of 1964 was yet another turning point in the relationship between French and English Canada, though of a very different kind from the pension *entente*. It provided an important public occasion for testing the anti-English feelings of Quebec's nationalists and demonstrated to the rest of the country that, while the separatists remained a minority, the moderates of French Canada were able to field little anti-separatist enthusiasm of their own.

In 1961 Walter Shaw, then Premier of Prince Edward Island, had suggested to Ottawa that the Queen should visit the island in October 1964 to mark the centennial of the Charlottetown Conference, where Canada East, Canada West and the three Maritime provinces had first met to discuss the terms of Confederation. When he heard about the projected visit, Jean Lesage reminded federal officials that the nation-building process had been completed in his capital with the Quebec Resolutions of October 27, 1864, and urged that Her Majesty should come to Quebec City as well. Later, during a visit to London, he personally urged the Queen to come. Between the tendering of these invitations and the time of the Queen's arrival, Lesage's province had become much more nationalistic but the Premier's genuine affection for the monarch had not changed. (During the Queen's visit, Lesage was so moved by her quiet courage that he several times burst into tears.)

Even six months before the visit, Ottawa's Quebec ministers didn't expect any real trouble. On March 13, 1964, Secretary of State

Maurice Lamontagne assured an audience at St Mary's University in Halifax: "It's always possible that something might happen to Queen Elizabeth – even in London or Scotland. But Quebec City was the warmest part of the 1939 Royal Tour and Quebec feelings do not change that rapidly."

At about the same time, however, separatist leaders Raymond Barbeau and Marcel Chaput issued warnings about the Queen's safety and admitted under questioning that Quebec City might be "another Dallas," referring to the assassination of President John F. Kennedy the previous year. What seemed remarkable later was how little appreciation there was in English Canada that the Queen's visit under the prevailing circumstances of burgeoning Quebec nationalism could only be an unpleasant reminder of the Conquest and, to many French Canadians, of coercion and injustice.

Because of mounting separatist threats, security preparations for the visit were unusually tight; they included a team of navy frogmen floating around the royal yacht *Britannia*, police dogs patrolling the city's parks, armoured cars and tough platoons of riot police. More than a thousand reporters converged on Quebec City. The CBC assigned a separate thirty-man crew to stand by in case an assassination occurred. A team of British television journalists filmed a so-called underground organization near an "arms cache," which yielded only three rusty rifles. IS IT A FLIGHT INTO DANGER? asked the Toronto *Telegram* in its main headline as the Queen flew in from Charlottetown.

The atmosphere of apprehension was so pervasive that only a few thousand people turned out to greet the monarch as she made a forlorn passage from the Quebec City docks to the legislature. Backs were turned, insults were hurled and riots broke out along her route. There were no attempts on the Queen's life but English Canadians who were accustomed to turning out in happy throngs to greet British monarchs were deeply shocked by Quebec's reaction. This was their first realization that Quebec separatism was not just the vague theorizing of Montreal intellectuals but a passionate movement of passionate men. The impact of the occasion on French and English Canadians was intensified by the brutality with which Quebec City police handled Laval University students who were protesting the visit. Even students shouting harmless slogans like *Vive Elizabeth* (pause) *Taylor!* were clubbed into silence and summarily arrested. London's *Daily Mail* called the visit "without doubt the most massive, most grievous insult ever offered the monarch." The editorial reaction of English Canada took two tacks: apoplexy and sorrow. "I'm not being entirely facetious when I suggest a rerun of the Battle of the Plains of Abraham – with the subsequent script rewritten to make more sense," wrote Richard Sanburn, editor of the *Calgary Herald*. A more moderate and more moving comment came from Scott Young, the *Globe and Mail* columnist, who wrote: "One of the difficulties in writing about the events that happened here Saturday is the need to keep calm and look at the violence as if it were happening in someone else's country. However, this was not someone else's country. And this was my throat that became choked with sadness and my eyes that became full of tears at some times on Saturday night. Not at blame for anyone, even the poor clods of police. They had received their orders to protect the Queen and were doing so within the limits of their understanding and their equipment, the gun, the riot car, the oak club."

Pierre Elliott Trudeau, then a professor of constitutional law at the University of Montreal, saw the Queen's visit and its attendant violence as having a profoundly important effect He believed it was a watershed in the history of Quebec separatism. "The love of law and order in a traditionally peaceful people turned the Quebec population against the rioting separatists," he said later. "The majority of Quebeckers don't draw much distinction between political and criminal violence."

DESPITE THE QUEBEC CITY RIOTS and the occasional flare-up of separatist violence in the province in the months that followed, fiscal negotiations between Jean Lesage and Lester Pearson continued. In addition to the twenty percentage points of personal income taxes already awarded to Quebec in return for contracting out of twenty-nine federal-provincial cost-sharing programs, three more points were turned over in 1964 to compensate for Quebec's non-participation in the federal youth allowance scheme. The impressive total of all the equalizing arrangements made between Ottawa and Quebec City showed up in a comparison of tax-sharing figures at the beginning and at the end of the Pearson Government's tenure. In 1963, Ottawa sent back to Quebec 17 per cent of income taxes collected within its borders, 9 per cent of corporation taxes and 50 per cent of succession duties. By the spring of 1968, the corresponding percentages were 50, 10 and 75.

None of this disturbed federal relations with the other provinces. They were extended similar arrangements, even if no premier actually took up the contracting-out offers. But the situation began to change in February of 1966, when Ottawa gave Quebec a small ($17 million) sum as the result of a federal increase from two to five dollars in per capita grants to universities. Lesage claimed that the money "had no strings attached" and that the province could spend it in any area it chose. Pearson admitted that it had been an unconditional grant but expressed the hope that Quebec would use the money for education. It was this exploitation by Lesage of the federal transfer as a political victory that finally stiffened Ottawa's position. Work began in the Finance Department on a new strategy that would jettison the vague generalities of co-operative federalism and substitute something more definite and much tougher. It was now evident to the Liberal Cabinet, especially to Mitchell Sharp, that the federal government had to find a more creative role than merely acting as a central bank for provincial enterprises. There could no longer be a vacuum at the centre without a loss of the ability to control the nation's fiscal direction.

Another factor that hardened Ottawa's posture was René Lévesque's stated determination that family allowances should come under provincial jurisdiction. This hit at the very core of the federal government's ability to spend money in the public interest. Family allowances were politically important because along with old-age security payments and unemployment insurance, they represented the main direct financial contact that Ottawa had with the people. (Nearly all other federal schemes provided assistance in the form of payments to provinces or institutions.) The federal Liberals felt that the Lévesque initiative was deliberately designed to place Quebec in the position of being the only government dealing directly with the people of the province, thereby putting Ottawa even more out of touch with the citizens of French Canada.

From the constitutional viewpoint, a Quebec takeover of family allowance payments would, according to the Ottawa argument, have left no line of demarcation remaining between federal and provincial jurisdictions. Family allowances (as well as old-age security payments and unemployment insurance, which Lévesque also designated as his eventual targets) were not shared-cost programs that would allow opting out by Quebec. They were, instead, federal responsibilities, and in the case of two of the measures (unemployment insurance in 1940 and old-age pensions in 1951), there were constitutional amendments to prove it.

Lesage backed up Lévesque's claims by declaring in the Throne Speech opening the 1966 legislative session that Quebec intended to take away the whole field of social legislation from the federal government. What the Quebec Premier was telling Pearson, in effect, was that he now intended to opt out of co-operative federalism. By stressing "the sustained evolution toward a new relationship between Quebec, the other provinces and the Government of Canada," Lesage was giving notice that he would press for an altered division of federal and provincial powers. Instead of co-operating with Ottawa in government programs, the Quebec administration now intended to move headlong into federal jurisdictions. These incursions would include family allowances, old-age pensions, mortgage lending, housing, offshore mineral rights and eventually indirect taxation revenues, as well as a greater share of direct tax funds.

Here was a profound change in tactics. Rather than merely conducting guerrilla raids on the federal treasury, Quebec was now switching to constitutional demands that would bring it both more money and a kind of special status within Confederation, requiring Ottawa to deal bilaterally with its demands.

Pearson had helped to make this climate possible by rhetorically endowing Quebec with a special status in some of his speeches. On August 17, 1963, speaking to the Canadian French-Language Weekly Newspapers Association at Murray Bay, Quebec, he had said: "While Quebec is a province in this national confederation, it is more than a province because it is the heartland of a people: in a very real sense it is a nation within a nation." Similarly, speaking on CBC television on January 5, 1964, he had called Quebec "in some vital respects not a province like the others but the homeland of a people." Now his government had to turn back the special-status tide.

THE LESAGE-PEARSON DIALOGUE BROKE OFF abruptly on June 5, 1966, when the Quebec Liberals were unexpectedly defeated in a provincial election. Lesage had gone to the Quebec electorate asking for "another mandate before pursuing our negotiations with Ottawa." In truth, his administration had launched so many reforms that he needed more funds to preserve the province's solvency. The generally poor state of the Canadian bond market plus the fact that Quebec had already borrowed an annual average of $500 millions during the three preceding years had diminished the province's capacity for further domestic borrowing. Access to the New York money market remained limited and provincial taxes could not be raised any further. As the Lesage administration's priorities shifted from social to economic requirements, the pressures for widening expenditures continued to mount. More money from Ottawa seemed to be the only alternative.

Lesage and his ministers had been so occupied with *la politique de grandeur* that they had neglected secondary issues of local concern. Reactionary elements in the church had turned against the government because its educational reforms had substantially weakened their influence in rural ridings. The Union Nationale adroitly exploited this discontent and its victory in the 1966 campaign was, to a large degree, a triumph for the local *curés*, notaries and the basically conservative core of Quebec's non-urban population. The sophisticates of the quiet revolution had done little to cope with the smouldering economic frustrations of the small towns and villages. Except for the 1962 nationalization of private power companies (which reduced electricity bills), few of the government's reforms had yet produced tangible results. Lesage, and even his most popular ministers, René Lévesque and Eric Kierans, had lost touch with the people. At one point during the campaign, Lesage actually called in an adviser and asked him to write the text of a speech to be delivered in Lévis the following evening that would stress, instead of local issues, the fact that his government needed a strong mandate to impress Harold Wilson, the Prime Minister of Great Britain. (The United Kingdom Parliament then had before it a request to approve a constitutional amendment to do away with Quebec's Legislative Council.)

The Union Nationale meanwhile was using a strategy quite remote from Lesage's grandiose approach. It had elected Daniel Johnson its leader in October of 1961 and had spent its energies in the intervening years on constituency organization. Lesage had treated the Union Nationale with utter contempt, convinced that it hadn't changed from its corrupt, paternalistic methods of the Duplessis era, and that its new leader was both harmless and a windbag.

Francis Daniel Johnson was neither. A Montreal lawyer, Johnson had entered politics as a fervent follower of Maurice Duplessis, who eventually appointed him Minister of Hydraulic Resources. Johnson was probably the only person in the country who wasn't surprised by his victory. He had planned his campaign carefully (using some of the same techniques that Lesage had pioneered in 1960) and had even brought in an American advertising agency to master-mind his image. Johnson's margin of victory was so narrow that for a while Lesage didn't want to give up power, and when he did he was so upset that he suffered a mild heart seizure.

To the many visitors who flocked into Quebec City to assess the new Quebec Premier in the next few weeks, Johnson gave the impression of a remarkably complex individual. Instead of the excitement of his predecessor's methods, there was an undercurrent of melancholy in his approach. His slim legislative majority was built on popular discontent and he was well aware that if he could not allay it, his power would vanish. During the election campaign, his plea had been to the poor and the alienated, the drop-outs from the quiet revolution. There was no trace in him of the arrogance that puffed up so many French-Canadian politicians of his vintage. Instead, he saw himself as a suave and courteous spokesman for those who needed protection from the impersonal grinding of modern society. He also had a quiet sense of humour. On February 16, 1965, when the Ottawa Liberals were being rocked by scandals, he started a speech to Montreal's *Chambre de Commerce* with the comment: "I wanted to talk about federal politics today. Then I realized that it's nearly all *sub judice* these days."

He was an oddly old-fashioned figure. His careful manners, his tight grip on his followers, his philosophy of government, even his car (a tug-size black Cadillac with provincial flags fluttering on its fenders) were all part of a vanishing tradition in Quebec politics. His view of the democratic process was deeply rooted in the concept that the essence of politics must be power, not law, and that Quebec could advance its case best by straining against the reality, not the legality, of each new situation.

He was firmly committed to an early and radical rewriting of Canada's constitution. While his opponents argued about the shades of meaning in the various clauses of the British North America Act, he dismissed the whole constitution as only one of five arrangements that had regulated French-English relations in Canada. (The others were those of 1763, 1774, 1791 and 1840.) "Too many people," he would say, "treat the BNA Act like a sacred cow, even though it's been violated many times in closed committee sessions and even in hotel rooms. So why not get rid of it and draft a sixth constitution?"

This sounded like a flippant way to dismiss the document on which the existence of the nation was based but it was entirely consistent with the line he had taken all of his adult life. He had always been convinced that Quebec must be able to create and control the economic and social institutions that constitute the true reflections of the French-Canadian spirit. He believed that the place of Quebec within the federal system inevitably inhibited English Canada from realizing its legitimate objectives, so that separation by mutual agreement into a loose alliance was the best way out for both groups. This was the theme of his book *Egalité ou Independance*, best expressed in its concluding paragraph: "Where the French-Canadian nation finds its freedom, there too will be its homeland."

This concept of two nations or "associate states" was foreign to English Canadians because it seemed to jeopardize the country's basic integrity, substituting a hybrid arrangement that had no modern precedents except for the madcap constitution of the Austro-Hungarian empire. But unlike Jean Lesage, Daniel Johnson had few sentimental

322

attachments to Ottawa or, indeed, to Canada. There was nothing vindictive about Johnson's stand, just a coldblooded assessment of the political realities as they struck him. "The trouble," he explained, "is that too many people equate Canada with Confederation as it is – that is, a confederation of ten provinces. I'm not advocating the disappearance of any province. But what's the formal element of Confederation? At the present time, it's the geographical dimension. I'd like to see a grouping under another dimension, which is the cultural one. We must have a new constitution. We can't leave the rights of any group to the whims of political struggle."

He was not a politician bound by ideology ("In a democracy you should have men to settle the problems that exist, not men who set out to prove philosophical ideals") but was determined on one point: that the question of a redistribution of tax revenues had to be tied in with constitutional reform. This made him a dangerous antagonist of the federal government because even if his province's dollar demands could be satisfied, the constitutional differences would remain. Unlike Lesage's brutal verbal assaults on the federal government, his briefs were drafted in moderate tones, never setting out ultimatums and always leaving himself an escape hatch. His contradictory pronouncements puzzled his supporters and baffled his critics. He would go to meet bond dealers on Wall Street and tell them: "Quebec won't separate, if we can live in Canada as a group." Then he would come home and tell a Quebec audience: "Unless Quebec can live in Canada as a group, we'll separate." Reporters would subtract one statement from the other, ending up with zero, and then Johnson would attack the press for misinterpreting his position.

In the late summer of 1966 a secret report was submitted to Johnson analysing the economic policies most conducive to Quebec's social and cultural objectives. It concluded that only full independence could guarantee these goals but that this was not immediately feasible. As a second-best policy it suggested reducing Quebec's participation in all joint federal-provincial programs through fiscal equivalents and the eventual expansion of this offensive into fields where Ottawa had either a mixed or even a clear jurisdiction of its own.

THE PEARSON GOVERNMENT, which had already been toughening its attitude toward Quebec, now was freed from the restraint of having to deal with fellow Liberals. In place of the vague generalities of cooperative federalism there began to emerge a new policy based on a consistent view of Canada both philosophically and constitutionally tenable. The main architect of this approach was A. W. Johnson, an economist of great originality who had been hired away from the Saskatchewan government as assistant deputy minister of Finance for federal-provincial relations. A Ph.D. from Harvard (where he had come under the influence of J. K. Galbraith), he had been appointed Deputy Provincial Treasurer in Saskatchewan in 1952 at the age of twenty-eight and had pioneered many of its enlightened policies. Johnson sympathized with Quebec's aspirations but he also recognized that within the Canadian confederation, Ottawa could not properly act merely as one of eleven governments. It had to sit across the table from the ten provincial administrations and could not subvert its own position by dealing privately with one of them.

At the same time, partly through the educational process triggered by the hearings of the Royal Commission on Bilingualism and Biculturalism, the federal government began to recognize French Canada as a cultural instead of a geographic concept. To differentiate it from the geopolitical entity of Quebec, Ottawa felt it necessary to become more of a spokesman for French (as well as English) Canada and to begin treating Quebec as a province with special problems instead of as a national entity on its own.

THE END OF CO-OPERATIVE FEDERALISM came about abruptly with two federal-provincial conferences held in Ottawa during the fall of 1966. It was replaced by a tough and explicit policy of decentralization that held the line on further tax abatements, charged the provinces – which had long been claiming fiscal adulthood – with the responsibility for running their own shared-cost social programs and left them responsible for collecting the new taxes to finance the schemes. The federal position, which Mitchell Sharp presented to the provinces at meetings on September 14 and October 24, had four main elements:

1. A radically new equalization formula, which took into account provincial tax yields from all sources;
2. The proposed termination of the long era of shared-cost programs, with the provinces being given an eventual seventeen points in personal income tax abatement in compensation and warned that the federal government would give up no more of its tax share;
3. Federal withdrawal from direct capital and operating grants to universities, with Ottawa providing unconditional grants based on 50 per cent of their operating costs;
4. The assertion by Ottawa of its financial responsibility for the occupational retraining of adults.

Significantly, these new arrangements granted Quebec no special status and left little room for the negotiation of any special arrangements with the province. Unlike most of the Pearson Government's other initiatives, these policies (except for the equalization formula) were presented to the provinces as a *fait accompli* without prior consultation.

Part of the reason for this unexpected toughness was that the federal position had come under the influence of Pierre Trudeau, elected to the Commons in 1965 and by this time the Prime Minister's parliamentary secretary.* Trudeau had long asserted that "the whole Canadian system of government would be improved by creative tensions between the central, the provincial and even the municipal administrations" and that the only important thing was that the Canadian people, wherever they lived, "clearly know which level of government is responsible for what area of legislation, so that they may be aroused to demand good laws from all their governments."†

Sharp's proposals to those autumn conferences in 1966 added up to a blunt warning that the provinces could no longer hope to raid the federal treasury and were received with cries of anguish from the provincial premiers. For the first time in memory, the meetings ended with the conference participants unable to agree on a final communiqué. The premiers looked toward Lester Pearson to make some last-minute retreat, but he let Sharp do most of the bargaining and backed up his Finance Minister in the new hard line. Given no choice, the premiers reluctantly agreed to a two-year test period for the new equalization and shared-cost programs and educational grants formula (which would yield them an extra $350 millions) and went home. When the meeting broke up and Sharp stepped out of the conference room, Eugene Forsey rushed up to the Finance Minister, all but embraced him and exclaimed with delight: "My God, at last somebody's standing up for Canada!"

No provincial premier was more upset than Daniel Johnson of Quebec. He had come to Ottawa with a brief asking for 100 per cent of the personal income tax collected in his province, 100 per cent of succession duties and 100 per cent of some corporate taxes. (This kind of tax-sharing, if applied to all provinces, would have deprived Ottawa of 45 per cent of its revenues and left it incapable of governing the country.) Johnson also set out in explicit detail the kind of constitutional powers his new Quebec would need:

*For the details of how Trudeau became a Liberal candidate in the 1965 election, see Chapter 26.

†From *Federalism and the French Canadians* (The Macmillan Company of Canada Limited, 1968).

As the mainstay of a nation, it wants free rein to make its own decisions affecting the growth of its citizens as human beings (i.e., education, social security and health in all respects), their economic development (i.e., the forging of any economic and financial tool deemed necessary), their cultural fulfilment (which takes in not only arts and literature but the French language as well) and the presence abroad of the Quebec community (i.e., relations with certain countries and international organizations). To this end, the new Quebec government is committed to the fundamental task of obtaining legal and political recognition of the French-Canadian nation; among other things this will require a new constitution to guarantee equal collective rights in our country to English-speaking and French-speaking Canadians, as well as to give Quebec the powers needed to safeguard its identity.

Johnson's brief concluded with the warning: "As of September 1966, Quebec's attitude toward Confederation is a waiting attitude. It is up to this gathering – particularly the federal government's representatives – to decide whether waiting is worth while." Although he limited himself to the exposition of an associate-state theory, the core of Johnson's demands was easy enough to detect: he wanted Ottawa to finance Quebec's journey to independence.

Johnson threatened and postured. He hinted that he might call a referendum on Quebec's place in Confederation and warned that he would immediately summon a constitutional assembly of his own. But in the end he was brought to bay by the sad state of his province's finances. At the time the Ottawa conference was being held, provincial bonds were selling scarcely at all, even in Quebec. Out of a $55 million issue floated on October 1, $25 millions' worth had to be taken up by the province's own pension fund and the only long-term bonds being placed outside the province were trades for older, outstanding Quebec issues. The Johnson Government's estimated 1966-67 revenues had become so dependent on federal transfers and tax abatements that fully 50 per cent of the $1.8 billion figure was made up of payments from Ottawa.

Johnson, who was above all a political pragmatist, realized that no matter how much he might be attracted to his associate-state theory or even to independence, he could not afford to surrender half his government's revenues. By mid November he was telling groups of Toronto and New York investment dealers that he had no intention of isolating Quebec or trying to weaken the federal government and was blandly portraying the threat of separatism as a tale to frighten little children.

THE NEXT INITIATIVE IN FEDERAL-PROVINCIAL RELATIONS came from an unexpected source: John Robarts of Ontario. Of all the provincial premiers, Robarts had the most difficult time striking a happy compromise between his function as a politician primarily concerned with the welfare of his province and his role as a statesman willing to defend the national interest.

Ontario was not a province like the others. An economic empire with a 1966 gross provincial product of $22.8 billions and a spending power exceeding that of half the member nations in the UN, the province in 1966 accounted for a third of Canada's population but half of the country's output of manufactured goods, with an aggregate personal income that was more than 40 per cent of the national total. Ontario's taxpayers contributed nearly as much to national revenues as all other Canadians put together.

In a very real sense, then, what was good for Canada was good for Ontario, so that it was always difficult for Robarts to champion national policies without at the same time appearing to be pushing his province's own cause. Robarts attempted to resolve this contradiction in two ways: by stressing that what was good for Ontario was also good for Canada (since the province's prosperity generated a higher gross national product) and by pioneering policies that he believed to be ahead of the thinking and planning being done in Ottawa.

His main complaint was that the federal government formulated its policies on tax revenues without adequate consultation with the provinces. What he advocated was a series of federal-provincial meetings that would make so many fundamental decisions they could, in effect, become constitutional conferences. It was to prepare for this kind of negotiation that John Robarts called together in Toronto during late November 1967 the Confederation of Tomorrow Conference. Quebec strongly supported the Ontario initiative, though the aims of the two governments were not identical. Daniel Johnson maintained that constitutional changes must take precedence, while Robarts and his advisers were more interested in analysing the modern requirements of the federal system, with constitutional reform being only a part of the exercise. Nevertheless, close co-operation between the Ontario and Quebec governments became one of the really significant trends in the evolution of Canadian federalism. This co-operation was quietly achieved at the senior civil service level between Claude Morin, now Deputy Minister of Intergovernmental Affairs, and Jacques Parizeau, the Quebec government's chief economist, on the one hand, and Ian Macdonald, chief economist for Ontario, and Don Stevenson, head of the federal-provincial co-ordinating secretariat, on the other. It was doubtful whether there had ever before been such a quartet of brilliant public servants operating in the provincial service. Together they managed to keep Ottawa's bureaucracy in a frenzy of activity just trying to respond to their initiatives.

As a result, Robarts was able to evade the choice that traditionally faced all premiers of Ontario: whether to become anti-Quebec or anti-Ottawa. He was neither. Although he frequently defended the prerogatives of the federal government, Robarts also believed it was essential for English Canada to recognize that Canada was a country of two societies and two founding peoples. The consequences of a staunchly Anglo-Saxon Ontario led by a man determined to resist the aspirations of French Canada could have been disastrous at this volatile point in Canadian history. But John Robarts' enlightened approach to the French-English problem earned him a large place in whatever agreement might finally be reached.

THE CONFEDERATION OF TOMORROW CONFERENCE was held in an Orwellian aerie on top of a Toronto skyscraper that was stocked with ad men's aids to patriotism, imbued with the aura of commerce and lit up with television klieg lights. Untheatrical as always, Daniel Johnson dominated the proceedings. He stressed that fifty countries had adopted new constitutions since World War II and wanted Canada to do the same. He demanded that this new constitution "acknowledge the existence in Canada of two nations, bound together by history, each enjoying equal collective rights." This meant that Quebec would exercise veto powers over national decisions. It was a frightening prospect and Joey Smallwood of Newfoundland demanded: "Where is the consensus in Canada that Quebec shall have anything all the other provinces don't have? Is one province to have rights the other nine don't enjoy? If so, you wouldn't have Canada, you'd have something else."

This was exactly the point. Finally the crisis in Canadian Confederation had been placed in proper perspective: to define the middle ground between the *status quo* and Quebec independence. The Robarts conference made it clear both that some new constitutional framework would have to be negotiated and how difficult the process was going to be. The governments of Newfoundland, Alberta, British Columbia and Saskatchewan remained firmly opposed to change of any kind. Ross Thatcher spoke for them all when he said: "In Saskatchewan, if we had a hundred problems, the constitution would be the one hundred and first."

The main benefit of the conference was that through its televised proceedings the whole nation could watch the ten men debating the future of the country. Each premier by the quality of his discourse revealed the essence of his being. Removed from the artificial aura of mystery that had surrounded all previous conferences of this kind, the meeting was able to achieve a rough consensus. By the time it adjourned, aware that the citizens of their own provinces wanted to be proud of them as Canadians, most of the premiers had revised their original obstructionist attitudes. Even Robert Bonner, who was sitting in for the Premier of British Columbia, managed to show traces of charm. Daniel Johnson left Toronto announcing that he had made "a bet on Canada" and that he was confident a new constitution would transform the country into "two equal partners as well as ten provinces."

A DIRECT OUTGROWTH OF THE ROBARTS MEETING was the first federal-provincial conference on the constitution, convened in Ottawa on February 5, 1968. Pierre Trudeau had, for most of the previous year, headed a small group studying the implications and techniques of constitutional reform. With Pearson's approval, Trudeau (who was named Minister of Justice on April 4, 1967) had chosen an entrenched Bill of Rights as the main federal policy for the conference. Had it been accepted by the provinces, the Bill of Rights would have brought about a basic change in Canada's system of government, placing a higher law in judgement over the federal parliament and each of the provincial legislatures.

The Trudeau approach would have allowed the Supreme Court (or its reconstituted version) to interpret the laws of all legislative assemblies in the country and judge the claims to inalienable rights (such as language equality) of Canadian citizens. Parliament and the legislatures would have been prevented from enacting measures that did not square with the rights bill. This would have represented a radical departure from the British system (which accepts the supremacy of Parliament) and a move to the American system, which uses its own supreme court to protect the inalienable rights of the individual). The constitutional function of Canada's Supreme Court had been limited to fixing the areas of jurisdiction between the federal and provincial levels of government.*

Trudeau described his new Bill of Rights as presupposing "a gigantic transformation of mentality. Should this happen, other useful constitutional reforms could be achieved without too much difficulty. If it cannot be achieved, on the other hand, it isn't worth while talking about other reforms, because Canada will be swept periodically by the ill wind of ethnic quarrels, and will become a sterile country for the mind, from which all peace and all greatness will be banished."

In the context of the 1968 federal-provincial conference, the main significance of the Bill of Rights was its effect on guaranteeing language rights to French Canadians outside Quebec. Here was a direct attempt by the federal government to differentiate between French Canada and Quebec. To Daniel Johnson, this was a secondary matter because he regarded Quebec as "the true national state" and realized that the success of such a policy would undermine his argument that Quebec needed special powers as the only government that French Canadians could trust. To Pierre Trudeau, equal language rights across the country formed the very basis of the genuine federalism he envisaged for Canada. By exposing Johnson's position to the conference, Trudeau succeeded in demonstrating for the first time that Quebec's real concern was not only the preservation of French culture in North America but the aggrandizement of its own powers.

With some exceptions, the premiers were dubious about Trudeau's bold initiative. But once again it was television that came to the rescue. The men charged with reshaping the constitution were aware that their electorates were watching, and none of them wanted to play the villain before a national audience. The compromises negotiated at the conference were based to a large degree on the awareness of its participants that their every speech, every aside, every gesture was being transmitted into the country's living rooms. Television also had the

*The new, entrenched Bill of Rights would have given the final word on many areas not covered by the Diefenbaker Bill of Rights, which became law on August 10, 1960. It was limited strictly to the federal jurisdiction and as a simple act of Parliament (rather than a constitutional amendment) it could be altered by any succeeding decision of the Commons. It was never meant as a law to protect Canadians from one another but simply as a set of instructions to the courts on how to interpret federal laws – a worthwhile codification of legal ideals. It was that and nothing more, since most of the abuses to civil liberties fall within provincial jurisdictions, which the Diefenbaker Bill could not touch.

effect of making the issues seem smaller, while magnifying the personalities involved. Consequently, the nation was deducing matter from manner, guiding its assessment of the conference according to its reactions to the participating politicians.

Daniel Johnson, never tougher in what he was demanding, generated a great deal of sympathy. He simply didn't look or behave like a man who would break up Canada. The image he projected was that of a thoughtful politician, anxious to please, troubled that he was always being misunderstood. Although his demands, if implemented, would have resulted in a divided Canada, his conduct seemed to imply that the whole thing was a semantic misunderstanding and that he was really a much-maligned patriot.

Lester Pearson came across as the ideal committee chairman. He seemed to know exactly when an appropriate quip or the call for a coffee break would drain the tension out of a potentially explosive confrontation.

On sight, G. I. Smith, the Nova Scotia Premier, seemed so restrained as to make Conservative Leader Robert Stanfield, his laconic predecessor, look like a personality kid. But he was a man preaching common sense, a concerned Canadian begging for attention to the mundane problems of regional economic inequalities. If it is true that TV cameras have remarkable fidelity in revealing a man's character, Walter Weir, the Premier of Manitoba, transmitted nothing. He was simply there.

Ross Thatcher came through as a troubled man who would rather have been somewhere else. He seemed to be making gargantuan efforts to be pleasant and his acceptance of the bilingualism and biculturalism commission's main recommendations was a gallant gesture. Yet there remained a sense of reserve about his commitment, and most viewers felt that he would have spent his time more profitably drumming up business for his province.

Premier Alex Campbell of Prince Edward Island emerged as the young statesman of the conference. Here was a man who had nothing to gain and little to lose from the subjects under discussion, but he rose above the parochial concerns of his province to show that his vision was wide enough to make him an important new father of Canada's reconfederation. Newfoundland's Premier Joey Smallwood, as always, was hamming it up for the folks back home. But his humour was infectious and at times irresistible. Premier Louis Robichaud of New Brunswick looked like a once-promising bantamweight boxer run to heft, but talked with the fervour of a reform Liberal.

John Robarts of Ontario acted as the conference's straight man. He sat reading his briefs like a lawyer handling dull litigation against a friendly witness. Occasionally he would blow through his moustache and make some sensible comment, but he seldom got excited enough to change the election-poster expression on his face. The non-heroes of the conference were Premiers Ernest Manning of Alberta and W. A. C. Bennett of British Columbia. Manning was the inflexible stand-patter, Bennett the cheerful malcontent. There was projected in Manning's statements the feeling that he had thought out his position carefully and was measuring his every word according to the dictates of his private gospel. He seemed to be a politician unwilling to gamble on progress, but his obstruction was rational and meticulously documented.

Bennett, on the other hand, recognized no crisis in Confederation and preferred discussing federal subsidies for paving British Columbia bridges to taking part in any nation-saving exercise. In his opening-day address he all but said that some of his best friends were French Canadians and openly wondered what all the commotion was about.

He had to be seen to be believed, and even then it wasn't easy. The highlight of Bennett's presentation was his introduction to the conference of one of his delegates, Peter Wing, the Chinese-Canadian mayor of Kamloops, to prove that even if he didn't respect Quebec's demands he wasn't really against minority rights as such.

The most magnetic television presence of all was Pierre Elliott Trudeau. Here was a cerebral man of action. Despite his obviously strong commitment to the issues being discussed, he seemed to be possessed by a sense of inner repose, the refusal to bend his personality into artificial political postures. When he got into a sharp exchange with Daniel Johnson and would not back down, Canadians had their first glimpse of the toughness in the man. The Quebec Premier at one point looked imploringly into the cameras and asked: "Watch out that you don't give the impression the Quebec delegation came here only to be cross-examined."

The conference ended with all governments agreeing that "as a matter of equity, French-speaking Canadians outside Quebec should have the same rights as English-speaking Canadians inside Quebec." The long process of drafting a new constitution for Canada had begun.

PART SIX   *Power Denied*

On November 8, 1965, Canadians went to the polls for the twenty-seventh time in their ninety-eight-year history. For those who follow federal politics with a passionate eye and hopeful spirit, it was not a happy contest.

An election freezes the political landscape of a nation at a given moment in time so that its results provide a temporal portrait of the emotions, tensions, and aspirations of its people. Reason fights impulse, the tug of the past competes with the pull of the future as voters cast their ballots. The 1965 election drew a portrait of Canada as a hard-bitten, provincial land digging for its soul, searching vainly for the potential of creative achievement that might illuminate its future.

In that perilous autumn of the nation's history most Canadians behaved as if they were caught up in a flight from politics and its exhaustion of ideologies. The generation gap was felt for the first time, as young Liberals and Tories found they had more in common with each other than with the elder statesmen of their own parties.

No basic recasting of party structures is possible in a democracy unless the subconscious, emotional loyalties of the voters are altered. In the 1965 campaign this would have required a politician central to his time, a man whose personality could have reached into a troubled nation to stir up new passions and create fresh allegiances. Yearning for such a leader, Canadians were instead confronted by the glazing spectacle of two aging men – John Diefenbaker and Lester Pearson – rasping out a litany of discontent as they swayed in the wind of their self-esteem.

The mood of the electorate, faced with this dismal prospect, seemed to oscillate between lethargy and disdain. So much so that a good deal of the campaign was conducted in a kind of abstract world of its own, as if it were not a national election at all, but a series of 265 by-elections that happened to fall on the same day. Faced with a choice between the shop-worn pioneer myths perpetuated by John Diefenbaker and the dispassionate mediocrities dispensed by Lester Pearson, Canadian voters withheld their confidence and voted according to their regional self-interests.

The Liberal and Conservative styles of electioneering were very different. The Diefenbaker campaign was all noise and jolting enunciations – the belching, lurching, howling CNR locomotive that pulled the train across the country its most appropriate symbol. The Pearson campaign functioned like some impersonal mechanism removed from the earthly yearnings of the electors, with the chartered CPA DC-6 – its shadow gliding over the countryside – a perfect personification.

At the end of that peculiar sixty-two-day battle for votes nearly eight million citizens paid the hesitant homage of their ballots, and the Liberals were granted a reluctant minority mandate. But the election campaign ended as it had begun, on a tentative note with issues unjoined, principles unclarified and power withheld.

CHAPTER 24

The Uncertain Trumpet Call

B Y THE SPRING OF 1965, THE PEARSON ADMINISTRATION had frittered away most of the public goodwill that had accompanied it into office two years before. On January 22 of that year, Yvon Dupuis had resigned from the cabinet amid allegations of bribery in high places; on March 2, Lucien Rivard had escaped from Bordeaux Jail, making the government an object of national ridicule; on June 29, Chief Justice Frédéric Dorion of the Quebec Superior Court had published his report on Conservative charges of corruption in the government, prompting the resignation of Guy Favreau as Minister of Justice. The House of Commons, still exhausted by the emotional splurge of the flag debate, stumbled listlessly through a few procedural reforms, then adjourned on the last day of June, its schedule of legislative priorities virtually untouched.

Many senior Liberals responded to this frustrating impasse by urging the Prime Minister to dissolve Parliament and call a general election. The chief advocate of this course of action was Walter Gordon, the Minister of Finance, who on April 26 had tabled a rosy budget that included a 10 per cent cut in personal income taxes. Gordon had already advised an election for October of 1964 and when that counsel was ignored had urged a vote on July 12, 1965.* But the publication of the

---

*The inner circle of the Liberal Party was actually gearing up for that date when somebody remembered it was the Orangemen's Glorious Twelfth, the anniversary of the Battle of the Boyne, and the election was hastily rescheduled for July 19.

Dorion Report put off the whole idea of a summer campaign, and just before Parliament adjourned Lester Pearson assured Members they would meet again on September 27.

Shortly afterwards, however, the election climate within the Liberal Party began to change. On July 8, the government announced the start of construction on the long-delayed Prince Edward Island causeway, a gesture most political veterans in Ottawa interpreted as a sure sign of an impending campaign. On July 19, the Pearson government presented its plans for a national medicare scheme to a federal-provincial conference in a manner that made it look like a hastily prepared election plank. The government was so badly informed that Health and Welfare Minister Judy LaMarsh clumsily told the provincial premiers that the total cost of the scheme would be lower by tens of millions of dollars than was actually the case. When Jean Lesage of Quebec indicated that his own studies showed Quebec's share alone would amount to her figure, Miss LaMarsh hastily said her cost accounting must be wrong.

Consideration of an election was delayed by a week-long national strike of postal workers in late July, which worried Pearson quite out of proportion to its long-term effects. "The Prime Minister," Walter Gordon recalled in a later interview, "got terribly worked up over the postal strike. He thought the country had stopped. I didn't think it had stopped, it just meant we wouldn't receive so many of those silly letters we get."

Gordon continued to push for an early election and gradually won some important converts, including Trade and Commerce Minister Mitchell Sharp and Lester Pearson himself. Sharp changed his position largely because of economic considerations, particularly the fear that balance of payments and anti-inflationary policy problems which he felt a minority government could not properly handle might come up in the late fall. DBS statistics showed that Canada's unfavourable balance of trade for the first quarter of 1965 was running at an annual rate of more than a billion dollars, compared with $453 millions in 1964. The spectacular bankruptcy of Atlantic Acceptance Corporation had shaken foreign investment confidence in Canada badly; prices of most Canadian resource exports were falling on world markets; the food component for June 1965 had driven the cost-of-living index up to 139, an unusual 3.7 points over the June 1964 level. There was still little evidence of the kind of massive inventory accumulation that precedes most business recessions, but Sharp began to feel that only a "stable" government (his euphemism for a Liberal majority) could deal with future economic problems.

Pearson's conversion to the pro-election position was a more complicated process. Fed up with the buffeting his government had received over the scandals, he saw an election victory as a symbolic washing-away of sin, a public vindication of his own honour and his administration's basic integrity. By the summer of 1965, he was a man who psychologically could take no more of the political pounding that goes with a minority government situation, and desperately wanted the release and relative security of a majority mandate. He blamed most of his administration's many difficulties on the hypertensions of its minority position.

Pearson's relationship with John Diefenbaker was another factor militating for an early election call. He shared the schizophrenic attitude most Liberals had toward the Conservative leader: they badly wanted him out of the Commons, where he tore most of their legislative attempts to shreds, but at the same time they half desired that he continue as head of his party because they felt he had become a liability to his cause, whereas with almost any other leader the Tories might win the next election. Talk of Conservative plans to depose Diefenbaker in the fall fitted perfectly into the government's scheme. The Liberal reasoning went this way: they would call an election while "the Chief" was still in command, beat him on the hustings, force his resignation, and form a majority government against a more reasonable Tory leader who would allow them to legislate at will.*

To gauge the public mood, Pearson set off on a nine-day western tour on August 19. In Vancouver he rode in a parade, participated in the *Vancouver Sun*'s fishing derby and addressed two meetings of local Liberals, sweetening his visit with outright political gifts. He announced a $2 million federal grant toward the construction of an exhibition-trade centre building in Vancouver that might also be used as a hockey arena, promised Ottawa would contribute to the development of west coast harbours for pleasure craft, and pledged his government would turn

---

*There was also a host of other, less significant considerations. Pearson had been advised that Jean Lesage intended calling a provincial election in 1966, and wanted a federal campaign out of the way first. New federal-provincial fiscal arrangements had to be negotiated, a task difficult for a minority administration facing a group of premiers all of whom had strong, majority mandates behind them. Canadian Institute of Public Opinion soundings showed the Liberals to be as much as 20 per cent ahead of the Conservatives, who had dipped to a ten-year low of 28 per cent of popular support. In mid August, Russia signed an unexpectedly large ($450 millions) wheat deal and the Liberals felt certain the time of their breakthrough in the West had come.

over to the city of Vancouver free of charge part of the defence base at Jericho Beach.*

Pearson spent the weekend of his west coast visit relaxing at Wood-wynn Farm, the Saanich estate of Mrs William Woodward of the department store family. There he met his old friend Bruce Hutchison and told him that an election would be called provided a private party survey being taken proved to be favourable, and that he would resign if his government didn't win a majority mandate. Another visitor was John Nichol, a prominent Vancouver Liberal, who came to warn Pearson against an early election call.† Meanwhile, in Vancouver, Keith Davey, the Liberal Party's National Organizer, was telling British Columbia Liberals that by the time their polls were heard from on election night he would be safely in bed asleep, serene in the knowledge of a Liberal majority.

At a Vancouver press conference, before continuing his trip by flying to Prince George, Banff and Edmonton, Pearson's intentions were finally pinned down, under intense questioning from Jack Webster, the crusading west coast radio and television commentator. The Prime Minister admitted that an announcement "one way or another" would be made within two weeks, and that the election would be called for either November of 1965 or late 1967. The rationale for this statement was based entirely on his view of the constituency boundaries redistribution timetable. "If redistribution were an over-riding factor, it would mean we couldn't have an election so far as the government is concerned until 1967," he said, "and I think the end of 1967 would be a better time than the beginning, in view of the nature of the [Centennial] year."

THIS LINE OF ARGUMENT – THAT A 1965 ELECTION was necessary because a 1966 campaign was impossible and a 1967 election undesirable

*The nature of Pearson's political largess was based on a report he'd received from his executive assistant, Mary Macdonald. She had gone to Vancouver for her holidays in July, had lunched with provincial Liberal Leader Ray Perrault, and asked him: "What shall we give Vancouver?" Perrault mentioned the hockey rink, the grant for small boat harbours and the Jericho Beach development – which turned out to be exactly what Pearson announced.
†Nichol had always disagreed with the view of the Liberal Party held by Walter Gordon and Keith Davey which he claimed was oriented "to that region of Canada visible on a clear day from the top of the Royal York Hotel." He once jokingly suggested to Gordon and Davey that they considered Canada's two founding races to be "the Toronto Maple Leafs and the Italians of Davenport riding."

– carried a lot of weight with the Prime Minister and he continued to justify his election call by repeating and embellishing it. But it was a false argument and Pearson had easy access to documents demonstrating its flaws.

The new Electoral Boundaries Readjustment Act had received Royal Assent on November 20, 1964. By late August of 1965 the representational commissions set up by the legislation had completed their preliminary task of preparing and publishing the new constituency maps based on the 1961 census. The final deadline for their reports was January 23, 1966, and the process of implementing them, it was estimated, would take at least another eighty-five days – to April 17. Polling divisions would then have to be reallocated, new returning officers appointed and trained. This required a minimum of another three months, taking the redistribution process well into the summer of 1966. Pearson's public claims to the contrary, there was nothing to prevent an election in the late fall of that year.

On July 5, 1965, at the request of Maurice Lamontagne, then the Secretary of State, Nelson Castonguay, Canada's Acting Chief Electoral Officer, had prepared a long memorandum which concluded that a November, 1966, election would be possible.* On August 4, O. G. Stoner, the assistant secretary to the cabinet, requested an opinion from the Justice Department on the Castonguay memorandum. The reply, signed by Acting Deputy Attorney General D. S. Maxwell, was returned to the PM's office on August 10, confirming the Castonguay timetable. On September 1, Pearson wrote to Castonguay directly, asking for a private estimate "of the earliest date [after redistribution] on which a general election could be held." Castonguay replied the following day that he had not changed his opinion since the July 5 memorandum. On September 3, Pearson, still not satisfied, wrote Castonguay again, sending him a further and more detailed Department of Justice opinion, which concluded with the statement: "Thus if all new returning officers were appointed immediately after the stages required by the redistribution legislation were completed, an election based on redistribution could be held after the end of September, 1966." Castonguay replied on September 7. He wrote that the Justice Department's legal opinion altered his timetable "only to the extent that it would be possible, in my opinion, to hold a general election in late October, 1966, instead of November as mentioned in the last paragraph of such [the July 5] memorandum."

*For this memorandum and copies of the correspondence that passed between Nelson Castonguay and Lester Pearson, see Appendix F.

This was the crystal-clear advice of the man who would have to be in charge of the mechanics of the election: a general election based on the new boundaries *could* be held by late October of 1966. Even though he had asked for that advice, and had confirmed it through this exchange of private correspondence, Pearson in public continued to insist that no election could be held in 1966 and he was therefore being *forced* into calling a vote for 1965.

The main points of opposition to the holding of an early election were expressed in an eloquent memorandum sent to the Prime Minister by John de B. Payne, a Montreal public relations consultant and former Pearson executive assistant. He delineated the five main reasons why a 1965 election should not be called, the last of them being that "the moral aspect of redistribution is too strong to be ignored."* At the same time, Leslie Roberts, the Montreal radio commentator and an old friend of Pearson's, wrote to him warning against an election and asking for a ten-minute appointment at any time to outline his reasons. The Payne memorandum was acknowledged on September 20; the Roberts letter ended up in Mary Macdonald's waste basket.

THE PARTY STRATEGISTS AT THIS TIME were engrossed in the confidential surveys being carried out for the Liberals by Oliver Quayle, head of New York's Oliver Quayle and Associates, the firm that had inherited the account when Lou Harris, the Kennedy pollster used by the Liberals for the 1962 and 1963 campaigns, left the private polling business to work for the Columbia Broadcasting System and *Newsweek*. In April of 1965 Quayle had warned the Liberals against an election, but by August his polls had changed slightly in the government's favour, as shown in this table of Quayle's private survey results:

	April, 1965	August, 1965
Liberals	41%	43%
Conservatives	32%	30%
NDP	15%	14%
Others	12%	13%

In his accompanying memorandum of advice, Quayle dismissed the redistribution issue: "We have never seen redistribution really cut with voters. They are not interested in such matters and usually don't understand what's involved." Quayle's conclusion was that "the risk of wait-

*For the text of the Payne memorandum, see Appendix G.

342

ing another year is that there will be a change in the Tory leadership, there will be more of Parliament moving at a desultory pace and/or there will be a downward trend in the economy." Quayle also noted that the government had "ridden out the storm" of the scandals and concluded: "We think [the Liberal Party] can win a majority, but it will certainly not be easy. Our own estimate is that at the present time there would be a total pickup of 11 to 15 seats, to make it 140-45 . . . but we will remain frightened until the day of the election and hope everyone runs scared."

On August 30, the day after Pearson returned from his western tour, Paul Martin asked him for a copy of the Quayle poll which he showed to a friend in his department who knew something about public opinion surveying. Martin then went back to see the PM and reported that it was not favourable enough to justify the calling of an election. Pearson agreed. The next day, Walter Gordon persuaded the Prime Minister to change his mind again. Finally, Pearson decided to poll the cabinet on each individual minister's preference at its regular meeting scheduled for September 1. The full Pearson ministry attended except for Arthur Laing and Jack Nicholson; Jack Pickersgill even flew in for the day from Newfoundland.

At the cabinet meeting seventeen ministers agreed to a fall election with varying degrees of enthusiasm. The exceptions were Paul Martin (who was asked first but replied simply, "Ask me last," then came out against an early vote), Paul Hellyer, Maurice Sauvé, and J. Watson MacNaught. Jack Pickersgill stayed neutral by coming down on both sides of the issue. He thought it would be a good thing for the Liberals, if they won, to be in a position of being able to tell the Quebec Government that they too represented French Canadians, but he also relayed Joey Smallwood's warning against an election call and refrained from giving his own advice. Walter Gordon, enthusiastic as ever, casually promised to resign if the Liberals didn't get their majority.

By the first week in September, Pearson had manoeuvred himself into an unenviable position. Sitting alone in the unnatural quiet that becalms the summit of political power, he now had to make the final decision. His long public dithering had put him in a spot where he appeared to have only two choices: to back down and call the election, or to back down and not call it.

The final choice of November 8 as polling day was made on the verandah of Pearson's summer residence, at a meeting on Friday, September 3, attended by the Prime Minister, Tom Kent, Walter Gordon, Keith Davey, Mary Macdonald, Richard O'Hagan and Mrs Pearson. To those sitting out in the bright sunlight at Harrington Lake that day, the world seemed full of promise for a Liberal majority, and as they broke up the members of the inner circle congratulated themselves on the wisdom of their decision.

AT THE END OF THE LABOUR DAY WEEKEND, on Tuesday, September 7, Pearson obtained the dissolution order from Governor General Georges Vanier and on the advice of his image-makers decided to make the actual election announcement over national television. After Richard O'Hagan got the necessary time reserved by the CBC, he telephoned CTV to get a similar commitment. Stuart Griffiths, the operating head of CJOH, the private network's Ottawa affiliate, promptly telephoned John Diefenbaker's office and invited him to comment on the PM's announcement. Tommy Douglas, Robert Thompson and Réal Caouette were also asked to stand by. Pearson was unaware of all this until he arrived at the CBC's studios to give his broadcast. Just before going on the air he was told that his seven-minute message would be followed by twenty-three minutes of criticism from the other party leaders. This so unnerved him that he botched his performance, making it sound as though he were still unsuccessfully trying to convince himself that a general election really was justified. Just before air time, Mary Macdonald hovered about, giving the PM last-minute advice. O'Hagan stood in the control room, gesturing with his hands like some entranced faith-healer trying to draw out of the TV monitors a more convincing performance than Pearson was able to deliver. That night on the nation's TV screens the Prime Minister looked like an unhappy puppet being manipulated by unseen influences though he was the one who had made the election decision.

John Diefenbaker came on immediately afterwards. "My fellow Canadians," he rumbled, "now we know. After days and weeks of hesitation and indecision, the Prime Minister has plunged this country into an election. I ask my fellow Conservatives to stand together. We have an appointment with destiny and I say, let us meet this improper challenge that has been dropped against us." When Fraser Kelly of the Toronto *Telegram* went up to the Conservative leader after his broadcast and asked what kind of campaign he intended running, Diefenbaker replied: "Young man, I never campaign, I just visit with the people."

The country's reaction to the election announcement was a national yawn. "Sir," wrote a reader to the *Montreal Star*, "Diefenbaker is impossible, Pearson is irresponsible. Douglas is impractical. Thompson is unbelievable. Caouette is incredible. What shall I do?" Richard Needham, in his *Globe and Mail* column, summed up the feelings of most of his readers:

> Well, here we go into still another federal election. Do you really care what is said or done in the campaign, who wins or who loses? Does it really matter to you whether we end up being governed by Lester Pathos or John Disaster or Tommy Handouts or Robert Zero or Réal the Unreal? For my own part, I'm about to turn the whole thing over to Eaton's or Simpson's or maybe the Bell Telephone. They couldn't run the country any worse, and from my experience with them, they'd run it a great deal better. Don't vote on November 8; eat an orange instead.

DURING THE NEXT FEW DAYS, the Liberals made the final strategic decisions that would hold throughout the campaign. Their choices were based on a series of secret memoranda written by Tom Kent on THE ISSUES (August 25), THE STRATEGY (September 3) and THE CAMPAIGN (September 6).

Kent's estimate was that the Liberals could win 150 seats, provided Pearson ran a non-partisan campaign in which he would, in effect, successfully project the image of a man trying to save Canada from its politicians. Kent judged the mood of the nation to be one of dulled anxiety, a time when the voters were seeking the comforts of political security rather than the excitement of a dramatic confrontation. He warned Pearson that he should on no account campaign against the Conservatives, because that would be "fighting on the Opposition's best ground" and the Liberals would be "helping to put in the forefront of people's minds just those things for which they don't like us." The Liberal line here seemed to be that, given free rein, John Diefenbaker would become revealed as a sort of baggy-kneed burlesque politician unfit for the smooth, sophisticated world of twentieth-century Canada, as conceived by the Liberal Party. "The Prime Minister should ignore him [Diefenbaker] utterly and completely," Kent advised. "That will make him so mad he'll get wilder and wilder. When he's really wild, the [National Liberal] Federation can put out a few really well-chosen answers and blow him up. But that must be done calmly, with an appearance almost of gentleness."

Kent, Gordon and Davey agreed the traditional pattern of electioneering in Canada should be broken by keeping Pearson in Ottawa for fully half of the campaigning time available. Instead of the standard election tour, they advised a series of two- and three-day forays, brief excursions into the electoral process. This strategy was outlined in Kent's final memo: "With any luck Diefenbaker will wear himself out during the campaign and towards the end of it will begin to look bedraggled especially on television. It will be very important, in contrast, for Mr Pearson to remain fresh." His suggested itinerary broke the Pearson timetable down into a series of "visits" from Ottawa, with long rest periods in between to allow the Prime Minister relief from the din, the tedium, the forced smiles and the lavish handshaking of the campaign. Instead of criss-crossing the nation advocating radical new initiatives, the Liberal leader would be presented to the electorate as a personification of the national consensus on all the broad basic issues.

The Liberals' approach seemed to be based on the somewhat arrogant assumption that scandals or not they alone could form a credible government. Asked by a Toronto *Telegram* reporter on September 10 why he had called the election, Pearson replied: "I have my reasons. And my reasons are very good." This was a remarkable nutshell summary of the Liberal view of the electorate – the attitude of the parent to a child too young to comprehend the subtleties of life.

FEW LIBERALS PAID MUCH ATTENTION to what John Diefenbaker was doing at the time they were busy making their final decisions. Smelling an election in the air, he had decided to make a late August exploratory journey into rural Quebec, which was supposed to be his weakest territory. Instead of debating constitutional issues, he used background papers prepared by Alvin Hamilton to announce policies that would give the hard-pressed farmers of eastern Canada some of the benefits the Diefenbaker Government had granted western agriculture. The tour was a success partly because it was expected to be a fiasco and partly because Diefenbaker was so well briefed. (At Louiseville, for example, during a brief reception in the auditorium of a high school run by the Brothers of Christian Instruction, he reminded the rector that as prime minister he had visited the order's new school in Tokyo and described in detail the Japanese trip.)

Clément Vincent, a local Conservative M.P.,* had spent $12 for a small advertisement to promote Diefenbaker's appearance at Fleur de Lys hall on August 24 in Ste Perpétue, a modest farming community of about eleven hundred, fifty miles east of Montreal. On the night of the meeting, twenty-five hundred people turned up, twice the village's population, and loudspeakers had to be set up on the streets to accommodate the overflow. Even more unusual was the fact that Diefenbaker spoke

*Later Minister of Agriculture in the Johnson administration.

for half an hour in almost faultless French, outlining his program of farm support. The audience listened to every word, gave him a standing ovation, then dispersed quickly and quietly into the night. Minutes after this stirring meeting, Ste Perpétue had turned back into a sleepy village and Diefenbaker never spoke French so well again. Ever afterwards that occasion was known among sceptical Conservatives and more sceptical newsmen as the Miracle of Ste Perpétue.

THE LIBERALS DISCOUNTED REPORTS of their opponent's dark magic. At a grand banquet for party candidates in the Chateau Laurier on September 21, Pearson spoke in lofty prime ministerial tones about his high office and asked for "the confidence of Canadians in all parts of the country." When the meeting broke up the candidates were herded into a private hall. Walter Gordon asked the campaign chairmen for each province to give their estimates of seats they would win. The total came to 164.*

And so the Liberals went to the electoral wars once more, armed with public opinion surveys, policy priorities, an elaborate strategy, a minutely worked out itinerary. All that the Pearson campaign lacked was a reason for being.

---

*The breakdown of the estimates given was as follows: Newfoundland, 7; New Brunswick, 6; Nova Scotia, 5; P.E.I., 2; Quebec, 64; Ontario, 62; Manitoba, 2; Saskatchewan, 2; Alberta, 6; B.C., 7; Yukon and N.W.T., 1.

CHAPTER 25

The Man Who Tried
to Become Canada

T HE ELECTION WAGED BY JOHN DIEFENBAKER in the fall of 1965
was not a campaign in the accepted sense. It was a guerrilla war,
fought along a four-thousand-mile front in treacherous circumstances with unreliable troops and intriguing generals. Victory was impossible; success would be measured by mere survival.

The Diefenbaker campaign style transcended ideology. To him, the
Conservative Party was little more than a front for his rhetoric. Even
more than winning the election, he seemed obsessed by a need to
propagandize his vision of Canada, to hold back, somehow, the mechanized urban society threatening to engulf his world.

From the beginning, John Diefenbaker refused to read the portents
or heed the omens of his defeat. In retrospect, only one explanation
seemed to fit the dimensions of his extraordinary campaign. It was as if,
sometime after Lester Pearson called the election, John Diefenbaker
decided to transform himself into an incarnation of the Canada he knew.
He became a figment of his own imagination, a man for whom nothing
was impossible, a politician without rivals, because he saw himself as
personifying the national will. In an age of political image-making, he
was the greatest pretender of them all.

John Diefenbaker had to lose. But the odds didn't seem fair. While
Lester Pearson was firing salvos of press releases from his Ottawa office
or the multigraph machines mounted in his campaign aircraft, John

Diefenbaker was jolting into small towns at twenty-minute intervals on a punishing coast-to-coast railway tour.*

AN AIR OF TIMELESSNESS HUNG over John Diefenbaker's campaign train as he whistle-stopped his way across the country. There was no taste of 1965 in the air, no sensation of progress or reality. The landscape on which the Diefenbaker train moved seemed like a sequence of Krieghoff tableaux run through a Cinerama lens.

Diefenbaker's advisers had warned him that campaigning by train could prove disastrous, because in the age of the automobile, railway stations were no longer a factor in most people's lives. During the first leg of his journey, from Halifax to Montreal, it looked as if his advisers had been right. At Matapédia, Quebec, only five off-duty trainmen and three stray dogs turned out to meet the Chief. At Rimouski, where seven lonely Tories were waiting on the platform, Diefenbaker asked one of them: "Who's the candidate here?" He replied: "I am, sir, my name is Gérard Ouellette." At Amqui, the Conservative leader was introduced to a Monsieur Legris, who in turn presented the young man beside him as "mon fils." Diefenbaker smiled and said: "Bonjour, Mon-seer Monfils."

It wasn't until the Diefenbaker train was being pulled into the rural way stations of southern Alberta that the campaign began to pick up. The signs that dotted most station platforms on the Prairies – sometimes printed, sometimes scrawled on fences – established the theme of the Diefenbaker campaign: HE CARED ENOUGH TO COME. Nothing else mattered. Diefenbaker cared, and had come. Pearson had not come and, by implication, did not care.†

John Diefenbaker moved like a legend over the land. Everywhere his train stopped, clusters of people would seek the sight of him under the cool Prairie sun. The men with hands hooked into the front of their broad belts gazed at the former prime minister, seeing him in a warm

---

*During the 1965 campaign, John Diefenbaker visited 196 places, Lester Pearson 32.

†The slogan had been adapted from the signs used by Nelson Rockefeller ("HE CARES ENOUGH TO COME") in the 1964 Oregon presidential primary to beat the absent Henry Cabot Lodge. It was spotted by Lowell Murray, a young Conservative adviser, on page 114 of *The Making of the President: 1964* by T. H. White and passed on to Tory headquarters, which ordered the signs printed for distribution throughout the West.

glow of recognition, as someone with whom they'd shared the experience of hard times. The wind fluttered the hair of the women as they shyly shook his hand to extend a mute blessing.

It was the presence of John Diefenbaker more than his words that excited the people. Here was a communion of instinct that no other politician could fully understand, much less duplicate. John Diefenbaker was the political poet who in his very being could evoke the pioneer virtues and the glories of a simpler past when the Red River carts still creaked along the Battleford Trail and buffalo bones littered the horizonless prairie. At Melville, Saskatchewan, he spoke to several old timers at the rear of the station platform, demanding: "When did you come here?" The oldest of them said, proudly, that he'd arrived in 1903. "But *when*?" Diefenbaker insisted. "In September," was the reply. A gleeful Diefenbaker shot back: "We came in August!"

The enthusiasm of the crowds was not essentially political. Most of the people who turned out to see the Chief (and they were nearly all in their late fifties, sixties or seventies) were revellers in a nostalgic rite. He stood there, reminding them of a time when they had been at the forefront of Canadian civilization. They had won this country and now they were being pushed aside by an alien world they had never made, losing their legacy to the slick, rootless generation of the big cities.

Out of his passion for the homely, awkward and shattering small truth came Diefenbaker's rapport with the people of these small, flat prairie towns, slanting across time. Here he could feel again the only role he had ever played well: the champion of society's downtrodden, assaulting the proud fortresses of the nation's various Establishments. He soaked up the mood of rural Canada and gave it off, like a hot swift fire that burns away the scrub of a hidebound life.

The Diefenbaker train went tumbling through the night of time, its press car filled with the noise of tapping typewriters, the tinkling of glasses and the slap of cards on a table. In his private car, Diefenbaker dictated and signed an average of three hundred letters a day, mostly to well-wishers along his route. Between whistle stops, particularly late in the day, fatigue would dissolve his face into deep creases and lines, like the topographical map of some rugged country. Occasionally he would relax by taking off his clothes and stomping around his car in a bathrobe, hunching his shoulders like a prize fighter flexing for the big bout.

The leader's entourage had picked up a canary from a supporter in Richmond Hill, Ontario, and Diefenbaker spent hours trying to coax the bird to whistle, as if its song were some omen of good fortune.

The bird never did sing, but on the morning of November 6, between Saskatoon and Prince Albert, the steward was imitating a canary whistle, and Diefenbaker, who thought it was the real thing, got very excited. No one ever told him the truth.

THE PRAIRIES BECAME A LAND TO FLEE ACROSS – every town, every village a destination. When would these place names – Rivers, Yarbo, Raymore, Watrous, Wadena, Mortlach, Morse, Maple Creek, Taber, Fort Macleod, Claresholm, Nanton, Vulcan, Barons, Three Hills, Findlater, Aylesbury, Lumsden, Gull Lake, Champion – ever again appear in reports of Canadian election campaigns?

The journey was illuminated with moments of lucid pathos. At Fort Macleod, 78-year-old Norman Grier confided to the Chief: "Heck, I wouldn't vote for that Pearson. He wants to give away Crowsnest Mountain to Quebec." At Stettler, two raggedy kids were holding up a huge, hand-lettered cardboard sign with the letters: DEIF FOR CHEIF. At Morse, local musicians serenaded him with a wavering version of *The Thunderer* and reporters couldn't file their copy because the telegrapher was playing the drums. As the train pulled out, the brave little aggregation struck up *God Be with You till We Meet Again* and John Diefenbaker cried. At Swift Current, twenty-one blue-gowned ladies on the back of a truck broke into *Land of Hope and Glory* and sang *Mademoiselle from Armentières* for an encore. At Taber, Diefenbaker told an audience of hushed school children: "I only wish that I could come back when you're my age to see the kind of Canada that you'll see. So dream your dreams, keep them and pursue them." Somewhere along the route, an old man sat by the tracks in the twilight, holding up a sign that read: JOHN, YOU'LL NEVER DIE.

WHAT GAVE DIEFENBAKER'S WHISTLE-STOP TOUR its substance was his delivery every weekday evening of a speech at some high school auditorium, Legion Hall, or community arena along the route. These speeches were grandiose, impressionistic spectacles, reminiscent in style of old-time Southern camp meetings, where the language of exhortation, graceless but emphatic by choice, took the place of logical discourse.

As the Old Chief rose each night, at first his manner would be halting, his voice muted, as if he were unwilling to give himself to the crowd. But once his listeners had committed their attention, the flow of his words would take on an infectious rhythm. His phrases would fan in and out, the alternation of clipped participles with long open vowel sounds giving the performance a biblical cadence. Gradually the immediacy of his language would be augmented by his limb movements, the right hand swooping down in accusing chops, the whole man swaying to the melody of his words, as if his body were without bones.

He used language not as a vehicle for concepts but as an instrument of provocation, a sensory agent for establishing accord with his audience. At one moment, he would take on a highly moralistic tone, like some gruff ship's captain reading from the Good Book during a burial at sea. The next instant, with an energy born of gloating, he would dance out his joy at some embarrassment suffered by his opponents, the wicked Grits. Words would appear to spring instinctively from him as he exulted in his dreams, blazing away against the invisible villains who, unlike himself, showed little concern for "the average Canadian." In a nightly recitation of recriminations and self-dramatizing confessions, he would hurl his defiance at the always unnamed, sombre forces which had sought his downfall, dropping each accusing phrase a tone at a time, as though throwing worthless coins into a canyon. By any contemporary standard Diefenbaker was a man clearly in conflict with his times, both as a reactionary who hankered for the past and as a visionary whose aims exceeded his grasp. Here was the "little man" writ large with massive determination to be just, to be virtuous, to be moral, and most of all, to be heard. His speeches were full of racing innuendos ("Mr Kent is the director of the war on poverty. They raised his salary to $25,000 – he won *his* war! What about the rest of us?"), invented words ("Those crimesters who support the Liberal Party . . . "), and improved clichés ("I never look a gift horse in the eye"). He was at his sarcastic best when dealing with the Liberal legislative record. "Just think of the pension plan," he said at a rally in Richmond Hill, Ontario, on October 25. "I recall so well when the Minister of Health came in with it and she said, 'This is a wonderful thing. Never has the mind of man ever produced anything like it.' Mr Lesage said it was no good. Mr Pearson said, 'I heard you the first time.' And out it went."

Through the sandstorm of words Diefenbaker's sense of occasion was unfailing. Addressing a rally of dock workers in the port city of Vancouver, he injected a topical note by claiming the first version of the Liberals' pension plan had been "put in dry dock." At the Prince George, B.C., Legion Hall, when the power suddenly went off in the middle of his speech, he looked around, raised his hands, and just before the electricity was restored, intoned: "Let there be light!" Speaking to a small, street-corner group in Beausejour, Manitoba, he was momentarily drowned out by a police siren, and rejoiced: "Oh, a lot of Liberals will be hearing that before we're through!" He could handle hecklers with a skill that left them uncomfortably twisting lumps of ebbing rebellion. At his rally in the Victoria, B.C., armouries, he declared: "In this election, we will increase the number of members in every province but one." When a heckler fell into his trap, and yelled out "Quebec!", Diefenbaker closed it. "No," he shouted back. "Saskatchewan, where we *have* all the seats."

As always, he tried in his speeches to reduce complicated national issues to simple slogans, in the process frequently distorting the facts. To prove that the Liberals didn't have much of a farm policy, he quoted Agriculture Minister Harry Hays as having said in the House of Commons that "if a Quebec farmer had two sows, six cows and a wife with a strong back, he can make $2,400 a year." Then, to give this accusation legitimacy, Diefenbaker asserted: "You wouldn't believe it unless you read it in Hansard. Here it is, Hansard, February 22, 1965, page 11580."*

JOHN DIEFENBAKER GRASPED THE INITIATIVE during the 1965 campaign by acting as though he'd never lost it. He decided to fight the election on one exclusive issue: the idea that the attitude really separating the Conservatives from the Liberals was their standard on integrity in politics. The names and dates of the many scandals charged to the Pearson administration gave the Tory leader a concrete focus for his cunning humour. He approached the subject in fun: "It was a warm night, just like this, when Rivard asked the warden for a hose to water the rink . . . " Then, just as his audience would join in his derision,

*Page 11580 of Hansard reveals no mention of a "wife with a strong back." Hays had used a documented version of the "two sows and six cows" argument to show that, DBS figures to the contrary, most farmers who could afford such animals would have a basic income of at least $2,400. His reasoning, completely ignored by Diefenbaker, went this way: "If a farmer has two sows they would each have two litters of pigs a year, and if they just made the national average of eight pigs per litter that would come to 32 pigs in a year. If they were sold on the Montreal market when they were five or six months old and weighed about 200 pounds they would bring something like $40 apiece. That is a gross income of $1,280, and he still has the two sows. If, in addition to the two sows, he has six cows each giving the national average of 8,000 pounds of milk per year, that is 48,000 pounds of milk. At the current Quebec price of $3.20 per cwt. that is a gross income of $1,536. So if you add the hog gross of $1,280 to the milk gross of $1,536 you get a total gross income of $2,816 for a farmer with two sows and six cows."

Diefenbaker's gladiatorial features would darken. His voice had the harsh sound of ripping canvas, his eyes blazed with frigid fire, as he leaned into the microphone and intoned: "Wrongdoing there will always be individually, but when it permeates the very soul and heart of an administration, when they conceal, when they deny and refuse to reveal until they can do no other, the time has come to restore in this nation new principles of honesty."

The Conservative leader sought to emphasize the sacredness of his mission by painting the Pearson ministers as men transformed by pride and power into enemies of his fellow Canadians. "The sacredness of the human personality must be preserved," he declared at Assiniboia, Saskatchewan, implying that the Grits were against it.

Every effective political stimulus must sit out its time lag, but John Diefenbaker was once more betrayed by his tendency to exaggeration. Instead of giving his scandal accusations a proper incubation period, he escalated them beyond the limits of credibility. The best example was his spiralling scale of references to Lucien Rivard, the Montreal narcotics smuggler. Early in the campaign, Diefenbaker contented himself by referring to Rivard as "a destroyer of the souls of men." But by the end of October he was calling Rivard "that worst, inhuman beast, walking around with seventy pounds of heroin, enough to degenerate almost a whole generation."

His attacks ballooned as the campaign wore on. At his Winnipeg rally he painted criminal activity as constituting the dominant philosophy of the Pearson Government, "that galaxy of wrongdoers . . . corruption has become a way of life for them." In Prince George, B.C., he said: "A vote for this Government is a vote for an open season for organized crime in Canada." At Hamilton, he portrayed Pearson as a politician who "contributes to the collapse of the whole moral fabric of the race he represents."

Instead of condemning the Pearson Government for its real (and grave) errors of ethics and judgement, these attacks reduced one of the election's legitimate issues to a carnival of meaningless charges. "Did you read the Prime Minister's code of ethics?" Diefenbaker would ask a rally. Then, in tones of mock confidence, he would whisper: "Did you read it? I'll tell you what's in it. It says: 'Be good. And if you can't be good, be careful.' "

In Diefenbaker's firecracker presentation the shady characters associated with the scandals became symbols of national disunity. "There are two flags, two pension plans and two laws," he said at most meetings. "One for us, and the other for the Bananas, the Mananas and the rest of that menagerie. They're waiting on the sidelines for the government to be returned: what a bonanza for them!"*

It was the effect of Diefenbaker's exploitation of the scandals in a way that seemed to reflect on the morality of French Canadians that made an already ugly issue much uglier. By constantly making fun of Rivard, Lamontagne, Favreau and Tremblay, he allowed English Canadians who really had strong anti-Quebec feelings to vote for their prejudices and for virtue at the same time. Three issues – the scandals, the new flag and relations with French Canada – became interchangeable in some WASP minds. The unsubstantiated but dramatic charges by Dr Guy Marcoux that the Liberals had bribed six Social Credit M.P.'s to support them in 1963 and the discovery by the Quebec Provincial Police, in mid campaign, of the corpses of several victims of a bankruptcy-racket gang war, all helped to provide Diefenbaker with ammunition.†

DESPITE DIEFENBAKER'S HEAVY-HANDED TREATMENT of the scandals, his accusations gravely subverted the Liberals' chances for a majority. Because Pearson had kept Favreau, Lamontagne and Tremblay in his cabinet despite a pre-election shuffle, the Liberal Leader had to maintain throughout his campaign that all was well within his government and that no further reforms were necessary. At first the Prime Minister and some of his supporters tried to make fun of the issue. In Edmonton Pearson told a rally: "I wonder that you'd want to be seen in the company of such a corrupt man!" On October 20, speaking at Chipman, N.B., Judy LaMarsh declared: "Generally speaking, people think all politicians are crooked. But if they were, they wouldn't go into politics. They could make more money as crooks."

*This was a doubtful proposition, since Mananas (Onofrio Minaudo) was dead and Bananas (Joe Bonanno) had disappeared. Minaudo, the Mafia gangster whose residence in Canada had been supported by both Conservative and Liberal politicians, had been shot dead on May 17, 1965, in his native village in Sicily. Joe Bonanno, the leader of a Brooklyn Cosa Nostra "family," had been kidnapped by a rival gang on a New York street on October 21, 1964. He had been in Canada for three months in 1964 before being deported.
†Diefenbaker tried to link Maurice Lamontagne and René Tremblay to the bankruptcy rackets and kept insisting that the government was holding back a secret report on bankruptcies. After the election Diefenbaker admitted in the Commons that he had been referring to the Mercier Report, submitted to the Quebec Government on July 30, 1965. It had dealt with the administration of bankruptcy legislation between November 1, 1959, and November 1, 1964, reflecting criticisms of both the Diefenbaker and Pearson governments.

355

What was really hurting the Liberals was not so much the past record of scandal allegations as a nagging doubt among the voters whether, once the grey cloak of a Liberal majority government enfolded Ottawa, there would be any way of determining how the Pearson administration might resolve future conflicts between public interest and private conscience. The scandals issue reinforced an already established image of the Prime Minister's weak leadership.

Pearson made one major television broadcast (on October 21) on this issue, in which he denied that scandals were a problem. "The facts are," he said, "first, that the attempt to influence justice failed completely; and, second, that the Government immediately severed connection with the people whose behaviour was questionable. The wrong-doing was dealt with, as it should have been. But I refused to go beyond the prevention and correction of such wrong-doing. I repeat, no charge has been made that has not been investigated. Nothing was revealed, that should have been dealt with, that was not dealt with. The rest is insinuation and misrepresentation." Significantly, John Diefenbaker's name was never mentioned in any of the Liberal counter-attacks. Harry Hays, the one minister who had planned to make a speech attacking the Conservative Leader, was ordered by Liberal campaign headquarters not to give it. Hays' undelivered text read, in part: "If John Diefenbaker honestly believes there is still wrong-doing to be corrected, I challenge him to take the honorable and courageous course and bring charges against those he accuses. I challenge him to use the tactics of men of honour. In his efforts to deceive Canadians into believing distortions instead of facts, I believe Mr Diefenbaker is guilty of the most dangerous and the most corrupting kind of political immorality. If he wanted to be serious about raising the moral standards of our politics, he would deal with the facts, he would deal with the truth, instead of indulging in all this smear-mongering."*

WHILE THEIR HANDLING OF THE SCANDALS helped to keep the Liberals from breaking through to a majority, Diefenbaker was similarly impeded by his failure to convince the voters that he believed in government as well as politics. Such an alchemy would have required him to become credible as the proponent of rational new priorities to light up the Canadian future. He could make the nerve ends twinge with his

*The most vicious attack on the Conservative Leader came from Bona Arsenault, the Provincial Secretary in the Lesage Government, who told a Quebec City rally on October 19: "The worst possible calamity in Canada at the present time is not the atomic bomb, cholera or rats, but Diefenbaker."

passions and indignations but his audiences invariably sat uneasy and disbelieving as he stumbled through an inept recital of his party's platform.

A political faith that purports to shape a real world must reconcile itself to the tedious study of administrative details. This Diefenbaker was never willing to attempt. Whenever he paused in rhetorical flight to spell out policies, his performance sagged, as though he were pitting his will against his impulse by stooping to mention such mundane matters. The end result was that Conservative policies, no matter how well thought out by his advisers, sounded like vague and unco-ordinated gropings.

One example was the Tory scheme for allowing house owners occupying their own homes to deduct up to five hundred dollars of their municipal taxes from their federal tax assessment. At nearly every press conference during the campaign, Diefenbaker was asked how much this plan would cost the federal treasury. He never answered, dismissing such questions by airily declaring: "We have the figures. I'll be dealing with that later." In Winnipeg, he baffled his audience by referring to the scheme as being limited to "home-occupied houses"; in Medicine Hat, he declared that "only home-owning owners" would qualify; and in Simcoe, Ontario, he talked of "home-owning occupying owners."

It seemed obvious that Diefenbaker never really understood what his own platform was all about.* His press conferences were tape-recorded by a party official and the tapes flown back to party headquarters in Ottawa, where they were transcribed and studied to decipher his latest policy commitment. To a press query about the meaning of one of Diefenbaker's policy statements, a harried headquarters official replied: "We'll give you the details when we think of them." During the twelve campaigning days between September 20 and October 5 Diefenbaker made promises that would have cost $1,848 millions to redeem – all the while attacking the evils of inflation and higher government expenditures. On October 14, in Stettler, Alberta, he began a speech by saying: "We have a national policy to develop the – what's the name of your river here?" When prompted by Eldon Woolliams, he added: "Oh yes, the Red Deer River."

*In an attempt to restrain Diefenbaker and to keep him briefed on the party's policies, Conservative headquarters had placed on the campaign train Richard Booth Rohmer, a bright young Toronto lawyer and personal adviser to John Robarts. Rohmer made a lot of good suggestions, but Diefenbaker seldom paid much attention. As the campaign wore on, Rohmer spent most of his time on station platforms frantically telephoning Conservative headquarters in Ottawa, begging Eddie Goodman, the party's national organizer, to let him get off the train.

One of his main concerns was to attack the Fulton-Favreau constitutional formula for patriating the constitution.* Although it had been his government that had written and advocated the original formula, he now proclaimed himself as the man who had single-handedly stood up against it. "I told the people of Quebec," he told a sea of uncomprehending faces in Prince Albert, "that if this thing goes through, they'd never have a right in kingdom come." When Diefenbaker kept repeating "we stood" (as in "we still have the coat of arms because we in the Conservative Party stood") it came out not as some courageous stand on a controversial issue, but simply as a position of immobility.

The one policy area where Diefenbaker did manage to make some impact was in his insistence that old-age pensions should immediately be boosted to one hundred dollars a month. His claim that such an increase could be financed from the contributory fund established under the Canada Pension Plan was denied by Pearson in a Charlottetown address, but it was Diefenbaker, not Pearson, who was believed.†

WHILE JOHN DIEFENBAKER WAS BARN-STORMING the country in his train another, almost independent, Conservative campaign was being waged from the party's Ottawa headquarters with rare zest and insight by a small group of dedicated Tories. This platoon of politically enlightened functionaries staged a brilliant rearguard action which had three main purposes: to maintain the Conservative Party as a viable political organism which would survive the Diefenbaker stewardship; to keep the Liberals from achieving their majority (which this group genuinely believed would jeopardize the national future); and to keep the Conservative campaign from going sour, so that John Diefenbaker would not be tempted to use, as a last resort, an open anti-Quebec appeal. These limited objectives were achieved.

The headquarters Tories tried to ignore what their leader was doing and saying. Since there was little they could do to control Diefenbaker, they just left him alone on his train (the Leader spent only five half-

---

*Few of the Conservatives running in Quebec could decipher where Diefenbaker stood on national unity. Most of them ignored the policy aspect of their campaigns. Gérard Vermette, the Conservative candidate in Labelle, invited his constituents instead to a free showing of a Brigitte Bardot film. He lost anyway.

†The Prime Minister's case wasn't helped much by the fact that just as he arrived in Prince Edward Island Judy LaMarsh was being quoted as having said in Preston, Ontario, that "a pensioner in Prince Edward Island doesn't need anything like a pensioner living in Toronto."

days in Ottawa once the campaign was under way) and, in effect, told their people: Forget about John Diefenbaker; vote for the future of the party.*

THE PROPELLING SPIRIT OF THE HEADQUARTERS campaign was Edwin "Fast Eddie" Goodman, a sometimes impetuous, always imaginative and unfailingly good-humoured Toronto lawyer whose genuine concern for the long-term future of Canadian Conservatism imbued his colleagues with rare *esprit de corps*. His grandfather had pushed a handcart around rural Ontario, selling gingham, and young Eddie had fought and yearned his way through Clinton Street Public School and Harbord Collegiate. Wounded as a tank commander in Normandy, he contested the 1945 provincial election against the Communist, Joe Salsberg, and lost. Ever since, he had kept to the back rooms of politics, acting as John Roberts' leadership campaign manager and the federal party's policy chairman (until he resigned in 1963 in protest against Diefenbaker's nuclear policy), all the while becoming one of the party's most influential power brokers. When Diefenbaker unexpectedly asked him to manage the 1965 campaign, Goodman moved into a suite at the Chateau Laurier and immediately ordered a refrigerator to keep available plentiful supplies of salami, dills and other foods he enjoyed. He insisted that all of his callers drink Labatt's beer, because he was the company's counsel. He could be tough but ran the campaign with an almost mischievous air of good fun.

One example was the fuss Goodman raised about Pearson's reluctance to campaign very hard. On October 4 Goodman called a press conference, expressly to declare: "Three weeks ago, Mr Pearson was ready to go to Pakistan as a cold-war mediator. Today he is unwilling to go to Lévis or Kelowna." This prompted a crotchety reply from the Liberal Leader, who primly asked: "Just who *is* Mr Goodman?"

"Fast Eddie" thought the whole exchange was hilarious. He waited for Pearson to reach Lévis, Quebec, just so he could send a wire to Liberal National Organizer Keith Davey, reading: "Glad you made Lévis, now try for Kelowna. I'll try for Pakistan."

Goodman's was an improvised campaign all the way. There was not much money to spend, because few businessmen wanted to help John

---

*When the mother of Terry Brennan, a young teacher from Vernon, B.C., who was a volunteer at Tory headquarters, phoned to say that even though she'd been a lifelong Conservative she couldn't bring herself to vote for John Diefenbaker, he was overheard begging her: "For God's sake, Mother, vote the Party this time."

Diefenbaker. Goodman had a total budget of less than two million dollars, half of it tagged for advertising.

Goodman got little aid in formulating Conservative policies (he worked out the party's science and trade policies on the back of an envelope during a two-hour break from the telephone one morning) but he did have valuable assistance from Flora MacDonald and a specially recruited young group of activists, including Lowell Murray, Del O'Brien, Paul Champagne, Doug Bassett, Kit Sampson, Marcel Bureau, Jim Johnston, Dave Jenkins, and Bill Dwyer. They provided the drive and ideas that turned a potential disaster into a qualified success.

Once a week Goodman and his young advisers would have a late-night session at the Chateau to discuss their tactics. At one such meeting on September 19, the question of a slogan for Diefenbaker came up. Someone suggested that most Canadians, disgusted with Pearson, would grit their teeth, look at Diefenbaker, and say to themselves: "Well, maybe we should give the old bugger another chance." Goodman crumpled up with mock delight: "That's it, that's our slogan: 'GIVE THE OLD BUGGER ANOTHER CHANCE!'" At another such gathering on October 2, when the Conservative campaign seemed to be going well and it looked as if Diefenbaker might have a chance of winning, Goodman looked around at his subalterns, most of whom had at one time or another opposed the Prince Albert politician, and said: "You know if Dief wins, there'll be the biggest political bloodbath this country has ever seen, and much of that blood is now running in the veins of those in this hotel room." The remark was greeted with shrieks of laughter and the assembled company immediately began to plan how they would act on election night following a Diefenbaker victory. It was agreed that Goodman would go on national television ("After all, I'll be something of an architect") and apologize to the people of Canada for having played such a monstrous practical joke on them. Then the entire Tory headquarters crew would join hands and leap off the roof of the Chateau Laurier.

ONE OF GOODMAN'S MAIN CONTRIBUTIONS was to co-ordinate the party's reunification effort. The disastrous Goldwater campaign in the United States the year before had convinced most thoughtful Tories that they could no longer accept the loss of national elections as the price of solving their leadership problem. They were determined to win as many seats as possible so that John Diefenbaker's successor would inherit a living political movement. This required not only an ordinance against

360

attacking Diefenbaker but more urgently a dramatic recruitment of anti-Diefenbaker rebels into active support of the Leader in the 1965 campaign. A dozen ex-Diefenbakerites came back without too much prompting: Davie Fulton abandoned the leadership of the defunct British Columbia Conservative Party to run federally in his old seat of Kamloops; Dalton Camp decided to take on Mitchell Sharp in Eglinton riding; Douglas Harkness not only ran in his Calgary seat but met Diefenbaker for a frosty exchange of greetings; George Hogan, his party's must outspoken young theorist, announced that he would run in the Toronto constituency of York West; Richard Bell won the nomination for his old Carleton seat; Frank McGee returned to York-Scarborough; Egan Chambers and Pierre Sévigny supported the party in Montreal; W. J. Browne, Diefenbaker's one-time solicitor general, ran in St John's; Senator Wallace McCutcheon made fourteen major speeches on behalf of the party and raised some badly needed funds.

Although Diefenbaker at first would have nothing to do with the return of these political prodigals ("I don't need them") he eventually came to recognize their value. But even as the efforts to reunite the party went on, Diefenbaker secretly recruited his own candidates to run against some of his enemies. The ploy didn't work, but there were some sticky moments. At one point Goodman was calling on the pro-Diefenbaker Tories in New Brunswick's Royal constituency to convince them that any attempt to ditch Gordon Fairweather for a Diefenbaker candidate would be a grave disfavour to Mr. Diefenbaker. After all, said Goodman, this was the "unity" election; Fulton was back in the party; Camp was running; there was a good chance Duff Roblin would be a candidate. At the end of his harangue, a taciturn Tory from Fairweather's riding asked the loquacious Goodman, "Have you spoken to Mr Diefenbaker about this?"

Goodman replied solemnly (lying in his teeth, as he said afterwards), "Of course."

"So have we," answered the Tory from Royal, "and he told us to go ahead."

What finally swung the Fairweather nomination was the intercession of Senator McCutcheon who bluntly told the New Brunswick organization that their election funds would be severely cut if they opposed their M.P.'s renomination.

THE TOUGHEST RECRUITING VENTURES were to bring into active federal Conservative ranks George Hees, the former Trade and Commerce minister who had resigned on the nuclear issue and was now president of the Montreal Stock Exchange, and Duff Roblin, the Premier of Manitoba. Gordon Churchill had called on Hees on July 4, 1965, to sound him out about a return, but the visit had been inconclusive. Gradually pressure began to build up from his friends, who thought he would make the best successor to Diefenbaker but would lose his place in line if he continued to stay out of politics. Besides Goodman, Senator McCutcheon, Richard Rohmer and Allister Grosart all urged Hees to make his re-entry. Probably the most persuasive influence was that of John Bassett, publisher of the Toronto *Telegram*, a lifelong friend of Hees' who bluntly told him that if he didn't run in the 1965 election, he would have no further call on his supporters in any future leadership convention. Bassett had supported the Liberals in the 1963 election because of Diefenbaker's nuclear stand, but had since switched back to his regular party under the influence of Lord Beaverbrook, the British press magnate. Beaverbrook had sent letters and telegrams from his villa at Cap d'Ail in the French Riviera, urging Bassett's return to his true political colours. "REBEL IF YOU MUST BUT RENEGADE NEVER – MAX" read one wire. In a long letter he advised Bassett against having "any truck with Pearson and the Liberals." Bassett had invited Hees to his summer estate at North Hatley, Quebec, where they played tennis, swam and drank together. Finally Hees was brought around to running against Pauline Jewett in the rural Ontario seat of Northumberland, where he had a summer home. (Hees' first reaction to the idea was: "I can't run there; I'd have all those farmers using my swimming pool.")

The Roblin operation was more complicated and less successful. On September 9, just two days after the election was called, Gordon Churchill had offered the Manitoba premier his seat, if he wanted to turn federal. Churchill also carried with him the hint that if Roblin did contest the 1965 election, John Diefenbaker would resign within eighteen months if he won or six months if he didn't. In either case, Diefenbaker was said to be willing to endorse Roblin as his successor. When Roblin expressed mild initial interest, Churchill and Alvin Hamilton rounded up forty-five M.P.'s to sign a wire urging him to run. A parade of Tory dignitaries and journalists had journeyed to Winnipeg over the preceding twelve months, trying to sound out Roblin as to his intentions, but this was the first concrete evidence that he might be persuaded. Robert Stanfield, Davie Fulton and John Robarts all called to urge his candidacy, though the Ontario premier also told him: "Be hard-headed about this. Don't let them panic you. It's not a last-chance proposition."

Roblin was still undecided when he met Diefenbaker, who was on his way to his Prince Albert nomination meeting, in a waiting room at the

Winnipeg airport. But when the Conservative Leader refused to admit a witness to the meeting, and when instead of discussing his impending retirement he merely talked about the carnage there would be in the party if he won, Roblin knew that he was being recruited not for any qualities of statesmanship he might bring to the party's inner councils, but merely as part of a power play by the Chief. By over-estimating Roblin's political ambitions, the Conservatives lost their chance of luring him into battle.

Goodman was furious. He considered that Roblin's entry might have been good for twenty extra seats in Ontario and Quebec and privately called his abstention "a kick in the party's testicles." He flew out to Winnipeg and extracted at least a promise from the Manitoba premier that he would speak for the national party at four important rallies outside his home province.

Roblin's refusal toppled the Conservatives' "domino" theory. The idea had been that once George Hees was hooked, Roblin would jump in because he was known to fear the possibility of Hees' becoming the next leader. Once Roblin was running it would have been easy to recruit Marcel Faribault, the Montreal financier, to give the party a strong Quebec lieutenant. But despite Senator McCutcheon's best efforts, Faribault decided to stay out, partly because he required a generous financial guarantee to offset his loss of private income. "Party Unity" remained the slogan of the Conservative campaign, but the only two men who would have had to make a major sacrifice to the cause – Duff Roblin and Marcel Faribault – stayed out.

The main expression of the party's new united front was a giant rally held at Toronto's Varsity Arena on October 1. Premiers Robarts, Roblin, Stanfield and Andrew MacRae (the Acting Premier of Prince Edward Island) all made loyal orations. Joseph Sedgwick, who for forty years had raised money and directed party policy in Toronto, spoke for the Establishment of his party when he said: "By calling this unnecessary election at a time when he thought the Conservatives were hopelessly divided, Mr Pearson has done more than any other man could have achieved in uniting our Party."

FOR ALL THE BRILLIANT PYROTECHNICS, energy and intelligence that went into his campaign, John Diefenbaker was never able to achieve the major breakthrough that would have returned him to power. He found himself pursued across the hustings by a political ghost. His most potent competitor in the election was not Lester Pearson but the John Diefenbaker who *had been*. Like any other virtuoso with a distinctive personal style, the Tory chief was being measured not so much against his opponents as against his younger self – the way he had been seven years before, when his charismatic campaign had produced the greatest electoral triumph in Canadian history. The gift of grace that he then possessed no longer was his to command in 1965.

CHAPTER 26

The Campaigner
Who Never Was

DEMOCRATIC ELECTIONS ARE A TUMBLE OF EVENTS that savage the poise of party leaders who must joust with one another far beyond the normal limits of physical and psychological endurance. Determined to impose some measure of civility on this process, Lester Pearson entered the 1965 campaign resolved to limit his commitment, maintain his distance and win the election.

From its slow beginning, the Liberal campaign proceeded according to a fixed interior logic which gave it an aura of comfort and confidence but provided no practical barrier to the onrushing confusion and frenzy generated by the unpredictable tactics of John Diefenbaker. Pearson and his advisers found themselves at moments of crisis prisoners of the Leader's itinerary and issue commitments, as outlined in the three Kent memoranda. They were locked into so many decisions that even those Liberal strategists sensitive to the ebb and flow, the real vibrations of the campaign, lacked the means or time to alter in any meaningful way the basic approach. Nearly everything that mattered had been decided before the election had really begun in earnest.

Lester Pearson performed exactly as he had been advised. In the two previous campaigns, his brain trust assured him, he had failed to triumph only because his campaign had "peaked too soon."

This time, Lester never peaked at all.

Pearson and his advisers read Canadian electoral history to mean that governments are not thrown out unless there is some clearly desirable alternative. Since they airily dismissed John Diefenbaker's Conservatives as not even potentially filling this role, they divined that Pearson could walk into power by waging a deliberately diffuse and unspectacular campaign.

There was a curious lack of application about his attitude toward the election, almost a disinterest, as though Pearson were once removed, watching some character whose performance he found mildly interesting doing the things he was supposed to do. When he was accused of talking above the voters' heads, it was an inexact metaphor, because he was really talking above their hearts – what he said could not be distilled into that mysterious chemistry that produces a sense of communion between the governors and the governed.

The Liberal Leader grinned until his cheek muscles gave out, but nothing danced in his eyes. His was the permanent, fixed smile of the dean of men at a small liberal arts college. In Edmonton, Pearson was approached by one of those Canadian old-timers who seem to emerge during elections expressly to provide one-paragraph stories for the Canadian Press overnight file. But his lines didn't come out quite the way his Liberal hosts had planned. "I heard Sir Wilfrid Laurier speak in 1911," the old man quavered, then added: "And he was a helluva lot better than you are!"

Pearson's staff still insisted on running a Kennedy-inspired campaign, using the techniques outlined in T. H. White's manuals on president-making right down to pouring Cutty Sark Scotch (Kennedy's favourite brand) on the press plane.

No one could doubt the Liberal Leader's serious concern with national problems. But his part-time campaigning confirmed him in the public mind as a disengaged politician who could not be brought to bay by the urgencies of the moment. Slowly he dragged his party down from the 48 per cent of national support the polls showed it had when the election was called to 40 per cent on polling day. Throughout his campaign, Pearson conjured up no broad concepts of the promise of Canadian life based on his own sense of national necessities.

Only occasionally, when he spoke about national unity, did sincerity burst the dikes of Pearson's normal restraint, such as this appeal he made during a rally at Orillia, Ontario, on October 13:

Last night, on the platform in Quebec City, we had a wonderful meeting. It was all in French, practically all, and at the end of the meeting we stood up and sang *O Canada* and on the platform I think my wife, and myself, Senator Connolly, Mr Nichol and a few others were the only people singing *O Canada* in English – everybody else was singing it in French. But we were singing the same song. They were singing it in one language, I was singing it in another, but the melody was the same, the harmony was the same and the spirit behind *O Canada* was the same. So it will be in the development of our country.

Until mid October, Pearson seldom left Ottawa to campaign. Instead he announced a wide variety of vote-catching bait, such as a $500 million health resources fund for the provinces, an increase in grants to provinces for student loans, and a study of Maritime tidal power. Eventually Pearson and his ministers made approximately one hundred and fifty specific electoral promises costing billions of dollars, including a pledge to maintain "in perpetuity" Newfoundland's annual $8 million subsidy for raising the standard of public services.

Jack Pickersgill, then senior minister for the Atlantic Provinces, distributed impending Liberal largess with such abandon that Patrick Nowlan, the Conservative candidate in the Nova Scotia riding of Digby-Annapolis-Kings, decided to have some fun. The Pickersgill offers of forthcoming federal expenditures took the form of telegrams from his ministerial office in Ottawa, timed to arrive at a key moment during a Liberal candidate's meeting. John Shaffner, the Port Williams, N.S., businessman who was running against Nowlan, had read such a message at one of his rallies. It contained Pickersgill's solemn pledge to maintain the economically dubious Saint John-Digby ferry service. Nowlan decided to liven up one of his meetings by reading a telegram of his own from "Transport Minister Pickersgill's executive assistant." This message went even further than the Minister's previous promise by fatuously pledging firm government support for the building of "a barge to help passengers get from the ferry to the land in Digby." Instead of ignoring the obvious poke at his fevered promising, Pickersgill reacted with a burst of pompous indignation. He actually sent a wire repudiating the barge contract joke, stating: "I am assured that neither my executive assistant nor anyone else in my office sent any such telegram and I would be very interested to see the telegram you claim to have read." Pickersgill earnestly requested Nowlan's official retraction, but the unrepentant Tory wired instead to the Transport Minister's office a paraphrase of Samuel Johnson: "I have provided you with a jest; I am not bound to provide you with understanding." Nowlan's prank served more effectively than all the thundering of John Diefenbaker to point up the indiscriminate nature of the Liberal promises.

The Liberal pledges were least persuasive in the Prairie Provinces where the party's agricultural platform included a commitment "to support Prairie farm income if grain marketings fall off." This was either meaningless rhetoric or it committed the federal government to an open-ended subsidy program for western agriculture which would have made Diefenbaker's generous treatment of the Prairies look stingy by comparison. The details of this grandiose promise were never explained. The agricultural program, devised by Harry Hays, also had as one of its planks subsidies for sheep ranchers even though there were fewer than a hundred flocks of sheep in Western Canada, and most of them were big, profitable operations.

Pearson's only appearance on a farm was near Dauphin, Manitoba, where he told the farmer's wife, in front of TV cameras: "I'm sorry to barge in like this . . ." and she promptly replied: "Oh, it's all right, I've been preparing all morning." It was a thoroughly phony visit staged by Toronto's MacLaren Advertising. His only speech in Saskatchewan was at Humboldt, which went Conservative anyway.

THE LIBERALS MADE MANY ERRORS, but the gravest of them was to base their election call on the majority issue. The idea of a parliamentary majority is a highly complex concept, certainly not one that can muster much public sympathy. Many minority governments were operating efficiently around the world at the time and on all the important issues in the previous Parliament, Social Credit had voted with the Liberals so that the jeopardy of imminent downfall never materialized. As the campaign progressed it seemed increasingly evident that a majority was necessary not for the welfare of the nation but only for the well-being of Liberal Cabinet ministers. Had this not been the case, it would have been Pearson's duty to explain exactly why he so desperately needed to have a majority mandate. He talked vaguely about the obscure tensions of a troubled future, but never outlined his intentions. Gradually it became clear that the Liberals were really asking for a majority not as a mandate for the future but as a vindication of the past.

The Liberal call for a majority government was unreal because it came at a time when public opinion in Canada was fractured in many directions. A majority government would have provided a welcome sanctuary for the troubled incumbents of the Liberal front benches but it would not have reflected accurately the nation's political alignments. When there is no consensus on any of the great issues there can be no majority mandate. Instead of attempting to create a mood of consensus through a vigorous and inspiring campaign, Pearson decided not to fight an election at all. He just warned the people that the nation's economic welfare depended on his re-election and that the choice was only between casting Liberal ballots or returning to the economic paralysis of the Diefenbaker Years. He tried to link continued prosperity with his wish for a majority mandate – even though that very prosperity had been achieved during a period of minority administration. In effect, the Liberals staged what amounted to a national plebiscite with one question on the ballot: Pearson or chaos? This could hardly be expected to work, since in the past two and a half years, Canada had experienced both Pearson *and* chaos. Once again, the root arrogance of the Liberals had broken through into public view.

Whenever he appeared, Pearson pleaded for a Liberal majority, abusing the issue by stretching it beyond the bounds of rational argument. In Peterborough he referred to a majority in power and a minority in opposition as "the British way of doing things"; in Winnipeg he had broadly hinted that Canada could not maintain her international commitments without a parliamentary majority and said that if one were not elected, "there would be no certainty that a minority government would last more than a week or two." At an Ottawa press conference he stated: "If the Liberal Party cannot obtain a majority – and I think it will – I would rather see some other party attain a majority." Perhaps the strangest reference of all came at the end of a luncheon for ethnic editors in Toronto when Pearson concluded his address by declaring: "The last action before I go to bed at night is to look across at the other bed and wave to my wife, and I ask her every night 'Do you still believe in the majority government issue?' and she replies that she does."

The Liberal ploy for a majority didn't work. The Toronto *Star*'s columnist, Ron Haggart, in a trenchant analysis of the situation, reminded the public that if the Liberals had been a majority government since 1963, the Dorion Inquiry might not have been set up and certainly would not have had such broad terms of reference; that the Canadian flag, the Canada Pension Plan and the first Gordon budget would all have been very different had the Liberals been able to master Parliament. Tommy Douglas killed the issue with one perceptive quip: "The Liberals talk about a stable government, but we don't know how bad the stable is going to smell." There was also the residue of memories from the late Fifties, when Liberal majorities were overbearing, acting only to please themselves. Statements like Walter Gordon's plea for "a *comfortable* majority" made it sound as though the Liberals believed Parliament existed for their personal comfort and convenience.

PROBABLY THE LIBERALS' GREATEST FAILURE – because the potential for success seemed so great – was their campaign in Quebec. Outside French Canada, Pearson's handling of Quebec was resented because many voters felt he had given up the federal prerogative too easily, and without developing any clear positions of his own. Inside Quebec, the old-line politicians were troubled by the results of the Dorion Inquiry, which seemed to threaten their way of doing things, while the new-wave Liberals remained uncertain about the extent of their influence. Guy Favreau had not been an effective Quebec lieutenant to the Prime Minister. The federal Quebec Liberal Party – waging its first election since splitting from the provincial body – was badly understaffed and poorly organized. At the same time, John Diefenbaker, with his hyperbolic policies for rural improvement, and Réal Caouette, with his still potent charm for the villagers of the economically depressed areas of the province, continued to exercise their appeal in the constituencies outside the large cities.

In the spring of 1965, three federal ministers – Guy Favreau, Maurice Sauvé and René Tremblay – had called a mass meeting at St Romuald, across the river from Quebec City. They drew only 350 people. The party badly needed new blood and it was the recruitment of three new members – Jean Marchand, then president of the Confederation of National Trade Unions, Pierre Elliott Trudeau, then a respected but not very widely known professor at the University of Montreal, and Gérard Pelletier, the ex-editor of *La Presse* – that provided the only excitement of the Liberals' Quebec campaign.

At the time no one could predict that in less than three years this trio would take over the Liberal Party and one of its members would be Prime Minister. But there was a feeling, even then, that the decision of the three middle-aging Quebec ex-revolutionaries to cast in their lot with the Liberal Party was an event of profound significance. It was no easy decision for the three men to make. The roots of their political concern stretched back to the 1949 Asbestos strike when French-Canadian intellectuals first came into open conflict with the crushing paternalism of the Duplessis administration. It was in the magazine *Cité Libre*, founded in the early 1950s by Pelletier and Trudeau, that the aspirations of the new Quebec were first articulated and it was the militancy of the unions under Jean Marchand's leadership which helped them to be realized. Now, the trio in effect was rejecting the notion that the government of Quebec should be the solitary custodian of French-Canadian rights. By joining the federal Liberal Party, the three men had pledged themselves to establish Ottawa as a second focus for the legitimate expression of Quebec's best interests.

Marchand had first encountered the federal Liberals at close quarters during the 1960 Kingston Conference, where he had been one of the featured speakers. His old friend and Laval University classmate

Maurice Lamontagne had been urging him to join the party ever since. Invited to run in the 1963 general election, he declined partly because he did not support the Liberals' pro-nuclear policy and partly because he was at the time trying to push a new labour code through the provincial house. Lamontagne flirted with the idea of trying to recruit André Laurendeau, the editor of *Le Devoir*, but no thought was given to either Trudeau (who was considered too radical and too academic) or Pelletier (who had earned the Liberals' enmity with his tough editorials in *La Presse*).

During the spring and summer of 1965, Lamontagne and Bob Guigère, the Liberal Party's chief Quebec organizer, three times entertained Marchand at the Laval sur le Lac golf course, trying to get a commitment from him for the next election. Marchand, whose mandate and power at the CNTU were fast running out, seemed favourably inclined. After one of the Lamontagne golfing sessions he had a chat with an old colleague, René Lévesque, who warned him: "Don't make the same mistake I did and go into politics alone. It's hell. Go in as part of a team."

Marchand had been meeting separately with Forestry Minister Maurice Sauvé, who wanted some help in his personal power struggle against Lamontagne and Guy Favreau. It was Sauvé who first suggested that Trudeau and Pelletier should be brought in with Marchand. He had discussed the possibility with Pelletier at that year's Couchiching Conference and on August 28 he telephoned Pierre Trudeau, who lived close to his Montreal home, and invited him in for a political chat the next morning. At the end of it when Sauvé asked whether he'd consider running, Trudeau replied: "Well, I won't say no, and I won't say yes." This was enough for Sauvé to set up a dinner for the following Tuesday (August 31) with Marchand, Pelletier and Trudeau, where their idea of a joint candidacy was discussed. This was one of the series of meetings that finally settled the three men on insisting that they join as a team. That was the only specific condition they set on their entry.

The next morning, back in Ottawa, Sauvé had lunch with the Quebec ministers and announced the trio's decision. There were immediate objections to Trudeau and Pelletier, but Favreau agreed to see them in Montreal during the evening of Thursday, September 9. The meeting which finally brought the three Quebeckers into the Liberal Party turned out to be an exercise in high farce. Marchand was staying at the Mount Royal Hotel in downtown Montreal at the time, Trudeau was at home in his apartment, Pelletier was in Winnipeg but was due to arrive back in Montreal later on the chosen evening. Sauvé was at home, waiting to be called in as a participant. Favreau was in Ottawa. His office had leaked a story that the meeting would be held during the supper hour at Montreal's Windsor Hotel, but when Favreau found out that the press intended to cover the affair, he immediately threatened to call it off. Finally, Favreau was persuaded to change his mind. He agreed to meet Marchand, but not the others, at the Windsor. Marchand promptly phoned Trudeau and asked him to come. Trudeau phoned Sauvé, but the Forestry Minister decided to wait until he heard from Favreau. When Trudeau arrived, he asked: "Where's Sauvé?" and Favreau said: "We've been trying to reach him all evening." So Marchand phoned Sauvé, who had spent the evening waiting anxiously by his silent telephone. Lamontagne and Guigère also arrived. Favreau began to put up some strenuous objections to Trudeau and Pelletier, but Marchand cut him off with the comment that the trio had talked about the prospects of entering the party among themselves and had decided they would only go in as a team, and that he himself would insist on confirmed constituency nominations for Trudeau and Pelletier before he would allow his own name to go forward as a Liberal candidate.

It was agreed to announce the Marchand candidacy the following morning but Favreau wanted Pelletier and Trudeau to arrange their own press conference on a separate occasion. Marchand insisted there would be a joint announcement. On September 10, the three friends made their commitment to the Liberal Party public. "After some consideration, I have decided to do something about the things I have been criticizing for the past fifteen years. If I succeed, then others can criticize me," Trudeau declared. "I consider the Liberal Party as an instrument for Quebec to stay within Confederation."

Five days later Jean-Paul Desbiens, the Quebec religious brother who had written *Les Insolences du Frère Untel*, sent a prophetic letter to Trudeau, which read in part: "With you three in Ottawa our options will become clarified. We are making the definitive test to see if Canada is viable. If you fail, we can turn squarely down the road to independence – without remorse and without bad conscience. Would it be too pompous to say that Canada itself is playing its last hand of cards? If you hadn't agreed to become involved, I ask myself how we would have been able to say that we had tried to use all the resources normally available in the democratic process."

There was little trouble finding seats for Marchand (who decided to fight for the Quebec West riding then held by Social Credit) and Pelletier (who took over Raymond Eudes' Hochelaga seat),* but Trudeau

*Eudes was rewarded by an appointment to the Senate in April, 1968.

was turned down by every French-speaking riding that was approached. He finally ended up competing for Mount Royal, the English seat being given up by Alan Macnaughton, the retiring Speaker of the Commons. He won the nomination, not because he gave a good speech at the nominating convention (the address by Dr Victor Goldbloom was better) but because he had done so well during the question-and-answer sessions that preceded the meeting. Also, it had been made very clear to the Mount Royal Liberal Association that Trudeau was favoured as the party's official choice.

THE ONLY MAJOR RECRUITMENT UNDERTAKEN by the Liberals in English Canada during the 1965 election was that of Robert Henry Winters, a former federal Public Works minister then head of Canadian operations for the Rio Tinto mining empire as well as a director of more than a dozen Canadian corporations with assets of well over $6 billions. A big, perpetually tanned, entirely uneccentric man, Winters was full of that good-natured arrogance which had marked the successful Liberal ministers of the St Laurent period. Always close to Pearson, he had been one of the few Canadian businessmen who openly campaigned for a political party. During the 1958 election, when Winters was officiating at the opening of the Panel uranium mill near Elliot Lake, Ontario, he drew some raised eyebrows by sporting a huge I LIKE MIKE button. In the 1962 and 1963 campaigns he had collected Liberal election funds and made a speaking tour of Eastern Canada on Pearson's behalf, referring to John Diefenbaker as "a national disease."

At a private meeting in Toronto's Park Plaza Hotel on September 13, 1965, Pearson had asked Winters to come back into federal politics. No firm offer of a cabinet post was made, but one of Winters' supporters later recalled that the Prime Minister had said: "No portfolio will be closed to you, including mine." Winters, on the other hand, was reported to have understood his entry would bring about the removal of Walter Gordon from the Finance portfolio and the transfer of Tom Kent from the prime ministerial entourage. The negotiations for Winters' return were designed to attract the votes and campaign fund contributions of the disillusioned members of the nation's business community who didn't want to support the Conservative Party as long as John Diefenbaker was in command, wouldn't help any party that was under the influence of Walter Gordon, but all loved Bob Winters.

Winters arranged to get a tax-free $499,000 pension settlement from his employers, lamented the fact that even though he'd just been elected to the board of the Chase Manhattan Bank he would not be able to attend any of its meetings, and set about getting a seat. Clem Neiman, a leading Toronto Liberal who had been set to run in York West, agreed to step down and Joe Potts, president of the Toronto and District Liberal Association, volunteered to show the new candidate his riding. Potts had his kids scrub the family's 1962 Chevrolet for the occasion, but when he arrived to pick up the ex-minister, Winters said he'd prefer to inspect his constituency from the back of his air-conditioned chauffeur-driven Lincoln Continental.

IT WAS ONLY AFTER THE ELECTION that the full implications of the Winters candidacy became clear.

Under Walter Gordon's influence, the Liberal Government had during its brief twenty-nine months in office managed to alienate almost every sector of the nation's business community. Bank presidents were mad because the government had refused to lift the 6 per cent interest-rate ceiling on loans; insurance company executives were mad because of the Canada Pension Plan; operators of American-owned subsidiaries were mad because of Gordon's nationalistic policies; most publishers were mad at the government's policy of forbidding sale of their enterprises to non-Canadians; the construction industry was mad at the 11 per cent sales tax on building materials; even the branch managers of chartered banks were mad because a month before the election the National Revenue Department had issued an edict that henceforth the expense of taking their wives to the annual meetings arranged for them at their head offices would no longer be considered tax deductible. Bank of Montreal President Arnold Hart spoke for many of his colleagues in the business community when he publicly attacked the Pearson Government for "taking pronounced moves in the direction of state socialism."

The day Pearson called the election, the National Liberal Federation in Ottawa was $250,000 in debt. The 1965 campaign was budgeted at about $4 millions.* When Senator John Aird, the party's chief fund raiser, made his initial contacts to try and raise that sum he was met by unprecedented resentment and resistance. During the week of September 6 some senior representatives of Canada's chartered banks urged Pearson through their intermediaries to recruit Robert Winters and drop Walter Gordon from the Finance portfolio. Jack Pickersgill and Senator John Connolly were among the cabinet ministers who supported this point of view. At the same time, a number of western Liberals organized by some Winnipeg businessmen connected with the Hudson's Bay

*Only $3,750,000 was raised. This was not a high budget for Liberal campaigns. In 1957, for example, the party had spent $7 millions.

Company and the Great-West Life Assurance Company, discreetly let out the word that they would bankroll any promising Conservative with a chance of defeating Walter Gordon in his home riding of Davenport. This group even approached Saskatchewan Premier Ross Thatcher with the idea of having him head a rump group of independent western Liberals in the federal House, but he dismissed their advances.

Whether or not Pearson acceded to the bankers' demands was never clear. But the bankers were left with the firm impression that the Liberal Leader had accepted their point of view, particularly since he had mentioned Robert Winters for the Trade and Commerce portfolio. Because Mitchell Sharp was then occupying this job, the bankers assumed that Pearson intended to move Sharp to Finance as Gordon's replacement. Following the Winters recruitment many Liberal fund raisers across the country, including James Sinclair, a former Fisheries minister in the St Laurent administration living in Vancouver, were openly promising their potential subscribers that Pearson had pledged to remove Gordon from the Finance portfolio after November 8.

Pearson didn't deny these rumours but he must have realized that Walter Gordon – then still his chief adviser and the party's national campaign chairman – was bound to hear them. On October 26, at a rally in Wallaceburg, Ontario, the Liberal Leader took the occasion of Gordon's rare presence on the platform with him to say: "There is a man here who is a candidate in Davenport in Toronto where they're trying awfully hard to beat him. But they won't be able to beat him because he is going to get elected and he is going to be the Minister of Finance."

The nation's financial community, which had been assured that Gordon's days were numbered, was severely shaken by the pronouncement. Winters sent Pearson a long, bitter telegram describing his position as "untenable" and demanding an immediate meeting.* Businessmen who had made pledges toward the Liberal campaign fund now renounced them. Even though the Liberal campaign had been paced to climax with saturation advertising coverage in the last two weeks, the money had stopped coming in and most of the preparations were abandoned. Candidates in the Maritime Provinces who had been promised as much as $20,000 actually got $5,000 and notes of apology for the last-minute cut. This was particularly damaging in Nova Scotia, where the purchasing of votes remained a not uncommon practice.

The cutback in the Liberals' campaign contributions was based on something more than an informal consensus. Several leading Mont-

*The two men met in the PM's suite at Toronto's Constellation Hotel, and what resulted, according to one witness, was "a shouting match which nobody won."

real, Toronto and Winnipeg businessmen were involved in organizing an active anti-Gordon lobby that urged business firms to severely limit their contributions to the Liberal Party. The chief moving spirit of this group was William Pearson Scott, chairman of Wood, Gundy and Company, the Toronto investment dealers.*

AS THE CAMPAIGN ENTERED ITS FINAL PHASE, the agents and activists of the Liberal Party were still encountering a strangely inaccessible electorate whose unpredictable temperament threatened to upset many of their favourite assumptions. In terms of national impact, the Diefenbaker campaign seemed the most successful. Tommy Douglas was flitting about the country, but no residual flowering of the NDP followed his trail. Lester Pearson's tactic of being placed on exhibit instead of actively campaigning was not working. Liberal strategy depended for its success on a last-minute escalation that would push the party into power with a majority mandate. This would have required a display of political magic that was simply not forthcoming. There was no evidence that any Pearson government – whether minority or majority – would display the strength of leadership that was required. "I've been told," John Diefenbaker commented, catching this sign of the public's mood, "that it's no use adding spokes to the wheel when the hub is gone."

*Although a Conservative, Scott had always been a close associate of Robert Winters. He succeeded Winters as chairman of the board at York University and during the 1968 Liberal leadership convention acted (along with J. G. Godsoe) as Winters' main financial collector.

CHAPTER 27

The Reluctant Reckoning

WHEN JOHN DIEFENBAKER HAD BEGUN his electoral journey on September 24, the trees were a russet glow against the landscape, a latent colour waiting momentarily for the departure of green. By the time the Diefenbaker train drew into its final destination of Prince Albert, on November 6, a foot of snow had fallen on northern Saskatchewan. It was not the same country in which the election campaign had started – in weather or in mood.

At Halifax, where Diefenbaker had given a lacklustre opening speech, his car had been escorted to the Queen Elizabeth High School Auditorium by only one motorcycle cop, a fat one at that. By the end of the election, as his train passed through the great cities of Western Canada, his campaign was on fire. He was being driven to the howling halls of his supporters in style, with three sleek outriders on each side of his car and saluting policemen waving it through intersections. During those last onrushing days it seemed to those who were with him that they were witnessing not a politician on the stump but a force of nature spending itself in one grand final effort.

Through that last crazy week John Diefenbaker's campaign began both to attract larger and more enthusiastic crowds and at the same time to take on an aspect of hysteria. In part, these crowds came out "to see Dief one last time"; there was an air of history about him already. Instead of bringing a message of political salvation to his listeners, the Conservative Leader gave the impression of a man searching for his elevation into glory. "Join with me. Join," he pleaded. "Join together to bring about in this country the attainment of the greatness that Almighty God has made possible."

Though his advisers exhaled despair, Diefenbaker never gave up, spending himself like a forest fire being starved by its own appetite. He moved from giant rallies in Hamilton, Montreal, Edmonton and Vancouver to Regina, where he held his last meeting on November 5. The next day, back on the train, Diefenbaker made his way at last through the mauve afternoon toward Prince Albert, and there was about him a suggestion of splendour.

THE LAST FEW DAYS OF THE LIBERAL CAMPAIGN inspired quite a different mood. Pearson's rallies at Vancouver, Winnipeg, Montreal, Toronto and Hamilton were modified disasters, but the Pearson entourage was bursting with confidence. Canadians, it seemed to them, were about to opt once again for the political centre and Pearson, whatever his political shortcomings, was the ideal man of the centre – the equilibrium-minded insider, while John Diefenbaker remained the eternal outsider challenging the settled order of things.

In Montreal, Guy Favreau managed to stage a rally that did not include among its speakers a single representative of the political New Guard, with neither Trudeau nor Marchand even being invited to attend. In a hall that could hold ten thousand, fewer than three thousand people had turned out to hear the Prime Minister. In Toronto, the sound system at the Yorkdale shopping plaza broke down, leaving 25,000 disappointed spectators.

The day after his Yorkdale meeting Pearson visited a Liberal committee room in the west end of Toronto where he gave a brief pep talk to campaign workers. "Now," he said, "it's very important to get the Liberals elected because we're the only party that has a chance of forming a majority government. And if we don't get a majority government, we're going to get another election in a year, in a year and a half – and who wants *that*?" Dave McIntosh of Canadian Press filed a story quoting these remarks and a tape-recording of them was played over CHUM, a Toronto radio station. Terry Grier, National Organizer for the NDP, was in the city at the time and heard the broadcast. He immediately telephoned Tommy Douglas, who was within ten minutes of leaving Vancouver airport for Victoria, and advised him to issue, the moment he landed, a statement attacking Pearson for threatening another election.

Pearson and his group, meanwhile, had climbed onto a transcontinental passenger plane for their own trip from Toronto to Vancouver.

378

The members of the national press corps, as well as Pearson's press secretary, Dick O'Hagan, were on the campaign plane following a similar route. The occupants of both aircraft were unaware that a controversy was developing over the PM's remarks. By the time Pearson had landed in Vancouver, Douglas' attack on his "election threat" was front-page news. As he stepped off his aircraft, Pearson was confronted by an insistent gaggle of local radio reporters demanding his comments on the Douglas accusations. O'Hagan had landed in time to be aware of what was happening but couldn't get through to his boss to prevent him from denying that he had ever made any statement threatening another election.

Pearson's original statement and his denial were immediately taped back-to-back by Ted Rogers, the owner of Toronto's CHFI and the Conservatives' chief radio adviser. He distributed the tapes to eighty radio stations in Ontario and Quebec which played the damagingly contradictory quotations nearly every hour for the next two days. Dr Eugene Forsey, the constitutional expert, jumped into the controversy by blasting the Liberals' arrogance in assuming that no government could carry on without a majority. "The electors need not be frightened by Mr Pearson's paper tiger," Forsey concluded in a three-page statement. "But his attempt to frighten them is nonetheless reprehensible." The tape-recorder episode was a minor flash of an event during a long election campaign. But it was highly significant, because it helped reinforce the public image of Lester Pearson as a weak, forgetful man who didn't seem to know his own mind.

Still, the Liberals were confident right to election night that they would win their much-touted majority. As their campaign jet glided over the countryside between the metropolitan complexes of southern Canada, the land lay lucent and promising underneath, like some great coral sea glimpsed through a glass-bottomed boat.

THE 1965 ELECTION HAD TAKEN TOMMY DOUGLAS across the country many times, but there was only limited response to his gallant campaign. His earnest digs at "the corporate élite" and attacks on a class system that no longer existed made the NDP leader seem a dated figure with little credibility as a man who could form and run a government. Despite the NDP's serious efforts to lash together a desirable set of policies, its three great crusades of the past – medicare, universal pensions and a federal labour code – had all been adopted by the Liberals. As a result, the NDP had to retreat to such mundane policy pledges as the establishment of a Department of Consumer Affairs in Ottawa, which would police the amount of soap flakes in soap-flake boxes. In the 1965 campaign, at least, the party that once dreamed of reforming Canadian society had been reduced to a sort of national Consumers' Complaint Society.

The Ralliement des Créditistes and the Social Credit became factions. Réal Caouette charged that the entry of Marchand-Trudeau-Pelletier into Liberal ranks represented "a flagrant infiltration of socialism and communism into the Liberal Party." Robert Thompson's Social Credit Party fell apart, with all of its Quebec members resigning to seek votes under other banners.

By election day, all of the major public opinion surveys were predicting a solid Liberal majority. The Gallup Poll showed a 44 per cent vote for the Liberals, 29 per cent for the Conservatives, 18 per cent for the NDP, 9 per cent for Social Credit and others.* Peter Regenstreif, writing in the *Toronto Daily Star*, predicted a Liberal majority of between 137 and 150 seats. The only reporter who correctly predicted the election results was Ron Collister, then with the Toronto *Telegram*. The only academic to forecast the voting trends accurately was John Wilson of the University of Waterloo.

The fortnight before election day was marked by an intense campaign on behalf of the Conservatives by Robert Stanfield in Nova Scotia. He made twelve speeches in the campaign's final thirteen days, criss-crossing the province as if he were running himself. Stanfield was annoyed with the federal Liberals for many reasons. He didn't like Ottawa's stand on offshore mineral rights and resented the fact that Allan MacEachen, Nova Scotia's representative in the cabinet, had never once paid a courtesy call on him. But most of all he was annoyed with MacEachen for promising that the Liberals would give the coal-mining industry $25 millions and open a new seam at Lingan, at a time when Stanfield suspected MacEachen had already read the draft recommendations of the Donald Report, which condemned the mining operations as uneconomical.

In contrast to Stanfield, John Robarts of Ontario did little to help his federal party. Some of his MLA's and full-time organizers worked hard for Diefenbaker, but the party machine was not placed on an electoral footing and Robarts' behaviour made it evident that he feared the possibility of a Diefenbaker victory. When Conservative Headquarters in Ottawa wanted to use for its Ontario campaign a postcard-size pamphlet with a picture of Diefenbaker and Robarts, the Ontario premier telephoned Goodman and threatened to dissociate himself publicly from the campaign if the idea wasn't dropped. It was.

*The actual result was Liberals, 40 per cent, Conservatives, 33 per cent, NDP, 17 per cent, Social Credit and others, 10 per cent.

ELECTION DAY IS THE TIME OF DECISION for the people, but for the politicians it is a frustrating moment of anticlimax. All the pressures have been applied, all of the arms twisted, all the IOU's collected. By evening, the regimented agony of the campaign has been reduced to an exercise in arithmetic. It is a time of inescapable drama. There are the intoxicating fumes in the air of power changing hands as the fragments of data are put together and national trends begin to emerge.

Newfoundland, still in the paternalistic grip of Joey Smallwood, proved no bell-wether that night. It was a straight Liberal sweep. Then the Nova Scotia mainland came in with ten Tory seats and only two Liberals. New Brunswick was unchanged but Quebec – where the Liberals had hoped to make substantial gains – returned only four more Liberals than in 1963, Trudeau, Pelletier and Marchand among them. In Ontario the Liberals dropped a seat and the Tory fortress in the Prairies held steady, contributing the defeat of two of the three Liberal survivors of 1963, including Agriculture Minister Harry Hays. British Columbia broke nearly the same as in 1963.

What it all meant was that despite the nearly two months of campaigning, the ballot boxes contained no verdict. Although the 1965 campaign had been viciously fought, it resulted in the smallest seat turnover of any electoral contest since Confederation. Of the 265 seats at stake, 223 did not change hands and the overall results gave the Liberals only two more seats, the Conservatives seven more and the New Democrats three more, with Social Credit absorbing most of the losses. A total of 150 M.P.'s had been elected with a minority mandate from their constituents.*

None of the party leaders had managed to mobilize the consent of a bewildered electorate. Neither Pearson nor Diefenbaker had been able to make much impression in each other's strongholds. The nation had been divided into two majorities; country had voted against city. There was the Liberal majority of urban Canada (only one Progressive Conservative had been elected in the fifty constituencies of Metropolitan Toronto, Montreal and Vancouver) and the Tory majority of rural Canada (only two non-Conservatives had won in sixty-four of the nation's least urbanized ridings).

*The overall result: Liberals, 131; Conservatives, 97; NDP, 21; Ralliement des Créditistes, 9; Social Credit, 5; Independent, 2. A study later carried out by the staff of the National Liberal Federation showed that the party would barely have achieved its majority had it waited for redistribution. By taking the results of the 52,000 polling stations and reapportioning them according to the redistributed constituency boundaries, the study showed the following results: Liberals, 136; Conservatives, 92; NDP, 24; Créditistes, 8; Social Credit, 4.

At Conservative Headquarters "Fast Eddie" Goodman was striding up and down in front of the tally boards like the coach of a winning football team. The pollster Peter Regenstreif telephoned David Greenspan, a friend of his who was a Liberal organizer in Toronto, and said, gloomily: "Ahh, you guys. Another eight seats and I would have been a genius." Tommy Douglas was wreathed in smiles, pleased with a showing that gave the NDP a 5 per cent boost in the popular vote. Even though his party came first in only twenty-one ridings, it had come second in thirty-five.

The real drama was going on at Liberal Headquarters on Ottawa's Cooper Street, where national organizer Keith Davey was trying to maintain his normal high spirits in the face of what was to him – and to Walter Gordon, his great friend and fellow enthusiastic advocate of this election – an unmitigated disaster. Upstairs in the old building Liberal functionaries and their wives, festooned with red corsages, watched a TV set stonily. (As one of them said morosely, "We've been waiting three and a half years and fought three bloody campaigns for a victory party that never came.") Downstairs, Davey kept frantically re-working his estimates, trying to show arithmetically that British Columbia would be sure to bring the majority.

At the Chateau Laurier, Pearson was sitting in a private suite, reckoning the toll of his humiliation. John Nichol, his amused good looks intact, said to nobody in particular: "We bombed." His wife Liz sat crying while Tom Kent, puffing his curved pipe, tried to comfort her. Outside in the hotel corridor newsmen stood around making jokes. Jack Pickersgill came ankling down the hall, the skin loose on his face, trying hard to smile, and, as the door to the PM's suite opened, somebody in the crowd yelled, "Hey, did you see Pearson? He's hiding under the bed."

At 11:30 p.m. Pearson finally went on national television and said: "My colleagues and I will naturally be assessing the situation in the light of the returns when they are final. In our assessment, we will be concerned with only one thing: that is, what's best for the country . . . It is our responsibility to carry on. We have very considerably the largest group in the House of Commons and we will have to assess our responsibilities in the light of that fact."

Asked about his campaign statement that, deprived of a majority, he would prefer to have another party lead the government, Pearson answered: "In this life you don't always get your preferences."

Later that night, an aide said to the PM: "We let you down." He smiled wryly and replied: "Oh no, the country let us down." The Liberals had tested the Canadian people and found them wanting.

IT WAS A GREAT NIGHT IN PRINCE ALBERT. Allister Grosart, John Diefenbaker's old companion in arms, flew up for the occasion. During the afternoon, when the Chief asked for Grosart's estimate of Tory strength, he gave his count at 107. "You're out about ten the other way," was the reply, making the Conservative Leader the best prophet of the night. He had voted earlier in the day at the home of Crist Sotos, a Prince Albert popcorn vendor, where the polling booth was a curtained-off alcove next to a large hand-stitched sampler of the Ten Commandments. The Diefenbaker railway cars were parked on a siding next to a stranded cattle train and all through the long evening the election results were punctuated by the bellowing of hungry steers. That, added to the klieg lights mounted on scaffolds to illuminate the Diefenbaker car for television, gave the scene a surrealistic glow under the polar moon of the northern Saskatchewan night.

Diefenbaker remained jubilant because he had deprived the Liberals of their majority. "Pearson said he was impotent without a majority," he remarked. "Well, his potency has not been intensified." On television he pointed out that the Liberals could not hold another election without bringing before the Governor General "the representatives of a second party which believes it can form an administration, a strong administration, to carry on the government of this country." When he returned from the television studios to his railway car he was presented with a cake made by Santo Bruno, a railway cook, which bore the iced inscription: ALWAYS THE CHIEF — TOUJOURS LE CHEF.

JOHN DIEFENBAKER HAD PATCHED TOGETHER a coalition of the politically discontented and socially dispossessed which had increased his party's parliamentary representation and humiliated the proud Liberals by keeping them in a minority position. Still, John Diefenbaker's defeat on November 8 was his own, final and irredeemable. It cost him not only an election but his last election as party leader, not just a dream, but his only dream: that history would grant him the rarest of its benefactions – a second chance.

Superficially, the 1965 election campaign had changed nothing. Canada remained a nation politically becalmed, with the federal parties still under the same leadership, drawing about the same degree of non-confidence from the electors. But despite the preservation of this superficial *status quo,* a fundamental shift in the future prospect of both the major parties did in fact take place. The end of the Diefenbaker-Pearson era of dominance over Canadian politics had finally come into view. Here, at last, was an opening up of the channels for the passage of power to new, younger hands. The succession of neither Robert Stanfield nor Pierre Elliott Trudeau would have been possible without the purge of the political system provided by the 1965 campaign.

Every election, even if it fails to confer a clear mandate on the winner, implies in its results advice from a democratic electorate. On November 8, the voters of Canada served very specific notice on the politicians. They made it clear that the realization of Canada's future potential lay not between Lester Pearson and John Diefenbaker, but beyond them.

PART SEVEN   *Abdication of Power*

During the twenty-five months between the election of November, 1965, and Lester Pearson's announcement in December of 1967 of his resignation as Prime Minister, most members of the Liberal Government behaved as though they were suffering from a low-grade fever. They were ambulatory but never quite sure of their equilibrium.

The political speeches continued to roll off the mimeograph machines and the partisan sallies and fatuous pronouncements still bloomed in the humid atmosphere of Parliament Hill. But few of the men who held national office had anything new to say and no one seemed certain any longer that anybody was listening. Outwardly confident as they tried to puff life into once appropriate clichés, spokesmen for all parties were privately bewildered by their inability to establish contact with the voters. Parliament became a kind of Disneyland-on-the-Rideau as most Canadians stopped believing that national problems had political solutions.

The *fin de siècle* mood that pervaded national politics was accentuated by the interminable feud between Lester Pearson and John Diefenbaker, which reached a climactic ugliness during the Munsinger affair. In the eyes of the nation these two old political warriors were intimately linked; their words and actions, their countenances and gestures filled the electorate with frustration and despair.

The inconclusive results of the 1965 campaign had marked the end of Pearson's effectiveness as a prime minister psychologically *capable of leading the country. He maintained the affectionate loyalty of most Liberals but his ambitious lieutenants openly set about seeking his job.*

This long season of Canada's political discontent was finally broken with the dramatic emergence of Pierre Elliott Trudeau, a politician who became a possibility as the country's leader because he appeared to be the very antithesis of the men who had gone before.

CHAPTER 28

The Munsinger Affair

T HE LOW POINT OF THE PEARSON GOVERNMENT'S FINAL TERM in office came during the mad month of March 1966, when Yvon Dupuis was being tried on charges of influence-peddling; an inquiry was hearing evidence that Mr Justice Leo Landreville, a Liberal appointee to the Ontario Supreme Court, had been given, before his appointment to the bench, $25,000 worth of natural-gas company stock that yielded him a personal profit of $117,000; and a jury was deliberating on the fate of Raymond Denis, the former executive assistant accused of offering a bribe in the Rivard case. But the grotesquerie before which these others paled – the event that held the nation enthralled and appalled that spring – was the Munsinger affair: the public revelation of the lurid misadventures of a $15-a-trick prostitute who had been involved with ministers of the Crown six years before.

Details of Gerda Munsinger's sex life, which eventually proved entirely irrelevant to the conduct of the country's business, were hardly made more edifying by the fact that they were aired through the deliberate disclosure by senior Liberals of confidential RCMP files on the private lives of Conservative ministers – that the whole episode was, in brief, a wilful act of political vengeance. In its grubby way, the Munsinger incident publicly displayed the deep neuroses engendered in federal politics by the long, unresolved feud between Lester Pearson's Liberals and John Diefenbaker's Tories. Both parties were exhibiting symptoms that in an individual would indicate a nervous breakdown. The politician who crumpled under this strain was Lucien Cardin, the Minister of Justice.

CARDIN WAS AN UNLIKELY CANDIDATE for the leading role in any political drama. Short, with a small moustache and an aptitude for self-effacement, he had been sitting in the Commons since 1952, saying little and doing less, one of that cadre of small-town Quebec lawyers who always warm the Liberal back benches. When he was promoted from Associate Defence Minister to Justice Minister, succeeding Guy Favreau, his own reaction of disbelief at being given such a senior portfolio was shared by many of his colleagues. Pearson explained Cardin's appointment by telling his cabinet that at least the new minister would keep the government out of trouble.

Despite his quiet demeanour, Lucien Cardin nurtured a bitter animosity toward John Diefenbaker. He saw the Conservative Leader as an enemy of French Canada, a destructive politician threatening national unity. Cardin's feelings for Diefenbaker had erupted only once in the Commons. On February 22, 1962, while sitting in a back row of the Liberal Opposition, Cardin had answered Diefenbaker's charge that Pearson had never raised his voice on behalf of "the beleaguered captives of the Soviet Ukraine" by saying it was "a blatant lie," "a Nazi-like lie," "a Fascist lie with strong overtones of McCarthyism." He accused Diefenbaker of arrogance and portrayed him as a silent-movie hero, "blasting his way through paper walls and open doorways, then waiting for applause." Diefenbaker didn't deign to reply but he filed the insults, along with the many others he had endured, in the back of his commodious mind.

WHEN CARDIN TOOK OVER JUSTICE on July 7, 1965, one of the urgent files on his desk concerned George Victor Spencer, a Vancouver mail clerk accused of spying for the Soviet Union. The case had turned into a smouldering political issue as a result of an unusual government press release issued the month before.

The RCMP, under heavy criticism for the slackness of their investigating methods as revealed during the Dorion Inquiry, were anxious to divert public attention to their prowess in guarding the nation's security. When their sleuthing caused two spy masters working out of the Soviet Embassy in Ottawa to be expelled from the country, the Mounties happily helped External Affairs draft a press release that went far beyond the usually terse details. It described an unnamed civil servant who had been paid "thousands of dollars" to "assist in the establishment of espionage activities in Canada and other countries."

Under questioning by the opposition in the House, Pearson refused to identify the suspected spy but admitted that he would probably not be charged because he was thought to be dying of cancer. The case was mentioned occasionally during the 1965 campaign but it might easily have slipped from public notice altogether except for the persistent interest shown in it by Tom Hazlitt, then a senior reporter for the *Vancouver Province*.

Late in October, 1965, Hazlitt published a speculative story suggesting that the spy was probably a minor government employee in Vancouver. He was promptly visited by a mysterious man calling himself "Mr Wilson" who wanted to know if he had any more details. Suspicious that his visitor might be the spy himself, Hazlitt ingeniously compiled a list of all the junior civil servants in Vancouver who had recently been operated on for cancer and eventually narrowed his search down to George Victor Spencer, a post office employee then on sick leave. On November 2, Hazlitt confronted Spencer with his suspicions and was rewarded by a confession, which he published in the *Province*.

Three weeks later, interviewed on the CBC television program *This Hour Has Seven Days*, Lucien Cardin confirmed the identification. He also imprudently disclosed an apparently contradictory government position on the matter: that, even though Spencer had not been convicted of – or even charged with – any criminal offence, he had been fired from his job and would be kept under surveillance by the RCMP for the rest of his life.

A relatively simple security case suddenly turned into a national issue. Cardin's disclosures outraged both the advocates of civil rights, who protested that Spencer was being convicted without a trial, and the country's ardent anti-Communists, who couldn't understand why a self-confessed spy was being allowed to remain at liberty.*

*The Commission of Inquiry that eventually investigated the case established that the government's attitude, inconsistent as it looked, was justified. Spencer could not be prosecuted because the information he had sold the Russians was not secret as defined by the Official Secrets Act. (The RCMP claimed that Spencer had received $3,500 from the Russians for supplying them with photographs of the Trans Mountain pipeline, names from Vancouver cemetery headstones that could be used for false passports, a list of farms for sale near the U.S. border, and similar trivial data.) But the inquiry found that Spencer deserved to be removed from his job because he had acted in a way not compatible with his loyalty oath as a civil servant.

At this stage Spencer himself was not protesting his treatment and regarded the RCMP officers assigned to him as friends.* His only quarrel with the government was over pension rights. Following a closed Civil Service Commission hearing, Spencer was notified that although his superannuation contributions would be returned to him, his pension and other rights were cancelled. Throughout January 1966, repeated requests by the Tories and the NDP for a full inquiry into the case were turned down on the ground that such a hearing would jeopardize the RCMP's security procedures. Cardin, on advice from the RCMP, convinced Cabinet this was indeed the case.

On January 31, when pressed further by the opposition, Cardin flatly declared that no judicial inquiry would be held. Cardin's statement reflected cabinet policy, but immediately after the Justice Minister had spoken, Lester Pearson rose to make the contradictory proposal that he would personally "give consideration" to such an inquiry. The results of this "consideration" were announced to the House on February 23, when the Prime Minister unequivocally stated: "I wish to confirm the view which has been given by the Minister of Justice that an inquiry into this matter is not necessary and would not be useful."

But opposition pressure continued. On February 25, Conservative Gerald Baldwin, Liberals Bryce Mackasey and Ralph Cowan, and New Democrat David Lewis all questioned the government's conclusion. Mackasey's appeal was the most emotional: "If a man like Spencer cannot have his case presented in the House of Commons, the highest court of the land, where can he turn for protection? If this high court becomes so callous that we are not interested in the rights of the individual, it is time for us to sit back and take stock."

The topic was raised in the Liberal caucus, where besides Mackasey and Cowan, Pierre Trudeau, Gérard Pelletier and Richard Cashin indicated that they might not support the government's stand against an inquiry. Still, the cabinet remained adamant on the issue. By an ironic set of circumstances, at this very point the Liberals needed Commons approval of Justice Department estimates in order to get a motion of supply passed. They began to discuss what means they could use to pressure the Conservatives into forgetting the Spencer case and allowing the Justice estimates through the House.

*Spencer's death was reported on April 10, 1966. Though he was still under RCMP surveillance at the time, his body was not discovered until three or four days after he died.

ON FEBRUARY 24, GUY FAVREAU, then President of the Privy Council, called Davie Fulton to his parliamentary office for a private talk. The two men were unusually close for members of opposing parties. At the Couchiching Conference the previous summer they had greeted each other with such effusive warmth that a bystander remarked: "That's the Fulton-Favreau formula in action." Now, Favreau issued a warning to his friend that if the Conservatives persisted in their demands for a judicial inquiry into the Spencer case, the Liberals would be forced to disclose the details of a scandal involving Conservatives. Fulton later quoted Favreau as saying: "If you keep fighting the Spencer case, things will probably blow up and we'll have to mention the Munsinger affair."

Rumours linking a sexy blonde from East Germany with Pierre Sévigny, the former Associate Minister of Defence in the Diefenbaker Government, had been circulating in the capital for years. Over drinks, irreverent Tories would make up for each other's amusement hilarious versions of how the suave Sévigny had succeeded in persuading the puritanical Diefenbaker that his interest in the woman was purely sexual and had nothing to do with the deployment of Bomarcs.

The facts of the case had first come to the official attention of the Liberals in 1964. A week after Erik Nielsen broke the Rivard affair in the Commons, when the Liberal Government seemed about to be swamped by a wave of scandals, Pearson summoned to his office George McClellan, the RCMP Commissioner. Also present were Guy Favreau and Gordon Robertson, the Clerk of the Privy Council. According to McClellan's later testimony, Pearson asked the Mountie if he had "information indicating any impropriety or anything of a scandalous nature involving any M.P. of any Party over the last ten years." When McClellan mentioned the Sévigny episode, the Prime Minister replied, "Well, I had better see it." A résumé of the Sévigny-Munsinger dossier was given to Favreau on December 1 and to Pearson the following day.

After reading the Munsinger file, Lester Pearson took an unusual step. He wrote a confidential letter to John Diefenbaker on December 4, 1964. It was considered to be such an important piece of correspondence that it was sent to the Opposition Leader's office by special messenger. When Mary Macdonald telephoned ahead to say it was on the way, she was informed Diefenbaker was at Stornoway, his official residence, but was assured the letter would be delivered promptly to him.*

*For the full text of this letter, see Appendix H.

After mentioning the Rivard affair and admitting he had asked "for a full report of instances in the last ten years or so in which political intervention was involved in investigations," Pearson wrote:

> One case (the Munsinger case) has given me very grave concern. It affects the security of the country. In 1960-61, a Minister who occupied a position of great responsibility in the Government was involved in a liaison which clearly endangered security. I have been greatly disturbed by the lack of attention which, in so far as the file indicates, this matter received. The Minister was left in his position of trust. . . .
>
> I recognize that the file before me may not disclose all the steps that were taken. In view of this, it is my duty to write you about the matter in case you might be in a position to let me know that the enquiries that were pursued and the safeguards that were taken reached further than the material before me would indicate. That material now indicates that the Minister of Justice brought the matter to your attention and that no action was taken. . . .
>
> If there is further information you can provide about the Munsinger case, I will be grateful if you will let me know.

John Diefenbaker didn't reply to the letter and even refused to confirm he had actually received it. But six days later he visited Pearson in his Centre Block office, stayed for thirty-five minutes and took part in a heated, if inconclusive, exchange about the Munsinger case.

AT THE TIME (and this was during the worst days of the Rivard scandals) Guy Favreau toyed with the idea of using the Munsinger information as a weapon against the Conservatives. But Walter Gordon served notice he would resign if such tactics were adopted. Later, when the Tories were making gleeful jokes about Liberal scandals in the 1965 campaign, Favreau and Cardin tried to persuade Pearson to release the Munsinger information. Pearson refused. But he hadn't returned the Munsinger file to the RCMP and in late February, 1966, when Favreau made his threats to Fulton, it was still lying in the Privy Council office safe.

ON WEDNESDAY, MARCH 2, George Victor Spencer's situation was altered in an important way. David Lewis, deputy leader of the NDP, telephoned Lucien Cardin and asked that the RCMP allow Spencer to meet a neutral lawyer so that it could be conclusively established whether Spencer himself wanted a judicial inquiry into his firing from the post office. Cardin, convinced that Spencer thought he had been fairly treated, agreed. Lewis arranged to have John Laxton, a Vancouver lawyer, meet Spencer on Thursday morning. Spencer told Laxton that he had been well treated by the RCMP but admitted that he did want a hearing into his pension situation. Laxton sent Lewis a wire about Spencer's decision, which arrived in Ottawa Thursday afternoon. Lewis decided to wait until the next day to make it public in the House of Commons.

WHEN THE HOUSE MET THAT FRIDAY, John Diefenbaker began to attack Cardin once more on the Spencer case, charging that the government had "erected a labyrinth of deception" and accusing the Justice Minister of "evasion, delusion and deception." Cardin kept jumping up to interrupt, becoming more and more agitated.

"The great executioner now is after my political neck," he shouted.

"You committed suicide yourself," Diefenbaker yelled back.

Cardin, so excited that he popped two tranquillizers into his mouth, then accused Diefenbaker of having "attained [such] a degree of political conceit that every time he decides to make loud noises, he expects the government, Parliament and everyone in it to jump." Cardin dramatically leaned over his parliamentary desk, shook his fist at Diefenbaker and cried, "Well, I refuse to jump!"

The two men stared at each other with an animosity so intense that the Commons hushed at the sight of them. Cardin pointed at Diefenbaker again and shrilled: "Of all the members he, I repeat *he*, is the very last person who can afford to give advice on the handling of security cases in Canada."

The Liberals banged their desks and Diefenbaker, who noticed that Pearson had joined in the clapping, yelled across the floor: "Applause from the Prime Minister. *I want that on the record.*"

In the fury of the moment, Cardin caught only the last phrase. At the same instant Favreau turned to Cardin and urgently whispered, *"Munsinger."* The Justice Minister, responding to what he thought was Diefenbaker's challenge to place his accusation "on the record," blurted out: "I want the right honourable gentleman to tell the House about his participation in the *Monseignor* case when he was prime minister of this country."

MEMBERS OF THE PARLIAMENTARY PRESS GALLERY rushed out of the Commons, trying to find out who or what the Monseignor case was all about. (It was rumoured the Monseignor in question was a Catholic prelate caught smuggling heroin.) The PM's office, besieged by calls, sent a representative to the Press Gallery who corrected Cardin's mispronunciation and briefly outlined the case. Correspondents who had heard stories about a beautiful German spy (erroneously named Olga and supposedly long since dead) immediately wrote speculative reports about an alleged love affair between Olga Munsinger and an unnamed minister in the Diefenbaker Cabinet.

In the Commons, meanwhile, David Lewis read his telegram from Spencer into the record. But the government held firm. There would be no inquiry. Cardin's erratic speech was followed by an emotional defence of the government position from Jean Marchand ("I am particularly concerned with this problem. I spent part of my life fighting for the right of an employee to be heard in cases of dismissal . . .") and a closely reasoned, legalistic view of the case by Solicitor General Larry Pennell.

While his ministers were speaking, Pearson was sitting in the parliamentary lobby with a group of Liberals, including Bryce Mackasey, the M.P. for Verdun, who had already stated his opposition to the government's handling of the Spencer case. Mackasey now reminded Pearson that the Lewis telegram added a new element to the situation. Pearson grabbed Cardin who was just coming out of the House and took him up to his Centre Block office. Allan MacEachen, Pearson's adviser on Commons procedure, was called up shortly afterwards.

Even though the Liberal Whip had assured Pearson earlier that the government could win the vote on Justice estimates with a safe margin, the PM wasn't sure how many of his own M.P.'s might vote against him now that Spencer's wishes were known. He decided to reverse his stand and grant Spencer a hearing after all. Cardin argued briefly and then gave his disheartened acquiescence. The Prime Minister arrived back in his Commons seat just after three of his ministers had reaffirmed the government's anti-inquiry position. Without warning anyone Pearson announced his reversal. He even offered to telephone Spencer to confirm his request for an inquiry, and did so that evening.

SEVERAL KEY ELEMENTS IN THE PEARSON STYLE were on display that dismal afternoon in the Commons. It was a moment of crisis. The Minister of Justice and the Leader of the Opposition were at each other's throats. Just as disaster seemed imminent, in rode the shining man of reason, smiling his boyish smile, under-reacting to the torrent of events threatening to engulf his government. His objective was admirable: Who could say it was wrong to grant a sick man the benefit of an inquiry into his dismissal from a job? Pearson did what he had always done. It seemed the perfect diplomatic compromise. By granting the inquiry, he thought he had once again reduced a self-generated crisis to reconcilable proportions.

But instead of genteel applause, the Prime Minister reaped unusual abuse from his own colleagues. By so suddenly reversing himself, he had cut the ground out from under three of his ministers guilty of nothing more than loyally and convincingly putting forward government policy. The Liberal caucus was furious that Pearson had betrayed the Justice Minister, the only member of the cabinet who had stood up to John Diefenbaker. Jean Marchand moved into a parliamentary desk near Pearson. Through clenched teeth he said, "If you ever do to me what you've just done to Cardin, all hell will break loose." Across the aisle, John Diefenbaker summed up the situation with a triumphant snort. "We stood," he declared, "and they folded."

The Pearson reversal on the Spencer case caught most Liberal cabinet ministers not only unprepared but out of town. On that day Paul Martin, Mitchell Sharp, Bud Drury, Joe Greene, Jean-Luc Pépin and Robert Winters were in Washington, attending the semi-annual meeting of the joint U.S -Canada committee on trade and economic affairs. Jack Pickersgill, Paul Hellyer, Jack Nicholson and Arthur Laing were in British Columbia on various assignments and Maurice Sauvé was at a forestry conference in Paris.

When these eleven men had left Ottawa, they had good reason to feel optimistic. Lucien Cardin seemed to be battling the Tories to a draw. The Spencer case was a diminishing factor on the national scene. At any rate, the ministers felt confident that this time there would be no change of position. The secret they shared was that when Cabinet had taken the decision against holding an inquiry into the Spencer case (in mid January of 1966) it had also very deliberately made a second, unanimous resolution: that this time, the government would stand firm and not change its mind, so that it could not be accused of yet another parliamentary retreat.

It was with these facts in mind that the travelling ministers received the news of Pearson's reversal. Ministerial executive assistants sent out rush telegrams, bearing the disturbing news. For once, the ministers could react, not as men who had been involved in the intricate machinations that produced a change of policy but as Canadians, viewing the actions of their government from a distance that lent objectivity to their appraisal.

The effect was shattering. At the Washington conference with the United States cabinet, the message was delivered to Paul Martin, who passed it around to his colleagues. As the piece of paper was circulated, one minister scribbled an oath beneath the message and the next one added his blessing.

Lucien Cardin, the man who felt most humiliated by the Pearson decision, went home to Sorel. After a weekend of discussion with his family he decided to hand in his resignation. When the Commons reassembled on Monday, Pearson again yielded to opposition demands and agreed to set up a judicial inquiry into intelligence procedures. On Tuesday morning Cardin sent a letter to the Prime Minister declaring his intention to quit politics. The Liberal Party's "resignation squad" (Walter Gordon, Maurice Lamontagne, and Guy Favreau) immediately swung into action to dissuade him. They argued that if Cardin left, most Quebec ministers would feel they could not stay in the government and without the support of the French Canadians in his cabinet, Pearson himself would have to resign. That, in turn, would cause an election, which might return John Diefenbaker to power, an idea that Cardin could scarcely cherish. It was never clear how many of the nine Quebec ministers would have resigned with Cardin but Jean Marchand, for one, decided he would leave politics with the Justice Minister and so informed the Prime Minister.

At a meeting of Quebec M.P.'s held on the Tuesday evening (March 8), René Tremblay, the deposed Minister of Immigration, attacked Pearson's handling of the Spencer affair and read out a motion of censure against the Prime Minister to be presented at next day's general caucus. It received support until Bryce Mackasey got up to speak: "Who's going to bell the cat?" he demanded. "Which one of you is going to get up and move that resolution? Why, you're so gutless that if I moved a standing ovation for Pearson, you'd all get up and clap." One M.P. suggested it could be tabled as a unanimous resolution of the Quebec caucus. But Mackasey butted in: "No. Because I vote against it, and if you try a trick like that I'm going to expose every one of you s.o.b.'s."

At about the same time that Tuesday evening, Pearson, who hadn't opened Cardin's resignation letter, was trying to talk his Justice Minister into withdrawing it. But Cardin just wanted to pack his bags and retreat from public view.

Next morning, on the way to his office, Cardin met James Walker, one of the most popular and compassionate members of the Liberal caucus. While the two men had coffee, Walker pleaded: "Don't desert those of us who see in you the only guy who's stood up on his feet and fought. As far as I'm concerned, the party's gone the moment you pull out. You're our last chance for a spark of guts." It was this appeal that finally persuaded Cardin not to resign. When he announced his decision to the caucus without hiding his disappointment in the Prime Minister's action but vowing that he would stay and fight, Cardin was cheered. The crisis seemed to be over.

THE FOLLOWING DAY, THURSDAY, MARCH 10, as a parting gesture before leaving for a holiday, Cardin held a press conference. He assured a worried Pearson that he intended only to explain why he had withdrawn his resignation. The PM's staff rushed a tape recorder to his office just in time to catch a whole new set of anti-Diefenbaker accusations. Though Cardin admitted he hadn't seen the RCMP's file, he claimed that the Munsinger affair was "worse than the Profumo case," that Mrs Munsinger had been engaged in espionage before coming to Canada, that her association with Conservative cabinet ministers (and he used the plural) had constituted a security risk, that both Fulton and Diefenbaker had been aware of the affair and that they had mishandled it by not referring it to the legal officers of the Crown. Cardin also confirmed that the woman in question had died of leukemia in East Germany. The Justice Minister left little doubt that the Munsinger disclosures were part of a Liberal plan to harass John Diefenbaker and his supporters. "There is a working arrangement," he told the press conference, "a working arrangement not only between the Prime Minister, myself and the members of Cabinet, but also all the [caucus] members, about what we are going to do. We are going to fight and fight hard and, if we have to, use the same methods that are being used and have been used against us for the past three years."

RALPH ALLEN, WHO WAS THEN MANAGING EDITOR of the *Toronto Daily Star*, had been highly suspicious about the rumoured death of the glamorous spy from the day the case broke. It seemed just too convenient for the politicians concerned. He assigned two crack *Star* reporters, Robert Reguly and Robert McKenzie, to look into the affair. They found an old Montreal telephone book in which she was listed and contacted some of her former neighbours, one of whom had the address of Gerda Munsinger's aunt. When Jack Granek, a German-speaking *Star* reporter, telephoned the aunt, he was assured that Gerda was working at a bar in Munich. Reguly flew across the Atlantic and three hours after landing at Munich airport was knocking on the woman's door. "I suppose you want to ask about Sévigny," she said, when he identified himself.

To prevent rival papers from copying the scoop, the *Star* kept the news out of its small first edition. Just after 1 p.m. on Friday, March 11, the second edition of the *Star* came out with a 120-point headline: STAR MAN FINDS GERDA MUNSINGER.

At 1:15, David Lewis cut into a debate on Cardin's allegations of the day before to announce Reguly's find. The news devastated an already over-excited Commons. Pearson suggested yet another judicial inquiry, which provoked angry retorts from the opposition. The sanest remarks came from Gordon Fairweather, who asked: "What in God's name have we been about here this week? We have been witnessing a conspiracy enjoyed by a frustrated minister who wishes to commit hara-kiri and is willing to take other people down with him. This man has demeaned and soiled this place and does not have the courage to stand up and make the charges [here] he loves to make when the press sits around his office. . . .This strange man likes to go about in other places making smears and statements; that is what he likes to do and that is why it will be hard to explain in the years ahead what we have been doing in these days."

In Montreal, cornered by newsmen, Pierre Sévigny denied any impropriety, vowed he would clear his name, and called Cardin "a cheap, despicable little man who has dishonoured his oath of office." That evening, accompanied by his wife and daughter, he went on national television and in an emotional outburst admitted he had seen Gerda "socially a few times," then based his defence on a distinguished war record: "I shall attack with every means that the law puts at my disposal to find out who is at the source of this infamous slander. I shall ask the soldiers who by the thousands fought and bled with me during World War II if they believe that Pierre Sévigny, or any Sévigny for that matter, could betray this Canada that the Sévignys love so much."

The mood of that incredible day in Canadian politics was best caught by Christopher Young, the editor of the *Ottawa Citizen*, who wrote: "Behind all the giggles, leers and knowing winks, behind the raging grassfire of tittle-tattle, behind the thunder in the Commons chamber, there was a deep and genuine sense of sorrow on Parliament Hill. It was indeed a sad occasion. For many years Parliament had been in a real sense a gentlemen's club. The comradeship of the club is a commonplace of political memoirs and the more human books of history. In Ottawa today, that kind of atmosphere is as dead as Gladstone and Disraeli. It has been dying for a long time, and the knowledge of its last convulsions was the reason for the unspoken mourning on the Hill."

400

THAT WEEKEND, LESTER PEARSON came close to resigning. The impact of what he had allowed to happen weighed heavily on his conscience. "This is a terrible precedent," he told a colleague on Sunday morning. "Good Lord, we can't have prime ministers investigated when they make a decision on their own. It's a prime minister's prerogative to make a wrong decision, and it's not subject to checks. We can't investigate a prime minister."

That afternoon he called to a meeting at 24 Sussex Drive Mitchell Sharp, Paul Martin and Paul Hellyer (each of whom suspected he was about to be asked to take over as Liberal Leader) as well as Lucien Cardin and Jack Pickersgill. But after listening to the smooth reassurances of Pickersgill, Pearson regained his composure and instead of discussing his resignation asked for advice on parliamentary strategy.

Next day in the Commons, Pearson announced the terms of reference for the Munsinger inquiry. George Hees, who had been named by Gerda as the second Tory minister of her acquaintance, made a dignified statement, acknowledging only that he had lunched with her twice. Davie Fulton affirmed that any RCMP reports he had seen on the case contained no suggestion that there had been any breach of security. Lucien Cardin added an odd comment of his own: "I'm not saying that I had not thought of it [dropping the Munsinger name into debate] before, but I had not intended to use it at that time [March 4]."

The mood of revenge pervading the Liberal benches that day was set by the Prime Minister himself, who said, "We've been subjected to this kind of treatment now for too long and reputations have been ruined over here [on the Liberal side of the House]. Now those gentlemen who have been so free with their accusations over the last few years are getting a little of it, and they don't like it."

FOR NEARLY TWO WEEKS OF RIOTOUS DEBATE, the House of Commons had been in a state of suspended degradation. Now, Parliament's self-protective devices began to operate. It was almost as though M.P.'s of all parties were possessed of an intuitive awareness of how much strain the system could stand. Realizing they had arrived near the breaking point, they drew back, collectively rallying to prevent Parliament's disintegration.

This sentiment was echoed from every corner of the chamber. Davie Fulton put it most bluntly: "If this course is persisted in, we are facing the ruination of our system and our institutions."

John Diefenbaker, who at that particular point in time probably had it within his power to cripple Parliament, drew back and staged one of his better summer-stock performances ("We do not snoop . . . we do not slither . . . ").

The terms of reference given to Mr Justice W. F. Spence of the Supreme Court, who was named to conduct the hearings, made it clear that the Liberals regarded the former Conservative Government's handling of the whole affair as having been a threat to the security of the state. As such, they felt the inquiry's ground rules should be as restrictive as possible, and used the 1946 hearings into the Gouzenko case as the closest parallel.

The Tories, on the other hand, viewed the hearing as something closer to a political exercise, and insisted that it should be conducted in a much more open manner. They recognized the Dorion Inquiry into the Rivard affair as the relevant precedent. Their main concern was that the terms of reference setting up the Spence Inquiry invited the Supreme Court judge to investigate mainly the charges that Justice Minister Lucien Cardin had made in a letter of March 11 to the Prime Minister. These were limited to two accusations: that the Conservatives "had failed to place the file on this case before the law officers of the Department of Justice for their advice," and that "the information given to the Leader of the Opposition when he was Prime Minister, concerned a case in which security risks were involved." Cardin ended his letter by declaring: "I have made and make no other charges."

But in his press conference of March 10, and in other private statements to parliamentary reporters, Cardin did, in fact, make several other accusations. He had described the Munsinger affair as being "worse than the Profumo case" and had referred to Gerda Munsinger as "a bona fide security case."

To substantiate the charges Cardin had made in his press statements, the Conservatives felt that the following facts would have to be clearly established before the Spence commission: that Gerda was a known spy; that she had been actively engaged in espionage in Canada; that she had compromised Conservative cabinet ministers; and that, despite the knowledge of all these facts, the Diefenbaker Government took no action, thereby compromising the security of Canada.

But instead of being referred to such specifics, Mr Justice Spence was requested to report only on whether or not the Munsinger case "constituted a risk to the security of Canada" and to investigate "the failure to seek the advice of the law officers of the Department of Justice."

Failure, in its dictionary sense, means the omission to perform an act. Fulton had already admitted that he didn't show the RCMP file to his departmental officials, but rushed it to Diefenbaker's attention. The former Minister of Justice claimed there was no reason to consult his officials, because no legal offence was involved, only the exercise of discretion by a prime minister on how he should discipline members of his cabinet.

Instead of broken security regulations, the point at issue seemed to be a matter of assessing John Diefenbaker's political judgement. That, according to the Conservative view, was something the electorate, not a judicial inquiry, should be asked to assess.

MEANWHILE IN MUNICH, MRS MUNSINGER was under siege, with fifty reporters from publications all over the world hammering at her apartment door. The CBC's national affairs reporter, Norman DePoe, negotiated an exclusive television appearance and on the evening of March 15 the nation sat bug-eyed as he conducted a twenty-minute interview with the somewhat haggard but still attractive Gerda.

In the newspapers the affair was blown up into an intrigue of glamour and passion. It was rumoured that the RCMP had taken pictures of Gerda and her lovers in action through a special light fixture in the ceiling of her bedroom, that the police had a tape-recording of a wooden leg going bump in the night, that DOT planes had been used for secret rendezvous and so on. To astonished Canadians it sounded as though the Diefenbaker Years had been one long champagne bash. Gil Purcell, general manager of the Canadian Press, won a limerick contest sponsored by *Maclean's* with the verse:

> *There was a young lady from Munich*
> *Whose bosom distended her tunic.*
> *Her main undertaking*
> *Was cabinet making*
> *In fashions bilingue et unique.*

Dennis Braithwaite summed up the whole affair in his *Globe and Mail* column with the comment: "However it turns out politically, *l'affaire Pierre* is a grand story. It provides, if only the Canada Council could recognize it, the ideal libretto for a great Canadian comic opera, offering besides such boffo ingredients as romance, mystery and international intrigue, the indispensable flavor of biculturalism."

IN MID APRIL, the ribald rumours were over and the Munsinger inquiry officially got under way. The setting gave the hearing the eerie atmosphere it deserved. The courtroom was a chamber on the main floor of the Centennial Towers, Ottawa's most modern office building. A windowless chamber, hermetically sealed from the traffic noises on busy Laurier Avenue, it had deep red broadloom muffling incidental sounds and a barrage of fluorescent light fixtures casting a shadowless pall on all present. Because the microphones were kept open, spectators·could hear over the earphones of the translation system the restless rustling of papers as the various lawyers and the judge himself leafed through the RCMP reports that constituted the heart of the inquiry.

The senior counsel for the Conservatives, C. F. H. Carson, looked fully as learned as the judge, though he seemed at times to be straining for composure in a situation which C. L. Dubin, his junior colleague, described as "singular in the annals of the parliamentary system of government."

And singular it was.

This was not only, as the official notices claimed, "The Commission of Inquiry into matters relating to one Gerda Munsinger"; it was also the political trial of one John George Diefenbaker.

But the trial was without climax and catharsis. The accused and the accusers never confronted one another.

The facts were easily established. On December 7, 1960, Clifford Harvison, then Commissioner of the RCMP, reported to Davie Fulton that Pierre Sévigny, the Associate Minister of National Defence, had an illicit sexual relationship with Gerda Munsinger, a Montreal prostitute with underworld connections. Harvison mentioned that Gerda, who had also been seen in the company of George Hees, had a doubtful security background. Five days later, Fulton received a written report on the case and immediately took it to the Prime Minister. On December 13, Diefenbaker confronted Sévigny with the RCMP charges. Brushing off Sévigny's denials, he told him to end the relationship and warned his minister that he would have to be satisfied there had been no breach of security. Two months later Sévigny told the Prime Minister that Gerda had returned to Germany. Nothing was ever done about the incident. Sévigny stayed in his position of trust and not even his superior, the Minister of National Defence, Douglas Harkness, was informed of his colleague's indiscretion.

Spence's assignment, five and a half years later, was to decide whether Diefenbaker and/or Fulton should have referred the matter to law officers of the Crown for guidance.

The Conservatives objected so strongly to the conduct of the inquiry that on May 18, Fulton and Diefenbaker withdrew their lawyers from the case in protest.

Secret RCMP files released by Mr Justice Spence showed that Gerda had first come to the attention of Western intelligence services in 1949 when she was arrested by German border police on charges of minor espionage activities for the Russians. Born Gerda Heseler, she had married Michael Munsinger, an American soldier, and was divorced from him in 1954, after her criminal record prevented her from following him to the United States. Admitted to Canada in August 1955, she became a prostitute in Montreal. Her first meeting with Pierre Sévigny took place at a Montreal golf course in August of 1958. Although he denied she had ever been his mistress, she admitted to the RCMP that he paid her apartment rent. RCMP testimony during the inquiry showed that the police considered Gerda a security risk but had no evidence she had tried to obtain secret information while in Canada or that she had committed any breach of security. Though it was not published at the time, the police case against Gerda Munsinger was strengthened by the fact that the Central Intelligence Agency in Washington passed on the information that it classed the woman as a definite security risk.

SPENCE'S REPORT ON THE MUNSINGER AFFAIR, published on September 23, 1966, found that Pierre Sévigny became a security risk through his affair with Gerda Munsinger although there was "no scintilla of evidence that there was any disloyalty involved." John Diefenbaker was censured for failing to dismiss his minister. "Doubt must always be resolved in favour of the 'national security,'" and the Conservative Leader had placed his personal assessment above national security. The judge also found fault with Diefenbaker for not seeking the advice or consent of his cabinet in arriving at his decision. The report commended Davie Fulton for the promptness with which he had reported the contents of the RCMP brief to Diefenbaker, but it criticized the former Minister of Justice for accepting the RCMP's conclusion that there had been no breach of security without further investigation. George Hees' "lack of discretion was slight but regrettable."

The Supreme Court judge's criticism did not extend to the Liberals. He found nothing reprehensible in Cardin's method of bringing up the case and nothing odd in the fact that the Prime Minister had kept the RCMP files for fifteen months. Spence neglected to mention that by searching the security files of the RCMP for ammunition against their political opponents, the Liberals established a precedent that could haunt Canadian politics long after the dreary details of the case itself had been forgotten.

Significantly, the Spence Inquiry recommended no action in the courts on any point of law. This raised the pertinent question whether a judge of the Supreme Court should be asked to give what are, in effect, political opinions. Criticizing the report, Dr Edward McWhinney, a McGill law professor, wrote: "Mr Justice Spence has accepted the most flimsy, uncorroborated hearsay evidence, which no respectable court of law would accept for more than one moment, as pointing to existence of wide-scale espionage activity in which prominent people in public life might be involved. Guilt by association, however indirect or far-fetched the association may be, is also not excluded from the ambit of the report."

Pierre Sévigny, asked by reporters to comment on the judge's findings, bellowed: "Spence, Spence, Spence. I suppose it takes all kinds to make a world. All I have to say is that the whole thing is bullshit." Told that this was not a quotable description, Sévigny tried again: "No? Well, what about horseshit?" Then he added: "All right, I'll settle for foolishness. Foolishness from A to Z."

But it was Gerda Munsinger herself who pronounced the most fitting epitaph to the affair. "I knew Pierre as a man," she said. "He knew me as a woman. That's all there was to it."

CHAPTER 29

Downhill All the Way

THE MUNSINGER AFFAIR WAS MERELY the most spectacular in the mind-boggling procession of blunders that marked the Pearson Government's last unhappy term in office. During those two years, Canada was like a country without a psychic centre or a recognizable leader. None of the issues for which the Liberals had so urgently demanded a majority in their 1965 campaign were resolved (or even joined) and everything that followed the election was really a setting of the political stage for the post-Pearson period.

Disillusioned with politicians and infected with a small dose of the revolutionary fever that was epidemic in western democracies, Canadians at all levels of the population began spontaneously – and quite uncharacteristically – to question authority. This mood spread from the post-adolescent group, where it could be expected, to the middle-class middle-aged and beyond to the old and the very young. Housewives organized boycotts of supermarkets to protest high food costs. Farmers climbed on their tractors and blocked highways to draw attention to their problems. A long series of labour disputes shook the economy, as union executives lost control over their members. Day and night on open-line radio programs Canadians gave voice to their pent-up resentment of "them," the people in charge, the managers of a society that no longer seemed able to satisfy the normal longings of its ordinary citizens.

Television was the national medium that fused these groups and the two programs that best expressed the general discontent and attracted the most viewers were *Wojeck*, a drama series about a big-city coroner crusading against the dehumanizing institutions of urban life, and *This Hour Has Seven Days*, a public affairs program that was not just the best television of the Sixties but the most dazzling creative expression of the temper of the times. (CBC management, assuming the role of the fat and outraged Establishment, ruthlessly and ineptly killed off *Seven Days* in the spring of 1966 despite the fact that it was the most popular serious program in the CBC's history and a real force for national unity.)

In Ottawa there was ample evidence every sitting day that the members of the House of Commons were baffled by what was going on in the country at large. They became an assembly of tired and angry men, removed from the rush of real events. "Canada's national political life has degenerated to a condition beyond patience," wrote Denis Smith, editor of *The Journal of Canadian Studies*. "The national parties should not, and need not, have brought us to this point, but they have done so. What further degradation must be endured before our myopic party leaders will understand the implications of the crisis? What further expression of outrage is necessary to convince these men that their leadership has failed and their inspiration has died? What signs of despair do they ask us to display?"

Typical of the frustration felt by the younger politicians in the House of Commons itself was a *cri de coeur* uttered on November 8, 1966, by Heward Grafftey, the young Tory M.P. from Brome-Missisquoi. After John Diefenbaker had run on interminably about a procedural point, Grafftey jumped to his feet, looked around wildly and, with the release of a decade's political frustration, declared: "Everybody who sits here knows that this establishment, particularly for the younger generation, is becoming absolutely meaningless. Let's get on with the public's business!" A group of Montreal high school students, occupying the visitors' galleries, broke into spontaneous cheers, a show of emotion strictly forbidden by House rules but accurately reflecting the national frustration.

It was one of those rare occasions when M.P.'s, looking up at the young faces in the gallery seats, were confronted for a fleeting moment by the true limitations of their mandate and left feeling like courtiers involved in some ceremonial rite that had long since lost its meaning. Demoralized by long years of minority government and the spectacle of scandals dragged through debates like tatty laundry, the politicians were snappish with each other and given to regarding the House proceedings with an aggrieved and weary air.

A small, silly incident that occurred during the first week of April 1967, while the House was debating Paul Hellyer's bill to unify the armed forces, was symptomatic of this mood. Bill Lee, the minister's jaunty executive assistant, was sitting in the Commons gallery one afternoon, bored rigid with the Tory filibuster. To amuse himself, he pulled out a three-foot-long telescopic ballpoint pen, which looked a little like the aerial of a walkie-talkie, and began to mutter into it, pretending to be relaying messages to Marcel Prud'homme (Liberal M.P. for Saint-Denis) on the floor of the Commons, who had a similar pen of his own. The Tories, already suspicious that Lee was ghost writing most of the government's unification speeches, came to life as soon as they spotted the by-play Gordon Churchill promptly called a dinner-hour caucus to plan a protest against Lee's temerity in using "an electronic spy device" to signal party strategy. That evening, just as Churchill was about to rise and make his motion, he noticed that two Conservative M.P.'s, Donald MacInnis and Michael Forrestall, had also been given trick pens by Lee. He sank back, bewildered and speechless. The debate droned on into the stale night, with the three M.P.'s and Lee jabbering like bad ten-year-olds into their pens.

LEE WAS ONE OF THE FEW LIBERALS still lively enough to show temerity. Most of the party had fallen into a protracted sulk. The activists of Pearson's first term were gradually drifting away from Ottawa. John Nichol summed up their feelings in the spring of 1966 when he told Keith Davey: "Listen, man, we're all turned off."

What Liberals of all ages and ideological stripes wanted was a quiescent period, a time to repair the party's fortunes and managerial image in order to make way for a new leader. They hoped to drift back to the good old attitudes and the best old times of the early Fifties, when only the CCF wanted to be radical and every piece of Liberal legislation worked. But they reckoned without Walter Lockhart Gordon.

By continuing to pretend that the Pearson Government was still a viable political force, malleable to his radical suggestions, Gordon achieved three things between 1965 and 1967: he prodded Pearson and his ministers out of their hopeful lethargy, he demolished the Liberal Party as it then existed and he destroyed his own position in it.

MINDFUL OF HIS CASUAL PROMISE to quit the cabinet if the Liberals failed to achieve their majority in the 1965 election, Gordon had gone through the motions of formally submitting his resignation to the Prime Minister immediately after polling day. To the Finance Minister's surprise, it was accepted with ill-concealed eagerness. At his farewell meeting with Pearson, Gordon angrily accused the Prime Minister of yielding to the big business lobbies that were after his scalp.

During the next twelve months ("my sabbatical year"), Gordon wrote a new book and functioned as a radical counterweight to incipient complacency inside the Liberal caucus. He was dropped from the Commons finance committee and humiliated when his successor, Mitchell Sharp, dismantled most of the nationalistic measures he had introduced. But he was undeterred by these rebuffs. In his book he demanded something that few Canadian politicians had previously dared to ask of their own party: an ideological showdown.* In every chapter Gordon documented his distaste for the neat, grey way in which Pearson was dealing with the nation's problems. Apart from his by now familiar alarums on behalf of economic nationalism, Gordon advocated such relatively radical measures as a major boost in unemployment insurance, the establishment of an income maintenance system to assist people whose work is interrupted by illness and free post-secondary education.

At this time, Gordon was also devoting his restless energies to the government's decennial review of the Bank Act. Its most controversial feature was Sharp's decision (taken at the urging of the chartered banks) to lift the 6 per cent ceiling on loan interest charges. Early in January 1966 Gordon sent Sharp a private letter, arguing against the lifting of the 6 per cent limit and suggesting there should be caucus consultation before the government proceeded. Sharp ignored the message and on January 26 Gordon launched an attack in the Liberal caucus against any lifting of the 6 per cent ceiling, urging members to join him in turning the party back from the abyss of reaction.

Gordon eventually lost the bank rate battle. But to head off the threatened resignation of Jean Marchand, who was supporting the Gordon stand, Sharp propitiated the Liberal left wing by raising payments to old-age pensioners instead. (He then had to propitiate the right wing by raising taxes to finance the pension increase.)

AT ABOUT THE SAME TIME, Gordon found a new if backhanded ally for his crusade on behalf of Canadian nationalism. Eric Kierans, who had so bitterly attacked Gordon's first budget, now joined him by levelling a blast against the continentalist tendencies of Mitchell Sharp.

On December 5, 1965, Sharp had announced an agreement with Washington that in return for repurchasing Canadian bonds in the

*A Choice for Canada: Independence or Colonial Status (McClelland and Stewart Limited, 1966).

410

United States whenever Ottawa's demand for American dollars reached a given level, Canada could preserve its access to the New York money market for new security issues. He made no mention of the fact that there was another rider on the agreement: Canada would have to accept restrictions on the expansion of U.S. subsidiaries. These were the so-called direct investment guidelines that set limits on how much American corporations could invest abroad.

Kierans, who was suspicious of the arrangements, got hold of the guidelines on December 9 and spent the next two weeks studying their implications. On December 23, in a Quebec City interview with Frank Howard of the *Globe and Mail,* he attacked Ottawa for failing to protect Canadian interests and placidly accepting the U.S. attitude. The next day, Louis Rasminsky, Governor of the Bank of Canada, telephoned Jean Lesage and asked him to restrain his rebellious Health Minister. When the Quebec Premier told Kierans about the telephone call, he immediately phoned Rasminsky back for a forty-minute discussion of the issue.

"At the end of the conversation," Kierans later recalled, "I was more discouraged as a Canadian than I've ever been before. I realized that the whole deal had been negotiated by Rasminsky and Bob Bryce [the Deputy Minister of Finance]. They're able enough, but how can they compete with the U.S. presidential power? It was at this point that I realized what would happen if I didn't act right away. Years from now some university professor in an obscure academic journal would analyse what had happened when we agreed to the guidelines, and conclude that Canada had lost a lot of sovereignty that day. At the same time I was getting reports from my friends who head large U.S. subsidiaries in Canada, telling me they were no longer sure whether their policies were being set by their home offices or by Washington."

So Kierans decided to attack. He told a friend that he regarded the issue as the greatest threat to Canadian independence since the War of 1812.

Kierans objected to the guidelines at two levels. One was their immediate effect of forcing many American subsidiaries to seek financing on the Canadian side of the border. This, he felt, could create havoc in Canada's capital market. But his more serious worry was the principle involved. Kierans was not concerned, as was Gordon, with Canadian ownership but only with Canadian sovereignty. Before the guidelines went into effect, the argument could be made that there was little essential difference between the way American- and Canadian-owned businesses operated, because both were presumably out to maximize the profits of their owners. But under the new guidelines, Kierans believed, U.S. subsidiaries in Canada would no longer be merely profit-seeking extensions of their parent companies, but instruments of Washington's external concerns. This view was confirmed by Secretary of the Treasury Henry Fowler who, in announcing the guidelines, emphasized that international companies based in the United States "have not only a commercial importance – but a highly significant role in U.S. foreign policy."

"This posed serious problems for Canada," Kierans commented later, "since the bulk of our manufacturing, mining and petroleum industries are foreign controlled. Such corporations would have to serve the aims of American policy and seek approval for the reinvestment-of-earnings, dividend and financial policies of their foreign subsidiaries. We were no longer dealing with the disparate and independent decisions of thousands of businessmen, but with hard government policy."

Kierans' initiative took the form of writing letters, in his capacity as Quebec's Acting Minister of Revenue, to U.S. Secretary of Commerce John Connor and Secretary of the Treasury Henry Fowler, protesting the new guidelines. His highly irregular and resolutely undiplomatic salvo was never officially acknowledged, but Washington quietly toned down its guidelines as they affected Canada.

THE LIBERAL PARTY'S NEXT INTERNAL SPASM involved the implementation of medicare, which had been included in the party platform as far back as 1919. Because it had been one of the main planks in the 1962 and 1963 campaigns, the Liberals felt compelled to introduce the measure and work started in the spring of 1965 on a comprehensive, portable, universal medical care program to go into effect on July 1, 1967. Despite objections from the provinces, which would have to share in the costs of the scheme, medicare by 1967 was plainly government policy. But as part of his over-all anti-inflationary program, Mitchell Sharp announced, in early September 1966, a one-year postponement of the starting date.

Inside the cabinet only Allan MacEachen and Jean Marchand were dismayed about the proposed delay. For months MacEachen had been fighting hard against the abandonment of the 1967 starting date and on September 8, when Sharp announced the postponement, MacEachen considered resigning from the cabinet. Marchand sent word to MacEachen that if he quit the government they would leave together.

On October 4, MacEachen, in a showdown with Pearson, informed him that he would not resign but also said that he felt he could not pilot the medicare bill through the House since he disagreed so fundamentally with the delay. Meanwhile, at a Liberal caucus the same day, the government's stand was attacked by Maurice Lamontagne, John Munro, Joseph Macaluso, Walter Gordon, Hugh Faulkner and Pierre Elliott Trudeau. But Mitchell Sharp carried the bulk of Liberal M.P.'s with him by holding up a book of spending estimates and asking the dissenting members exactly which items they would like to see eliminated in order to implement medicare. The Prime Minister then stepped in to announce that the medicare postponement had been his decision and that if the caucus didn't agree with it they had better plan on a leadership convention. On the morning of October 7 the issue came before Cabinet, where the first signs of a compromise began to emerge. It was suggested that the Finance Minister might be able to find some wording for the medicare bill that would allow it to be implemented earlier than July, 1968, provided economic conditions changed. MacEachen and Marchand were delighted.

That afternoon, however, Sharp told the Prime Minister that in his opinion there was no way of fulfilling the cabinet's instructions to change the wording of the bill without giving the appearance that the government was making yet another retreat. Pearson immediately tried to contact Allan MacEachen, who had flown out to Vancouver on a speaking engagement. When they finally reached each other, the Health Minister returned to his original position, saying that he would not take the bill into the House. In that case, the Prime Minister informed MacEachen testily, he would take it himself.

The next day (Saturday, October 8) MacEachen met Sharp in Ottawa. No agreement was reached and the Finance Minister made it clear that the government would not back down from its new hard line.

Jean Marchand was not told of the change. He had fulfilled a long-standing speaking engagement in Toronto on Saturday, and as far as he was aware the Friday morning cabinet decision still stood: the wording of the bill would be changed to allow for earlier implementation. It wasn't until the morning of Monday, October 10, when the Prime Minister opened a Liberal Party policy conference in the Chateau Laurier by announcing that the July 1, 1968, medicare date was firm government policy that the Manpower Minister realized what was happening. He immediately decided to hand in his resignation.

When he was informed of Marchand's threat, Pearson called the minister to his hotel suite. The two men talked for ninety minutes and had another long confrontation that afternoon. At one point Marchand, very excited over not having been consulted about the medicare policy change, told Pearson: "I'm not going to be treated as a puppet. I'm no *roi nègre*. There are already too many messenger boys down here from French Canada."

Finally, after Marchand was assured that he would, from then on, be consulted on all major policy changes, the resignation crisis was settled.

The party's internal medicare dispute erupted again that same afternoon during one of the conference's workshop sessions. Liberals from the four western provinces were committed both to the postponement of medicare and to the establishment of a North American free-trade area. They left home determined that the conference would, once and for all, rid the party of Walter Gordon and his ideas. Their position was best summed up by Dr Pat McGeer, the British Columbia MLA. "Mr Gordon has drawn the plans for a Fortress Canada," he said. "All through time there have been those who have erected bastions to secure and protect what they have gained. Europe is studded with these curiosities of the past. But history has never been made by those who erected bastions and sheltered behind them. Rather it has been made by adventurers who scorned protection in order to explore and open up new territories. Canada was founded and developed by such adventurers."

When the western Liberals arrived in Ottawa they combined with Sharp's anti-medicare, anti-nationalist forces to dominate the discussions, including the Monday afternoon workshop in the Chateau's ornate ballroom. It was a strange setting for political combat, all gilt-and-cream elegance, lit by tiers of television lights, crowded with Liberals who had come to witness the knockout fight between Mitchell Sharp in the right corner and Walter Gordon in the left.

Most of the delegates were young, as politicians go, well dressed and still slightly tanned from the summer sun. They looked as fresh as the people depicted in the new car ads, but they sounded about as sympathetic as a heavyweight-bout audience at Madison Square Garden. They rushed up to one another, eyes darting through the crowd, repeating eagerly the wisdom of the moment ("Gordon will be clobbered . . . it's going to be a real blood-letting . . . it's a Greek tragedy . . . Walter has a death wish . . .").

But the blood-letting never really came, for this was, after all, a Liberal crowd, and the drama was badly staged and not tragic but merely sad.

Under the glare of the klieg lights, delegates lined up at microphones, waiting to have their say on a compromise resolution dealing with Canadian economic nationalism. Mitchell Sharp was sixth in line behind the first microphone and he stood there patiently, demo-cratically, the good man who had no doubt been a model boy, wait-ing to say his rational piece with the lights glancing off his faded red hair and the strong planes of his face. "One of the really great faces," murmured an entranced would-be power broker. "One of your really great television faces. Even McLuhan says so."

Sharp was shortly moved, by popular request, to the head of his microphone line, and he made a Mitchell Sharp speech ("Let me suggest to this workshop that our approach should be Canadian and Liberal . . . it should be positive, outward-looking . . ."). He was for U.S. investment and for Canadian enterprise at the same time. We must, he warned, not allow our brain power to be drained, but we cannot, on the other hand, take a narrow nationalistic approach, for everything would be lost and nothing would be gained in a world growing increasingly interdependent . . .

He defended his decision to postpone medicare with accustomed cool. "It would be illiberal and irresponsible," he said, "to proceed with medicare in 1967 when in the view of the government this would seriously undermine the position of the country and the budgetary position of the government. The only result of proceeding in 1967 as we see it now would be to greatly increase the likelihood that the rising prices and inflationary pressures we face today would continue indef-initely into the future and to ensure that we ran a budgetary deficit that would be neither justifiable nor sustainable in economic terms." The delegates stood up and cheered, because he sounded as though he knew what he meant. It was not a brilliant speech, but there was just enough chauvinism, enough partisanship and, above all, enough strength in it to make it rousing.

Walter Gordon was then called, and he was his awkward public self, polite, a little abashed, a little apologetic, a little sad. He was not, he said, of the extreme, and he was not really so far from Mitchell Sharp.

But he was further than he knew or could admit, for he was a marked loser and Sharp was with the winners. Further apart than that in politics you cannot get. Gordon sat down to small applause, a man who was once a power and was now a fading force. What he had stood for in the green springtimes of 1962 and 1963 seemed remote in the sadder fall of 1966. In those brave early days he was the Leader's confidant, the moulder of great victories, the maker of political miracles, but now he was dispossessed and alone.

The Liberal policy conference buried the myth that Walter Gordon still controlled the organizational heart of his party. The Gordon supporters thought they could rally a conference majority on behalf of their policies, but their strategy caucuses never attracted more than two hundred of the conference's two thousand delegates. It was only because of the strenuous efforts of Keith Davey, lobbying for his old friend Walter Gordon, that even this many supporters turned up. The resolution on economic nationalism that finally came out of the conference was as toothless as an endorsement of motherhood. The medicare postponement was passed without significant dissent.

Summing up the results of the policy conference, Bruce Hutchison wrote in the *Vancouver Sun*: "This was the final destruction of Walter Gordon. So long as the myth of his power remained, so long as his presence haunted the Prime Minister in personal friendship and political ambivalence, there was no chance of unity or strength in the government. Now that he has gone and can never return as a real force in the Liberal Party, the government (and doubtless the Prime Minister himself) feels like a man released from an iron mask. The sense of liberation is profound, almost pathetic, though never admitted, of course, in public."

During the weeks that followed, it really did seem as though Walter Gordon, the leader-in-exile of the Liberal Party's nationalistic left wing, had exhausted his political usefulness. On October 29, 1966, at a private lunch with Pearson at the York Club in Toronto, Gordon told the PM that he intended to resign his seat and take his wife on a holiday to Leningrad. The Prime Minister, dismayed at the prospect of yet another party ruction, persuaded him to hold off until Christmas.

As soon as word of this conversation reached federal Liberal members from Ontario, the last bastion of Gordon's support, they organized a private Gordon-must-stay dinner for November 9. It was a highly emotional affair, with fourteen speakers (including Dr Harry Harley, John Munro, Larry Pennell, James Walker and Keith Davey) making passionate appeals to ward off the former Finance Minister's resignation. Highlights of the evening were the speeches given by Gordon himself and by the Prime Minister who, carried away by the occasion, warmly summed up his former colleague's accomplishments in a tone that he hadn't been heard to use since before the 1965 election.

The next day, Gordon called on the Prime Minister but Pearson had regained his composure and no resolution about his future was reached. Then, on November 16, the Ontario caucus met again. After considerable debate and some opposition, a majority of its members decided that a delegation should go to Pearson to urge him to keep Gordon in the party by taking him back into Cabinet. Several members of the Quebec caucus, including Jean Marchand and Pierre Elliott Trudeau, also sent word to Gordon, encouraging him to stay.

416

The men who eventually acted as chief intermediaries in these touchy negotiations were Keith Davey, the former national organizer who was by then a senator, and James Walker, the former government whip, then parliamentary secretary to the Minister of National Revenue. When Pearson seemed immune to their appeals, they made certain the PM realized that if Gordon went, he would not depart without delivering an impassioned valedictory, blaming his exodus on the fact that the Liberal Party had become a refuge for right-wing anti-nationalists.

What took over at this point was the tendency to close ranks that had kept the Liberals in power for thirty-five of the preceding forty-six years. Unlike the Conservatives, who had always reacted to internal differences of opinion by destroying each other, the Liberals prided themselves on being rational middle-of-the-roaders endowed with the capacity to swallow the rare right- or left-wing extremist who occasionally challenged the party's finely balanced power structure. Since Gordon had made it obvious he wouldn't go quietly, he had to be absorbed.

Finally, on December 29, over yet another lunch Pearson invited Gordon back into the cabinet. It was decided that they would each write a job description for the new role the former Finance Minister would play and meet again early in the new year. Gordon was satisfied to re-enter Cabinet as a Minister without Portfolio, but he wanted an early promotion and broad terms of reference for his eventual position, which he visualized as a kind of deputy prime ministership in charge of government policy. Pearson wanted Gordon's physical presence and little more.

It was Davey and Walker who actually arranged the details of the return. By telling Gordon that Pearson really wanted him back (to which Gordon would reply: "Okay. But only on my terms") and then telling Pearson that Gordon really wanted to come back (to which Pearson would say: "Okay. But only on my terms"), they made both men believe that the reconciliation was much more strongly desired than it actually was. Pearson met Gordon again on January 3, this time with Mitchell Sharp, who was allowed a veto over his former colleague's reinstatement but chose not to exercise it.

Next day Pearson informed the full cabinet of his decision and immediately afterwards held a joint press conference with Gordon to announce the prodigal's return. It was an over-hearty, somehow false occasion, with Pearson blandly confessing how close he felt to Gordon's strong pro-Canadian views and Gordon sheepishly releasing the news that he really had no policy differences with anybody.

The move was made so suddenly that Liberal ministers who were out of town that day received no warning. Senator John Connolly and George McIlraith, holidaying together in Florida, sent a joint wire to the Prime Minister, demanding: "What the hell is going on?" Robert Winters, flabbergasted by the move, said in the first cabinet meeting after Gordon's return: "If things get much worse around here, I may have to resign." To which Gordon gently replied: "Well, Bob, some of us thought you shouldn't have run in the first place."

THE FIRST CLASH OF ARMS TO ATTRACT GORDON'S INTEREST after his return to Cabinet was the dispute over a clause in the proposed revision of the Bank Act aimed at limiting the future growth in Canada of the Mercantile Bank, a subsidiary of the First National City Bank of New York (Citibank). This complex, protracted battle by American business interests to win a preferential position that might have allowed them to dominate Canada's banking system eventually caused the sharpest confrontation in U.S.-Canadian relations of the entire Pearson period.

Citibank, the world's third largest banking institution, had come into Canada through acquisition of the assets of the Mercantile, Canada's smallest and only foreign-owned bank, formerly controlled by the Nationale Handelsbank of Amsterdam. The purchase, part of the American bank's expansion program (it had 192 branches in sixty countries), was made under unusual circumstances.

On June 20, 1963, R. P. MacFadden, a senior Citibank vice-president, had informed Louis Rasminsky that his firm intended to buy the small Dutch bank's holdings as their Canadian operating base. When the Bank of Canada Governor strongly advised MacFadden to consult Walter Gordon, the Finance Minister, before proceeding with the purchase, MacFadden agreed and in a private memorandum about this meeting sent to James S. Rockefeller, chairman of Citibank, he wrote: "I assured [Rasminsky] we would come back to him when the deal is firm and before signing, and at the same time to clear with the Minister of Finance." But six days later Citibank purchased Mercantile in a manner Rockefeller later described as "irrevocable and legally enforceable." The two Americans didn't go to Ottawa for their consultation with Gordon until July 18, more than three weeks after they took control of Mercantile.

When Rockefeller and MacFadden walked into Gordon's office, they found him flanked by Bob Bryce, his deputy minister, and C. F. Elderkin, Canada's Inspector General of Banks. According to notes of the conversation taken by Elderkin (and signed by Bryce), Rockefeller assured Gordon that no commitment to the Dutch owners had yet been made and he was merely calling to test the Canadian government's reaction to such a deal. Gordon reminded Rockefeller of his strongly held views against the expansion of American financial interests in Canada and said he was glad no firm arrangements had been made because he would feel it quite proper to alter the Bank Act retroactively against such a purchase. Rockefeller was outraged by the suggestion. "You mean," he demanded, "that we'll be coming in at our own peril?" Gordon gave a calm answer: "I wouldn't use those words, but I certainly don't think you should commit yourself to anything until you know what the rules are going to be."

Quite apart from his personal feelings against more American investment, Gordon's objections were based on the grounds that free entry of Citibank would have opened the way for charter applications from competing American banks and that the confidential nature of the relations between the Governor of the Bank of Canada and domestic chartered banks would be disrupted by the presence of a large American financial institution that would report the substance of these discussions to its head office. Gordon also felt that by having access to the $16 billions in assets of its parent bank, Mercantile would be able to afford to disregard the monetary policies laid down by the Bank of Canada for domestic institutions without outside drawing accounts.

Despite Gordon's warning, Citibank publicly announced its takeover of Mercantile soon afterwards and began to expand the bank's assets and operations, confident that, like *Time* and *Reader's Digest*, it would receive an exemption from any legislation that might affect its status since it was already established in the country.

The decennial review of the Bank Act was delayed until 1966 and when Mitchell Sharp presented his revised version to the Commons it included a clause restricting non-Canadian holdings in any chartered bank to 25 per cent and limited to 10 per cent the holdings of any shareholder. The violation of either of these provisions – and Mercantile violated them both – called for prohibition of the offending bank from increasing its assets to more than twenty times its authorized capital. (At September 30, 1966, Mercantile's total assets were $226,067,000, a figure already over the limit of twenty times its authorized capital of $10 millions.)*

To strengthen its entrenched position, Citibank enlisted the aid of the U.S. State Department. On April 7, 1966, Ambassador Butter-

*The ratio between authorized capital and total assets of other Canadian banks was then between forty and sixty-two to one.

worth handed a strong note of protest to the External Affairs Depart
ment, objecting to "discrimination against American-owned banks"
and containing a veiled threat that retaliatory action might be take
against Canadian-owned bank agencies operating in the United States.

The Canadian government's reply was handed to C. G. Wootton,
counsellor in the U.S. Embassy, on June 29 by A. E. Ritchie, then th
Deputy Undersecretary of State for External Affairs. The note cate
gorically rejected the American protest by pointing out that the ne
bank-ownership regulations would apply to domestic as well a
foreign-owned banks.† On November 11, 1966, Nicholas Katzenbac
the U.S. Undersecretary of State, called in Ritchie (who had in th
meantime been named Canadian Ambassador to the United States
and handed him the toughest diplomatic note ever sent by the Unite
States to Canada. It was based on official American acceptance c
Rockefeller's contention that Walter Gordon had been told the Cit
bank purchase of Mercantile stock was an accomplished fact during th
July 18, 1963, meeting, so that any later action was by definition
punitive and retroactive step.‡

The American message specifically threatened retaliation again
Canadian banking operations in the United States and other measure
At the same time the Canadian directors of Mercantile, includin
Senator Louis Gélinas (former treasurer of the Quebec federal Liber
Party) and A. T. Seedhouse, president of the Toronto-based Manufac
turers Life Insurance Company, lobbied furiously for a governme
retreat on the issue. Officials of the American Embassy in Ottaw
turned themselves into unpaid agents of Citibank, fighting Mercantile
battle at Ottawa cocktail parties, at lunches with civil servants and i
a round of talks with Liberal cabinet ministers. It was their hardes
fought lobby since they had won the battle for *Time* and *Reader
Digest*. On December 9 Walton Butterworth roundly denounce
Walter Gordon at a Washington meeting of a seminar on Canadia
American relations. Robert Estabrook of the *Washington Post* reporte

*For the full text of this note, see Appendix I. Five Canadian banks ma
tained agencies in New York. Unlike regular U.S. banks, they were n
limited in the interest they could pay. By accepting deposits (outside Ne
York State) at interest rates marginally higher than the prevailing maximum
they had been able to attract substantial deposits. This in turn had allowe
them to enter the active "call loan" market (very short-term borrowings b
stockbrokers) and by 1966 they were handling nearly half of this lucrati
quick-turnover business on Wall Street. The assets of Canadian bank agencie
in New York were then $1.6 billions.
†For the text of this note, see Appendix J.
‡For the text of Ritchie's cable to Ottawa on this meeting, see Appendix K

420

that senior Canadian officials were demanding Butterworth be replaced "because he was throwing his weight around and treating Canada like a banana republic."

The Mercantile issue was at the top of the agenda when Gordon rejoined the cabinet early in 1967. At two stormy sessions on February 23 and 24, Gordon said he would resign (just seven weeks after being sworn in again) unless the restrictions against Mercantile were retained in the Bank Act. He pointed out that to retreat would mean giving the American bank the advantage of being able to own 25 per cent of Mercantile's shares while individual holdings in Canadian-owned banks were limited to 10 per cent. Sharp, who was trying to work out a compromise agreement, vaguely threatened that *he* would resign if the stand on Mercantile wasn't softened. Gordon was defended by E. J. Benson, sharply attacked by George McIlraith and Senator Connolly. The Prime Minister sided with Gordon, the man he judged to be most determined to resign if he didn't get his way. Anxious to regain for his party the image of a government serenely united in pursuit of national goals, the PM told his gathered ministers: "Don't tell your deputies about this [cabinet split], don't tell your executive assistants, or even your wives. If this leaks out, I'll fire you all!" Not quite twenty-four hours later the news made the papers.

An independent conciliation effort had meanwhile been launched by Bryce Mackasey, then a Liberal backbencher. He had been shocked by Rockefeller's statement to the House of Commons finance committee that he would under no circumstances share his ownership of Mercantile with Canadian investors and impulsively decided to go to New York in an unofficial capacity to see what, if any, compromise might be negotiated. After he had registered at the Waldorf, he arranged to have dinner with Ward Stevenson, one of Citibank's vice-presidents. The next day (Sunday, January 29), he met at 10 a.m. with Stevenson, Robert MacFadden (the president of Mercantile), Henry Hartfield (a Citibank lawyer) and Stewart Clifford (Mercantile's executive vice-president).

During a long day's talking, Mackasey suggested that Mercantile might be able to sell its shares to Canadians in stages over a ten-year period with the government allowing periodic increases in authorized capital to let the bank's business grow accordingly. By Sunday evening the beginnings of an agreement seemed to emerge, but the Canadian M.P. insisted that he take back with him a letter signed by Rockefeller, agreeing to sell the shares in Canada. When he returned to Citibank's offices at eleven the next morning, Mackasey was informed by the gloomy quartet of bankers that Rockefeller would rather pack up the whole operation than sell Mercantile shares to Canadians. At this point, Mackasey blew his Irish cork and declared that he personally would lead the fight on the floor of the House of Commons against Mercantile unless he got a fair hearing from Rockefeller.

After considerable hesitation, an audience was arranged for Mackasey, and he went into Rockefeller's office. Rockefeller worked in an oversized chair behind an enormous desk and visitors approaching his dazzling presence were waved imperiously to an oddly placed seat at one end of it. Mackasey, built like a fullback, forthrightly moved the chair so he could confront Rockefeller head-on and declared: "I'm not a banker and I don't claim any particular talents except that I've never met a man I was afraid of. The only reason I'm here is to see whether that stupid statement you made before the banking committee in Ottawa was such that there is no possibility of you people conforming to Canadian laws."

Rockefeller grumped away for several minutes, comparing Canada to Mexico and complaining that his bank was being discriminated against. Mackasey shot back that Mexicans had a right to run their own affairs, as did Canadians. Gradually he persuaded Rockefeller out of his implacable mood and at one point even inspired a wintry smile on the bank chairman's face when he suggested that he didn't suppose Rockefeller had made it into that big chair "by picking up his marbles whenever things got rough." After a great deal of plain talk on both sides, Rockefeller finally conceded that he could visualize a situation where Canadians could own shares in his bank and that he was willing to send some officials to Ottawa to work out a solution. Rockefeller then called in MacFadden, repeated his instructions, and took a cordial leave of Mackasey.

Mackasey's initiative helped to bring about the final compromise, which granted Mercantile a temporary five-year exemption from the Canadian ownership provisions of the Bank Act, subject to annual cabinet review. This arrangement angered Mercantile executives because they thought the bank deserved less severe treatment. They reacted by issuing a statement accusing the Canadian government of "a forced sale, tantamount to nationalization." It was a Gordon victory but it was based less on cabinet support of his policies than on the fact that by using the threat of resignation as a meaningful weapon he managed to outmanoeuvre the Minister of Finance in the political powerplay involved.

AWARE THAT HIS RESIGNATION TACTIC was growing less alarming by the month, Gordon now settled back quietly to wait for the report on the effects of foreign investment that he had commissioned from a team of eight young economists under Professor Melville Watkins of the University of Toronto. Booked to speak at a management conference in Toronto on May 13, 1967, Gordon decided to stay away from the economic nationalism controversy and picked what he thought was a fairly safe subject instead, the war in Vietnam.

Although his speech was fairly mild and by no means original – considering the fact that he was discussing the most important moral issue of the times – it went far beyond what any member of the government had previously had the courage to say. He deplored Canada's neutralist attitude toward the struggle, which he called "a bloody civil war which cannot be justified on either moral or strategic grounds" and demanded that the American President stop the bombing of North Vietnam without calling for any compensating concessions from Hanoi. At the time, the official Canadian position was that the United States was fighting in Vietnam not a civil war but a defensive action against communist aggression from the North, and that Canada had to keep quiet about the conflict because of its membership in the International Control Commission.*

Pearson swiftly and firmly repudiated Gordon's stand. At the next meeting of the Liberal caucus not a man stood up to defend the errant minister's outburst. Gordon accepted the rebuke and left Ottawa for a long fishing holiday. Recognizing that his political power was gone, he decided to remain in Cabinet only until the Watkins task force report was published.† Washington dealt him the ultimate insult. Realizing that Gordon was no longer a threat, it didn't even bother to ask its Ottawa Embassy for a copy of his Vietnam speech.

THE NATIONALISTIC FERVOUR THAT WALTER GORDON had never personally been able to stir in Canadians erupted of its own accord during celebrations marking the 1967 centennial year. It was a brief shimmering season in the long wash of history, a mass rite that managed to expose the latent patriotism in even the most cynical Canadians, leaving them a little embarrassed at their sentiment, a little surprised by their tears.

*Ironically, only four months later, on September 27, Paul Martin, expressing the Canadian government's official stand at the United Nations, called for a similar unilateral halt by the United States of its bombing of the North.
†Gordon resigned from Cabinet quietly on March 11, 1968, a few weeks after the Watkins Report was published, and did not contest the 1968 election.

It was a wild, happy, crazy year. Canadians bought and waved a million flags, climbed mountains, burned privies, built new community halls and centennial sewage plants, jumped from airplanes, grew beards, dressed up in period costumes, raced canoes, enjoyed singing Bobby Gimby's lively *CA-NA-DA*, all in the Whoopee-we're-a-hundred-years-old spirit.

The focus for the celebrations was Montreal's Expo 67, which turned out, to most Canadians' surprise, to be a wow of a fair. All of it. Not just one building or one exhibit, but everything.

Goaded on by the inspired stubbornness of Jean Drapeau, the energetic mayor of Montreal, Expo officials turned two small islands in the St Lawrence River into a magic exhibition that made most visitors feel that if this little sub-arctic, self-obsessed country could put on this marvellous show, it could do anything. Expo was flooded with girls in mini-skirts and boys with long hair, a place so full of youth and gaiety that it made the old and the middle-aged spill laughter. On the evening of its opening day a throng of teenagers, strangers to one another, linked arms as they left the fair site and broke spontaneously into *O Canada*.

Some sixty state visitors – kings, queens, presidents, prime ministers, princes and princesses – came to Expo and to Ottawa. Lester Pearson gave lavish banquets for them all and even though he spent at least an hour a day pedalling a reducing bicycle, he gained nine pounds consuming *mousses centenaires*.

FOR THE FIRST THREE MONTHS OF THE EXPO CELEBRATIONS, the Liberals shared the national euphoria, certain that public goodwill would accrue to them long after the fair was over, that things would at last "return to normal." And then came Charles de Gaulle.

The last giant of the pre-atomic world, De Gaulle was a hero handmade to inflame the French-Canadian imagination. In a province that prided itself on having withstood two hundred years of onslaught from the English, De Gaulle was the resister-incarnate, the great liberator, the world's foremost guardian of the precious French fact. "The reason De Gaulle's effect was out of all reasonable proportion," wrote R. D. Mathews after the visit in *The Journal of Canadian Studies*, "was that he legitimized the abandonment of a contractual relation on the part of French-speaking Canadians to the facts of Canadian history. He invited them to make history whatever they want it to be. In a word, he abetted their revolutionary tendencies. He asked them to jump backwards and forwards over the facts of history to a francophone 'eternal present.' He helped to give their revolution a basis; a reconstituted past upon which to base a break with the present."

IN THE PROFUSION OF CAUSES SERVED by the De Gaulle visit, the unstated purposes of the French President were the most fascinating of all. According to the savants in the External Affairs Department, it was all part of a French conspiracy to help establish Quebec as an independent country, which through its control of access to the St Lawrence Seaway and other facilities would prove a costly liability to the United States, English Canada, Great Britain and the rest of the Anglo-Saxon world. The diplomats were convinced that Quebec was co-operating fully in this venture, hoping to repeat history by following the same route to independence taken by Canada itself forty years before.* They thought that Quebec, by signing more and more treaties on its own in ever-widening jurisdictions, intended to reach out for *de facto* international recognition.

Quebec never officially admitted to such a goal, insisting instead that it was merely interested in closer cultural and industrial ties to France and an expression of the province's "international personality." In 1961, Quebec opened a *délégation générale* in Paris and when Jean Lesage flew over to open it he was greeted at the airport by a seventy-two-man guard of honour, cheered along the Champs-Elysées and toasted in champagne by De Gaulle at a glittering formal dinner party. Three years later the provincial government established a division for *délégations étrangères* within its Commerce Department and a large-scale youth and teacher exchange program was worked out with France. On November 17, 1965, Ottawa issued an *accord-cadre*, a framework agreement allowing Quebec to negotiate its own cultural agreements with France under the umbrella of federal sanctions. The really significant step was the creation, in April 1967, of a Department of Intergovernmental Affairs in Quebec, headed by Claude Morin, which was, in effect, an embryo external affairs office.

The new department's first confrontation with the federal government was won by Ottawa. Belgium had been offered an *accord-cadre*

---

*Although Canada was officially declared a nation in 1867, it wasn't until the years between 1923 and 1931 that Canadian sovereignty was given final recognition through a series of treaty negotiations that first allowed the country's diplomats to negotiate independently of British auspices. This process began with the Halibut Treaty of 1923 and culminated in the Statute of Westminster of 1931, which provided that no Canadian treaty could be voided, even if it were incompatible with British law.

similar to the one signed by France but, because of internal problems with their Flemish nationalists, the Belgians turned it down in favour of a bilateral treaty with Canada's federal administration. In May 1967, just before the centennial visit to Canada of Belgium's Prince Albert and Princess Paola, Pearson sent a letter to all provincial premiers advising them that a treaty would be signed between the two countries, but noting that it would be limited to fields within federal jurisdiction.* It was at this point that Quebec began to put pressure on Belgian embassy officials in Ottawa, urging them not to sign the treaty until after the royal visit to Quebec (on May 9 and 10) so that it could at least appear as though the Quebec government had been involved in its drafting. The embassy replied that it was not engaged in any act of wilful provocation, but that the presence of the royal personages in the national capital merely seemed the ideal occasion for the signing ceremonies. On Sunday, May 7, Premier Daniel Johnson sent a telegram to the Prime Minister stating that signing of the agreement with the Belgian government without consultation with his province "raised the general astonishment of Quebec" and that his government would be obliged to "dissociate itself from such a gesture." The next morning an even stiffer telegram was sent by André Patry, chief of protocol in Johnson's office, to General Robert Moncel, Ottawa's man in charge of state visits, requesting Moncel to inform the Department of External Affairs that the presence of Paul Tremblay, Canada's ambassador to Belgium, who was accompanying the royal party, would not be welcome in Quebec City under the circumstances. The federal cabinet considered the Patry request and rejected it out of hand. Patry was warned that the royal visit to Quebec would be cancelled on twelve hours' notice and that the cancellation would have implications for future state visits as well. The federal reply asserted further that visitors of state were guests of Canada and that it was clearly within the rules of international protocol that Canada's ambassador to the country involved accompany the distinguished visitors.

The Canada-Belgium agreement was signed in Ottawa on Monday, May 8, with the royal couple, Paul Martin, Paul Tremblay and Guy Daufresne de la Chevalerie (Belgium's ambassador to Canada) in attendance. The following afternoon Marc Lalonde, the Prime Minister's policy adviser, flew to Quebec City to persuade Daniel Johnson that he had no choice but to back down and allow the Canadian ambassador to Belgium to accompany the royal couple. By nine o'clock the same night Lalonde had obtained a withdrawal of the threat from

*The eleven-point treaty dealt mostly with matters involving the CBC, the Canada Council, the National Research Council and other federal agencies.

Johnson and carried it back with him to Ottawa. Although Daniel Johnson charged the next day in the Quebec legislature that Belgian royalty had been used as dupes in a federal campaign to crush Quebec's rights, the visit of the prince and princess to Quebec City was relatively uneventful.

ALL THIS WAS A MERE DRESS REHEARSAL for the visit of the French President. The original schedule called for him to arrive with his flotilla of warships at Quebec City on July 23, to be greeted by the Governor General and the Quebec Premier, to hold a reception aboard the cruiser *Colbert* and then to attend a dinner given in his honour by the Quebec government. The following day he was to drive to Montreal, where he would be welcomed at City Hall by Mayor Jean Drapeau. After one day at Expo, he was scheduled to spend the next thirty-six hours in Ottawa before flying back to Paris.

The French maintained an active intelligence network in Canada, directed by forty diplomats in eleven consulates and the embassy in Ottawa. De Gaulle's agents had been carefully studying the Canadian situation for two years before his arrival. Jacques Parizeau, then the Quebec government's senior economist, was astonished during one of his trips to Paris when a functionary in the President's office was not only able to describe the exact intensity of nationalism in various parts of Quebec but could brief Parizeau on the grievances of French Canadians in the various counties of eastern Ontario.

Everything that happened during De Gaulle's visit was meticulously planned. Weeks in advance External Affairs officials warned the Prime Minister that the French President would never actually visit Ottawa though they could not predict which circumstances would allow his premature departure.

The first day of the visit went smoothly enough. De Gaulle landed on Canadian soil and shouted, *"Vive le Canada dans son ensemble! Vive la France!"* He laid a wreath at the Basilica in Sainte Anne de Beaupré and toured Quebec City. That afternoon at his reception aboard the *Colbert*, when Paul Martin came up to shake his hand, De Gaulle leaned down and whispered in French, "How do you think it went?"

Next day, De Gaulle drove to Montreal over *le chemin du Roy* to the sound of loud cheering every time his cavalcade slowed down. When he reached the city hall in Montreal, he was greeted by a crowd variously estimated at between five thousand (by the *Globe and Mail*) and fifteen thousand (by *La Presse*). In a brief speech he said that his journey had made him feel much as he had so many years before on his triumphant entry into Paris. Then he raised his long arms and shouted, *"Vive Montréal! Vive le Québec! Vive le Québec libre!"*

De Gaulle's use of the French-Canadian separatist slogan was no spontaneous outburst but the climax of a theatrical performance staged by a master tactician fully in command of himself, a man who knew exactly what he was saying and what its impact would be. Several times at stops made during his journey from Quebec City, he was seen breaking away from his entourage to shake hands with pickets carrying *Québec libre!* signs. As he spoke at city hall, he looked down fixedly at a group of young separatist placard carriers, giving the impression of deliberately encouraging them.

De Gaulle's declaration placed the federal government in a difficult diplomatic position. Paul Martin, who had been listening to the speech on the radio, telephoned Jules Léger, Canada's ambassador to France, who was accompanying De Gaulle. When Martin couldn't get Léger in his room at the Queen Elizabeth Hotel, he telephoned the office of Paul-Emile Cardinal Léger, the ambassador's brother. He wasn't there either but the Cardinal's secretary told the External Affairs Minister that His Eminence had been displeased with the President's speech and was considering being terse with him during a reception later at the University of Montreal.*

The cabinet met at Ottawa the next day and after considerable discussion Pearson went on television at six o'clock to condemn "certain statements by the President [which] tend to encourage the small minority of our population whose aim is to destroy Canada; and, as such, they are unacceptable to the Canadian people and its government."

De Gaulle, who had spent the evening at a lavish dinner in the French pavilion given by Robert Bordaz, France's Commissioner General to Expo, was not told of the Prime Minister's statement until 11:30 p.m. He immediately called a meeting of his staff and at 1:15 a.m. Foreign Minister Maurice Couve de Murville informed Jules Léger that the President's Ottawa visit was being cancelled.

*All through the De Gaulle crisis, in fact in all of the dealings between Quebec and Ottawa on France-Canada relations, Paul Martin deliberately downgraded the importance of French intrusion into Canadian affairs, presumably because he recognized that a harsh reaction might cost him political support in Quebec. In its official bulletin, *External Affairs*, his department limited its report of the General's visit to the following paragraph: "The President of the Republic of France and Mme de Gaulle accompanied by French Foreign Minister, M. Couve de Murville, paid an official visit to Canada starting at Quebec City on July 23. They also visited Montreal on July 25 and took part in the celebration of France's national day at Expo 67."

Pearson replied with a dignified statement, which said simply, "The Canadian government has been informed that General De Gaulle has decided not to come to Ottawa as planned but will be returning immediately to Paris by air after completion of his programme today in Montreal. General De Gaulle's decision to cut short his visit to Canada is understandable in the circumstances. But those circumstances, which are not of the government's making, are greatly to be regretted."

De Gaulle spent one more day in Montreal before flying home. It was Jean Drapeau who made the most effective reply to the General's divisive comments in a luncheon speech. Speaking without a text, Drapeau pointed out, with passion swelling in his voice, how small a part France had played in the history of Quebec. He said:

> We practised resistance before it was a word and if it was to be redone we would start over again because if there is no sentiment of gratitude to underline regarding successive French governments, there is, however, a nation's gratitude toward one's mother for having inherited the virtues of the language and culture of French civilization. . . .
>
> [However] it must be admitted that for hundreds of years we have had no connection with France. Almost five generations had no connection with France. . . .
>
> How many are there [in France] who know the immense possibilities of French Canada? In the end, it is to them that my confidences are addressed, Mr President. It is because of the virtues which we inherited from our ancestors that challenges have never scared us and that we think it is possible to play a role in Canada which I hope is comparable in terms of North America to that which France plays in Europe. We are attached to this immense country, and whatever be our way of serving it, if we serve our country better because we serve it as Canadians of French origin, then we will be of greater service to France and humanity.

BY EARLY OCTOBER, THE LAST OF THE OFFICIAL VISITORS had departed and with them vanished the final wispy remnants of the Liberals' centennial summer elation. Rarely during its convulsive four years in office was the government's mood so gloomy. At the Conservative Party's September convention Robert Stanfield had won the Tory leadership, providing the country at last with a creditable head for an alternative government. The Pearson Cabinet started to decompose. Jack Pickersgill scurried for cover as head of the Canadian Transport

Commission. Senior Liberals began to talk fatalistically about losing the next election, debating the merits of a period in Opposition and brooding about how they might have done things differently.

But there was little time for introspection. Overnight, or so it seemed, the nation was plunged into a financial crisis and the spectre that began to haunt Ottawa was that unless some effective action was quickly taken, a psychologically damaging emergency devaluation of the Canadian dollar might become inevitable.

Superficially, the economy seemed to be in a healthy state. The gross national product was growing at an annual rate of 7 per cent, unemployment was down to 4 per cent of the labour force, bank savings accounts were at record levels and exports were reaching toward a high of $11¼ billions. But another set of statistics – a steadily climbing bank rate and an NHA mortgage rate of 8¼ per cent – indicated that serious inflationary problems had been created by the nation's prosperity. Inflation, it seemed, had become the occupational hazard of Liberal governments in very much the same way as high unemployment plagued Conservative administrations. It had been the threat of serious inflation in the spring of 1957 that caused Walter Harris to table a budget which, despite its $282 million surplus, gave the old-age pensioners a raise of only $6 a month, and cost the Liberals the election that followed.

When the Liberals returned to power in the spring of 1963, they attempted to offset the high unemployment of the Diefenbaker Years with a Kennedy-like promise of "getting the economy moving again." The part of Walter Gordon's first budget that survived was full of expensive measures to accelerate the country's economic expansion. But the economy was already rolling, partly because of the boost in exports that followed the Diefenbaker Government's devaluation of the dollar the previous spring.

The Liberals, like the Conservatives before them, added massive new expenditures to the federal budget, and the economy's growth turned out to be faster than they expected. (The 1964 budget estimated an increase in the gross national product of 5.5 per cent, which turned out to be 8.9 per cent; the 1965 budget predicted a 7 per cent jump, which turned out to be just over 9 per cent.) Finally, in August of 1965, the Prime Minister, worried about the overheated economy, announced a cut-back in government spending, and urged private industry to do likewise. But a month later he hit the election trail, scattering hockey arenas, causeways and various other capital projects across the country, thus negating his own policy. During that campaign, Mitchell Sharp had sent a letter to his constituents in Toronto-

Eglinton proclaiming that majority government was essential because of "the tough decisions which must be taken to ensure steady economic progress. These decisions must be taken without delay or Canada will suffer." Though Sharp never identified his tough decisions, he had obviously been referring to anti-inflationary measures. But when the government was returned, Liberal policy-makers, shocked into immobility by their minority mandate, did nothing for more than three months about inflation or any other economic problem. Then on February 21, 1966, representatives of the International Monetary Fund arrived in Ottawa, looked over Canada's national accounts and in private sessions with several ministers cautioned against inflation. The first Sharp budget, which followed on March 29, took up this warning. It raised taxes (through a special 5 per cent refundable levy on business profits), pledged a 10 per cent cut in government construction amounting to $34,800,000 and called for a halt to new government spending programs. This was a relatively mild dose of anti-inflationary medicine, but Sharp hoped it would reduce capital expansion by at least $300 millions.

But government expenditures went on spiralling, expensive wage contracts (expanding at twice the rate of productivity gains) were signed by both Ottawa and private industry, and by late fall the Finance Department found itself in the embarrassing position of not being able to raise enough money to run the government. During the 1966-67 fiscal year, Ottawa had to cover a budgetary deficit of $740 millions plus another $850 millions in non-budgetary items – a total cash requirement of nearly $1.6 billions, the highest since 1946.

The trouble was that governments can raise money in only two ways, through taxation or through borrowing, and that the acceptable limits had been reached in both directions. Despite the highest interest structure in the country's history, bond buyers showed little enthusiasm for new government issues. One offering of $525 millions would have flopped had not the Bank of Canada taken up $175 millions of the total. The tightness of the money market seemed to be based not on any shortage of available funds, but on a wait-and-see attitude by wary investors dubious about the government's ability to carry out its promises of restraining future expenditures. The result was the unhealthy combination of readily available credit and high interest rates.

All of these trends coming together in the late fall of 1967 meant that the government, for once, was being forced to deal not just with the politics of inflation but with inflation itself. Most inflationary threats to the economy in the past had been successfully countered by the influence the Bank of Canada was able to exert on the nation's money markets. Even when such actions hurt the voters through higher interest rates, the politicians were able to shrug, piously point to the other side of Wellington Street, and explain that since nobody wanted to launch another Coyne affair, the Bank could not be interfered with. But this time, monetary policy had been exhausted as an effective anti-inflationary weapon. The root of the trouble was that the Bank of Canada had been increasing the nation's money supply at an unprecedented rate (11.3 per cent since the beginning of 1967). Governor Louis Rasminsky had felt compelled to do this in an attempt to hold down interest rates so that American funds wouldn't suddenly gush across the border, breaking Canada's reserve agreement with the United States, which, in turn, would have cut off Canadian access to the New York money market.

The strategy did not work. Despite the higher money supply, interest rates shot up anyway. At the same time, investors had divested themselves of $502 millions in government bond holdings during the year and for the first time since 1947 Canada was having genuine trouble financing itself.

The only recourse was a tough anti-inflationary budget plus some deep cuts in government expenditures and a halt in the growth of the civil service.* The Pearson Government (like the Diefenbaker Government before it) was now caught in the classic dilemma of having tried to do too much at one time, subscribing to the opportunistic notion that political parties can spend their way into power.

On November 30, 1967, Mitchell Sharp presented his final budget. It was a hard-line, anti-inflationary document placing a 5 per cent surtax up to a limit of $600 on individual taxpayers, as well as a 10 per cent increase in taxes on liquor and tobacco. The changes meant a $520 million annual boost in government revenues, helping to lower Ottawa's demands on the overstrained capital market.

The fiscal crisis, which came so late in the Pearson administration, finally made both the Prime Minister and his colleagues realize what was wrong with the management of cabinet affairs. By not having any system of policy priorities, by succumbing to most of the pressures exerted on the administration, they had lost command and had found themselves being controlled by events instead of controlling them.

*During the Pearson Government's time in office, the federal public service expanded by about 71,000 and annual interest charges on the national debt rose from $822 millions to $1,274 millions.

432

THE LIBERAL PARTY NOW BEGAN to move out from under Lester Pearson's command.

The real source of any prime minister's power, as distinguished from his constitutional authority, is the respect he draws from his followers. While there was little loss of personal affection for Pearson, the realization set in at all levels of the Liberal Party that by delaying the process of succession they might be forfeiting the next election. They realized that when a prime minister retires, he takes his good qualities with him and bequeaths only his weaknesses to the party he leaves behind.

The jarring discord of the previous four years had left Pearson's admirers convinced that he could never run an orderly administration. Many of his close friends still found it difficult to reconcile the fact that such a shabby political spectacle as the Munsinger affair could have come about under the auspices of an avowed intellectual, a man who had on other occasions stood out against immoderation, sensationalism and slander. Of the four most influential groups within the Liberal Party – the parliamentary caucus, the Quebec organization, the Toronto power clique and the western wing – only French-Canadian Liberals still gave him unquestioning support.

A Gallup Poll published on November 8, 1967, showed that 47 per cent of Canadians wanted Pearson to resign and an earlier public opinion survey had indicated that the Conservatives, under their new leaders, had a 9 per cent edge in cross-country popularity over the Liberals. Robert Stanfield's succession had robbed Lester Pearson of his political immunity. "Seldom has an administration decayed so fast," wrote Anthony Westell in the *Globe and Mail*. "With three years of its mandate still to run, the Pearson Cabinet is showing symptoms of disintegration that may be the prelude to collapse." On November 28, the government was humiliated in the Commons by being defeated on a resolution raising postal rates. Postmaster General Jean-Pierre Côté, who could have kept the debate going until enough Liberals had turned up to win the vote, seemed to doze through the proceedings.

As Pearson's prestige declined, the underground race for his succession gained in both vigour and visibility. Mitchell Sharp, Paul Martin, Paul Hellyer, Allan MacEachen, Joe Greene and John Turner gradually began to build up their personal leadership organizations and quietly to recruit delegates. Sharp and Hellyer had already taken the precaution of enrolling themselves in crash Berlitz courses to learn Canada's third official language: Election French.

On December 11 Pearson presided over a federal-provincial conference on housing. Poorly planned by Labour Minister Jack Nicholson, it broke up a day ahead of schedule, having accomplished nothing beyond angering the premiers who attended. "They were the worst twenty-four hours in my life," Pearson told one of his ministers after the meeting. That same week Pearson was feeling unwell. Dr Peter Burton, his physician, detected an unusual jump in blood pressure and suggested that it might be dangerous for him to continue in his post.

At a small family party celebrating Mrs Pearson's birthday on the evening of Wednesday, December 13, the Prime Minister gave her the gift she had wanted for so long: a firm promise to retire from politics. Next morning, during a routine cabinet meeting, when the agenda called for a discussion of adjustment assistance, Pearson broke into the proceedings. "Speaking of adjustment assistance," he said, "I want to read you a letter I've just sent to Senator Nichol [president of the Liberal Federation]." It was his resignation.

Later, in a hastily called press conference, the Prime Minister read his resignation letter to astonished reporters. At the end of a brief question-and-answer session, as correspondents sat there looking at him in awkward silence, Lester Pearson stretched out both arms with the palms of his hands facing upwards, shrugged and said, with one of those crooked smiles for which he had been famous for forty years, "Well, *c'est la vie*."

Back in his office, he was immediately besieged by telephone calls from various anxious heirs-apparent who wanted to discuss the future. But Pearson gracefully turned them aside and invited only two ministers to join him in the study at 24 Sussex Drive that evening: Jean Marchand and Pierre Elliott Trudeau.

CHAPTER 30

The Flowering of Pierre

PIERRE ELLIOTT TRUDEAU'S CONQUEST of the Liberal Party appeared in retrospect like a royal procession predestined to glory, with the other contenders for the leadership serving as mere flag-bearers in the dramatic elevation of a once and future king. But in the bleak chill of December just after Lester Pearson's resignation, Trudeau's victory seemed far from inevitable; in fact, it was scarcely credible. To most Liberals, he was an untested outsider, a disturbing presence not easily encompassed by the collective party mind.

Rideau Club denizens were fond of telling each other the story about the time he turned up on a Saturday morning at the Privy Council office dressed in desert boots and a boiler suit and the commissionaire on duty, convinced he was a plumber who had his worksheets jumbled, turned him away at the door. When his name was mentioned casually in the early speculative talk about candidates, it was dismissed as a joke. ("How could anybody who combs his hair like that be a *Canadian* prime minister?")

In this uncertain preliminary stage, the contest for the succession was little more than a sentiment in search of a leader. Many Liberals felt they wanted a dramatic change from the Pearson brand of politics, a candidate who could re-establish public trust in the party and the party's confidence in itself. But it was difficult to identify this urge with any of the men so eagerly offering themselves for the job. Privately, several of the party's power brokers were expressing the gloomy opinion that there wasn't anybody who could beat Stanfield anyway and what the Liberals should concern themselves with was the healing of party wounds and the choosing of an effective Leader of the Opposition, who could regain power in the election after next.

Certainly the serene consensus that had so smoothly bestowed the Liberal leadership on Lester Pearson (and on Louis St Laurent before him) was conspicuously absent. To head off any unseemly power struggle, a few aging Liberals left over from the Mackenzie King era gathered secretly at Vincent Massey's great country house near Port Hope. They considered themselves positively reckless when they decided that the best man for the job would be "young Davie Dunton," the 55-year-old president of Carleton University and former head of the CBC. No one, Dunton included, took the suggestion seriously.

The trouble, as the prospective contenders were discovering on their first forays into the country, was that in the disturbing decade since Pearson's anointment, changes in the Canadian social structure had splintered the party hierarchy. The machine politicians, smoky-room lawyers, bagman senators and cabinet ministers with a talent for back-concession politicking who had once been able to "deliver" whole provinces could no longer be trusted to do so. Party authority at the constituency level had been disseminated among large groups of younger political activists who were not so readily predictable or so easily controllable.

These new politicians, the men in their thirties and forties who were taking over the party apparatus from the men in their late fifties and sixties, had already rejected the old Pearson-St Laurent Liberal values. As a generation, they had come to maturity in the smug Fifties without a strong ethos of their own. But now in their young middle age they were facing (as were all but the most reactionary adults in every other part of the Western world) the necessity to heed the disaffection of the very young – that vibrant generation of the Sixties that was questioning the traditionalist's view of every human exchange from the sex act to the political rally, marching to rhythms as different from those of their elders as their own electrified guitars and the old pols' wailing bagpipes.

Because the politicians of the post-Pearson generation were, like all true Liberals, more interested in success than in ideology, they recognized instinctively that they could not pick a man of the old school and expect him to be a winner. They surveyed with understandable chagrin the field of eight who entered the leadership race within five weeks of Lester Pearson's resignation. All of them, it was agreed, had some important political assets. But in each one there was a serious flaw that prevented him from being what the activists felt the party needed or the country wanted.

THE FIRST BRAVE BANNER RAISED belonged to Eric William Kierans. In the four careers he had already adorned (president of a glue company, director of the McGill School of Commerce, head of the Montreal Stock Exchange, cabinet minister in the Lesage administration) Kierans had always been tempted by – and had proved able to conquer – seemingly insurmountable odds. A deceptively ordinary-looking man, with a hound-dog face on which deep lines of compassion were permanently etched, Kierans was set apart in any company by his volatile Irish nature, the intensity of his blue-eyed gaze and a strong existentialist streak that made him feel any retreat from challenge amounted to a destruction of self.

After winning a bitter battle with René Lévesque in the late fall of 1967, Kierans decided to abandon provincial politics for the federal field.* In early January, with characteristic charm and glowing confidence, Kierans announced his candidacy for the federal party leadership and set out on an arduous cross-country tour during which he planned to meet most of the convention's 2,500 delegates personally and persuade the country that he was the man of the hour.

Kierans saw his great advantage in the fact that, unlike the other expected contenders, he was not encumbered by the Pearson record. He determined to carve out a distinguishable position on all the crucial issues and hoped to solidify the scattered dissatisfaction with the existing regime into support for himself. But Kierans' strength – the fact that he was an outsider of proven ability – was also his weakness. He had no real friends in the federal Liberal Party and no access to its apparatus.

NEXT THERE MARCHED SMARTLY ONTO THE FIELD the impressive all-too-upright figure of Paul Theodore Hellyer, who at the moment of announcing his candidacy on January 11 saw himself as ideally programmed to win the race. He was the minister who had unified the armed forces, the supreme doer among the Pearsonian compromisers, the technocrat politician who was still young (forty-four, though he looked fifty-four) but already experienced (he had been in the House since 1949) and a party man with a loyal following in urban Ontario that could be used as a base to win the nation. Hellyer was convinced the delegates wanted efficient government above all and he hoped to place the blame for Pearson's difficulties on the Ottawa bureaucrats

*He had been able to carry the provincial Liberals' policy convention with him on a resolution opposing Quebec independence and had driven Lévesque into establishing his own separatist movement.

with whom he would shortly cope in much the same way as he had with the navy's apoplectic admirals. For months his superbly organized campaign machine, set up by his ubiquitous assistant, Bill Lee, had been humming, ready to be turned on high.

But for all their careful reckoning, the Hellyer boosters were hampered by a maddening imperfection in their candidate's personality. Likeable and relaxed in private, he was incapable in public of showing the human warmth required of politicians in dealing with large groups of people. He had the misfortune of looking like a cavalry captain in Kaiser Wilhelm's army and in his speeches he talked like a mechanical man, standing as though his shoulder blades were pulling him backwards, delivering the too-perfect mélange of solutions in a manner that chilled the soul.

THE REASONING BEHIND ALLAN MACEACHEN'S DECISION to declare himself available the following day was never really clear but it must have had something to do with his conviction that Maritime Liberals should put forward a favourite son to counter Stanfield's regional strength. As an avowed left-wing Liberal, MacEachen also seemed to believe that Walter Gordon's remaining support might accrue to his stocky Scottish self. Yet even down east, he was assessed as a handy fellow to have at your political elbow but no leader by a league. Despite (or was it because of?) his decision to hire half the unemployed pipers in the country to swirl and skirl in his wake, his campaign had about it from the very beginning a melancholy air of futility.

JOHN TURNER JOGGED INTO THE RACE five days later with a list of professional and personal attributes that made him sound like a story-book prime minister, or at least a story-book prince. He was young (thirty-eight), handsome (with silver in his thick black hair), rich (his stepfather had been the Lieutenant-Governor of British Columbia, his lovely wife was a peaches-and-creamy child of privilege), bilingual, a Rhodes Scholar, an Olympic-class sprinter, a graduate in civil and common law who had lived in British Columbia, Ontario and Quebec, and had an easy familiarity with the disparate worlds of the Anglo-Saxon business establishment and the technocratic élite of the new Quebec. His discourse had a McLuhanesque ring, his approach projected a Kennedyesque pragmatism and he could even claim to be among those Liberals touched by the legend of Mackenzie King. (During World War II, when Turner was a small boy living in Ottawa with his mother, he used to walk his dog occasionally in the company of the Incredible Canadian.) But somehow these shimmering parts didn't add up to a convincing whole. For all his lithe vitality and youthful ardour (he once described Princess Margaret as "an interesting chick"), he had, during the five years he had spent in the House, gained a reputation for trying too hard and was said to be more anxious to please his elders than to display his own convictions. At the very end of the campaign, in circumstances unforeseeable at the beginning, he was to come of political age and show for the first time his true, tough, impressive self. But by then he couldn't turn back the delegates' general feeling that he was not quite ready to lead.

MITCHELL SHARP, THE MANDARIN CANDIDATE INCARNATE, calmly presented himself on January 19, a man full of confidence in the primacy of his days. His intention was to wage a miniature one-man election campaign across the country, displaying his competent self to the public as well as to convention delegates in a blitz of short tours. He would develop policy proposals as he went so that he could enter the prime minister's office with something close to a genuine mandate, behaving throughout as though he were, if not the prime minister already, at least the natural heir to the Liberal succession. His chief adviser, Mike McCabe, went so far as to have black-and-white matchbooks and pencils imprinted with the stark slogan: MITCHELL SHARP 6/4/68, as though, on that last important day of the convention, Sharp would come into his own. The plan was a good one and, if a parliamentary error and a shaky Canadian dollar had not unexpectedly intervened, it might very well have worked.

THE SAME DAY JOHN JAMES "JOE" GREENE, Osgoode Hall lawyer turned hayseed minister of agriculture, also became a candidate. Folksy as a fox, awkward as Abe Lincoln, Greene planned to gain delegates by making cracker-barrel speeches and developing a cogent personal theory of Liberalism. But he must have known when he started his gallant campaign that what he stood to gain was not the leadership but a national reputation. He lacked the essential ingredients of solid financial backing and a power base in the party.

THE MAN WHO HAD THE POWER BASE – his shoulders rounded by a lifetime spent hunching over lecterns, speech-making to the party faithful – chose the same day to glide into the Press Gallery conference theatre in Ottawa and announce that he, Paul Martin, was heeding a loud clear call to fill the nation's highest political office. His hair dyed black for the occasion, Martin made a point of dismissing as unworthy of consideration the fact that he was sixty-four. "Age is not a question of years," he said, "but of health, vitality and ideas. Why, some of the greatest men of our time – not that I want to place myself in their class – undertook responsibility at a later age; Mr Pearson for one, John XXIII for another, Churchill, Adenauer." In this press meeting and throughout the campaign Martin was displaying his conviction that ideologies and issues are minor diversions from the real business of politics: the handshake. All his life he had been the supreme vote-hustler, the great master of brick-by-brick political masonry, and now he intended to concentrate his efforts on collecting the many IOU's he had amassed during forty years of partisan labour. He saw no real reason why he should not win since he had a quarter of a million dollars to spend and public and private opinion polls taken before and immediately after Pearson's resignation showed him with a decisive edge in delegate support.*

Martin's trouble was not that he was too old but that he had been around for so long. He had known Sir Wilfrid Laurier, had served as a delegate to the League of Nations. His habit of resolutely avoiding straightforward pronouncements made him easy to caricature if difficult to oppose. In brief, he made no demands on the delegates' curiosity and his very familiarity and flexibility instead of being strengths, as he fully expected, were to prove pathetic detriments.

ROBERT WINTERS HAD ALREADY DECLARED HUFFILY that he would *not* be a candidate, a decision he was to reverse later on. A smiling, self-charmed, big-businessman, he once revealed the secret of his appeal to so many Liberals by answering a question about where he placed himself on the left-right spectrum with the good-humoured retort, "Tell me where the centre is and I'll tell you where I stand."

All through the rocky reform days of the Pearson period Winters had been regarded by the C. D. Howe school of Liberals as the party's last hope. But since his return to Ottawa in 1965, he himself had been notably unhappy, finding it difficult to fit into the new dynamics of Canadian politics. Eight years spent as a tycoon on Bay Street had so

*The other Pearson ministers, who knew him well, saw many reasons why he should not win. The only one who supported him, more out of stubbornness than conviction, was Maurice Sauvé.

solidified his thinking that he was always expressing either shock or amazement at the differences that cropped up between the running of a government and the operation of a large corporation.* Winters genuinely believed that the main function of government was to create the kind of economic climate in which private enterprise could flourish. "The more good decisions made in boardrooms . . . the fewer will have to be made in cabinet chambers," he maintained. At one 1966 cabinet meeting he surprised even his most reactionary colleagues by flatly declaring that there was no such thing as poverty in Canada.

Dismayed by what he considered to be the Pearson Government's socialistic leanings and appalled by the fact that the Liberal leadership campaign was turning into a democratic free-for-all, he told a press conference on January 12, "In business, when you want a man for an important job, you turn to the man you want, not the job seekers. The job should seek the man, not vice versa . . . I can't recall other leadership conventions in which the candidates have been called on to debate public issues during the course of the campaign." He condemned the Pearson administration for its budget deficits and made it clear that he could have balanced the accounts. Asked about dissension within the Pearson Cabinet, he replied: "I can't imagine any businessman accepting the chairmanship of a board that was so divided."

Curiously, this spoiled-boy announcement of his decision to abandon the government prompted the nearest thing to a genuine draft that was to appear during the Liberal leadership race. Letters and petitions flowed into Winters' office, urging him to change his mind. Two Nova Scotia senators – Donald Smith and J. J. Kinley – headed a Maritimes committee for Winters. Toronto and Winnipeg businessmen organized similar campaigns. Persuaded by these appeals that he could win after all, Winters on February 28 resigned from Cabinet ("I have always believed that if you don't agree with the policies of a firm, you either get out or take it over") and on March 1 announced his belated candidacy.

Winters was sure that by criss-crossing the country and reminding delegates of the trouble-free St Laurent days he would impress everyone with his ability to resurrect the "sound" government that was now only a memory. But his hesitation in entering the race was to prove costly and many of the delegates who could easily have been his early in

---

*Commenting on C. D. Howe's cavalier treatment of the Commons, Winters once told a reporter, "I think C.D. really missed a bet by not appreciating how Parliament works. I always found it salutary to take something and have it approved by Parliament – it's the same feeling as having your board and shareholders behind you."

January were already committed to other candidates by the beginning of March. Despite Winters' great attractiveness to the acquisitive urge in every Liberal soul, the support couldn't all be gathered up again.

The other candidates in the meantime had been parading their virtues and their ideas across the country, leaving in their wake amazement that Lester Pearson had been able to govern (more or less) with a cabinet of such contradictory personalities. Early in the campaign, when the Prime Minister lectured the aspirants on the importance of cabinet solidarity, they responded by accelerating their daily output of platitudes. Still, none of them could claim to have broken free of the pack and they were all casting nervous glances over their shoulders at an unexpected newcomer to the race, Pierre Elliott Trudeau, who at the time had been a Liberal for only twenty-nine months and a member of the cabinet for less than a year.

PIERRE TRUDEAU'S UNEXPECTED PROMOTION TO CABINET the previous April as Lucien Cardin's successor in the Justice ministry puzzled the Ottawa sages who had expected Larry Pennell, the popular Solicitor General, to be given the honour. Unknown to most of them, a close relationship had developed between Pearson and Trudeau. The Prime Minister had appointed Trudeau his parliamentary assistant on January 9, 1966, at a time when he was coming around to the view that his own policy of co-operative federalism should be abandoned for a tougher, more defensible approach. During long evenings of discussion in the privacy of the study at 24 Sussex Drive, Trudeau provided the Prime Minister not just with a rationale for a practical new concept of Canadian federalism but with perceptive insights into Quebec society. Pearson, in turn, gave Trudeau a crash course in the politics of statesmanship. He sent him to the United Nations as part of the Canadian delegation, dispatched him on a fact-finding tour of Africa, and placed him in charge of a task force studying the possibility of changing Canada's constitution. At the same time, because Pearson had fallen into the habit of discussing important issues with his parliamentary assistant, Trudeau began to perceive the nature of the problems that confront a Canadian prime minister and the limitations on the powers with which he is endowed to deal with them. During these months there developed a strong feeling of respect and affection between the two men and on the day Pearson resigned Trudeau was seen with tears in his eyes.

Pearson recognized in Trudeau a man very different in style and temperament from his fellow Quebec M.P's. In the freshness of his thoughts and in the intuitive leaps of logic that marked his conversation, Trudeau was of a different breed from the many florid French Canadians who had preceded him. Despite Trudeau's deliberate eccentricities of dress, he possessed many of the qualities that Pearson admired. He was the product of a rich and cultivated home, he had been educated abroad, had travelled widely, was an avowed intellectual, a sometime reformer and a convinced internationalist. In addition, the Prime Minister saw in Trudeau a personal toughness and an ability to respond to the political forces in play, both attributes Pearson himself lacked.

When Trudeau was appointed Minister of Justice, he settled in for what he hoped would be a long tenure. He had always considered himself an agent of ferment, questioning the collective conventional wisdom of his society, testing his ideas through personal experience. He felt there would exist in the Justice Department the opportunity to put to practical use ideas he had developed during thirty years of action and reflection. As Justice Minister he could expand the creative use of law, which had always been his predominant interest. He told a reporter shortly after taking over Justice, "This should be regarded more and more as a department planning for the society of tomorrow, not merely acting as the government's legal adviser. It should combine the function of drafting new legislation with the disciplines of sociology and economics, so that it can provide a framework for our evolving way of life. Society is throwing up problems all the time – divorce, abortions, family planning, LSD, pollution – and it's no longer enough to review our statutes every twenty years. If possible, we have to move the framework of society slightly ahead of the times, so there is no curtailment of intellectual or physical liberty."

During the first eight months in his new portfolio Trudeau made little public impact except as an odd character with eccentric pursuits. John Diefenbaker attacked him for wearing a yellow ascot into the House of Commons. A few stories were published about his Mercedes convertible and the apparently unending parade of beautiful young women with whom he shared his leisure. There were anecdotes repeated about his many exploits: his part in the 1949 Asbestos strike, his attempts to swim the Hellespont and row a boat to Cuba, his trip to Moscow and his interview with Mao Tse-tung. But he ignored the gossipy dinner-party circuit where Ottawa reputations are made and maintained an air of reserve, an almost fawnlike shyness, in everything he did. He had yet to make the adjustment that faces intellectuals who assume public office, the difficult transition between seeking truth and exercising power.

His first major legislation dealt with the broadening of grounds for divorce to include mental and physical cruelty, bigamy, sexual deviation, desertion and marriage breakdown. On December 5, 1967, during second reading of the bill, he gave a speech that impressed even opposition members of the House. "We are now living in a social climate," he said, "in which people are beginning to realize, perhaps for the first time in the history of this country, that we are not entitled to impose the concepts which belong to a sacred society upon a civil or profane society. The concepts of the civil society in which we live are pluralistic, and I think this parliament realizes that it would be a mistake for us to try to legislate into this society concepts which belong to a theological or sacred order. These are very important concepts no doubt, but they should not by themselves be considered as the sole guide for a government."

Two weeks later, Trudeau tabled his proposed amendments to the Criminal Code, which included some reasons for permissible abortion and the legalizing of homosexual acts between consenting adults. On television Trudeau described these reforms as "legislation by tolerance. I want to separate sin from crime. You may have to ask forgiveness for your sins from God, but not from the Minister of Justice." Then he added, "There's no place for the state in the bedrooms of the nation."

This was hardly a startling proposition. But it made a disproportionate impact on a nation whose citizens had been numbed by generations of politicians talking obtusely about the gross national product and the difficulties of federal-provincial relations. It was a human remark in a field where incomprehensible statements were the norm, and the response to it was the first intimation of how close Trudeau was to the people's mood.

A few days later, on December 26, he left Ottawa for a fortnight's holiday in Tahiti.

BY THIS TIME THE UNOFFICIAL LEADERSHIP RACE was twelve days old. Sharp, Martin and Hellyer were the recognized front-runners, although Jean Marchand's name was occasionally bandied about as a possible entry from Quebec. The party had alternated French and English prime ministers since Confederation. But the commonly held view of the moment was that the concessions demanded by Quebec would be more acceptable to the rest of Canada if they were put forward by an English-speaking leader. At the same time, it was said that if a French Canadian did try for the succession and lost (or won the leadership but was defeated in the election to follow) it would be interpreted as a serious insult to French Canada. Most Ottawa Liberals argued that the Quebec ministers, instead of putting up a candidate of their own, should form a block, pick an English-speaking minister to back, and bargain off their support in return for some specific policy commitments and the promise of at least two senior economic portfolios in the new leader's cabinet.

This was not the view held by a small but resolute band of Quebec Liberals who had started to meet at informal weekly sessions in Montreal the previous September. If the group had a leader it was Claude Frenette, an unusually talented young lawyer with a rare flair for organization. Frenette had been Maurice Sauvé's principal assistant and was now, at twenty-nine, a senior executive with Power Corporation, the large Montreal holding company. Also in the group were Fernand Cadieux, who was often described by his friends as "the Marshall McLuhan of French Canada" and had been one of the original planners of Expo 67; Jim Davey, a politically astute British physicist and computer specialist then employed by Chemcell Limited; Harold Gordon, an articulate and amusing Montreal lawyer who had also served a term in Sauvé's office; Jean-Pierre Goyer, the Liberal M.P. for Dollard; André Ouellette, a forceful, red-bearded radical who was yet another Sauvé assistant; and Marc Lalonde, Prime Minister Pearson's policy secretary.

They were all friends, reform minded, warm, lively and young and they treated politics not as a profit-seeking venture but as an exercise in idealism. The group had been convened originally by Jean Marchand, when he took over as Pearson's French-Canadian lieutenant, to serve as his advisory body in reorganizing Quebec's federal Liberals. Their first decision was to hire, as the party's regional executive director, Pierre Levasseur, a 28-year-old graduate in business administration from Laval and the University of Western Ontario who was then Secretary General of the Directorate of Collegiate Studies in the Quebec Department of Education. Levasseur quickly became an important member of the group, which fell into the habit of meeting most Friday evenings during the fall of 1967 in the boardroom of Power Corporation, on the top floor of Place Ville Marie.

Although they vaguely talked about the problem of the succession, their discussions were mostly about the Quebec Liberal Federation annual meeting scheduled for late January of 1968. But on December 15, the day after Pearson made his announcement, the group decided to set out the specific qualities it wanted in the next party leader and to pick a candidate it could support. The criteria were these: that he could unite the country; that he could unite the party; that he could win the next election; that he could master the House of Commons; and that he was a demonstrably inspiring leader. After a discussion that lasted long into the night, the group decided the only man who could meet these tests was Pierre Elliott Trudeau.

At about the same time several Liberal M.P.'s from Toronto, including James Walker, Robert Stanbury and Donald Macdonald, had approached Marc Lalonde, as a close friend of Trudeau's, to ask what he thought about the availability of the Justice Minister. Television broadcasters Pat Watson and Roy Faibish also wrote personal letters to Trudeau, urging him to run. Gordon Gibson, executive assistant to Indian Affairs Minister Arthur Laing, resigned his job and offered to help organize a Trudeau campaign. Eddie Rubin, a bright and bushy-tailed young lawyer serving as Trudeau's executive assistant, met Lalonde several times, anxious to launch a leadership drive for his minister.

Back in November of 1967, when Marc Lalonde was a federal observer at John Robarts' Confederation of Tomorrow Conference, he had a talk with Professor Ramsay Cook. Lalonde brought up the idea of a Trudeau candidacy and Cook was instantly enthusiastic. Later, when the leadership race was under way, Cook talked to Professor William Kilbourn, head of the humanities faculty at York University, a one-time Sharp supporter who was sounding out his colleagues' reactions to Trudeau on his own. The two professors, quickly joined by John Saywell, York University's Dean of Arts and Science, circulated a petition to the faculties of Canadian universities advocating a Trudeau draft. They eventually obtained six hundred signatures. The Canadian academic community had admired Pierre Trudeau for years mainly because of his articles in *Cité Libre* and the *Canadian Forum* as well as his appearances at scholarly meetings. He was one of their own. After Trudeau's entry into politics in 1965, Kenneth McNaught, the University of Toronto historian, had written: "His political fate will likely be the political fate of Canada."*

When Lalonde returned to Ottawa from the Robarts conference, he asked Pearson's permission to organize a national tour for Trudeau during January to brief provincial premiers on the forthcoming constitutional conference. The original plan was to have the Justice Minister deliver major speeches in every provincial capital as part of the tour, but Trudeau later vetoed the idea.

The Trudeau campaign was still only a phantom movement among enthusiasts who had no solid assurance they would end up with a

*Nationalism in Canada, edited by Peter Russell (McGraw-Hill Company of Canada Limited, 1966).

candidate. Trudeau himself was at first amused, then troubled, by the idea of contesting the leadership. Quite apart from feeling that he was so new to politics that it would be presumptuous to consider the leadership, he feared that he could never win the party over to his ideas. At the same time, he had doubts whether the double constraints of the existing cabinet structure and the entrenched power of Ottawa's bureaucracy would allow him to lead a government according to his own style and in his own direction. Just before Christmas he confided to a few close friends, "You know, before I make my decision, I've got to find out whether it's really possible to *do* anything once you get into the prime minister's office." Another important restraint was his feeling that Quebec's candidate for the leadership should be not himself but Jean Marchand.

Marchand was in political difficulties at the time. At his urging the government had proposed a bill (C-186) to alter the makeup of the Canada Labour Relations Board in favour of his former union federation in jurisdictional disputes by breaking up national bargaining units. The bill was never really debated, since it drew such embarrassing opposition criticism. Marchand also felt that his health was unequal to the rigours of running, that he had an inadequate command of English and no power base outside Quebec and that his almost certain defeat would be a blow to national unity. During a winter holiday in Florida with Bob Giguère, Marchand tentatively decided that he would probably not contest the leadership himself but would urge Trudeau to run. Soon after his return to Montreal Giguère began quietly to collect financial pledges to pay for Trudeau's campaign, if he decided to run.*

EARLY IN JANUARY OF 1968, before any money was collected and while the Justice Minister was still in Tahiti, Eddie Rubin and Gordon Gibson decided on their own to rent office space in Ottawa for the expected Trudeau candidacy. Rubin spent a thousand dollars of his own money for the first month's rent. Jim Davey took a vacation from his company and moved in to begin setting up the organization. A few girls joined up as volunteer switchboard operators, but they carefully answered incoming calls with only the number (237-6460). Officially, the Trudeau headquarters didn't yet exist.

When Trudeau returned to Canada on January 10, he discovered that what had been a vague idea was now a blossoming reality. He

---

*Individual contributions were deliberately held down so that no single donation exceeded 2½ per cent of the total budget, which was eventually set at about $300,000.

conferred several times with Lalonde and Marchand but refused to commit himself before setting off on his tour of the provinces in connection with the constitutional conference. In Newfoundland he received a surprising public endorsement from Joey Smallwood. The Premier later recounted his first meeting with the Justice Minister:

> I had hardly heard of the man but I invited him to lunch and asked him what he wanted. He said he wanted my views on the constitution. So I told him, for Quebec – nothing. Nothing. I don't mean almost nothing. I mean nothing whatsoever, Quebec should have nothing that Prince Edward Island doesn't have – that Newfoundland doesn't have. But I said, for the French people in Canada, anywhere in Canada – everything. Everything. Everything that the English Canadians have, rights, education, everything. Trudeau listened and then remarked that he might as well go home because I had expressed his views so clearly and so forcefully. And he told me he only wished he could have made his views so clear, that as a French Canadian he wished he could use the English language like that. And I didn't know that I was talking to a man with such facility, such powers of exposition in the English language. Why there aren't four or five men in the country who can express themselves in English like this man and here I was, using my meat axe like a clumsy elephant with arthritis and he tells me he wished he could express himself so clearly!

IN EVERY SUCCESSFUL POLITICAL CAMPAIGN, there is an identifiable moment when it catches fire, a time when a kind of natural momentum overtakes the candidate and propels him into the lead. For Pierre Trudeau, that moment arrived on January 28, at the Quebec Liberal Federation meeting at the Hotel Bonaventure in Montreal. Jean Marchand, as Quebec lieutenant, had craftily made sure that none of the leadership candidates would be allowed to address the federation, even though Quebec would be sending 626 delegates to the April convention. Since he was not yet a candidate and because federal-provincial relations was the main theme of the meeting, Trudeau could appropriately deliver the conference's keynote address. Using a back-slide illuminated screen that listed all of Quebec's options (from separatism to absolute monarchy) Trudeau, in crystal-clear prose, demonstrated why federalism would ensure the most attractive future for the province. It was the first time the delegates had been given a policy they could understand and support. At the end of Trudeau's speech they stood up and cheered, sang *Il a gagné ses épaulettes*, and one M.P. yelled out,

"THE NEXT PRIME MINISTER!" Trudeau appeared embarrassed by the acclaim. He bowed, waved his hand in a self-depreciating gesture and sat down. Whatever doubts had existed among his supporters about the willingness of Quebec delegates to support his leadership bid vanished.

Their confidence was confirmed by Claude Frenette's defeat of Yves Paré, an Old Guard candidate, for the presidency of the Quebec Liberal Federation. After the votes had been counted and the tally showed a four-to-one margin for Frenette, Trudeau walked into his room, hugged him and said, "Well, we beat the bastards. Now it's possible for us to do things."

At the annual meeting of the Ontario Liberals in Toronto in early February Trudeau was carried through the meeting hall on delegates' shoulders and, for the first time, there was evidence of Trudeaumania – the spectacle of pretty young girls in mini-skirts squealing at the sight of him. An Ontario-for-Trudeau committee (organized by Robert Stanbury, Tim Reid, a provincial Liberal MPP, and Charles Caccia, a Toronto alderman) assured him of wide support among the province's delegates.

Everywhere Trudeau went he was followed by television crews, recording his shrugs and diffident comments. He had appeared on the CBC program *Newsmagazine* on January 23, in an interview with Norman DePoe and Ron Collister, and later had been a guest on *The Public Eye, The Way It Is* and CTV's *W5*. The more he was seen on the screen, the more entranced Canadians were by his style and demeanour. There was about him a subtle, indefinable intensity, a suggestion of pent-up power and hidden dimensions that fascinated the nation's TV viewers.

Trudeau's image took on an even sharper focus during the constitutional conference held in Ottawa from February 5 to 7, which featured him in a television duel with Daniel Johnson. Sitting at Pearson's right hand, the Justice Minister took control of the confrontation. He managed to paint the Quebec Premier as a politician more interested in the aggrandizement of his personal power than dedicated to advancing the interests of French Canada.

On the night the conference ended, Trudeau held a meeting in his office with Jim Davey, Pierre Levasseur, Gordon Gibson and Eddie Rubin. With mounting excitement they showed him organizational charts for his leadership campaign and outlined some strategy suggestions. Trudeau thanked them but still did not commit himself. The following Tuesday (February 13) Trudeau spent the evening discussing the idea with Marc Lalonde and a senior civil servant. The same day E. J. Benson, Bryce Mackasey and Russell Honey, the Liberal M.P. for

Durham (Ontario), assured Trudeau of their support. The final decision was made two days later at a meeting attended by Jean Marchand, Benson, Honey, Lalonde, Goyer, Gibson, Rubin, Levasseur and Jim Davey. Trudeau asked them about the regional spread of his potential delegates. He seemed particularly anxious to find out whether or not Bud Drury, a Sharp supporter, might be persuaded to come out for him. At the end of the meeting, when Rubin demanded: "So what's the decision?" Trudeau replied: "I guess we all know what it is."

Next day the Justice Minister called a press conference to announce his candidacy. Seven television cameras, seventeen photographers and nearly a hundred reporters attended the meeting. Asked why he had decided to run, Trudeau gave this unorthodox explanation:

> If I try to assess what happened in the past two months, I have a suspicion you people [the press] had a lot to do with it. If anybody's to blame I suppose it's you collectively. If there's anybody to thank, it's you collectively. To be quite frank, if I try to analyse it, well, I think in the subconscious mind of the press I think it started out like a huge practical joke on the Liberal Party. I mean that, because, in some sense, the decision that I made this morning and last night is in some ways similar to that I arrived at when I entered the Liberal Party. It seemed to me, reading the press in the early stages a couple of months ago, it seemed to me as though many of you were saying, you know, "We dare the Liberal Party to choose a guy like Trudeau. Of course, we know they never will, but we'll just dare them to do it and we'll show that this is the man they could have had as leader if they had wanted. Here's how great he is."

> But you wouldn't have said that if you'd known the Liberal Party or myself would have taken up the challenge. I don't want to read interpretation into your mind, but this is the way I saw events in the past month or month and a half: it was a good joke on the Liberal Party, and after somebody else had won – it would be a good man, because they are all good men in the field – the press would sit back and the public would sit back and say, "Oh well, you know they didn't have the guts to choose a good guy," because the good guy in your hypothesis really wouldn't be running – and in mine, too.

> I mean, some good guys would, but this good guy wouldn't. And what happened, I think, is that the joke blew up in your faces and in mine. You know, people took it seriously. I saw this when – not when the press thought I had a chance, and that I should go, and so on – but when I saw the response from political people, from

members of the party and responsible members of parliament. This is when I began to wonder if, oh, you know, this whole thing was not a bit more serious than you and I had intended. And when members of parliament formed committees to draft me, and when I got responsible Liberals in responsible positions in different parts of the country telling me seriously that I should run, I think what happened is that the joke became serious, and I tried to analyse it, and as I say, it looks a bit like when I tried to enter the party. I didn't think the Liberal Party would take – I think I've told that story sometimes – and suddenly, they did. So I was stuck with it. Well, now you're stuck with me.

When one journalist asked about the charge being made by Trudeau's competitors that he had not served any political apprenticeship for the prime ministership, the Justice Minister gave a long, thoughtful reply. "Most of today's problems are not solved by experience," he said. "The further we advance into the modern age, the less important experience will become. It's much more important to have the necessary adaptability with which to face and solve new problems." By the end of his press conference Trudeau had made it clear that if the Liberals should pick him as their next leader, they would also be subscribing to a managerial revolution in Canadian politics. That night Trudeau went to the Press Club Ball at the Chateau Laurier and was mobbed as he frugged on the dance floor.

THREE DAYS LATER, THE LEADERSHIP CONTEST became a secondary issue as the Liberal Government stumbled into an accidental parliamentary defeat. On February 19, as a half-empty House debated Mitchell Sharp's budget resolutions, the Liberals were aware that an unusually high proportion of their members were away. During the late afternoon a key section of Sharp's bill had carried by a voice vote of only 65 to 62. At 8:10 p.m., when Herman Batten, the Deputy Speaker, called out, "When shall the said bill be read a third time?", a few Liberals replied: "At the next sitting."* But Batten did not seem to hear them and called for third reading. Allan MacEachen, sensing the danger, objected, but Conservative House Leader Michael Starr insisted that the Commons was now committed to a vote.

Sharp, thoroughly confused by the proceedings, did not think to

*Without unanimous consent, bills normally do not pass more than one stage per sitting.

intervene. The division bells rang for seventy-eight minutes and in the vote that followed, with forty-eight Liberals absent, the government went down, 82 to 84. The defeat was an accident, partly owing to the usual low turnout on Monday nights and the fact that three leadership contenders (Paul Martin, Joe Greene and John Turner) and some of their supporters were out hustling delegates. But that such a situation was allowed to develop emphasized in an unexpectedly dramatic way what had been a major flaw in the Pearson Government from the beginning: that it consisted of a group of self-willed politicians who had little faith or interest in Parliament and preferred to transact the nation's business in the serene sanctuary of the cabinet chamber and the ministerial office. The Liberals appeared to view the House of Commons as a conveyor belt to ratify what they decided among themselves, not as a forum where public men are daily made accountable for their actions to the people who elected them. This attitude was evident in Pearson's discomfort on the floor of the Commons. Leaving his office for the question period, he would often sigh and say to Mary Macdonald, "Well, here I go, back into the trenches." He was never able to control or dominate the House as a Prime Minister should and was not very familiar with its workings. Because External Affairs sponsors little legislation of its own, Pearson had never actually had the experience of steering a bill through all stages and retained only a vague impression of the House rules. He once asked a colleague: "Can we introduce a financial bill in the Senate?" even though it is one of the elementary tenets of parliamentary procedure that no money bills can be started in the upper chamber. When moving an important motion he would occasionally forget that it required a seconder. Because of the Prime Minister's inexperience and lack of interest in Parliament, most of the Pearson Government's legislative journeys turned into bruising, bumpy rides of occasionally incredible confusion.

Pearson had never been capable of imposing on his colleagues the kind of tight discipline that might be expected in a minority government situation. But since the announcement of his resignation any remaining traces of control vanished. On February 19, Pearson was on a holiday in Jamaica. After the defeat on the crucial vote, Robert Winters, who was Acting Prime Minister, called a late-night cabinet meeting. The ministers acted sheepish and confused; only Judy LaMarsh treated the incident as a joke and wanted an election called immediately.

The Prime Minister was hastily summoned back to Ottawa and as soon as he returned asked Opposition Leader Robert Stanfield for a twenty-four-hour adjournment. He went on national television to plead that the mishap had been "a hazard of minority government" and did not constitute a true defeat. The opposition argued just as strongly that a lost vote on a major money bill was by definition a motion of no confidence and that Pearson had little choice except to dissolve the House. The Liberals began to search around desperately for precedents and on February 21 Pearson presented a motion to the effect that the defeat had not really constituted "a vote of non-confidence in the Government." The more militant Conservatives refused to attend committee meetings, taking the stand that Parliament no longer existed. Robert Stanfield, bewildered but determined to be the statesman, allowed the Liberals to rally their forces. Paul Martin applied pressure on the Ralliement des Créditistes and won reluctant agreement from Réal Caouette, who didn't want an immediate election, to support the government position. On February 28, the Liberals were sustained, 138-119.* The crisis had been resolved, but it left a bitter legacy. It meant that a government defeated on a major money bill was no longer presumed to have lost the confidence of the House of Commons and thus denied Parliament one of its important prerogatives.

THE INCIDENT HAD A SOBERING EFFECT on the leadership race. Certainly the argument of Trudeau's competitors – that experience was what counted – had been destroyed. If experienced politicians could make such a mess of things, the country needed all the inexperienced politicians it could get. The events of February 19 also showed that the authority of this particular parliament had been exhausted and Liberal delegates suddenly realized they were choosing not just a new leader, but one who would have to face the people soon after his selection.

In this context, Pierre Trudeau's astonishing rapport with the public began to impress the delegates and frighten the contenders. Few of the candidates actually attacked the Justice Minister.† But they began to measure themselves against his contemporary appeal, trying to alter their own personalities to fit the restless groping for consensus within the Liberal Party. Robert Winters kept stressing that he had been born in Lunenburg, Nova Scotia, the son of a fishing-boat captain, and

*In protest against allowing the government's motion to come to a vote, Gordon Churchill resigned from the caucus of the Conservative Party.

†One exception was Paul Martin who privately told delegates, when they asked about Trudeau that the candidacy was comparable to George Bernard Shaw's running for the Conservative leadership in Britain. Presumably this was an intimation in Martinese that the Justice Minister was both a dilettante and a Fabian socialist.

wondering out loud how that could possibly make him a right-winger. John Turner was trying to act older and wiser than he was, Paul Martin younger and more carefree. Allan MacEachen and Joe Greene were both attempting to project themselves as national figures with regional power bases instead of regional figures with national ambitions. Paul Hellyer was passing sandwiches, pretending he was the Good Guy writ large. Eric Kierans was simply being himself: a brave man bent on an impossible mission, doing his best.

Mitchell Sharp, haunted by his image as a stuffy civil servant, was playing the piano, smoking cigars and giving highly partisan pep talks. Sharp's handlers remained confident their man would still emerge as a last-ballot compromise winner. But the fact that he had borne the brunt for the government's defeat on February 19, as well as his long absence from the campaign made necessary by the weakness of the Canadian dollar, caused even committed supporters to question his suitability for the prime ministership.* Members of the business community, sensing Sharp's troubles, quietly withdrew their pledges to finance his campaign and Sharp, who had already spent $100,000 and was budgeting for a total expenditure of $225,000, suddenly found himself short of cash. "Mitchell Sharp," wrote Gordon Pape, an associate editor of the Montreal *Gazette*, "will probably never become prime minister of Canada: he knows it and the men close to him know it. A devastating series of events have in the last three weeks dropped him far down on the list of contenders. His closest associates are saddened and demoralized by the course events have taken, the more so because Sharp is a man who commands intense loyalty and who, his backers fervently believe, is by far the best equipped to take over the country at this critical juncture."

*During the first two and a half months of 1968, Mitchell Sharp had to battle almost daily against a devaluation of Canada's currency, caused both by an international gold-buying rush and by the investment guidelines issued by President Lyndon Johnson at the turn of the year. These called for a cut to 65 per cent of the 1965-66 level in direct investments by American corporations operating abroad and an acceleration in the return to the United States of profits and dividends earned by foreign subsidiaries. The American move, prompted by the devaluation of the British pound, resulted in an immediate withdrawal of U.S. funds from Canada and this, in turn, triggered a wave of downward trading in the Canadian dollar. The Bank of Canada was forced to spend $342 millions of its exchange reserves during January alone to help shore up the nation's currency. Sharp eventually was forced to fly to Washington and beg Treasury Secretary Henry Fowler to exempt Canada from the American investment guidelines. This exemption plus emergency drawings from the Bank for International Settlements and other standby credits finally stabilized Canada's dollar.

454

But even without his unexpected travail, Sharp and all the other contenders were suffering because of Pierre Trudeau's broad and expanding appeal. Suddenly it had become Trudeau against the rest. The Liberal professionals running against him, earnestly spelling out the details of their policy commitments, seemed to be treating the many difficult issues facing the nation as segments of public opinion to be assuaged. Trudeau, even though he was the least specific of all the candidates in the pledges he made, projected the determination of a man who views politics as a moral commitment. He began to evolve his ideas for turning Canada into what he labelled a "just society." Here, it seemed, was a politician who promised to end the long, exhausted era of "postwar Canada" and to launch a time, still nameless, filled with challenges the nation was aching to undertake.

Barry Callaghan, literary editor of the Toronto *Telegram*, in a review of Trudeau's book, *Federalism and the French Canadians*, best caught the essence of the man.

Trudeau has made a special mark, not only in his willingness to engage unpleasant facts, but in his ability to see through the traditional racial smokescreens. If one accepts Arthur Miller's judgment that "the task of the real intellectual consists of analyzing illusions in order to discover their causes," then M. Trudeau is distinguished for this reason alone. . . . There are absolutes in Pierre Elliott Trudeau's world – the individual free unto himself who is pitted against totalitarian tyranny. The release into freedom is through the intellect, while enslavement is the fate of those who trust their emotions. It is the old Jansenist dichotomy: the spirit struggling against the flesh. Of course, M. Trudeau is not hobbled by the struggle. But in his own way, he is a true believer; in the intellect; in his intellect. This makes Trudeau a potentially great man. It also makes him a potentially dangerous man, for in the refusal to recognize emotional responses, in the belief that one is always acting rationally, lies possible self-deception. In no way do I mean to suggest that Pierre Elliott Trudeau is necessarily a victim of self-deception. I believe him to be the most articulate, analytical, and creative federal politician of my lifetime. But there is this curious streak in Trudeau, a streak that is an integral part of his strength, and I suspect that M. Trudeau's unique understanding of the authoritarian nature of his country stems from the tensions that exist within himself. Or, to put it another way, it has been said that English and French Canadians do not have opinions, they merely have emotions. It seems that Pierre Elliott Trudeau is determined to prove that there is nothing merely emotional about himself, nor about the people of Canada, if only they will learn to have an honest opinion of themselves.

RIDING A CHARTERED JET and wearing a leather coat, Trudeau travelled twenty thousand miles, making thirty stops, during his leadership campaign. His every appearance brought standing ovations. He seemed able, without strain, to establish personal contact with his audiences, operating on a private wave length the other candidates couldn't jam. In Victoria, where the monarchy was still an important issue, local Liberals closely questioned Trudeau on a topic he had previously dismissed as irrelevant. He won the crowd over with a shrug and the comment: "I was in Saskatoon last night and crowned a very lovely queen, so I feel very warm toward the monarchy."

There was a certain shock value in his appearances. The delegates came prepared to be fascinated and scandalized by a wild man in sandals spouting socialist slogans. Instead they found an immaculate, demure professor delivering proposals that *sounded* exciting but would not have been out of place in any Canadian Manufacturers' Association brief. "The truth," wrote Paul Fox, the University of Toronto political scientist, in the *Toronto Daily Star*, "is that beneath his dashing image Pierre Trudeau is conservative. His attitude on many matters is cautious and conventional – on the constitution, for instance, on medicare, on the sale of war material to the United States, on NATO and other matters, as his public statements during the current campaign are now beginning to make clear. That is the source of his appeal to many English Canadians. They like his conservative, hard line on Quebec. It is just what they have been waiting to hear from anyone and, coming from a French Canadian, it is all the sweeter to their ears."

Unable to classify him as a man of either the political right or the political left, most of Trudeau's listeners seemed happy to regard him simply as a man of the future.

Trudeau's organization in Ottawa was now operating at full tilt, with an executive committee consisting of Jim Davey, Pierre Levasseur, Jean-Pierre Goyer, Gordon Gibson, Donald Macdonald and Gérard Pelletier. It had attracted a swarm of hip young women, including Gwen Clark, Merle Shain, Jennifer Rae and Allison Gordon, who wrote press releases, designed cheerleaders' costumes for the convention and added pizazz to the scene. Despite its outward appearance of amateurish gaiety, the inner core of the Trudeau organization was tough and businesslike. Every step of the campaign was plotted on a critical-path flow chart, each delegate's loyalties and wavering potential were tabulated by computers. There was even a "war room" to which the organization's spies (pretty girls in clinging dresses who had infiltrated the other candidates' organizations) came to be debriefed. The main strategy of the Trudeau backers was simply "the campaign is the man." His advisers – gambling on the impact Trudeau would have on delegates as compared with that of his opponents – believed that little hard-sell was needed. Great care was taken to avoid attacking the other candidates. The secret Trudeau campaign manual stated explicitly:

At the end of the Convention it will be necessary to have a united Party. With this in mind:

1. Maximum care should be exercised to avoid any attacks or action that will hurt or damage other candidates.

2. Confrontations with them should be avoided if at all possible.

3. The best way to achieve this is to run a campaign that, as far as possible, ignores the presence of other candidates. If comment on them is required, it should be to the effect that they are fine, competent men who clearly believe they have something to offer the Party and the country. It is good and healthy for the Party that they are presenting themselves. The delegates will have the opportunity to hear points of view and make a choice.

THE FACT THAT TRUDEAU'S CANDIDACY, which at the beginning of the race had no roots within the party apparatus – and indeed, was hardly more than a seed of speculation in the minds of a few friends – could burst into full flower within weeks indicated a great deal about the country and the Liberal Party. It meant that national politics was passing through one of its periodic upheavals when a relatively non-partisan outsider moves in to reform and recharge the system. Within the Liberal ranks there was still formidable opposition to Trudeau but the group that opposed him as an interloper no longer controlled the party. More realistic and more modern Liberals admitted only that Trudeau was difficult to categorize. His manner was certainly ostentatiously anti-Establishment, as was his connection with trade unionism. But his upbringing, background and education gave him an Establishment aura. Any die-hard doubters who confided their qualms to Lester Pearson found the departing Prime Minister enthusiastic about Trudeau. One visitor who brought up some personal doubts about the Justice Minister's ideological position was assured by Pearson that he had taken the trouble of sending for Trudeau's RCMP file and had found nothing in it that would cast doubt on his character.

THE DIFFERENCE BETWEEN THE CANADA that created Lester Pearson and the Canada that overwhelmed him was nowhere more poignantly visible than in the contrast between the way he was chosen leader in 1958 and the way Pierre Elliott Trudeau gained power in 1968. In that decade, the nation had undergone a revolution and the world that had bestowed the leadership of his party on Lester Pearson like a garland had vanished.

In January 1958, Pearson had run his leadership campaign without leaving Ottawa. He had taken rooms at the Chateau Laurier Hotel, met key delegates and exchanged confidences without ever actually giving the impression that he was campaigning. Paul Martin, his only serious rival, was criticized at the time for boldly turning up at the Ottawa railway station to shake the hands of arriving dignitaries. The convention itself was held in the Ottawa Coliseum, still fragrant from a recent livestock show and decorated for the occasion with bunting and large portrait-studio blow-ups of Laurier, St Laurent and King. It was a low-key spectacle, where backrooms and senators still counted and the only touch of colour was provided by a few University of Toronto students in sober business suits and pearly girls in cashmere sweaters shouting "Hurrah for Mike!" Television coverage was subdued and limited mainly to Pearson's acceptance speech delivered after his easy first-ballot win.

But the convention in 1968 was a very different occasion. The senators were still moving imperiously through the convention proceedings in Ottawa's vast new Civic Centre but they seemed somehow irrelevant to the action. The delegates were mostly big-city contemporaries with decisive jaws and narrow lapels, their women mod-ishly chic beside them. But what really changed the environment was the importance given to television. The candidates, bathed in the beams of hand-held klieg lights, seemed larger than life, their faces taking on that incandescent glow which can transform modern politicians into stars or snuff out their careers in one ninety-second take.

Because television screens can accommodate only one image at a time and tend to give all events equal significance, Trudeau stood to gain most from the TV coverage. From the moment he entered the race, the managers of the electronic media made an instinctive decision that he would be the winner, and their message was not lost on the delegates.

Throughout the convention eight camera crews clustered about the Justice Minister, ignoring most of the other candidates much of the time, giving Trudeau the advantage of built-in excitement and bathing him in a constant halo of artificial light.

TRUDEAU IN TURN WAS ABLE TO PROVIDE the cameras with two vital elements, the magic of his television presence and some important dramatic action:

The first plot twist comes on the morning of Wednesday, April 3, the day most delegates are arriving in Ottawa, when Mitchell Sharp folds up his own campaign and declares for the Justice Minister.* This sudden switch not only transfers a group of extra delegates (as well as three ministers) to Trudeau, it also adds to the Justice Minister's candidacy an aura of solid strength and legitimacy.† Now he has at his side an accredited member of the Liberal Establishment whose redheaded presence acts as a talisman of responsibility, quieting the fears of cautious delegates afraid to gamble on an unorthodox man. Equally important, the Trudeau organization is strengthened by its merger with the smooth and efficient Sharp convention team. Sharp makes it clear that no deals had been offered to him nor had he asked for any. "I am backing Mr Trudeau not because I think he's going to win," he says, "but because I *want* him to win."

The publicity given to Trudeau's impressive delegate commitments now begins to have a self-generating effect. There are few political tricks

*The previous Sunday, Mike McCabe, Sharp's campaign manager, had counted the delegates committed to the Finance Minister and arrived at a figure of only 275 – not enough to generate second-ballot support. To test the loyalty of these delegates, McCabe hired a Toronto polling organization to do a quick telephone check on how they really intended to vote. By Monday night he had his answer: many of them liked Sharp but intended to vote for Trudeau; if he ran, the Finance Minister would be humiliated, probably running sixth on the first ballot. By Tuesday noon Sharp and his senior advisers had decided to withdraw in Trudeau's favour. In the early afternoon the Finance Minister informed Pearson, who approved the move. Late that evening Sharp telephoned Trudeau in Montreal with his decision.
†Industry Minister Bud Drury, National Revenue Minister Jean Chrétien and Energy Minister Jean-Luc Pépin switched with Sharp to Trudeau. Senator John Connolly, a Minister without Portfolio, went to Robert Winters. Walter Gordon came out for Trudeau.

more difficult than prying delegates loose from a man who looks as though he has the nomination virtually won. For a delegate to stick with a loser for ideological or personal reasons is an honourable, soul-stirring decision. But few can contemplate the possibility of going from a winner to a loser and for that reason, if no other, the Trudeau commitments hold and multiply despite the blandishments of the other candidates. The Trudeau organization takes advantage of the situation by gradually shifting its emphasis from the wooing of individual delegates to persuading the workers who surround each major candidate that Trudeau should become their option after their own man is lopped off.

The emotional impact the Justice Minister has been generating for weeks is demonstrated once more Wednesday afternoon when Trudeau arrives in Ottawa by train. Teen-age girls throw wedding rice, wave valentines, squeal in delight as he comes near them. The crowds burst the police barriers, gasping for the sight of him. "Something happens to people's faces when they see Trudeau," Ron Haggart writes in the *Toronto Daily Star*. "You can manufacture noise and screaming kids, but you cannot manufacture that excitement in the eyes, that glistening look of rapturous excitement which is on the faces Trudeau now sees when he makes his little speeches, saying nothing, in the hotel ballrooms where the delegates gather to see him. It is not madness, not in these excited matrons and lawyers. It is belief. It is belief, perhaps at this stage only shallow belief in one man's shy appeal, but it is belief, too, that an interesting and uniquely intermingled Canadian society produced this man."

Later in the evening at a jammed dance in the Chaudière Golf and Country Club, near Ottawa, Joey Smallwood elbows his way to the bandstand, declares for Trudeau and with characteristic hyperbole boasts: "Pierre is better than medicare – the lame have only to touch his garments to walk again."

The other candidates are still behaving as though the Trudeau phenomenon may vanish if only they ignore it manfully enough. The only one who openly defies the coalition formed through the Sharp declaration for Trudeau is John Turner. Standing before his cheering supporters at a pre-opening party held in the ballroom of the Skyline Hotel, he denounces "the Liberal Establishment" and "backstage deals" that are "taking away the democratic character of the convention."

THE FOLLOWING MORNING (THURSDAY, APRIL 4) delegates in hotels all over Ottawa read with their breakfast coffee a warm editorial endorsement of Trudeau in the *Globe and Mail* and then set out for the

Civic Centre in the rain to watch the candidates arrive for the convention's opening session.

First Paul Hellyer's troops goose-step into the arena, band blaring a march tune, red-and-white straw hats waving in time; then comes John Turner looking resolutely confident, surrounded by stomping, cheering, big-wheel-on-campus, middle-aged young; Paul Martin slides by, raising his arms in premature victory salutes, calling out thirty first-name greetings a minute; Bob Winters waltzes down the aisle to the strains of *Walking in a Winter Wonderland.* All these carefully planned demonstrations are suddenly made to look old-fashioned and contrived when Trudeau, as Frank Walker, editor of the *Montreal Star*, puts it, "creeps in like Jesus Christ," slipping unheralded into his seat followed only by a few homemade banners and some very young and pretty girls.

The crowd rises and roars at the sight of him and the other contenders grow rigid with nerves. They cluster with their advisers, trying to divine the source of Trudeau's political magic, suspicious that he has some special trick that can be mastered. They send emissaries to observe him, talk to him, touch him. But the couriers come back as puzzled as ever, variously reporting that it must be his looks, or his youth, his money, his suspected radicalism, or maybe his reputation as an intellectual. But Turner is younger, Winters handsomer, Kierans more radical, Hellyer richer and Martin has more degrees.

Still Trudeau goes serenely on, maintaining his inner repose, refusing to dissolve his personality or lend himself to the gravitational pull of the convention. And the more he holds back, the more the crowd wants a piece of him. "I made him get a haircut!" boasts an excited assistant. "What if I faint when he comes by?" a vibrating young matron asks her husband. He gives her a look of sheer disgust but when Trudeau appears his eyes turn moist and he impulsively hugs his wife.

It's as though Trudeau is performing what Norman Mailer once described as "the indispensable psychic act of a leader, who takes national anxieties so long buried and releases them to the surface where they belong." This is the mystery that makes him the source of such fascination, the trick that professionals can't duplicate.

In Trudeau's offhand statements ("What we need are new guys and new ideas"), in his very presence, the delegates think they recognize that Canada under his leadership would no longer be a tired nation clinging to the past, fearful of change. He seems to hold out the promise that the process of discovering Canada has not come to an end, that Expo 67 wasn't just a momentary phenomenon, that this is a young nation with vast, unexploited possibilities. He personifies the hoped-for sophistication of the perfectly bicultural Canada of tomorrow. Not only

461

is he flawlessly fluent in both English and French, but his manner combines Gallic touches that come out in his shrugs, with something of the phlegm of the British upper class, the unflappability that once built an empire.

Trudeau's grace and gaiety are on public display that afternoon at a series of policy workshops. During his first appearance, the platoon of television technicians and newspaper photographers following his every move block the view of the delegates. Finally, an exasperated delegate stands up and yells, "Down in front!" Trudeau instantly asks, "How far in front?" quizzically implying that they want *him* to sit down. It's a small joke but it relaxes the audience, persuades the photographers to move back and wins a round of applause.

At another workshop, in presenting his views on the constitution Trudeau explains that Daniel Johnson must oppose Ottawa because he is under pressure from the separatists.

"So are you," shouts a delegate.

"No, you're not very well informed," Trudeau replies.

"Yes, you are," the heckler persists.

"So's your old man," Trudeau snaps back.

The other candidates' presentations at the workshops are not so much ineffectual as predictable. Paul Hellyer promises it will take less time to get to airports if he's elected prime minister; John Turner pledges that his government would sponsor hot-line radio programs; Paul Martin boasts that he is being supported by the second youngest M.P. in the Commons; Robert Winters talks about pollution and says that governments can't legislate bilingualism since "the reality is going to come from commercial and industrial Canada."

By Thursday evening it's obvious that Trudeau will be out in front on the first ballot. But Martin, Hellyer and Winters still think there is some way to control the convention if only they can negotiate a coalition among themselves. Their difficulty is that each of them is convinced he is in second place and wants the others to join *him*. No formal agreement is reached but there is a loose understanding that the two trailing candidates will back whoever clearly holds down second place.

ALL DAY FRIDAY TRUDEAU CONTINUES to divide and conquer. While the other candidates generously dispense food and liquor in their hospitality rooms to all comers, the Justice Minister rushes through the day, holding a working breakfast for delegates quartered at the Talisman Motor Hotel; meeting a group of farmers in the West Block; entertaining women delegates and delegates' wives at a noontime sherry-and-roses party in the National Library.* The stock of 40,000 Trudeau buttons runs out and 10,000 more are ordered. (Only hours after Winters' organization issues green buttons that read "IT'S WINTERSTIME," the Trudeau girls have designed attractive tags that proclaim "IT'S SPRING!")

All the candidates spend the day pursuing delegates, trying to sew up support, building up to the scheduled main event – the speech each of them must make to the assembled convention that evening. Trudeau's assistants move into the Civic Centre in mid afternoon and conduct a "total simulation" exercise to test the arena's acoustics, adjust the microphones to Trudeau's height, and run through his text, marking it up with timing pauses to ensure maximum impact.

The evening proceedings begin with Paul Martin marching toward the stage at the head of an enormous bugle-corps band. An old pro to the end, he betrays no lack of confidence. His speech is a mixture of on-stage politics, off-stage bunkum, high-minded inanities, partisan ploys and unctuous compliments. His clichés blow up like bubbles, getting thinner and thinner, vanishing before anyone can discover what, if anything, they mean. He equates the U S. civil rights movement with the aspirations of French Canada and makes it all sound uninteresting and uninvolving though not entirely illogical. He keeps stressing his experience and says that he offers the best of everything. He delivers a "do-not-reject-this man" speech about himself, while his aides circulate a press release claiming a final count for him of 525 first-ballot delegates. "Democracy," he concludes, "is not a system where truths are implemented by philosopher-kings."

NEXT UP IS BOB WINTERS, handsome, confident, a little touch of Back Bay Boston in his voice. He pays tribute to Pearson (though the two men have hardly spoken for a year) in a manner that implies the departing prime minister should feel himself honoured by the gesture. He makes a few remarks in pre-Berlitz French. The total effect is that of a board chairman delivering his annual report – a rundown of Canada's assets – our fisheries, forests and wheat fields. "Already we have the

*Each of these events seemed like a casual happening. But Trudeau's organization planned them to the last minute detail. For an example, see Appendix L, which is a section from the Trudeau convention manual setting up the Talisman breakfast.

second highest living standard in the world. But we can be first!" He comes across as a cartoon capitalist, actually saying, "We can win the war on poverty by making the poor richer," then proposing to do so by "keeping the economy on an even keel." He ends with the ringing declaration that only mediocrity is satisfied with itself. Bob Winters is the most satisfied man in the hall.

THE MOOD CHANGES ABRUPTLY as Joe Greene ambles up to the stand, picks up a hand microphone and delivers, without a text, the best speech of the evening. His language is reminiscent of a waterfall with sunlight coming through it – beautiful, but as much froth as substance. He does the old meeting hall trick of making a statement, then asking his audience: "Do any of you agree with that?" and gets a good response. This is a decent man, the Alvin Hamilton of the Liberal Party. He praises the farmers, talks about the need for a grassroots political structure, wipes his brow country-style, goes back to his seat and hugs his kids.

PAUL HELLYER STRIDES UP, looking like an automated reproduction of himself. His cheering section is led by Judy LaMarsh in a pair of knee-high boots and ninety-year-old Senator Arthur Roebuck in a wing collar, both incongruously waving white boaters. Hellyer's speech is delivered in the tone of a United Chuch steward reading the collection plate receipts. It is jammed with such pork-barrel promises as: "A fairer application of anti-dumping laws to take into account seasonal average prices for fruits and vegetables in the United States, and not just end-of-season prices." His aides later estimate that his performance has cost him at least 150 delegate votes.

THEN THE BAGPIPES WAIL and Allan MacEachen comes on, looking hot and nervous, constantly examining his watch in a manner uncomfortably like that of the sweating PR man in the old Humphrey Bogart film, *The Barefoot Contessa*. He has a strong voice but he is too heavy for television and makes a poor speech. This is the authentic voice of the party's left wing ("I don't want the Liberals to become a second Conservative Party – that's the way to oblivion"), giving the most strongly felt and easily the most boring speech of the evening.

ERIC KIERANS TAKES HIS TURN, preceded by lively cheerleaders and the engineering students' band from Queen's University. The music is ragged and loud; they're playing the Irish Fighting Song and they mean it. Kierans can't control his kids, so he laughs at them, and they laugh back. He comes on as he is: an intelligent, impassioned and good man. He asks the delegates to vote with their consciences and then describes exactly where he stands on all the seminal issues. He points out that we live in a brutal, mechanistic, materialistic age. He praises gentleness and says "we must bend all our policies to preserve the gentleness that is in our society."

He is one of those rare Canadian politicians who is a convincing and convinced nationalist without being anti-American. He promises courage. It is a quality that he has to spare and the audience is a little embarrassed in its recognition of it.

NOW THE SIEGE OF PHOTOGRAPHERS, REPORTERS AND TV MEN around his box lifts briefly to allow Pierre Trudeau an entrance. As if pulled by a single string, Trudeau signs are silently lifted in every part of the crowded arena.* The delegates, instead of applauding, let out a collective "AAAHH," like the salute to a daring high-wire trapeze artist doing his star turn. Although the demonstration has been carefully planned, it *looks* spontaneous, as though the Liberal Party has reached its pro-Trudeau consensus at this exact moment. Trudeau waits in the stands for precisely five minutes, then moves toward the platform.† It is not a great speech, but the delegates listen in awed silence. He talks about a "just society," about strife in the world, Canada's internal divisions, about each man's share of the eternal burden. "As Liberals,"

---

*At the suggestion of Trudeau himself, the banners were strategically placed throughout the Civic Centre and passed out by hard-core Trudeau supporters at widely spaced intervals. Robert Kaplan (later the Liberal M.P. for Don Valley) opened fire-escape doors before the speeches started to allow into the hall those Trudeau enthusiasts who couldn't get entrance passes. Had the demonstration *not* succeeded a recording of *Vive La Canadienne* was ready to be played over the Centre's sound system, to accompany Trudeau to the stage.

†Each candidate had been allotted thirty minutes. Trudeau's speech was the shortest (nineteen minutes), allowing a build-up beforehand and a six-minute "spontaneous" demonstration at its conclusion. The other candidates used up their time speaking and had their reception cut off by the gavel of the chairman enforcing the time limit.

he says, "we rely on that most unlikely bulwark against chaos – you and me, the individual citizen, the young and the old, the famous and the unknown, the Arctic nomad and the suburbanite." He confirms his belief in the triumph of reason over passion in politics: "For many years I have been fighting for the protection of individual freedoms against the tyranny of the group, and for a just distribution of our national wealth. It was my concern with these values which led me to the Liberal Party. We are no longer satisfied with vague generalizations or adroit evasions. Those who resort to them betray a lack of confidence in democracy and in the judgement of the people," he continues. This is the sober, not the witty Pierre, softly blowing his own horn and at the end of his speech he stands there, smiling, in his rounded Edwardian collar, a daffodil in his buttonhole.

LAST UP, SENTENCED TO ANTI-CLIMAX, is John Turner, who makes a tough, gutsy speech – the toughest and gutsiest in a deliberately bland career. "I'm not just in this race so you will remember my name at some future date," he says. "I'm not here now for some next time; I'm not bidding now for your consideration at some vague convention in 1984 perhaps when I've mellowed a bit. My time is now, and now is not the time for mellow men."

HOLY KINGSMERE! ON SATURDAY MORNING, Edna Poole, an Ottawa grandmother who was once Mackenzie King's favourite spiritualist, announces she has "a terrific feeling" Trudeau will win the leadership. The Justice Minister's campaign newspaper, its cover decorated with a poetic line-drawing of Trudeau by Harold Town, claims that seven ministers and thirty-three M.P.'s now support his candidacy. Arieh Eshel, the Israeli ambassador to Canada, telephones Trudeau headquarters to ask what the new PM's policy will be on the Middle East situation. Trudeau's delegate logistic data centre gives its final reading at 7 a.m.: 702 votes on the first ballot. Two hundred Trudeau workers converge on the Civic Centre, carrying computer-tabulated lists separated according to voting machines. They are linked by telephones, walkie-talkies and short-wave radios. A secondary communications system, the legacy of Mitchell Sharp's defunct campaign, is standing by in case of sabotage.

The balloting begins at 1:45. Paul Hellyer, who is getting his own computer "readouts" every two hours, is told he'll have 562 votes on the first count. Fourteen hundred telephones have been installed in the building, and nearly all of them are in use as workers relay last-minute instructions. Young girls wearing Trudeau's Buddhist-orange mini-skirts, with faces like flowers and shapes like fence pickets, are being fondled by a thousand eyes. "They're learning about politics," somebody explains. A burly Scot from Nova Scotia's Pictou County parades gravely around the corridors, kilt swirling, bearing a banner with the strange device: ALLAN MACEACHEN – CHEF DE FILE. The Turner boys turn up in construction helmets, as if expecting the heavy artillery of the establishment to rain down on them.

"Anybody who dropped turds on the party two years ago and then expects to lead it will never get my vote," Judy LaMarsh confides to Val Sears of the *Toronto Daily Star*. Walter Gordon, sitting in the Trudeau box, says: "I've come all this way, I might as well vote," and goes to do so.

Trudeau reaches over, grabs a grape from Jean Marchand, throws it up in the air and catches it in his mouth. A TV producer who misses the performance asks for a repeat, sticks a microphone into Trudeau's face, and says: "Could we hear the crunch, please?" Lester Pearson jokes that he is wearing a Trudeau button under his lapel and calculates the Justice Minister will get seven hundred votes on the first count. Mike McCabe, the Sharp man, predicts that Trudeau will start with 750 votes. He is almost dead on. The first-ballot result is announced by Senator John Nichol: Trudeau, 752; Hellyer, 330; Winters, 293; Turner, 277; Martin, 277; Greene, 169; MacEachen, 165; Kierans, 103; Henderson, 0.*

Kierans quietly withdraws and Paul Martin, with a grace and courage few expected, follows. The low Martin score is the surprise of the first vote. As his abdication is announced, Maurice Sauvé sprints for the Trudeau box. Eddie Rubin nudges Trudeau and whispers, "Clap!" Trudeau moves his hands mechanically, pins a button on Sauvé and later walks over to shake Martin's hand. "We Liberals," Martin says, "whether we run against one another for party office, we always stick together." Martin and Kierans release their delegates without naming their preferences, but MacEachen joins Trudeau. The Scot from Pictou County, kilt flying, jumps up and down, yelling "Go, Pierre, Go!" Hellyer struggles through the pandemonium of the convention floor toward Turner and advises him obscurely: "Fight the Establish-

---

*Lloyd Henderson, a Presbyterian minister and former mayor of Portage la Prairie, Manitoba, obtained the required fifty signatures to get his name on the ballot but he was not a voting delegate.

ment, John!" The second ballot is counted: Trudeau, 964; Winters, 473; Hellyer, 465; Turner, 347; Greene, 104; MacEachen, 11.*

The Winters surge is suddenly on. It looks as though Trudeau may be stopped after all. This is exactly the kind of situation the anti-Trudeau coalition has been set up to exploit. Now Robert Winters tries to set the agreement in motion by approaching Hellyer.

"Is there anything we should do, Paul?" he asks.

"Well, I think we have to . . . I don't know. I really don't know what we should do."

"Do you want to think about it and talk some more?"

"Might do."

"All right, I'll be available."

Judy LaMarsh huddles with Hellyer, pleading with him to come out for Winters: "He's all right. You know him, Paul, and he knows you. You're all right with him. It's tough, but what the hell's the point of going down and letting that bastard be there. Come on, Paul, you're forty-four and we've still got lots of time."

But Hellyer, still unable to believe that his computers are wrong, refuses to budge. He turns to the rows of his supporters behind him and starts yelling: "Fight! Fight! Fight!"

Joe Potts, a Hellyer booster with a voice like a moose call and inextinguishable optimism, now proposes an ingenious – if naive – compromise. Winters should flip a coin and if he loses, join Hellyer against Trudeau. But Winters is doubtful: "I'm a front-runner. People would say I was nuts. I'm ahead. You can't stop when you're ahead."

"Only eight votes . . . it couldn't matter less now."

"I know, but there's psychology in this . . . "

"There's a whole damned election for Trudeau in it."

"Now, Joe, if you were advising me, you'd advise me to stay in."

"I would like hell . . . I would like hell . . . "

As voting on the third ballot begins, Trudeau is noticed reading notes from a piece of paper. "Is it your acceptance speech?" asks an excited reporter. "No," he whispers back. "It's a love letter." He seems to be paying little attention to the convention's tumult, withdrawing into himself, becoming remote from the crowd. The next ballot is announced: Trudeau, 1,051; Winters, 621; Hellyer, 377; Turner, 279; Greene, 29.

Greene joins Trudeau and Hellyer rushes over to the Winters stands shrieking: "GO, BOB, GO! BEAT THE ESTABLISHMENT! LET'S

*MacEachen's withdrawal notice reached Senator Nichol too late and his name was included on the second ballot.

HAVE A LIBERAL LEAD THE PARTY!" Winters and Hellyer search out Turner. Having pledged that he would make no deals, the young minister informs them he's staying in. Most of the Hellyer supporters put on Winters buttons, but Keith Davey leads about seventy-five Hellyer delegates to Trudeau. Now the party is polarized between Winters and Trudeau. Suddenly scared, the Trudeau workers, led by Bryce Mackasey, swarm out, applying pressure to the delegates. The arena erupts into a frenzy of excitement. Bud Drury, that well-known swinger from Westmount, is standing behind Trudeau, leading the cheers: "Gimme a 'T' . . . Gimme an 'R' . . . " Mike McCabe tells a friend, "If Trudeau doesn't win, the entrails of the Liberal Party will be left all over this hall." Mrs Pearson is restrained from rushing onto the convention floor to wave a Trudeau banner.

As the fourth-ballot results are being read, the chant "TRU – DEAU, CANA – DA!" deafens the hall. Trudeau has 1,203 ballots; Winters, 954; Turner, 195.

It's over.

Lester Pearson rises from his seat, freed of power at last. A wedge of policemen arrive to escort the winner on stage. Pierre Elliott Trudeau's face, which might have been carved in alabaster to commemorate some distant war of the Crusades, closes in mask-like as he walks into the future, burdened with hope.

Appendices

Chronology

Acknowledgements

Appendix A

The following private memorandum was written to Lester Pearson by Paul Hellyer after his return to Ottawa from the North Atlantic Treaty Organization Parliamentary Conference held in Paris, November 8-20, 1962. It became the main document on which the Liberal Leader based his party's dramatic switch in policy on Canada's acquisition of nuclear warheads.

When Hellyer visited Canadian troops in Western Europe he found their morale at the breaking point because they were being asked to man weapons systems without the nuclear warheads that made them effective. At the political level, Hellyer was told, it would be only a matter of weeks before the North Atlantic Council formally took note of the Canadian government's unwillingness to discharge its commitments. The military information in the memo was based on a private, ninety-minute briefing Hellyer was given on November 14 by General Lauris Norstad, the NATO Supreme Commander, in which he convinced the Canadian politician of his country's defaulted responsibilities.

Pearson checked the facts in the Hellyer memo with his own contacts at NATO by trans-Atlantic telephone and on January 23, 1963, made the Scarborough, Ontario, speech that committed the Liberal Party to the acquisition of nuclear warheads — a stand that eventually brought about the downfall of the Diefenbaker Government and led to the 1963 general election.

MEMORANDUM TO: The Honourable L. B. Pearson

NATO Strategy

The official U.S. view is that the conventional power of NATO in Europe should be increased. This is consistent with their abandonment of the theory of massive retaliation and with the published views of General Maxwell Taylor. A greater conventional capacity permits a doctrine of "measured choice" and thereby minimizes the risk of nuclear incineration.

From the military standpoint all members are being urged to accept

473

the recommended force goals for 1966. If goals are reached, NATO will have 30 – 33 divisions in being in Europe. The chance of reaching this goal is very slim indeed but member countries will be under increasing pressure to produce. (Unless the goals are fully met we are subjecting ourselves to unnecessary risk in the process of this defence – Norstad.)

NATO has now adopted a forward strategy which has been a goal from the outset but which has been unrealistic until now. It involves moving forward to defend all NATO territory rather than retiring to predetermined lines. This plan involves some risk. It is felt that from a morale standpoint a forward strategy is desirable and that the availability of stronger forces now makes the step possible as well. To minimize the risk and maximize the effectiveness of a forward strategy it is imperative that the 1966 force goals be met in full. So far the U.S.A. is the only country which has met its commitments in full. We have said that Canada, too, has met its commitments but according to the military people at SHAPE, we have not.

The Canadian Commitment

GROUND FORCES – We have committed one division. As far as I know we have never accepted the NATO definition of a division. It is two mechanized infantry brigades and one armoured brigade. Our interpretation has been two brigade groups consisting of three infantry battalions, an armoured regiment, a reconnaissance squadron, an artillery regiment, a surface to surface missile battery, an engineer squadron, a signals squadron and supporting "service" units for each.

Of this "division" we have agreed to keep one third in Europe and the remainder in reserve in Canada for use in an emergency. Our brigade in Europe is considered first rate. The professional soldiers are amongst the best in the alliance and set a high standard in their training and capability. Most of their equipment is considered satisfactory. Much of it is getting old, however, and soon will have to be replaced. For example, the small radio sets carried by soldiers in the field are old, unreliable and forever breaking down. They could use heavy helicopters, light aircraft, etc., which they do not have but these deficiencies are not considered critical. The critical deficiency is an armoured personnel carrier. The development of the Bobcat has been delayed and its supply to the brigade is long overdue. Present mobility is confined to wheeled vehicles which can only operate successfully on roads. The brigade does not have, and desperately needs, the capacity to take to the fields. An armoured personnel carrier is the most serious deficiency of the brigade group at this time. Stores and supplies fairly well meet the minimum requirements laid down by SACEUR.

The reserve part of our commitment is largely a "paper" reserve. Not only have we not accepted the NATO definition of a division, we do not have the equipment necessary for our version.

We do have the men to man another brigade but not the heavy equipment they would require to "go active." Consequently the time required to field our reserve is so great that it would most likely not be available to SACEUR in time to be useful in the event of hostilities.

The remedy suggested by SACEUR is as follows. The heavy equipment and supplies required for the reserve should be stockpiled in appropriate places in Europe so that in time of crisis the soldiers could be moved "as an airline passenger carrying with him little more than his hat, his rifle, and 20 kilos of baggage." The United States is doing this in respect to its reserve commitments and with satisfactory results. Seconded airline capacity lifted soldiers from Fort Lewis in the State of Washington to Frankfurt, Germany, in ten and one half hours during an exercise last February. The NATO conference passed a resolution recommending this policy to the governments of other members of the alliance. In order for Canada to implement this policy, it would be necessary, of course, to acquire quite a bit of new hardware.

THE AIR DIVISION – Our air division presently consists of eight (8) squadrons of day fighters and four (4) squadrons of all-weather interceptors stationed at four (4) wings – two located in Germany and two in France. In 1958, we (Canada) undertook to replace the eight (8) squadrons of F-86's with CF-104's and to undertake the strike attack role. This role consists of forward reconnaissance with an atomic capability to deal with special targets. It is considered an essential role particularly for the next five years until the question of medium-range ballistic missiles and possible NATO control of such a force is decided and acted on. SACEUR feels that a strike attack capability adds greatly to the credibility of the defence and particularly in the case of a situation where reference to all-out war would not be taken seriously. We also promised to maintain the four (4) all-weather fighter squadrons until the planes wore out and this has been done. They will be retired from service at the year end and not replaced. The eight (8) strike attack squadrons will operate from four bases with a reduced number of planes (eighteen) in each squadron. SACEUR has agreed to this because the CF-104 is a very sophisticated aircraft and requires greater maintenance and other facilities than the present squadrons.

ARMAMENT – The CF-104 is designed to carry atomic bombs. The first squadron at No. 3 Wing (Zweibrucken) will be flying in December and ready to go active at the end of April. The other squadrons will be equipped within twelve (12) months after that. The infrastructure required to accommodate the CF-104 has been given the highest NATO priority and is now underway. Runways are being extended and storage facilities built. I am advised that it takes six months from the time a bi-lateral agreement is signed to work out the necessary details including supply of the weapons and training required to handle them. Working back six months from April 30th, makes the decision critical November 1st, 1962, which is now past. The military people at SHAPE are very concerned about the indecision of the Canadian government. So far (when we were in Paris) they have not reported to the Council in a way which will bring the matter into the international political arena. If a decision is not reached, it will not be long before they will consider such a report unavoidable.

ALTERNATIVES – It was my opinion that the arming of the Honest John rocket while it is considered desirable is not absolutely essential in order for the brigade to continue to play an important role. The question of the air division is a different matter. If it is not armed with nuclear bombs, the consequences are far-reaching. SACEUR is counting on this capacity. If we do not fulfil our commitment, there will be intense pressure on us to withdraw and turn the facilities over to others. Our influence in NATO will be reduced to negligible. There is no question but that we could have adopted a non-nuclear role four years ago and still have made a real contribution to the total effort. To make that choice now, however, for immediate implementation would involve a very great disruption and immediate expenditure of hundreds of millions of dollars on new equipment. It would be a decision of such magnitude that I do not believe it practicable.

PROLIFERATION OF ATOMIC WEAPONS – The signing by Canada of a bi-lateral agreement with the United States and the acceptance by us of atomic devices is not, in fact, proliferation of control. The weapons would still be under the control of the United States and this is logical in view of the fact that they have the ultimate responsibility in any event. We would only be joining those of our allies who have already joined in similar arrangements. Italy, Greece, Turkey, Holland, England, Germany, Belgium, Denmark and Norway have already signed agreements. Not all of these countries actually have the weapons on their soil but the majority do.

DANGER TO PEACE AND DISARMAMENT – In my opinion acceptance by Canada of its responsibility would not in any way increase the possibility of hostilities. On the contrary to the extent that we contribute to a greater collective strength in Europe we would be increasing the likelihood of peace and the chances of success in negotiation. As far as disarmament is concerned the more we have to throw on the table the greater the likelihood of success. The weaker we are in Europe, the less likely the Soviets are to redress the balance through disarmament. Agreement is only possible if it is in the interests of both parties and not likely to disturb the status quo.

NORAD

If we decide to fulfil those commitments which we have undertaken in NATO, I cannot see why we should not do the same in NORAD. The one agreement would permit both. I have not changed my opinion about the usefulness of the Bomarc missile, but if there is one thing that is more useless than an armed Bomarc it is an unarmed Bomarc. Similarly, I cannot see the logic of surveillance by planes which, if they did discover an enemy attack, would be helpless except to warn the United States. Surely we have not withdrawn from collective responsibility to the point where we would only clutter up the skies and impede our friends in their task.

Economic Consequences

These are considerable. If we don't fulfil our agreements the Americans are almost certain to reduce or terminate their production sharing arrangements with us. This case is discussed at some length in *The Financial Post*, December 1st, 1962, "Now we pay the Piper for our Defence Tune."

Political Consequences

The great majority of the Canadian people would want their country to fulfil its obligations. We are on sound ground in the fact that we have consistently recommended a different course at a time when a different choice was feasible. Now, however, our choice is limited by the circumstances. Furthermore, we are not bound by the present circumstances for all time. If we wished to play a different role this could be negotiated and implemented over a period of years in a responsible way. Now, however, we must uphold the honour and integrity of our word as a nation.

Recommendation

In view of all the circumstances, particularly the fact that we as a nation have undertaken, of our own free will, certain commitments which we are now expected to fulfil, and the implementation of which is now a critical necessity in the alliance of which we are a part, I recommend that the Liberal Party state categorically that Canada should sign a bi-lateral agreement with the United States and fulfil its commitments forthwith.

PAUL T. HELLYER

Appendix B

A puzzle of the Pearson style of governing was the extent to which members of the parliamentary caucus continued their unquestioning support of the Liberal Leader, despite his government's many pratfalls. One explanation of the basis for this unwavering loyalty was advanced in a letter to the author from John R. Matheson, Member of Parliament for Leeds and parliamentary secretary to the Prime Minister.

Ottawa
September 16, 1966

Dear Peter:

The other day you asked for an explanation of the almost mystical attachment of Liberal Members to our Leader. Pearson is one of those rare persons possessed of an authority over others. If you get close enough you are committed. As my wife puts it: "He glows."

This attachment is not physical, although he carries the natural attraction of the athlete. His earthiness would delight Abraham Lincoln. His reactions are instinctive, even in spleen he puts you at ease. He is immensely human.

Nor is this attachment intellectual, although most of us are sympathetic with Pearson's views which tend to be objective, long range, generous. He is a man without frontiers. He is unchained and his outreach is oftentimes exciting to behold. He takes us on voyages. Like T. E. Lawrence he could never bore.

This attachment of which you spoke is spiritual – the authority of goodness. Avoiding piety, freely acknowledging his imperfections, he walks towards light. His caucus is a band of happy warriors differing on means but never on ends. In spite of the stress of politics, Pearson retains the blithe spirit of the boy who soldiered in the desert, the Dardanelles, the Royal Flying Corps. He is the most courageous man I know.

Favoured always with popularity, he matured as few men to recognize popularity as cheap coin and no substitute for excellence. In his abundant caring for others he, developed the habit of self denial. In a selfish society he stands as a man apart. Without pretension he has allowed himself to become an instrument of Providence. When he says "come" there is no choice. We know all the failures resulting from his lack of worldliness and pride. They do not matter.

I know these are the views of many others.

Sincerely yours,

JOHN R. MATHESON

Appendix C

*The following memorandum, written by Davie Fulton to John Diefenbaker,
compared the Favreau constitutional patriation formula with the procedure
originally worked out by the Conservative administration.*

October 26, 1964
322 Seymour St.
Kamloops, B.C.

MEMORANDUM RE: CONSTITUTIONAL AMENDMENT FORMULA

I have read the draft bill attached to the Federal Provincial Conference
communique of October 16, 1964, and have carefully compared that
proposal with the one we worked out and submitted for approval by the
Provinces in a draft dated November 6, 1961. In this memo I shall designate
them the 1964 proposal and the 1961 proposal respectively.

This comparison establishes that the 1964 proposal, with the exception
of Clauses 6, 7 and 8 thereof, Clause 12 thereof, and Part III thereof (and
except for minor textual amendments which do not alter the effect), is
precisely similar to the 1961 proposal.

Clauses 6, 7 and 8, Clause 12, and Part III of the 1964 proposal are
new; none of them were contained in the 1961 proposal. The important
question is therefore whether these additions make such changes in effect
that the 1961 proposal as a whole is substantially altered. I shall examine
these provisions separately.

1. *Clause 6*

Clause 6 of the 1964 proposal, while it is a substantial addition to the
1961 proposal, does not in my view alter the amending formula contained
therein. What it does is to place defined limits on the already existing power
of the Federal Parliament, under Sec. 91 (1) of the BNA Act, to amend the
Constitution in those aspects of purely Federal concern. As such, this does
not affect the formula for making amendments of joint concern worked out
and embodied in the 1961 proposal.

There may be some question whether the powers of the Federal Parliament hitherto contained in Sec. 91 (1) would be overly circumscribed by Clause 6. This is a question of policy which I have not had time to study fully, and on which therefore I express no opinion as yet, beyond saying that I do feel it has to be carefully considered. But the important points in the context of a comparison between the 1961 and 1964 proposals are the following:

a. Clause 6 does not create a new power of amendment but is rather an amendment or modification of an existing power of amendment;

b. It does not alter or modify the amending formula embodied in the 1961 proposal;

c. It does not transfer any head of legislative authority, as distinct from amending authority, from the Parliament of Canada to the Provincial legislatures;

d. What it does is to require a degree of Provincial consent not hitherto by written law required, for any amendment to this part of the Federal Constitution coming within the eight classes of exceptions therein specified. As far as I can determine, on the basis of the study I have so far given it, amendments coming within those exceptions would require to be approved by the legislatures of two thirds of the Provinces, under Clause 5 of the proposal. Amendments not within the exceptions could continue to be made by the Federal Parliament exclusively. Whether this is too great a circumscribing of the exclusive Federal power of amendment is the matter of policy requiring determination to which I have referred. It could be argued that an amendment falling within the exceptions would be of so fundamental a nature as to make a degree of Provincial consent a reasonable prerequisite.

2. *Clause 7*

Clause 7 of the 1964 proposal is also new in terms of the 1961 proposal, but does not alter or transfer either a present legislative power or a present amending power. In fact it does nothing more than re-enact present head 1 of Sec. 92 of the BNA Act.

3. *Clause 8*

Clause 8 of the 1964 proposal is new in terms of the 1961 proposal. It seems to me, however, on the basis of the study I have so far been able to give it, that it does not alter or affect the basic formula contained in the 1961 proposal, but is rather a clarification as to which of the amending processes contained therein is applicable to the various types of amendments which may be contemplated, and is made necessary by the inclusion in the 1964 proposal of new Clauses 6 and 7.

It has been suggested that the new Clause 8 puts all the heads of Sec. 91 of the BNA Act (other than head 1) under Clause 5 requiring the two-thirds plus 50% consent provision for amendment, and that this is different from the 1961 proposal. In my view this is not well founded. The 1961 proposal contained both Clause 1 and Clause 5 found in the 1964 proposal in identical form, and it is these two Clauses which have that result. Clause 8 merely clarifies the position in the light of the new Clauses 6 and 7.

(NOTE: It should be observed that the reason why this position was accepted by us, and reflected in the 1961 proposal, is because it is difficult if not impossible to see how any amendment to the other heads of Sec. 91 can be made which would not have the effect of transferring and/ or distributing the powers to or among the Provinces and it seems reasonable that such a far-reaching change should require the consent of a two-thirds majority to be effective.)

4. *Clause 12*

This Clause is also new but as it is entirely consequential upon the inclusion of Clauses 6 and 7 it has no effect beyond what they have and requires no further comment.

5. *Part III*

Part III is also new but does not in any way add to or alter the result of the 1961 proposal itself.

In summary, therefore, I would say the following:

a. The 1964 proposal differs from the 1961 proposal to the extent that it now includes Clauses 6, 7 and 8, Clause 12, and Part III, which are new.

b. These new provisions do not, however, alter in principle or effect the amending formula as embodied in the 1961 proposal.

c. Insofar as there is now incorporated by Clause 6 a new provision which limits the Federal power of amending the Constitution in those respects which are of exclusively Federal concern (which power was contained in Sec. 91 (1) BNA Act), by attempting to define the limits of what is of exclusively Federal concern, there is a new policy question for consideration: are the limits thus defined reasonable, or are they unduly restrictive? But this is a question which does not, it seems to me, affect the integrity of the remainder of the amending formula as contained in the 1961 proposal.

As to the delegation provisions, which are contained in Clause 13 of Part II of the 1964 proposal, these are absolutely identical with the delegation provisions which were contained in Clause 9 of Part II of the 1961 proposal, with the exception of a substitution only of two new expressions in the entire text, which do not in the slightest degree vary or alter the effect. (To be precise, the substitutions are, firstly, of the word "classes" for "heads" in one place, and of the words "coming within" for the words "that is otherwise within" in another.)

It is important to bear in mind that:

a. The delegation provisions are thus exactly as they were embodied in the 1961 proposal; and

b. That these provisions do not confer any new jurisdiction or power on the Provinces, nor do they have the effect of diminishing the Federal jurisdiction or power in the slightest.

They provide only the means by which reciprocal delegations of authority to exercise a power may be made. And such delegation of authority cannot be made by mere inter-governmental agreement nor by unilateral act of Provincial legislatures; it is expressly provided that there must be a legislative act of the Federal Parliament in every case.

E. Davie Fulton

Appendix D

This memorandum, written by Erik Nielsen, the M.P. from the Yukon, set out the reasoning behind John Diefenbaker's "One Canada" policy. It was rejected by the Conservative parliamentary caucus following a series of stormy sessions.

March 1, 1965

The opting-out formula cannot be considered apart from the general pattern of Liberal policies, the effect of which is to give political expression to the theory of "Two Nations."

Considered in abstract or academic terms, the theory of "Two Nations" can be tolerated as a descriptive reference relating to two cultures and two languages being accorded constitutional recognition in a single state.

When carried into the political field through the advancement of policies deliberately designed to give reality to a theoretical abstraction it means the end of the Federal system as we know it.

Had it not been for Confederation, there would be no French Canada today.

Had it not been for those, both French- and English-speaking, who fought to keep Canada free, united and independent, our fate would have been simply to become an annex of the United States.

This could have been the result in 1775, in 1812 and in 1849, when a movement for annexation was launched in Montreal.

There are more than 4,000,000 persons of French extraction in the United States today.

Of these less than 15 per cent have managed to preserve and keep alive their culture and language.

In Canada, of 6,000,000 French-speaking Canadians, the proportion is precisely the opposite.

The question is no longer one of survival.

And survival is no longer enough.

The question is whether French Canada shall be free to preserve and safe-guard its culture outside of Quebec; or whether that freedom shall be restricted to that province.

The policies of the Liberal Government, including "opting out," the throwing open of Federal powers, the pension plan, delegation, and the rest – are based on the assumption that French Canada is to be restricted to one province; and that that province is to be progressively set apart from the rest of Canada.

The effect of the policies, as a number of commentators, including Mr Pelletier in *La Presse*, have pointed out, is to progressively isolate Quebec.

Is Quebec to be regarded as something apart from Canada – something foreign – something to be treated as a depressed nation under some sort of domestic Colombo Plan – but not to be included in the mainstream of Canadian political life?

This is the effect of the Liberal policies – and this is something about which the people of Quebec must make their decision.

To those who believe in the dream of the Fathers of Confederation – One Canada – united from sea to sea, the prospect of the isolation and setting aside of one province tends to promote disunity and division, rather than that unity which is essential if we are to survive in freedom and independence.

I turn to the words of Winston Churchill – in a speech pronounced as long ago as 1938 – called "The Choice for Europe" – when he said this:

> But what is the purpose which has brought us all together? It is the conviction that the life of Britain, her glories and message to the world, can only be achieved by national unity and national unity can only be preserved upon a cause which is larger than the nation itself.

In Britain's case, the cause was the defence of civilization against tyranny and aggression; in Canada's it is the defence of our national structure, national identity and national sovereignty against powerful external pressures and internal divisions.

To do this we must remain strong, we must remain united.

We must have a central Government with the capacity to act; we must have a clear line of demarcation between Federal and provincial powers – without this, we are opening the door to chaos and confusion.

These issues are not new, nor are they peculiar to Canada.

They arose in the United States as early as 1830, based on no difference of culture or language but on the principle of States Rights, which the framers of our constitution wisely sought to avoid.

In 1832, South Carolina refused to accept Federal legislation on tariffs and the President of the United States, Andrew Jackson, issued a proclamation on Nullification which set out the principle of Federal Union in these words:

> I consider then, the power to annul a law of the United States, assumed by one state, incompatible with the existence of the Union, contradicted

expressly by the letter of the constitution, unauthorized by its spirit, inconsistent with every principle on which it was founded, and destructive of the great object for which it was formed.

It is noteworthy that he did not base himself exclusively on the constitution, which differs from ours, but to a great extent on the principle that such a procedure would be destructive of the Union.

Consent by the Federal Government to the principle makes it no less destructive in its application.

What is a constitution in a Federal State but the setting forth of the distribution of powers as between the Federal and provincial parts?

A constitution that does not do this is not a constitution; it is a pious hope.

An invertebrate constitution leads to an invertebrate national structure.

An invertebrate national structure leads to a loss of national identity and integrity and the absorption of our sovereignty.

This is the danger of the policies now being pursued by the Pearson Government.

You have one Pension Plan for Canada, another for Quebec.

There is nothing to say that within ten years, both plans may not have drifted apart through changes in rates of premiums and benefits, imposed by economic differences.

Anyone who doubts this need only to refer to Mr Kent's reply to that question before the committee. (He said there was no constitutional or legal obstacle to this.)

Opting out places a premium on non-participation in Federal programs.

Sums are levied upon the taxpayers of Canada by one Government and dispensed by another.

In certain fields, exclusively under provincial jurisdiction, such as education, this can be permitted; but it should not be erected into a general policy.

There is a simple test to be applied.

Should all provinces avail themselves of the provisions, in the same way as Québec, would there not be a weakening of national structure?

If only one province follows that course, the others abstaining, do we not set up, in fact, two entities, two nations, politically as well as culturally?

Whether we do it on the instalment plan or immediately, the end is the same.

I come to the constitution.

The Liberal program is all of a piece.

It is a program of legislation, designed to accomplish in steps that which could not be accomplished in a single act.

You cannot consider the parts separately.

Opting out, the constitution, the Pension Plan, the Two Flags, all tend in one direction.

I am not going to get into the argument about whether it is the same formula as in 1961.

This is disproved by the simple fact that it was not acceptable in 1961, because of Section 91 (1); and it became acceptable in 1964, when that section was removed.

That section would have retained for Parliament the right to exercise a final veto. That is gone, watered down to the point where Parliament becomes a bystander at the fragmentation of a nation.

But Parliament, if it does not voice its views in a decided and positive way, will not be an *innocent* bystander.

The simple fact about the constitution is that, under the guise of repatriation, we have produced an amended constitution — a new constitution — under which any four provinces can move into the fields of Federal jurisdiction, with the consent of Parliament.

Some will say, this will not happen.

If it is not intended to happen, why have it?

Certainly the constitution is subject to examination and subject to change.

But is it subject to changes that, at one stroke, remove the dividing line between what is Federal and what is provincial and throw the powers into the market place for the highest bidder, or the most powerful combination of forces?

Is it subject to changes that remove or reduce the powers of the Federal Government, while conferring those powers on all or some of the provinces?

Is Parliament silently to acquiesce?

Are we as a party to acquiesce in a policy of dismemberment?

You cannot give power to one without taking from the other.

Are you going to have a situation where some provinces have powers that others do not?

Where the Federal writ runs in some provinces and stops at the boundaries of others?

Is that a nation?

Or is it a loose conglomeration of semi-autonomous states?

Is that what the people want?

If it is not what the people want — and I am sure it is not — that party which tamely subscribes to what it knows is wrong will write its own epitaph in history.

Our job is to stand for Canada.

Pearson will not do it.

Our whole history as a party points to this stand.

It is a stand which our leader, by instinct, by conviction, by the record of his whole life, is compelled to take — without equivocation or illusion.

There are some who by compromise and acquiescence see the possibility of momentary popularity.

I say to them that there is not only one side to this question — even in Quebec.

Mr Faribault is on record against opting out.

One of the major parties in Quebec is prepared to wage a last-ditch stand against tampering with the constitution. Professor Morin is one of the authorities who believes that the changes will freeze the rights of French Canada for all time.

In the face of this, why follow the Liberals?

Mr Fulton has his own reasons for accepting the formula. He is personally identified with it in his own mind.

The Liberals are using his name less and less in that connection.

You can bet that if it goes through, it will be the Favreau Formula – not the Fulton Formula.

In Quebec, it is Mr Gérin-Lajoie who is recognized as the original author. (Claude Ryan, *Le Devoir*.)

There are some in this party who have consistently sought to accommodate the Liberals in these measures.

They are no doubt well meaning and sincere.

Do they think they will receive any credit for their attitude?

This has not historically been the case of those who proved to be followers, not of their own principles, but of the principles of others.

Surely if the conviction is that the policies advocated outside this party are policies to build a stronger, more united Canada, then the course to follow is clear.

But how can a course of attack and public criticism directed against the party and the leader, while remaining within the ranks of that party, in any way be justified?

Policies accepted by the majority of caucus and the majority of the party are party policies.

Those who remain, even if they do not subscribe, should at least cease from public outcry.

That is the least that can be demanded within a political party.

But they do not take a stand on the basis of Canada.

They do not say how it can prosper Canada to demolish piece by piece a constitutional structure that has served this nation well for 100 years – that has preserved it in peace, freedom and independence.

When you consider that in the place of that constitutional structure nothing is being put back except an arrangement open at both ends, revocable at any time by any of the parties, and having the effect of removing the dividing line in the demarcation of powers – then it is to this that you must look, rather than to the pious platitudes of those who for political advantage are prepared to bring about the rise of regionalism and the dangerous weakening of the Federal structure.

We are decentralizers.

That is our tradition.

How can you speak of centralization or decentralization when the centre is removed?

Decentralization is giving to the provinces what is theirs.

At the same time it means preserving for the Federal authority the capacity to fill its commitments.

When there is no clear statement of those commitments and those powers – then what is there left to preserve?

We must adopt a positive stand.

Insofar as French Canada is concerned, this can be done by securing the rights of the French language in Canada, so that those outside Quebec will have their cultural freedom preserved.

This can only be done by reaching an understanding with the provinces through Federal-provincial conferences on this matter, as suggested by the Leader of the Opposition.

Anything other than this is merely illusory and destructive.

Insofar as economic problems are concerned, those in Quebec – high unemployment and rural misery – must be recognized as national problems by a Federal Government prepared to place its resources at the disposal of proper and adequate solutions.

Without this there can be no effective hope for a reasonable living standard in those areas.

Twenty-two years of Liberal centralization removed from Quebec the power to deal adequately with these problems.

Are we to blame for this?

We will decentralize but not deconfederate.

We will recognize and deal with the problems.

But no adequate solutions can be proposed by a Federal Government shorn of the power to act.

In this connection it must be remembered that rural poverty is not restricted by provincial boundary lines.

It exists in Eastern Ontario and the Maritimes as well, affecting almost one-third of the nation.

On this basis, our course is clear.

We must continue to stand for the preservation of the national structure, the national identity and the power of the Federal Government to deal with regional problems.

Failing this, as Mr St Laurent pointed out in 1949, it is not only our identity but our sovereignty itself which will be in danger.

Finally, in a matter about which there is so much division, we as a party must remain united.

Those who are not prepared to stand must be at least prepared to support or, failing that, to go where their convictions lead them.

One thing is clear – an election with divided voices in our own ranks is a betrayal not only of our party but of the many thousands of Canadians who look to this party for a strong and clear voice of leadership.

Their betrayal will not be forgiven or forgotten.

ERIK NIELSEN, M.P.

Appendix E

This list gives an indication of how the Pearson Cabinet was divided into standing, special and ad hoc committees. Membership in these committees was altered from time to time, but this roster, made up in January 1966, is a fairly typical example of how cabinet duties were assigned.

January 24, 1966

STANDING COMMITTEES OF THE CABINET

Membership	*Terms of Reference*

1. EXTERNAL AFFAIRS AND DEFENCE

Membership		Terms of Reference
Prime Minister	(Chairman)	External relations including external aid; defence policy and programs (excluding emergency planning and security and intelligence).
Mr. Martin	(Vice-Chairman)	
Mr. Winters		
Mr. Hellyer	(Vice-Chairman)	
Mr. Sharp		
Mr. MacEachen		
Mr. Drury		
Senator Connolly		
Mr. Cadieux		
Mr. Pépin		

Membership	Terms of Reference

2. LEGISLATION

Mr. Cardin   (Chairman)
Mr. Pickersgill
Mr. McIlraith
Mr. Favreau
Mr. Nicholson
Senator Connolly
Mr. Pennell
Mr. Greene
Mr. Turner

Reviewing the drafting of legislation and recommending bills for cabinet approval.

3. SESSIONAL

Prime Minister   (Chairman)
Mr. McIlraith
Mr. Cardin

Ordering of government business for each session of Parliament; legislative priorities; drafting priorities.

4. FINANCE AND ECONOMIC POLICY

Mr. Sharp   (Chairman)
Mr. Martin
Mr. Winters
Mr. MacEachen
Mr. Drury
Mr. Nicholson
Mr. Sauvé
Mr. Benson
Mr. Pépin
Mr. Marchand

Economic policy generally; domestic and external financial policy; taxation; tariff policy and customs administration; industry policy; defence production; area development; business regulations.

Membership	*Terms of Reference*

5. RESOURCES AND TRADE

Mr. Laing (Chairman)	Northern development;
Mr. Martin	parks and tourism; energy,
Mr. Winters	mines and other resources;
Mr. Sharp	water use; trade policy
Mr. Robichaud	and trade promotion;
Mr. Drury	export credits.
Mr. Pépin	
Mr. Greene	
Mr. Turner	

6. COMMUNICATIONS AND WORK

Mr. Pickersgill (Chairman)	Transportation; communications
Mr. Winters	other than broadcasting;
Mr. Hellyer	postal services; public works
Mr. McIlraith	and construction programs
Mr. Robichaud	generally.
Mr. Drury	
Mr. Benson	
Mr. Côté	
Mr. Turner	

7. MANPOWER, SOCIAL DEVELOPMENT AND LABOUR

Mr. MacEachen (Chairman)	Social security and welfare;
Mr. Sharp	health programs; labour
Mr. Robichaud	relations and labour
Mr. Teillet	standards; employment problems;
Miss LaMarsh	vocational training;
Mr. Drury	unemployment insurance;
Mr. Favreau	the national employment service;
Mr. Nicholson	immigration; Indian affairs;
Mr. Sauvé	Eskimo affairs; rural development
Mr. Pennell	
Mr. Marchand	

8. AGRICULTURE, FORESTRY AND FISHERIES

Membership		Terms of Reference
Mr. Sauvé	(Chairman)	Agricultural policy and programs; forestry and fisheries.
Mr. Winters		
Mr. Laing		
Mr. Robichaud		
Mr. Teillet		
Mr. Nicholson		
Mr. Cadieux		
Mr. Greene		
Mr. Côté		

9. CULTURAL AND OTHER MATTERS

Membership		Terms of Reference
Miss LaMarsh	(Chairman)	The National Film Board; the National Gallery; the Public Archives; the National Library; the Canada Council; the National Museum and the Queen's Printer; National Centre for the Performing Arts; citizenship; universities and education.
Mr. Pickersgill		
Mr. Hellyer		
Mr. Favreau		
Mr. Benson		
Mr. Turner		

10. FEDERAL-PROVINCIAL RELATIONS

Membership		Terms of Reference
Prime Minister	(Chairman)	Federal-provincial aspects of government policies; federal-provincial consultative arrangements; preparations for federal-provincial conferences.
Mr. Pickersgill		
Mr. Sharp		
Mr. MacEachen		
Mr. Teillet		
Mr. Favreau	(Vice-Chairman)	
Mr. Nicholson		
Mr. Sauvé		
Mr. Benson		
Mr. Pépin		
Mr. Marchand		

SPECIAL AD HOC COMMITTEES OF THE CABINET

COLLECTIVE BARGAINING IN THE PUBLIC SERVICE

Mr. Benson   (Chairman)
Mr. Winters
Mr. McIlraith
Mr. Cardin
Miss LaMarsh
Mr. Nicholson
Mr. Marchand
Mr. Côté

CRIMINAL AND PENAL MATTERS

Mr. Pennell   (Chairman)
Mr. Martin
Mr. Cardin
Mr. Favreau
Mr. Benson
Mr. Marchand

EMERGENCY PLANNING

Mr. Drury   (Chairman)
Mr. Pickersgill
Mr. Hellyer
Mr. McIlraith
Mr. MacEachen
Mr. Pennell

GOVERNMENT ORGANIZATION

Mr. Benson   (Chairman)
Mr. Pickersgill
Mr. Hellyer
Mr. McIlraith
Miss LaMarsh
Mr. Drury
Mr. Sauvé

PRIVY COUNCIL COMMITTEE ON
SCIENTIFIC AND INDUSTRIAL RESEARCH

Mr. Drury   (Chairman)
Mr. Martin
Mr. Winters
Mr. Hellyer
Mr. Sharp
Mr. MacEachen
Mr. Robichaud
Mr. Sauvé
Mr. Pépin
Mr. Greene

SECURITY AND INTELLIGENCE

Prime Minister   (Chairman)
Mr. Martin
Mr. Hellyer
Mr. Cardin
Mr. Drury
Mr. Benson
Mr. Pennell   (Vice-Chairman)
Mr. Marchand

SPECIAL COMMITTEE OF COUNCIL

Mr. Favreau   (Chairman)
Mr. Robichaud
Mr. Teillet
Mr. Nicholson
Senator Connolly
Mr. Pennell
Mr. Greene
Mr. Côté
Mr. Turner

SPECIAL PROGRAM COMMITTEE

Prime Minister   (Chairman)
Mr. Pickersgill
Mr. Sharp
Mr. MacEachen   (Vice-Chairman)
Mr. Drury
Mr. Nicholson
Mr. Sauvé
Mr. Marchand

TERRITORIAL WATERS

Mr. Martin   (Chairman)
Mr. Laing
Mr. Cardin
Mr. Robichaud
Mr. Favreau
Mr. Pépin
Mr. Turner

TREASURY BOARD

Mr. Sharp	(Chairman)	*Alternates*
Mr. McIlraith		Mr. Cardin
Mr. Laing		Mr. Robichaud
Mr. Nicholson		Mr. Teillet
Mr. Benson	(Vice-Chairman)	Mr. Drury
Mr. Sauvé		Senator Connolly
		Mr. Pennell
		Mr. Côté
		Mr. Turner

VETERANS AFFAIRS

Mr. Teillet	(Chairman)
Mr. Winters	
Mr. MacEachen	
Miss LaMarsh	
Mr. Cadieux	

1967 COMMITTEE

Prime Minister	(Chairman)
Mr. Winters	
Mr. McIlraith	
Mr. Laing	
Mr. Robichaud	
Mr. Teillet	
Miss LaMarsh	
Mr. Drury	
Mr. Favreau	(Vice-Chairman)
Mr. Pépin	

Appendix F

This exchange of private correspondence between senior Liberals and Nelson Castonguay, the Acting Chief Electoral Officer, established that, despite the redistribution problem, a general election based on the new boundaries could have been held in late October, 1966.

Memorandum to the Honourable Maurice Lamontagne, Secretary of State.

It is difficult at this time to know

(1) when all Boundaries Commissions will have their reports (section 18 of the Electoral Boundaries Readjustment Act) ready for translation and printing. The Province of Newfoundland completed its sittings on July 1st; the last sitting will be on October 5th for the Province of British Columbia;

(2) the problems that may arise as to (a) the translation and printing of such reports, and (b) the printing of the maps to be included;

(3) if the reports are given to the Speaker of the House of Commons during a session of Parliament or in the interval between sessions (section 19 of the afore-mentioned Act) which would have a bearing on the time factor.

For such reasons, it is impossible for anyone to predict with accuracy the exact date when the new electoral maps for Canada will be in force. However, there is every reason to believe that all Commissions will have presented their reports to the Speaker by the completion date which is on or about January 21, 1966.

If no objections (section 20 of the afore-mentioned Act) are made in the House of Commons to any of the reports of the Commissions, the new electoral maps for Canada should be in force by April, 1966. If objections are made to one or more of such reports, the time factor can be measured by the provisions of sections 20 and 21 of the afore-mentioned Act.

After the coming into force of all Representation Acts up to 1952, no appointment of returning officer was made for an electoral district whose name *did not* change and in which the returning officer continued to reside. The only appointments of returning officers made were in the case of new electoral districts or of electoral districts whose names had changed, or in the case of a returning officer who had ceased to reside in the electoral district due to the changes made to the boundaries of that electoral district.

A survey made on the basis of the proposed maps of the ten Commissions indicates that there are 130 new electoral districts or electoral districts whose names have changed and 32 electoral districts whose names have not changed but in which the present returning officers cease to reside, making it a cause for removal from office under section 8 of the Canada Elections Act.

There is reason to believe that the course followed in the past had no support in law, because, with the coming into force of the new electoral maps, the Representation Act, 1952, is repealed, and the electoral districts established by that Act, as well as the offices of the returning officers appointed for such districts, cease to exist (sections 24 and 27 of the Electoral Boundaries Readjustment Act and section 8 of the Canada Elections Act). Since, as you know, the question of the appointment and tenure of office of returning officers rests exclusively with the Governor in Council and that you look after such question for the Governor in Council, I would respectfully suggest that you obtain an opinion on the subject from the Department of Justice and if Justice support that view, the appointment of 264 returning officers will have to be made after the new electoral maps come into force. If Justice do not support that view, then the appointment of approximately 160 returning officers will have to be made.

The setting up of polling divisions is a task that can only be performed by returning officers. The staff of the Chief Electoral office commenced on July 2, 1965, to re-allocate existing polling divisions into the new electoral districts, which re-allocation will take about six months to complete. When the report of a Commission is approved, final re-allocation of such polling divisions will then be made before the preliminary material is supplied to returning officers.

It must be borne in mind that the Commissions did not consider existing polling divisions as it was not one of the criteria set out in section 13 (c) of the Electoral Boundaries Readjustment Act. Since the boundaries of the new electoral districts have split many of the existing polling divisions, the material being prepared by the staff of the Chief Electoral office can only be of small assistance to the returning officers in setting up the polling division arrangements of their new electoral districts. Moreover, the existing polling divisions were last brought up to date in the Fall of 1964, and the shift of electors in such polling divisions between the Fall of 1964 and the Spring of 1966 would be considerable in many of them.

The time required for a returning officer to complete the setting up of the polling division arrangement of his electoral district depends on the following factors:

(1) If the former returning officer is re-appointed, he should be able to complete his task in approximately two months.

(2) If a person is appointed returning officer with no experience as federal returning officer, it is essential that he first be given a course of instructions in the duties of returning officer and then be directed to revise the polling division arrangement of his electoral district. After such course, a new returning officer could then also complete his task in approximately two months.

Therefore, to complete the above-mentioned redistribution of approximately 50,000 polling divisions, two or three months will be required after the last of the 264 returning officers is appointed. Experience, after the re-enactment of the Dominion Elections Act of 1934 and of 1938 and in 1960 of the Canada Elections Act, when the positions of all returning officers became vacant, and after the Representation Act of 1947 and of 1952, clearly shows that a period of at least one year elapsed before the last returning officer was appointed.

If the new electoral maps for Canada come into force in April, 1966, and a general election is contemplated or becomes necessary in late November, 1966, it is imperative that the appointment of *all 264 returning officers* be made by the Governor in Council *within thirty (30) days* after such maps come into force. A period of five months to give courses of instructions to new returning officers and to supervise the redistribution of the polling divisions in 264 electoral districts will place a very heavy strain on the small staff of the Chief Electoral office, which staff will be required to do a considerable amount of overtime to complete such work in that period of time.

Respectfully submitted.

NELSON CASTONGUAY
Acting Chief Electoral Officer.

Ottawa, July 5, 1965.

Ottawa
September 1, 1965

Mr N. J. Castonguay,
Acting Chief Electoral Officer,
39 McArthur Avenue,
Eastview, Ontario.

Dear Sir:

As you know, there is a certain amount of controversy at the present time concerning the earliest date at which a general election could be held following redistribution in accordance with the Electoral Boundaries Readjustment Act.

May I request a statement from you indicating the date by which you expect redistribution to be completed and giving your estimate of the earliest date thereafter on which a general election could be held?

I need not add that this letter is not intended to be construed as indicating that I have decided to ask His Excellency the Governor General to dissolve the twenty-sixth Parliament. Rather, I would hope that your opinion as the official who is most directly concerned and who has had the most experience with these matters might end any controversy respecting the time table for prospective completion of the tasks entrusted to you by the redistribution legislation.

Yours sincerely,

L. B. Pearson

Ottawa
September 2, 1965

The Right Honourable L. B. Pearson,
Prime Minister of Canada,
House of Commons,
Ottawa.

Dear Mr Prime Minister:

On July 5th last, I sent to the Honourable Maurice Lamontagne, Secretary of State, a memorandum with regard to the subject matter of your letter of September 1st.

From the information I have available at this time, I have nothing to add or delete from what is set out in that memorandum, copy of which I am enclosing.

Yours respectfully,

N. Castonguay
Chief Electoral Officer.

Mr N. J. Castonguay,
Acting Chief Electoral Officer,
39 McArthur Avenue,
Eastview, Ontario.

Dear Sir:

I have received your letter of September 2nd, with the enclosed memorandum of July 5th to the Honourable Maurice Lamontagne.

I have been advised that the office of the Secretary of State recently forwarded to you a copy of a legal opinion in which the Acting Deputy Attorney General dealt with the matter raised in the second page of the July 5th memorandum. Since it is possible that this copy of the legal opinion reached you after September 2nd, I would be glad if you could advise me further whether this legal opinion alters the time table set out in the July 5th memorandum.

I enclose a copy of the opinion of the Acting Deputy Attorney General.

Yours sincerely,

L. B. PEARSON

Ottawa
September 7, 1965

The Right Honourable L. B. Pearson,
Prime Minister of Canada,
House of Commons,
Ottawa.

Dear Mr Prime Minister:

The legal opinion of the Acting Deputy Attorney General referred to in your letter of September 3 alters the time table, set out in my memorandum to the Honourable Maurice Lamontagne, only to the extent that it would be possible, in my opinion, to hold a general election in late October, 1966, instead of November as mentioned in the last paragraph of such memorandum.

Yours respectfully,

N. CASTONGUAY
Representation Commissioner.

Appendix G

This memorandum was sent to Lester Pearson in August of 1965 to urge that no election be held until after redistribution by John de B. Payne of Montreal, a former executive assistant to the Prime Minister.

NOTES ON A FEDERAL GENERAL ELECTION

The purpose of a general election, with a mandate barely half expired, would be to:

   a) Settle an issue of national importance and significance,
   b) obtain a majority in the House in order to govern more effectively,
   c) acquire a Parliamentary wing which would be truly national in composition.

We have, at the moment, no real issue. And, I seriously doubt, in the present political climate, we could attain either of the other two objectives.

We have been robbed of issues by two events of the past few months. The conduct of the House improved considerably after the Easter recess and a good amount of business was transacted. The most recent federal-provincial conference failed to generate a major issue, let alone a contentious one.

Without an issue, it is difficult to seek a new mandate. We cannot excite the public nor create in their minds the sense of urgency which could be translated, at the polls, into a majority Liberal government. The simple request for a majority so that we could govern more effectively has no political sex appeal. There is no challenge and voters would be inclined to vote on regional attitudes and interests.

Our record would be as great a disadvantage as it would be an advantage. Our achievements are such that people would have every reason to question the need for a majority government – and the need for an election – when a government had done so well under the most trying circumstances. And, the prospects are that we can do as well or better in the future because of the rule changes. All of this may not have been true seven months ago but it is certainly true today.

The public is not concerned with our difficulties and discomfitures in Parliament. Their disgust with Parliament has not been dissipated. The Tories may be the villains, but our image – and we must be frank with ourselves – has been tarnished too. The scandals have hurt. But our real problem is the damage to our reputation as "the Great Administrators" by a series of incidents during the past two years. Our recovery is slow, in part because our most effective work has been in a sphere that is hard for the public to understand and is paved with prejudice – the evolvement of a sound and practical approach to federal-provincial relations.

The prospects of acquiring a truly national Parliamentary wing seem remote. We need at least a minimal representation of three from each of the provinces and I doubt we could reach this objective on the Prairies where we might lose rather than gain seats. The price of wheat will be a factor with the Tories talking two-dollar wheat, the Sauvé comments about the Wheat Board will not be forgotten and the "back-lash" will certainly affect the attitude of some voters.

The economic factor – the prospect of an economic recession in early 1966 – is debatable as there seems no unanimity of opinion that one will occur nor is there any firm opinion as to its possible severity. But if an economic slow-down did take place we could take the initiative in adopting the required policies for the cure and if the Opposition became balky we could use those policies as the platform for an election.

The remedial measures ought not to be too severe nor unpalatable if the economy is properly managed in the interim – and all the evidence suggests that this is the case.

A constant question of any government is the manœuvrability it possesses to call an election at a time of its own choosing and the selection of the issue. A minority never enjoys this to the full. The conditions of 1958 were a rare exception – the demand for a majority government. In other instances, minority governments have gone to the country on a major issue – the 1926 constitutional crisis is the classic example.

At the moment, with the House in recess, the government has a certain manœuvrability – it could dissolve the House. But it lacks the other ingredient – the issue. In other words, the manœuvrability is relative and minor. The government would have almost as much if the House were in session and would also have the prospect of generating or selecting an issue. The risk, of course, is that the Opposition may select the issue and set the timing. But that can be controlled, to a degree, by the legislative program and the management of the business of the House. The new rules of the House will be of immense help in this regard.

The real advantage of manœuvrability is the ability to exploit it in a political climate which is favourable to the government. In my view the present political climate is too unsettled and not necessarily favourable to us.

The public opinion polls do not show any significant change from those of 1962 and 1963 which would suggest that the composition of the House would be different than it is or that a majority government would emerge. The NDP is the only party at which the public is not mad.

The risk of an election now is that the Liberal Party could gain a small majority, at the best, but in the process become a French and Roman Catholic Party without true national representation. This equation results from the prospects of heavy gains in Quebec, minor gains in the Atlantic Provinces and a status quo or slight loss in Ontario and western Canada. This could mean the end of the Party as a dominant political force in the country.

There is, too, the risk that an election, with Diefenbaker loose on the hustings, may split the country beyond repair. This risk will always exist as long as Diefenbaker leads the Tories. While, as a responsible party, we cannot ignore its dangers, on the other hand we cannot allow it to tie our hands forever. This, as much as anything else, makes the requirement of a valid issue essential.

Redistribution is the hard core of the government's decision. The imbalance of representation in the Commons is an irritant. If an election was held prior to redistribution, then the current redistribution would be out of date and have a life of less than three years (1969-1972) because of the next decennial census. The disfranchisement has been creeping upon us for 15 years; and it could continue in its present extreme form for 18 years to 20 years if an election were held now. While the present redistribution has corrected the major imbalance between the rural representation on the one hand and the urban and suburban electors on the other, adjustments will have to be made due to the changing patterns of development in the cities and suburbs in 1971.

The ethical question cannot be dismissed casually nor solely in the possible interest of the party. We have a moral obligation to those electors who do not enjoy full enfranchisement because of the current imbalance in representation.

We were critical of the Tories for failing to act. We were even louder in our criticism at the time of Diefenbaker's filibuster. And, we have been vocal about redistribution and the financing of political campaigns since 1959. We have placed great importance on the need for prompt action on legislation relating to redistribution and other electoral matters.

We can maintain some pressure on the opposition to behave if we make it stated government policy, through the Prime Minister, that we do not intend to call an election until redistribution is feasible. The risk of such a policy is far less now than six months ago – and here again, life for the government ought to be easier in the House under the new rule changes. It would not affect our manœuvrability.

But the moral issue of calling an election without the accepted criteria remains a primary consideration. A minister of the government [Jack Pickersgill] has stated, in the House, that it would be immoral to call an election before redistribution. The moral posture of a government seeking to ease the parliamentary role of its ministers, through the calling of an election the reasons for which, beyond those of self-interest, would be difficult to state, would be offensive to many Canadians and many of our partisans. It would be a sorry historical commentary if a party, which has always placed public interest above those of privileged groups and always above its own, should call an election which would be self-seeking.

If redistribution were not so close at hand, a little more than a year at most and, perhaps, a few months less, the moral issue would not exist. The government would have more freedom to decide.

The polls, to return to them for a moment, do not indicate that we could expect anything other than a minority government or a very narrow majority. The undecided vote is too great (30%) to draw any other conclusion. We do not know where the weight of the decided vote exists – urban, rural, western, central or eastern. In instances where the undecided vote was substantial (in excess of 11%), strange electoral results have occurred. In 1962, the undecided vote in Quebec was 18% and the Social Credit did very well indeed. An election ought not to be called until the significance of the undecided factor has been thoroughly analysed and the prospects translated into a potential majority.

I have mentioned the change in the rules of the House several times and this has been deliberate. We were prepared to fight an election if the House failed to pass it. During the debate, and for months prior to it, we made the point in the strongest possible terms that the business of the nation could not be properly managed unless the antiquated rules of the House were changed. Now we propose to call an election without the rules being tested. In my view the public would have the right to question the validity of our arguments and also ask that we at least try them out through a full session. The failure to test the new rules weakens our claim that we need a majority to govern.

The moral aspect of redistribution coupled with the need to test the opposition's behaviour under the new rules make it extremely dangerous to call an election which the public does not want. We might acquire a small majority but we might suffer over the long term by the unwillingness of the people to forgive us for getting them to the polls at a time when they feel we should get on with the job of running the country.

There are other aspects to the calling of an election now.

The sale of wheat to Russia is a stroke of luck. But it may not have the full political impact which some expect. We reduced the price of wheat, and with reason, earlier in the year. The cost of shipments will increase with the new wage rates of the grain handlers. The potential prosperity of the farmer can be exaggerated. The Tories could make a case on what the sale will mean in terms of payments to farmers, and they could renew their call for two-dollar wheat.

A fall election would eliminate any freedom the Prime Minister might have in terms of cabinet shuffles and the strengthening of the cabinet through new appointments. It would be wrong to imply that the old team was not too effective, but here is a new one which can do better. In other words the government would have to support its present team, unless some members do not choose to seek re-election. New members of a cabinet ought to be allowed to prove themselves in the House before taking to the hustings.

The NDP will undoubtedly make much of their proposal that the old-age pension be 100 dollars a month, citing the defeat of their amendment in the House during the Pension debate. While our arguments are strong regarding our pension proposals in respect to our plan and those already retired, the NDP approach might have a great deal of appeal because of the increasing cost of living which is considered severe by many people.

Without an issue, Diefenbaker will wander over the full oratorical range. He will charge the government, in his most persuasive hustings style, with weakness and indecisiveness, ignoring all the time historical and political reality. He will attempt to show that the Pearson team has been no better than his motley crowd. But he will be his most dangerous in terms of national interests when he will preach of his concept of "One Canada." This theme will provide him with the weapon to rouse the backlash in the hope of translating it into Diefenbaker votes. If he becomes as irresponsible as he has been at times in the past, he could succeed in dividing the country beyond future salvation.

In summary there seem to be more disadvantages than advantages in holding an election in the fall.

1. We have no issue of national importance and significance.
2. A plea that we need a majority to govern is offset by our legislative record and the fact that the new rules of the House have not been truly tested.
3. We have no indication that we could achieve a majority without an imbalance between Quebec representation and that of the rest of the country. As a matter of fact we have no indications that we can improve the national representation of our parliamentary wing.
4. The undecided factor in the recent polls suggests that the prospects of improving our position are poor, that we would be taking a risk beyond that which is normal in what is a business of unknowns.
5. The moral aspect of redistribution is too strong to be ignored.

My judgement may fail me, and cause me to pull a prize political boner, but I cannot see where we have anything to gain in calling an election now. I think too many ingredients have not been studied in depth through polling and analysis for us to decide that our prospects of gaining a majority, based upon a sound national representation, are good or better than average.

I have taken into account the problem of a provincial election in Quebec next year and that Lesage might well fight City Hall (the Federal Government). Many people would not agree with me but I think a confrontation at the polls might resolve the history of our country for many years to come rather than allowing it to drift in a vacuum as it is at present. In terms of the Quebec voter it would allow him to declare himself in terms of confederation – and I feel that he would opt to stay in confederation. Lesage has his problems at home and they will not be cured by fighting Ottawa. He has a record to support and discontent to deal with in the rural and depressed areas of the province. He might find Social Credit a thorn in his side as we did in 1962. Lesage might be in for some surprises. If we have strong Quebec leadership, we might repeat Mr Lapointe's tour-de-force in 1940. I think the prospects of a confrontation at the polls (the election need not be held at the same time) is a risk worth taking.

But the main reasons for my opposition to an election at this time are – the moral issue of redistribution and the changes in the rules of the House and the uncertainties of other factors which I believe require more study in depth.

JOHN DE B. PAYNE

Appendix H

This private letter, one of the rare pieces of correspondence passed between Lester Pearson and John Diefenbaker and written during the parliamentary debates on the Rivard scandal, contained the first official mention of the "Munsinger affair." It was neither acknowledged nor answered by the Opposition Leader.

Ottawa
December 4, 1964

The Right Honourable J. G. Diefenbaker, M.P.
Leader of the Opposition
House of Commons, Ottawa.

Dear Mr Diefenbaker:

In discharge of my constitutional duty as Prime Minister, I am writing this letter to you as a Privy Councillor and former Prime Minister.

I have been much concerned, not only about allegations made recently in a particular case, the Rivard case, but, even more, about an attitude toward the operation of the law that certain evidence in this case discloses. This attitude is not widespread but the Rivard case illustrates the need to take thorough action to remove it.

The problem has not sprung up suddenly. In order to assess the need for corrective action, I have asked for a full report of instances in the last ten years or so in which political intervention was involved in investigations. This information will enable me to see how such matters could and should be dealt with.

One case (the Munsinger case) has given me very grave concern. It affects the security of the country. In 1960-61, a Minister who occupied a position of great responsibility in the Government was involved in a liaison which clearly endangered security.

I have been greatly disturbed by the lack of attention which, in so far as the file indicates, this matter received. The Minister was left in his position of trust.

I have decided that I cannot, in the public interest, let the matter lie where it was left and that I must ask the R.C.M. Police to pursue further enquiries.

I recognize that the file before me may not disclose all the steps that were taken. In view of this, it is my duty to write you about the matter in case you might be in a position to let me know that the enquiries that were pursued and the safeguards that were taken reached further than the material before me would indicate. That material now indicates that the Minister of Justice brought the matter to your attention and that no action was taken.

Because national security is involved, this is the most serious and disturbing of the matters that have been brought to my attention. But I assure you that all incidents during the last ten years are being thoroughly examined, and will be followed up without fear or favour if and when the evidence requires it.

If there is further information you can provide about the Munsinger case, I will be grateful if you will let me know.

Yours sincerely,

L. B. PEARSON

Appendix I

This diplomatic note, the first official American protest against Canadian legislation that might affect the U.S.-owned Mercantile Bank, was handed to a representative of the External Affairs Department on April 7, 1966, by the American Embassy in Ottawa.

No. 340

The Embassy of the United States of America refers to the recent meeting in Washington of the Joint Committee on Trade and Economic Affairs, and in particular to the statement of the Minister of Finance that the Government of Canada expects to introduce new banking legislation during the current session of Parliament.

The Embassy has been instructed to remind the Government of Canada of the concern with which the United States Government viewed certain aspects of the banking legislation introduced in Parliament last year but not enacted (Bill C-102 of May 6, 1965), and to express the hope that the banking legislation to be introduced this year will not contain provisions discriminating against American-owned banks.

The United States Government wishes to remind the Government of Canada that Canadian banks are not subject to discrimination in their United States operations. Indeed, in some respects they enjoy a privileged position relative to United States banks in that their banking operations are not restricted to one state. As a result of favorable United States treatment, major Canadian banks play a significant role in United States banking activities, particularly in New York City's financial market.

The United States Government recognizes the right of the Government of Canada to regulate all banking carried on in Canada. However, there is nothing in the operations of American-owned banks in Canada which would appear to justify the adoption of regulations that discriminate against them. In view of the important interrelationships of capital markets in the two countries and the substantial benefits derived by Canadian banks from operations in the United States, it is hoped that the Government of Canada would agree that it is desirable to avoid placing unnecessary restrictions on such mutually beneficial activities.

[Embassy of the United States of America, Ottawa, April 7, 1966]

Appendix J

This is the text of the Canadian reply to the American note on the Mercantile Bank. It was handed to C. G. Wootton, a counsellor of the United States Embassy, at 5:05 p.m. on June 29, 1966, by A. E. Ritchie, Canada's Deputy Undersecretary of State for External Affairs. It rejected the American protest.

No. E-270

The Department of External Affairs presents its compliments to the Embassy of the United States of America and has the honour to refer to the Embassy's Note No. 340 of April 7 concerning the possible contents of the new Canadian banking legislation which will be presented to Parliament during the current session. In this connection the Canadian authorities note the concern with which the United States Government viewed certain aspects of the bill which was introduced in 1965 to revise the Bank Act. They further note the hope expressed by the Embassy that the legislation to be introduced this year will not contain provisions which discriminate against usa-owned banks. The Canadian authorities have carefully considered the Embassy's representations on these matters.

It is the intention of the Government of Canada to introduce shortly another bill to revise the Bank Act under which the powers of the existing banks expire on November 30 of this year. It is intended to include in this legislation provisions relating to the ownership and control of Canadian banks. In particular, it will be provided that save for existing holdings, no shareholder or group of associated shareholders may own more than ten per cent of the shares of a bank, and that save for existing holdings, not more than 25 per cent of the shares of a bank may be owned by non-residents. The bill will also provide that where one shareholder or associated group of shareholders owns more than 25 per cent of the shares of a bank, that bank may not have outstanding total liabilities exceeding twenty times its authorized capital stock.

These provisions are intended to ensure that the ownership of the relatively few banks in Canada will be broadly dispersed among a large number of shareholders who are predominantly Canadian residents. While the Government of Canada recognizes that exceptions to this general rule may be appropriate in the case of new and small banks, it believes that the statute should contain a measure to enable the Government to control the growth of any bank with concentrated ownership which may tend to become a major unit in our banking system.

It will be seen that the proposed provisions will not discriminate against United States-owned banks. The limits on ownership by a single shareholder or associated group of shareholders will apply both to residents and non-residents. The limits on the proportion of shares to be held by non-residents will apply to all non-residents and not merely to those of any particular country or category. The limitation on total liabilities in relation to authorized capital where more than 25 per cent of the shares are held by a single shareholder or associated group of shareholders will apply whether the major shareholding is Canadian or non-resident. The one existing bank to which this provision will apply happens to be one which is owned by an American bank, although it may well apply to a new bank by the time the new Bank Act comes into force. This measure of control in any case need not involve any inequity since increases in authorized capital can be approved. Furthermore, it is intended that this limitation on total outstanding liabilities will not come into effect until 1968, which will provide ample opportunity to deal with any request for an increase in authorized capital that may be submitted before then.

The Canadian Government has taken note of the Embassy's reminder that Canadian banks are not subject to discrimination in their operations in the United States. It must be pointed out, however, that the situations in the two countries are not parallel. The role of the United States dollar as the major trading and reserve currency in the world attracts a great deal of short-term banking and other financial transactions to the United States. Since Canada is an important user of the United States dollar as both a trading and reserve currency, it is not surprising that Canadian banks, as well as other Canadians, would have a very large volume of financial transactions in the United States and would find it convenient to have their own agencies and branches there.

Moreover, the United States agencies of Canadian banks are generally precluded by State banking legislation and regulations from engaging in the business of receiving deposits, although they may maintain credit balances incidental to or arising out of other authorized operations. As a result of this, in part at least, these agencies have a relatively small volume of deposits from United States residents. By far the largest part of the funds which these agencies and branches have at their disposal is supplied from the head offices and branches of Canadian banks elsewhere in the world and is derived from deposits held outside the United States. The volume of such assets financed by these deposits has undergone a substantial increase since the end of 1964. In this way, the Canadian banks through their agencies and branches in the United States are making a valuable contribution to the United States balance of payments.

Notwithstanding the general conditions that lead Canadians and Canadian banks to wish to carry on banking transactions in the United States, and despite the fact that Canadian banks may operate agencies and branches in more than one State, the Canadian banks have not become a major element in the total United States banking picture. Agencies have been opened in only a few large cities, in most cases where substantial export-import and foreign exchange business involving Canadians is available, and the total deposits of all agencies of the Canadian banks appear to be only about one per cent of the total United States bank deposits, with a substantial part originating outside the United States. The one United States-owned bank in Canada now has deposits amounting to nearly this same proportion of the total deposits of the Canadian banks.

It should also be noted that the circumstances governing the ownership and control of banks in Canada differ in one fundamental respect from those in the United States. In the United States there are more than 14,000 banks, with no one bank controlling more than a relatively small share of the total banking business. Canada has only eight banks, most of which have a significant share of the total business. Consequently, it is not unreasonable that the Canadian authorities should be relatively more concerned with problems of ownership and control than would a government in a country whose banking system is as large and diversified as that of the United States.

While the Canadian authorities recognize that there may be no restriction on the ownership of banks in the United States, they note that national banks in the United States may have only United States citizens as directors. This even applies in the case of the so-called Edge Act corporations, organized for the purpose of engaging in international or foreign banking. There are similar provisions in the bank acts of most States. It would therefore appear that, even in the very different circumstances in which banking activities are carried on in the United States, the question of control by non-residents of banks in the United States is of some concern to the United States Government.

The Government of Canada hopes that the United States Government will recognize that the proposals relating to the ownership and control of Canadian banks which will be laid before Parliament are reasonable in the special circumstances of Canada, and that they are being brought forward only after the most careful consideration of the views of the United States Government.

Appendix K

Here is the text of a priority cable message sent to the External Affairs Department by A. E. Ritchie, then Canadian Ambassador to the United States, on November 11, 1966. After describing his unsuccessful attempts to soften the American attitude on the Mercantile issue, Ritchie transmitted the text of the State Department note — one of the sharpest protests ever sent to Canada by the United States.

[FM Wash DC Nov. 11/66 Confd.]

I am reproducing below text of USA note on this subject which Under-Sec. Katzenbach gave to me this afternoon. He indicated that he in fact had this note in his possession when he saw me on another matter other day but that he had decided to go into the matter more thoroughly himself before giving it to me, as he realized that it was a rather severe communication. He hoped that we would appreciate from note just how serious USA Govt. regarded matter. They were concerned about many aspects of situation including strong political criticism which would be expressed in this country if present Cdn. measures were to go ahead. They were also disturbed at use that might be made by other countries of our action as a precedent. Katzenbach hoped it might be possible to meet our needs without raising all problems and emotions that were bound to be aroused by proceeding with provision now in bill.

2. I replied that his was indeed a very rough note. I asked him if he had really read our June note. I thought this reply contained numerous inaccuracies and some lines of reasoning which seemed highly questionable on a first reading. I thought it also sounded very threatening. Moreover authors still seemed unable to grasp fundamental differences between USA and Cdn. situations. If no rpt. no limitations were to be imposed on size of a foreign-controlled bank with vast resources behind it Cdn. monetary policy could be all too easily frustrated. Cdn. financial system was relatively small in size and a big foreign-owned bank which did not rpt. not necessarily accept same guidance or discipline as domestic banks could make it

515

very difficult for Cdn. financial and monetary authorities to carry out their policies effectively in interests of Cdn. economy. Cdn. agencies in NY were in a different category and incidentally brought substantial benefits to USA financial position.

3. I asked Mr Katzenbach whether he really thought we could accept a complete absence of any limitation on size of an outside bank. He replied that he hoped that whatever needed to be done could be done in a manner which would not rpt. not provoke criticisms which were bound to accompany our present measure. I mentioned practical flexibility provided by Treasury Board authority.

4. On factual inaccuracies in USA draft I questioned retroactivity and noted that according to our records reps. of USA banks in Cda. had been fairly warned when they were in process of acquiring Mercantile Bank. Katzenbach interrupted to say that their version of these earlier exchanges was obviously rather different from ours. I agreed that accounts seemed to be divergent but I thought he would recognize that Cdn. authorities had to proceed on basis of their own direct knowledge of what had happened or what had been said. I also questioned accuracy of suggestions in note that only an American bank would likely be affected. I thought it was clear that other banks with concentrated ownership could be involved and I mentioned case of Bank of Western Cda. Another inaccuracy seemed to me to be indication halfway through note that Cdn. banking operations in USA are "many times larger" than Mercantile's operations in Cda. I thought that on basis which we would normally make comparison they were roughly same.

5. Katzenbach said that if of course there were any inaccuracies in their note he would welcome any info that might make it possible to correct them.

6. I reverted to point in note about our not rpt. not taking any action when Mercantile Bank had been under other foreign ownership. I thought there was a substantial difference on one hand between a bank owned by a Dutch institution and operating on kind of scale contemplated when its charter was secured and on other hand a bank owned by an institution as large and aggressive as National City. On matter of "discrimination" I referred to limitations on nationality of directors of federally incorporated USA banks including National City.

7. At several points in conversation Katzenbach referred to "political" problem. I said that we were aware of interest of Senator Javits and some others in case. I emphasized however that there was an extremely political problem on Cdn. side as well which tended to reinforce other arguments for maintaining provision now in bill. Mr Rufus Smith who was also present remarked that according to his info. Cdn. Bankers' Association were critical

of this provision in act. I replied that Cda. had a variety of views on this and other provisions of legislation. I knew that at least some of larger banks strongly supported proposed provision.

8. I concluded by saying that I would report contents of note to Cdn. Govt.

Following is text of note:

Govt. of USA refers Govt. of Cda. to note No. 340 April 7 from USA Emb. in Ottawa and Dept. of External Affairs note No. E-270 of June 29 in reply concerning discriminatory treatment of USA banks in Cda. Govt. of USA cannot agree with contention in Dept. of External Affairs note that Bank Act Bill of 1966 will not rpt. not discriminate against USA-owned banks. While it is true that provisions of bill imposing a limitation on growth of only USA-owned bank in Cda. could apply in theory to other banks that either residents or non-residents might wish to establish in future, in fact only existing bank to which they would apply is USA-owned Mercantile Bank. USA Govt. is particularly recognizant of fact that Cdn. Govt. did not rpt. not attempt to impose discriminatory restrs. on Mercantile Bank until its acquisition by American interests, even though its previous ownership was also foreign, and, of course, it was chartered by act of Parliament.

Previous US note pointed out that Cdn. banks are not rpt. not subject to discrimination in their USA operations. In reply to this statement of fact, Dept. of External Affairs asserted that agencies of Cdn. banks in USA are generally precluded by state banking legislation and regs. from receiving deposits. This appears in part to be a ref. to conditions under which agencies of Cdn. banks operate in state of NY. It should be pointed out that this condition obtains owing to their status as agencies and would not rpt. not apply if they were chartered as branches, as they could be under NY law on basis of reciprocity. Moreover, two of Cdn. banks with agencies in NY also have banking subsidiaries in state which are now allowed to accept deposits. In addition there are Cdn.-owned banks in California, Washington, Oregon, Puerto Rico and USA Virgin Islands, all of which are permitted to accept deposits. Cdn. banking operations in USA are many times larger than Mercantile bank operation in Cda. Five Cdn. agencies in NY alone are estimated to account for over $2 billion in assets, or ten times asset ceiling Govt. of Cda. proposes to impose on Mercantile Bank. In all, five Cdn. banks operating in USA have upward of 35 offices. Counting only states in which they are now operating, they have access to a market for banking services in USA which is substantially larger than their home market. USA Govt. considers that it has made clear its view that retroactive discrimination in Bank Act Bill violates a fundamental principle that has heretofore guided both govts. in their conduct with respect to foreign-owned enterprises within their borders; namely, that an enterprise established in accordance with law is henceforth entitled to equal protection of law and to equality of treatment with other like or similar enterprises organized under same law, and should not rpt. not be subjected to discrimination because of its foreign ownership.

While USA Govt. appreciates that Govt. of Cda. has given careful consideration to its views, it cannot accept suggestion in Cdn. note that it consider discriminatory proposals under discussion as reasonable in special circumstances of Cda.

USA Govt. understands that Govt. of Cda. is considering possibility of allowing establishment of foreign bank agencies in Cda. While USA Govt. in principle would welcome such a development, it would in no rpt. no way change retroactive and discriminatory aspect of proposed legislation affecting Mercantile Bank. For its part, USA Govt. continues to hold view that it is not rpt. not reasonable to expect that privileged position now enjoyed by Cdn. banks in USA would continue unimpaired if only USA-owned bank in Cda. is subjected to retroactive and discriminatory treatment.

In this connection, Govt. of Cda. will be aware of legislation which has been introduced before USA Congress which would provide means of giving practical effect to principle of reciprocity through federal control of foreign-owned banks. In addition, since action contemplated by Cdn. Govt. will not rpt. not only adversely affect Mercantile Bank but will also undermine ground rules on which all American-owned firms operating in Cda. must rely, USA Govt. has under exam. a number of other courses of action consistent with very serious view it takes of issue.

Dept. of State, Wash DC Nov. 11, 1966

Appendix L

Although the leadership campaign of Pierre Elliott Trudeau appeared to be a people's movement, spontaneously executed by a gaggle of happy amateurs, it was actually a professional, minutely planned operation, outlined in a secret, 65-page Convention Organization Manual. *Typical examples of the planning involved were the candidate's breakfasts held daily during the leadership convention. They appeared to be informal affairs, relaxed occasions for the delegates to meet Trudeau. As the following excerpt from the* Manual *illustrates, every detail of these meetings was meticulously arranged beforehand; little was left to chance.*

SPECIAL PROJECTS REPORT

1. *Name of Event:* Breakfast With Trudeau.

2. *Place of Event:* Talisman Motor Hotel, East-West Dining Rooms.

3. *Date and Time of Event:* Friday, April 5 from 8:00 - 9:00 a.m.

4. *Description of Event:*

   "Breakfast With Trudeau" will be an informal occasion and will provide delegates from Nova Scotia, Saskatchewan and British Columbia with an opportunity to meet Mr Trudeau, ask him questions and to chat with one another.
   A sit-down breakfast; there will be ten waiters on hand to serve the 26 circular tables placed randomly throughout the room. Bright yellow table cloths, gay flowers and decorations, and soft music playing in the background will facilitate the development of the informal atmosphere we wish to create.

5. *Contacts:*

   CAMPAIGN COMMITTEE: Judy Holland.
   TALISMAN MOTOR HOTEL: Mr Samson, tel. 722-7601.
   M.P. CONTACT: Bryce Mackasey, tel. 996-5234.

6. *Publicity and Press Details:*

Delegates will be made aware of the event by:
- personalized invitations issued to them immediately as they sign into the hotel;
- large posters advertising the event which will be situated on bulletin boards in the main foyer of the hotel.

Don Peacock has assumed responsibility for informing Press and News Media of the event and for ensuring that adequate coverage is given to it.

To accommodate a good Press turn-out:
- ample space between tables will allow a free flow of movement;
- Mr Trudeau's table will be equipped with a microphone and telephone;
- another telephone will be situated by the dining-room entrance;
- a special table will be set up for Press and staff writers;
- a raised platform for cameras and other equipment will be set up in a central location of the dining room.

7. *Invitations:*

Invitations for the Talisman Breakfast are being sent to all delegates scheduled to remain in the Talisman Motor Hotel and the Bruce Mac-Donald Hotel during the Convention.

A special courier will convey the sealed, personalized invitations to the hotels – it is hoped by Wednesday afternoon at the latest – and they will be handed to each of the delegates as they sign in.

8. *Refreshments:*

Orange Juice   Tomato Juice

Scrambled Eggs

Bacon   Ham

Muffins   Sweet Rolls   Toast

Coffee   Tea

9. *Decorations:*

Bright yellow table cloths will complement the predominant colour of orange of our decorations:
- large floral centre pieces from Scrim's Florist;
- orange, yellow and white streamers around the room;
- large blow-ups of Trudeau on the walls, surrounded by crepe sunflowers and orange balloons;
- Trudeau serviettes, Trudeau monogrammed penny-matches, a supply of cigarettes and maple sugar on the tables; and,
- small orange crepe lapel buttons to be worn by each of the delegates.

10. *Security Guards and Guides:*

Merle Shain will be responsible for providing six Guides, to perform the following duties:
- two to stand in the main foyer of the Talisman to escort delegates downstairs to the dining room;
- one to stand at the entrance of the dining room to greet delegates as they arrive, to provide them with an orange lapel button and to take their names. The latter function will act as a form of security check for us and ensure that *only* delegates enter the dining room;
- two to circulate in the dining room to ensure delegates are being looked after and to act as liaisons with the Head Waiter; and,
- one to circulate through the dining room with a supply of newspapers from the home towns of each of the delegates.

11. *Budget:*

(a) Menu:	$2.00 x 300 people plus 5% sales tax plus 10% gratuity	$690.00
(b) Centre Pieces:	$4.00 x 26 tables	$104.00
	TOTAL	$794.00

12. *Transportation:*

A memorandum was submitted to the Transportation Committee with the following requirements:
- cars to transport decorations, a six-man volunteer decorating team and staff organizers to the Talisman the evening of Thursday, April 4th, and, after the room has been set up, to convey them home;
- a car to transport staff organizers to the same location the morning of Friday, April 5th.

Transportation requirements of the Guides are being looked after by Merle Shain.

Transportation requirements of Mr Trudeau are being looked after by Gordon Gibson.

13. *Role of Regional Organization and M.P.'s:*

Bryce Mackasey will assume responsibility for:
- locating regional people in key positions throughout the dining room;
- escorting Mr Trudeau to the tables and introducing him to delegates;
- ensuring that an informal atmosphere is preserved and that no delegate is left stranded or forgotten.

14. *Candidate's Role:*

Mr Trudeau is to arrive promptly at 8:00 a.m. to greet delegates as they arrive for breakfast. As the room is filled and delegates seat themselves to be served, Mr Trudeau, accompanied by Bryce Mackasey, will circulate through the dining room to chat with delegates.

15. *Official Programme:*

Thursday, April 4th,	7:00 p.m.	– Decoration of room.
Friday, April 5th,	7:00 a.m.	– Setting of tables.
	7:30 a.m.	– Briefing and stationing of Guides.
	8:00 a.m.	– Mr Trudeau arrives,
8:00 a.m. -	8:30 a.m.	– Delegates arrive.
		– Breakfast is served.
8:30 a.m. -	9:00 a.m.	– Coffee.
		– Distribution of local newspapers.
	9:30 a.m.	– Breakfast officially ends.

Chronology

1963

APRIL

8 Federal election returns Liberals as largest party, with 129 seats to Conservatives' 95.

17 John Diefenbaker announces his resignation as Prime Minister.

20 FLQ bomb blast kills Wilfrid O'Neill, night watchman at Montreal armoury.

22 Lester Pearson assumes office; cabinet is sworn in.

MAY

1 Quebec government takes over privately owned hydro-electric companies.

1-3 Pearson visits Prime Minister Macmillan in London.

10-11 Pearson visits President Kennedy at Hyannis Port, Massachusetts.

16 Parliament meets.

17 Sergeant-Major Walter Leja injured dismantling FLQ bomb planted in Westmount mailbox.

21 Liberals win non-confidence vote on nuclear arms.

22-24 NATO meetings in Ottawa.

JUNE

4 Pearson announces unilateral extension of offshore fishing limits from three to twelve miles.

7 Commons approves establishment of defence committee.

10 Municipal Winter Works Incentive Program established.

12 Alleged FLQ terrorists found criminally responsible by Montreal coroner's jury for night watchman's bomb death.

13 Walter Gordon brings down first budget.

14 Gordon reveals names of "the bright boys," three young Toronto businessmen brought in to help prepare budget.

19 Gordon announces withdrawal of 30 per cent takeover tax proposed in budget.

20	Sixtieth Day of Decision. Gordon offers resignation, which is not accepted.
24	Government survives Conservative motion of non-confidence in Minister of Finance.
27	Salvas Report on Union Nationale corruption released in Quebec.

JULY

8	Walter Gordon tables revised version of budget.
10	Governments of Canada and B.C. announce agreement on Columbia River Treaty.
15	Norris Report on Great Lakes labour dispute released.
18	President Kennedy announces U.S. equalization tax; stock market collapse threatened in Canada.
21	Canada gains exemption from U.S. equalization tax.
22	Names of the chairmen of Royal Commission on Bilingualism and Biculturalism announced. Department of Industry established.
26-27	Federal-provincial conference on municipal loan fund.
29	Commons approves raising members' salaries to $18,000 a year.

AUGUST

2	Communist China agrees to buy 112 to 187 million bushels of Canadian wheat over next three years. Municipal development and loan bill passed by Commons. Economic Council of Canada established.
5-6	Interprovincial premiers' conference meets at Halifax.
6-9	NDP convention meets in Regina.
8	Canada signs nuclear test-ban treaty.

SEPTEMBER

2	Social Credit split; Commons seats now Ralliement des Créditistes under Réal Caouette, 13, Social Credit under Robert Thompson, 11.
6	Pierre Dupuy appointed commissioner general of Expo 67.
16	Largest Russian wheat deal announced; to buy $500 millions' worth within next twelve months.
19	Pearson addresses UN General Assembly.
25	Eric Kierans elected to Quebec Legislature.
30	Parliamentary session resumes.

OCTOBER

9	Pearson announces U.S.-Canadian agreement on nuclear warheads.
16	Old-age security raised from $65 to $75 a month, phasing to include all those over 65 by 1970.
23	Proclamation of legislation for trusteeship for Seafarers' International Union.

24   Paul Hellyer begins defence cutbacks with cancellation of frigate-building program.

10   War disability pensions increased 10 per cent, effective September 1, 1964.
22   Assassination of John F. Kennedy.
26   Health Minister LaMarsh mounts campaign against smoking.
26-29   Federal-provincial fiscal conference.

19   Hal Banks ordered to stand trial.
27   Lionel Chevrier and Azellus Denis resign from Pearson Cabinet.
31   Nuclear warheads reach North Bay.

1964

9   George Hees named president of Montreal and Canadian stock exchanges.
13   Canadian-U.S. negotiators reach agreement on Columbia River project.
14   Chevrier appointed Canadian High Commissioner in London.
15-17   Pearson visits Paris, confers with De Gaulle; announces at press conference willingness to sell uranium to France; later denies this.
20   Reconstruction of Liberal Cabinet.
20-23   Federal-provincial Fisheries Development Conference in Ottawa.
21-22   Pearson visits Washington, meets Lyndon Johnson.
24   Canada-USSR agreement on exchange of information on atomic power.
25-26   Convention of Ralliement des Créditistes decides to enter provincial politics.
30   Les Fusiliers Mont Royal armoury in Montreal robbed of 100 weapons and 20,000 rounds of ammunition.

1-5   PC annual convention in Ottawa, where proposal for secret-ballot vote of confidence on Diefenbaker's leadership defeated.
5   Léon Balcer accepted by John Diefenbaker as Quebec Conservative lieutenant.
     Quebec Legislative Assembly approves bill to set up education ministry.
8   Russia defeats Canada 3 to 2 to win Olympic hockey gold medal; Canada finishes fourth.

18	Eighty-five arrested in Montreal during anti-Victoria Day demonstrations.
21	Federal cabinet approves proposed flag design, three red maple leaves on white background flanked by vertical blue bars.
22	Ross Thatcher takes office as Premier of Saskatchewan.
25-26	U Thant visits Ottawa.
27	Pearson announces proposed design of new Canadian flag to Commons.
28	Pearson and Lyndon Johnson talk in New York.

JUNE

3	Beginning of strike at Montreal *La Presse*.
4	Official name changeover from Trans-Canada Air Lines to Air Canada.
5	Commons approves Columbia River Treaty.
15	Flag debate begins in Commons.
19	Volume I of Royal Commission on Health Services tabled.
25	Washington meeting of U.S.-Canada cabinet committee on defence.
26	Ten thousand farmers march on Quebec Legislature.
	Pearson tells Commons study being conducted of economic, social and political effects on Canada of Quebec secession.

JULY

6	Roland Michener appointed Canadian High Commissioner to India.
9	Commons approves legislation extending Canada's coastal fishing limits to twelve miles.
13	Pearson proposes Commonwealth declaration of racial equality at Commonwealth Prime Ministers' Conference.
22	Conservative caucus adopts flag filibuster.
27-28	Malaysian Prime Minister visits Ottawa.
28	Student Loans Act established offering university students loans up to $5,000.

AUGUST

3-4	Third interprovincial premiers' conference at Jasper.
8-9	Ralliement des Créditistes convention demands associate state or secession.
20	Roosevelt Campobello International Park in New Brunswick opened by Mrs L. B. Pearson and Mrs Lyndon Johnson.
21	Inauguration of Commonwealth Conference on Education in Ottawa.

SEPTEMBER

| 1 | Centennial celebration of Charlottetown Conference of 1864. Federal-provincial conference in Charlottetown. |

9-12	Conservative Conference on Canadian Goals in Fredericton.
10	Deadlock in Commons flag debate temporarily broken with decision to place question in hands of fifteen-man committee.
16	Pearson, Bennett and Lyndon Johnson sign Columbia River Treaty at Blaine, Washington.
23	Walter Gordon introduces legislation to guard against foreign take-over of certain Canadian financial institutions.

OCTOBER

1	Hal Banks found aboard yacht in New York by *Toronto Daily Star* reporter Robert Reguly.
5-12	Queen Elizabeth visits Canada to commemorate one-hundredth anniversary of Charlottetown and Quebec conferences. French-Canadian separatists demonstrate in protest in Quebec City on October 10.
14	Federal-provincial conference of attorneys general accepts draft recommendation for constitutional amendments without approval by British Parliament.
29	Commons committee (by vote of ten to four with English-speaking Conservatives opposed) recommends Canadian flag design of single red maple leaf on white background with vertical red bars at either end.
30	George McIlraith succeeds Guy Favreau as House Leader.

NOVEMBER

2-6	UN peace-keeping conference in Ottawa.
3	Defence Minister Hellyer announces mass reorganization of army reserve forces.
16	Kennedy-round negotiations begin in Geneva.
20	Quebec Royal Commission on Education calls for radical transformation of classical college system. Electoral Boundaries Readjustment Act given Royal Assent.
23	Conservative M.P. Erik Nielsen breaks Rivard scandal.
24	Guy Favreau announces Dorion judicial inquiry on Rivard charge. Guy Rouleau resigns as parliamentary assistant to Lester Pearson after admitting he made representations in the case.
27	Government agrees to widen terms of Dorion Inquiry.
30	Flag debate resumes. Pearson's letter on political morality to cabinet.

DECEMBER

5	PC executive council meets in Ottawa.
11	Government announces closure on flag debate.
14	Senate committee rejects Bank of British Columbia.
15	Beginning of Dorion hearings. Commons approves flag at 2.13 a.m.

528

18 Share of succession duties rebated to provinces increased from 50 per cent to 75 per cent.
Parliament adjourns.

21 Léon Balcer hints he may leave Progressive Conservatives.

22 Paul Hellyer announces $1.5 billions new equipment for armed forces.
Labour dispute that shut down Montreal *La Presse* settled after 202 days.

1965

JANUARY

11 First annual review of Economic Council of Canada published.

14 Ten Quebec PC M.P.'s demand leadership convention.

16 Pearson and Lyndon Johnson sign auto agreement at LBJ ranch.

22 Pearson makes public Yvon Dupuis' letter of resignation.

FEBRUARY

6 PC national executive meets in Ottawa; Léon Balcer's call for a leadership convention rejected.

11 Jean-Paul Deschatelets resigns from federal cabinet.

14 Guy Rouleau resigns as chairman of Liberal caucus.

15 New Canadian flag raised in Ottawa for first time.

16 Commons reassembles.

18 M.P. Rémi Paul leaves Conservatives to sit as independent as protest against Diefenbaker leadership.

25 Royal Commission on Bilingualism and Biculturalism issues interim report on "greatest crisis in [Canada's] history."

27 Quebec-France cultural agreement signed.

MARCH

2 Lucien Rivard escapes from Bordeaux jail.

5 Pearson addresses Canadian Society of New York on Vietnam.

11 Ontario Legislature approves Fulton-Favreau formula.

26 John Diefenbaker's twenty-fifth anniversary in federal politics.

29 Commons approves Canada Pension Plan.

APRIL

3 Prorogation of Parliament.

5 Third session of twenty-sixth Parliament opens.

7 Léon Balcer leaves Conservative Party to sit as independent M.P.

26 Third Gordon budget.

MAY

1 Bomb explodes at U.S. consulate in Montreal.

7 Two Soviet officials expelled from Ottawa.

11-12 NATO meeting in London.

JUNE

2 Legislation enacted requiring retirement from Senate at age 75 for senators appointed after this date.

17 Atlantic Acceptance Corporation goes into receivership.

23 Arnold Smith appointed Commonwealth Secretary General.

28 Dorion Report submitted to government.

29 Guy Favreau resigns as Justice Minister as result of criticism contained in Dorion Report.

JULY

7 Minor Liberal Cabinet shuffle.

8 Pearson announces beginning of P.E.I. causeway.

16 Lucien Rivard arrested.

19 Federal-provincial conference opens in Ottawa.

22 Rivard extradited to U.S.

29 A national postal strike ends after seven days.

AUGUST

2-3 Interprovincial premiers' conference at Winnipeg.

19 Pearson begins nine-day western tour.

24 Diefenbaker, touring rural Quebec, gets standing ovation at Ste Perpétue.

SEPTEMBER

7 Pearson calls general election for November 8.

9 Fowler Report on Broadcasting released.

10 Gérard Pelletier, Jean Marchand and Pierre Elliott Trudeau decide to run as Liberals in Quebec.

21 Liberal candidates meet in Ottawa for election briefing sessions.

23 Provincial health ministers convene in Ottawa to discuss medicare.

OCTOBER

1 Conservatives hold giant "unity" rally in Toronto's Varsity Arena.

6 Bladen Commission report released.

26 Pearson makes statement in Wallaceburg, Ontario, that Walter Gordon will still be Minister of Finance after election.

28 Pearson meets Robert Winters in Toronto in row over promise to reappoint Gordon.

8 Liberals fail to gain majority in federal election, winning 131 seats to Conservatives' 97.

9 Power failure blacks out eastern North America including much of Ontario; later traced to failure in Canadian power plant.

11 Finance Minister Walter Gordon resigns from cabinet, citing bad advice given to Prime Minister in calling election.

17 Paul Martin and French Ambassador to Canada sign umbrella agreement enabling provinces to make *"ententes"* with France.

26 Meeting of NATO defence ministers.

DECEMBER

1 Cost-of-living index reaches record high of 140.8.

5 Bank rate increased from 4¼ per cent to 4¾ per cent.

6 Announcement of new guide lines on foreign investment by American firms.

16 Maurice Lamontagne and René Tremblay resign from cabinet.

17 Lester Pearson announces major cabinet reorganization, appoints, among other new ministers, Jean Marchand and Robert Winters.

23 Progressive Conservatives contest Maurice Sauvé's election on Magdalen Islands.

1966

JANUARY

6 Eric Kierans makes public letter sent to U.S. Commerce Secretary Connor protesting American economic guidelines.

17 Bilateral air agreement signed between Canada and U.S.

18 Commons reassembles.

FEBRUARY

23 Pearson announces in House that no inquiry will be held in case of George Victor Spencer, Vancouver postal clerk accused of selling information to Russian officials in Ottawa.

MARCH

4 Pearson announces judicial inquiries into counter-espionage methods and treatment of George Victor Spencer.

10 Lucien Cardin raises Munsinger charges against Conservatives in press conference.

11 Gerda Munsinger found in Munich by *Toronto Daily Star* reporter Robert Reguly.

14 Pearson establishes judicial inquiry into Munsinger affair under Supreme Court Justice Wishart Spence.

18 External Affairs Minister Paul Martin announces Canada to give up Marville and Metz air bases in France.

29 First Mitchell Sharp budget.

APRIL

5 Commons votes 143 to 112 to retain death penalty.

18-24 Munsinger Inquiry hearings.

19 Government orders review of Steven Truscott conviction for rape-murder of Lynne Harper, 12, in 1959.
Flora MacDonald fired from PC National Headquarters by Diefenbaker appointee James Johnston.

MAY

9 Quebec civil servants strike.

18 Paul Joseph Chartier blown up by bomb he tried to bring into House of Commons.

JUNE

5 Union Nationale defeats Liberals in Quebec provincial election; Daniel Johnson becomes Premier.

28 Company of Young Canadians established.

JULY

4 White Paper on broadcasting tabled.

6-8 Commonwealth-Caribbean Conference in Ottawa.

8 Canada Assistance Plan passed.

11 Canada-USSR agreement providing for Montreal-Moscow air-flights announced.
General A. G. L. McNaughton dies.

16 Lieutenant-General Jean V. Allard becomes Chief of Canadian defence staff.

29 Civil servants' strike ends in Quebec.

AUGUST

1-2 Interprovincial premiers' conference in Toronto.

12 Opening of western Liberal Party policy conference in Saskatoon.

21 Gilles Grégoire elected president of separatist Ralliement National of Quebec.

26 CPR and CNR workers strike.

SEPTEMBER

6-15 Commonwealth Conference in London, England.

8 Postponement of medicare until July 1, 1968, announced.

14-15 Tax Structure Committee meeting in Ottawa.

| 20 | Dalton Camp calls for reappraisal of PC leadership in speech to Toronto Junior Board of Trade. |
| 23 | Spence Report on Munsinger scandals released. |

OCTOBER

5	Carrothers Report on Northwest Territories tabled. Parliament reassembles.
6	Quebec and Newfoundland agree to development of Churchill Falls hydro-electric power in Labrador.
10-12	Liberal national policy conference in Ottawa.
11	Donald Report on Cape Breton coal industry released.
18	Canada-United Kingdom uranium sale announced.
24-26	Conference on higher education in Ottawa.
27	Arthur Maloney states his intention of contesting PC presidency against Dalton Camp.
28	Opening of federal-provincial fiscal conference.

NOVEMBER

11	Canada elected to UN Security Council.
14	Air Canada machinists strike.
13-16	PC National Convention in Ottawa; Dalton Camp wins leadership reassessment motion.
22	Canada calls for seating of both nationalist and communist Chinese governments in UN General Assembly with Peking government in Security Council.
28	Air Canada resumes service.

DECEMBER

| 19 | Second Sharp budget. |
| 21 | Medical Care Insurance Act authorizing federal government to pay approximately half cost of provincial medicare plans approved, to come into effect July 1, 1968. Amendment of Old Age Security Act (Guaranteed Income Supplement) approved, legislation guaranteeing monthly income of $105 to aged. |

1967

JANUARY

1	Centennial Year begins.
4	Walter Gordon returns to cabinet.
9	Confederation Train unveiled at Victoria by State Secretary Judy LaMarsh.
12	Guy Favreau resigns as leader of federal Liberal Party in Quebec.

13 Strikes by Roman Catholic teachers close more than four hundred schools in Province of Quebec.

18 Jean Marchand named leader of federal Liberal Party in Quebec.

23 Gordon named head of special committee to study implications of foreign investment in Canada.

FEBRUARY

3 Royal Commission on Status of Women announced.

12 Conservative leadership convention called for September.

13 Dr Timothy Leary, former Harvard professor and founder of LSD religious cult in U.S., denied entry to Canada.

14 Davie Fulton officially enters PC leadership race.

16 George Hees officially enters PC leadership race.

20 Montreal Roman Catholic teachers vote to obey provincial legislation ordering them back to work after five-week strike.
Mike Starr officially enters PC leadership race.

24 Carter Royal Commission recommends new tax base including capital gains tax and levy on all family income from any source.

MARCH

5 Governor General Georges Vanier, 78, dies in Ottawa.

9 Robert Thompson resigns as national Social Credit leader.

15 Commons committee votes 12 to 4 to recommend that Parliament remove Mr Justice Leo Landreville from Ontario Supreme Court.

26 Nancy Greene wins world skiing championship.

APRIL

4 Roland Michener, High Commissioner to India, named Governor General.
Pierre Elliott Trudeau and Jean Chrétien named to federal cabinet; Lucien Cardin and Guy Favreau resign.

25 Commons approves bill to unify armed forces.

27 Expo 67 opened at Montreal by Governor General Michener.

MAY

4 Supreme Court of Canada dismisses appeal of Steven Truscott.

11 Wallace McCutcheon officially enters PC leadership race.

22 Daniel Johnson announces in Paris that governments of France and Quebec have agreed to co-operate on several financial and cultural projects.

24 Farmers march on Parliament Hill.

25 President Johnson visits Expo 67, then confers with Pearson on international problems at Harrington Lake, Quebec.

26 Alvin Hamilton officially enters PC leadership race.

28 Canadian forces begin emergency withdrawal from Gaza Strip.

29 Liberals win four federal by-elections in Quebec and Conservatives win one in Ontario.

30 Robert Stanfield's Progressive Conservative Government re-elected in Nova Scotia with 40 of 46 seats.

JUNE

1 Federal budget brought down.

7 Donald Fleming enters PC leadership race.

JULY

1 Canada observes one-hundredth anniversary of Confederation; Queen Elizabeth addresses Parliament.

3 Queen Elizabeth and Prince Philip visit Expo 67.

7 Parliamentary session ends; Diefenbaker's last day in House as Conservative Leader.
Ninety Canadians named to first honours list of Order of Canada.

11 Guy Favreau dies.

19 Robert Stanfield enters PC leadership race.

24 Charles de Gaulle of France shouts *"Vive le Québec libre"* at Montreal reception.

26 Charles de Gaulle cancels visit to Ottawa and returns to France following diplomatic rebuke from Pearson for his support of Quebec separatists.

AUGUST

3 Duff Roblin enters PC leadership race.

7-10 "Thinkers' Conference" held by Conservative Party at Montmorency, Quebec.

SEPTEMBER

5-9 Progressive Conservative convention in Toronto; Robert Stanfield, Nova Scotia Premier, elected leader succeeding John Diefenbaker.

18 Defense Secretary McNamara announces U.S. will start building limited $5 billion anti-ballistic missile system by end of 1967.
J. W. Pickersgill resigns as Transport Minister to become president of new Canadian Transport Commission; succeeded by Paul Hellyer.

27 Paul Martin at United Nations calls on United States to stop bombing of Vietnam.

OCTOBER

14 René Lévesque resigns from Quebec Liberal Party.
New Broadcasting Act introduced in Commons.

29 Expo 67 closes at Montreal; final attendance total: 50,306,648.

3 Hal Banks ordered extradited from U.S. to Canada. Appeals proceedings.

6 PC leader Robert Stanfield wins federal by-election in Colchester-Hants.

23 Commons gives second-reading approval in principle to bill to eliminate death penalty for murder for trial five-year period, except for murder of police or prison guards.

27 President Charles de Gaulle in press conference calls for Quebec to be raised to rank of a sovereign state.

28 Pearson denounces De Gaulle's stand on Quebec as intolerable.

30 Mitchell Sharp imposes 5 per cent surcharge on income tax and raises liquor and tobacco taxes in mini-budget.
Confederation of Tomorrow Conference of provincial leaders ends in Toronto with decision to set up four-man committee of premiers to be called Continuing Committee on Confederation.

5 Report of Royal Commission on Bilingualism and Biculturalism calls for equality for English and French languages in federal operations; asks Ontario and New Brunswick to give French-speaking minorities same rights as extended to English-speaking population of Quebec.

11 Paul-Emile Cardinal Léger leaves for African leper colony as missionary after resigning as archbishop of Montreal.

14 Pearson announces his resignation as Leader of Liberal Party; will continue in office until leadership convention chooses successor.
Lloyd Henderson enters Liberal leadership race.

21 Abolishment of capital punishment for experimental period of five years legislation passed.
Commons receives proposals for massive overhaul of Criminal Code of Canada, with changes to affect homosexuality, abortion, weapons possession, lotteries, etc.
Department of Consumer and Corporate Affairs established.

30 Vincent Massey dies in London.

1968

9 Eric Kierans enters Liberal leadership race, followed by:

11 Paul Hellyer,

12 Allan MacEachen,

13 John Turner.
Jean Chrétien appointed Minister of Revenue.

19 Paul Martin, Mitchell Sharp and Joe Greene enter Liberal leadership race.
George Davidson named president of CBC.

22   Bank rate increased to 7 per cent.

1   Divorce legislation broadening grounds to become effective July 2.
     1968, receives Royal Assent.
5-7 Constitutional conference in Ottawa.
7   New Broadcasting Act passed.
9   Bryce Mackasey appointed Minister without Portfolio.
16   Pierre Elliott Trudeau enters Liberal leadership race.
19   Liberals defeated on major tax bill while Pearson out of country.

1   Robert Winters enters Liberal leadership race.
4   Pearson announces ties with Gabon suspended since February 19.
14   U.S. State Department refuses to extradite Hal Banks.
15   Bank rate increased to 7½ per cent.
30   Five-year extension to NORAD agreement signed.

3   Mitchell Sharp drops out of Liberal leadership contest to support
     Pierre Elliott Trudeau.
4   Martin Luther King assassinated in Memphis. Tennessee.
     Pearson gives farewell address to Liberal convention.
6   Pierre Elliott Trudeau chosen new Liberal Leader in Ottawa.

Acknowledgements

As I finish this book, the faces and voices of my collaborators crowd around me and I am reminded of how much I owe them. Unhappily, anonymity is the price of candour about incumbent politicians and since most of my research involved off-the-record interviews, acknowledgement of my sources by name is not possible. Where no printed source is indicated, direct quotations are from my on-the-record conversations.

This book bears the imprint – as does everything I have written or ever will write – of the long and happy apprenticeship I served under Ralph Allen. As my mentor and friend first at *Maclean's* magazine and then at the *Toronto Daily Star*, Ralph inspired me and indeed a whole generation of Canadian journalists to strive for a stylistic excellence and an editorial integrity that he alone achieved.

I am most grateful for the encouragement, wise counsel and precious gift of writing time so generously proffered by Beland Honderich, president and publisher of the *Toronto Daily Star*.

My greatest debt is to Christina McCall Newman for being a demanding, creative and perceptive partner in this undertaking as in all the others of our shared life. During the years when "this damn book" was being written, she was funnier, gloomier, kinder and more generous with her talents than any man has a right to expect or any woman has a reason to be.

Martin Lynch, assistant news editor of the Toronto *Globe and Mail*, and Carol Lindsay, chief librarian of the *Toronto Daily Star*, have been invaluable editors and friends. I also want to thank Bernice Anderson for her cheerful and immensely capable secretarial assistance. I would like to acknowledge as well the publishers who have allowed me to quote brief excerpts from their books as identified by footnotes in the text.

Distemper owes its existence to the aid and encouragement of many others not mentioned here; only the responsibility for its imperfections is fully my own.

PETER C. NEWMAN

OTTAWA,
April 22, 1963– April 6, 1968

Index

Index

Suggestions for Further Reading

The following is a selection of publications pertinent to the events and personalities covered in this volume.

Bothwell, Robert. *Pearson: His Life and World.* Toronto: McGraw-Hill Ryerson, forthcoming.

Careless, Anthony, G. S. *Initiative and Response: The Adaptation of Canadian Federalism to Regional Economic Development.* Montreal: McGill-Queen's University Press, 1977.

Creighton, D. G., *Canada's First Century, 1867-1967.* Toronto: Macmillan, 1970.

Diefenbaker, John G. *One Canadian: Memoirs of the Rt. Honourable John G. Diefenbaker.* Volume III. Toronto: Macmillan, 1977.

Gwyn, Richard J. *The Shape of Scandal: A Study of a Government in Crisis.* Toronto: Clarke, Irwin & Co., 1965.

La Marsh, Judy. *Memoirs of a Bird in a Guilded Cage.* Toronto: McClelland and Stewart, 1968.

Meisel, John. *Working Papers on Canadian Politics.* 2nd rev. ed. Montreal: McGill-Queen's University Press, 1975.

Monro, John A. and Inglis, Alex I. (eds.). *Mike: The Memoirs of the Right Honourable Lester B. Pearson,* Vol. III. Toronto: University of Toronto Press, 1972.

Nicholson, Patrick. *Vision and Indecision.* Toronto: Longmans, 1968.

Pearson, Lester B. *Words and Occasions.* Toronto: University of Toronto Press, 1970.

Shakleton, Doris F. *Tommy Douglas.* Toronto: McClelland and Stewart, 1975.

Simeon, Richard. *Federal-Provincial Diplomacy.* Toronto: University of Toronto Press, 1972.

Smith, Denis. *Gentle Patriot: A Political Biography of Walter Gordon.* Edmonton: Hurtig, 1973.

Stursberg, Peter. *Diefenbaker: Leadership Gained, 1956-1962.* Toronto: University of Toronto Press, 1975.

Stursberg, Peter. *Diefenbaker: Leadership Lost, 1962-65.* Toronto: University of Toronto Press, 1976.

Thordarson, Bruce M. *Lester Pearson: Diplomat and Politician.* Toronto: Oxford University Press, 1974.

THE CARLETON LIBRARY